DOMESDAY BOOK

Somerset

History from the Sources

P-7
(890)

DOMESDAY BOOK

A Survey of the Counties of England

LIBER DE WINTONIA

Compiled by direction of

KING WILLIAM I

Winchester
1086

DOMESDAY BOOK

General editor

JOHN MORRIS

8

Somerset

edited by
Caroline and Frank Thorn

from a draft translation prepared by
Caroline Thorn

PHILLIMORE
Chichester
1980

1980

Published by

PHILLIMORE & CO. LTD.,
London and Chichester

Head Office: Shopwyke Hall,
Chichester, Sussex, England

ISBN 0 85033 367 9 (case)
ISBN 0 85033 368 7 (limp)

Printed in Great Britain by
Titus Wilson & Son Ltd.,
Kendal

SOMERSET

History from the Sources
General Editor: John Morris

The series aims to publish history written directly from the sources for all interested readers, both specialists and others. The first priority is to publish important texts which should be widely available, but are not.

DOMESDAY BOOK

The contents, with the folio on which each county begins, are:

Domesday Book is termed *Liber de Wintonia* (The Book of Winchester) in column 332c

INTRODUCTION

The Domesday Survey

In 1066 Duke William of Normandy conquered England. He was crowned King, and most of the lands of the English nobility were soon granted to his followers. Domesday Book was compiled 20 years later. The Saxon Chronicle records that in 1085

> at Gloucester at midwinter ... the King had deep speech with his counsellors ... and sent men all over England to each shire ... to find out ... what or how much each landholder held ... in land and livestock, and what it was worth ... The returns were brought to him.[1]

William was thorough. One of his Counsellors reports that he also sent a second set of Commissioners 'to shires they did not know, where they were themselves unknown, to check their predecessors' survey, and report culprits to the King.'[2]

The information was collected at Winchester, corrected, abridged, chiefly by omission of livestock and the 1066 population, and fair-copied by one writer into a single volume. Norfolk, Suffolk and Essex were copied, by several writers, into a second volume, unabridged, which states that 'the Survey was made in 1086'. The surveys of Durham and Northumberland, and of several towns, including London, were not transcribed, and most of Cumberland and Westmorland, not yet in England, was not surveyed. The whole undertaking was completed at speed, in less than 12 months, though the fair-copying of the main volume may have taken a little longer. Both volumes are now preserved at the Public Record Office. Some versions of regional returns also survive. One of them, from Ely Abbey,[3] copies out the Commissioners' brief. They were to ask

> The name of the place. Who held it, before 1066, and now?
> How many *hides*?[4] How many ploughs, both those in lordship and the men's?
> How many villagers, cottagers and slaves, how many free men and Freemen?[5]
> How much woodland, meadow and pasture? How many mills and fishponds?
> How much has been added or taken away? What the total value was and is?
> How much each free man or Freeman had or has? All threefold, before 1066,
> when King William gave it, and now; and if more can be had than at present?

The Ely volume also describes the procedure. The Commissioners took evidence on oath 'from the Sheriff; from all the barons and their Frenchmen; and from the whole Hundred, the priests, the reeves and six villagers from each village'. It also names four Frenchmen and four Englishmen from each Hundred, who were sworn to verify the detail.

The King wanted to know what he had, and who held it. The Commissioners therefore listed lands in dispute, for Domesday Book was not only a tax-assessment. To the King's grandson, Bishop Henry of Winchester, its purpose was that every 'man should know his right and not usurp another's'; and because it was the final authoritative register of rightful possession 'the natives called it Domesday Book, by analogy

---

[1] Before he left England for the last time, late in 1086.   [2] Robert Losinga, Bishop of Hereford 1079-1095 (see *E.H.R.* 22, 1907, 74).   [3] *Inquisitio Eliensis*, first paragraph.   [4] A land unit, reckoned as 120 acres.   [5] *Quot Sochemani.*

from the Day of Judgement'; that was why it was carefully arranged by Counties, and by landholders within Counties, 'numbered consecutively ... for easy reference'.6

Domesday Book describes Old English society under new management, in minute statistical detail. Foreign lords had taken over, but little else had yet changed. The chief landholders and those who held from them are named, and the rest of the population was counted. Most of them lived in villages, whose houses might be clustered together, or dispersed among their fields. Villages were grouped in administrative districts called Hundreds, which formed regions within Shires, or Counties, which survive today with minor boundary changes; the recent deformation of some ancient county identities is here disregarded, as are various short-lived modern changes. The local assemblies, though overshadowed by lords great and small, gave men a voice, which the Commissioners heeded. Very many holdings were described by the Norman term *manerium* (manor), greatly varied in size and structure, from tiny farmsteads to vast holdings; and many lords exercised their own jurisdiction and other rights, termed *soca*, whose meaning still eludes exact definition.

The Survey was unmatched in Europe for many centuries, the product of a sophisticated and experienced English administration, fully exploited by the Conqueror's commanding energy. But its unique assemblage of facts and figures has been hard to study, because the text has not been easily available, and abounds in technicalities. Investigation has therefore been chiefly confined to specialists; many questions cannot be tackled adequately without a cheap text and uniform translation available to a wider range of students, including local historians.

Previous Editions

The text has been printed once, in 1783, in an edition by Abraham Farley, probably of 1250 copies, at Government expense, said to have been £38,000; its preparation took 16 years. It was set in a specially designed type, here reproduced photographically, which was destroyed by fire in 1808. In 1811 and 1816 the Records Commissioners added an introduction, indices, and associated texts, edited by Sir Henry Ellis; and in 1861-1863 the Ordnance Survey issued zincograph facsimiles of the whole. Texts of individual counties have appeared since 1673, separate translations in the Victoria County Histories and elsewhere.

This Edition

Farley's text is used, because of its excellence, and because any worthy alternative would prove astronomically expensive. His text has been checked against the facsimile, and discrepancies observed have been verified against the manuscript, by the kindness of Miss Daphne Gifford of the Public Record Office. Farley's few errors are indicated in the notes.

6*Dialogus de Scaccario* 1,16.

The editor is responsible for the translation and lay-out. It aims at what the compiler would have written if his language had been modern English; though no translation can be exact, for even a simple word like 'free' nowadays means freedom from different restrictions. Bishop Henry emphasized that his grandfather preferred 'ordinary words'; the nearest ordinary modern English is therefore chosen whenever possible. Words that are now obsolete, or have changed their meaning, are avoided, but measurements have to be transliterated, since their extent is often unknown or arguable, and varied regionally. The terse inventory form of the original has been retained, as have the ambiguities of the Latin.

Modern English commands two main devices unknown to 11th century Latin, standardised punctuation and paragraphs; in the Latin, *ibi* ('there are') often does duty for a modern full stop, *et* ('and') for a comma or semi-colon. The entries normally answer the Commissioners' questions, arranged in five main groups, (i) the place and its holder, its hides, ploughs and lordship; (ii) people; (iii) resources; (iv) value; and (v) additional notes. The groups are usually given as separate paragraphs.

King William numbered chapters 'for easy reference', and sections within chapters are commonly marked, usually by initial capitals, often edged in red. They are here numbered. Maps, indices and an explanation of technical terms are also given. Later, it is hoped to publish analytical and explanatory volumes, and associated texts.

The editor is deeply indebted to the advice of many scholars, too numerous to name, and especially to the Public Record Office, and to the publisher's patience. The draft translations are the work of a team; they have been co-ordinated and corrected by the editor, and each has been checked by several people. It is therefore hoped that mistakes may be fewer than in versions published by single fallible individuals. But it would be Utopian to hope that the translation is altogether free from error; the editor would like to be informed of mistakes observed.

The maps are the work of Jim Hardy and Frank Thorn.

The preparation of this volume has been greatly assisted by a generous grant from the Leverhulme Trust Fund.

This support, originally given to the late Dr. J. R. Morris, has been kindly extended to his successors. At the time of Dr. Morris's death in June 1977, he had completed volumes 2, 3, 11, 12, 19, 23, 24. He had more or less finished the preparation of volumes 13, 14, 20, 28. These and subsequent volumes in the series were brought out under the supervision of John Dodgson and Alison Hawkins, who have endeavoured to follow, as far as possible, the editorial principles established by John Morris.

Conventions

*   refers to a note to the Latin text

[ ]   enclose words omitted in the MS.   ( )   enclose editorial explanations.

EXTRACTS TO SHOW COMPARISON BETWEEN
EXON. AND EXCHEQUER DB ENTRIES

SOMERSET DB 10,1 *For the Latin see the main text*

St. Peter's Church, Athelney, holds ILTON. Before 1066 it paid tax for 8 hides.
Land for 12 ploughs. In lordship 4 hides; 3 ploughs there; 4 slaves;
 10 villagers and 6 smallholders with 4 ploughs.
 A mill which pays 7s 6d; meadow, 40 acres; pasture, 30 acres; woodland 1
  league long and another in width.
Value 100s.
 The Count of Mortain holds 2 hides of this manor's land, which were in (the
lands of) this church before 1066. Land for 4 ploughs. Value 30s.

Exon. 191 a 1

Abbas adelinienſis hŧ. ɪ. manſ q̇ uocat. Atiltona. 7 redđ gildũ p. vɪɪɪ. hidis.

die q̇ rex. e. f. u. 7 m. has poſsŧ arare. xɪɪ. carr. ĩde hŧ. A. ɪɪɪɪ. hid. 7. ɪɪɪ. carr

7 uiłł. ɪɪ. hid. 7. ɪɪɪɪ. carr. ibi hŧ. A. x. uiłł. 7. vɪ. bord. 7. ɪɪɪɪ. feruo 7. ɪɪ. roncino.

&. vɪ. animal. 7. x. porco. 7. xl. oues. 7. ɪ. molendiñ q̇ redđ. vɪɪ. ſol 7 vɪ. nũmos

7. ɪ. leucã nemoris ĩ longitud. 7. aliã ĩ latitud. 7. xl. agŗ pti. 7. xxx. agŗ paſcuę.

7 ualet p anñ. v. libras. de hac manſ sŧ ablate. ɪɪ. hid de his prediċtis. vɪɪɪ. hid.

de cartrai.

q̇ erant de ipſa ęccła die q̇ rex. e. f. u. 7 m. has tenet malgerˢ de comite de

moritanio. has poſsŧ arare. ɪɪɪɪ. carr. 7 ualet p anñ. xxx. ſol.

The Abbot of Athelney has a manor called ILTON; it paid tax for 8 hides in 1066*.
12 ploughs can plough these. The Abbot has there 4 hides and 3 ploughs and the
villagers (have) 2 hides and 4 ploughs. The Abbot has there 10 villagers, 6 smallholders, 4 slaves, 2 cobs, 6 cattle, 10 pigs, 40 sheep, a mill which pays 7s 6d, 1
league of woodland in length and another in width, 40 acres of meadow and 30
acres of pasture. Value £5 a year. From this manor have been taken away 2 hides
of the said 8 hides; they were (part) of this church('s lands) in 1066*. Mauger of
Carteret holds them from the Count of Mortain. 4 ploughs can plough them.
Value 30s a year.

Exon. 512 a 1 *(Terrae Occupatae)*

V Abb ædelingenſis aecłae. hŧ. ɪ. ñi quę uocat. Hiltona.

quę ſemp fuit de aecła 7 redđ gueldũ p vɪɪɪ. hid de his. vɪɪɪ. funt

ablatę. ɪɪ. hid quę erant de ipſa aeccła die q̇ rex. E. f. v. 7 ñi. has

tenet. Come de moritonio. & Malgeru de cartrai. de eo. & 7 ualet

p annũ. xxx. ſoł.

The Abbot of Athelney Church has a manor called ILTON which was always (part)
of the church('s lands); it paid tax for 8 hides. Of these 8 (hides) 2 hides have
been taken away which were (part) of this church('s lands) in 1066*. The Count
of Mortain holds them and Mauger of Carteret from him. Value 30s a year.

* *die qua rex Edward fuit vivus et mortuus* ('on the day on which King Edward was alive
and dead'); it is always translated in this edition as 'in 1066' and is equivalent to DB *TRE*,
'before 1066'.

THE EXETER DOMESDAY

For the South Western counties there is another set of returns, the Exeter Book (*Liber Exoniensis*), differently set out, for Somerset, Devon and Cornwall, part of Dorset and one Wiltshire holding. Compared with the Exchequer version Exon. omits some information, e.g. the rest of Wiltshire, much of Dorset and some entries for Devon. Arrangement is by fiefs, and within these by counties (not always in the same order). Within each county places are often grouped in Hundreds, although without the Hundred name given, and frequently the Hundreds occur in the same order under different holders. This provides evidence for the identification of places and in part supplies the lack of Hundred headings in Exchequer DB here. Information is often duplicated; for example in Somerset certain manors and lands held in 1066 by Glastonbury Church, but alienated in 1086, are listed both under that church's lands (folios 171b-173a) and under the lands of the 1086 holders (folios 137a; 139b; 145b; 197b; 266b-267b; 278b; 435a). After the fiefs in Exon. come details for Devon, Cornwall and Somerset of 'Appropriated Lands' (*Terrae Occupatae*), folios 495-525: condensed entries of manors, which had had land taken from them, or added, or had been held as two or more manors before 1066 by one or more holders, or had not paid their customary dues, or were unusual in some other way (see the introduction to the Exon. Notes p. 310). The information almost always repeats that in the main Exeter Domesday, but occasionally adds to it. In this edition the whole of the corresponding entry in the *Terrae Occupatae* is only given when it differs from, or adds to, the DB entry; but the reference to it is always given. Exon. also includes the returns of the tax levied in 1084 for all five counties, which it is hoped will be published in a separate volume. The Exon. folios dealing with Somerset are 75a-82b; 88b-91b; 103a-107b; 113a-116b; 136b-175b (with one Devon entry); 185a-193b; 196a-198b; 265a-283a; 286b-287a; 315a-b; 344a; 350a-365a (with one Devon entry); 369a-b; 371b-375a; 380a; 382b-386a; 422a-454a; 462b-467a; 473b; 477a-480b; 490a-493b; 508b-527a; 528a and 530b (parts only).

The MS, in Exeter Cathedral library, was published in 1816 by Sir Henry Ellis in the third volume of the Record Commission's edition of DB, from a transcript by Ralph Barnes, Chapter Clerk. No facsimile edition exists for Exon. The MS is of 532 parchment folios, (measuring about 6½ by 9¾ inches (16.5 by 25 cms.), a single column on each side of about 20 lines) in quires, varying between one and twenty folios. Generally a new quire was started for each major landholder, and a new side for most tenants. This led to many blanks, increased by spaces sometimes left for information not to hand. There is no indication of the original sequence of quires, the present order dates from the last rebinding in 1816. The MS is by about a dozen scribes, the hand changes often between entries and even within them.

The text cannot be economically reproduced here; nine-tenths of it repeats the DB survey, differing only a fraction of one per cent in tens of thousands of figures. Ellis's edition has been used here, but the MS has been checked where Exon. and DB differ, and elsewhere. The principal corresponding Exon. reference is given beside each entry in the translation, with other references in the Exon. Notes; the last number refers to the order of the entry on each side, as indicated in the MS generally by gallows marks. All discrepancies and additional facts are given, either in small type in the translation or in the Exon. Notes, the table of lordship and villagers' land and ploughs, or the table of details of holdings not given in DB, marked E, L or D respectively in the right margin of the translation. A specimen opposite, with the DB equivalent, shows the differences in formulae. The substance, though not the wording, of the whole of the Exeter Domesday returns is therefore here reproduced.

For further details see V. H. Galbraith *Domesday Book*, Oxford 1974, pp. 184-88; R. Welldon Finn, *The Liber Exoniensis*, London 1964; N. R. Ker, *Medieval Manuscripts in British Libraries*, vol. ii, pp. 800-807; Sir Henry Ellis, *DB3*, Introduction, pp. ix ff.

The editors would like to thank Mrs. A. M. Erskine of Exeter Cathedral Library for her help in making available the Exon. MS.

SŪMERSETE.

HIC ANNOTANTVR TENENTES TERRAS IN SUMMERSETE.

.I. REX WILLELMVS

.II. Eps Wintonienſis.

.III. Eps Sariſberienſis.

.IIII. Eps Baiocenſis.

.V. Eps Conſtantienſis.

.VI. Eps Wellenſis.

.VII. Æccła de Bada.

.VIII. Æccła de Glaſtingberiens.

.IX. Æccła Micelenienſis.

.X. Æccła Adelingienſis.

.XI. Æccła Romana S PETRI.

.XII. Æccła de Cadom.

.XIII. Æccła de Monteburg.

.XIIII. Æccła de Scefteſberie.

.XV. Eps Mauricius.

.XVI. Clerici tenentes de rege.

.XVII. Comes Euſtachius

.XVIII. Comes Hugo.

.XIX. Comes Moritonienſis.

.XX. Balduin de Execeſtre.

.XXI. Rogerius de Corcelle.

.XXII. Rogerius Arundel.

.XXIII. Walterius gifard.

.XXIIII. Walterius de douuai. *uel Walſcin*

XXV. Willelmus de Moion.

XXVI. Willelm de Ow.

XXVII. Willelm de Faleiſe.

.XXVIII. Willelm fili Widonis.

XXIX. Radulf de Mortemer.

.XXX. Radulf de Pomerei.

.XXXI. Radulf pagenel.

XXXII. Radulf de Limeſi.

.XXXIII. Robt filius Giroldi.

.XXXIIII. Alured de Merleberge.

.XXXV. Alured de Iſpania.

.XXXVI. Turſtin filius Rolf.

.XXXVII. Serlo de Burci.

.XXXVIII. Odo filius Gamelin XXXIX Oſbnus *gifard*

.XL. Eduuard de Sariſberia.

.XLI. Ernulfus de Heſding.

.XLII. Gisłebtus filius Turold

.XLIII. Godebold. XLIIII. Mathi de More *tania*

.XLV. Hunfrid camerarius.

.XLVI. Robt de Odburuile 7 alij ſeruient *regis.*

XLVII. Taini regis.

SOMERSET

LIST OF LANDHOLDERS IN SOMERSET

1	King William	23	Walter Giffard
2	The Bishop of Winchester	24	Walter, or Walscin, of Douai
3	The Bishop of Salisbury	25	William of Mohun
4	The Bishop of Bayeux	26	William of Eu
5	The Bishop of Coutances	27	William of Falaise
6	The Bishop of Wells	28	William son of Guy
7	Bath Church	29	Ralph of Mortimer
8	Glastonbury Church	30	Ralph of Pomeroy
9	Muchelney Church	31	Ralph Pagnell
10	Athelney Church	32	Ralph of Limesy
11	St. Peter's Church, Rome	33	Robert son of Gerald
12	Caen Church	34	Alfred of Marlborough
13	Montebourg Church	35	Alfred of 'Spain'
14	Shaftesbury Church	36	Thurstan son of Rolf
15	Bishop Maurice	37	Serlo of Burcy
16	The Clergy who hold from the King	38	Odo son of Gamelin
		39	Osbern Giffard
17	Count Eustace	40	Edward of Salisbury
18	Earl Hugh	41	Arnulf of Hesdin
19	The Count of Mortain	42	Gilbert son of Thorold
20	Baldwin of Exeter	43	Godbold
21	Roger of Courseulles	44	Matthew of Mortagne
22	Roger Arundel	45	Humphrey the Chamberlain
		46	Robert of Auberville and others of the King's servants
		47	The King's Thanes

Terra Regis.

Rex tenet *Svmertone* . Rex . E . tenuit . Nunq̄
geldauit . neq̄ scit q̄t hidæ sint ibi . Tra . ē . L . car̄.
In dñio st̄ . v . car̄ . 7 IIII . serui . 7 q̄t xx . uitti . 7 XXVIII.
borđ cū . XL . car̄ . Ibi . c . ac̄ pti . 7 una leu pasturæ
in lḡ . 7 dimiđ leū lat̄ . Silua . I . leū lḡ . 7 una q̄ lat̄.
Ibi Burgū qđ uocat̄ *Lanporth* . in quó manej̄ . xxx
IIII . burḡfes redđ . xv . foliđ . 7 II . pifcariæ redđ . x . fot̄.
Reddit p̄ anñ . LXX.IX . liḃ 7 x . foliđ 7 VII . denar̄.
de . xx . in ora.

Huic c̄ additæ st̄ . III . træ q̄s teneḃ . III . taini . T.R.E.
Brifnod 7 Aluric 7 Sauuin . 7 gelđ p̄ . v . hiđ 7 dimiđ.
Ibi st̄ . VII . uitti 7 v . borđ cū . IIII . car̄ . Redđ . VII . liḃ 7 xv.
De hoc c̄ . ē ablata dimiđ hida *Denesmodes*   ⌐foliđ.
Welle . q̄ fuit de dñica firma regis . E . Aluredus
de hifpania teñ . 7 ualet . x . foliđ.

Rex teñ *Cedrē* . Rex . E . tenuit . Nunq̄ geldauit.
nec fcit q̄t hidæ sint ibi . Tra . ē . xx . car̄ . In dñio
st̄ . III . car̄ . 7 II . serui . 7 uñ colibt̄ . 7 XVII . uitti 7 xx.
borđ cū . XVII . car̄ . 7 VII . gablatores redđ . XVII . fot̄.
In *Alsebrvge* . XXXII . burḡfes redđ . xx . foliđ.
Ibi . II . molini redđ . XII . foliđ 7 VI . denar̄ . 7 III . pif
cariæ redđ . x . foliđ . 7 xv . ac̄ pti . Paftura . I . leū lḡ.
7 tñtđ lat̄ . Redđ p̄ anñ . xxi . liḃ 7 II . den 7 obolū
de . xx . in ora . Silua . II . leū lḡ . 7 dīm leū lat̄.
De hoc c̄ teñ Gifo eṗs uñ mēbrū *Wetmore* . qđ
ipfe tenuit de rege . E . Pro eo cōputat Witts uicecom
in firma regis . XII . liḃ . unoq̄q̄ anno.
De ipfo c̄ . ē ablata dimiđ v̄ træ . q̄ fuit de dñica
firma regis . E . Robt̄ de Otburguile teñ . 7 xv . deñ uat̄.
Hæc . II . c̄ *Svmertone* 7 *Cedre* . cū appenđ fuis.
reddeḃ firmā unius noctis T.R.E.

The King holds
1 SOMERTON. King Edward held it. It has never paid tax,
nor is it known how many hides are there. Land for 50
ploughs. In lordship 5 ploughs; 4 slaves;
    80 villagers and 28 smallholders with 40 ploughs.   89
    Meadow, 100 acres; pasture, 1 league in length and ½   b5
      league wide; woodland 1 league long and 1 furlong wide.
    A town which is called LANGPORT in which 34 burgesses live   E
      who pay 15s; 2 fisheries which pay 10s. 2 cobs; 9 pigs; 500 sheep. E
It pays £79 10s 7d a year at 20 (pence) to the *ora*.
    To this manor 3 lands have been added which three thanes,   E 90
Brictnoth, Aelfric and Saewin, held before 1066; they paid   D a2
tax for 5½ hides.
    7 villagers and 5 smallholders with 4 ploughs.
They pay £7 15s.
    From this manor ½ hide, DEADMANS WELL, has been taken   E
away which was (part) of the lordship revenue of King Edward.   89
Alfred of 'Spain' holds it. Value 10s.   b5

2 CHEDDAR. King Edward held it. It has never paid tax, nor
is it known how many hides are there. Land for 20 ploughs.
In lordship 3 ploughs; 2 slaves; 1 freedman;
    17 villagers and 20 smallholders with 17 ploughs.   90
      7 people who pay 17s in tribute. In Axbridge 32   a1
      burgesses who pay 20s.
    2 mills which pay 12s 6d; 3 fisheries which pay 10s;
      meadow, 15 acres; pasture 1 league long and as wide.
      6 cattle; 15 pigs; 100 sheep.
It pays £21 2½d a year at 20 (pence) to the *ora*.
Woodland 2 leagues long and ½ league wide.
    Of this manor Bishop Giso holds 1 member, WEDMORE, which   E
he held himself from King Edward. William the Sheriff
accounts £12 for it in the King's revenue every year.
    From this manor ½ virgate of land has been taken·away
which was (part) of the lordship revenue of King Edward.
Robert of Auberville holds it. Value 15d.

These 2 manors of SOMERTON and CHEDDAR, with their dependencies,   90
paid one night's revenue before 1066.   a2

Rex ten⁊ NORT/PERET . Rex . E . tenuit . Nunq̄ geldauit.

nec ſciť q̃t hidæ ſť ibi . Tra . ē . xxx . car̄ . In dñio ſť . iii .

car̄ . ⁊ xx . uiłłi ⁊ xix . borđ . ⁊ xx . porcarij cū . xxiii . car̄ .

Ibi moliñ redđ . xv . denar̄ . ⁊ c . ãc p̃ti . ⁊ ii . leū paſturæ .

redđ . xx . ſoł p añ .   /in ora.

Redđ hoc m̄ . xlii . liꝑ ⁊ viii . ſoł ⁊ iiii . den⁊ de . xx .

Rex ten⁊ SVDPERET . Rex . E . tenuit . Nunq̄ gel

dauit . nec ſciť q̃t hidæ ſť ibi . Tra . ē . xxviii . car̄ .

In dñio ſť . ii . car̄ . ⁊ v . ſerui . ⁊ xxii . coliꝑti . ⁊ lxiii .

uiłłi ⁊ xv . borđ cū . xxvi . car̄ . Ibi moliñ redđ . xx .

ſoliđ . ⁊ l . ãc p̃ti . Silua . xi . q̃rent⁊ lḡ . ⁊ x . q̃ꝗ lať .

Redđ . xlii . liꝑ ⁊ c . denar⁊ de . xx . in ora .

De hoc m̄ tenuit Merleſuain . ii . hiđ in STRATONE .

T . R . E . ⁊ erat tainlande . Reddit m̄ . lx . ſoł in firma regis .

De ipſo m̄ ablata . ē dimiđ hiđ . Norman tenet de

Rogerio de curcelle . ⁊ ualet . xvi . ſoliđ .

Huic m̄ reddebaṫ T . R . E . de Cruche p añ c̄ſuetudo .

hoc . ē . vi . oues cū agnis totiđ . ⁊ q̃ſꝗ liꝑ hō . i . blomā .

ferri . Turſtin ten⁹ de comite moritoñ . ſed c̄ſuetudinē

ñ reddiđ poſtꝗ comes tr̄a⁊ habuit .

Rex ten⁊ CHVRI . Rex . E . tenuit . Nunq̄ geldau⁊ .

nec ſciť q̃t hidæ ſť ibi . Tra . ē . xiii . car̄ . In dñio

ſť . iii . car̄ . ⁊ v . ſerui . ⁊ xx . uiłłi . ⁊ ii . borđ . cū . x . car̄ .

Ibi . xl . ãc p̃ti . ⁊ Silua . ii . leū lḡ . ⁊ una leū lať .

Redđ . xxi . liꝑ ⁊ l . den⁊ de . xx . in ora .

De hoc m̄ eſt ablata una v⁊ tr̄æ⁊ . Bretel ten⁊ de comite

moritoñ⁊ . ⁊ ualet . x . ſoliđ ⁊ viii . denar⁊ .

H̄ . iii . Maner⁊ Nordperet ⁊ Sudperet ⁊ Churi T . R . E

reddeꝑ firm̄a uni⁹ noctis cū c̄ſuetudinibꝗ ſuis .

3 NORTH PETHERTON. King Edward held it. It has never paid
tax, nor is it known how many hides are there. Land for 30   E
ploughs. In lordship 3 ploughs;
    20 villagers, 19 smallholders, 6 slaves and 20 pigmen   E
      with 23 ploughs.   88
    A mill which pays 15d; meadow, 100 acres; pasture, 2 leagues,   b1
      which pays 20s a year. 2 cattle; 100 sheep.
This manor pays £42 8s 4d at 20 (pence) to the *ora*.

4 SOUTH PETHERTON. King Edward held it. It has never paid
tax, nor is it known how many hides are there. Land for 28
ploughs. In lordship 2 ploughs; 5 slaves; 22 freedmen;   88
    63 villagers and 15 smallholders with 26 ploughs.   b2
    A mill which pays 20s; meadow, 50 acres; woodland 11
      furlongs long and 10 furlongs wide. 2 cobs; 1 cow; 12 pigs; 63 sheep.
It pays £42 100d at 20 (pence) to the *ora*.
    Of this manor Merleswein held 2 hides in (Over) STRATTON before
1066; it was thaneland. It now pays 60s in the King's revenue.   E
    From this manor ½ hide has been taken away. Norman holds   E
from Roger of Courseulles. Value 16s.
    Before 1066 a customary due was paid every year to this
manor from Cricket (St. Thomas); that is 6 sheep with as   E
many lambs, and each free man (paid) 1 bloom of iron. Thurstan E
holds from the Count of Mortain; but he has not paid the
customary due since the Count has had the land.

5 CURRY (Rivel). King Edward held it. It has never paid   E
tax, nor is it known how many hides are there. Land for 13
ploughs. In lordship 3 ploughs; 5 slaves;   89
    20 villagers and 2 smallholders with 10 ploughs.   a1
    Meadow, 40 acres; woodland 2 leagues long and 1 league wide.
      1 cob; 8 cattle; 11 pigs; 64 sheep.
It pays £21 50d at 20 (pence) to the *ora*.
    From this manor 1 virgate of land has been taken away.
Bretel holds from the Count of Mortain. Value 10s 8d.

These 3 manors, NORTH PETHERTON, SOUTH PETHERTON and CURRY
(Rivel), paid one night's revenue with its customary dues
before 1066.

Rᴇx teñ *WILLETONE*. 7 *CANDETONE* 7 *CARENTONE*.

Rex.E.tenuit. Nunq geldaueř.nec ſciꝉ q̃t hidæ ibi ſꝉ.

Tra.ē.c.cař. In dñio ſꝉ.xi.cař 7 dimiđ.7 xi.ſerui.

7 xxx.colibti.7 xxxviii.uiłłi 7 l.borđ cũ.xxxvii.cař

7 dimiđ.Ibi.ii.molini redđ.v.ſoꝉ.7 ciiii.ãc p̃ti.

Paſtura.v.leũ in l̅g̅.7 iii.leũ   in laꝉ.Silua.iiii.

leũ in l̅g̅.7 ii.leũ 7 dim in laꝉ.   Ꝼ in ora

Redđit.c.libꝰ 7 cxvi.ſoliđ 7 xvi.denař 7 obolũ de.xx.

T.R.E.reddeꝋ firmã unius noctis.

Huic Ɱ Welletone.ē addita dimiđ hida.Saric tenuit

T.R.E.ꝑ.ii.Maṅ.7 ꝑ dim hida geldꝋ.Tra.ē.v.cař.Ibi

vi.uiłłi 7 iiii.borđ hñt.iii.cař.7 iiii.ãc p̃ti ibi.Silua

iiii.q̃ꝫ in l̅g̅.7 una q̃ꝫ in laꝉ.Redđ.xxxi.ſoꝉ 7 viii.deñ.

Eiđ Ɱ addita.ē alia dimiđ hida.*WAISTOV*.quã tenuit

Aluuiñ T.R.E.7 ꝑ dimiđ hida geldꝋ.Tra.ē.i.cař.Redđ

xl.deñ.Adhuc ipſi Ɱ addita.ē dimiđ hida.

7 redđ in firma regis.vii.ſoꝉ.De *SELVERE* Ɱ Aluredi

addita.ē huic Ɱ una cſuetudo.id eſt.xviii.oues in anno.

Ħ ñ p̃tinuit in Welletone T.R.E.

Rᴇx teñ *BEIMINSTRE*.Rex.E.tenuit.Nunq

geldau.nec ſciꝉ q̃t hidæ ſꝉ ibi.Tra.ē.xxvi.cař.In dñio

ſꝉ.iii.cař.7 iii.ſerui.7 xxv.uiłłi 7 xxii.borđ cũ.x.cař.

Ibi moliñ redđ.v.ſoꝉ.7 xxxiiii.ãc p̃ti.Silua.ii.leũ l̅g̅.7 una

leũ laꝉ.Redđ.xxi.libꝰ.7 ii.denař 7 obolũ de.xx.in ora.

Pꝋr huj Ɱ teñ trã ad.i.cař.7 ualet.xx.ſoliđ.

De hoc Ɱ teñ eꝑs cſtantiens.cxii.acs p̃ti 7 ſiluæ.

Rᴇx teñ *FROME*.Rex.E.tenuit.Nunq geldauit.

nec ſciꝉ q̃t hidæ ſꝉ ibi.Tra.ē.l.cař.In dñio ſꝉ.iii.cař.

7 vi.colibti.7 xxxi.uiłłs 7 xxxvi.borđ cũ.xl.cař.

6   WILLITON, CANNINGTON and CARHAMPTON.   King Edward held   86 c
them. They have never paid tax, nor is it known how many   E
hides are there. Land for 100 ploughs. In lordship   89
11½ ploughs; 11 slaves; 30 freedmen;   a2
     38 villagers and 50 smallholders with 37½ ploughs.
     2 mills which pay 5s; meadow, 104 acres; pasture 5 leagues
        in length and 3 leagues in width; woodland 4 leagues in
        length and 2½ leagues in width.   2 cobs; 11 pigs; 350 sheep.
It [pays] £100 116s 16½d at 20 (pence) to the *ora*. Before   E
1066 it paid one night's revenue.
     To this manor of Williton ½ hide has been added. Saeric   E
held it before 1066 as two manors; it paid tax for ½ hide.
Land for 5 ploughs.   89
     6 villagers and 4 smallholders have 3 ploughs.   b1
     Meadow, 4 acres; woodland 4 furlongs in length and 1
        furlong in width.
It pays 31s 8d.
     To the same manor has been added another ½ hide, WESTOWE,   E
which Alwin held before 1066; it paid tax for ½ hide.   89
Land for 1 plough. It pays 40d.   b2
     A further ½ hide has been added to this manor; it pays   E 89
7s in the King's revenue.   b3
     From Alfred's manor of MONKSILVER has been added to this   E
manor 1 customary due, that is 18 sheep a year. This did   89
not belong to Williton before 1066.   b4

      To Williton has been added 1 virgate of land called *Ledforda* , which Dunn   509
      held in 1066; value 2s a year.   b 9

7   BEDMINSTER. King Edward held it. It has never paid tax,   E
nor is it known how many hides are there. Land for 26 ploughs.
In lordship 3 ploughs; 3 slaves;   90
     25 villagers and 22 smallholders with 10 ploughs.   b1
     A mill which pays 5s; meadow, 34 acres; woodland 2 leagues
        long and 1 league wide.   1 cob; 9 cattle; 22 pigs; 115 sheep.
It pays £21 2½d at 20 (pence) to the *ora*.   E
     A priest of this manor holds land for 1 plough. Value 20s.   E
     Of this manor Bishop Geoffrey of Coutances holds 112 acres of   E
meadow and woodland.

8   FROME. King Edward held it. It has never paid tax, nor   E
is it known how many hides are there. Land for 50 ploughs.
In lordship 3 ploughs; 6 freedmen;   90
     31 villagers and 36 smallholders with 40 ploughs.   b2

Ibi.iii.molini redd.xxv.folid.7 mercatū redd.xlvi.

folid 7 viii.denar.Ibi.xxx.ac p̃ti.7 l.ac pafturæ.

Silua.i.leū lḡ.7 tntd laƚ.

Redd.liii.liƀ 7 v.denar de.xx.in ora.

De hoc m̃ tenet æccƚa S̃ Joḣis de Froma.viii.car træ

7 fimiliƚ tenuit T.R.E.Reinbald ibi.ē p̃br.

REX ten̄ BRVMETONE.Rex.E.tenuit.Nunq̨

geldauit.nec fciƚ q̃t hidæ ſƚ ibi.Tra.ē.l.car̄.

In dn̄io ſƚ.iii.car̄.7 v.ferui 7 iiii.coliƀti.7 xxviii.

uiƚƚi 7 xxvi.bord cū.xviii.car̄.Ibi.v.burḡfes

7 un porcari.Ibi.vi.molini redd.xx.folid.7 xxx

viii.ac p̃ti.7 cl.ac pafturæ.Siluæ.v.leū in lḡ.

7 una leū in laƚ.

Redd.liii.liƀ 7 v.denar de.xx.in ora. ⌐noƈtis.

Hoc m̃ cū fupiori FROME:T.R.E.reddeƀ firmā uni

De hoc m̃ ſƚ ablati.ix.agri.q̃s ten̄ Breteƚ de comite

moriton.7 uaƚ xviii.denar.

De eod m̃.ē ablata dimiḋ hida in CILEMETONE.Serlo

de burci ten̄ 7 ualet.x.folid.De dn̄ica firma fuer̄.

De ipfo m̃.ē ablata.i.hida.Gozelin ten̄ de Roƀto filio

Giroƚd.Tra.ē.iii.car̄.Valƀ.xl.folid.Modo.xx.folid.

REX ten̄ MILEBVRNE.Rex.E.tenuit.Nunquā

geldauit.nec fciƚ q̃t hidæ ſƚ ibi.Tra.ē.l.car̄.In dn̄io

ſƚ.iiii.car̄.7 v.ferui.7 lxx.uiƚƚi 7 xviii.bord.cū.lxv.

car̄.Ibi.vi.molini redd.lxxvii.folid.7 vi.denar̄.

7 c.lxx.ac p̃ti.Silua.ii.leū in lḡ.7 ix.q̃ƶ laƚ.Paftura

iiii.q̃ƶ lḡ.7 ii.q̃ƶ laƚ.7 una leū Moræ.

In hoc m̃ ſƚ.lvi.burḡfes.7 mercato Reddtes.lx.foƚ.

IN GIVELCESTRE funt.cvii.burḡfes redd xx.folid.

Mercatū cū fuis append.redd.xi.liƀ.

3 mills which pay 25s; a market which pays 46s 8d;
meadow, 30 acres; pasture, 50 acres; woodland
1 league long and as wide. 24 pigs; 100 sheep, less 7.
It pays £53 5d at 20 (pence) to the *ora*.

Of this manor St. John's Church, Frome, holds 8 carucates E
of land; it held them similarly before 1066. Reinbald is a E
priest there. E

9 BRUTON. King Edward held it. It never paid tax, nor
is it known how many hides are there. Land for 50 ploughs.
In lordship 3 ploughs; 5 slaves; 4 freedmen;
28 villagers and 26 smallholders with 18 ploughs. 5 burgesses;
1 pigman who pays 5 pigs a year. 90
6 mills which pay 20s; meadow, 38 acres; pasture, b3
150 acres; woodland, 5 leagues in length and
1 league in width. 80 sheep; 13 goats.
It pays £53 5d at 20 (pence) to the *ora*.

This manor with the above one, Frome, paid one night's E
revenue before 1066.

From this manor 9 acres have been taken away, which Bretel E 91
holds from the Count of Mortain. Value 18d. a1

From the same manor ½ hide in KILMINGTON has been taken E 91
away. Serlo of Burcy holds it. Value 10s. It was (part) of the a2
lordship revenue.

From this manor 1 hide has been taken away. Jocelyn of Rivers E
holds from Robert son of Gerald. Land for 3 ploughs. 91
The value was 40s; now 20s. a3

10 MILBORNE (Port). King Edward held it. It has never paid tax, E
nor is it known how many hides are there. Land for 50 91
ploughs. In lordship 4 ploughs; 5 slaves; a4
70 villagers and 18 smallholders with 65 ploughs. E
6 mills which pay 77s 6d; meadow, 170 acres; woodland
2 leagues in length and 9 furlongs wide; pasture 4
furlongs long and 2 furlongs wide; moor, 1 league.
2 cobs; 22 pigs; 153 sheep.
In this manor 56 burgesses who pay 60s with the market. E
In ILCHESTER 107 burgesses who pay 20s. The market with 91
its dependencies pays £11 into the King's revenue. b1

Toť *MELEBVRNE* cū p̄dictis append .redd q̇ṫ xx.liƀ
de albo argento ix.ſoliď 7 v.deñ miñ.T.R.E.reddeƀ
dimiď firmā noctis 7 quadrantē.　　　　Ｆſoliď.
Reinbalď teñ æcclam cū.i.hida.Ibi h̄ṫ.i.caῥ.Val xxx.

86 d

Ｒex teñ *BRVNETONE*.Ghida tenuit T.R.E.7 gelďƀ p̣ x.hiď.
Ṫra.ē.lx.caῥ.De ea sī in dñio.iii.hidæ.7 ibi.iii.caῥ.7 vii.ſerui.
7 l.uiłłi 7 xvii.borď.cū.xx.caῥ.Ibi.ii.molini redď.iii.ſoliď.7 lx.ãc
p̄ti.Paſtura.iii.leū lḡ.7 una leū laῥ.7 tn̄tď Siluæ in lḡ 7 laῥ.
Redď.xxvii.liƀ 7 xii.ſoł 7 uñ deñ de albo argento.
De his.x.hiď teñ p̄br.i.elemoſina de rege.Ibi h̄ṫ.i.caῥ.7 iiii.uiłł
cū.i.caῥ.7 iii.acs p̄ti.Valet.xx.ſoliď.
De hoc m̄ teñ Com̄ moriť.i.hiď in *PRESTETVNE*.q̇ fuit de dñica
firma.T.R.E.Ṫra.ē.iiii.caῥ.Ibi sī.ii.caῥ.Val.xl.ſoliď.7 ualuit.
De hoc m̄ ablaṫ.ē tcius denaῥ de *MILVERTONE*.qui reddebaṫ ibi
Ｒex teñ *DOLVERTVNE*.Herald tenuit T.R.E.7 gelďƀ　Ｆ T.R.E.
p̣.ii.hiď 7 dimiď.Ṫra.ē.xi.caῥ.De ea.ē in dñio.i.hida.7 ibi sī.ii.caῥ.
7 vi.ſerui.7 xvii.uiłłi 7 vi.borď cū.iii.caῥ 7 dim.Ibi.iii.ac p̄ti.Paſtura
una leū lḡ.7 dim leū laῥ.7 tn̄tď ſiluæ.
Reddit.xi.liƀ.7 x.ſoliď.de albo argento.
Huic m̄ sī additæ.ii.hidæ ṫræ dimiď ferding miñ.Duodeci̇ taini te
neƀ T.R.E.Ṫra.ē.x.caῥ.Ibi sī.viii.uiłłi cū.iiii.caῥ 7 dimiď.7 iii.ãc
p̄ti.7 paſtura dimiď leū lḡ.7 iiii.q̇ł̇ laῥ.Silua.i.leū lḡ.7 dimiď leū laῥ.
Valet.lxiiii.ſoliď.7 ii.deñ.
De hoc m̄.ē ablata c̄ſuetudo de m̄ comiṫ moritoñ *BRIGEFORD*.hoc.eſt
xxiiii.oues p̄ añ.q̇ ibi reddebanṫ.T.R.E.Malgerius detiñ p̄ comiṫē.

The whole of Milborne (Port) with the said dependencies pays £80 of white silver, less 9s 5d. Before 1066 it paid ½ and ¼ night's revenue.

    Reinbald holds the church with 1 hide; he has 1 plough. Value 30s.

E 91
b2

11 BROMPTON (Regis). Gytha held it before 1066; it paid tax for 10 hides. Land for 60 ploughs, of which 3 hides are in lordship; 3 ploughs there; 7 slaves;

    50 villagers and 17 smallholders with 20 ploughs & 5 hides.

      15 pigmen who pay 32s a year.

    2 mills which pay 3s; meadow, 60 acres; pasture 3 leagues long and 1 league wide; woodland, as much in length and width.

86 d

103
a 1

E

It pays £27 12s 1d of white silver.

    A priest holds 1 of these 10 hides in alms from the King. He has 1 plough & 3 virgates in lordship.

    4 villagers with 1 plough & 1 virgate.

    Meadow, 3 acres. 4 cattle; 9 pigs; 30 sheep; 7 goats.

Value 20s.

    Of this manor the Count of Mortain holds 1 hide in PRESTON, which was (part) of the lordship revenue before 1066. Land for 4 ploughs. 2 ploughs there. The value was and is 40s.

Hugh of Vautortes now holds it from the Count of Mortain.

    From this manor has been taken away the third penny of MILVERTON, which was paid there before 1066 as a customary due.

E

E
L
E

12 DULVERTON. Earl Harold held it before 1066; it paid tax for 2½ hides. Land for 11 ploughs, of which 1 hide is in lordship; 2 ploughs there; 6 slaves;

    17 villagers and 6 smallholders with 3½ ploughs & 1½ hides.

    Meadow, 3 acres; pasture 1 league long and ½ league wide; woodland, as much. 6 cattle; 30 sheep.

103
b 1

It pays £11 10s of white silver.

    To this manor have been added 2 hides of land, less ½ furlong. Thirteen thanes held them before 1066. Land for 10 ploughs.

    8 villagers with 4½ ploughs.

    Meadow, 3 acres; pasture ½ league long and 4 furlongs wide; woodland 1 league long and ½ league wide.

E
E

Value 64s 2d.

    From this manor has been taken away a customary due of Brushford, the Count of Mortain's manor, that is 24 sheep a year, which were paid there before 1066. Mauger keeps it back through the Count.

E

Rex ten CLIVE. Herald tenuit T.R.E.7 geldb p.IIII.hid 7 una v træ.
Tra.e.xxxiii.car.De ea.e in dnio.I.hida.7 ibi.III.car.7 IIII.ferui.7 xix.
uilli.7 ix.bord cu.xviii.car.Ibi.ii.molini redd.LIIII.denar.7 xxiiii.
ac pti.Silua.I.leu lg.7 dimid leu lat.Redd.xxiii.lib de albo argto.
Huic M adjacuit tcius denar de Burgherift 7 Caretone 7 Willetone
7 Cantetone.7 Nordpereth.

Rex ten NETELCVBE.Goduin tenuit T.R.E.7 geldb p.ii.hid 7 iii.v træ.
Tra.e.xii.car.De ea.e in dnio una v 7 dimid.7 ibi.ii.car.7 iii.ferui.
7 xv.uilli 7 iiii.bord cu.vii.car.Ibi.vi.ac pti.7 c.ac pafturæ.
rq 7 l.ac filuæ.Redd   lib xii.folid.de albo argento.

Rex ten CAPINTONE.Herald tenuit 7 geldb p una hida.Tra.e
.v.car.De ea.e dimid hida in dnio.7 ibi.i.car.7 v.uilli cu.i.car.
Ibi.viii.ac pti.7 xx.ac pafturæ.7 x.ac filuæ.

Redd.xLvi.folid de albo argento.

Rex ten LANGEFORD.Goduin tenuit T.R.E.7 geldb p.v.hid.
Tra.e.x.car.De ea.e in dnio.I.hida 7 dimid.7 ibi.i.car.7 iiii.ferui.7 xxi.
uilt 7 iiii.bord cu.viii.car.Ibi molin redd.vii.fot.7 vi.den.7 viii.ac pti.
7 c.ac pafturæ.7 xxx.ac filuæ.Redd.iiii.lib 7 xii.folid.

Rex ten WINESFORD.Tofti tenuit T.R.E.7 geldb p.iii.hid 7 dimid.
Tra.e.Lx.car.De ea.e in dnio dim hida.7 ibi.ii.car.7 ix.ferui.7 xxxviii.
uilti cu|.xiii.car.Ibi molin redd.vi.den.7 viii.ac pti.7 xL.ac filuæ.
Paftura.iiii.leu lg.7 ii.leu lat.Redd.x.lib 7 x.fot.de albo argento.
Huic M.e addita dimid hida.Tres taini teneb T.R.E.7 feruieb ppofito
M p cfuetud abfq omi firma donante.Tra.e.iiii.car.Ibi.ft.iii.uilli
7 xxiii.bord.Redd.xx.folid.

13 (Old) CLEEVE.   Earl Harold held it before 1066; it paid
tax for 4 hides and 1 virgate of land. Land for 33 ploughs,
of which 1 hide is in lordship; 3 ploughs there; 4 slaves;
    19 villagers and 9 smallholders with 18 ploughs & the rest of the land.
    2 mills which pay 54d; meadow, 24 acres; woodland 1 league
       long and ½ league wide. 1 cob; 14 pigs; 300 wethers; 50 goats.
It pays £23 of white silver; when William of Mohun acquired it, as much.
    To this manor was attached the third penny of the 'borough -
right' (of) Carhampton, Williton, Cannington, and North Petherton.

103
b 2

14 NETTLECOMBE.   Godwin son of Harold held it before 1066; it
paid tax for 2 hides and 3 virgates of land. Land for
12 ploughs, of which 1½ virgates are in lordship; 2 ploughs
there; 3 slaves;
    15 villagers and 4 smallholders with 7 ploughs & 1½ hides & 1 virgate.
    Meadow, 6 acres; pasture, 100 acres; woodland, 50 acres. 1 cob.
It pays £... 12s of white silver; when William acquired it, as much.

104
a 1

15 CAPTON.   Earl Harold held it; it paid tax for 1 hide. Land for
5 ploughs, of which ½ hide is in lordship; 1 plough there;
    5 villagers with 1 plough & ½ hide.
    Meadow, 8 acres; pasture, 20 acres; woodland,
      10 acres. 4 cattle; 50 sheep.
It pays 46s of white silver; when William acquired it, as much.

104
a 2

16 LANGFORD (Budville).   Godwin son of Harold held it before 1066;
it paid tax for 5 hides. Land for 10 ploughs, of which 1½ hides
are in lordship; 1 plough there; 4 slaves;
    21 villagers and 4 smallholders with 8 ploughs & 3½ hides.
    A mill which pays 7s 6d; meadow, 8 acres; pasture, 100
      acres; woodland, 30 acres. 1 cob; 3 cattle; 10 pigs; 30 sheep; 18 goats.
It pays £4 12s; when William acquired it, as much.

104
a 3

17 WINSFORD.   Earl Tosti held it before 1066; it paid tax
for 3½ hides. Land for 60 ploughs, of which ½ hide is
in lordship; 2 ploughs there; 9 slaves;
    38 villagers and 11 smallholders with 13 ploughs & the rest of the land.
    A mill which pays 6d; meadow, 8 acres; woodland, 40
      acres; pasture 4 leagues long and 2 leagues wide. 52 sheep.
It pays £10 10s of white silver; when William acquired it, as much.
    To this manor ½ hide has been added. Three thanes held it
before 1066 and served the reeve of the manor as a customary
due without giving any revenue. Land for 4 ploughs.
    3 villagers and 23 smallholders.
It pays 20s into the King's revenue; when William of Mohun acquired it, as much.

104
b 1

E
E

REX ten̄ *CRICE*. Gunnild tenuit T.R.E. 7 geldб p. x. hid̄ 7 dimid̄.
Tra. ē. VIII. car̄. De ea st̄ in dn̄io. VI. hidæ. 7 ibi. II. car̄. 7 VI. ſerui. 7 XX.
uitti. 7 X. bord̄ cū. VI. car̄. Ibi molin̄ redd̄. VIII. den̄. 7 VIII. ac̄ pti.
Paſtura. I. leū lḡ. 7 tntd̄ lat̄. Silua. I. q̄z lḡ. 7 tntd̄ lat̄.
Redd̄. IX. lib 7 IIII. ſolid̄ de albo argento. Ibi. ē piſcaria. ſ3 n̄ ptin̄ ad firmā.
REX ten̄ *NORTCVRI*. Herald com tenuit T.R.E. 7 geldб p. XX. hid̄. Tra. ē
XL. car̄. De ea st̄ in dn̄io. V. hidæ. 7 ibi. V. car̄. 7 XVIII. ſerui. 7 XXIII.
colibi. 7 C. uitti V. min̄. 7 XV. bord̄ cū. XXX. car̄. Ibi. LX. ac̄ pti. 7 L. ac̄
ſiluæ. paſtura. II. leū lḡ. 7 una leū lat̄. Huic m̄ ptin̄. V. burḡſes
in Langporth. redd̄. XXXVIII. den̄. 7 XVIII. ſerui. 7 IIII. porcarij. 7 II. cot̄.
Tot̄ Redd̄. XXIII. lib de albo argento. Ibi. ē piſcaria ſ; n̄ ptin̄ ad firmā.
7 VII. ac̄ uineæ.
Æcclam huj m̄ ten̄ Mauricī eps. cū. III. hid̄ de ead̄ tra. Ibi ht̄. VII. uitt̄.
7 XI. bord̄ 7 II. ſeruos cū. IIII. car̄. 7 XVIII. acs pti. 7 V. acs paſturæ.
7 XII. acs ſiluæ. Redd̄. LX. ſolid̄.
De ead̄ tra huj m̄ ten̄ Anſger. I. hid̄ de comite morit̄. Val̄. XX. ſol̄.
REX ten̄ *CRVCHE*. Eddeua tenuit T.R.E. 7 non geldб. nec ſcitur q̄t
ibi hidæ habent̄. Tra. ē. XL. car̄. In dn̄io st̄. V. car̄. 7 XII. ſerui. 7 XXVI.
colibti. 7 XL. II. uitti 7 XLV. bord̄. cū. XX. car̄. Ibi. IIII. molini redd̄
XL. ſolid̄. 7 Mercat̄ redd̄. IIII. lib. Ibi. LX. ac̄ pti. Paſtura dim̄ leū lḡ.
87 a
7 IIII. q̄z lat̄. Silua. IIII. q̄z lḡ. 7 II. q̄z lat̄.
Redd̄. XLVI. lib de albo argento.
De hoc m̄ eſt ablat̄ *ESTHAM*. T.R.E. fuit de firma m̄. 7 n̄ poterat
inde ſeparari. Turſtin̄ ten̄ de comite moriton̄. Val̄. L. ſolid̄.

18 CREECH (St. Michael), Gunhilda held it before 1066; it
paid tax for 10½ hides. Land for 8 ploughs, of which 6
hides are in lordship; 2 ploughs there; 6 slaves;
> 20 villagers and 10 smallholders with 6 ploughs & 4½ hides.   104
> A mill which pays 8d; meadow, 8 acres; pasture 1   b 2
> league long and as wide; woodland 1 furlong long
> and as wide. 1 cob; 10 cattle; 10 pigs; 48 sheep.

It pays £9 4s of white silver; when William acquired it, as much.
> A fishery there, but it does not belong to the revenue.

19 NORTH CURRY. Earl Harold held it before 1066; it paid tax
for 20 hides. Land for 40 ploughs, of which 5 hides are
in lordship; 5 ploughs there; 18 slaves; 23 freedmen;
> 100 villagers, less 5, and 15 smallholders with 30 ploughs   105
> & 11 hides.   a 1
> Meadow, 60 acres; woodland, 50 acres; pasture 2 leagues
> long and 1 league wide. 1 cob; 20 cattle; 20 pigs; 100 sheep.
> To this manor belong 5 burgesses in Langport who pay 38d;
> 18 slaves; 4 pigmen; 2 cottagers.

The whole pays £23 of white silver; when William acquired it, as much.
> A fishery there, but it does not belong to the revenue;

vineyard, 7 acres.
> Bishop Maurice holds this manor's church with 3 hides of   E

this land. He has
> 7 villagers, 11 smallholders and 2 slaves with 4 ploughs;
> meadow, 18 acres; pasture, 5 acres; woodland, 12 acres.

It pays 60s.
> Ansger the Breton holds 1 hide of this manor's land from   E

the Count of Mortain. Value 20s.

20 CREWKERNE. Edeva held it before 1066; it did not pay tax,
nor is it known how many hides are reckoned there.
Land for 40 ploughs. In lordship 5 ploughs; 12 slaves;   105
26 freedmen;   b 1
> 42 villagers and 45 smallholders with 20 ploughs.
> 4 mills which pay 40s; a market which pays £4; meadow,
> 60 acres; pasture ½ league long and 4 furlongs wide;   87 a
> woodland 4 furlongs long and 2 furlongs wide.
> 2 cobs; 8 unbroken mares; 9 cattle; 40 pigs; 400 sheep; 64 goats.

It pays £46 of white silver.
> EASTHAMS has been taken away from this manor. Before 1066

it was (part) of the manor's revenue and could not be
separated from it. Thurstan holds it from the Count of Mortain.
Value 50s; when the Count acquired it, as much.

Rex ten̄ *CVNGRESBERIE*. Herald tenuit T.R.E.⁊ geldb̄ ᵽ.xx.hid̄.
Tra.ē.L.car̄.De ea st̄ in dn̄io.v.hidæ.⁊ ibi.vi.car̄.⁊ xii.ſerui.
⁊ xxxiiii.uilli.⁊ xxxiiii.bord.cū xxxiiii.car̄.Ibi.ii.molini redd̄
xvii.ſol ⁊ vi.den̄.⁊ cc.L.ac̄ p̄ti.Paſtura.ii.leū lḡ.⁊ dim̄ leū lat̄.
Silua.ii.leū ⁊ dim̄ lḡ.⁊ dimid̄ leū lat̄.

Redd̄ xxviii.lib̄ ⁊ xv.ſol de albo argento.

De hac t̄ra huj ꝋ ten̄.iii.taini Aluuard Ordric ⁊ Ordulf.iii.hid̄.
⁊ iii.virg t̄ræ.Ipſi teneb̄ T.R.E.nec poterant á Dn̄o ꝋ ſeparari.
Ibi st̄ in dn̄io.iii.car̄.⁊ iiii.ſerui.⁊ vi.uilli.⁊ xvii.bord cū.iii.car̄.
⁊ dim̄.Ibi.xx.ac̄ p̄ti.⁊ xxx.ac̄ ſiluæ.Totū ual̄.Lx.ſolid̄.

Huj ꝋ eccłam ten̄ Mauricius eᵽs cū dimid̄ hida.Val̄.xx.ſolid̄.

De ipſa t̄ra.huj ꝋ ablatæ st̄.ii.hidæ.q̄ ibi jacuer̄ T.R.E.

Giſo eᵽs ten̄ unā.⁊ ual̄.iiii.lib̄.Serlo de burci ⁊ Giſlebt̄.f.Turoldi
ten̄ aliā hid̄.⁊ ual̄.xL.ſolid̄.

Rex ten̄ *CAMEL*.Ghida tenuit T.R.E.⁊ geldb̄ ᵽ viii.hid̄ ⁊ dimid̄.
Ibi st̄ tam̄.xv.hidæ.Tra.ē.xv.car̄.De ea st̄ in dn̄io.v.hidæ.⁊ ibi.iiii.car̄.
⁊ vi.ſerui.⁊ xxviii.uilli.⁊ x.bord cū.xi.car̄.Ibi.ii.molini redd̄.xx.
ſolid̄.⁊ c.ac̄ p̄ti.⁊ c.ac̄ paſturæ.⁊ c.ac̄ ſiluæ.

Redd̄.xxiii.lib̄.de albo argento.

Rex ten̄ *COCRE*.Ghida tenuit T.R.E.Ibi st̄.xv.hidæ.⁊ geldb̄ ᵽ.vii.
hid̄.Tra.ē.xv.car̄.De ea st̄ in dn̄io.v.hide ⁊ dimid̄.⁊ ibi.iii.car̄.
⁊ vii.ſerui.⁊ iiii.colibti.⁊ xxxv.uilli.⁊ xL.ii.bord.cū.xii.car̄.
Ibi molin̄ redd̄.v.ſolid̄.⁊ c.ac̄ p̄ti.Paſtura.i.leū lḡ.⁊ dim̄ leū lat̄.
Silua.viii.q̄ lḡ.⁊ vi.q̄ lat̄.Redd̄.xix.lib̄.⁊ xii.den̄ de albo ar

Rex ten̄ *HARDINTONE*.Gunnild tenuit T.R.E.⁊ ibi st̄   ſgento.
x.hidæ.⁊ geld̄ ᵽ.v.hid̄.Tra.ē.x.car̄.De ea st̄ in dn̄io.v.hidæ ⁊ dim̄.

21 CONGRESBURY. Earl Harold held it before 1066; it paid
tax for 20 hides. Land for 50 ploughs, of which 5 hides
are in lordship; 6 ploughs there; 12 slaves;
    34 villagers and 34 smallholders with 34 ploughs & 9½ hides.   106
    2 mills which pay 17s 6d; meadow, 250 acres; pasture   a 1
        2 leagues long and ½ league wide; woodland 2½ leagues
        long and ½ league wide. 2 cobs; 20 cattle; 40 pigs; 200 sheep; 40 goats.
It pays £28 15s of white silver; when William the Sheriff acquired it, as much.
    Of this manor's land three thanes, Alfward, Ordric and   D
Ordwulf, hold 3 hides and 3 virgates of land. They held them   E
themselves before 1066; they could not be separated from   E
the lord of the manor. In lordship 3 ploughs; 4 slaves;
    6 villagers and 17 smallholders with 3½ ploughs.
    Meadow, 20 acres; woodland, 30 acres.
Value of the whole, 60s.
    Bishop Maurice holds this manor's church with ½ hide.
Value 20s.
    From this manor's land have been taken away 2 hides which lay
there before 1066. Bishop Giso holds 1; value £4; when he acquired
it, as much.
Serlo of Burcy and Gilbert son of Thorold hold the other   E
hide; value 40s; when they acquired it, as much.

22 (Queen) CAMEL. Countess Gytha held it before 1066; it paid
tax for 8½ hides; 15 hides there, however. Land for 15
ploughs, of which 5 hides are in lordship; 4 ploughs there; 6 slaves; E
    28 villagers and 10 smallholders with 11 ploughs & 10 hides.   106
    2 mills which pay 20s; meadow, 100 acres; pasture, 100   b 1
        acres; woodland, 100 acres. 1 cob; 12 cattle; 20 pigs; 300 sheep.
It pays £23 of white silver; when William the Sheriff acquired it, as much.

23 COKER. Countess Gytha held it before 1066. 15 hides. It
paid tax for 7 hides. Land for 15 ploughs, of which 5½ ·   107
hides are in lordship; 3 ploughs there; 7 slaves; 4 freedmen;   a 1
    35 villagers and 42 smallholders with 12 ploughs & the rest of
    the land. 1 pigman who pays 10 pigs.
    A mill which pays 5s; meadow, 100 acres; pasture 1
    league long and ½ league wide; woodland 8 furlongs
    long and 6 furlongs wide. 1 cob; 3 cattle; 20 pigs; 150 sheep; 48 goats.
It pays £19 12s of white silver; when William the Sheriff acquired it, as much.

24 HARDINGTON (Mandeville). Gunhilda daughter of Earl Godwin held it
before 1066. 10 hides. It paid tax for 5 hides. Land for
10 ploughs, of which 5½ hides are in lordship; 2 ploughs   107
    a 2

7 ibi.ii.car.7 vii.ſerui.7 xvi.uiłłi.7 xvi.borđ cū.viii.car.Ibi.xl.ac
p̃ti.Silua.v.q̃ɀ łg.7 iiii.q̃ɀ lat.

Redđ.xii.lib 7 xiiii.ſoł de albo argento.

Rex teñ *HESTERIGE*.Herald tenuit.T.R.E.7 geldb̄ ꝑ.x.hiđ.
Tra.ē.xvi.car.P̃ter has.x.hidas.ē tra ad.viii.car.q̃ nunq̃
geldauit.Ibi ſt in dñio.v.car.7 viii.ſerui.7 xxxvii.uiłłi 7 xv.borđ
cū.xvi.car.Ibi moliñ redđ.xxx.den.7 clx.ac p̃ti.Paſtura una
leū łg.7 dimiđ leū lat.7 tñtđ ſiluæ.Redđ.xxiii.lib de albo argto.
In hoc ꟽ tenuit uñ lib hõ.ix.acs træ.7 ii.acs ſiluæ.Vał xxx.den.
Non ſe poterat a dño ꟽ ſeparare.

Has Svbter Scriptas ᴛerras Tenvit Eddid Regina.
Rex teñ *MILVERTONE*.T.R.E.geldb̄ ꝑ dimiđ uirg træ.Tra.ē.xvi.
car.In dñio.ē.i.car.7 iii.ſerui.7 iii.cotar.7 xvi.uiłłi.7 vii.borđ
cū.ix.car.Ibi moliñ redđ.vii.ſoliđ.7 vi.den.7 vi.ac p̃ti.7 c.ac
paſturæ.7 c.ac ſiluæ modicæ.Ibi Mercatū redđ.x.ſoliđ.

Totū redđ.xxv.lib ad numerū.T.Eddid reginæ.reddb̄.xii.lib.

Rex teñ *MERTOCII*.Ibi ſt.xxxviii.hidæ.T.R.E.geldb̄ ꝑ.xiii.
hiđ.Tra.ē.xl.car.De ea ſt iñ dñio.viii.hidæ.7 ibi.iii.car.7 vi.ſerui.
7 xiiii.colibti.7 lxv.uiłłi 7 xxiiii.borđ cū.xxviii.car.Ibi.ii.molini
redđ.xxxv.ſoliđ.7 l.ac p̃ti.Paſtura.i.leū łg.7 tñtđ lat.Silua
ſeptuag ᵘuna leū łg.7 ii.q̃ɀ lat.Piſcaria redđ.v.ſoliđ
·LXX· Redđ.lxx.lib ad numeꝛ.7 c.ſoliđ plus ſi eṕs Walcheł teſtat̄ fuerit.

Huic ꟽ ſt additæ.iii.hidæ.Has teneb̄.iii.taini T.R.E.

Redđ in Mertoch.iiii.lib 7 x.ſoliđ.

there; 7 slaves;
    16 villagers and 16 smallholders with 8 ploughs & the rest of the land.
    Meadow, 40 acres; woodland 5 furlongs long and 4
        furlongs wide. 1 cob; 5 cattle; 100 sheep.
It pays £12 14s of white silver; when William the Sheriff acquired it, as much.

25 HENSTRIDGE.   Earl Harold held it before 1066; it paid
tax for 10 hides. Land for 16 ploughs. Besides these 10
hides, land for 8 ploughs, which has never paid tax.   107
In lordship 5 ploughs; 8 slaves;   a 3
    37 villagers and 15 smallholders with 16 ploughs & 10 hides.
    A mill which pays 30d; meadow, 160 acres; pasture 1 league   E
        long and ½ league wide; woodland, as much. 3 cobs; 1 cow;
        22 pigs; 438 wethers.
It pays £23 of white silver; when William the Sheriff acquired it, as much.
    In this manor 1 free man held 9 acres of land and 2 acres
of woodland. Value 30d. He could not separate himself   E
from the lord of the manor.

             QUEEN EDITH HELD THE LANDS MENTIONED BELOW   E

26 MILVERTON. Before 1066 it paid tax for ½ virgate of land.   E
Land for 16 ploughs. In lordship 1 plough; 3 slaves;   E
    3 cottagers, 16 villagers and 7 smallholders with
        9 ploughs & the rest of the land.   113
    A mill which pays 7s 6d; meadow, 6 acres; pasture,100   a 1
        acres; a small wood, 100 acres. A market which pays   E
        10s. 1 cob; 40 sheep; 11 goats.
Value of the whole, £25 at face value; in Queen Edith's
time it paid £12 at face value.

27 MARTOCK. 38 hides. Before 1066 it paid tax for 13 hides.
Land for 40 ploughs, of which 8 hides are in lordship; 3
ploughs there; 6 slaves; 14 freedmen;   113
    65 villagers and 24 smallholders with 28 ploughs & 30 hides. a 2
    2 mills which pay 35s; meadow, 50 acres; pasture 1 league
        long and as wide; woodland 1 league long and 2 furlongs
        wide; a fishery which pays 5s. 2 cobs; 23 cattle; 36 pigs;
        300 sheep, less 16.
It pays £70 at face value and 100s more if Bishop Walkelin
has testified.
    To this manor 3 hides have been added. Three thanes held   E
these before 1066. They pay £4 10s in Martock.

De hoc M̄ eſt ablata.I.hida 7 una v̇ træ in *CONTONE*.Aniger ten.

Tra.ē.II.car.Ibi.IIII.hões hn̄t.I.car.Valuit.L.ſot.Modo.xxx.ſot.

De ipſo eċd M̄ eſt ablata hida 7 dimid.Aluric tenet.7 uat.XL.ſolid.

REX ten *CAINESHAM*.T.R.E.geldb̄ ꝓ.L.hid.Tra.ē.c.car.De ea

ſt in dn̄io.xv.hidæ 7 dim.7 ibi ſt.x.car.7 xx.ſerui.7 xxv.colibti.

7 LxX.uiłłi.7 xL.bord cū.Lx.III.car.Ibi.vI.molini redd.Lx.ſolid.

7 c.āc p̄ti.7 c.āc paſturæ.Silua.I.leū łḡ.7 tn̄td lat.

87 b

Redd.cvIII.lib ad numerū.Reddeb q̇t xx.lib.

Huic M̄ p̄tin.vIII.burḡſes in *BADE*.redd.v.ſot ꝑ annū.

De ipſis.L.hid ten Euſtachius in *BELETONE*.IIII.hid.

7 Alured de eo.Toui tenuit ꝓ uno M̄.T.R.E.Ibi in dn̄io.I.car

7 dim.cū.I.ſeruo.7 v.uiłłi 7 II.bord cū.II.car.Ibi molin̄ redd

xv.ſolid.7 xxII.āc p̄ti.7 xx.āc paſturæ.Silua.III.q̊ż łḡ.7 II.

q̊ż lat.Valuit.III.lib.Modo.IIII.lib.

De ead tra ipſius M̄ ten Rogerius.x.hid in *STANTONE*.

Ibi ht̄ in dn̄io.I.car.7 xv.uiłłi 7 xIII.bord.hn̄t.vII.car.

Ibi molin̄ redd.x.ſolid.7 xv.āc p̄ti.Paſtura.IIII.q̊ż łḡ.7 una

q̊ż 7 dim lat.7 tn̄td ſiluæ.Valet.c.ſolid.

De ipſa tra ten eƥs conſtantienſis dimid hid.7 ibi ht̄ dimid

car.Valet.v.ſolid.Vluuard tenuit.nec poterat a M̄ ſepari.

Vxor ipſius Vluuard ten.I.hid de ſuƥdictis.L.hid.7 ibi ht̄

IIII.car cū.III.ſeruis.7 III.uiłłis.7 IIII.bord.Ibi.xII.āc p̄ti.

7 IIII.āc ſiluæ minutæ.Valuit 7 uat.IIII.lib.

Aluric ten de ead tra.I.hid.quā tenuit Vlmar T.R.E.

nec poterat a M̄ ſepari.Ibi.ē.I.car.7 xvII.āc p̄ti.7 II.āc

paſturæ.Valet.xx.ſolid.

From this manor have been taken away 1 hide and 1 virgate
of land in COMPTON (?Durville). Ansger Cook holds them. Land
for 2 ploughs. Four men have 1 plough there.
The value was 50s; now 30s.   E

Also from this manor 1½ hides have been taken away. Aelfric   E
Little of Hampshire holds them. Value 40s; when Aelfric acquired them,
as much.

28 KEYNSHAM. Before 1066 it paid tax for 50 hides. Land for 100
ploughs, of which 15½ hides are in lordship; 10 ploughs there;
20 slaves; 25 freedmen;
    70 villagers and 40 smallholders with 63 ploughs & 17 hides.   113
    6 mills which pay 60s; meadow, 100 acres; pasture, 100 acres;   b 1
        woodland 1 league long and as wide. 4 cobs; 10 cattle; 44 pigs;
        700 sheep; 70 goats.
It pays £108 at face value; it paid £80, when William Hussey acquired   87 b
it in the revenue.
    To this manor belong 8 burgesses in Bath who pay 5s a year.   E
    Of these 50 hides Count Eustace holds 4 hides in BELLUTON, and   E
Alfred from him. Tovi held them as 1 manor before 1066.
In lordship 1½ ploughs & 2½ hides & ½ virgate, with 1 slave;   114
    5 villagers and 2 smallholders with 2 ploughs & 1 hide & 1½ virgates.   a 2
    A mill which pays 15s; meadow, 22 acres; pasture, 20
    acres; woodland 3 furlongs long and 2 furlongs wide.
    10 cattle; 13 pigs; 47 sheep; 10 goats.
The value was £3; now £4.
    Also of this manor's land Roger holds 10 hides in STANTON   E
(Drew); he has 1 plough in lordship & 5½ hides.
    15 villagers and 13 smallholders have 7 ploughs & 4½ hides.   113
    A mill which pays 10s; meadow, 15 acres; pasture 4 furlongs   b 1
    long and 1½ furlongs wide; woodland, as much. 87 sheep.
Value 100s; when Roger acquired them, £4.
    The Bishop of Coutances holds ½ hide of this land; he has ½   E
plough. Value 5s. Wulfward held it and could not be separated
from the manor.
    The wife of the same Wulfward holds 1 hide of the said   E
50 hides; she has 4 ploughs, with 3 slaves and   L
    3 villagers and 4 smallholders.   114
    Meadow, 12 acres; underwood, 4 acres. 6 pigs; 100 sheep.   a 1
The value was and is £4.
    Of this land Aelfric holds 1 hide which Wulfmer held before   E
1066; he could not be separated from the manor. 1 plough there.   E
    Meadow, 17 acres; pasture, 2 acres. 100 sheep.   113
Value 20s.   b 1

Rex ten̄ *CIWETVNE*. Ibi s̄t . xxix . hidæ . T . R . E . geldb̄ ꝓ . xiiii.
hid̄ . Tra . ē . xl . car̄ . De ea s̄t in dn̄io . xviii . hidæ . 7 ibi . ix.
car̄ . 7 xx . ſerui . 7 ii . colib̄ti . 7 xviii . uilti . 7 xxv . bord̄ cū . xix.
car̄ . Ibi . v . molini redd̄ . xxx . ſot . v . denar min . 7 c . ac̄ p̄ti.
Paſtura . ii . leū lḡ . 7 una leū lat̄ . Silua . i . leū in lḡ 7 lat̄.
In Bade . iiii . burḡſes redd̄ . xl . denar̄.
Redd̄ . l . lib̄ ad numerū . T . E . regine . reddeb̄ . xxx . lib̄.
Ecctam huj m̄ ten̄ abb̄ de Gēmetico cū dim hida træ.
Ibi s̄t . ii . car̄ 7 dim̄ . 7 ii . ſerui . 7 ii . uilti . 7 viii . bord̄ 7 viii . cotar̄.
Valuit 7 uat̄ . xl . ſolid.
Rex ten̄ *ESTONE* . Ibi s̄t . ii . hidæ . 7 geld̄ ꝓ una hida . Tra . ē
x . car̄ . In dn̄io . ē . i . car̄ . 7 ii . ſerui . 7 vii . colib̄ti . 7 xiii . uilti.
7 iii . bord̄ 7 iii . cotar cū . v . car̄ . Ibi . ii . molini redd̄ . c . denar̄.
7 l . ac̄ p̄ti . 7 ii . leū ſiluæ minutæ . in lḡ 7 lat̄.
Hæ . ii . hidæ fuer̄ 7 s̄t de dn̄ica firma burgi *BADE*.
Rex ten̄ *BADE* . T . R . E . geldb̄ ꝓ . xx . hid̄ . qdo ſcira
geldb̄ . Ibi h̄t rex . lxiiii . burḡſes . reddtes . iiii . lib̄ . 7 q̄t xx
7 x . burḡſes alioꝫ hōum redd̄t ibi . lx . ſolid.
Ibi h̄t rex . vi . uaſtas dom̄.
Iſtud burgū cū p̄dicta *ESTONE* . redd̄ . lx . lib̄ ad numerū.
7 unā mark̄ auri . P̄ter hoc redd̄ moneta . c . ſolid.
Eduuard̄ redd̄ . xi . lib̄ de tcio denario huj burgi.
De ipſo burgo . ē una dom̄ ablata . Hugo ten̄ . 7 uat̄ . ii . ſolid.
De tcio denario *GIVELCESTRE* . redd̄ Wilts . vi . lib̄ de xx . in ora.
De *MELEBVRNE* . xx . ſolid . De *BRAVETONE* . xx . ſolid . ſ v . ſolid.
De *LANPORT* . x . ſolid . De *AISSEBRIGE* . x . ſot . De *FROME*.
Has infra scriptas terras . Tenvit Vlward alb.
Rex ten̄ *CORFETONE* . T . R . E . geldb̄ ꝓ . vii . hid̄ . Tra . ē . vii.
car̄ . De ea s̄t in dn̄io . iii . hidæ 7 dimid̄ 7 i . ferding . 7 ibi . i . car̄.
7 iii . ſerui . 7 x . uilti 7 viii . bord̄ . cū . iii . car̄ . Ibi . vi . ac̄ p̄ti.
Silua . ii . q̄ꝫ lḡ . 7 una q̄ꝫ lat̄ . Valuit 7 uat̄ . vii . lib̄.

29 CHEWTON (Mendip). 29 hides. Before 1066 it paid tax for 14 hides. Land for 40 ploughs, of which 18 hides are in lordship; 9 ploughs there; 20 slaves; 2 freedmen;
    18 villagers and 25 smallholders with 19 ploughs & 11 hides.
    5 mills which pay 30s, less 5d; meadow, 100 acres;
        pasture 2 leagues long and 1 league wide; woodland
        1 league in length and width. 1 cob; 35 pigs, 800 sheep; 50 goats.
In Bath 4 burgesses who pay 40d.
It pays £50 at face value; in Queen Edith's time it paid £30.
    The Abbot of Jumièges holds this manor's church with ½ hide
of land. 2½ ploughs there; 2 slaves; 2 villagers; 8 smallholders;
8 cottagers. The value was and is 40s.

114
b 2

E
L

30 BATHEASTON. 2 hides. It paid tax for 1 hide. Land for 10 ploughs. In lordship 1 plough; 2 slaves; 7 freedmen; 1 hide.
    13 villagers, 3 smallholders and 3 cottagers with
    5 ploughs & 1 hide.
    2 mills which pay 100d; meadow, 50 acres; underwood,
        2 leagues in length and width. 150 sheep; 24 goats.
  These 2 hides were and are (part) of the lordship revenue of the Borough of Bath.

114
a 3

31 BATH. Before 1066 it paid tax for 20 hides when the Shire paid tax. The King has 64 burgesses who pay £4; 90 burgesses of other men pay 60s there. The King has 6 derelict houses.
This Borough, with the said BATHEASTON, pays £60 at face value and 1 gold mark. Besides this, the mint pays 100s.
    Edward the Sheriff pays £11 of the third penny of this Borough.
  From this Borough 1 house has been taken away. Hugh the Interpreter holds it; value 2s.
    Of the third penny (of) ILCHESTER William of Mohun pays £6 at 20 (pence) to the *ora;* of MILBORNE (Port) 20s; of BRUTON 20s; of LANGPORT 10s; of AXBRIDGE 10s; of FROME 5s.

E

E

114
E *b 1*
E

107
E *b 1*

      WULFWARD WHITE HELD THE LANDS MENTIONED BELOW   *E*

32 CORTON (Denham). Before 1066 it paid tax for 7 hides. Land for 7 ploughs, of which 3½ hides and 1 furlong are in lordship; 1 plough there; 3 slaves;
    10 villagers and 8 smallholders with 3 ploughs & the rest of the land.
Meadow, 6 acres; woodland 2 furlongs long and 1 furlong wide.
    1 cob; 4 pigs; 150 sheep.
The value was and is £7.

116
a 1

Rex ten WITECVBE.T.R.E. geldb̄ p̄.v. hid.Tra.ē.iiii.car̄.

De ea sꝫ in dn̄io.iii.hidæ 7 iii.virg træ.7 ibi.i.car̄ 7 ii.ſerui.

7 iii.uilti 7 iii.bord hn̄tes.ii.car̄.Ibi.vi.ac̄ p̄ti.Silua.iiii.

q̃ꝫ lḡ.7 una q̃ꝫ lat̄.Redd.iiii.lib̄.

Rex ten PETENIE.T.R.E.geldb̄ p̄.i.hida.Tra.ē.i.car̄ 7 dim̄.

Hunfrid ten ibi dimid hid.7 ibi hꞇ.i.car̄.7 vi.ac̄s p̄ti.7 iii.ac̄s

ſiluæ.Valuit 7 ual̄.xx.ſolid̄.Rex qd hꞇ ibi.ual̄.x.ſolid̄.

Warmund ten MVNDIFORD in Vadimonio de Vluuardo.teſtimo

nio breuis regis.T.R.E.geldb̄ p̄.v.hid.Tra.ē.v.car̄.De ea sꝫ in dn̄io

ii.hidæ.7 ibi.ii.car̄.Ibi.xii.ac̄ p̄ti.7 tntd paſturæ.Valuit 7 ual̄.iii.lib̄.

87 c

TERRA EP̄I WINTONIENSIS.

Ep̄s WINTONIENSIS ten TANTONE.Stigandus

tenuit T.R.E.7 geldb̄ p̄.liiii.hid 7 ii.virg træ

7 dimid.Tra.ē.c.car̄.Præt hanc hꞇ ep̄s in dn̄io

tram ad.xx.car̄.quæ nunq geldauit.7 ibi hꞇ.xiii.car̄.

Ibi q̃ter xx.uilti 7 quat xx 7 ii.bord.7 lxx.ſerui.7 xvi.

colibti.7 xvii.porcarij.redd.vii.lib̄.7 x.ſot.Int om̄s

hn̄t.lx.car̄.Ibi.lxiiii.burḡſes redd.xxxii.ſolid̄.

Ibi.iii.molini redd.c.ſolid̄.lx.denar̄ min.Mercatū

redd.l.ſot.7 de Monetá.l.ſolid̄.Ibi.xl.ac̄ p̄ti.Paſtu

ra.ii.leū lḡ.7 una leū lat̄.Silua una leū lḡ.7 tntd lat̄.

Quando Walchelin ep̄s recep̄.reddeb̄.l.lib̄.Modo

reddit.cliiii.lib̄.7 xiii.denar̄.cū om̄ibꝫ appendic̄

7 c̄ſuetudinibꝫ ſuis.

Iſtæ c̄ſuetudines p̄tinent ad TANTONE.Burgheriſth.Latro

nes.Pacis infractio.Hainfare.Denarij de Hundret.

7 Denarij S̄ Petri.Circieti.Ter in anno teneri placita ep̄i

ſine ammonitione.p̄fectio in exercitū cū hominibꝫ ep̄i.

33 WHITCOMB. Before 1066 it paid tax for 5 hides. Land for 4 ploughs,
of which 3 hides and 3 virgates of land are in lordship; 1 plough
there; 2 slaves;

> 3 villagers and 3 smallholders who have 2 ploughs & the rest of
> the land.

Meadow, 6 acres; woodland 4 furlongs long and 1 furlong wide.
It pays £4.

116
a 2

34 PITNEY. Before 1066 it paid tax for 1 hide. Land for 1½ ploughs. E
Humphrey holds ½ hide there; he has 1 plough and

> meadow, 6 acres and woodland, 3 acres.

The value was and is 20s; value of what the King has there, 10s.

116
a 4-5

35 Warmund holds MUDFORD in pledge from Wulfward by witness of
the King's writ. Before 1066 it paid tax for 5 hides. Land for 5
ploughs, of which 2 hides are in lordship; 2 ploughs there; 2 slaves.

> 4 villagers and 8 smallholders with 3 ploughs and 3 hides.

Meadow, 12 acres; pasture, as much. 1 cob.
The value was and is £3.

116
a 3

[2]   LAND OF THE BISHOP OF WINCHESTER

87 c

1 The Bishop of Winchester holds TAUNTON. Archbishop Stigand
held it before 1066; it paid tax for 54 hides and 2½ virgates of E
land. Land for 100 ploughs. Besides this, the Bishop has in E
lordship land for 20 ploughs, which has never paid tax; he has
13 ploughs there.

> 80 villagers, 82 smallholders, 70 slaves, 16 freedmen and
> 17 pigmen who pay £7 10s. Between them they have
> 60 ploughs & 37 hides. 64 burgesses who pay 32s.
> 3 mills which pay 100s, less 60d; a market which pays 50s;
> from the mint, 50s. Meadow, 40 acres; pasture 2 leagues
> long and 1 league wide; woodland 1 league long and as wide.
> 8 cobs; 30 cattle; 24 pigs; 100 sheep.

When Bishop Walkelin acquired it, it paid £50; now it pays
£154 13d with all its dependencies and customary dues. E

173
b 4

2 These customary dues belong to TAUNTON: 'borough right';
thieves; breach of the peace; house-breaking; Hundred pence;
St. Peter's pence; Church taxes; three times a year the Bishop's
pleas to be held without summons; setting out on military
service with the Bishop's men.

173
b 4

Has denominatas c̄suetudines redd̄t in *TANTONE* .hǽ trǽ.

Talanda. Acha. Holeforde .7 Vbcedene 7 Succedene.

Maidenobroche. Laford. Hilla 7 Hela. Nichehede.

Nortone. Bradeforde. Halſa 7 Hafella.

Scobindare 7 Stocha. Hǽ duǽ trǽ n̄ debent exercitū.   ⌐turā.

Eaſd c̄ſuetudines debeɴ̄ illi de Bauueƀga. p̄t exercitū 7 ſepul

De his om̄ib꜋ tris faɔuri ſacramtū uel judiciū porta

turi.́ad *TANTONE* ueniunt. Cū dn̄i de his tris moriunt.́

in Tantone ſepeliuntur.

Hilla 7 Hela n̄ poteraɴ̄ a Tantone ſeparari. T. R. E.

De ſuꝑdiɔis. LIIII. hid̄ 7 dim̄.7 dim̄ virg trǽ.́ten modo

de eꝑo. Goisfrid̄. IIII. hid̄ 7 unā v trǽ. Roƀt. IIII. hid̄

7 dim̄. Hugo. II. hid̄ 7 dim̄.

Ibi ſt in dn̄io. x. car̄.7 XII. ſerui.7 xx. uilli.7 XXXVII. bord̄ cū. x.

car̄. Ibi. XXXVII. ac pti.7 XL. III. ac ſiluǽ.7 Molin̄ de. III. ſol.

iſtud. ē Hugonis.   -   Int totū ual. XXVII. liƀ.

Ite de ſuꝑdiɔis hid̄ ten de eꝑo Goduin. II. hid̄. dimid̄ v trǽ

min. Leueua. II. hid̄. Aluuard̄. I. hid̄ 7 unā v trǽ 7 dimid̄.

Aluric 7 Edmer. III. hid̄. Leuui. dim̄ virg trǽ.

Ibi in dn̄io. VII. car̄.7 XIII. ſerui.7 XIII. uilli.7 xx. bord̄. cū. III.

car̄ 7 dimid̄. Ibi. II. molini. redd̄. VI. ſolid̄.7 VIII. den̄.7 XL. v. ac

pti.7 LXI. ac ſiluǽ.   Int totū ual. VIII. liƀ.7 III. ſolid̄.

Qui has tras teneƀ T. R. E.́n̄ poterant ab ǽccla ſeparari.

Ite de ſuꝑdiɔis hid̄ ten comes moriton. I. hid̄. Aluredus

. I. hid̄. Joħs. II. hid̄.7 dim̄ v trǽ. In dn̄io ſt ibi. II. car̄.7 VI.

ſerui.7 XII. uilli.7 XVII. bord̄ cū. III. car̄.7 dim̄. Ibi. II. molini

redd̄. XIIII. ſol.7 II. den̄.7 XIX. ac pti.7 c. ac paſturǽ.7 xx. ac ſiluǽ.

Hǽ. III. trǽ ꝑtineƀ ad *TANTONE*. T. R. E.7 ualeƀ. LXX. ſolid̄.

Modo redd̄. VI. liƀ 7 x. ſolid̄.

3   These lands pay these specified customary dues to TAUNTON: E

Tolland, Oake, Holford, Upper Cheddon, Cheddon (Fitzpaine),   173

Maidenbrooke, Ford, Hillfarrance, Hele, Nynehead, Norton   E   b 4

(Fitzwarren), Bradford (on Tone), Halse, Heathfield, Shopnoller

and Stoke (St. Mary). These two lands do not owe military service.

The people of Bagborough owe these customary dues, except for

military service and burial.

4   From all these lands those who have to make an oath or bear   173

judgment come to TAUNTON. When the lords of these lands die   b 4

they are buried in Taunton.

5   Hillfarrance and Hele could not be separated from Taunton   173

before 1066.   b 4

6   Of the said 54½ hides and ½ virgate of land Geoffrey now holds   E

from the Bishop 4 hides and 1 virgate of land; Robert 4½ hides;   D   173

Hugh de uillana 2½ hides. In lordship 10 ploughs; 12 slaves;   b 4

    20 villagers and 37 smallholders with 10 ploughs.   174

    Meadow, 37 acres; woodland, 43 acres; a mill at 3s: it is Hugh's.   b 1

In total, value £27.

7   Also of the said hides Godwin holds from the Bishop 2 hides,   D

less ½ virgate of land; Leofeva 2 hides; Alfward 1 hide and 1½

virgates of land; Aelfric and his brother Edmer 3 hides; Leofwy   D   174

½ virgate of land. In lordship 7 ploughs; 13 slaves;   E   b 3-4

    13 villagers and 20 smallholders with 3½ ploughs.

    2 mills which pay 6s 8d; meadow, 45 acres; woodland, 61 acres.   E

In total, value £8 3s.

    The holders of these lands before 1066 could not be separated

from the church.

8   Also of the said hides the Count of Mortain holds 1 hide;   E

Alfred of 'Spain' 1 hide; John the Usher 2 hides and ½ virgate of land.   E

In lordship 2 ploughs; 6 slaves;   D

    12 villagers and 17 smallholders with 3½ ploughs.   174

    2 mills which pay 14s 2d; meadow, 19 acres; pasture,   b 4

        100 acres; woodland, 20 acres.   E

    These three lands belonged to Taunton before 1066.   E

The value was 70s; now they pay £6 10s.

Huic M̄ Tantone additæ s̄t.ii.hidæ 7 dim̃ in Lidiard 7 Lega.
quas teneḃ un̄ tain parit T.R.E.7 potuit ire ad quēlibet dn̄m.
Modo ten̄ de ep̄o Wluuard 7 Aluuard p̄ c̄ceſſionē regis. W.
Tra.ē.v.car̄.Ibi s̄t.vi.uiłłi.7 iii.bord̄.7 iiii.ſerui.7 xi.ac̄ p̄ti.
7 c.ac̄ paſturæ.7 xlix.ac̄ ſiluæ.   Valḃ 7 uał.xlv.ſolid̄.
De his tris sēp jacuer̄ c̄ſuetudines 7 ſeruitiū in *TANTONE*.
7 rex.W.c̄ceſſit iſtas tras habendas S̄ Petro 7 Walchelino ep̄o.
ſicut ipſe recognouit apud Sarisḃiam audiente ep̄o dunel
menſi.cui p̄cepit.ut hanc ipsā c̄ceſſionē ſuā in breuiḃ ſcribet.
I̋d ep̄s ten̄ *PIPEMINSTRE*.Stigand tenuit 7 geldḃ p̄.xv.hid̄.Tra.ē.xx.
car̄.De ea s̄t in dn̄io.v.hidæ.7 ibi.ii.car̄.7 xvii.uiłłi 7 viii.bord̄ cū.xii.car̄.
Ibi.vi.ac̄ p̄ti.7 cccc.ac̄ paſturæ.7 totid̄ ac̄ ſiluæ.Valuit.xiii.liḃ.M.xvi.liḃ.

87 d

I̋dē ep̄s ten̄ *BLEDONE*.De uictu monachoꝝ fuit 7 eſt.T.R.E.geldḃ p̄ xv.hid̄.
Tra.ē.xvii.car̄.De ea s̄t in dn̄io.x.hidæ.7 ibi.iii.car̄.7 viii ſerui.7 xvi.uiłłi.
7 x.bord̄ cū.xi.car̄.Ibi.l.ac̄ p̄ti.7 paſtura.i.leū łḡ.7 dim̃ leū łat̄.Valuit
De his.x.hid̄ ten̄ Saulf de ep̄o.i.hid̄.7 ibi ht̄.i.car̄.cū.i.ſeruo⨍ 7 uał.xv.liḃ.
7 i.bord̄.7 xvi.ac̄s p̄ti.7 una ac̄ ſiluæ minutæ.Vał.xx.ſolid̄.
I̋d ep̄s ten̄ *RINTONE*.Stigand tenuit.T.R.E.7 geldḃ p̄.v.hid̄.Tra.ē.v.car̄.
De ea s̄t in dn̄io.ii.hidæ.7 una virg tre 7 dim̃.7 ibi.iii.car̄.7 ii.ſerui.7 viii.uiłłi.
7 vii.bord̄ cū.iii.car̄.Ibi x.ac̄ p̄ti.Silua.iiii.q̊ꝝ łḡ.7 una q̊ꝝ łat̄.Valuit 7 uał
⨍ vii.łiḃ.

87 c, d

9 To this manor (of) Taunton have been added 2½ hides in LYDEARD   E
(St. Lawrence) and LEIGH, which a thane held jointly before 1066;
he could go to whichever lord he would. Now Wulfward and   D
Alfward hold them from the Bishop with the assent of King   E
William. Land for 5 ploughs.   174
> 6 villagers, 3 smallholders and 4 slaves.   E   b 4
> Meadow, 11 acres; pasture, 100 acres; woodland, 49 acres.   E
The value was and is 45s.
> The customary dues and service of these lands have always
> lain in Taunton.
> King William granted these lands for St. Peter's and Bishop
> Walkelin to have, as he acknowledged himself at Salisbury in
> the hearing of the Bishop of Durham, whom he ordered to write
> down this grant of his in the records.

10 The Bishop also holds PITMINSTER. Archbishop Stigand held it; it
paid tax for 15 hides. Land for 20 ploughs, of which 5 hides are
in lordship; 2 ploughs there; 4 slaves.
> 17 villagers and 8 smallholders with 14 ploughs & 10 hides. 1 pigman.   173
> Meadow, 6 acres; pasture, 400 acres; woodland, as many.   b 1
> A mill which pays 16d. 1 cob; 20 pigs; 36 goats.
The value was £13; now £16.

11 The Bishop also holds BLEADON. It was and is for the monks'   E   87 d
supplies. Before 1066 it paid tax for 15 hides. Land for
17 ploughs, of which 10 hides are in lordship; 3 ploughs there;
8 slaves;   E
> 16 villagers and 10 smallholders with 11 ploughs & 4 hides.   173
> Meadow, 50 acres; pasture 1 league long and ½ league wide.   b 3
> 18 cattle; 10 pigs; 250 sheep.
The value was and is £15.
> Of these 10 hides Saewulf holds 1 hide from the Bishop;   E
> he has 1 plough there, with 1 slave and   E
> 1 smallholder.
> Meadow, 16 acres; underwood, 1 acre.   7 cattle; 6 pigs; 100 sheep.
Value 20s; when the Bishop acquired it, 10s.

12 The Bishop also holds RIMPTON. Bishop Stigand held it before
1066; it paid tax for 5 hides. Land for 5 ploughs, of which 2
hides and 1½ virgates of land are in lordship; 3 ploughs there;
2 slaves;   173
> 8 villagers and 7 smallholders with 3 ploughs & the rest of the land.   b 2
> Meadow, 10 acres; woodland 4 furlongs long and 1 furlong
> wide.   1 cob; 20 cattle; 24 pigs; 60 sheep.   E
The value was and is £7.   E

TERRA EPI SARISBERIENSIS.

Eps Sarisber teñ SEVEBERGE. Aluuard tenuit.T.R.E.7 geldb
ꝑ hida 7 dim.Tra.e.i.car 7 dim.Tam st ibi.ii.car.7 ii.uilti.7 iiii.bord.
7 ii.ſerui.Ibi dim moliñ redd.x.deñ.7 ix.ac ꝑti.7 x.ac ſiluæ.Paſtura
dim leu lg.7 dim q̃ƶ lat.Huic ꝏ eſt addita alia SEVEBERGE.Aluer
tenuit.T.R.E.7 geldb ꝑ hida 7 dim.Ibi st.ii.car cu uno uitto.7 v.bord.7 dim
moliñ redd.x.deñ.7 ix.ac ꝑti.7 x.ac ſiluæ.Paſtura dim leu lg.7 dim q̃ƶ lat.
He.ii.træ ñ st de epiſcopatu Sariſberie.Oſmund ten ꝑ uno ꝏ.
7 Walter de eo.Valeb 7 uat.lx.ſolid.T.R.E.jacuer in CRVCHE ꝏ
regis.7 qui teneb inde ñ poteraꝗ ſepari.7 reddeb in CRVCHE ꝑ cſuetud
xii.oues cu agnis.7 una bloma ferri de uno q̃q̃ libo homine.
Ide eps ten CONTONE.7 Walter de eo.Aluuard tenuit T.R.E.7 geldb
ꝑ v.hid.Tra.e.iii.car.In dñio st.ii.car.7 ii.ſerui.7 v.uitti.7 iiii.bord
7 vii.cotar cu.ii.car.Ibi moliñ redd.xxx.deñ.7 xiiii.ac ꝑti.7 q̃t xx.
ac ſiluæ.7 una leu paſturæ.Valuit 7 uat lx.ſolid.

TERRA EPI BAIOCENSIS.

Eps Baiocensis ten COME.7 Sanſon de eo.Leuuin tenuit
T.R.E.7 geldb ꝑ.viii.hid.Tra.e.viii.car.De ea st in dñio.v.hidæ.
7 ibi.iii.car.7 vii.ſerui.7 x.uitti 7 vi.bord cu.ii.car.Ibi.xl.ac ꝑti.
7 xl.ac paſturæ.7 lx.ac ſiluæ minutæ.Valuit 7 uat.x.lib.
Huic ꝏ adjunctæ st.iii.uirg træ in TORNIE.Aluuard tenuit
T.R.E.ꝑ uno ꝏ.7 ꝑ tanto geldb.Tra.e dim car.Valuit 7 uat.xiii.ſot.

[3]   LAND OF THE BISHOP OF SALISBURY

1   The Bishop of Salisbury holds SEABOROUGH. Alfward held it
    before 1066; it paid tax for 1½ hides. Land for 1½ ploughs;
    2 ploughs there, however.   L
            2 villagers, 4 smallholders and 2 slaves.   E
    ½ mill which pays 10d; meadow, 9 acres; woodland, 10 acres;
            pasture ½ league long and ½ furlong wide. 7 cattle; 5 pigs;   154
            68 sheep.   a 1
    Another SEABOROUGH has been added to this manor. Alfhere   E
    held it before 1066; it paid tax for 1½ hides. 2 ploughs there, with   L
            1 villager and 5 smallholders.   154
    ½ mill which pays 10d; meadow, 9 acres; woodland, 10 acres;   a 2
            pasture ½ league long and ½ furlong wide. 4 pigs; 58 sheep.
    These two lands are not (part) of the bishopric of Salisbury.
    Bishop Osmund holds them as one manor, and Walter Tirrell
    from him.
    The value was and is 60s.
            Before 1066 they lay in (the lands of) Crewkerne, a manor of
    the King's. The holders could not be separated from it.   E
    They paid to Crewkerne as a customary due 12 sheep with their
    lambs and 1 bloom of iron from every free man.

2   The Bishop also holds CHILCOMPTON, and Walter Tirrell from him.
    Alfward held it before 1066; it paid tax for 5 hides. Land for 3
    ploughs. In lordship 2 ploughs; 2 slaves; 3 hides & 3½ virgates.
            5 villagers, 4 smallholders and 7 cottagers with   154
            2 ploughs & the rest of the land.   a 3
    A mill which pays 30d; meadow, 14 acres; woodland, 80 acres;
            pasture, 1 league. 3 cattle; 8 pigs; 100 sheep; 20 goats.
    The value was and is 60s.

[4]   LAND OF THE BISHOP OF BAYEUX

1   The Bishop of Bayeux holds (Temple) COMBE, and Samson the   E
    Chaplain from him. Earl Leofwin held it before 1066; it paid tax
    for 8 hides. Land for 8 ploughs, of which 5 hides are in lordship;
    3 ploughs there; 7 slaves;   153
            10 villagers and 6 smallholders with 2 ploughs & 3 hides.   b 1
    Meadow, 40 acres; pasture, 40 acres; underwood, 60 acres.
            2 cobs; 6 cattle; 20 pigs; 100 sheep; 25 goats.
    The value was and is £10.
            To this manor have been joined 3 virgates of land in 'THORENT'.
    Alfward held them before 1066 as one manor; they paid tax   E
    for as much. Land for ½ plough.
    The value was and is 13s.   E

TERRA EƤI CONSTANTIENSIS.

Eᴘꜱ Constantiens̃ ten *Dovles*. Aluuard tenuit T.R.E.

7 geldb̄ ⱷ.ɪɪ.hid 7 una v̄ træ.Tra.ē.ɪ.car̃ 7 dim.quæ ibi sᷓ cū.ɪɪɪ.

uittis.7 ɪɪɪ.bord.7 ɪ.ſeruo. Valuit 7 uaƚ.xxɪɪɪɪ.ſolid.

Huic m̃ additæ sᷓ.vɪɪ.hidæ.q̃s teneb̄ tres taini T.R.E.ⱷ.ɪɪɪ.Man̄.

Ibi sᷓ in dn̄io. ɪɪ.car̃.7 ɪɪ.ſerui.7 xɪ.uitti.7 xɪ.bord cū.v.car̃.

Ibi.xLɪɪɪɪ.ac̃ p̃ti.7 ɪɪɪɪ.q̃ɀ paſturæ in lg̃.7 tn̄td in laᷓ.7 xx ac̃ plus.

Silua.vɪɪɪ.q̃ɀ lg̃.7 ɪɪɪ.q̃ɀ laᷓ.7 xx.ac̃ inſuᵽ. Vaƚ.vɪ.lib̄ 7 x.ſoƚ.

Hanc tra̅ ten Witts de eᵽo.

Id̃ eᵽs ten *CAFFECOME*.7 Radulf⁹ de eo.Duo taini tenuer̃ T.R.E.

7 geldb̄ ⱷ.ɪɪɪ.hid 7 dim̃.Tra.ē.ɪɪɪ.car̃.In dn̄io.ē una.7 ɪɪ.uitti

7 vɪ.bord.hn̄t.ɪ.car̃.Ibi Silua.vɪɪɪ.q̃ɀ lg̃.7 tn̄td laᷓ.Vaƚ.xL.ſoƚ.

Huic m̃ addita.ē.ɪ.hida 7 ɪɪɪ.virg̃ træ.Duo taini tenuer̃ T.R.E.

ⱷ.ɪɪ.m̃.Tra.ē.ɪɪ.car̃.Has hn̄t ibi.ɪɪɪ.uitti.Vaƚ.xx.ſolid.

Idem eᵽs ten *HASECVBE*.7 Witts de eo.Quattuor taini tenuer̃

T.R.E.7 geldb̄ ⱷ.ɪɪ.hid 7 ɪɪɪ.virg̃ træ.Tra.ē.ɪɪɪ.car̃.In dn̄io sᷓ.ɪɪ.car̃.

cū.ɪ.ſeruo.7 ɪɪɪɪ.uitti 7 vɪɪɪ.bord cū.ɪɪ.car̃.Ibi.xxx.ɪ.ac̃ p̃ti.7 x.ac̃

ſiluæ minutæ. Valuit.xL.ſolid. Modo. L.ſolid.

Id̃ eᵽs ten *STOCHES*.Aluied tenuit T.R.E.Ibi sᷓ.v.hidæ 7 una virg̃

træ.7 ⱷ.ɪɪɪɪ.hid geld.Tra.ē.v.car̃.De ea sᷓ in dn̄io.ɪɪ.hidæ.7 dimid.

7 ibi.ɪɪ.car̃.7 ɪɪɪ.ſerui.7 ɪx.uitti.7 ɪɪɪ.bord cū.ɪɪɪɪ.car̃.7 dimid.

Ibi molin̄ redd.ɪɪɪ.ſolid.7 xv.ac̃ p̃ti.Paſtura.ɪɪ.leū lg̃.7 una leū laᷓ.

[5] LAND OF THE BISHOP OF COUTANCES

1 The Bishop of Coutances holds DOWLISH. Alfward held it
before 1066; it paid tax for 2 hides and 1 virgate of land.
Land for 1½ ploughs, which are there, with   L
    3 villagers, 3 smallholders and 1 slave.   136
    4 cattle; 7 pigs; 32 sheep.   b 1
The value was and is 24s.   E
    To this manor have been added 7 hides which three thanes held   E
before 1066 as three manors. In lordship 2 ploughs; 2 slaves;   D
    11 villagers and 11 smallholders with 5 ploughs.
    Meadow, 44 acres; pasture, 4 furlongs in length and as much
       in width and 20 acres more; woodland 8 furlongs long
       and 3 furlongs wide and 20 acres in addition.
Value £6 10s.
William of Monceaux holds this land from the Bishop.

The Bishop also holds
2 CHAFFCOMBE. Ralph Rufus holds from him. Two thanes held   E
it before 1066; it paid tax for 3½ hides. Land for 3 ploughs.
In lordship 1; 3 hides & ½ virgate.   136
    2 villagers and 6 smallholders have 1 plough & 1½ virgates.   b 2
    Woodland 8 furlongs long and as wide. 8 cattle; 24 pigs; 65 sheep.
Value 40s; when the Bishop acquired it, as much.
    To this manor have been added 1 hide and 3 virgates of land.
Two thanes held them before 1066 as two manors. Land for 2
ploughs; 3 villagers have them there.
Value 20s; when the Bishop acquired them, as much.

3 'HISCOMBE'. William of Monceaux holds from him. Four thanes   E
held it before 1066; it paid tax for 2 hides and 3 virgates
of land. Land for 3 ploughs. In lordship 2 ploughs & 1½ hides,
with 1 slave;   137
    4 villagers and 8 smallholders with 2 ploughs & 1 hide & 1 virgate.   a 1
    Meadow, 31 acres; underwood, 10 acres. 10 cattle; 20 pigs; 143 sheep.
The value was 40s; now 50s.

4 (Rodney) STOKE. Alfgeat Puttock held it before 1066. 5 hides
and 1 virgate of land. It paid tax for 4 hides. Land for
5 ploughs, of which 2½ hides are in lordship; 2 ploughs
there; 3 slaves;   137
    9 villagers and 3 smallholders with 4½ ploughs & 1½ hides.   a 2

7 II .foliđ defup plus . Silua . I . leū lg̅ .7 una q̃ǥ lat̅ . Valuit . VI . liƀ . Modo

I̅d̅e̅ ep̅s ten ESSETVNE .7 Drogo de eo . Eduiñ tenuit T . R . E .ʃ IIII . liƀ.

7 geldƀ ₽ . III . hiđ 7 uno ferding . Tra . e̅ . XII . car̅ . In dn̅io fi̅ . II . car̅.

7 VI . ferui .7 XX . uiłti .7 XIII . borđ . cū . VII . car̅ . Ibi . VIII . a̅c p̅ti.

7 LX . a̅c filuæ . Paftura . I . leu lg̅ .7 tn̅tđ lat̅ . Vał . VI . liƀ.

De hac eađ tra T . R . E . jacueɼ . III . virg̅ træ in NETECVBE m̅ regis.

I̅d̅e̅ ep̅s ten WINEMERESHA̅ .7 Drogo de eo . T . R . E . geldƀ ₽ . I . hida

7 una v̅ træ . Tra . e̅ . V . car̅ . De ea fi̅ in dn̅io . III . v̅ .7 ibi . I . car̅.

7 III . ferui .7 V . uiłti 7 III . borđ cū . I . car̅ . Ibi . cc . a̅c pafturæ.

7 tn̅tđ filuæ . Valet . XXX . foliđ.

I̅d̅e̅ Drogo ten de ep̅o CHETENORE . T . R . E . geldƀ ₽ . I . hida 7 una v̅.

Tra . e̅ . II . car̅ . Ibi fi̅ . II . uiłti 7 I . borđ 7 I . feru cū . I . car̅ .7 L . a̅c pa

fturæ .7 c . a̅c filuæ . Valet . XV . foliđ . H̅ . II . m̅ tenuit Ofmunđ T . R . E.

E̅dmer ten de ep̅o WIDICVBE . Alnod tenuit 7 ₽ . III . hiđ geldƀ

T . R . E . Tra . e̅ . X . car̅ . In dn̅io fi̅ . II . car̅ .7 VI . ferui .7 XIIII . uiłti 7 VII.

borđ cū . VIII . car̅ . Ibi . X . a̅c p̅ti .7 q̅ngentæ 7 L . a̅c pafturæ

7 c . a̅c filuæ . IIII . min . Valuit . IIII . liƀ . Modo . VI . liƀ.

A̅zelin ten de ep̅o HARPETREV . Alric 7 Vluuɼ tenueɼ T . R . E.

₽ . II . m̅ .7 geldƀ ₽ . V . hiđ . Tra . e̅ . V . car̅ . De ea fi̅ in dn̅io . III . hidæ.

7 ibi . II . car̅ .7 II . ferui .7 IX . uiłti 7 I . borđ 7 IIII . cotar̅ . cū . III . car̅.

Ibi moliñ de . V . foliđ .7 XL . a̅c p̅ti . Paftura . VIII . q̃ǥ lg̅ .7 v̅.

q̃ǥ lat̅ . Silua . IIII . q̃ǥ lg̅ .7 II . q̃ǥ 7 dim̅ lat̅ . Valuit 7 uał . XL . fot.

A mill which pays 3s; meadow, 15 acres; pasture 2 leagues
    long and 1 league wide and 2s in addition; woodland   E
    1 league long and 1 furlong wide. 20 mares; 5 cows; 20 pigs;
     65 sheep; 68 goats.
The value was £6; now £4.
    Roger Whiting holds it now from the Bishop.

5 EXTON. Drogo holds from him. Edwin held it before 1066;
it paid tax for 3 hides and 1 furlong. Land for 12 ploughs.
In lordship 2 ploughs; 6 slaves; 1 furlong.
    20 villagers and 13 smallholders with 7 ploughs & 3 hides.   139
    Meadow, 8 acres; woodland, 60 acres; pasture 1 league   a 1
       long and as wide. 6 pigs; 60 sheep.
Value £6; when the Bishop acquired it, 40s.
    Also of this land 3 virgates of land lay in Nettlecombe,   E
a manor of the King's, before 1066. Value 15s; when the Bishop
acquired them, as much.

6 WILMERSHAM. Drogo holds from him. Before 1066 it paid tax   88 a
for 1 hide and 1 virgate of land. Land for 5 ploughs, of
which 3 virgates are in lordship; 1 plough there; 3 slaves;   139
    5 villagers and 3 smallholders with 1 plough & 3 virgates.   a 2
    Pasture, 200 acres; woodland, as much. 5 cattle; 40 sheep; 30 goats.
Value 30s.

7 Drogo also holds CULBONE from the Bishop. Before 1066 it
paid tax for 1 hide and 1 virgate. Land for 2 ploughs.   L
    2 villagers, 1 smallholder and 1 slave with 1 plough.   E 139
    Pasture, 50 acres; woodland, 100 acres.   a 3
Value 15s; when the Bishop acquired it, 5s.
 Osmund Stramin held these two manors before 1066.

8 Edmer holds WITHYCOMBE from the Bishop. Alnoth held it;
it paid tax for 3 hides before 1066. Land for 10 ploughs.
In lordship 2 ploughs; 6 slaves; 1 hide.   139
    14 villagers and 7 smallholders with 8 ploughs & 2 hides.   a 4
    Meadow, 10 acres; pasture, 550 acres; woodland, 100 acres,   E
       less 4. 1 cob; 3 cattle; 10 pigs; 40 sheep; 30 goats.
The value was £4; now £6.

9 Azelin holds (East) HARPTREE from the Bishop. Alric and   E
Wulfwy held it before 1066 as two manors; it paid tax for 5 hides.
Land for 5 ploughs, of which 3 hides are in lordship; 2 ploughs
there; 2 slaves;   139
    9 villagers, 1 smallholder and 4 cottagers with 3 ploughs & 2 hides.   b 1
    A mill at 5s; meadow, 40 acres; pasture 8 furlongs long
       and 5 furlongs wide; woodland 4 furlongs long and
       2½ furlongs wide. 1 cob; 3 cattle; 12 pigs; 46 sheep; 20 goats.
The value was and is 40s.

Azelin ten de epo *HOTVNE* . Duo taini tenuer T.R.E .ꝑ.II. ꝏ̄.
7 geldb̄ ꝑ.v.hid . Tra . ē.v.car . In dnio.ē.I.car.7 v.uilti 7 vI.
bord hnt.II.car.Ibi.xxx.ac̄ p̄ti.7 cc.ac̄ pasturæ.7 xv.acræ
filuæ minutæ . Valuit . IIII .lib̄.Modo.LX .folid.

Azelin ten de epo *LILEBERE* . Aluuard tenuit T.R.E.7 geldb̄
ꝑ.III. hid . Tra.ē.IIII.car.In dnio st̄.II.car.cū.I.feruo 7 I.uilto.
7 v.bord cū.I.car.Ibi.xx.ac̄ p̄ti.7 XL.ac̄ pasturæ.
Valuit.LX.fol.Modo.XL.folid.

Herluin ten de epo Wintreth. Briſtric tenuit T.R.E.7 geldb̄
ꝑ.I. hida.Tra.ē.II.car.Ibi st̄ cū.II.uiltis 7 II. bord 7 II.feruis.
Ibi.vIII.ac̄ p̄ti.7 III.ac̄ filuæ modicæ.Valuit 7 ual.xx.folid.
H̄.III.Maner erant de æccla Glaſtingb̄ie.T.R.E.Qui teneb̄
non poterant ab æccla feparari.

Herluin ten de epo *AISECOME* . Briſtric tenuit T.R.E.7 geldb̄
ꝑ.III.hid 7 dim.Tra.ē.v.car.In dnio st̄.II.car.7 vII.ferui.7 vI.
uilti 7 v.bord cū.III.car.Ibi.XL.ac̄ p̄ti.7 III.ac̄ filuæ minutæ.
7 c.ac̄ pasturæ.Valuit 7 ual.c.folid.

Wilts ten de epo *CLVTONE*.Turchil tenuit T.R.E.7 geldb̄ ꝑ.x.hid.
Tra.ē.vIII.car.In dnio st̄.III.car.cū.I.feruo.7 x.uilti 7 xII.
bord cū.vI.car.Ibi moliñ redd.xxx.denar.7 cvII.ac̄ p̄ti.
Paſtura.x.q̄ʒ lḡ.7 IIII.q̄ʒ lat̄.Silua dimid leu lḡ.7 tntd lat̄.
Valuit.III.lib̄.Modo.vI.lib̄.

Wilts ten de epo *TEMESBARE* .Ape tenuit T.R.E.7 geldb̄ ꝑ.III.
hid.Tra.ē.III.car.In dnio.ē.I.car.7 II.ferui.7 II.uilti 7 I.bord
cū.I.car.Ibi.II.partes molini redd.III.folid.7 xxvI.ac̄ p̄ti.
7 tntd pasturæ.Valuit.xxvI.folid.Modo.L.folid.

10   Azelin holds HUTTON from the Bishop. Two thanes held it before   E
1066 as two manors; it paid tax for 5 hides. Land for 5 ploughs.
In lordship 1 plough; 3½ hides.   139
    5 villagers and 6 smallholders have 2 ploughs & 1½ hides.   b 2
    Meadow, 30 acres; pasture, 200 acres; underwood, 15 acres.
The value was £4; now 60s.

11   Azelin holds ELBOROUGH from the Bishop. Alfward held it before   E
1066; it paid tax for 3 hides. Land for 4 ploughs. In lordship
2 ploughs, & 2½ hides, with 1 slave and   139
    1 villager and 5 smallholders with 1 plough & ½ hide.   b 3
    Meadow, 20 acres; pasture, 40 acres.   10 cattle; 12 pigs; 200 sheep.
The value was 60s; now 40s.

12   Herlwin holds WINTERHEAD from the Bishop. Brictric held
it before 1066; it paid tax for 1 hide. Land for 2 ploughs.   L
They are there, with   140
    2 villagers, 2 smallholders and 2 slaves.   a 1
    Meadow, 8 acres; a small wood, 3 acres.   8 cows; 40 sheep.
The value was and is 20s.   E
  These three manors were the Church of Glastonbury's before 1066.
The holders could not be separated from the church.

13   Herlwin holds ASHCOMBE from the Bishop. Brictric held it
before 1066; it paid tax for 3½ hides. Land for 5 ploughs.
In lordship 2 ploughs; 7 slaves;   2 hides & 1 virgate.   140
    6 villagers and 5 smallholders with 3 ploughs & 1 hide & 1 virgate.   a 2
    Meadow, 40 acres; underwood, 3 acres; pasture, 100 acres.
        30 cattle; 18 pigs; 136 sheep; 60 goats.
The value was and is 100s.

14   William holds CLUTTON from the Bishop. Thorkell held it
before 1066; it paid tax for 10 hides. Land for 8 ploughs.
In lordship 3 ploughs & 5½ hides, with 1 slave;   140
    10 villagers and 12 smallholders with 6 ploughs & 4½ hides.   a 3
    A mill which pays 30d; meadow, 107 acres; pasture
        10 furlongs long and 4 furlongs wide; woodland ½ league
        long and as wide.   1 cob; 12 cattle; 26 pigs; 176 sheep.
The value was £3; now £6.

15   William holds TIMSBURY from the Bishop. Ape held it
before 1066; it paid tax for 3 hides. Land for 3 ploughs.
In lordship 1 plough; 2 slaves; 1½ hides.   140
    2 villagers and 1 smallholder with 1 plough & 1½ hides.   b 1
    2 parts of a mill which pay 3s; meadow, 26 acres; pasture,
        as much.   1 cob; 9 cattle; 14 pigs; 60 sheep.
The value was 26s; now 50s.

Huic M̄ additæ s̄t.ii.hidæ.q̄s teneb̄ Sibe T.R.E.p̄ uno M̄.7 pro
tanto geldb̄.Tra.ē.ii.cař.q̄ ibi s̄t cū.i.feruo.7 i.uitto 7 iii.bord
Ibi tcia pars molini redd.ii.folid.7 xvi.ac̄ p̄ti.7 tn̄td̄ pafturæ.
Valuit.xiiii.folid.Modo.xxx.folid.

Vlueua teñ de ep̄o NORTONE.Aluuold tenuit T.R.E.7 geldb̄
p̄.v.hid.Tra.ē.viii.cař.In dn̄io.ē.i.cař.7 iii.ferui.7 v.uitti
7 xi.bord cū.iii.cař.Ibi moliñ redd.xl.deñ.7 xxxiiii.ac̄ p̄ti.
7 vi.ac̄ filuæ minutæ.7 una leū Siluæ in lḡ.7 tn̄td̄ in lař.
Valuit.c.fot.Modo.lx.folid.

Folcheran teñ de ep̄o CLIVEHA.Gonnil tenuit T.R.E.7 geldb̄ p̄.ii.
hid.Tra.ē.iii.cař.In dn̄io.ē.i.cař.cū.i.feruo.7 iii.uitti.7 xii.bord.
cū.ii.cař.Ibi.vii.ac̄ p̄ti.Silua.i.q̄ȝ lḡ.7 tn̄td̄ lař.Silua mo
dica dimid̄ leū lḡ.7 tn̄td̄ lař.Valuit.xx.fot.Modo.xxx.fot.

Witts teñ de ep̄o FERENBERGE.Edric tenuit T.R.E.7 geldb̄
p̄.v.hid.Tra.ē.v.cař.In dn̄io s̄t.ii.cař.7 v.ferui.7 iiii.uitti
7 iii.bord cū.ii.cař.Ibi.lxxvii.ac̄ p̄ti.7 lxxiiii.ac̄ pafturæ.
Valuit 7 uat.iiii.lib.

Huic M̄ additæ s̄t.v.hidæ.Alúric tenuit T.R.E.p̄ uno M̄.

88 b

7 p̄.v.hid̄ geldb̄.Tra.ē.v.cař.Nigel teñ de ep̄o.
In dn̄io s̄t.ii.cař.cū.i.feruo.7 i.uitto.7 v.bord.
Ibi.lxxvii.ac̄ p̄ti.7 lxxiiii.ac̄ pafturæ.Valuit 7 uat
Fulcran 7 Nigett teñ de ep̄o CLIVEWARE.⌞iiii.lib.
Turchil tenuit T.R.E.7 geldb̄ p̄.iii.v̄ træ uno ferding
min.Tra.ē.ii.cař.q̄ ibi s̄t cū.vi.uittis.7 x.ac̄ p̄ti.
Herluiñ teñ de ep̄o BICHEVRDE. ⌞Valet.xv.fot.
Algar tenuit T.R.E.7 geldb̄ p̄.ii.hid.Tra.ē.ii.cař.

To this manor have been added 2 hides which Sibbi held as
one manor before 1066; they paid tax for as much. Land for 2
ploughs, which are there, with 1 slave and
  1 villager and 3 smallholders.
  The third part of a mill which pays 2s; meadow, 16 acres;
    pasture, as much. 5 cattle; 6 pigs; 40 sheep.
The value was 14s; now 30s.

16 Wulfeva holds NORTON (Malreward) from the Bishop. Alfwold
held it before 1066; it paid tax for 5 hides. Land for 8 ploughs.
In lordship 1 plough; 3 slaves; 4 hides.
  5 villagers and 11 smallholders with 3 ploughs & 1 hide.
  A mill which pays 40d; meadow, 34 acres; underwood, 6
    acres; woodland, 1 league in length and as much in width.
    1 cob; 9 cattle; 18 pigs; 147 sheep.
The value was 100s; now 60s.

17 Fulcran holds CLAVERHAM from the Bishop. Gunhilda held it
before 1066; it paid tax for 2 hides. Land for 3 ploughs.
In lordship 1 plough & 1 hide, with 1 slave;
  3 villagers and 12 smallholders with 2 ploughs & 1 hide.
  Meadow, 7 acres; woodland 1 furlong long and as wide;
    a small wood ½ league long and as wide. 1 cob; 4 cattle.
The value was 20s; now 30s.

18 William holds FARMBOROUGH from the Bishop. Edric held it
before 1066; it paid tax for 5 hides. Land for 5 ploughs.
In lordship 2 ploughs; 5 slaves; 2½ hides.
  4 villagers and 3 smallholders with 2 ploughs & 2½ hides.
  Meadow, 77 acres; pasture, 74 acres. 1 cob; 14 cattle, 215 sheep.
The value was and is £4.
  To this manor 5 hides have been added. Aelfric held them
before 1066 as one manor; they paid tax for 5 hides. Land for
5 ploughs. Nigel holds from the Bishop. In lordship 2 ploughs
& 4 hides, with 1 slave and
  1 villager and 5 smallholders & 1 hide.
  Meadow, 77 acres; pasture, 74 acres. 21 cattle; 14 pigs; 68 sheep.
The value was and is £4.

19 Fulcran and Nigel hold CLEWER from the Bishop. Thorkell
held it before 1066; it paid tax for 3 virgates of land, less 1
furlong. Land for 2 ploughs, which are there, with
  6 villagers.
  Meadow, 10 acres.
Value 15s; when they acquired it, as much.

20 Herlwin holds BISHOPSWORTH from the Bishop. Algar held it
before 1066; it paid tax for 2 hides. Land for 2 ploughs.

E
L

140
b 2

140
b 3

141
a 1
E

E
141
a 2

E
88 b
141
a 3

141
L b 1
E

In dñio.ē.ı.caŕ.7 ııı.ſerui.7 ıı.borđ.Ibi.xıı.ãc p̃ti.

Silua.vı.q̃ʒ l̃g.7 una q̃ʒ lat̄.In Briſtou.x.dom̃.

In Bade.ıı.dom̃ redđ.x.den̄.Valuit.xx.ſot.M̊.xL.ſot.

Azelin teñ de·ep̃o BISCOPEWRDE.Edric tenuit

T.R.E.7 geldb̃ ꝑ.ı.hida 7 dim̄.Tra.ē.ıı.caŕ.q̃ ibi

ſt̄ cū.ıııı.uittis.7 ıııı.borđ 7 ıııı.cotar̄.Ibi.x.ãc p̃ti.

7 xLv.ãc paſturæ.Valuit.xx.ſolid̄.Modo.xxx.ſot.

Azelin teñ de ep̃o WESTONE.Britnod tenuit T.R.E.

7 geldb̃ ꝑ.vıı.hid̄.Tra.ē.vı.caŕ.In dñio ſt̄.ııı.caŕ.

7 ıı.ſerui.7 vı.uitti 7 vıı.borđ cū.ııı.caŕ.Ibi.xxxııı.

ãc p̃ti.Paſtura.xıı.q̃ʒ l̃g.7 vııı.q̃ʒ lat̄.Silua.

vıı.q̃ʒ l̃g.7 ııı.q̃ʒ lat̄.Valuit 7 uat.ıııı.libֿ 7 x.ſot.

Rogeri teñ de ep̃o SANFORD.Quattuor taini tenuer̄

T.R.E.7 geldb̃ ꝑ.ıııı.hid̄.Tra.ē.vı.caŕ.In dñio ſt̄

.ııı.caŕ.7 vı.ſerui.7 vıı.uitti 7 x.borđ cū.ıııı.caŕ.

Ibi moliñ redđ.xıı.ſot.7 vı.den̄.7 xxx.ıı.ãc p̃ti.

Valuit 7 uat.vı.libֿ.

Roger teñ de ep̃o ESTONE.Ailric tenuit T.R.E.7 geldb̃

ꝑ.xıı.hid̄.Tra.ē.ıx.caŕ.In dñio ſt̄.ıı.caŕ.7 ııı.ſerui.

7 xıııı.uitti 7 vıı.borđ cū.vıı.caŕ.Ibi moliñ redđ

.L.denaŕ.7 xxxvı.ãc p̃ti.7 xxx.ãc ſiluæ.7 c.ãc paſturæ.

Valuit.x.libֿ.Modo.vıı.libֿ.

Witts teñ de ep̃o PORTESHE.Aluric tenuit T.R.E.

7 geldb̃ ꝑ.vııı.hid̄.Tra.ē.vııı.caŕ.In dñio ſt̄.ıı.caŕ.

cū.ı.ſeruo.7 ıx.uitti 7 ıııı.borđ cū.v.caŕ.Ibi moliñ

redđ.vııı.ſolid̄.7 xx.ãc p̃ti.7 c.ãc paſturæ.Silua

minuta.xıı.q̃ʒ l̃g.7 ııı.q̃ʒ lat̄.Valuit 7 uat.Lxx.ſot.

In lordship 1 plough; 3 slaves;
   2 smallholders.
   Meadow, 12 acres; woodland 6 furlongs long and 1 furlong wide;
      in Bristol 10 houses; in Bath 2 houses which pay 10d.
The value was 20s; now 40s.

141
b 2

21 Azelin holds BISHOPSWORTH from the Bishop. Edric held it
before 1066; it paid tax for 1½ hides. Land for 2 ploughs,
which are there, with
   4 villagers, 4 smallholders and 4 cottagers.
   Meadow, 10 acres; pasture, 45 acres.
The value was 20s; now 30s.

L
141
E b 3

22 Azelin holds WESTON (in Gordano) from the Bishop. Brictnoth
held it before 1066; it paid tax for 7 hides. Land for 6 ploughs.
In lordship 3 ploughs; 2 slaves; 5½ hides.
   6 villagers and 7 smallholders with 3 ploughs & 1½ hides.
   Meadow, 33 acres; pasture 12 furlongs long and 8 furlongs
      wide; woodland 7 furlongs long and 3 furlongs wide.
     1 cob; 8 cattle; 7 pigs; 67 sheep; 24 goats.
The value was and is £4 10s.

141
b 4

23 Roger Whiting holds SALTFORD from the Bishop. Four thanes held
it before 1066; it paid tax for 4 hides. Land for 6 ploughs.
In lordship 3 ploughs; 6 slaves; 1½ hides.
   7 villagers and 10 smallholders with 4 ploughs & 2½ hides.
   A mill which pays 12s 6d; meadow, 32 acres. 1 cob; 13 pigs; 120 sheep.
The value was and is £6.

E

142
a 1

24 Roger son of Ralph holds EASTON (in Gordano) from the Bishop.
Alric held it before 1066; it paid tax for 12 hides.
9 ploughs. In lordship 2 ploughs; 3 slaves; 5 hides & 3 virgates.
   14 villagers and 7 smallholders with 7 ploughs & 6 hides & 1 virgate.
   A mill which pays 50d; meadow, 36 acres; woodland,
     30 acres; pasture, 100 acres. 2 cobs; 3 unbroken mares;
     12 cattle; 20 pigs; 200 sheep.
The value was £10; now £7.

142
a 2

25 William of Monceaux holds PORTISHEAD from the Bishop.
Aelfric Young held it before 1066; it paid tax for 8 hides.
Land for 8 ploughs. In lordship 2 ploughs & 6 hides, with 1 slave;
   9 villagers and 4 smallholders with 5 ploughs & 2 hides.
   A mill which pays 8s; meadow, 20 acres; pasture, 100 acres;
     underwood 12 furlongs long and 3 furlongs wide. 8 cattle;
     10 pigs; 60 goats.
The value was and is 70s.

142
a 3

Wills teñ de eṕo *WESTONE* . Algar tenuit T.R.E . 7 geldb
p.iii.hiđ 7 una v̓ træ.Tra.ē.iii.car̄. In dñio sẽ.ii.car̄.
7 ii.ſerui.7 iiii.uilli 7 iiii.borđ cũ.ii.car̄. Ibi.xvii.ac̄
p̃ti.7 xii.ac̄ ſiluæ minutæ . paſtura.xii.q̃ʒ lḡ.7 ii.q̃ʒ
lat̄.7 vi.q̃ʒ moræ. Valuit 7 ual.lx . ſolid.

Herluin teñ de eṕo *CLOTVNE* . Algar tenuit T.R.E.
7 geldb p.v.hiđ 7 dim̓.Tra.ē.v.car̄. In dñio sẽ.ii.car̄.
7 ii.ſerui.7 x.uilli 7 x.borđ cũ.iii.car̄. Ibi.l.ac̄ p̃ti.
Paſtura.xviii.q̃ʒ lḡ.7 iii.q̃ʒ lat̄.Silua.vii.q̃ʒ lḡ.
7 una q̃ʒ lat̄.Valuit.xl.ſolid.Modo.lxx.ſolid.

Brungar teñ de eṕo *ATIGETE*. Tidulf tenuit T.R.E
7 geldb p hida 7 dim̄.Tra.ē.i.car̄.q̄ ibi.ē in dñio.
cũ.iii.borđ.Ibi.x.ac̄ p̃ti.7 xx.ac̄ ſiluæ. Valuit 7 ual

Ipſe eṕs teñ unā trā q̄ uocat̄ *CHEN*.Ibi.ē ⌐ xx.ſol.
dimiđ hida.7 ibi hẽ.i.ſeruũ.Valet.v.ſoliđ.

Fulcran 7 Nigel teñ de eṕo *BACOILE*. Turchil tenuit T.R.E.
7 geldb p.x.hiđ.Tra.ē.xiiii.car̄. Has hñt ibi.xxxii.
uilli 7 xxi.borđ 7 ii.ſerui. Ibi moliñ redđ.iiii.ſoliđ.
7 xxiiii.ac̄ p̃ti.Paſtura.i.leũ lḡ.7 dimiđ leũ lat̄.Silua
minuta.i.leũ lḡ.7 ii q̃ʒ lat̄.Valuit 7 ual.viii.lib.

Fulcran teñ de eṕo *BVDICOME*.Eluuard tenuit T.R.E.
7 geldb p.iii.hiđ.Tra.ē.iii.car̄.In dñio.ē.i.car̄.7 ii.
ſerui.7 xi.uilli 7 iiii.borđ cũ.v.car̄.Ibi moliñ redđ
xx.denar̄.7 x.ac̄ p̃ti.7 xxx.ac̄ ſiluæ.Valuit 7 ual.iiii.lib.

Nigel teñ de eṕo *BERVE*.Edric tenuit T.R.E.7 geldb
p.x.hiđ.Tra.ē.xiiii.car̄.In dñio sẽ.ii.car̄.7 iii.ſerui.

26 William holds WESTON (in Gordano) from the Bishop. Algar held
   it before 1066; it paid tax for 3 hides and 1 virgate of land. Land
   for 3 ploughs. In lordship 2 ploughs; 2 slaves; 2½ hides & 1½ virgates.   E
       4 villagers and 4 smallholders with 2 ploughs & ½ hide & ½ virgate.   142
       Meadow, 17 acres; underwood, 12 acres; pasture 12 furlongs   b 1
           long and 2 furlongs wide; moor, 6 furlongs. 100 sheep.
   The value was and is 60s.

27 Herlwin holds CLAPTON (in Gordano) from the Bishop. Algar held   E
   it before 1066; it paid tax for 5½ hides. Land for 5 ploughs.
   In lordship 2 ploughs; 2 slaves; 3½ hides.
       10 villagers and 10 smallholders with 3 ploughs & 2 hides,
       less 1 virgate.   142
       Meadow, 50 acres; pasture 18 furlongs long and 3 furlongs   b 2
           wide; woodland 7 furlongs long and 1 furlong wide.
       1 cob; 16 cattle; 40 pigs; 50 goats.
   The value was 40s; now 70s.

28 Brungar the Englishman holds HAVYATT from the Bishop. Tidwulf   E
   held it before 1066; it paid tax for 1½ hides. Land for 1 plough,
   which is there, in lordship, with
       3 smallholders.   142
       Meadow, 10 acres; woodland, 20 acres. 4 cows; 5 pigs; 100 sheep;   b 3
       50 goats.
   The value was and is 20s.

29 The Bishop himself holds one land called KENN. ½ hide.
   He has 1 slave.   143
   Value 5s.   a 1

30 Fulcran and Nigel hold BACKWELL from the Bishop. Thorkell
   held it before 1066; it paid tax for 10 hides. Land for 14 ploughs.
       32 villagers, 21 smallholders and 2 slaves have them there.
       A burgess who lives in Bath & pays 32d a year.   143
       A mill which pays 4s; meadow, 24 acres; pasture 1 league   a 2
           long and ½ league wide; underwood 1 league long and 2
           furlongs wide. 23 pigs.
   The value was and is £8.

31 Fulcran holds BUTCOMBE from the Bishop. Alfward held it before
   1066; it paid tax for 3 hides. Land for 3 ploughs. In lordship 1
   plough; 2 slaves; 1 virgate.   143
       11 villagers and 4 smallholders with 5 ploughs & 3 hides,less 1 virgate.   a 3
       A mill which pays 20d; meadow, 10 acres; woodland, 30 acres.
       1 cob; 6 cattle; 2 pigs; 124 sheep.
   The value was and is £4.

32 Nigel of Gournai holds BARROW (Gurney) from the Bishop. Edric
   held it before 1066; it paid tax for 10 hides. Land for 14
   ploughs. In lordship 2 ploughs; 3 slaves; 5 hides.   143
                                                                            a 4

88 b

7 xv . uitti 7 vii . borđ . Ibi moliñ redđ . v . ſolid . 7 xxxv .

ac p̄ti . 7 xxx . ac paſturæ . Silua . i . leū lḡ . 7 una q̃z lat̄ .

Valuit 7 uat̄ . x . liƀ .

Ipſe ep̄s teñ *Porberie* . Goduin tenuit T . R . E . 7 geldƀ

p̃ . viii . hiđ . Tra . ē . xviii . car̄ . In dñio ſt̄ . ii . car̄ . 7 xiii .

ſerui . 7 xx . uitti 7 xvii . borđ cū . xvi . car̄ . Ibi . ii . molini

redđ . vi . ſolid . 7 cl . ac p̄ti . Paſtura . xvii . q̃z lḡ . 7 ii .

q̃z lat̄ . Silua . i . leū lḡ . 7 v . q̃z lat̄ . Valuit 7 uat̄ . xv . liƀ .

Ipſe ep̄s teñ *Estvne* . Tres taini tenuer̄ T . R . E . 7 geldƀ

p̃ . xx . hiđ . Tra . ē . xxx . car̄ . In dñio ſt̄ . ii . car̄ . 7 v . ſerui .

7 xii . uitti 7 vi . borđ cū . vii . car̄ . Ibi moliñ redđ . xl .

den . 7 xxv . ac p̄ti . Paſtura . i . leū lḡ . 7 dimiđ leū lat̄ .

7 ċ . ac ſiluæ . Valuit . xii . liƀ . Modo . x . liƀ .

De hac tra huj M teñ Roge de ep̄o . vii . hiđ . 7 ibi h̄t

in dñio . ii . car̄ . 7 iiii . ſeruos . 7 viii . uitt 7 x . borđ cū . v .

car̄ . Ibi . xviii . ac p̄ti . 7 xxx . ac ſiluæ . Valet . vii . liƀ .

De eađ tra ejđ M teñ Widó . iii . hiđ . 7 ibi h̄t . ii . car̄ .

7 ii . ſeruos . 7 iii . uitt 7 ii . borđ cū . ii . car̄ . Valet . c . ſot̄ .

Ad æcctam huj M ptiñ una virḡ de eađ tra .

Roger teñ de ep̄o *Firford* . Toui tenuit T . R . E . 7 geldƀ

p̃ . ii . hiđ 7 dimiđ . Tra . ē . iii . car̄ . In dñio ſt̄ . ii . car̄ .

7 viii . borđ cū . i . car̄ . Ibi dimiđ moliñ redđ . v . ſot̄ . 7 xii .

ac p̄ti . 7 xxx . ac paſturæ . 7 xii . ac ſiluæ minutæ .

Valuit . xl . ſolid . Modo . lx . ſolid .

15 villagers and 7 smallholders (have) 12 ploughs & 5 hides.
A mill which pays 5s; meadow, 35 acres; pasture, 30 acres;
woodland 1 league long and 1 furlong wide.
2 cobs; 27 cattle; 14 pigs; 152 sheep, 50 goats.
The value was and is £10.

33 The Bishop holds PORTBURY himself. Godwin held it before
1066; it paid tax for 8 hides. Land for 18 ploughs. In
lordship 2 ploughs; 13 slaves; 1 hide & 1 virgate.
    20 villagers and 17 smallholders with 16 ploughs
      & 6½ hides & 1 virgate.
    2 mills which pay 6s; meadow, 150 acres; pasture 17 furlongs
      long and 2 furlongs wide; woodland 1 league long and
      5 furlongs wide. 2 cobs; 14 unbroken mares; 15 cattle; 18 pigs; 216 sheep.
The value was and is £15.

    88 c

    143
    b 1

34 The Bishop holds (Long) ASHTON himself. Three thanes held it
before 1066; it paid tax for 20 hides. Land for 30 ploughs.
In lordship 2 ploughs; 5 slaves; 6 hides, less 1 virgate.
    12 villagers and 6 smallholders with 7 ploughs & 4 hides & 1 virgate.
    A mill which pays 40d; meadow, 25 acres; pasture 1
      league long and ½ league wide; woodland, 100 acres.
      1 cob; 14 cattle; 12 pigs; 27 sheep; 20 goats.
The value was £12; now £10.
  Roger the Bursar holds 7 hides of this manor's land from the
Bishop. He has 2 ploughs in lordship and 4 slaves; 4 hides,
less 1 virgate.
    8 villagers and 10 smallholders with 5 ploughs & 3 hides.
    Meadow, 18 acres; woodland, 30 acres. 2 cobs; 14 cattle; 22 pigs;
      36 sheep; 14 goats.
Value £7; when Roger acquired them, 100s.
  Guy the priest holds 3 hides of this manor's land. He has
2 ploughs and 2 slaves;
    3 villagers and 2 smallholders with 2 ploughs.
    2 cobs; 13 cattle; 60 unbroken mares; 22 pigs; 80 sheep; 30 goats.
Value 100s; when he acquired them, 20s.
  1 virgate of this land belongs to this manor's church; a priest holds it.
The Bishop holds these three manors as one manor.

    E

    143
    b 2

35 Roger Whiting holds FRESHFORD from the Bishop. Tovi held
it before 1066; it paid tax for 2½ hides. Land for 3 ploughs.
In lordship 2 ploughs; 1½ hides & ½ virgate.
    8 smallholders with 1 plough & 1 hide, less ½ virgate.
    ½ mill which pays 5s; meadow, 12 acres; pasture, 30 acres.
      underwood, 12 acres. 2 cobs; 8 cattle; 15 pigs; 44 sheep.
The value was 40s; now 60s.

    144
    a 1

Azelin teñ̄ de epo *LANCHERIS*. Ælſi tenuit T.R.E.

7 geldɓ ꝑ.ii.hiɗ 7 dim. Tra.ē.v.caɍ.In dñio ſt.iii.

caɍ.7 iii.ſerui.7 v. uiłłi 7 vii.borɗ.cū.ii.caɍ.Ibi mo

liñ redɗ.xl.deñ.7 iiii.ac ꝑti 7 dimiɗ.7 cxxx.ac

paſturæ.Valuit.xl.ſoliɗ.modó.lx.ſoliɗ.

Ipſe eps teñ *WICHE*. Aluric tenuit T.R.E.7 geldɓ

ꝑ.iiii.hiɗ.Tra.ē.iiii.caɍ.In dñio ſt.iii.caɍ.7 iiii.ſerui.

7 uñ uiłłs 7 x.borɗ.Ibi moliñ redɗ xxxv.ſoł.7 l.ac

ꝑti.7 cxx.ac paſturæ.Valet.vii.liɓ.

Huic Ꝏ addita.ē una hida in *WILEGE*.quã teneɓ Aluric

T.R.E.ꝑ uno Ꝏ.7 ꝑ.i.hida gelɗ.Ibi ſt.ii.caɍ.7 vi.ſer

ui.7 ix.borɗ cū.i.caɍ.Ibi.ii.molini redɗ.ii.ſoliɗ.

7 xx.ac ſiluæ minutæ.Valuit 7 uał.lx.ſoliɗ.

Nigel teñ de epo *WICHE*. Alured tenuit T.R.E.7 geldɓ

ꝑ.i.hida.Tra.ē.i.caɍ.Valuit 7 uał.xx.ſoliɗ.

Ipſe eps teñ *CONTONE*. Edric tenuit T.R.E.7 geldɓ ꝑ.x.

hiɗ.Tra.ē.xiiii.caɍ.In dñio.ē.i.caɍ.7 iiii.ſerui.7 xvi.

uiłłi.7 vi.borɗ.cū.vi.caɍ.Ibi.ii.molini redɗ.xxv.

ſoliɗ.7 xv.ac ꝑti.7 c.ac paſturæ.7 xv.ac ſiluæ.

Valuit 7 uał.x.liɓ.

Ipſe eps teñ *WEROCOSALE*. Aluric tenuit T.R.E.7 gelɗ

ꝑ.xx.hiɗ.Tra.ē.xxvi.caɍ.In dñio.ē.i.caɍ.7 ii.ſerui.

7 xxxiiii.uiłłi 7 xxx.borɗ cū.xxv.caɍ.Ibi.ii.molini

redɗ.xii.ſoliɗ 7 vi.deñ.7 cl.ac ꝑti.7 tñtɗ ſilue.

Paſtura.ii.leū lḡ.7 vii.q̃ lat.Valuit 7 uał xv.liɓ.

De eaɗ tra huj Ꝏ teñ uñ miles.iiii.hiɗ 7 diñ de epo.

7 ibi hɓ.ii.caɍ cū.iii.uiłł 7 iiii.borɗ.Valuit 7 uał.l.ſoł.

36 Azelin holds LANGRIDGE from the Bishop. Alfsi held it
before 1066; it paid tax for 2½ hides. Land for 5 ploughs.
In lordship 3 ploughs; 3 slaves; 1 hide.
    5 villagers and 7 smallholders with 2 ploughs & 1½ hides.   144
    A mill which pays 40d; meadow, 4½ acres; pasture,   a 2
        130 acres. 17 cattle; 4 pigs; 200 sheep, less 6.
The value was 40s; now 60s.

37 The Bishop holds BATHWICK himself. Aelfric held it before 1066;   E
it paid tax for 4 hides. Land for 4 ploughs. In lordship 3
ploughs; 4 slaves; 3 hides & 11 acres.
    1 villager and 10 smallholders who have 1 hide, less 11 acres.   144
    A mill which pays 35s; meadow, 50 acres; pasture,   a 3
        120 acres. 2 cobs; 14 pigs; 250 sheep.
Value £7.
    To this manor has been added 1 hide in WOOLLEY which Aelfric   E
held before 1066 as one manor; it paid tax for 1 hide. 2
ploughs there, in lordship, & 1 virgate less 3 acres; 6 slaves.
    9 smallholders with 1 plough & 3 virgates.
    2 mills which pay 2s; underwood, 20 acres. 1 cob; 14 pigs;   E
        106 sheep; 33 goats.
The value was and is 60s.
The Bishop holds these two manors from the King as one manor.

38 Nigel of Gournai holds SWAINSWICK from the Bishop. Alfred held
it before 1066; it paid tax for 1 hide. Land for 1 plough.   144
The value was and is 20s.   b 1

39 The Bishop holds COMPTON (Dando) himself. Edric Young held it
before 1066; it paid tax for 10 hides. Land for 14 ploughs.
In lordship 1 plough; 4 slaves; 3 hides & 3 virgates.   144
    16 villagers and 6 smallholders with 6 ploughs & 6 hides & 1 virgate.   b 2
    2 mills which pay 25s; meadow, 15 acres; pasture, 100 acres;
        woodland, 15 acres. 1 cob; 16 cattle; 14 pigs; 120 sheep.
The value was and is £10.

40 The Bishop holds WRAXALL himself. Aelfric held it before 1066;
it paid tax for 20 hides. Land for 26 ploughs. In lordship 1
plough; 2 slaves; 7½ hides.   144
    34 villagers and 30 smallholders with 25 ploughs & 8½ hides.   b 3
    2 mills which pay 12s 6d; meadow, 150 acres; woodland,
        as much; pasture 2 leagues long and 7 furlongs wide.
        2 cobs; 2 unbroken mares; 24 cattle; 19 pigs; 100 sheep, less 4.
The value was and is £15.
    A man-at-arms holds 4½ hides of this manor's land from the
Bishop; he has 2 ploughs there, with   E
    3 villagers and 4 smallholders. 70 sheep.
The value was and is 50s.

Huic M̄ addita.ē una hida.quā tenuit un̊ tain̊ T.R.E.

Tra̅.ē.ɪ.car̅.Valet.x.ſoliđ.

Eps ten̅ *WENFRE*.Aluuold tenuit T.R.E.7 geldb

đ.x.hiđ.Tra̅.ē.xxɪɪ.car̅.De ea ten̅ Roger.ɪɪɪɪ.hiđ

Folcran.v.hiđ.Colſuain.ɪ.hiđ.In dn̄io hn̄t.v.car̅.

7 ibi.vɪɪ.ſerui.7 xɪx.uiłłi.7 xɪɪ.borđ.cū.xɪɪɪɪ.car̅.

Ibi molin̅ redđ.xʟ.den̅.7 xx.ãc p̃ti.Paſtura.ɪɪ.q̃ꝝ l̄g.

7 una q̃ꝝ lat̅.Silua.ɪ.ℓcu l̄g.7 ɪɪ.q̃ꝝ lat̅.

Totū ualuit.ɪx.lib 7 v.ſot.Modo.xx.ſot plus.

Huic M̄ addita.ē una hida quā tenuit Aluric T.R.E.

N̄c ten̅ Colſuain de epo.7 ibi ht̅.ɪɪ.car̅ 7 ɪɪ.borđ.

Valuit 7 uat.xxv.ſoliđ.

Wiłłs ten̅ *FVSCOTE*.Aldida tenuit T.R.E.7 geldb

đ.v.hiđ.Tra̅.ē.ɪɪɪɪ.car̅.In dn̄io ſt̅.ɪɪ.car̅.7 ɪɪɪ.ſerui.

7 ɪɪ.cotar̅.7 ɪɪɪ.uiłłi.7 vɪ.borđ cū.ɪɪ.car̅.Ibi molin̅ redđ

x.ſoliđ.7 xɪx.ãc p̃ti.7 vɪ.ãc paſturæ.7 xx.ãc ſiluæ minutæ.

Valuit 7 uat.ɪɪɪɪ.lib.

☞ Idē.W.ten̅ de epo *STRATONE*.Aluuold tenuit T.R.E.de
æccła Glaſtingłe ie.nec poterat ab ea ſeparari.7 gełd đ.ɪɪɪ.hiđ.

88 d

.Tra̅.ē.ɪɪɪ.car̅.In dn̄io ſt̅.ɪɪ.car̅.7 ɪɪɪ.ſerui.7 v.uiłłi 7 vɪ.borđ cū car̅

7 dimiđ.Ibi molin̅ redđ.v.ſoliđ.7 xx.ãc p̃ti.Paſturæ.ɪɪɪɪ.q̃ꝝ int

l̄g 7 lat̅.Silua.ɪɪɪ.q̃ꝝ l̄g.7 ɪɪ.q̃ꝝ lat̅.Valuit.ʟ.ſot.Modo.ɪɪɪɪ.lib.

Huic M̄ addita.ē.ɪ.hida 7 dim in *PICOTE*.Wlmar teneb T.R.E.

7 poterat ire q̊ uoleb.Tra̅.ē.ɪ.car̅.Ibi ſt̅.ɪɪ.uiłłi 7 ɪɪ.borđ cū.ɪ.ſeruo.

Ibi molin̅ redđ.xʟ.den̅.7 vɪɪ.ãc p̃ti.7 ɪɪ.q̃ꝝ paſturæ.7 una q̃ꝝ

ſiluæ.Valuit 7 uat.xx.ſoliđ.Wiłłs ten̅ de epo.

To this manor has been added 1 hide which a thane held
before 1066. Land for 1 plough.
Value 10s.

E

41 The Bishop holds WINFORD. Alfwold held it before 1066;
it paid tax for 10 hides. Land for 22 ploughs, of which Roger
Whiting holds 4 hides, Fulcran 5 hides, Colswein 1 hide.
They have 5 ploughs in lordship; 7 slaves there;
    19 villagers and 12 smallholders with 14 ploughs.
    A mill which pays 40d; meadow, 20 acres; pasture 2
        furlongs long and 1 furlong wide; woodland 1 league
        long and 2 furlongs wide.
The value of the whole was £9 5s; now 20s more.
    To this manor has been added 1 hide which Aelfric held
before 1066. Now Colswein holds from the Bishop; he has
2 ploughs there, and
    2 smallholders. 5 pigs; 60 sheep.
The value was and is 25s.

D

145
a 1

E
E

E

42 William of Monceaux holds FOXCOTE. Aldith held it before 1066;
it paid tax for 5 hides. Land for 4 ploughs. In lordship
2 ploughs; 3 slaves; 3 hides & 3 virgates.
    2 cottagers, 3 villagers and 6 smallholders with
        2 ploughs & 1 hide & 1 virgate.
    A mill which pays 10s; meadow, 19 acres; pasture, 6 acres;
        underwood, 20 acres. 20 cattle; 29 pigs; 177 sheep.
The value was and is £4.

145
b 1

† 43 William of Monceaux also holds STRATTON (on the Fosse) from
the Bishop. Alfwold held it before 1066 from Glastonbury
Church; he could not be separated from it. It paid tax for 3
hides. Land for 3 ploughs. In lordship 2 ploughs;
3 slaves; 2½ hides.
    5 villagers and 6 smallholders with 1½ ploughs & ½ hide.
    A mill which pays 5s; meadow, 20 acres; pasture, 4 furlongs
        in both length and width; woodland 3 furlongs long and
        2 furlongs wide. 1 cob; 10 cattle; 27 unbroken mares; 21 pigs;
        317 sheep; 43 goats.
The value was 50s; now £4.
    To this manor have been added 1½ hides in PITCOTE. Wulfmer
held them before 1066; he could go where he would.
Land for 1 plough. In lordship 1 hide & 1 virgate.
    2 villagers and 2 smallholders with 1 slave; 1 virgate & ½ plough.
    A mill which pays 40d; meadow, 7 acres; pasture, 2
        furlongs; woodland, 1 furlong.
The value was and is 20s.
    William Hussey holds from the Bishop.
    The Bishop holds these two manors as one manor.

E

88 d

145
b 2

E
E

E
E

E

88 c, d

Nigel ten de epo *ENGLISCOME*. Vn̄ tain tenuit T.R.E.7 geldb̄
p.x.hid.Tra.ē.x.car̄.In dn̄io st̄.iii.car̄.7 vi.ferui.7 iii.uilli
7 xvii.bord cū.vi.car̄.Ibi.ii.molini redd.xi.fol 7 vii.denar̄.
Ibi.xii.ac pti.7 c.ac filuæ minutæ.Valuit 7 ual.x.lib.

Idē.N.ten de epo *TVVERTONE*.Tres taini tenuer̄ T.R.E.7 geldb̄
p.vii.hid 7 dimid.Tra.ē.x.car̄.In dn̄io st̄.iii.car̄.7 vi.ferui.
7 vii.uilli 7 xiii.bord.cū.vi.car̄.Ibi.ii.molini redd.xxx.fol.
7 xv.ac pti.Valuit 7 ual.x.lib.

Goisfrid ten de epo *TVVERTONE*.Vn̄ tain tenuit T.R.E.7 geldb̄
p.ii.hid.7 dim.Tra.ē.ii.car̄ 7 dim.q̄ ibi st̄ in dn̄io cū.iiii.bord
7 ii.feruis.Ibi.ii.molini redd.xxx.fol.7 vii.ac pti.7 iii.ac filuæ
minutæ.Valuit 7 ual.lx.folid.   ſut dicit.
Hanc tr̄a tenuit Alured de Eddid regina.Modo ten eps de rege

Rogeri ten de epo *STOCHE*.Aluied Aluuin 7 Ælgar tenb̄ T.R.E.
7 geldb̄ p.vii.hid 7 iii.virg.Tra.ē.ix.car̄.In dn̄io st̄.iii.car̄.
7 ii.ferui.7 ix.uilli 7 xii.bord 7 iii.cotar cū.iiii.car̄.Ibi mol.n̄
redd.xiii.folid.7 xii.ac pti.Valuit 7 ual.vii.lib.

Radulf ten de epo *HARDINTONE*.Tres taini tenuer̄ T.R.E.
7 geldb̄ p.iiii.hid.Tra.ē.iiii.car̄.In dn̄io st̄.ii.car̄.7 iiii.ferui.
7 un uilts 7 vii.bord cū.iii.car̄.Ibi.xxx.vi.ac pti.7 xii.ac filuæ mi
nutæ.Valuit 7 ual.iiii.lib.In hoc m̄.ē una hida ptin ad *HAMINTONE*.
Balduin tenet.7 ht̄ comune paftura huic m̄.

Azelin ten de epo *BABINGTONE*.Duo taini tenuer̄ T.R.E.7 geldb̄
p.v.hid.Tra.ē.iiii.car̄.In dn̄io st̄.ii.car̄.7 vii.ferui.7 ii.uilli 7 ii.
bord cū.iii.car̄.Ibi molin̄ redd.xl.denar̄.7 xii.ac pti.7 xv.ac pa

44 Nigel of Gournai holds ENGLISHCOMBE from the Bishop. A thane   E
held it before 1066; it paid tax for 10 hides. Land for 10 ploughs.
In lordship 3 ploughs; 6 slaves; 6½ hides & 1 virgate.   146
    3 villagers and 17 smallholders with 6 ploughs & 4 hides & 1 virgate.   a 1
    2 mills which pay 11s 7d. Meadow, 12 acres; underwood,
       100 acres.   2 cobs; 9 cattle; 24 pigs; 137 sheep.
The value was and is £10.

45 Nigel of Gournai also holds TWERTON from the Bishop. Three thanes   E
held it before 1066; it paid tax for 7½ hides. Land for 10
ploughs. In lordship 3 ploughs; 6 slaves; 3½ hides.   146
    7 villagers and 13 smallholders with 6 ploughs & 3 hides.   a 2
    2 mills which pay 30s; meadow, 15 acres.   2 cobs; 11 cattle; 17 pigs;
      200 sheep.
The value was and is £10.

46 Geoffrey Malregard holds TWERTON from the Bishop. A thane   E
held it before 1066; it paid tax for 2½ hides. Land for 2½
ploughs, which are there, in lordship, with
    4 smallholders and 2 slaves.   146
    2 mills which pay 30s; meadow, 7 acres; underwood,   b 1
      3 acres.   2 cobs; 6 cattle; 18 pigs; 200 sheep.
The value was and is 60s.
    Alfred the Steward held this land from Queen Edith.
Now the Bishop holds from the King, as he states.

47 Roger holds RADSTOCK from the Bishop. Alfgeat, Alwin and Algar   E
held it before 1066; it paid tax for 7 hides and 3 virgates.   146
Land for 9 ploughs. In lordship 3 ploughs; 2 slaves; 3½ hides.   b 2
    9 villagers, 12 smallholders and 3 cottagers with   . E
      4 ploughs & 4 hides & 1 virgate.
    A mill which pays 13s; meadow, 12 acres.   1 cob; 5 cattle; 22 pigs;   E
      210 sheep.
The value was and is £7.

48 Ralph Rufus holds HARDINGTON from the Bishop. Three thanes   E
held it before 1066; it paid tax for 4 hides. Land for 4 ploughs.
In lordship 2 ploughs; 4 slaves; 3 hides & 1 virgate.   147
    1 villager and 7 smallholders with 3 ploughs & 3 virgates.   a 1
    Meadow, 36 acres; underwood, 12 acres.   1 cob; 6 cattle;
      28 pigs; 26 sheep; 2 asses.
The value was and is £4.
    In this manor is 1 hide which belongs to Hemington.   E
Baldwin holds it; he has common pasture in this manor.

49 Azelin holds BABINGTON from the Bishop. Two thanes held   E
it before 1066; it paid tax for 5 hides. Land for 4 ploughs.
In lordship 2 ploughs; 7 slaves; 4 hides & 1 virgate.   147
    2 villagers and 2 smallholders with 3 ploughs & 3 virgates.   a 2
    A mill which pays 40d; meadow, 12 acres; pasture, 15 acres;   E

sturæ.Silua.vi.q̃ʒ lḡ.7 ii.q̃ʒ lat̄.Valuit.xl.fol.Modo.lx.folid.

☞ Azelin ten̄ de epo *MILLESCOTE*.Duo taini tenuer̄ de æccl̄a Glaf
tingbie.nec poterant ab ea feparari.7 geldb̄ ꝓ.v.hid.7 dimid.
Tra.ē.v.car̄.In dn̄io.ē.i.car̄ 7 dim.7 iii.ferui.7 ix.uiłłi 7 vi.bord
7 v.cotar cū.v.car̄.Ibi molin̄ redd.vi.foł 7 vi.den.7 iii.ac̄ p̄ti.
Paftura.iiii.q̃ʒ lḡ.7 ii.q̃ʒ lat̄.7 tnt̄d filuæ.Valuit.xl.fol.Modo
Ipfe ep̄s ten̄ *LOLIGTONE*.Herald tenuit T.R.E.7 geldb̄ ⌐ iiii.lib.
ꝓ.vii.hid.Tra.ē.v.car̄.In dn̄io ft̄.ii.car̄.7 ii.ferui.7 vii.uiłłi
7 x.bord cū.iiii.car̄.Ibi molin̄ redd.xx.folid.7 xx.ac̄ p̄ti.
Silua.vi.q̃ʒ lḡ.7 ii.q̃ʒ lat̄.Valuit.iiii.lib.Modo.c.folid.
Ipfe ep̄s ten̄ *HORCERLEI*.Tres taini tenuer̄ T.R.E.7 geldb̄ ꝓ.v.
hid.Tra.ē.iiii.car̄.In dn̄io ft̄.iiii.car̄.7 ii.ferui.7 iii.uiłłi.7 ix.
bord cū.ii.car̄.Ibi molin̄ redd.xii.folid.7 vi.den.7 xxiiii.ac̄ p̄ti.
Silua.vi.q̃ʒ lḡ.7 ii.q̃ʒ lat̄.Valuit 7 uał.iiii.lib.
Moy̆fes ten̄ de epo *TABLESFORD*.Eduuard tenuit T.R.E.7 geldb̄
ꝓ.ii.hid.Tra.ē.iii.car̄.In dn̄io ft̄.ii.car̄.7 v.cotar 7 iiii.bord cū
una car̄ 7 dim.Ibi dimid molin̄ redd.vii.foł 7 vi.denar.7 vii.ac̄
p̄ti.7 x.ac̄ pafturæ.7 una ac̄ filuæ 7 dimid.Valet.xxx.folid.
Huic M̃ ft̄ additæ.iii.hidæ.Aluiet tenuit T.R.E.7 ꝓ tanto geldb̄
Tra.ē.iiii.car̄.In dn̄io.ē.i.car̄.7 iii.ferui.7 iii.uiłłi 7 viii.bord
cū.ii.car̄.Ibi dim molin̄ redd.ix.foł.7 xi.ac̄ p̄ti 7 dimid.7 xxx.
ac̄ pafturæ.7 iiii.ac̄ filuæ 7 dimid.Valuit lx.foł.Modo.xl.fol.

woodland 6 furlongs long and 2 furlongs wide. 2 cobs; 1 (head of) cattle; 13 pigs; 200 sheep.
The value was 40s; now 60s.

50 Azelin holds 'MIDDLECOTE' from the Bishop. Two thanes held it ⸕E
from Glastonbury Church; they could not be separated from it; E
it paid tax for 5½ hides. Land for 5 ploughs. In lordship 1½
ploughs; 3 slaves; 2½ hides. 147
    9 villagers, 6 smallholders and 5 cottagers with 5 ploughs & 3 hides. b 1
    A mill which pays 6s 6d; meadow, 3 acres; pasture 4 furlongs
      long and 2 furlongs wide; woodland, as much. 2 cattle;
    9 pigs, 30 sheep.
The value was 40s; now £4.

51 The Bishop holds LULLINGTON himself. Earl Harold held it
before 1066; it paid tax for 7 hides. Land for 5 ploughs.
In lordship 2 ploughs; 2 slaves; 4 hides. 147
    7 villagers and 10 smallholders with 4 ploughs & 3 hides. b 2
    A mill which pays 20s; meadow, 20 acres; woodland 6 furlongs
      long and 2 furlongs wide. 2 cobs; 4 cattle; 16 pigs; 220 sheep.
The value was £4; now 100s.

52 The Bishop holds ORCHARDLEIGH himself. Three thanes held it E
before 1066; it paid tax for 5 hides. Land for 4 ploughs.
In lordship 3 ploughs; 2 slaves; 3 hides. 147
    3 villagers and 9 smallholders with 2 ploughs & 2 hides. b 3
    A mill which pays 12s 6d; meadow, 24 acres; woodland 6
      furlongs long and 2 furlongs wide. 3 cobs; 14 goats.
The value was and is £4.

53 Moses holds TELLISFORD from the Bishop. Edward held it
before 1066; it paid tax for 2 hides. Land for 3 ploughs.
In lordship 2 ploughs; 1½ hides. 148
    5 cottagers and 4 smallholders with 1½ ploughs & ½ hide. a 1
    ½ mill which pays 7s 6d; meadow, 7 acres; pasture, 10 acres;
      woodland, 1½ acres. 7 cattle; 13 pigs; 100 sheep, less 5; 29 goats.
Value 30s; when the Bishop acquired it, 20s.

    To this manor 3 hides have been added. Alfgeat held them E
before 1066; they paid tax for as much. Land for 4 ploughs.
In lordship 1 plough; 3 slaves; 1 hide & 3 virgates.
    3 villagers and 8 smallholders with 2 ploughs & the rest of the land.
    ½ mill which pays 9s; meadow, 11½ acres; pasture, 30 acres;
      woodland, 4½ acres. 12 pigs; 65 sheep; 24 goats.
The value was 60s; now 40s.
    Roger holds from the Bishop.
    The Bishop has these two manors as one manor.

Eps ten *RODE* ꝓ.iii.ⒸⓂ.Septē taini tenuer̃ T.R.E.⁊ geldb̃ ꝓ.ix.
hid̃.Tra.ē.ix.car̃.De ea ten de eꝑo Rob̃t.i.hid̃.Moẏſes dim̃
hidã.Rob̃t.i.hidã ⁊ dimid.Roger.ii.hid̃ ⁊ dim̃.Sireuuold
.ii.hid̃ ⁊ dim̃.Ricard.i.hid̃.In dñio ſt.vii.car̃.⁊ vi.ſerui.⁊ iii.
uiłłi ⁊ xxix.bord cũ.iiii.car̃ ⁊ dim̃.De molinis exeũt.xxvii.ſolid̃.
⁊ xxxiii.aͨ p̃ti.⁊ xxxiii.aͨ ſiluæ.⁊ xxv.aͨ paſturæ.
Toͭ ualuit.vii.lib̃ ⁊ x.ſoł.Modo inͭ om̃s uaͭ.viii.lib̃ ⁊ v.ſoł.

Nigel ten de eꝑo *CAIVEL*.Leuedai tenuit T.R.E.⁊ geldb̃ ꝓ una
hida ⁊ una v̄ træ.Tra.ē.i.car̃.ꝗ ibi.ē in dñio cũ.xii.cotar̃.
Ibi molin̄ redd.xxx.denar̃.⁊ vi.aͨ p̃ti.⁊ v.aͨ paſturæ.
valuit.x.ſolid̃.Modo.xv.ſolid̃.

Oſmund ten de eꝑo *LITELTONE*.Gõduin tenuit T.R.E.⁊ geldb̃
ꝓ.ii.hid̃.Tra.ē.ii.car̃.ꝗ ibi ſt·in dñio cũ.i.bord ⁊ vi.ſeruis.
Ibi molin̄ redd.x.ſolid̃.⁊ ii.aͨ p̃ti.⁊ vi.aͨ paſturæ.Valet.xl.ſolid̃.

Ipſe eꝑs ten *NIWETONE*.Aluric tenuit T.R.E.⁊ geldb̃ ꝓ.iii.hid̃.
Tra.ē.iiii.car̃.In dñio ſt.ii.car̃.⁊ iiii.ſerui.⁊ iiii.uiłłi ⁊ iii.bord
cũ.ii.car̃.Ibi molin̄ redd.vii.ſolid̃ ⁊ vi.den̄.⁊ ix.aͨ p̃ti.⁊ xl.aͨ
ſiluæ minutæ.Valuit.lx.ſoł.ͭ.Modo.c.ſolid̃.

Huic ⒸⓂ ſt additæ.vii.hidæ.quas teneb̃.ii.taini T.R.E.Tra.ē.viii.
car̃.Ibi ſt.xiiii.uiłłi ⁊ viii.bord ⁊ vii.ſerui.cũ.vi.car̃.⁊ xxiii.
aͨ p̃ti.Valuit.c.ſolid̃.Modo.x.lib̃.

Azelin ten de eꝑo *FERENTONE*·Briſmar tenuit T.R.E.⁊ geldb̃
ꝓ.v.hid̃.Tra.ē.vii.car̃.In dñio ſt.iii.car̃.⁊ iiii.ſerui.⁊ vii.uiłłi.
⁊ vii.bord cũ.iiii.car̃.Ibi.c.aͨ p̃ti.Valuit.l.ſoł.modo.iiii.lib̃.

54 The Bishop holds RODE as three manors. Seven thanes held   E
    it before 1066; it paid tax for 9 hides. Land for 9 ploughs,
    of which Robert holds 1 hide from the Bishop, Moses ½ hide,   D
    Robert 1½ hides, Roger 2½ hides, Sheerwold 2½ hides, Richard
    the Interpreter 1 hide. In lordship 7 ploughs; 6 slaves;   E
      3 villagers and 29 smallholders with 4½ ploughs.   148
      From mills come 27s; meadow, 33 acres; woodland, 33 acres;   E a 2
        pasture, 25 acres.
    The value of the whole was £7 10s; value now between them £8 5s.   E

55 Nigel holds KEYFORD from the Bishop. Leofday held it before
    1066; it paid tax for 1 hide and 1 virgate of land.
    Land for 1 plough, which is there, in lordship, with   149
      12 cottagers.   a 1
      A mill which pays 30d; meadow, 6 acres; pasture, 5 acres.
        2 cattle; 13 pigs; 26 sheep; 18 goats.
    The value was 10s; now 15s.

56 Osmund holds (Stony) LITTLETON from the Bishop. Godwin held   89 a
    it before 1066; it paid tax for 2 hides. Land for 2 ploughs, which
    are there, in lordship, with
      1 smallholder and 6 slaves.   149
      A mill which pays 10s; meadow, 2 acres; pasture, 6 acres.   a 2
        1 cob; 5 cattle; 15 pigs; 200 sheep.
    Value 40s; when he acquired it, 30s.

57 The Bishop holds NEWTON (St. Loe) himself. Aelfric held it
    before 1066; it paid tax for 3 hides. Land for 4 ploughs.
    In lordship 2 ploughs; 4 slaves; 2½ hides.   149
      4 villagers and 3 smallholders with 2 ploughs & ½ hide.   a 3
      A mill which pays 7s 6d; meadow, 9 acres; underwood,
        40 acres. 2 cobs; 12 cattle; 40 pigs; 100 sheep, less 7.
    The value was 60s; now 100s.
      To this manor have been added 7 hides which two thanes held   E
    before 1066. Land for 8 ploughs. (In lordship) 3½ hides & ½ virgate.   E
      14 villagers, 8 smallholders and 7 slaves with
        6 ploughs & 3 hides & 1½ virgates.
      Meadow, 23 acres.
    The value was 100s; now £10.

58 Azelin holds FARRINGTON (Gurney) from the Bishop. Brictmer
    held it before 1066; it paid tax for 5 hides. Land for 7 ploughs.
    In lordship 3 ploughs; 4 slaves; 3 hides.   149
      7 villagers and 7 smallholders with 4 ploughs & 2 hides.   b 1
      Meadow, 100 acres. 2 cobs; 7 cattle; 7 pigs; 100 sheep.
    The value was 50s; now £4.

Azelin ten de epo ESTONE. Tres taini tenuer T.R.E.7 geldb p.iiii.
hid 7 dimid. Tra.e.vi.car. In dnio st.iii.car.7 iiii.ferui.7 v.uilti
7 iiii.bord 7 ii.cotar cu.iiii.car. Ibi molin redd.xxx.denar.7 xl.
ac pti.7 xl.ac pafturæ. Valuit 7 ual.lxx.folid.

Azelin ten de epo HERPETREV. Edric tenuit T.R.E.7 geldb p.v.
hid. Tra.e.iiii.car. In dnio.e dim car.7 vii.uilti 7 iiii.bord.
7 v.cotar cu.iii.car. Ibi molin redd.v.fol.7 lviii.ac pti.7 xlii.
ac filuæ. Paftura.i.leu lg.7 dimid leu lat. Valuit 7 ual.xl.folid.

Robt ten de epo AMELBERGE. Duo taini tenuer T.R.E.7 geldb
p.iii.hid. Tra.e.iiii.car. In dnio st.ii.car.7 ii.ferui.7 vi.uilti
7 iiii.bord cu.v.car. Ibi.xxix.ac pti. Valuit.xx.fol.M.lxx.fol.

Ipfe eps ten CAMELEI. Duo taini tenuer T.R.E.7 geldb p.ix.
hid 7 dim v træ. Tra.e.ix.car. In dnio st.iii.car.7 xiii.ferui.
7 ix.uilti 7 i.bord.7 vii.cotar cu.iiii.car. Ibi molin redd.v.fol.
7 cxx.ac pti.7 xxx.ac pafturæ.7 l.ac filuæ minutæ.
Valuit.vii.lib.Modo.x.lib.
De hac tra huj co ten Hunfrid.i.hid.7 ibi ht.i.car.7 iii.uilt
7 i.cotar cu.i.car. Ibi.xl.ac pti. Valet.xx.folid.

Witts ten de epo CHINGESTONE. Eldred tenuit T.R.E.7 geldb
p.i.hida. Tra.e.xvii.car. In dnio st.iii.car.cu.i.feruo.7 xviii.
uilti 7 iiii.bord cu.xi.car. Ibi.xl.ac pafturæ. Valuit 7 ual.vi.lib.

59 Azelin holds (Ston) EASTON from the Bishop. Three thanes held it   E
before 1066; it paid tax for 4½ hides. Land for 6 ploughs.
  In lordship 3 ploughs; 4 slaves; 3 hides.   149
    5 villagers, 4 smallholders and 2 cottagers with   b 2
      4 ploughs & 1½ hides.
  A mill which pays 30d; meadow, 40 acres; pasture, 40 acres.
    1 cob; 1 cow; 6 pigs.
  The value was and is 70s.

60 Azelin holds (West) HARPTREE from the Bishop. Edric held it
before 1066; it paid tax for 5 hides. Land for 4 ploughs.
  In lordship ½ plough; 3 hides.   150
    7 villagers, 4 smallholders and 5 cottagers with   a 1
      3 ploughs & 2 hides.
  A mill which pays 5s; meadow, 58 acres; woodland, 42 acres;
      pasture 1 league long and ½ league wide. 5 cattle; 4 pigs; 24 goats.
  The value was and is 40s.

61 Robert holds EMBOROUGH from the Bishop. Two thanes held it   E
before 1066; it paid tax for 3 hides. Land for 4 ploughs.   150
  In lordship 2 ploughs; 2 slaves; 1 hide & 3 virgates.   a 2
    6 villagers and 4 smallholders with 5 ploughs & 1 hide & 1 virgate.   E
    Meadow, 29 acres. 1 cob; 23 cattle; 25 pigs; 158 wethers.
  The value was 20s; now 70s.

62 The Bishop holds CAMELEY himself. Two thanes held it before 1066; E
it paid tax for 9 hides and ½ virgate of land. Land for 9 ploughs.
  In lordship 3 ploughs; 13 slaves; 4 hides & 3 virgates.
    9 villagers, 1 smallholder and 7 cottagers with 4 ploughs
      & 3 hides & 1½ virgates.   150
  A mill which pays 5s; meadow, 120 acres; pasture, 30 acres;   b 1
    underwood, 50 acres. 2 cobs; 12 cattle; 21 pigs; 150 sheep.
  The value was £7; now £10.
    Humphrey holds 1 hide of this manor's land; he has 1
  plough there, in lordship.
    3 villagers and 1 cottager with 1 plough.
    Meadow, 40 acres. 12 cattle; 14 pigs; 70 sheep.
  Value 20s.

63 William of Monceaux holds KINGSTON (Seymour) from the Bishop.
Aldred held it before 1066; it paid tax for 1 hide. Land for
17 ploughs. In lordship 3 ploughs & 1 virgate, with 1 slave;   150
    18 villagers and 4 smallholders with 11 ploughs & 3 virgates.   b 2
    Pasture, 40 acres. 20 cattle; 31 pigs; 120 sheep.
  The value was and is £6.

De hac ʼtra huj⁹ ⊙̃ ten̓ Fulcran de eṕo.Trã.ɪ.caɼ.⁊ ibi hɍ.ɪɪ.borđ.

Idē.W.ten̓ *CHINGESTONE* de eṕo.Quatuor   *L̸* Valet.ɪɪɪ.ſoł.
taini tenueɼ T.R.E.⁊ geldɓ ᵱ.ɪɪɪɪ.hiđ ⁊ dim̓.Tra.ē.vɪɪ.caɼ.Ibi
sɼ.ɪx.uiłti ⁊ vɪɪɪ.borđ cũ.ɪ.ſeruo hñtes.vɪ.caɼ ⁊ dimiđ.
Valuit ⁊ uał.ʟx.ſoliđ.Hoc ⊙̃ T.R.E.n̄ geldɓ niſi ᵱ una hida.

Roger̓ ten̓ de eṕo *HELGETREV*.Quatuor teini tenueɼ T.R.E.
⁊ geldɓ ᵱ.v.hiđ dimiđ v̓ trǽ min̓.Tra.ē.vɪ.caɼ.In dñio.ē
una caɼ ⁊ dim̓.⁊ ɪɪɪɪ.uiłti ⁊ ɪɪɪ.borđ ⁊ ɪɪɪ.cotar̓ cũ.ɪɪ.caɼ.
Ibi.xxvɪɪ.ãc p̃ti.⁊ xxxɪɪɪ.ãc paſturǽ.Valuit ⁊ uał.ʟx.ſoliđ.

Radulf⁹ ten̓ de eṕo *LITELTONE*.Aluuold tenuit T.R.E.⁊ geldɓ
ᵱ.v.hiđ.Tra.ē.v.caɼ.In dñio sɼ.ɪɪ.caɼ.cũ.ɪ.ſeruo.⁊ ɪɪɪɪ.uiłti
⁊ vɪ.borđ cũ.ɪɪɪ.caɼ.Ibi moliñ redđ.ʟ.den̓.⁊ xxxɪɪ.ãc p̃ti.⁊ ʟxvɪ.ãc
paſturǽ.In Bada.ɪ.burḡſis redđ.xv.denaɼ.Valuit ⁊ uał.ʟx.ſoł.

Idē Rađ ten̓ de eṕo *OPETONE*.Lefmer tenuit T.R.E.⁊ geldɓ ᵱ.ɪɪɪ.
hiđ.Tra.ē.ɪɪɪ.caɼ.In dñio.ē.ɪ.caɼ.⁊ ɪɪ.ſerui.⁊ v.uiłti ⁊ ɪɪɪɪ.borđ
⁊ ɪɪ.cotaɼ.cũ.ɪɪɪ.caɼ.Ibi.v.ãc p̃ti.Silua dimiđ leũ lḡ.⁊ ɪɪɪɪ.q̃₂ lat̓
Valuit ⁊ uał.ʟx.ſoliđ.

Leuuin̓ ten̓ de eṕo *MEGELE*.Almar̓⁹ tenuit T.R.E.⁊ geldɓ ᵱ.ɪ.hida.
Tra.ē.ɪɪ.caɼ.q̄ ibi sɼ cũ.ɪɪ.uiłtis.⁊ ɪɪɪ.borđ ⁊ ɪ.ſeruo.⁊ vɪ.ãc p̃ti.
Valuit.ɪɪɪɪ.ſoliđ.Modo.xx.ſoliđ.

Radulf⁹ ten̓ de eṕo *WEREGRAVE*.Tres taini tenueɼ T.R.E.⁊ geldɓ
ᵱ.ɪɪ.hiđ.Tra.ē.ɪ.caɼ.q̄ ibi.ē.in dñio.⁊ ɪɪ.ſerui.⁊ uñ uiłts.⁊ v.borđ
⁊ ɪɪ.cotar̓ cũ dim̓ caɼ.Ibi moliñ redđ.ɪɪɪ.ſoliđ.⁊ ɪɪɪ.ãc p̃ti.⁊ v.ãc
filuǽ.Valuit.xx.ſoliđ.Modo.xxx.ſoliđ.

Of this manor's land Fulcran holds land for 1 plough from the Bishop. He has
2 smallholders.
Value 4s; when he acquired it, as much.

64 William of Monceaux also holds KINGSTON (Seymour) from the   E
Bishop. Four thanes held it before 1066; it paid tax for   E
4½ hides. Land for 7 ploughs. In lordship 2 hides.   151
9 villagers and 8 smallholders with 1 slave who have   a 1
6½ ploughs & the rest of the land.
The value was and is 60s.
Before 1066 this manor did not pay tax except for 1 hide.

65 Roger holds HALLATROW from the Bishop. Four thanes held it   E
before 1066; it paid tax for 5 hides, less ½ virgate of land.
Land for 6 ploughs. In lordship 1½ ploughs; 3½ hides.   151
4 villagers, 3 smallholders and 3 cottagers with   a 2
2 ploughs & the rest of the land.
Meadow, 27 acres; pasture, 33 acres. 1 cob; 17 sheep.
The value was and is 60s.

66 Ralph Rufus holds (High) LITTLETON from the Bishop. Alfwold held E
it before 1066; it paid tax for 5 hides. Land for 5 ploughs.
In lordship 2 ploughs, & 4 hides & 1½ virgates, with 1 slave;   151
4 villagers and 6 smallholders with 3 ploughs & the rest of the land. b 1
A mill which pays 50d; meadow, 32 acres; pasture, 66 acres;
In Bath 1 burgess who pays 15d. 6 cattle; 2 pigs; 83 sheep.
The value was and is 60s.

67 Ralph Rufus also holds UPTON (Noble) from the Bishop. Leofmer   E
held it before 1066; it paid tax for 3 hides. Land for 3 ploughs.
In lordship 1 plough; 2 slaves; 2 hides & 1 virgate.   151
5 villagers, 4 smallholders and 2 cottagers with   b 2
3 ploughs & 3 virgates.
Meadow, 5 acres; woodland ½ league long and 4 furlongs wide.
4 cattle; 21 pigs; 30 sheep; 11 goats.
The value was and is 60s.

68 Leofwin holds MIDGELL from the Bishop. Aelmer held it before
1066; it paid tax for 1 hide. Land for 2 ploughs, which are   L
there, with
2 villagers, 3 smallholders and 1 slave.   151
Meadow, 6 acres. 4 cattle; 1 pig.   b 3
The value was 4s; now 20s.

69 Ralph holds WEATHERGROVE from the Bishop. Three thanes held it   E
before 1066; it paid tax for 2 hides. Land for 1 plough, which
is there, in lordship; 2 slaves; 1½ hides.   152
1 villager, 5 smallholders and 2 cottagers with ½ plough & ½ hide.   a 1
A mill which pays 3s; meadow, 3 acres; woodland, 5 acres.
The value was 20s; now 30s. 2 pigs; 66 sheep.

Azelin ten de epo STANWELLE . Turmund tenuit T.R.E.7 geldb ꝑ.III.

hid.Tra.ē.IIII.caȓ.In dñio sȓ.II.caȓ.7 II.ſerui.7 v.uilli 7 VII.borđ

7 II.cotar cū.II.caȓ.Ibi.XVI.ãc p̃ti.7 v.ãc paſturæ.7 VI.ãc ſiluæ

minutæ.Valuit.XL.ſoliđ.Modo.LX.ſoliđ.

.VI. TERRA EPI WELLENSIS.

Eᴘꜱ WELLENSIS ten WELLE.Ipſe tenuit T.R.E.

7 geldb ꝑ.L.hiđ.Tra.ē.LX.caȓ.De ea sȓ in dñio.VIII.

hidæ.7 ibi.VI.caȓ.7 VI.ſerui.7 xx.uilti 7 XIIII.borđ.

cū.XV.caȓ.Ibi.IIII.molini redđ.xxx.ſoliđ.7 ccc.ãc p̃ti.

Paſtura.III.leū lḡ.7 una leū laȓ.Silua.II.leū lḡ.

7 II.q̃ʒ laȓ.7 III.leū moræ.Valet.xxx.lib ad oꝑ eꝑi.

De hac ȓra ejđ M ten canonici.XIIII.hiđ.Ibi hñt

in dñio.VI.caȓ.7 VIII.ſerui.7 XVI.uilti.7 XII.borđ.

cū.VIII.caȓ.Ibi.II.molini redđ.L.den.Valet.XII.lib.

De eađ ȓra ejđ M ten de epo Faſtrad.VI.hiđ.Ricarđ

v.hiđ.Erneis.v.hiđ.Ibi sȓ in dñio.VI.caȓ.7 x.ſerui.

7 XVII.uilli.7 xVI.borđ.cū.XI.caȓ.7 II.molini redđ

.x.ſoliđ.Inȓ oms ualet.XIII.lib.

De ipſa ȓra ipſi M ten de epo Faſtrad.II.hiđ.Radulf

II.hiđ.Hæ.IIII.hidæ sȓ de dñio eꝑi.Ibi in dñio.II.caȓ.

7 III.ſerui.7 v.uilti 7 v.borđ.cū.I.caȓ.Ibi moliñ redđ

VII.ſoliđ 7 VI.denaȓ.Totū ualet.LXX.ſoliđ.   ſ xx.ſot.

De eiſđ.L.hiđ ten uxor Manaſſe.II.hiđ.ſed ñ de epo.Vat

Præt has.L.hiđ hȓ epſ.II.hiđ q̃ nunꝗ geldaueȓ T.R.E.

Aluuarđ 7 Edric ten de epo.Valent.xxx.ſoliđ.

Iđē epſ ten CVMBE.Azor tenuit T.R.E.7 geldb ꝑ.xx.

hiđ.Tra.ē.XVI.caȓ.De ea sȓ in dñio.VIII.hidæ.7 ibi.III.

caȓ.7 XII.ſerui.7 xv.uilti 7 XIII.borđ cū.XII.caȓ.

70 Azelin holds STOWELL from the Bishop. Thormund held it before
1066; it paid tax for 3 hides. Land for 4 ploughs. In lordship 2
ploughs; 2 slaves; 1½ hides.   152
    5 villagers, 7 smallholders and 2 cottagers with 2 ploughs   a 2
      & the rest of the land.
    Meadow, 16 acres; pasture, 5 acres; underwood, 6 acres.
      2 cobs; 6 cattle; 20 pigs; 140 sheep.
The value was 40s; now 60s.

6   LAND OF THE BISHOP OF WELLS   89 b

1 The Bishop of Wells holds WELLS. He held it himself before 1066;   E
it paid tax for 50 hides. Land for 60 ploughs, of which 8 hides
are in lordship; 6 ploughs there; 6 slaves;   157
    20 villagers ànd 14 smallholders with 15 ploughs & 6 hides.   b 1
    4 mills which pay 30s; meadow, 300 acres; pasture 3 leagues
      long and 1 league wide; woodland 2 leagues long and 2
      furlongs wide; moor, 3 leagues. 2 cobs; 22 cattle; 30 pigs;
      150 sheep; 24 goats.
Value £30, for the Bishop's use.
    The Canons of St. Andrew's Church hold 14 hides of this manor's
land. They have 6 ploughs in lordship; 8 slaves; 6 hides.
    16 villagers and 12 smallholders with 8 ploughs & 8 hides.
    2 mills which pay 50d. 2 cobs; 12 cattle; 10 pigs; 100 sheep.
Value £12, for the Canons' use.
    Also of this manor's land Fastrad holds 6 hides from the Bishop,   D
Richard 5 hides, Erneis 5 hides. In lordship 6 ploughs; 10 slaves;   E
    17 villagers and 16 smallholders with 11 ploughs.   E
    2 mills which pay 10s.
Value between them £13.
    Of this manor's land Fastrad holds 2 hides from the Bishop,   D
Ralph 2 hides. These 4 hides are of the Bishop's lordship.
In lordship 2 ploughs; 3 slaves;
    5 villagers and 5 smallholders with 1 plough.
    A mill which pays 7s 6d.
Value of the whole 70s.
    Also of these 50 hides Manasseh's wife holds 2 hides, but not   E
from the Bishop. Value 20s.
    Besides these 50 hides the Bishop has 2 hides which never paid   E
tax before 1066. Alfward Croc and Edric hold from the Bishop .
Value 30s.

  The Bishop also holds
2 COMBE (St. Nicholas). Azor son of Thorold held it before 1066;
it paid tax for 20 hides. Land for 16 ploughs, of which 8 hides
are in lordship; 3 ploughs there; 12 slaves;   156
    15 villagers and 13 smallholders with 12 ploughs & 12 hides.   a 1

Ibi . xii . ãc p̃ti . 7 dimid leũ pasturæ int̃ lḡ 7 lat̃ . 7 una
leũ siluæ int̃ lḡ 7 lat̃ . Valuit . x . lib̃ . Modo . xviii . lib̃ .

Idẽ ep̃s teñ *CHINGESBERIE* . Ipse tenuit T . R . E . 7 geldb̃
p̃ . xx . hid̃ . T̃ra . ẽ . xxiiii . car̃ . De ea st̃ in dñio . vi . hidæ .
7 ibi . ii . car̃ . 7 iiii . serui . 7 xvi . uitti 7 iiii . bord cũ . xi . car̃ .
Ibi . ii . molini redd . xxx . solid . 7 c . ãc p̃ti . Pastura
una leũ lḡ . 7 iii . q̃ƺ . lat̃ .

De ead̃ tra huj M̃ teñ tres milites 7 uñ cleric̃ . viii . hid̃ .
Valet ad op̃ ep̃i . xii . lib̃ . Ad op̃ militũ . viii . lib̃ .

Idẽ ep̃s teñ *CERDRE* . Ipse tenuit T . R . E . 7 geldb̃ p̃ . viii .
hid̃ . T̃ra . ẽ . xx . car̃ . De ea st̃ in dñio . ii . hidæ . 7 ibi . ii .
car̃ . 7 xi . serui . 7 xx . uitti cũ . xiiii . car̃ . Ibi molĩ redd
xxx . denar̃ . 7 xx . ãc p̃ti . Silua . ii . leũ lḡ . 7 iiii . q̃ƺ lat̃ .
7 tñtd pasturæ . De ead̃ tra teñ uñ tain . ii . hid̃ .
qui ñ potest separari ab æccta . Tot̃ ualet . xvi . lib̃ .

Idẽ ep̃s teñ *LITELANDE* . Ipse tenuit T . R . E . 7 geldb̃ p̃ . ii .
hid̃ . T̃ra . ẽ . viii . car̃ . De ea . ẽ . i . hida in dñio . 7 ibi . ii . car̃ .
7 ii . serui . 7 iii . uitti 7 vi . bord cũ . ii . car̃ . Ibi . xii . ãc
p̃ti . 7 c . ãc pasturæ . 7 xx . ãc siluæ . Valuit 7 ual̃ . xl . sot .

Idẽ ep̃s teñ *WIVELESCOME* . Ipse tenuit T . R . E . 7 geldb̃
p̃ . xv . hid̃ . T̃ra . ẽ . xxx.vi . car̃ . De ea st̃ in dñio . iii . hidæ .
7 ibi . iiii . car̃ . 7 viii . serui . 7 xvi . uitti 7 iii . bord cũ
vii . car̃ . Ibi molĩ redd . l . den . 7 xxxiiii . ãc p̃ti .
7 cc . ãc pasturæ . 7 q̃t xx . ãc siluæ .

De hac tra huj M̃ teñ . iii . milites de ep̃o . ix . hid . 7 ibi hñt
. xvi . car̃ . H̃ tra ẽ de dñio episcopat̃ . nec potest ab ep̃o separi .
Valet ep̃o . x . lib̃ . Militib; . xv . lib̃ .

Idẽ ep̃s teñ *WALINTONE* . Ipse tenuit T . R . E . 7 geldb̃
p̃ . xiiii . hid̃ . T̃ra . ẽ . xxx . car̃ . De ea st̃ in dñio . iii . hidæ .
7 ibi . iiii . car̃ . 7 xxxi . seru̍ . 7 liii . uitti 7 lxi . bord cũ . xxv .

Meadow, 12 acres; pasture, ½ league in both length and width;
woodland, 1 league in both length and width.
12 cattle; 18 pigs; 315 sheep; 1 cob.
The value was £10; now £18.

3 KINGSBURY (Episcopi). He held it himself before 1066; it paid
tax for 20 hides. Land for 24 ploughs, of which 6 hides are in
lordship; 2 ploughs there; 4 slaves;
16 villagers and 4 smallholders with 11 ploughs & 6 hides.
2 mills which pay 30s; meadow, 100 acres; pasture 1 league
long and 3 furlongs wide. 1 cob; 2 cattle; 4 pigs; 30 sheep.
3 men-at-arms and 1 clerk hold 8 hides of this manor's land.
Value £12, for the Bishop's use; £8, for the men-at-arms' use.

156
a 2

4 CHARD. He held it himself before 1066; it paid tax for 8 hides.
Land for 20 ploughs, of which 2 hides are in lordship;
2 ploughs there; 11 slaves;
20 villagers with 14 ploughs & 6 hides.
A mill which pays 30d; meadow, 20 acres; woodland 2 leagues
long and 4 furlongs wide; pasture, as much. 1 cob; 13 cattle;
20 pigs; 300 sheep; 24 goats.
A thane holds 2 hides of this land; he cannot be separated
from the church.
Value of the whole £16.

156
a 3
E

5 'LITNES'. He held it himself before 1066; it paid tax for 2 hides.
Land for 8 ploughs, of which 1 hide is in lordship; 2 ploughs
there; 2 slaves;
3 villagers and 6 smallholders with 2 ploughs & 1 hide.
Meadow, 12 acres; pasture, 100 acres; woodland, 20 acres. 1 cob.
The value was and is 40s.

156
b 1

6 WIVELISCOMBE. He held it himself before 1066; it paid tax for 15
hides. Land for 36 ploughs, of which 3 hides are in lordship; 4
ploughs there; 8 slaves;
16 villagers and 3 smallholders with 7 ploughs & 3 hides.
A mill which pays 50d; meadow, 34 acres; pasture, 200 acres;
woodland, 80 acres. 1 cob; 15 cattle; 12 pigs; 70 sheep; 36 goats.
3 men-at-arms hold 9 hides of this manor's land from the
Bishop; they have 16 ploughs. This land is of the Bishopric's
lordship; it cannot be separated from the Bishop.
Value to the Bishop £10; to the men-at-arms £15.

156
b 2
E
E

7 WELLINGTON. He held it himself before 1066; it paid tax for 14
hides. Land for 30 ploughs, of which 3 hides are in lordship; 4
ploughs there; 31 slaves;
53 villagers and 61 smallholders with 25 ploughs & 9 hides.

156
b 3

caŕ.Ibi.11.molini redd.xv.fot.7 cv.ãc p̃ti.Paſtura
una leu l̄g.7 dim̄ leū lat̄.Silua.111.q̃z l̄g.7 tntd̄ lat̄.
De hac tra huj m̃ ten Joħs de ep̃o.11.hid̄.de tra uillanoz.
Totū ualet xxv.liɓ.

Huic m̃ addita.ē.1.hida.quā tenuit p m̃ Alueua T.R.E.
Tra.ē.111.caŕ.q̃ ibi st̄ cū.v111.uiłłis.7 1111.bord̄ 7 1.feruo.
Ibi.v.ãc p̃ti.Silua.111.q̃z l̄g.7 tntd̄ lat̄.Valet.xxx.fot.

Idē ep̃s ten̄ LIDEGAR.Ipfe tenuit T.R.E.7 geldɓ p.x.hid̄.
una v min.Tra.ē.xvi.caŕ.De ea st̄ in dn̄io.111.hidæ.
7 ibi.11.caŕ.7 v.ferui.7 xx.viłłi.7 x11.bord̄ cū.v1.caŕ.
Ibi molin̄ redd̄.xxx1.denaŕ.7 xxx.ãc p̃ti.Paſtura.1.leū
l̄g.7 111.q̃z lat̄.7 tntd̄ filuæ.⎰De hac tra huj m̃ ten.11.milit̄
.111.hid̄ de tra uiłłoz.7 ibi hn̄t.111.caŕ.Tot̄ ualet.x111.liɓ.

89 c

Idē ep̃s ten̄ BANWELLE.Herald com̄ tenuit T.R.E.7 geldɓ
p.xxx.hid̄.Tra.ē.xl.caŕ.De ea st̄ in dn̄io.v1.hidæ.
7 ibi.111.caŕ.7 v.ferui.7 xx1111.uiłłi.7 x11.bord̄ cū
xv111.caŕ.Ibi.c.ãc p̃ti.Paſturæ.1.leū l̄g.7 lat̄.
Silua.11.leū 7 dim̄ in l̄g 7 lat̄.
De hac tra huj m̃ ten de ep̃o Serlo.111.hid̄.Radulf
v.hid̄ 7 dim.Rohard.v.hid̄ 7 dim.Faſtrad.1.hid̄.
Bono.1.hid̄.Eluui.1.hid̄.Ibi st̄ in dn̄io.1x.caŕ.7 v.ferui.
7 xxv.uiłłi 7 xv.bord̄ hn̄tes.x111.caŕ 7 dim.
Ibi.11.molini Rohardi redd̄.x.folid̄.Ordulf.1.molin̄
Tot̄ m̃ ualet.xv.liɓ ad opus ep̃i.   ⎰ redd̄ xl.den̄.
Ad opus hominū.xv.liɓ.fimiliter.
Idē ep̃s ten̄ EVRECRIZ.Ipfe tenuit T.R.E.7 geldɓ
p.xx.hid̄.Tra.ē.xx.caŕ.De ea st̄ in dn̄io.111.hidæ.
7 ibi.111.caŕ.7 v1.fcrui.7 111.uiłłi 7 x.bord̄ cū.11.caŕ.
Ibi molin̄ redd̄.v11.folid̄.7 v1.den̄.7 lx.ãc p̃ti.7 cc.ãc
paſturæ.Silua.1.leū l̄g.7 una q̃z lat̄.Valet.x.liɓ.

2 mills which pay 15s; meadow, 105 acres; pasture 1 league
long and ½ league wide; woodland 3 furlongs long and
as wide. 1 cob; 17 cattle; 3 pigs; 110 sheep.
Of this manor's land John the Usher holds 2 hides of the
villagers' land from the Bishop.
Value of the whole £25.   E
    To this manor has been added 1 hide which Aelfeva held as a   E
manor before 1066. Land for 3 ploughs, which are there, with
8 villagers, 4 smallholders and 1 slave.
    Meadow, 5 acres; woodland 3 furlongs long and as wide.
Value 30s.

8 (Bishops) LYDEARD. He held it himself before 1066; it paid tax
for 10 hides, less 1 virgate. Land for 16 ploughs, of which 3
hides are in lordship; 2 ploughs there; 5 slaves;
    20 villagers and 12 smallholders with 6 ploughs & 4 hides.   157
    A mill which pays 31d; meadow, 30 acres; pasture 1 league   a 1
        long and 3 furlongs wide; woodland, as much. 1 cob;   E
        10 cattle; 20 pigs; 150 sheep.
    Of this manor's land 2 men-at-arms hold 3 hides of the
    villagers' land; they have 3 ploughs.
    Value of the whole £13.   E

9 BANWELL. Earl Harold held it before 1066; it paid tax for   89 c
30 hides. Land for 40 ploughs, of which 6 hides are in lordship;
3 ploughs there; 5 slaves;
    24 villagers and 12 smallholders with 18 ploughs & 7 hides.   E
    Meadow, 100 acres; pasture, 1 league long and wide; woodland   157
        2½ leagues in length and width. 15 cattle; 15 pigs; 30 sheep; 20 goats.   a 2
    Of this manor's land Serlo of Burcy holds 3 hides from the Bishop, D
    Ralph Crooked Hands 5½ hides, Roghard 5½ hides, Fastrad 1 hide,   D
    Bofa 1 hide, Alfwy son of Banna (?) 1 hide. In lordship 9 ploughs;
    5 slaves;
        25 villagers and 15 smallholders who have 13½ ploughs.   E
        2 mills of Roghard's which pay 10s; Ordwulf, 1 mill which
            pays 40d.
Value of the whole manor £15, for the Bishop's use; for the
men's use, £15 likewise.

10 EVERCREECH. He held it himself before 1066; it paid tax for 20
hides. Land for 20 ploughs, of which 3 hides are in lordship; 3
ploughs there; 6 slaves;   158
    3 villagers and 10 smallholders with 2 ploughs & 2 hides.   a 1
    A mill which pays 7s 6d; meadow, 60 acres; pasture, 200
        acres; woodland 1 league long and 1 furlong wide.
    1 cob; 25 cattle; 30 pigs; 200 sheep.
Value £10, for the Bishop's use.

De ead tra ejd $\widetilde{m}$ ten de epo Erneis . vii . hid . Machari
hid 7 dim . Ildebt . i . hid . In dnio st . iiii . car . 7 iiii . ferui.
7 v . uitti 7 iiii . bord cu . ii . car . Int oms ual . cx . folid.
De ead tra . ten pbr 7 ii . alij angli . v . hid 7 una v træ.
Valet . iiii . lib.

Ide eps ten *WESTBERIE* . Ipfe tenuit T.R.E. 7 geldb ρ . vi.
hid . Tra . e . viii . car . De ea st in dnio . iii . hidæ . 7 ibi . ii.
car . 7 ii . ferui . 7 vi . uitti 7 x . bord cu . v . car . Ibi . xxx . ac
pti . 7 Silua . i . leu lg . 7 ii . q$\tilde{z}$ lat . Valet . viii . lib.

Ofmund ten de epo *WINESHA* . Elfi tenuit T.R.E.
7 geldb ρ . x . hid . Tra . e . xvi . car . De ea st in dnio . iiii.
hidæ . 7 ibi . iii . car . 7 xii . ferui . 7 L . uitti cu . ix . car.
Ibi . ii . molini redd . xx . folid . 7 vi . ac pti . Silua dim
leu lg . 7 una q$\tilde{z}$ 7 dimid lat . Valuit . vi . lib . m . x . lib.

Ipfe eps ten *CHIVVE* . Ipfe tenuit T.R.E. 7 geldb ρ . xxx.
hid . Tra . e . L . car . De ea st in dnio . iiii . hidæ . 7 ibi . vi . car.
7 xiiii . ferui . 7 xxx . uitti 7 ix . bord cu . xxiiii . car.
Ibi . iii . molini redd . xx . fol . 7 c . ac pti . 7 L . ac pafturæ.
Silua . ii . leu lg . 7 dim leu lat . Valet epo . xxx . lib.

De hac tra huj $\widetilde{m}$ ten de epo Ricard . v . hid . Rohard
vi . hid . Stefan . v . hid . Aluric . vii . virg . Vluric . ii . hid.
In dnio st ibi . vii . car . 7 viii . ferui . 7 xviii . uitti 7 xxvii.
bord cu . x . car . Ibi . ii . molini redd . x . fol.
Int oms ualet . xiii . lib.

Ide eps ten *LATVNE* . Johs dan tenuit T.R.E. 7 geldb
ρ . xx . hid . Tra . e . xxii . car . De ea st in dnio . vi . hidæ.
7 ibi . ii . car . 7 iii . ferui . 7 x . uitti 7 xiiii . bord cu . vi . car.
Ibi . xxxii . ac pti . Silua . i . leu lg . 7 ii . q$\tilde{z}$ lat . Moræ
una lcu in lg 7 lat . Valet epo . vi . lib.

Also of this manor's land Erneis holds 7 hides from the   D
Bishop, Maghere 1½ hides, Hildebert 1 hide. In lordship 4
ploughs; 4 slaves;
    5 villagers and 4 smallholders with 2 ploughs.
Value between them, 110s.
    Also of this land a priest and 2 other Englishmen hold 5 hides   E
and 1 virgate of land. Value £4.

11 WESTBURY (sub Mendip). He held it himself before 1066; it paid
tax for 6 hides. Land for 8 ploughs, of which 3 hides are in
lordship; 2 ploughs there; 2 slaves;   158
    6 villagers and 10 smallholders with 5 ploughs & 3 hides.   b 1
    Meadow, 30 acres; woodland 1 league long and 2 furlongs wide.
        1 cob; 10 cattle; 18 pigs; 200 sheep.
Value £8.

12 Osmund holds WINSHAM from the Bishop. Alfsi held it before 1066;
it paid tax for 10 hides. Land for 16 ploughs, of which 4 hides
are in lordship; 3 ploughs there; 12 slaves;   158
    50 villagers with 9 ploughs & 6 hides. 1 pigman who pays 12 pigs.   b 2
    2 mills which pay 20s; meadow, 6 acres; woodland ½ league long
        and 1½ furlongs wide. 2 cobs; 13 cattle; 13 pigs; 270 sheep.
The value was £6; now £10.

13 The Bishop holds CHEW (Magna) himself. He held it himself
before 1066; it paid tax for 30 hides. Land for 50 ploughs,
of which 4 hides are in lordship; 6 ploughs there; 14 slaves;
    30 villagers and 9 smallholders with 24 ploughs & 6 hides.   159
        2 pigmen who pay 24 pigs.   a 1
    3 mills which pay 20s; meadow, 100 acres; pasture, 50 acres;
        woodland 2 leagues long and ½ league wide. 1 cob; 9 cattle;
        36 pigs; 148 sheep; 46 goats.
Value to the Bishop £30.   E
    Of this manor's land Richard holds 5 hides from the Bishop,   D
Roghard 6 hides, Stephen 5 hides, Aelfric of Stowey 7 virgates,   E
Wulfric 2 hides. In lordship 7 ploughs; 8 slaves;
    18 villagers and 27 smallholders with 10 ploughs.   E
    2 mills which pay 10s.   E
Value between them £13.

14 The Bishop also holds YATTON. John the Dane held it before
1066; it paid tax for 20 hides. Land for 22 ploughs, of which
6 hides are in lordship; 2 ploughs there; 3 slaves;   159
    10 villagers and 14 smallholders with 6 ploughs & 2 hides.   b 1
    Meadow, 32 acres; woodland 1 league long and 2 furlongs wide;
        moor, 1 league in length and width. 11 cattle; 15 pigs.
Value to the Bishop £6.   E

De hac tra huj ꝿ ten de epo Faftrad . v . hid . Ildebt

.IIII . hid . In dnio ſt ibi . III . car . 7 IIII . ſerui . 7 XVIII . uilli

7 XXIII . bord cu . XI . car . Int eos ualet . IX . lib.

Vna paſtura Waimora dicta ibi . e . q̄ T.R.E . ꝑtineb

ad Congreſbie ꝿ regis.

Æcclam huj ꝿ cu . I . hida ten Benthelm de epo . Val . XX . ſol.

Ide eps ten WEDMORE . Ipſe tenuit T.R.E . 7 geldb ꝑ . X.

hid . St tam ibi . XI . hidæ . Tra . e . XXXVI . car . De ea ſt

in dnio . v . hidæ . una v min . 7 ibi . IIII . car . 7 IIII . ſerui.

7 XIII . uilli 7 XIIII . bord cu . IX . car . 7 XVIII . cotar.

Ibi . LXX . ac pti . 7 II . piſcariæ redd . X . ſol . 7 L . ac ſiluæ.

7 una leu paſturæ int lg 7 lat.

Valuit . XX . lib . Modo . XVII . lib.

Canonici S. Andreæ ten de epo WANDESTREV . Ipſi teneb

T.R.E . 7 geldb ꝑ . IIII . hid . Tra . e . IIII . car . De ea ſt in dnio

II . hidæ . 7 ibi . II . car . 7 IIII . ſerui . 7 v . uilli 7 II . bord cu . III.

car . Ibi . XII . ac pti . Silua . III . q̊ʒ lg . 7 II . q̊ʒ lat . Valet

Ipſi ten LITVNE . Ipſi teneb T.R.E . 7 geldb ſ III . lib.

ꝑ . VIII . hid 7 dim . Tra . e . VII . car . De ea ſt in dnio . VI . hidæ

7 dimid . 7 ibi . II . car . 7 VI . ſerui . 7 VIII . uilli 7 VII . bord cu

IIII . car . Ibi . III . molini redd . X . ſolid . 7 LX . ac pti . 7 mille ac

paſturæ . 7 III . q̄rent ſiluæ in lg 7 lat . Valet . C . ſolid.

89 d

Rex ten . . ꝿ MILVERTVNE . Gﻧo tenuit T.R.E . 7 geldb ꝑ una v træ.

Roger Arundel ten un ꝿ AISSA . 7 jaceb T.R.E . in LEDIART ꝿ epi.

Giſo eps teneb . 7 geldb ꝑ . III . hid 7 una v . Roger ten de rege injuſte

ſ Valet . III . lib.

89 c, d

Of this manor's land Fastrad holds 5 hides from the Bishop,   D
Hildebert 4 hides. In lordship 3 ploughs; 4 slaves;   E
   18 villagers and 23 smallholders with 11 ploughs.
Value between them £9.
   A pasture called WEMBERHAM is there, which before 1066
belonged to Congresbury, a manor of the King's.
   Benzelin the Archdeacon holds this manor's church with 1 hide   E
from the Bishop. Value 20s.

15 The Bishop also holds WEDMORE. He held it himself before 1066.
It paid tax for 10 hides; however there are 11 hides there.
Land for 36 ploughs, of which 5 hides, less 1 virgate,   159
are in lordship; 4 ploughs there; 4 slaves;   b 2
   13 villagers and 14 smallholders with 9 ploughs & 5 hides & 1 virgate.
     18 cottagers.   E
  Meadow, 70 acres; 2 fisheries which pay 10s; woodland, 50
    acres; pasture, 1 league in both length and width. Moors which pay
    nothing. 6 unbroken mares; 17 cattle; 3 pigs.
The value was £20; now £17.

16 The Canons of St. Andrew's hold WANSTROW from the Bishop.
They held it themselves before 1066; it paid tax for 4 hides.   E
Land for 4 ploughs, of which 2 hides are in lordship; 2 ploughs
there; 4 slaves;   160
   5 villagers and 2 smallholders with 3 ploughs & 2 hides.   a 1
  Meadow, 12 acres; woodland 3 furlongs long and 2 furlongs
    wide. 12 pigs.
Value £3; when the Bishop acquired it, £4.

17 They hold LITTON themselves. They held it themselves before   E
1066; it paid tax for 8½ hides. Land for 7 ploughs, of which
⌄½ hides are in lordship; 2 ploughs there; 6 slaves;   160
   8 villagers and 7 smallholders with 4 ploughs & 2 hides.   a 2
   3 mills which pay 10s; meadow, 60 acres; pasture, 1,000 acres;   E
    woodland, 3 furlongs in length and width. 13 cattle; 40 goats.
Value 100s.

18 The King holds .... manor of MILVERTON.   Bishop Giso held it   89 d
before 1066; it paid tax for 1 virgate of land.   160
    a 4

19 Roger Arundel holds a manor, ASH (Priors); it lay in (the lands   E
of) the Bishop's manor of (Bishops) Lydeard before 1066.
Bishop Giso held it; it paid tax for 3 hides and 1 virgate.   160
Roger holds from the King, wrongfully.   a 3
Value £3.   E

TERRA ÆCCLÆ DE BADE.

Eccla S̃ Petri de Bada h̃ in Burgo ipfo . xxiiii . burgenſes
redd . xx . folid . Ibi moliñ redd . xx . fol . 7 xii . ãc p̃ti . Toť ual xl . fol
Ipfa æccla teñ PRISCTONE . T.R.E. geldb̃ ꝑ . vi . hid̃ . T̃ra . ẽ . viii .
car̃ . De ea s̃t in dñio . ii . hidæ . 7 ibi . i . car̃ . 7 iii . ſerui . 7 vii . uiłłi
7 vliii . bord cũ . vi . car̃ . Ibi moliñ redd . vii . fol 7 vi . den̄ . 7 xx . ãc
p̃ti . 7 qť xx . ãc paſturæ . Valuit 7 ual . vi . lib̃ .
Ipfa æccla teñ STANTONE . T.R.E. geldb̃ ꝑ . iii . hid̃ . T̃ra . ẽ . iii . car̃ .
De ea . ẽ in dñio dimid̃ hida . 7 ibi . i . car̃ . 7 v . ſerui . 7 iiii . uiłłi 7 iii .
bord cũ . ii . car̃ . Ibi . xii . ãc p̃ti . 7 xxx . ãc paſturæ . 7 xxx . ãc filuæ
minutæ . Valuit 7 ual . iii . lib̃ .
Wₐlter teñ de æccla WIMEDONE . Vñ taiñ tenuit de æccla T.R.E.
7 geldb̃ ꝑ . iii . hid̃ . T̃ra . ẽ . iiii . car̃ . In dñio s̃t . ii . car̃ . 7 ii . ſerui . 7 vii .
bord cũ . i . car̃ . Ibi moliñ redd . v . folid̃ . 7 x . ãc p̃ti . 7 x . ãc paſturæ .
Valuit 7 ual . lx . folid̃ .
Ipfa æccla teñ WESTONE . T.R.E. geldb̃ ꝑ . xv . hid̃ . T̃ra . ẽ . x . car̃ .
De ea s̃t in dñio . viii . hidæ 7 dimid̃ . 7 ibi . ii . car̃ . 7 vii . ſerui . 7 vii .
uiłłi 7 x . bord cũ . vi . car̃ . Ibi moliñ redd . x . folid̃ . 7 xx . ãc p̃ti .
Siluæ minutæ una leũ int lg̃ 7 lať . Valuit . viii . lib̃ . Modo . x . lib̃ .
Ipfa æccla teñ FORDE . T.R.E. geldb̃ ꝑ . x . hid̃ . T̃ra . ẽ . ix . car̃ . De ea
s̃t in dñio . v . hidæ . 7 ibi . ii . car̃ . 7 vi . ſerui . 7 v . uiłłi . 7 vii . bord cũ
vi . car̃ . Ibi moliñ redd . x . folid̃ . 7 xii . ãc p̃ti . 7 una leũ filuæ minutæ
int lg̃ 7 lať . Valuit 7 ual . x . lib̃ .
Ipfa æccla teñ CVME . T.R.E. geldb̃ ꝑ . ix . hid̃ . T̃ra . ẽ . viii . car̃ . De ea s̃t
in dñio . vi . hidæ . 7 ibi . iii . car̃ . 7 vi . ſerui . 7 vi . uiłłi 7 viii . bord . cũ . v . car̃ .

LAND OF BATH CHURCH

1 The Church of St. Peter of Bath has in this Borough   E
     24 burgesses who pay 20s.   185
     A mill which pays 20s; meadow, 12 acres.   a 4
     Value of the whole 40s.

one hide 120 acres

2 The Church holds PRISTON itself. Before 1066 it paid tax for 6
     hides. Land for 8 ploughs, of which 2 hides are in lordship; 1
     plough there; 3 slaves;   185
       7 villagers and 8 smallholders with 6 ploughs & 4 hides.   a 1
       A mill which pays 7s 6d; meadow, 20 acres; pasture, 80 acres. 1 cob.
     The value was and is £6.

3 The Church holds STANTON (Prior) itself. Before 1066 it paid
     tax for 3 hides. Land for 3 ploughs, of which ½ hide is in
     lordship; 1 plough there; 5 slaves;   185
       4 villagers and 3 smallholders with 2 ploughs & 2 hides.   a 2
       Meadow, 12 acres; pasture, 30 acres; underwood, 30 acres.
         1 cob; 50 sheep.
     The value was and is £3.

4 Walter Hussey holds WILMINGTON from the church. A thane held
     it from the church before 1066; it paid tax for 3 hides.
     Land for 4 ploughs. In lordship 2 ploughs; 2 slaves; 2 hides & 1 virgate.
       7 smallholders with 1 plough & 3 virgates.   185
       A mill which pays 5s; meadow, 10 acres; pasture, 10 acres.   a 3
         1 cob; 300 sheep.
     The value was and is 60s.

5 The Church holds WESTON itself. Before 1066 it paid tax
     for 15 hides. Land for 10 ploughs, of which 8½ hides are in
     lordship; 2 ploughs there; 7 slaves;   185
       7 villagers and 10 smallholders with 6 ploughs & 6½ hides.   b 1
       A mill which pays 10s; meadow, 20 acres; underwood, 1 league
         in both length and width. 1 cob; 200 sheep.
     The value was £8; now £10.

6 The Church holds BATHFORD itself. Before 1066 it paid tax
     for 10 hides. Land for 9 ploughs, of which 5 hides are in
     lordship; 2 ploughs there; 6 slaves;   185
       5 villagers and 7 smallholders with 6 ploughs & 5 hides.   b 2
       A mill which pays 10s; meadow, 12 acres; underwood, 1 league
         in both length and width. 1 cob; 12 cattle; 8 pigs; 112 sheep.
     The value was and is £10.

7 The Church holds (Monkton) COMBE itself. Before 1066 it paid
     tax for 9 hides. Land for 8 ploughs, of which 6 hides are   E
     in lordship; 3 ploughs there; 6 slaves;   185
       6 villagers and 8 smallholders with 5 ploughs & 3 hides & 1 virgate.   b 3

Ibi.II.molini redd.XIII.fol 7 VI.den.7 XXXII.ac pti.7 una leu filuæ minutæ in lg 7 lat . Valuit.VII.lib.Modo.VIII.lib.

Witts ten de æccta CERLECVME.Vn tain tenuit T.R.E.de æccta. 7 geldb p.IIII.hid.Tra.e.IIII.car.In dnio ft.II.car.7 III.ferui.7 v.uitti 7 IIII.bord cu.II.car.Ibi.v.ac pti.7 x.ac filuæ minutæ. Valuit.L.folid.Modo.VI.lib.

Ipfa æccta ten LINCVME.T.R.E.geldb p.x.hid.Tra.e.VIII.car. De ea ft in dnio.VII.hidæ.7 ibi.III.car.7 VIII.ferui.7 IIII.uitti 7 x. bord cu.III.car.Ibi.II.molini redd.x.folid.7 xxx.ac pti.7 cc.ac pafturæ.Valuit.VI.lib.Modo.VIII.lib.

Walteri ten de ipfa æccta ESTONE.Vluuard abb tenuit T.R.E. 7 geldb p una hida 7 dim.Tra.e.II.car.In dnio.e.I.car.cu.I.uitto 7 VIII.bord cu.I.car.Ibi.II.molini redd.VI.folid.7 VIII.denar. Ibi.II.ac pti.Valuit.xxx.fol.Modo.xl.folid.

Hugo .III.hid 7 Colgrim .II.hid ten de ipfa æccta HANTONE.Duo taini tenuer T.R.E.nec poteran ab æccta feparari.7 geldb p.v.hid.Tra.e.VI.car. In dnio ft.III.car.7 III.ferui.7 III.uitti 7 VI.bord.cu.III.car. Ibi.xxVIII.ac pti.7 VI.q̃ pafturæ int lg 7 lat.7 x.qrent filuæ minutæ in lg 7 latit.Valet.cx.folid.

Rannvlf flabard ten de ipfa æccta VNDEWICHE.Vn monach de eod monafterio tenuit T.R.E.7 geldb p.II.hid 7 dim.Tra.e.III.car. Ibi ft.v.bord.7 dimid molin redd.v.folid.7 XII.ac pti.7 xxx.ac pafturæ.Valuit 7 ual.xx.folid.

Ipfa æccta ten CORSTVNE.T.R.E.geldb p.x.hid.Tra.e.IX.car. De ea ft in dnio.v.hid.7 ibi.II.car.7 IIII.ferui.7 v.uitti 7 VIII.bord cu.III.car.Ibi molin redd.xxx.den.7 VI.ac pti.Valet.VIII.lib.

2 mills which pay 13s 6d; meadow, 32 acres; underwood, 1
    league in length and width. 1 cob; 12 pigs; 72 sheep.
The value was £7; now £8.

8 William Hussey holds CHARLCOMBE from the Church. A thane held it
before 1066 from the Church; it paid tax for 4 hides. Land for 4
ploughs. In lordship 2 ploughs; 3 slaves; 2 hides & 3 virgates.
    5 villagers and 4 smallholders with 2 ploughs & 1 hide & 1 virgate.
    Meadow, 5 acres; underwood, 10 acres. 1 cob; 200 sheep.
The value was 50s; now £6.

    186
    a 1

9 The Church holds LYNCOMBE itself. Before 1066 it paid tax
for 10 hides. Land for 8 ploughs, of which 7 hides are in
lordship; 3 ploughs there; 8 slaves;
    4 villagers and 10 smallholders with 3 ploughs & 2 hides.
    2 mills which pay 10s; meadow, 30 acres; pasture, 200 acres.
        1 cob; 8 pigs; 180 sheep.
The value was £6; now £8.

    186
    a 2

10 Walter Hussey holds BATHEASTON from this church. Abbot Wulfwarc
held it before 1066; it paid tax for 1½ hides. Land for 2
ploughs. In lordship 1 plough & 1 hide & 1 virgate, with
    1 villager and 8 smallholders with 1 plough & 1 virgate.
    2 mills which pay 6s 8d. Meadow, 2 acres. 250 sheep.
The value was 30s; now 40s.

    186
    a 3

11 Hugh the Interpreter, 3 hides, and an Englishman called Colgrim, 2
hides, hold BATHAMPTON from this church. Two thanes held it
before 1066; they could not be separated from the church.
It paid tax for 5 hides. Land for 6 ploughs. In lordship
3 ploughs; 3 slaves;
    3 villagers and 6 smallholders with 3 ploughs.
    Meadow, 28 acres; pasture, 6 furlongs in both length and
        width; underwood, 10 furlongs in length and width.
Value 110s.

    D

    186
    a 4

    E

12 Ranulf Flambard holds 'WOODWICK' from this church. A monk of
this monastery held it before 1066; it paid tax for 2½ hides.
Land for 3 ploughs.
    5 smallholders.
    ½ mill which pays 5s; meadow, 12 acres; pasture, 30 acres.
The value was and is 20s.

    186
    b 1

13 The Church holds CORSTON itself. Before 1066 it paid tax
for 10 hides. Land for 9 ploughs, of which 5 hides are in
lordship; 2 ploughs there; 4 slaves;
    5 villagers and 8 smallholders with 3 ploughs & 5 hides.
    A mill which pays 30d; meadow, 6 acres. 1 cob; 6 pigs; 62 sheep.
Value £8; when the Abbot acquired it, £7.

    186
    b 2

Ipſa æccła ten *EVESTIE*.T.R.E.geldb ꝑ una hida.Tra.ē.ɪ.caꝝ.q̄ ibi.ē in dn̄io.7 ɪɪɪ.ſerui.7 ɪɪɪɪ.ac̄ p̄ti.Valet.xx.ſolid.

Ipſa æccła ten *ESCEWICHE*.T.R.E.geldb ꝑ dimid hida.Tra.ē dimid caꝝ.Ibi.ē un̄ ſeruus.7 ɪɪ.uiłłi redd.xlɪɪ.den.7 xɪɪ.ac̄ p̄ti. 7 ɪɪɪ.ac̄ ſiluæ minutæ.Valet 7 ualuit.xlɪɪ.denaꝝ.

Tota ħ tra jacuit in ipſa æccła T.R.E.nec poterat inde ſepararari.

.VIII. TERRA SC̄Æ MARIÆ GLASTINGBERIENSIS.

Eccła GLASTINGBER habet in ipſa uilla.xɪɪ.hid q̄ nunq̄ geldaueꝝ.Tra.ē.xxx.caꝝ.De ea ſt in dn̄io.x.hidæ.dimid virg min.7 ibi.v.caꝝ.7 xvɪɪ.ſerui.7 xxɪ.uiłłs.7 xxxɪɪɪ.bord cū.v. caꝝ.Ibi.vɪɪɪ.fabri.7 ɪɪɪ.arpenz uineæ.7 lx.ac̄ p̄ti.7 cc.ac̄ pa ſturæ.7 xx.ac̄ ſiluæ.7 ccc.ac̄ ſiluæ minutæ.Valet.xx.lib.

Huic ꝏ adjacet inſula q̄ uocat *MERE*.Ibi ſt.lx.ac̄ træ.Tra. .ɪ.caꝝ q̄ ibi.ē.7 x.piſcatores.7 ɪɪɪ.piſcariæ redd.xx.den.7 vɪ. ac̄ p̄ti.7 vɪ.ac̄ ſiluæ.7 ɪɪ.arpenz uineæ.Valet.xx.ſolid.

Alia inſula ꝑtiñ ibi q̄ uocat *WADENEBERIE*.Ibi ſt.vɪ.ac̄ træ. 7 ɪɪɪ..arpenz uineæ.7 un̄ bord.Valet.ɪɪɪɪ.ſolid.

Tercia inſula adjacet ibi 7 uocat *EDERESIGE*.In qua ſt.ɪɪ.hidæ q̄ nunq̄ geldaueꝝ.Ibi.ē.ɪ.caꝝ cū.ɪ.bord.7 ɪɪ.ac̄ p̄ti.7 una ac̄ ſiluæ minutæ.Valet.xv.ſolid.Goduin ten de abbe.

Ipſa æccła ten *WINESCOME*.T.R.E.geldb ꝑ.xv.hid.Tra.ē.xxx.caꝝ. De ea ſt in dn̄io.v.hidæ una v min.7 ibi.ɪɪ.caꝝ.7 ɪɪɪ.ſerui.7 xxvɪɪɪ. uiłłi 7 vɪ.bord cū.ɪx.caꝝ.Ibi moliñ redd.v.ſolid.7 lx.ac̄ p̄ti. 7 una leū paſturæ in łg 7 lat.Silua.ɪɪ.leū łg.7 una leū lat.

14 The Church holds 'EVERSY' itself. Before 1066 it paid tax for 1 hide.
   Land for 1 plough, which is there, in lordship; 3 slaves.   186
     Meadow, 4 acres.   b 3
   Value 20s.

15 The Church holds ASHWICK itself. Before 1066 it paid tax
   for ½ hide. Land for ½ plough. 1 slave.   187
     2 villagers who pay 42d.   a 1
     Meadow, 12 acres; underwood, 3 acres.
   The value is and was 42d.
The whole of this land lay in (the lands of) this church before   E
1066; it could not be separated from it.   E

8   LAND OF ST. MARY'S OF GLASTONBURY   90 a

1 Glastonbury Church has in that town 12 hides which have never
  paid tax. Land for 30 ploughs, of which 10 hides, less ½ virgate,
  are in lordship; 5 ploughs there; 17 slaves;
     21 villagers and 33 smallholders with 5 ploughs & the rest of the land.
     8 smiths.   E
     Vineyard, 3 *arpents;* meadow, 60 acres; pasture, 200 acres;   172
       woodland, 20 acres; underwood, 300 acres. 5 cobs; 58 cattle; 20 pigs;   a 1
       20 sheep; 50 goats.
   Value £20; when Abbot Thurstan acquired it, £10.
     An island called MEARE is attached to this manor. 60 acres of
  land. Land for 1 plough, which is there.
     10 fishermen.
     3 fisheries which pay 20d; meadow, 6 acres; woodland, 6 acres;
       vineyard, 2 *arpents.* 1 cob; 13 cattle; 4 pigs.
   Value 20s; when the Abbot acquired it, as much.
     Another island called PANBOROUGH belongs there. 6 acres of land.
     Vineyard, 3 *arpents.*
     1 smallholder.
   Value 4s; when the Abbot acquired it, as much.
     A third island is attached to it and is called 'ANDERSEY', on which   E
  are 2 hides which have never paid tax. 1 plough there, with   E
     1 smallholder.
     Meadow, 2 acres; underwood, 1 acre.
   Value 15s; when the Abbot acquired it, as much.
     Godwin holds from the Abbot.

2 The Church holds WINSCOMBE itself. Before 1066 it paid tax   E
  for 15 hides. Land for 30 ploughs, of which 5 hides, less 1
  virgate, are in lordship; 2 ploughs there; 3 slaves;   161
     28 villagers and 6 smallholders with 9 ploughs & 5 hides, less 1 virgate.   a 2
     A mill which pays 5s; meadow, 60 acres; pasture, 1 league
       in length and width; woodland 2 leagues long and 1 league
       wide. 8 cows; 16 pigs; 30 sheep; 31 goats.

De hac tra huj ᵭ ten de abƀe Rogeri.11.hiᵭ 7 dim.Radulf.1.hiᵭ.
7 unā v.Pipe dim hiᵭ.Ibi sᵵ.v.cař.

Hoc ᵭ ualet abƀi.viii.liƀ.Hōib; ej.Lv.foliᵭ.

De tra huj ᵭ ten eps ᵭftantiens de rege.1.hiᵭ.7 ual.xx.foliᵭ.
Brictric liƀe tenuit T.R.E.fed n̄ poterat ab æccla feparari.

Ipfa æccla ten MIDELTONE.T.R.E.geldƀ ꝓ.vi.hiᵭ.Tra.ē.vi.cař.
De ea sᵵ in dn̄io.1111.hidæ.7 vii.ac.7 ibi.11.cař.7 viii.uiili 7 vi.borᵭ
cū.1111.cař.Ibi.l.ac p̄ti.7 c.ac pafturæ.Valuit 7 ual.vi.liƀ.

Rogeri ten de æccla LIDEFORD.Aluuard tenuit T.R.E.nec pote
rat ab æccla feparari.7 geldƀ ꝓ.1111.hiᵭ.Tra.ē.v.cař.De ea sᵵ
in dn̄io.111.hidæ.7 dimiᵭ v træ.7 ibi.11.cař.7 vi.ferui.7 vi.uiili.
7 111.borᵭ cū.1.cař 7 dim.Ibi molin̄ redᵭ.x.fol.7 xl.ac p̄ti.
Valuit 7 ual.1111.liƀ.

Ipfa æccla ten SAPESWICH.T.R.E.geldƀ ꝓ xxx.hiᵭ.Tra.ē.xl.
cař.Præt hanc hᵵ abƀ trā.xx.cař.q̄ nunq̄ gelᵭ.Ibi sᵵ.xii.cař. uillanor'
7 alibi.1111.cař in dn̄io.7 vi.ferui.7 v.coliƀti.7 xv.uiili 7 xvi.borᵭ.
Ibi.lx.ac p̄ti.7 lx.ac pafturæ.7 lvii.ac filuæ minutæ.

De his.xxx.hiᵭ ten Rogeri de abƀe.v.hiᵭ in Sutone.7 v.hiᵭ
in Eduuinetone.7 v.hiᵭ in Ceptone.7 v.hiᵭ in Caldecote.

Has teneƀ.xiiii.taini T.R.E.7 n̄ poterant ab æccla feparari.

Ibi sᵵ in dn̄io.1x.cař.7 x1.ferui.7 x1x.uiili 7 xx111.borᵭ cū.viii.
cař 7 dimiᵭ.Ibi.c.ac p̄ti.una min.7 xxx1.ac filuæ minutæ.

De eifᵭ.xxx.hiᵭ ten Alured.v.hiᵭ in Hvnlauintone.7 ibi hᵵ
11.cař.Ibi.v.ferui.7 x11.uiili 7 viii.borᵭ cū.vi.cař.Val.x.fol.

De eaᵭ tra ten Warmund hiᵭ de abƀe.7 ibi hᵵ.1.cař 7 1111.borᵭ.

Hoc ᵭ ualet abƀi.xii.liƀ.Rogerio.x1x.liƀ.Aluredo.vii.liƀ.

Of this manor's land Roger of Courseulles holds 2½ hides from the Abbot, Ralph Crooked Hands 1 hide and 1 virgate. Pipe ½ hide. 5 ploughs there.   E

Value of this manor to the Abbot £8; to his men, 55s.   E

The Bishop of Coutances holds 1 hide of this manor's land   E from the King; value 20s. Brictric held it freely before 1066, but he could not be separated from the church.

3 The Church holds PODIMORE itself. Before 1066 it paid tax   E for 6 hides. Land for 6 ploughs, of which 4 hides and 7 acres are in lordship; 2 ploughs there;   161

   8 villagers and 6 smallholders with 4 ploughs & 2 hides, less 7 acres.   b 1

   Meadow, 50 acres; pasture, 100 acres. 1 cob; 3 sheep.

The value was and is £6.

4 Roger of Courseulles holds (East) LYDFORD from the church. A thane by the name of Alfward held it before 1066; he could not be separated from the church. It paid tax for 4 hides. Land for 5 ploughs, of which 3 hides and ½ virgate of land are in lordship; 2 ploughs   161 there; 6 slaves;   b 2

   6 villagers and 3 smallholders with 1½ ploughs & 1 hide, less ½ virgate.

   A mill which pays 10s; meadow, 40 acres. 1 cob; 6 cattle;

     13 pigs; 160 sheep.

The value was and is £4.

5 The Church holds SHAPWICK itself. Before 1066 it paid tax for 30   E hides. Land for 40 ploughs. Besides this the Abbot has land for 20 ploughs, which has never paid tax. 12 villagers' ploughs   E there; elsewhere 4 ploughs in lordship; 6 slaves; 5 freedmen;

   15 villagers and 16 smallholders.   161

   Meadow, 60 acres; pasture, 60 acres; underwood, 57 acres.   b 3

     2 cobs; 23 cattle; 11 pigs; 100 sheep.

Of these 30 hides Roger of Courseulles holds 5 hides in SUTTON   D (Mallet) from the Abbot, 5 hides in EDINGTON, 5 hides in CHILTON (Polden) and 5 hides in CATCOTT. Fourteen thanes held   E them before 1066; they could not be separated from the church. In lordship 9 ploughs; 11 slaves;

   19 villagers and 23 smallholders with 8½ ploughs.

   Meadow, 100 acres, less 1; underwood, 31 acres.   E

Also of these 30 hides Alfred of 'Spain' holds 5 hides in WOOLAVINGTON; he has 2 ploughs & 3 hides in lordship. 5 slaves.   E

   12 villagers and 8 smallholders with 6 ploughs & 2 hides.

     11 cattle; 13 horses; 33 pigs; 151 sheep.   E

Warmund holds ½ hide of this land from the Abbot; he has 1   E plough in lordship. 4 smallholders. Value 10s.

Value of this manor to the Abbot £12; to Roger £19; to Alfred £7.   E

Ipſa æccta teñ *SOWI*.T.R.E.geldb ꝑ.xii.hid.Tra.ē.xx.cař.

De ea ſt in dñio.v.hidæ.7 ibi.ii.cař.7 ii.ſerui.7 xii.colibti.7 xxvii.

uitti.7 xiii.borđ.cū.xiiii.cař.Ibi.xxx.ãc ꝑti.7 xii.ãc ſiluæ

minutæ.Valuit.x.lib.Modo.xxiiii.lib.

Walteri teñ de abbe *COSINTONE*.Aluuin tenuit de abbe

T.R.E.7 geldb ꝑ.iii.hid.Tra.ē.vi.cař.De ea.ē in dñio.i.hida

7 ibi.i.cař.7 iiii.ſerui.7 ix.uitti 7 ix.borđ cū.v.cař.Ibi.x.ãc

ꝑti.7 ii.ãc ſiluæ minutæ.Valuit 7 uat.vi.lib.

Rogeri teñ de abbe *DEREBERGE*.Oſuuald tenuit de abbe

T.R.E.7 geldb ꝑ.ii.hid.Tra.ē.iii.cař.Ibi ſt.iii.uitti 7 iii.borđ

cū.ii.cař.7 in dñio dimiđ cař.7 xi.ãc ꝑti.7 xx.ãc paſturæ.

7 x.ãc ſiluæ.Vat.xxx.ſoliđ Cū recep.xl.ſoliđ ualb.

Ailuuacre teñ de abbe *BLACHEFORD*.Alnod tenuit de abbe.

T.R.E.7 geldb ꝑ.iiii.hid.Tra.ē.vi.cař.In dñio ſt.iii.cař.7 v.

ſerui.7 vii.uitti 7 x.borđ cū.iiii.cař.Ibi.xv.ãc ꝑti.7 xliii.ãc

paſturæ.7 xlvii.ãc ſiluæ.Valet.c.ſot.Q̃do recep.iiii.lib.

Godeſcal teñ de abbe *STAWELLE*.Aluuard tenuit T.R.E.7 geldb

ꝑ.ii.hid 7 dimiđ.Tra.ē.ii.cař 7 dim.In dñio.ē.i.cař.7 iii.ſerui.

7 iii.borđ cū.i.cař.7 xx.ãc ꝑti.Valet.xl.ſot.Q̃do recep.v.ſoliđ.

90 b

Ipſa æccta teñ *WALTONE*.T.R.E.geldb ꝑ.xxx.hid.

Tra.ē.xl.cař.De ea ſt in dñio.x.hidæ.7 ibi.iiii.cař.

7 iiii.ſerui.7|xvii.uitti 7 xii.borđ cū.xviii.cař.

Ibi.l.ãc ꝑti.Paſtura.vii.q̃ʒ lḡ.7 una q̃ʒ lat.

Silua.vii.q̃ʒ lḡ.7 iii.q̃ʒ lat.Valet abbi.xv.lib.

6 The Church holds MIDDLEZOY itself. Before 1066 it paid tax   E
for 12 hides. Land for 20 ploughs, of which 5 hides are in
lordship; 2 ploughs there; 2 slaves; 12 freedmen;   162
   27 villagers and 13 smallholders with 14 ploughs & 7 hides.   b 1
   Meadow, 30 acres; underwood, 12 acres. 17 cattle; 18 pigs; 50 sheep.
The value was £10; now £24.

7 Walter of Douai holds COSSINGTON from the Abbot. Alwin Pike held
it from the Abbot before 1066; it paid tax for 3 hides. Land for   162
6 ploughs, of which 1 hide is in lordship; 1 plough there; 4 slaves;   b 2
   9 villagers and 9 smallholders with 5 ploughs & 2 hides.
   Meadow, 10 acres; underwood, 2 acres. 1 cob; 6 cattle; 26 pigs; 26 sheep.
The value was and is £6.   E

8 Roger of Courseulles holds DURBOROUGH from the Abbot. Oswald held E
it from the Abbot before 1066; it paid tax for 2 hides. Land for
3 ploughs.
   3 villagers and 3 smallholders with 2 ploughs & 1 hide.   163
   In lordship ½ plough & 1 hide.   a 1
   Meadow, 11 acres; pasture, 20 acres; woodland, 10 acres. 6 pigs.
Value 30s; value when he acquired it, 40s.

9 Alwaker holds BLACKFORD from the Abbot. Alnoth held it from the
Abbot before 1066; it paid tax for 4 hides. Land for 6 ploughs.
In lordship 3 ploughs; 5 slaves; 2½ hides.   163
   7 villagers and 10 smallholders with 4 ploughs & 1½ hides.   a 2
   Meadow, 115 acres; pasture, 43 acres; woodland, 47 acres.
      1 cob; 9 unbroken mares; 30 cattle; 24 pigs; 84 sheep.
Value 100s; when he acquired it, £4.

10 Godescal holds STAWELL from the Abbot. Alfward held it before
1066; it paid tax for 2½ hides. Land for 2½ ploughs. In lordship 1
plough; 3 slaves; 2 hides & 1 virgate.   163
   3 smallholders with 1 plough & 1 virgate.   a 3
   Meadow, 20 acres. 5 cobs; 8 cattle; 200 sheep.
Value 40s; when he acquired it, 5s.

11 The Church holds WALTON itself. Before 1066 it paid tax for   E 90 b
30 hides. Land for 40 ploughs, of which 10 hides are in
lordship; 4 ploughs there; 4 slaves;   163
   27 villagers and 12 smallholders with 18 ploughs & 4½ hides.   b 1
   Meadow, 50 acres; pasture 7 furlongs long and 1 furlong wide;
      woodland 7 furlongs long and 3 furlongs wide.   E
      2 cobs; 10 cattle; 18 pigs; 100 sheep; 30 goats.
Value to the Abbot £15; when Abbot Thurstan acquired it, 100s.

De his . xxx . hiđ teñ de abбej. v . hiđ in *CONTONE*. Rogerius

Walteri̓ . III . hiđ in *AISSECOTE* .7 III . hiđ in *PEDEWELLE*.

Qui teneƀ T . R . E . ñ poterant ab æccła feparari.

In dñio sƚ ibi . III . caŕ .7 vi . ferui .7 xv . uilłi 7 xII.

borđ cū . vIII . caŕ . Rogeri̓ hƚ . xx . aĉs p̃ti .7 vi . q̃ƺ

Siluæ in łǥ .7 una q̃ƺ laƚ . Walteri̓ . xII . aĉ p̃ti .7 xL.

aĉ filuæ minutæ . Inƚ eos ualet . vIII . liƀ.

Rogeri̓ teñ de abбe *BODESLEGE* . Winegod tenuit

T . R . E .7 geldƀ p̧ . III . v̓ træ . Tra . ē . I . caŕ 7 dim̓ . q̃ ibi sƚ

cū . vII . borđ . Ibi . vi . aĉ p̃ti .7 II . aĉ filuæ . Valet . x . foliđ.

Idē . Ro . teñ de abбe *DONDEME* . Algar tenuit T . R . E.

7 geldƀ p̧ . v . hiđ . Tra . ē . IIII . caŕ . De ea sƚ in dñio . III . hidæ

7 dim̓ . v̓ træ .7 ibi . II . caŕ .7 IIII . ferui .7 v . uilłi 7 x . borđ

cū . III . caŕ . Ibi . xL . aĉ p̃ti .7 x . aĉ filuæ . Valet . c . foliđ.

Idē Ro . teñ de abбe *AISSECOTE* .7 p̃tiñ ad *WALTONE*

m̃ abбis . T . R . E . geldƀ p̧ . II . hiđ . Tra . ē . III . caŕ . Ibi sƚ

II . uilłi 7 III . borđ 7 II . ferui . cū . I . caŕ .7 IIII . aĉ p̃ti.

Valuit 7 uaƚ . xL . foliđ.

Girard̓ teñ de abбe *GRAINTONE* . Vlmer tenuit T . R . E.

7 geldƀ p̧ . II . hiđ .7 dim̓ . Tra . ē . II . caŕ .7 dimid . In dñio

esƚ . I . caŕ .7 v . ferui .7 II . borđ 7 II . coliƀti . cū . I . caŕ.

Ibi . xx . aĉ p̃ti .7 III . aĉ filuæ . Valet 7 ualuit . L . foliđ.

Ip̃fa æccła teñ *LEGA* . T . R . E . geldƀ p̧ IIII . hiđ . Tra . ē . x.

caŕ . De ea sƚ in dñio . II . hidæ . Vna ex his fuit teinland.

ñ tam̃ poterat ab æccła feparari . In dñio sƚ . IIII . caŕ.

cū . I . feruo .7 vII . uilłi 7 x . borđ cū . v . caŕ . Ibi . xxxv . aĉ

p̃ti .7 xxx . aĉ pafturæ .7 vi . aĉ filuæ . Valet . vIII . liƀ.

Of these 30 hides Roger of Courseulles holds 5 hides in COMPTON   D
(Dundon) from the Abbot, Walter of Douai 3 hides in ASHCOTT
and 3 hides in PEDWELL. The holders before 1066 could not be   E
separated from the church. In lordship 3 ploughs; 6 slaves;
   15 villagers and 12 smallholders with 8 ploughs.
   Roger has meadow, 20 acres; woodland, 6 furlongs in length
      and 1 furlong wide.
   Walter (has) meadow, 12 acres; underwood, 40 acres.
Value between them £8.   E

12 Roger of Courseulles holds ?BUTLEIGH from the Abbot. Winegot the
priest held it before 1066; it paid tax for 3 virgates of land.   E
Land for 1½ ploughs, which are there, with   L
   7 smallholders.   164
   Meadow, 6 acres; woodland, 2 acres. 4 cattle; 2 pigs.   a 1
Value 10s; when he acquired it, 6s.

13 Roger of Courseulles also holds DUNDON from the Abbot. Algar held
it before 1066; it paid tax for 5 hides. Land for 4 ploughs, of
which 3 hides and ½ virgate of land are in lordship; 2 ploughs   164
there; 4 slaves;   a 2
   5 villagers and 10 smallholders with 3 ploughs & the rest of the land.
   Meadow, 40 acres; woodland, 10 acres. 5 unbroken mares; 2 cobs; 9 pigs.
Value 100s; when he acquired it, £6.

14 Roger of Courseulles also holds ASHCOTT from the Abbot; it belongs to
the Abbot's manor of Walton. Before 1066 it paid tax for 2 hides.
Land for 3 ploughs. In lordship 1½ hides & 2 oxen in a plough.   164
   2 villagers, 3 smallholders and 2 slaves with   b 1
      1 plough & the rest of the land.
   Meadow, 4 acres. 1 cob; 2 cows; 7 pigs; 42 sheep; 8 goats.
The value was and is 40s.

15 Gerard Ditcher holds GREINTON from the Abbot. Wulfmer held it   E
before 1066; it paid tax for 2½ hides. Land for 2½ ploughs.
In lordship 1 plough; 5 slaves; 2 hides.   164
   2 smallholders and 2 freedmen with 1 plough & ½ hide.   b 2
   Meadow, 20 acres; woodland, 3 acres. 4 cattle; 6 pigs.
The value is and was 50s.

16 The Church holds OVERLEIGH itself. Before 1066 it paid tax for 4   E
hides. Land for 10 ploughs, of which 2 hides are in lordship. One
of these was thaneland; however it could not be separated from   E
the church. In lordship 4 ploughs, with 1 slave;   164
   7 villagers and 10 smallholders with 5 ploughs & 2 hides.   b 3
   Meadow, 35 acres; pasture, 30 acres; woodland, 6 acres.
      2 cobs; 8 cattle; 20 pigs; 55 sheep.
Value £8; when Abbot Thurstan acquired it, 60s.

Ipſa æccła ten̄ *HAME* . T.R.E. geldb̄ ℣p. xvii . hiđ.

Tra . ē . xx . car̄ . De ea ſt in dn̄io . v . hidæ .7 ii . v̄ 7 dim̄.

7 ibi . iii . car̄ .7 v . ſerui .7 xxii . uiłłi 7 xxi . borđ cū . viii.

car̄ . Ibi . xxx . ac̄ p̄ti .7 xvi . ac̄ ſilúæ . Valet . x . lib̄.

De hac tra huj M̄ ten̄ de abb̄e Rob̄t . i . hiđ 7 un̄a v̄.

7 Serlo . v . hiđ . Girard . iii . virḡ træ . Leuric 7 Aluuold

7 Almar tenuer̄ T.R.E. nec poterant ab æccła ſepari.

In dn̄io ſt . ii . car̄ .7 iiii . ſerui .7 ii . uiłłi 7 xiiii . borđ

cū . ii . car̄ . Ibi . xxx . ac̄ p̄ti .7 xx . ac̄ paſturæ.

Valet int̄ tot̄ . cx . ſoliđ.

Ipſa æccła ten̄ *BODVCHELEI* .T.R.E. geldb̄ ℣p . xx . hiđ.

Tra . ē . xx . car̄ . De ea ſt in dn̄io . v . hidæ .7 ibi . v . car̄ .7 vii.

ſerui .7 xi . uiłłi 7 vii . borđ cū . vi . car̄ . Ibi . l . ac̄ p̄ti.

7 c . ac̄ ſiluæ . Valet abb̄i . x . lib̄.

De hac tra huj M̄ ten̄ Turſtin . viii . hiđ . Rogeri . ii.

hiđ . Duo taini teneb̄ de æccła T.R.E .7 n̄ poteraɴ inde

ſeparari . In dn̄io ſt ibi . iiii . car̄ .7 vi . ſerui .7 xi . uiłłi

7 vi . borđ cū . iii . car̄ . Ibi . xiiii . ac̄ p̄ti .7 xii . ac̄ ſiluæ

minutæ . Valuit 7 ual̄ . vii . lib̄ int̄ eos.   ꟿValet . x . ſoł.

De ead̄ tra ten̄ Aleſtan de abb̄e . . ᵈⁱᵐⁱᵈ hiđ .7 ibi hr̄ . i . car̄.

Hunfrid ten̄ de rege . ii . hiđ in *LODREFORD* .7 p̄tin huic M̄

Aluric teneb̄ T.R.E. nec poterat ab æccła ſeparari.

Tra . ē . ii . car̄ . Valet . xx . ſoliđ.

Ipſa æccła ten̄ *PILTONE* . T.R.E. geldb̄ ℣p . xx . hiđ . Tra . ē

xxx . car̄ . P̄ter hanc hr̄ abb̄ ibi tram . xx . car̄ . quæ nunq̄

geldau . In dn̄io ſt . x . car̄ .7 xv . ſerui .7 xxi . uiłłs 7 xlii.

borđ cū . x . car̄ ſup tr̄a n̄ geldant . Ibi . ii . molini redđ

x . ſoliđ .7 xlvi . ac̄ p̄ti .7 xl . ac̄ paſturæ . Silua . i . leū

lḡ .7 dim̄ leū lat̄ . De tra q̄ n̄ geld̄ ten̄ Alnod monꞏch . i . hiđ

17 The Church holds HAM itself. Before 1066 it paid tax for 17 hides.　E
Land for 20 ploughs, of which 5 hides and 2½ virgates are in
lordship; 3 ploughs there; 5 slaves;　165
　　22 villagers and 21 smallholders with 8 ploughs & 3 hides & 1½ virgates.　a 1
　　Meadow, 30 acres; woodland, 16 acres. 2 cobs; 17 cattle; 10 pigs; 150 sheep.
Value £10; when Abbot Thurstan acquired it, £4.
　　Of this manor's land Robert of Auberville holds 1 hide and 1　E
virgate from the Abbot, Serlo of Burcy 5 hides, Gerard Ditcher 3　D
virgates of land. Leofric, Alfwold and Aelmer held them before　E
1066; they could not be separated from the church. In lordship
2 ploughs; 4 slaves;
　　2 villagers and 14 smallholders with 2 ploughs.　E
　　Meadow, 30 acres; pasture, 20 acres.
In total, value 110s.

18 The Church holds BUTLEIGH itself. Before 1066 it paid tax for 20　E
hides. Land for 20 ploughs, of which 5 hides are in lordship;
5 ploughs there; 7 slaves;
　　11 villagers and 7 smallholders with 6 ploughs & 2½ hides.　165
　　Meadow, 50 acres; woodland, 100 acres. 2 cobs; 12 cattle;　b 1
　　　　25 pigs; 120 sheep.
Value to the Abbot £10; when Thurstan acquired it, 60s.　E
　　Of this manor's land Thurstan son of Rolf holds 8 hides, Roger　D
of Courseulles 2 hides. Two thanes held them from the church before　E
1066; they could not be separated from it. In lordship 4 ploughs;
6 slaves;
　　11 villagers and 6 smallholders with 3 ploughs.
　　Meadow, 14 acres; underwood, 12 acres.
The value was and is £7 between them.　E
　　Alstan holds ½ hide of this land from the Abbot; he has 1 plough. E
　　　　1 cob; 60 sheep.
Value 10s; when he acquired it, 5s.

19 Humphrey the Chamberlain holds 2 hides in LATTIFORD from the King;　E
they belong to this manor. Aelfric held them before 1066; he　165
could not be separated from the church. Land for 2 ploughs.　b 2
Value 20s.　E

20 The Church holds PILTON itself. Before 1066 it paid tax for 20　E
hides. Land for 30 ploughs. Besides this the Abbot has land
there for 20 ploughs, which has never paid tax. In lordship
10 ploughs; 15 slaves;　165
　　21 villagers and 42 smallholders with 10 ploughs on the　b 3
　　　land which does not pay tax.
　　2 mills which pay 10s; meadow, 46 acres; pasture, 40 acres;
　　　woodland 1 league long and ½ league wide.　E
　　　　4 cobs; 35 cattle; 56 pigs; 500 sheep; 42 goats.
　　Of the land which does not pay tax Alnoth the monk holds 1 hide

libalit de abbe cceſſu regis . H̅ tainland fuit.7 nec poteſt
ab æccła ſeparari . Tot ualet.xxiiii . lib̄ . Valuit . xvi . lib̄.
De hac tra huj ꝏ ten Rogeri in SEPETONE . vi . hid
7 dimid .7 In CORISTONE . iii . hid . Vluert 7 Elmer te
nuer T . R . E . 7 n̅ poterant ab æccła ſeparari.

In dn̅io ſt . iii . car .7 viii . ſerui .7 xiii . uiłłi 7 xix . bord
cu̅ . vi . car . Ibi . ii . molini redd . vi . ſolid 7 iii . denar.
7 l . ac pti .7 xlii . ac ſiluæ minutæ . Paſtura . iii . q̃ȝ
lg̅ .7 una q̃ȝ lat . Valet tot . ix . lib̄.
De ead tra ejd ꝏ ten de abbe Adret . v . hid in VRONE.
7 Serlo . v . hid in PILLE .7 Radulf . ii . hid in ipſa PILTONE.
Qui teneb T . R . E . n̅ poterant ab æccła ſeparari.
Iu dn̅io ſt ibi . iiii . car 7 dimid .7 viii . ſerui .7 viii . uiłłi
7 xviii . bord cu̅ . iii . car . Ibi . ii . molini redd . iiii . ſol
7 vi . den .7 xxxvi . ac pti 7 dimid .7 xx . ac paſturæ.
7 iiii . ac ſiluæ . Tot ualet . vii . lib̄ 7 x . ſol . int eos.
Ipſa æccła ten PENNARMINSTRE . T . R . E . geldb̄
ꝑ . x . hid . Ibi ſt tam . xx . hidæ . Tra . e̅ . xii . car.
De ea ſt in dn̅io . xii . hidæ .7 ibi . v . car .7 iiii . ſerui.
7 xvii . uiłłi 7 ix . bord 7 x . cotar . cu̅ . vi . car.
Ibi . xxx . ac pti .7 xl . ac paſturæ . Silua . i . leu̅|lg̅.⁷ᵈⁱᵐⁱᵈ
7 iiii . q̃ȝ lat . Valet abbi . xii . lib̄
De hac tra huj ꝏ ten Serlo de abbe . i . hid.
Ailmar tenuit T . R . E . Ibi ſt . iiii . uiłłi hn̅tes . ii . car.
7 viii . ac pti .7 xxx . ac ſiluæ . Valuit 7 ual . xxx . ſol.
Ipſa æccła ten BALTVNESBERGE . T.R.E . geldb̄ ꝑ . v.
hid . Tra . e̅ . vi . car . De ea ſt in dn̅io . iiii . hidæ .7 una v̅.
7 ibi . ii . car .7 iiii . ſerui .7 v . uiłłi .7 ix . bord .7 iii . cotar
cu̅ . ii . car . Ibi moliñ redd . v . ſolid .7 xxx . ac pti . Silua
una leu̅ 7 dim lg̅ .7 dimid leu̅ lat . Valuit 7 ual . vi . lib̄.

freely from the Abbot with the King's assent. It was thaneland;
it cannot be separated from the church.
Value of the whole £24; the value was £16.

Roger of Courseulles holds 6½ hides of this manor's land in   D
SHEPTON (Mallet) and 3 hides in CROSCOMBE. Wulfred and Aelmer   E
held them before 1066; they could not be separated from the church.
In lordship 3 ploughs; 8 slaves;   90 c
   13 villagers and 19 smallholders with 6 ploughs.
   2 mills which pay 6s 3d; meadow, 50 acres; underwood,
      42 acres; pasture 3 furlongs long and 1 furlong wide.
Value of the whole £9.

Also of this manor's land Edred holds 5 hides in (North)   D
WOOTTON from the Abbot, Serlo of Burcy 5 hides in PYLLE and
Ralph Crooked Hands 2 hides in PILTON itself. The holders before   E
1066 could not be separated from the church. In lordship
4½ ploughs; 8 slaves;
   8 villagers and 18 smallholders with 3 ploughs.
   2 mills which pay 4s 6d; meadow, 36½ acres; pasture, 20
     acres; woodland, 4 acres.   E
Value of the whole £7 10s between them.   E

21 The Church holds PENNARD itself. Before 1066 it paid tax for   E
10 hides. However there are 20 hides there. Land for 12 ploughs,
of which 12 hides are in lordship; 5 ploughs there; 4 slaves;
   17 villagers, 9 smallholders and 10 cottagers with   166
     6 ploughs & 7 hides.   b 1
   Meadow, 30 acres; pasture, 40 acres; woodland 1½ leagues long
     and 4 furlongs wide. 2 cobs; 42 cattle; 25 pigs; 55 sheep.
Value to the Abbot £12; when Abbot Thurstan acquired it, £4.

Serlo of Burcy holds 1 hide of this manor's land from the Abbot.   E
Aelmer held it before 1066.
   4 villagers who have 2 ploughs & 1 hide.
   Meadow, 8 acres; woodland, 30 acres.
The value was and is 30s.

22 The Church holds BALTONSBOROUGH itself. Before 1066 it paid tax   E
for 5 hides. Land for 6 ploughs, of which 4 hides and 1 virgate
are in lordship; 2 ploughs there; 4 slaves;
   5 villagers, 9 smallholders and 3 cottagers with   167
     2 ploughs & 3 virgates.   a 1
   A mill which pays 5s; meadow, 30 acres; woodland 1½ leagues
     long and ½ league wide. 2 cobs; 16 cattle; 14 pigs; 33 goats.
The value was and is £6.

Ipſa æccła ten̄ *DOLTIN*. T.R.E. geldƀ p̱. xx. hid̄. Tra. ē xx. car̄. De ea ſt̄ in dn̄io. XII. hidæ. 7 ibi. II. car̄. 7 v. ſerui. 7 x. uiłłi 7 VI. bord̄ 7 IIII. cotar̄ cū. VI. car̄. Ibi. xxx. ac̄ p̄ti. 7 LX. ac̄ paſturæ. 7 LX. ac̄ ſiluæ minutæ. Valet abƀi. XIIII. lib̄.

De hac tra ten̄ Rogeri᷒. III. hid̄ 7 unā v̄ træ in *CER LETONE*. 7 alibi. II. hid̄ 7 III. v̄ træ. In dn̄io. ē una car̄. cū. I. ſeruo. 7 VIII. uiłłi 7 VI. bord̄ cū. II. car̄. Ibi molin̄ redd̄. IX. denar̄. 7 XXIII. ac̄ p̄ti. 7 x. ac̄ paſturæ. 7 xxx. ac̄ ſiluæ minutæ. Valet. c. ſolid̄.

Ipſa æccła ten̄ *BATECVBE*. T.R.E. geldƀ p̱. xx. hid̄. Tra. ē. XVI. car̄. De ea ſt̄ in dn̄io. IX. hidæ 7 III. v̄ træ. 7 ibi. II. car̄. 7 VI. ſerui. 7 IIII. uiłłi 7 XIIII. bord̄ cū. III. car̄. Ibi molin̄ redd̄. v. ſolid̄. 7 xx. ac̄ p̄ti. 7 VI. ac̄ paſturæ. 7 XL. ac̄ ſiluæ. Valet abƀi. VII. lib̄.

De hac tra huj᷒ co̅ ten̄ Rogeri᷒. II. hid̄. Vluui tenuit T.R.E. 7 n̄ poterat ab æccła ſeparari. Ibi hₜ. I. car̄. cū. I. ſeruo. 7 III. bord̄. Ibi. XII. ac̄ p̄ti. 7 x. ac̄ paſturæ. Valet xx. ſolid̄.

De ipſa tra ejd̄ co̅ ten̄ Azelin᷒ in *WESTCVBE* VII. hid̄ 7 III. v̄ træ. Alfhilla tenuit T.R.E. 7 n̄ poterat ab æccła ſeparari. In dn̄io ſt̄. IIᵉ. car̄. 7 VI. uiłłi 7 VII. bord̄ 7 VI. cotar̄ cū. I. ſeruo hn̄t. II. car̄ 7 dimid̄. Ibi. II. molini redd̄. v. ſolid̄. 7 XII. ac̄ p̄ti. 7 XII. ac̄ paſturæ. 7 XVI. ac̄ ſiluæ. Valet. IIII. lib̄ 7 x. ſolid̄. Duæ hidæ de hac tra fuer̄ de tra uiłłoꝝ. 7 aliæ. v. eraɴ̄ tainland.

Ipſa æccła ten̄ *MVLLE*. T.R.E. geldƀ p̱. xx. hid̄. Tra. ē. xx. car̄. De ea ſt̄ in dn̄io. x. hidæ. 7 ibi. II. car̄. 7 II. ſerui.

23 The Church holds DOULTING itself. Before 1066 it paid tax   E
for 20 hides. Land for 20 ploughs, of which 12 hides are
in lordship; 2 ploughs there; 5 slaves;
> 10 villagers, 6 smallholders and 4 cottagers with   167
> > 6 ploughs & 2 hides.   a 2
>
> Meadow, 30 acres; pasture, 60 acres; underwood, 60 acres.
> > 1 cob; 4 cattle; 15 pigs; 340 sheep.

Value to the Abbot £14; when Thurstan acquired it, £6.   E
Of this land Roger of Courseulles holds 3 hides and 1 virgate of land   D
in CHARLTON, and 2 hides and 3 virgates of land elsewhere.   E
In lordship 1 plough, with 1 slave;
> 8 villagers and 6 smallholders with 2 ploughs.
> A mill which pays 9d; meadow, 23 acres; pasture, 10 acres;
> > underwood, 30 acres.

Value 100s.

24 The Church holds BATCOMBE itself. Before 1066 it paid tax   E
for 20 hides. Land for 16 ploughs, of which 9 hides and 3 virgates
of land are in lordship; 2 ploughs there; 6 slaves;
> 4 villagers and 14 smallholders with 3 ploughs & ½ hide.   167
> A mill which pays 5s; meadow, 20 acres; pasture, 6 acres;   b 1
> > woodland, 40 acres.   2 cobs; 8 cattle; 9 pigs; 150 sheep; 17 goats.

Value to the Abbot £7; when Abbot Thurstan acquired it, 40s.
Roger of Courseulles holds 2 hides of this manor's land.
Wulfwy held them before 1066; he could not be separated from
the church. He has 1 plough, with 1 slave;
> 3 smallholders.
> Meadow, 12 acres; pasture, 10 acres.   1 cob; 2 pigs.

Value 20s; when he acquired them, 40s.
Of this manor's land Azelin holds 7 hides and 3 virgates of
land in WESTCOMBE. Alfhild, the Abbot's mother, held them
before 1066; she could not be separated from the church.
In lordship 2 ploughs; 5 hides & 1 virgate.
> 6 villagers, 7 smallholders and 6 cottagers with 1 slave
> > have 2½ ploughs & the rest of the land.
> 2 mills which pay 5s; meadow, 12 acres; pasture, 12 acres;
> > woodland, 16 acres. 1 cob; 11 cattle; 10 pigs; 100 sheep.

Value £4 10s; when he acquired them, 20s.
> Two hides of this land were villagers' land; the other five   E
were thaneland.

25 The Church holds MELLS itself. Before 1066 it paid tax for 20   E
hides. Land for 20 ploughs, of which 10 hides are in
lordship; 2 ploughs there; 2 slaves;

7 VIII . uitti 7 VII . bord 7 v . cotar cū . III . car . Ibi moliñ
redd . v . folid .7 xv . ac pti .7 XII . ac pafturæ . Silua . I . leū
lḡ .7 II . q̃ lat Valet abbi . x . lib.

De hac tra huj ḿ ten Godeue de abbe . I . hid . Vir ej
tenuit T . R . E . nec poterat ab æccta feparari . Valet . LXXVIII.

Eps cftantienſ ten de rege . v . hid 7 dim ptinent ⌐ den
huic ḿ . Duo taini teneɓ T . R . E . fed ñ poterant ab æccta
feparari . Azelin ten de epo.

Walteri ten de abbe in WATELEI . IIII . hid . Vlgar monac°
tenuit T . R . E .7 ñ poterat ab æccta feparari . Tra . ē . IIII . car.
De ea ſt in dñio . II . hidæ 7 dimid .7 ibi . II . car .7 IIII . ferui.
7 VIII . uitti 7 v . bord cū . II . car . Ibi moliñ redd . v . fol.
7 VI . ac pti .7 L . ac pafturæ .7 XIIII . ac filuæ . Val . LXX . fol.
In eod ḿ ten Joħs de abbe . I . hidā de tra uillanoɀ.
Tra . ē . I . car . q̃ ibi . ē cū . II . uittis . Valet . xv . folid.

90 d

Ipfa æccta ten WERITONE . T . R . E gelɗɓ p . xx . hid . Tra . ē . xxxII.
car . De ea ſt in dñio . xi . hidæ .7 ibi . vi . car .7 VII . ferui .7 xLI . uitts
7 XII . bord cū . xx . car . Ibi . III . molini redd . xIIII . fol 7 II . denar.
7 xLIIII . ac pti .7 cc . ac pafturæ . Silua . II . leū lḡ .7 tntd lat.
Valet abbi . xxx . lib.

De hac tra huj ḿ ten Rogeri . I . hid 7 dimid de abbe . Vñ tain
tenuit T . R . É .7 ñ poterat ab æccta fepari . Ibi ſt . III . car .7 II . uitti
7 VI . bord . Valet . xxx . folid.

De ipfa tra ten Saulf . I . hid 7 dim . Ipfe tenuit T . R . E . Ibi hɫ . I . car
7 dimid .7 uñ uitts cū . IIII . cotar hñt . I . car . Valet . xxx . folid.

90 c, d

8 villagers, 7 smallholders and 5 cottagers with
  3 ploughs & 3½ hides.

A mill which pays 5s; meadow, 15 acres; pasture, 12 acres;
  woodland 1 league long and 2 furlongs wide. 1 cob; 7 cattle;
  15 pigs; 100 sheep, less 9.

Value to the Abbot £10; when Abbot Thurstan acquired it, 100s.

Godiva holds 1 hide of this manor's land from the Abbot.
Her husband held it before 1066; he could not be separated
from the church. Value 78d.

The Bishop of Coutances holds 5½ hides from the King which
belong to this manor. Two thanes held them before 1066, but
they could not be separated from the church. Azelin holds from
the Bishop. Value 25s; when the Bishop acquired them, as much.

26 Walter Hussey holds 4 hides in WHATLEY from the Abbot. Wulfgar,
a monk, held them before 1066; he could not be separated
from the church. Land for 4 ploughs, of which 2½ hides are in
lordship; 2 ploughs there; 4 slaves;
  8 villagers and 5 smallholders with 2 ploughs & 1½ hides.

A mill which pays 5s; meadow, 6 acres; pasture, 50 acres;
  woodland, 14 acres. 8 cattle; 100 sheep.

Value 70s; when he acquired it, 30s.

John the Usher holds 1 hide of villagers' land in this manor
from the Abbot. Land for 1 plough, which is there, with
  2 villagers.
Value 15s; when John acquired it, as much.

27 The Church holds WRINGTON itself. Before 1066 it paid tax
for 20 hides. Land for 32 ploughs, of which 11 hides are in
lordship; 6 ploughs there; 7 slaves;
  41 villagers and 12 smallholders with 20 ploughs & 6 hides.

3 mills which pay 14s 2d; meadow, 44 acres; pasture, 200
  acres; woodland 2 leagues long and as wide. 46 cattle; 30 pigs;
  278 sheep; 47 goats.

Value to the Abbot £30.

Roger of Courseulles holds 1½ hides of this manor's land from
the Abbot. A thane held them before 1066; he could not be
separated from the church. 3 ploughs there.
  2 villagers and 6 smallholders.
Value 30s.

Saewulf holds 1½ hides of this land. He held them himself
before 1066. He has 1½ ploughs there.
  1 villager with 4 cottagers have 1 plough.
Value 30s.

Margin: 168 a 1; E; E; 168 b 1; E; E 90 d; 169 a 1; E; E; E

Ipſa æccła ten̄ MONECHETONE. T.R.E. geldb̄ ꝑ. xv. hiđ. Tra. ē. xx. caꝛ.
De ea ten̄ Walchet epſ de abb̄e. v. hiđ 7 unā v̄ træ in dn̄io. 7 ibi. III.
caꝛ. 7 VII. ſerui. 7 xx. uiłłi 7 VII. borđ cū. VII. caꝛ. Ibi. xx. ać ꝑti. 7 c. ać
paſturæ. 7 xxIIII. ać ſiluæ. Valet. VII. lib̄.

In ipſa uilla ten̄ Rogeri de abb̄e. IIII. hiđ 7 III. v̄ træ. 7 Serlo. II. hiđ
7 dimiđ. Qui teneb̄ T.R.E. n̄ poteraꝗ ab æccła ſeparari. Ibi ſꝽ. IIII.
caꝛ in dn̄io. 7 III. ſerui. 7 VIII. uiłłi. 7 xI. borđ cū. II. caꝛ 7 dimiđ.
7 xIx. ać ꝑti. 7 xL. ać paſturæ. Valet int eos. IIII. lib̄ 7 x. ſoliđ.

Ipſa æccła ten̄ MERCESBERIE. T.R.E. geldb̄ ꝑ. x. hiđ. Tra. ē. VIII.
caꝛ. De ea ſꝽ in dn̄io. IIII. hiđ 7 dim. 7 ibi. II. caꝛ. 7 v. ſerui. 7 VI. uiłłi
7 v. borđ cū. III. caꝛ. Ibi. xIx. ać ꝑti. 7 xL. ać ſiluæ. Valet. x. lib̄.
De hac t̄ra ten̄ un̄ tain̄. II. hiđ 7 dimiđ. Valet. xx. ſoliđ.
Oſuualđ tenuit T.R.E. 7 n̄ potuit ab æccła ſeparari.

Ipſa æccła ten̄ DICESGET. T.R.E. geldb̄ ꝑ. xxx. hiđ. Tra. ē. xxx.
caꝛ. De ea ſꝽ in dn̄io. III. hidæ. 7 ibi. III. caꝛ 7 dimiđ. 7 II. ſerui.
7 xIII. uiłłi 7 xVIII. borđ 7 III. coſcez. cū. VII. caꝛ. Ibi molin̄ redđ
VII. ſoliđ 7 v. den̄. 7 xL. ać ꝑti. 7 paſtura. VI. q̃ꝗ lḡ. 7 II. q̃ꝗ lat̄. Silua
una leū 7 dim lḡ. 7 II. q̃ꝗ lat̄. Valet abb̄i. xII. lib̄.

De hac t̄ra huj ꝏ ten̄ de abb̄e Serlo. v. hiđ 7 dim in HORBLAWE
TONE. Radulf. vI. hiđ 7 dim̄ in ALENTONE. Nigell. v. hiđ 7 dimiđ
in LAMIETA. Qui teneb̄ T.R.E. n̄ poterant ab æccła ſeparari.
In dn̄io ſꝽ. IIII. caꝛ. 7 IIII. ſerui. 7 xxIx. uiłłi 7 xII. borđ 7 III. coſcez.
cū. xv. caꝛ. Ibi. III. molini redđ. xIII. ſoł 7 IIII. den̄ 7 Lv. ać ꝑti.
7 xx. ać paſturæ. Silua. Ix. q̃ꝗ lḡ. 7 una q̃ꝗ 7 dimiđ lat̄.
Tot̄ ual int eos. xIIII. lib̄ 7 x. ſoliđ. Valuit xI. lib̄.

28 The Church holds (West) MONKTON itself. Before 1066 it paid   E
tax for 15 hides. Land for 20 ploughs, of which Bishop Walkelin
holds 5 hides and 1 virgate of land from the Abbot in lordship;
3 ploughs there; 7 slaves;   169
    20 villagers and 7 smallholders with 7 ploughs & 2½ hides.   a 2
    Meadow, 20 acres; pasture, 100 acres; woodland, 24 acres.
        1 cob; 22 cattle; 12 pigs; 50 sheep.
Value £7, for Walkelin's use.
    In this village Roger of Courseulles holds 4 hides and 3 virgates of   D
land from the Abbot, and Serlo of Burcy 2½ hides. The holders   E
before 1066 could not be separated from the church. 4 ploughs
in lordship; 3 slaves;
    8 villagers and 11 smallholders with 2½ ploughs.
    Meadow, 19 acres; pasture, 40 acres.
Value between them £4 10s.   E

29 The Church holds MARKSBURY itself. Before 1066 it paid tax   E
for 10 hides. Land for 8 ploughs, of which 4½ hides are in
lordship; 2 ploughs there; 5 slaves;   169
    6 villagers and 5 smallholders with 3 ploughs & 3 hides.   b 1
    Meadow, 19 acres; woodland, 40 acres. 1 cob; 29 pigs; 85 sheep.
Value £10 to the Abbot.
    A thane holds 2½ hides of this land; value 20s.
Oswald held them before 1066; he could not be separated
from the church.

30 The Church holds DITCHEAT itself. Before 1066 it paid tax   E
for 30 hides. Land for 30 ploughs, of which 3 hides are in
lordship; 3½ ploughs there; 2 slaves;   169
    13 villagers, 18 smallholders and 3 Cottagers with   b 2
       7 ploughs & 2 hides.
    A mill which pays 7s 5d; meadow, 40 acres; pasture 6 furlongs
      long and 2 furlongs wide; woodland 1½ leagues long and
      2 furlongs wide. 2 cobs; 12 cattle; 20 pigs; 123 sheep; 23 goats.
Value to the Abbot £12.   E
    Of this manor's land Serlo of Burcy holds 5½ hides in   D
HORNBLOTTON from the Abbot, Ralph Crooked Hands 6½ hides in   170
ALHAMPTON, Nigel the Doctor 5½ hides in LAMYATT. The holders   E a 1-2
before 1066 could not be separated from the church. In
lordship 4 ploughs; 4 slaves;
    29 villagers, 12 smallholders and 3 Cottagers with 15 ploughs.   E
    3 mills which pay 13s 4d; meadow, 55 acres; pasture, 20
      acres; woodland 9 furlongs long and 1½ furlongs wide.   E
Value of the whole between them £14 10s; the value was £11.   E

De eiſd.xxx.hid teñ de rege Alfric 7 Eurard⁹.ı.hid.Hanc tenuit

uñ taiñ T.R.E.nec potuit ab æccła ſeparari.Valet.xx.ſolid.

De eiſd xxx.hid teñ Comes morit de rege.vıı.hid.Has tenebat

uñ taiñ de abbe T.R.E.nec poterat ab æccła ſepari.Valet.c.ſoł.

Ipſa æccła teñ CAMELERTONE.Edmer   tenuit T.R.E.7 geldb

p.x.hid.Tra.ē.x.car.De ea ſt in dñio.vıı.hidæ.7 ibi.ıı.car.

7 vııı.ſerui.7 vı.uiłłi 7 vı.bord cū.ıı.car.Ibi.ıı.molini redd

v.ſolid.7 qt xx.ac pti.7 xx.ac paſturæ.7 xl.ac ſiluæ.Valet

De hac tra huj M teñ Rogeri de abbe.ı.hid.7 ibi ſvıı.lib.

ht.ı.car.cū.ı.ſeruo 7 ı.bord.Ibi.x.ac pti.7 vı.ac ſiluæ.Vał x.ſoł.

Hoc M ded com moritoñ abbi p excābio TVTENELLE.

Harding teñ de abbe CRENEMELLE.Ipſe tenuit ſimilit T.R.E.

7 geldb p xıı.hid.Tra.ē.x.car.De ea ſt in dñio.vı.hidæ.7 ibi

una car.7 vı.ſerui.7 vııı.uiłłi 7 ıı.bord 7 vıı.cotar cū.ııı.car.

Ibi moliñ redd.xxx.den.7 l.ac pti.7 lx.ac paſturæ.7 c.ac

ſiluæ.Valet.ıııı.lib.H tra ñ poteſt ſepari ab æccła.

Ipſa æccła teñ BRENTEMERSE.T.R.E.geldb p xx.hid.Tra.ē

xxx.car.De ea ſt in dñio.ıııı.hidæ.7 ibi.vııı.car.7 v.ſerui.7 l.uiłłi.

7 xlvıı.bord.cū.xvı.car.7 xx.ac pti.Valet abbi.l.lib.

De his.xx.hid teñ de abbe Rogeri.ı.hid.Radulf⁹.v.uirg.

Alfric.v.uirg.Goduiñ.ı.hid 7 dim.Qui teneb de abbe T.R.E.

ñ poterant ab æccła ſeparari.In dñio ſt ibi.ıııı.car.cū.ı.ſeruo.

Also of these 30 hides Aelfric and Evrard hold 1 hide from the
King. A thane held it before 1066; he could not be separated
from the church. Value 20s.

E
170
a 3

Also of these 30 hides the Count of Mortain holds 7 hides
from the King. A thane held them from the Abbot before 1066;
he could not be separated from the church. Value 100s; when the
Count acquired them, £7.

E
170
a 4

31 The Church holds CAMERTON itself. Edmer Ator held it before 1066;
it paid tax for 10 hides. Land for 10 ploughs, of which 7 hides
are in lordship; 2 ploughs there; 8 slaves;
   6 villagers and 6 smallholders with 2 ploughs & 2 hides.

E
E

   2 mills which pay 5s; meadow, 80 acres; pasture, 20 acres;
      woodland, 40 acres. 1 cob; 13 pigs; 154 sheep.

170

Value £7; when Abbot Thurstan acquired it, £6.

a 5

   Roger holds 1 hide of this manor's land from the Abbot; he
has 1 plough in lordship, with 1 slave;

E

   1 smallholder.
   Meadow, 10 acres; woodland, 6 acres.
Value 10s; when he acquired it, as much.
   The Count of Mortain gave this manor to the Abbot in ·
exchange for Tintinhull.

32 Harding holds CRANMORE from the Abbot. He held it himself
likewise before 1066; it paid tax for 12 hides. Land for 10
ploughs, of which 6 hides are in lordship; 1 plough there; 6 slaves;
   8 villagers, 2 smallholders and 7 cottagers with
      3 ploughs & 6 hides.

170
b 1

   A mill which pays 30d; meadow, 50 acres; pasture, 60 acres;
      woodland, 100 acres. 1 cob; 16 goats.
Value £4.
   This land cannot be separated from the church.

33 The Church holds BRENT itself. Before 1066 it paid tax for 20
hides. Land for 30 ploughs, of which 4 hides are in lordship;
8 ploughs there; 5 slaves;

E

   50 villagers and 47 smallholders with 16 ploughs & 11 hides.
   Meadow, 20 acres. 1 cob; 73 cattle; 60 pigs; 82 sheep.

170
b 2

Value to the Abbot £50; when the Abbot acquired it, £15.

E

   Of these 20 hides Roger of Courseulles holds 1 hide from the

D

Abbot, Ralph of Conteville 5 virgates, Aelfric son of Everwacer 5 virgates,
Godwin the priest 1½ hides. Those who held from the Abbot before

E

1066 could not be separated from the church. In lordship 4 ploughs,
with 1 slave;

7 III.uilli 7 v.borđ 7 x.cotař cū.III.cař.Valet int́ eos.IIII.lib̄ 7 x.ſol.

Walcin̅ ten̅ de abb̅e *LODENWRDE*.Vn̅ tain̅ tenuit T.R.E.nec po

terat ab æccła ſepari.7 geldb̄ p.II.hiđ.Tra.ē.v.cař.In dn̅io ſt́.II.cař.

7 IIII.ſerui.7 IIII.uilli.7 v.borđ 7 v.cotař cū.IIII.cař.Valet.XL.ſol.

Erneis ten̅ de abb̅e *DVNEHEFDE*.Vlgar monac̅ tenuit T.R.E.

7 geldb̄ p.III.hiđ.T́ra.ē.v.cař.De ea ſt́ in dn̅io.II.hidæ.7 ibi.III.cař.

cū.v.uilłis 7 IIII.borđ.Ibi.v.ac̅ pti.Paſtura.v.q̊ꝛ lḡ.7 II.q̊ꝛ lat́.

Silua dimiđ leū.lḡ.7 tn̅tđ lat́.Valuit 7 ual.XL.ſolid.

Siuuard ten̅.III.uirǵ træ de æccła Glaſtingb̅ie.in c̅ꝺ qđ uocat́

DINNITONE.Valet.XIII.ſolid 7 II.den̅.

91 a

S Andree

Mauricius ep̅s ten̅ æcciam de Giuelceſtre cū.III.hiđ t́ræ.de rege.

Hanc teneb̄ Brictric T.R.E.de æccła Glaſtingb̅ie.nec ab ea poterat ſepari.

Ep̅s c̅ſtant ten̅ de rege Hutone.~~Eleberie~~.Eleberie.Hetſecome.

7 Stretone.Hæ t́ræ erant tainland T.R.E.nec poterant ab æccła

ſeparari.Valent.c.ſolid.7 āplius.Æccła ſeruitiū inde n̅ habet.

Comes moriton̅ ten̅ de rege h̅ c̅ꝺ.Stane.Stoca 7 Stoca.Dreicote.

Hæ t́ræ fueř tainlande in Glaſtingb̅ie T.R.E.nec poteraꝗ ab ea ſepari

Valent.XIII.lib̄.   ꝼin Glaſtingb̅ie T.R.E.

Idē com̅ ten̅ in c̅ꝺ Bodcchclic.II.q̊ꝛ filuæ in lḡ.7 una q̊ꝛ lat́.qđ fuit

Rogeri de Corcelle h̅t́ uñ c̅ꝺ Limingtone.p quo deđ pat́ ej

.v.hiđ in excābio q̊s teneb̄ de æccła Glaſtingb̅ie.nec inde poteraꝗ ſepari.

De his æccła ſeruitiū pdit.

3 villagers, 5 smallholders and 10 cottagers with 3 ploughs. E
Value between them £4 10s.

34 Walscin of Douai holds EDINGWORTH from the Abbot. A thane held
it before 1066; he could not be separated from the church.
It paid tax for 2 hides. Land for 5 ploughs. In lordship 2
ploughs; 4 slaves; 1 hide. 171
4 villagers, 5 smallholders and 5 cottagers with a 1
4 ploughs & 1 hide.
1 cob; 15 cattle; 5 pigs; 5 sheep.
Value 40s; when Walscin acquired it, as much.

35 Erneis holds DOWNHEAD from the Abbot. Wulfgar, a monk, held E
it before 1066; it paid tax for 3 hides. Land for 5 ploughs,
of which 2 hides are in lordship; 3 ploughs there, with E
5 villagers and 4 smallholders (who have) 1 hide. 171
Meadow, 5 acres; pasture 5 furlongs long and 2 furlongs b 2
wide; woodland ½ league long and as wide.
The value was and is 40s.

36 Siward holds 3 virgates of land from Glastonbury Church in the E
manor called DINNINGTON. 172
Value 13s 2d. b 2

37 Bishop Maurice holds St. Andrew's Church of ILCHESTER with 3 E 91 a
hides of land from the King. Brictric held it before 1066 from 171
Glastonbury Church; he could not be separated from it. b 1
Value of this church, 100s; when Maurice acquired it, as much.

38 The Bishop of Coutances holds HUTTON, ELBOROUGH, 'HISCOMBE' E
and STRATTON (on the Fosse) from the King. These lands were E 172
thaneland before 1066; they could not be separated from the church. b 1;
Value 100s and more. 6-7
The church does not have service from them. E

39 The Count of Mortain holds these manors from the King: ? KINGSTONE, E
STOKE (sub Hamdon), STOKE (sub Hamdon), DRAYCOTT. These lands E 172
were thaneland in Glastonbury (lands) before 1066; they could E b 3-5
not be separated from it.
Value £13.

40 The Count also holds in the manor of BUTLEIGH woodland, 2 E
furlongs in length and 1 furlong wide; it was in Glastonbury (lands) 173
before 1066. a 1

41 Roger of Courseulles has a manor, LIMINGTON, for which his father E
gave in exchange 5 hides which he held from Glastonbury 172
Church; they could not be separated from it. The church loses a 2
service from them. E

TERRA ÆCCLÆ DE MICELENIE.

Eccla S Petri de Micelenẏe. hr̄. IIII. carucatas trǽ q̄ nunq̄
geldaueꝛ̄. in his. III. inſulis. Michelenie. Midelenie. 7 Torleie.
Ibi ſꝓ in dn̄io. II ꞏ car̄. 7 un̄ arpent uineæ. Ibi. IIII. ſerui. 7 III. uilli
7 XVIII. borđ cū. II. car̄. Ibi. II. piſcariæ redđ. VI. Mill anguillaꝛ̄.
7 XXV. ac̄ pti. 7 XII. ac̄ ſiluæ. 7 c. ac̄ paſturæ. Valuit 7 ual. III. liƀ.
Ipſa æccla ten CIPESTAPLE. Celric tenuit T.R.E. 7 geldƀ ꝑ. II.
hiđ 7 dim. Tra. e. VI. car̄. De ea. e in̄ dn̄io dim hida. 7 ibi. I. car̄.
7 II. ſerui. 7 XVI. uilli. 7 II. borđ cū. V. car̄. Ibi dimiđ ac̄ pti. 7 c. ac̄
paſturæ. Silua dim leū lḡ. 7 II. q̄ꝫ lat̄. Valet. L. ſoliđ.
Ipſa æccla ten ILEMINSTRE. Liuuard tenuit T.R.E. 7 geldƀ
ꝑ. XX. hiđ. Tra. e. XX. car̄. De ea ſꝓ in̄ dn̄io. IX. hidæ. 7 una v 7 dim.
7 ibi. III. car̄. 7 X. ſerui. 7 XXV. uilli 7 XXII. borđ. cū. XX. car̄.
Ibi. III. molini redđ. XXII. ſoliđ 7 VI. den̄. 7 qt xx. ac̄ pti. Silua
.III. leū lḡ. 7 una leū 7 dim lat̄. Ibi mercatū redđ XX. ſoliđ.
De hac tra ten. II. taini. I. hiđ 7 dimiđ. q̄ n̄ pot̄ ab æccla ſepari.
Tot̄ ualet. XX. liƀ. Q̄do abƀ obijt̄ ualƀ XXVI. liƀ.
Ipſa æccla ten ILE. Godric tenuit T.R.E. 7 geldƀ ꝑ. V. hiđ.
Tra. e. V. car̄. De ea ſꝓ in dn̄io. III. hidæ. 7 ibi. II. car̄. 7 VI. ſerui.
7 XII. uilli 7 V. borđ cū. II. car̄. Ibi molin̄ redđ. XV. ſoliđ. 7 XL.
ac̄ pti. 7 VII. ac̄ paſturæ. Silua. III. leū lḡ. 7 una leū 7 dim lat̄.
Valuit 7 ual. IIII. liƀ.
Ipſa æccla ten ILE. Eduin tenuit T.R.E. 7 geldƀ ꝓ una hida 7 dimiđ.
Tra. e. I. car̄ 7 dim. Ibi ſꝓ. III. borđ tenent̄. XV. ac̄s. alia. e in dn̄io.
7 X. ac̄ pti. 7 VII. ac̄ paſt̄. Silua. III. q̄ꝫ lḡ. 7 una q̄ꝫ lat̄. Valet. XVI. ſot.

1 St. Peter's Church, Muchelney, has 4 carucates of land which have   E
   never paid tax in these 3 islands: MUCHELNEY, MIDELNEY and THORNEY.
   In lordship 2 ploughs; vineyard, 1 *arpent*. 4 slaves.
       3 villagers and 18 smallholders with 2 ploughs.   189
       2 fisheries which pay 6,000 eels; meadow, 25 acres; woodland,   a 1
           12 acres; pasture, 100 acres. 1 cob; 21 cattle; 6 pigs; 30 goats.
   The value was and is £3.

   The Church itself holds

2 CHIPSTABLE. Ceolric held it before 1066; it paid tax for 2½
   hides. Land for 6 ploughs, of which ½ hide is in lordship; 1
   plough there; 2 slaves;   188
       16 villagers and 2 smallholders with 5 ploughs & the rest of the land. a 1
       Meadow, ½ acre; pasture, 100 acres; woodland ½ league long
           and 2 furlongs wide.
   Value 50s.

3 ILMINSTER. Abbot Leofward held it before 1066; it paid tax for 20
   hides. Land for 20 ploughs, of which 9 hides and 1½ virgates
   are in lordship; 3 ploughs there; 10 slaves;   188
       25 villagers and 22 smallholders with 20 ploughs & 10½ hides   a 2
           & ½ virgate.
       3 mills which pay 22s 6d; meadow, 80 acres; woodland 3
           leagues long and 1½ leagues wide. A market which pays 20s.   E
           2 cobs; 27 cattle; 33 pigs; 40 sheep.
       Two thanes held 1½ hides of this land; they could not be   E
       separated from the church.
   Value of the whole £20; value when the Abbot died £26.

4 ISLE (Abbotts). Godric[A] held it before 1066; it paid for 5   E
   hides. Land for 5 ploughs, of which 3 hides are in lordship; 2
   ploughs there; 6 slaves;   188
       12 villagers and 5 smallholders with 2 ploughs & 2 hides.   a 3
       A mill which pays 15s; meadow, 40 acres; pasture, 7 acres;
           woodland 3 leagues long and 1½ leagues wide. 1 cob;
           25 cattle; 15 pigs; 60 sheep, less 1.
   The value was and is £4.

5 ISLE (Abbotts). Edwin[B] held it before 1066; it paid tax for 1½   E
   hides. Land for 1½ ploughs.
       3 smallholders who hold 15 acres; another one in lordship.   E 188
       Meadow, 10 acres; pasture, 7 acres; woodland 3 furlongs   b 1
           long and 1 furlong wide.
   Value 16s; when the Abbot died, as much.

Ipſa æccła teñ *DRAITVNE*.T.R.E.geldb ꝓ.xx.hiđ.Tra.ē.xv.caꞃ.

De ea ſꞇ in dño.xɪ.hidæ.7 ɪɪ.uirg træ 7 dim.7 ibi.vɪ.caꞃ.7 x.ſerui.

7 xvɪ.uilłi 7 xɪɪɪɪ.borđ cū.ɪx.caꞃ.Ibi.ʟ.aͨ ꝓti.7 paſtura.ɪɪ.leū

lḡ.7 una leū laꞇ.Silua.ɪɪ.leū lḡ.7 una leū 7 dim łaꞇ.

De his.xx.hiđ teñ Celric 7 Vluuard.ɪɪ.hiđ.Has teneb Briͨtuin

7 Leuing de abbatia T.R.E.nec inde poteraꝗ ſepari.Ibi ſꞇ.ɪɪɪɪ.borđ

7 ɪɪɪ.aͨ ꝓti.7 xxxv.aͨ paſturæ.7 vɪɪ.aͨ ſiluæ.

Toꞇ ualeꞇ.x.libṫ.

Ipſa æccła teñ *CAMELLE*.T.R.E.geldb ꝓ.x.hiđ.Tra.ē.xvɪ.caꞃ.

De ea ſꞇ in dño.ɪɪɪɪ.hidæ 7 dimiđ.7 ibi.ɪɪɪɪ.caꞃ.7 v.ſerui.7 vɪɪ.uilłi

7 vɪɪɪ.borđ cū.vɪ.caꞃ.Ibi moliñ redđ.x.ſoliđ.7 ʟx.aͨ ꝓti.7 ʟx.aͨ

De his.x.hiđ teñ Dodeman de abbe.ɪ.hiđ.7 ibi hꞇ.ɪ.caꞃ.ꝭ paſturæ.

7 ɪɪɪ.uilł cū.ɪ.caꞃ.7 ɪɪ.aͨs ꝓti.

Toꞇ ualeꞇ.x.libṫ.7.x.ſołđ.

Ipſa æccła.teñ *CATHANGRE*.Wadel tenuit T.R.E.7 geldb ꝓ.ɪ.hida

7 dimiđ.Tra.ē.ɪ.caꞃ 7 dim.Ibi.ē uñ uilłs cū.ɪ.borđ.tenent.xv.aͨs.

De hac tra teñ Ingulf.ɪ.hiđ.7 ibi hꞇ.ɪ.caꞃ.cū.ɪɪɪ.borđ.

Ibi.vɪ.aͨ ꝓti.7 xv.aͨ ſiluæ.Valet.xx.ſoliđ.Pars monacoꝛ⁊vɪɪ.ſoł.

ꝭGodric 7 Eduin 7 Wadel ñ ꝓtinueꞃ abbatiā T.R.E.

.X. ## TERRA ÆCCLÆ DE ADELINGI.

Eccła S PETRI de ADELINGYE.teñ *ATILTONE*.T.R.E.geldb

ꝓ.vɪɪɪ.hiđ.Tra.ē.xɪɪ.caꞃ.In dño ſꞇ.ɪɪɪɪ.hidæ.7 ibi.ɪɪɪ.caꞃ.7 ɪɪɪɪ.

ſerui.7 x.uilłi 7 vɪ.borđ cū.ɪɪɪɪ.caꞃ.Ibi moliñ redđ.vɪɪ.ſoł 7 vɪ.deñ.

7 xʟ.aͨ ꝓti.7 xxx.aͨ paſturæ.Silua.ɪ.leū lḡ.7 alia in łaꞇ.Valet.c.ſoł.

De tra huꝗ ꟓ teñ comes moriton.ɪɪ.hiđ.ꝗ eraꝗ in ipſa æccła T.R.E.

Tra.ē.ɪɪɪɪ.caꞃ.7 ual.xxx.ſoliđ.

6 DRAYTON. Before 1066 it paid tax for 20 hides. Land for 15 ploughs, of which 11 hides and 2½ virgates of land are in lordship; 6 ploughs there; 10 slaves;

> 16 villagers and 14 smallholders with 9 ploughs & 5 hides.   188

> Meadow, 50 acres; pasture 2 leagues long and 1 league wide;   b 3
> woodland 2 leagues long and 1½ leagues wide.   3 cobs; 22 pigs;
> 107 sheep.

> Ceolric and Wulfward hold 2 hides of these 20 hides. Brictwin   D
> and Leofing held them from the Abbey before 1066; they
> could not be separated from it.

> 4 smallholders.

> Meadow, 3 acres; pasture, 35 acres; woodland, 7 acres.

Value of the whole £10.   E

7 (West) CAMEL. Before 1066 it paid tax for 10 hides. Land for 16 ploughs, of which 4½ hides are in lordship; 4 ploughs there; 5 slaves;

> 7 villagers and 8 smallholders with 6 ploughs & 4½ hides.   189

> A mill which pays 10s; meadow, 60 acres; pasture, 60 acres.   a 2
> 2 cobs; 7 cows; 1 pig; 100 sheep, less 9.

> Of these 10 hides Dodman holds 1 hide from the Abbot; he has
> 1 plough & 1 virgate in lordship.

> 3 villagers with 1 plough & 3 virgates.   E

> Meadow, 2 acres.   4 cattle; 100 sheep.

Value of the whole £10 10s.   E

8 CATHANGER. Waddell^C held it before 1066; it paid tax for 1½ hides.   E
Land for 1½ ploughs. The monks have in lordship ½ hide, less 15 acres.

> 1 villager with 1 smallholder who hold 15 acres.   188

> Ingulf holds 1 hide of this land; he has 1 plough, with   b 2
> 3 smallholders.

> Meadow, 6 acres; woodland, 15 acres. 5 cattle; 9 pigs; 25 sheep.

Value of Ingulf's part 20s; of the monks' part, 7s; when the Abbot died, as much.

Godric^A , Edwin^B , Waddell^C did not belong to the Abbey before 1066.

10   LAND OF ATHELNEY CHURCH

1 St. Peter's Church, Athelney, holds ILTON. Before 1066 it paid   E
tax for 8 hides. Land for 12 ploughs. In lordship 4 hides; 3
ploughs there; 4 slaves;   191

> 10 villagers and 6 smallholders with 4 ploughs & 2 hides.   a 1

> A mill which pays 7s 6d; meadow, 40 acres; pasture, 30 acres;
> woodland 1 league long and another in width.
> 2 cobs; 6 cattle; 10 pigs; 40 sheep.

Value 100s.

> The Count of Mortain holds 2 hides of this manor's land, which   E
> were in (the lands of) this church before 1066.
> Land for 4 ploughs. Value 30s.

Ipſa æccła teñ SVTVNE . T.R.E geldb ꝑ.x.hid . Tra.ē
xvi.car̃.De ea ſt in dñio.iiii.hidæ.7 ibi.ii.car̃.7 iiii.
ſerui.7 viii.uiłi 7 vi.bord cũ.vi.car̃. Ibi.xl.ac̃ p̃ti.
7 c.ac̃ paſturæ.Valet abbi.viii.lib.

De ipſa tra teñ Rogeri brito. dimid hid 7 h̄.i.car̃.

De ead tra huj ꝏ teñ Rogeri de Corcel.ii.hid inuito
abbe.Duo taini teneb de æccła T.R.E.nec inde poteraꝓ
ſeparari.Tra.ē.ii.car̃.q̃ ibi ſt in dñio.7 vi.ac̃ p̃ti.
Valet.l.ſolid Duo hões teñ de Rogerio.

Ipſa æccła teñ SEOVENAMENTONE .T.R.E.geldb
ꝑ.ii.hid.Tra.ē.ii.car̃.q̃ ibi ſt cũ.vii.uiłt 7 iii.bord
7 ii.ſeruis.Ibi.vi.ac̃ p̃ti.Valet.xxx.ſolid.

Ipſa æccła teñ HAME .T.R.E.geldb ꝑ una hida.Tra.ē
.iiii.car̃.In dñio.ē.i.car̃.7 iiii.ſerui.7 i.uiłt 7 vii.bord
cũ.i.car̃.Ibi.xv.ac̃ p̃ti.7 iii.ac̃ ſiluæ minutæ.Valet

Ipſa æccła teñ LEGE .Ibi.ē.i.hida ſed ñ geld ſ xxx.ſolid.
T.R.E.In dñio ſt ibi.ii.car̃.7 vi.ſerui.7 iii.uiłti.7 iiii.
bord cũ.ii.car̃.Ibi.xii.ac̃ p̃ti.7 l.ac̃ ſiluæ.Valet

Comes moritoñ teñ.ii.hid | de ꝏ abbis q̃uocat ſ xl.ſolid.
in AISSELLE .7 Rogeri de Corcelle teñ.ii.hid de ꝏ SVTONE.
7 Radulf de Limeſi teñ.i.hid in de ꝏ BOSINTONE.

Hæ træ jaceb in Adelingi T.R.E.7 ñ poterant inde ſeparari.

.XI. TERRA ÆCCLÆ ROMANÆ.

Eccła Romana beati PETRI apłi teñ de rege
PERITONE .Eddid regina teneb T.R.E.Ibi ſt.vi.
hidæ.ſed ñ geld niſi ꝑ.v.hid.Tra.ē.xii.car̃.
De ea ſt in dñio.iii.hidæ.7 ibi.ii.car̃.7 iiii.ſerui.7 xi.
uiłti 7 iiii.bord cum.vi.car̃.Ibi.cl.ac̃ p̃ti.7 cl.ac̃
paſturæ.Redd ꝑ annũ.xii.lib.

The Church itself holds

2 (Long) SUTTON. Before 1066 it paid tax for 10 hides. E
Land for 16 ploughs, of which 4 hides are in lordship; 2
ploughs there; 4 slaves; 191
    8 villagers and 6 smallholders with 6 ploughs & 3½ hides. a 2
Meadow, 40 acres; pasture, 100 acres. 6 cattle; 15 pigs; 102 sheep.
Value to the Abbot £8. E
    Roger the Breton holds ½ hide of this land; he has 1 plough.
    Roger of Courseulles holds 2 hides of this manor's land, E
against the Abbot's will. Two thanes held them from the E
church before 1066; they could not be separated from it.
Land for 2 ploughs, which are there, in lordship;
    Meadow, 6 acres. 8 cattle; 2 pigs; 80 sheep. E
Value 50s. E
    Two men hold from Roger. E

3 SEAVINGTON. Before 1066 it paid tax for 2 hides. Land for E
2 ploughs, which are there, with L
    7 villagers, 3 smallholders and 2 slaves. 191
    Meadow, 6 acres. 1 cob; 9 pigs; 40 sheep. a 3
Value 30s.

4 HAMP. Before 1066 it paid tax for 1 hide. Land for 4 ploughs. E
In lordship 1 plough; 4 slaves; ½ hide. 191
    1 villager and 7 smallholders with 1 plough & ½ hide. b 1
    Meadow, 15 acres; underwood, 3 acres. 2 cattle.
Value 30s.

5 LYNG. 1 hide, but it did not pay tax before 1066. In lordship E
2 ploughs; 6 slaves; ½ hide. 191
    3 villagers and 4 smallholders with 2 ploughs & ½ hide. b 2
    Meadow, 12 acres; woodland, 50 acres. 1 cob; 2 cattle; 10 pigs; 30 sheep.
Value 40s.

6 The Count of Mortain holds 2 hides *from the Abbot's manor* E
called in ASHILL, Roger of Courseulles holds 2 hides from the
manor of (Long) SUTTON, and Ralph of Limesy holds 1 hide 191
from the manor in BOSSINGTON. b 3-5
    These lands lay in (the lands of) Athelney (Church) before 1066;
they could not be separated from it.

11   **LAND OF THE CHURCH OF ROME** E
1 The Church of Rome of the Blessed Apostle Peter holds PURITON
from the King. Queen Edith held it before 1066. 6 hides, but they
did not pay tax, except for 5 hides. Land for 12 ploughs,
of which 3 hides are in lordship; 2 ploughs there; 4 slaves; 197
    11 villagers and 4 smallholders with 6 ploughs & 3 hides. b 3
    Meadow, 150 acres; pasture, 150 acres. 2 cows; 60 sheep.
It pays £12 a year.

.XII. TERRA cadom SCI STEFANI DE CADOM.

* Eccla S Stefani ten de rege æcclam *CRVCHE*.Ibi st.x.hidæ.
Tra.ē xiii.car.De ea st in dnio.ii.hidæ.7 ibi.i.car.
cū.i.feruo.7 xi.uilli 7 ii.colibti 7 xvii.bord cū.vi.car.
Ibi.x.ac pti.7 dimid leu pafturæ in lg 7 in lat
De his.x.hid ten un miles de abbe.iii.hid.7 ibi ht
ii.car.cū.i.feruo.7 vi.uilli 7 ii.bord cū.iiii.car.
habet molin redd.v.folid.7 x.acs pti.7 dim leu paf
turæ in lg 7 in lat.Valet abbi.vii.lib.Militi.iiii.lib.

.XIII. TERRA SCÆ MARIÆ DE MONTEBVRG.

Eccla S Mariæ de Monteburg tenet de rege unū
Maneriū dono Nigelli medici.Spirtes pbr teneb T.R.E.
7 geldb p.v.hid.Tra.ē.iii.car.De ea st in dnio.ii.
hidæ 7 dimid.7 ibi.ii.car.7 ii.ferui.7 v.uilli.7 xii.bord
cū.ii.car.Ibi molin redd.xxx.denar.7 xx.ac pafturæ.
Silua dimid leu lg.7 tntd lat.Oli 7 modo ual.iiii.lib.

.XIIII. TERRA SCI EDWARDI.

Eccla S Edwardi ten *CVMBE*.T.R.E.geldb p.v.hid.
Tra.ē.v.car.De ea st in dnio.ii.hidæ 7 dim.7 ibi.ii.car.
7 iiii.uilli 7 vii.bord cū.ii.car.In Meleburne.vi.burgfes.
redd.l.denar.Pratū.iiii.q̊ꝫ lg.7 ii.q̊ꝫ lat.Silua.iii.q̊ꝫ
lg.7 ii.q̊ꝫ lat.Paftura.ii.q̊ꝫ lg.7 una q̊ꝫ lat.
Valuit 7 ual.vi.lib.

.XV. QD MAVRICIVS EPS TENET.

Eps Mauricius ten de rege æcclam S *ANDREÆ*.Brictric tenuit
T.R.E.7 geldb p.iii.hid.Tra.ē.iii.car.In dnio st.ii.car.7 iii.
ferui.7 un uills.7 vi.bord cū.i.car.Ibi molin redd.xx.folid.
7 xxx.ac pti.Valuit 7 ual.c.folid.

12   **LAND OF ST. STEPHEN'S OF CAEN**   E

1   St. Stephen's Church, Caen, holds CREWKERNE church from the King.   E
10 hides. Land for 13 ploughs, of which 2 hides are in lordship;
1 plough there, with 1 slave;
> 11 villagers, 2 freedmen and 17 smallholders with
> > 6 ploughs & 4½ hides.   197
>
> Meadow, 10 acres; pasture, ½ league in length and in   a 3
> > width. 1 cob; 25 sheep.
>
> Of these 10 hides a man-at-arms holds 3 hides from the
> Abbot; he has 2 ploughs & 1½ hides in lordship, with 1 slave.
> > 6 villagers and 2 smallholders with 4 ploughs & 1½ hides.
> > He has a mill which pays 5s; meadow, 10 acres; pasture
> > ½ league in length and in width. 1 cob; 5 cattle;
> > > 14 pigs; 150 sheep.

Value to the Abbot £7; when the Abbot acquired it, as much.   E
Value to the man-at-arms £4; when he acquired them, as much.

13   **LAND OF ST. MARY'S OF MONTEBOURG**   E

1   St. Mary's Church of Montebourg holds one manor from the King
by gift of Nigel the Doctor. Spirtes the priest held it before 1066;   E
it paid tax for 5 hides. Land for 3 ploughs, of which 2½ hides
are in lordship; 2 ploughs there; 2 slaves;   198
> 5 villagers and 12 smallholders with 2 ploughs & the rest of the land.   a 4
> A mill which pays 30d; pasture, 20 acres; woodland ½ league   E
> > long and as wide. 10 pigs; 60 sheep; 18 goats.

Value formerly and now £4.

14   **LAND OF ST. EDWARD'S**

1   St. Edward's Church holds (Abbas) COMBE. Before 1066 it paid   E
tax for 5 hides. Land for 5 ploughs, of which 2½ hides are
in lordship; 2 ploughs there;   193
> 4 villagers and 7 smallholders with 2 ploughs & 2½ hides.   b 1
> In Milborne (Port) 6 burgesses who pay 50d.
> Meadow 4 furlongs long and 2 furlongs wide; woodland 3
> furlongs long and 2 furlongs wide; pasture 2 furlongs
> long and 1 furlong wide. 1 cob; 7 cows; 40 sheep.

The value was and is £6.

15   **WHAT BISHOP MAURICE HOLDS**   E

1   Bishop Maurice holds St. Andrew's Church (ILCHESTER) from the
King. Brictric held it before 1066; it paid tax for 3 hides. Land
for 3 ploughs. In lordship 2 ploughs; 3 slaves; 1 hide & 3 virgates.   197
> 1 villager and 6 smallholders with 1 plough & 1 hide & 1 virgate.   b 2
> A mill which pays 20s; meadow, 30 acres. 2 cobs; 9 cattle; 50 sheep.

The value was and is 100s.

.XVI Rᴇɪɴʙᴀʟᴅ ten æcclam de *Fʀᴏᴍᴇ* . cū . VIII . carucat́ træ.

In dn̄io st́ . II . car̄ 7 dim . 7 IIII . ſerui . 7 VIII . uilti 7 XII . bord́

cū . VI . car̄ . Ibi molin̄ redd́ . V . ſolid́ . 7 XXXV . ac̄ p̄ti . Silua.

VI . q̄ʒ lḡ . 7 II . q̄ʒ lat̄ . Valet . VI . lib̄.

Rɪcʜᴇʀɪᴠꜱ ten æcclam de *Wᴀʀᴠᴇʀᴅɪɴᴇꜱᴛᴏcʜ* de rege.

T . R . E . geldb̄ .p . II . hid́ . Tra . ē . IIII . car̄ . Ibi st́ . V . uilti 7 IIII.

bord́ 7 II . ſerui . cū . II . car̄ . Ibi . III . ac̄ p̄ti . 7 XX . ac̄ paſturæ.

7 IIII . ac̄ ſiluæ . Valet . III . lib̄ 7 IIII . uaccas.

91 c

Eʀcʜᴇɴɢᴇʀ ten de rege in æccla de *Cᴀɴᴛᴇᴛᴏɴᴇ*

II . virǵ træ 7 dimid́ . Tra . ē . II . car̄ . In dn̄io . ē dimid́

car̄ . cū . I . uilto 7 VI . bord́ . Ibi . VII . ac̄ paſturæ.

7 XXX . ac̄ p̄ti . 7 IIII . ac̄ ſiluæ minutæ . Valet . XXX . ſol.

Sᴛᴇꜰᴀɴ capellan ten æcclam de *Mɪʟᴠᴇʀᴛᴏɴᴇ* . cū

una v træ 7 uno ferding . Tra . ē . I . car̄ . Ibi . X . ac̄ ſiluæ.

Aʟᴠɪᴇᴛ p̄br ten de rege . I . hidam ☖ Val . XL . ſol.

in *Sᴠᴅᴘᴇʀᴇᴛᴏɴᴇ* . Tra . ē . I . car̄ . q̄ ibi . ē cū . I . bord́

7 uno ſeruo . Ibi . VIII . ac̄ p̄ti . Valet . XX . ſolid́.

Iɴ æccla *Cᴀʀᴇɴᴛᴏɴᴇ* jacet . I . hida 7 dim . Ibi . ē in

dn̄io . I . car̄ 7 dimid́ . cū p̄bro 7 I . uilto . 7 VIII . bord́.

Ibi . XL . ac̄ paſturæ . 7 XV . ac̄ ſiluæ . Valet . XXX . ſolid́.

Iɴ æccla de *Pᴇʀᴇᴛᴠɴᴇ* . jacent . III . virǵ træ . Tra . ē

.I . car̄ . q̄ ibi . ē . Valet . XX . ſolid́. ☖ regis.

Has . II . æcclas tenuit Petrus ep̄s . Modo st́ in manu

Lɪᴏꜰᴜꜱ ten *Bᴇʀᴀ* . q̄ 7 tenuit de rege . E . 7 geldb̄

.p una v træ . Tra . ē . I . car̄ . q̄ ibi . ē cū . I . ſeruo . 7 II . bord́.

WHAT THE KING'S CLERGY (HOLD)

E

E

1 Reinbald holds FROME church with 8 carucates of land.
In lordship 2½ ploughs; 4 slaves;
    8 villagers and 12 smallholders with 6 ploughs.
    A mill which pays 5s; meadow, 35 acres; woodland 6 furlongs
        long and 2 furlongs wide. 1 cob; 3 cattle; 30 pigs; 228 sheep.
Value £6.

198
a 3

2 Richere of Les Andelys holds STOGUMBER church from the King.
Before 1066 it paid tax for 2 hides. Land for 4 ploughs.
In lordship 1½ hides & 3 furlongs.
    5 villagers, 4 smallholders and 2 slaves with
      2 ploughs & 1 virgate & 1 furlong.
    Meadow, 3 acres; pasture, 20 acres; woodland, 4 acres.
Value £3 and 4 cows; when Richere acquired it, 30s.

E

197
a 1

3 Erchenger the priest holds from the King 2½ virgates of land
in (the lands of) CANNINGTON church. Land for 2 ploughs.
In lordship ½ plough & ½ hide, with
    1 villager and 6 smallholders (who have) ½ virgate.
    Pasture, 7 acres; meadow, 30 acres; underwood, 4 acres.
      3 cows; 9 pigs; 10 wethers.
Value 30s; when he acquired it, as much.

91 c

E

196
b 1

4 Stephen the chaplain holds MILVERTON church with 1 virgate
of land and 1 furlong. Land for 1 plough.
    Woodland, 10 acres.
Value 40s.

197
a 2

5 Alfgeat the priest holds 1 hide in SOUTH PETHERTON from the
King. Land for 1 plough, which is there, with
    1 smallholder and 1 slave.
    Meadow, 8 acres. 8 cattle; 11 pigs; 50 sheep.
Value 20s.

E

196
b 2

6 In (the lands of) CARHAMPTON church lie 1½ hides.
In lordship 1½ ploughs & ½ hide, with
    a priest, 1 villager and 8 smallholders (who have) 1 hide & 1½ ploughs.
    Pasture, 40 acres; woodland, 15 acres. 1 cob.
Value 30s; value when the Bishop died, 40s.

196
b 3

7 In (the lands of) (North) PETHERTON church lie 3 virgates of land.
Land for 1 plough, which is there.
Value 20s.

E

196
a 2

Bishop Peter held these two churches; now they are in the King's hands. E

8 Leofa holds BEERE, which he also held from King Edward; it paid
tax for 1 virgate of land. Land for 1 plough, which is there,
with 1 slave and
    2 smallholders.

L

196
a 3

Ibi moliñ redđ . vi . deñ . 7 . vi . ac p̃ti . Valet . x . foliđ.

Turſtiñ teñ *Lege* . Pat ej tenuit T.R.E . 7 geldb ꝓ . i.

hida . Tra . ē . i . car̃ . Ibi ſt . ii . borđ . Valet . x . foliđ.

Goduiñ teñ dimiđ hiđ in cõ qđ uocat̃ Ragiol.

de rege in elemoſina . Valet . i·iii . fol . ⌐ Valet . xii . fol.

In æccła de *Cvri* . ē dimiđ hida . Ibi ht̃ p̃br . i . car̃.

Eddida monialis teñ in elemoſina de rege . xii . acs

træ . Ibi ht̃ q̃t xx . acs ſiluæ 7 paſturæ . Vał . v . foliđ.

Duæ nonnæ teñ de rege in elemoſina . ii . v̄ træ

7 dimiđ in *Honecote* . Tra . ē . ii . car̃ . Ibi . ē . i . car̃.

7 v . ac p̃ti . Valet . v . foliđ.

In *Chenemeresdone* . ē dimiđ hida træ . Vał . x . fol.

Petrus ep̃s tenuit . Modo . ē in manu regis.

.XVII.   TERRA COMITIS EVSTACHIJ.

COMES EVSTACHIVS tenuit de rege *Newentone*.

Leuuiñ tenuit T.R.E . 7 geldb ꝓ una hida 7 una v̄ træ.

Tra . ē . iiii . car̃ . De ea ſt in dñio . ii . virg træ 7 dim . 7 ibi . i.

car̃ . 7 ii . ferui . 7 vii . uiłłi . 7 vi . borđ cū . iii . car̃ . Ibi moliñ

redđ . xv . deñ . 7 vii . ac p̃ti . 7 xxxiii . ac paſturæ . 7 xvii . ac

ſiluæ . Valuit 7 uał . iiii . lib . Alured⁹ teñ de comite.

Idē Alured teñ de . co . *Cõmiz* . Leuuiñ tenuit T.R.E . 7 geldb

ꝓ . i . hida 7 dim . Tra . ē . vi . car̃ . In dñio . ē . i . car̃ . 7 ii . ferui.

7 ii . uiłłi 7 i . borđ cū . ii . car̃ . Ibi xxvi . ac p̃ti . 7 x . ac

paſturæ . 7 ii . ac ſiluæ . Valuit . l . fol . Modo . xl . foliđ.

Eurard teñ de . Co . *Lecheswrde* . Aluuard tenuit

T.R.E . 7 geldb ꝓ una v̄ træ . Tra . ē . ii . car̃ . In dñio . ē

dimiđ car̃ . 7 iiii . ferui . 7 iiii . uiłłi 7 iii . borđ cū . i . car̃

A mill which pays 6d; meadow, 6 acres. 4 cattle; 5 pigs; 5 sheep.
Value 10s.

9 Thurstan holds (Abbots) LEIGH. His father held it before 10bɔ;
it paid tax for 1 hide. Land for 1 plough.
    2 smallholders. 2 cattle; 6 pigs.
Value 10s.

> 198
> a 1

10 Godwin holds ½ hide in the manor called RIDGEHILL in alms from
the King. He had the whole manor before, in 1066.
Value 3s.

> E 198
> a 2

11 In (the lands of) CURRY (Rivel) church is ½ hide. A priest
has 1 plough there.
Value 12s.

> 197
> b 1

12 Edith, a nun, holds 12 acres of land in alms from the King. She has
woodland and pasture, 80 acres. 4 cattle; 4 pigs; 11 sheep.
Value 5s.

> 196
> a 3

13 Two nuns hold 2½ virgates of land in ?HOLNICOTE in alms from
the King. Land for 2 ploughs. 1 plough there, in lordship.
    Meadow, 5 acres.
Value 5s; when they acquired them, 10s.

> E
> 196
> b 4

14 In KILMERSDON is ½ hide of land.
Value 10s.
    Bishop Peter held it; now it is in the King's hands.

> E
> 198
> b 1

17   LAND OF COUNT EUSTACE

1 Count Eustace held (holds) NEWTON from the King. Leofwin held
it before 1066; it paid tax for 1 hide and 1 virgate of land. Land
for 4 ploughs, of which 2½ virgates of land are in lordship; 1 plough
there; 2 slaves;
    7 villagers and 6 smallholders with 3 ploughs & the rest of the land.
A mill which pays 15d; meadow, 7 acres; pasture, 33 acres;
    woodland, 17 acres. 2 pigs; 35 sheep.
The value was and is £4.
Alfred (of) Marlborough holds from the Count.

> 282
> a 1

2 Alfred also holds COMBWICH from the Count. Leofwin held it
before 1066; it paid tax for 1½ hides. Land for 6 ploughs.
In lordship 1 plough; 2 slaves; ½ hide & 1 virgate.
    2 villagers and 1 smallholder with 2 ploughs & the rest of the land.
    Meadow, 26 acres; pasture, 10 acres; woodland, 2 acres.
The value was 50s; now 40s.

> 282
> a 2

3 Evrard holds LEXWORTHY from the Count. Alfward held it
before 1066; it paid tax for 1 virgate of land. Land for 2 ploughs.
In lordship ½ plough; 4 slaves; ½ virgate.
    4 villagers and 3 smallholders with 1½ ploughs & ½ virgate.

> 282
> a 3
> E

7 dimiđ.Ibi.ıı.molini redđ.ıı.plūbas ferri.7 ııı.ac̃ p̃ti.

7 xx.ac̃ filuæ.Valuit 7 uał.xxx.foliđ.

Ipfe.Comes ten̋ *LOCHESTONE*.Vlueua tenuit T.R.E.

7 gelđƀ ,p.v.hiđ.Tra̋.ē.vıı.car̃.De ea s̃t in dñio.ıııı.

hidæ.7 ibi.ıı.car̃.7 ıı.ferui.7 v.uiłłi 7 vı.borđ cū.ııı.

car̃.Ibi moliñ redđ.vı.den̄.7 L.ac̃ p̃ti.7 Lx.ac̃ paf

ture.7 vı.ac̃ filuæ minutæ.Valuit 7 uał.c.foliđ.

Aluređ ten de.Co.*CELEWORDE*.Thuri tenuit T.R.E.

7 gelđƀ ,p.ııı.hiđ.Tra̋.ē.ııı.car̃.De ea s̃t in dñio.ıı.

hidæ 7 dim̋.7 ııı.uiłłi 7 ıı.borđ cū.ı.car̃.7 in dñio alia

Ibi.v.ac̃ p̃ti.Silua.v.q̂ӡ lg̃.7 una q̂ӡ lat̃.Valet.Lx.foł.

Aluređ ten de.Co.*BELGETONE*.Toui liƀe tenuit T.R.E.

7 gelđƀ ,p.ıııı.hiđ.Tra̋.ē.ıııı.car̃.In dñio.ē.ı.car̃ 7 dim̋.

cū.ı.feruo.7 v.uiłłi 7 ıı.borđ cū.ıı.car̃.Ibi molinū

redđ.xv.foliđ.7 xxıı.ac̃ p̃ti.7 xx.ac̃ pafturæ.Silua

ıııı.q̂ӡ lg̃.7 ıı.q̂ӡ lat̃.Valuit.ııı.liƀ.Modo.ıııı.liƀ.

91 d

Comitiffa Ida ten̋ de rege bolonienſ̛. *CHINWARDESTVNE*.Vlueua tenuit

T.R.E.7 gelđƀ ,p.v.hiđ.Tra̋.ē.vııı.car̃.De ea s̃t in dñio.ıı.hide

7 ııı.uirg̋.7 ibi.ıı.car̃.7 vı.ferui.7 vııı.uiłłi.7 vııı.borđ.cū.v.car̃.

Ibi.xxv.ac̃ p̃ti.7 xxıı.ac̃ pafturæ.Silua.ııı.q̂ӡ lg̃.7 una ac̃ lat̃.

Valuit 7 uał.vı.liƀ.

Mathildis ten de.Co.*CONTITONE*.Wlnođ tenuit T.R.E.7 gelđƀ

,p.v.hiđ.Tra̋.ē.v.car̃.De ea s̃t in dñio.ııı.hidæ.7 ibi.ıı.car̃.7 ıııı.

ferui.7 v.uiłłi 7 x. borđ.cū.ııı.car̃.Ibi moliñ redđ.Lxıııı.den̋.

7 v.ac̃ p̃ti.Paftura.ıııı.q̂ӡ lg̃.7 ıı.q̂ӡ lat̃.Valet.c.foliđ.

2 mills which pay 2 blooms of iron; meadow, 3 acres;
woodland, 20 acres. 6 cattle; 5 pigs.
The value was and is 30s.

4 The Count holds LOXTON himself. Wulfeva held it before 1066;
it paid tax for 5 hides. Land for 7 ploughs, of which 4 hides
are in lordship; 2 ploughs there; 2 slaves;
    5 villagers and 6 smallholders with 3 ploughs & 1 hide.
    A mill which pays 6d; meadow, 50 acres; pasture, 60 acres;
      underwood, 6 acres. 3 cattle; 3 pigs.
The value was and is 100s.

    282
    b 1

5 Alfred holds CHELWOOD from the Count. Thori held it
before 1066; it paid tax for 3 hides. Land for 3 ploughs,
of which 2½ hides are in lordship;
    3 villagers and 2 smallholders with 1 plough & ½ hide;
    another (plough) in lordship.
    Meadow, 5 acres; woodland 5 furlongs long and 1 furlong wide.
      15 pigs; 80 sheep.
Value 60s; when the Count acquired it, 40s.

    282
    b 2

6 Alfred holds BELLUTON from the Count. Tovi held it freely
before 1066; it paid tax for 4 hides. Land for 4 ploughs.
In lordship 1½ ploughs & 2½ hides & ½ virgate, with 1 slave.
    5 villagers and 2 smallholders with 2 ploughs & 1 hide & 1½ virgates.
    A mill which pays 15s; meadow, 22 acres; pasture, 20 acres;
      woodland 4 furlongs long and 2 furlongs wide.
      10 cattle; 13 pigs; 47 sheep; 10 goats.
The value was £3; now £4.

    282
    b 3
    E

7 Countess Ida of Boulogne holds KINGWESTON from the King.
Wulfeva held it before 1066; it paid tax for 5 hides.
Land for 8 ploughs, of which 2 hides and 3 virgates are
in lordship; 2 ploughs there; 6 slaves;
    8 villagers and 8 smallholders with 5 ploughs & 2 hides, 1 virgate
    & 5 acres.
    Meadow, 25 acres; pasture, 22 acres; woodland 3 furlongs
      long and 1 acre wide. 12 cattle; 12 pigs.
The value was and is £6.

    E 91 d

    283
    a 1

8 Matilda holds COMPTON (Durville) from the Count. Wulfnoth
held it before 1066; it paid tax for 5 hides. Land for 5
ploughs, of which 3 hides are in lordship; 2 ploughs there;
4 slaves;
    5 villagers and 10 smallholders with 3 ploughs & the rest of the land.
    A mill which pays 64d; meadow, 5 acres; pasture 4 furlongs
      long and 2 furlongs wide. 2 cows; 140 sheep.
Value 100s; when the Count acquired the manor, £4.

    283
    a 2

TERRA HVGONIS COMITIS.

COMES HVGO.teñ de rege *TEDINTONE*.7 Wills de eo.Ednod
tenuit T.R.E.7 geldb ꝑ una hida.Tra.ē.IIII.car.In dñio.ē
una car.7 IIII.ſerui.7 v.uilli 7 VIII.bord cū.II.car.Ibi.v.ać ꝓti.
7 c.ać paſturæ.7 XL.ać ſiluæ.Valuit 7 ual.XL.ſolid.

Wills teñ de.Co.*SANFORD*.T.R.E.geldb ꝑ.II.hid.Tra.ē.v.car.
In dñio.ē.I.car.cū.I.ſeruo.7 VIII.uilli cū.I.car.Ibi.IX.ać ꝓti.
7 L.ać ſiluæ.7 moliñ.   Valuit 7 ual.III.lib.

Wills teñ de Co.*ALRE*.Ednod tenuit T.R.E.7 geldb ꝑ dim hida.
Tra.ē.II.car.cū.I.ſeruo.7 I.bord 7 I.uillo.7 I.ać ꝓti.7 XXXVI.ać
paſturæ.7 VI.ać ſiluæ.Valuit.XX.ſol.Modo.XV.ſol.

Æccła S SEVERI teñ de.Co.*HENGESTERICH*.Ednod tenuit T.R.E.
7 geldb ꝑ.IIII.hid.Tra.ē.III.car.De ea ſt in dñio.III.hidæ 7 dim.
7 ibi.II.car.7 IIII.ſerui.7 VI.bord cū.I.car.Ibi.XXX.ać ꝓti.7 XXX.
ać paſturæ.7 ſilua.IIII.q̇ꝝ lg.7 I.q̇ꝝ lat.Valet.IIII.lib.7.X.ſol.

TERRA COMITIS MORITONIENS.

COMES MORITON.teñ de rege *CRVCHE*.7 Turſtiñ de eo.Sireuuold
tenuit T.R.E.7 geldb ꝑ.VI.hid.Tra.ē.v.car.De ea ſt in dñio.IIII.
hidæ.7 ibi.III.car.7 II.ſerui.7 VI.uilli 7 v.bord cū.III.car.
Ibi moliñ redd.XII.ſolid.7 una ać ꝓti 7 dimid.Silua.VII.q̇ꝝ lg.
7 II.q̇ꝝ lat.Valuit.IIII.lib.Modo.c.ſolid.

Malger teñ de.Co.*SEVENEHANTVNE*.Aluuard tenuit T.R.E.7 geld
ꝑ.VII.hid.Tra.ē.VII.car.De ea ſt in dñio.v.hidæ 7 dim.7 ibi.III.
car.7 VI.ſerui.7 VIII.uilli 7 VII.bord cū.III.car.Ibi moliñ redd.v.
ſolid.7 XL.ać ꝓti.Valuit.VIII.lib.Modo.c.ſolid.

18   LAND OF EARL HUGH

1   Earl Hugh holds TETTON from the King, and William from him.
Ednoth held it before 1066; it paid tax for 1 hide.
Land for 4 ploughs. In lordship 1 plough; 4 slaves; ½ hide.
    5 villagers and 8 smallholders with 2 ploughs & the rest of the land.
    Meadow, 5 acres; pasture, 100 acres; woodland, 40 acres.   286
       8 cattle; 6 pigs; 60 sheep.   b 1
The value was and is 40s.

2   William holds SAMPFORD (Brett) from the Earl. Before 1066 it   E
paid tax for 2 hides. Land for 5 ploughs. In lordship 1   286
plough & 1 hide & 3 furlongs, with 1 slave;   b 2
    8 villagers with 1 plough & the rest of the land.   E
    Meadow, 9 acres; woodland, 50 acres; a mill. 3 cattle; 4 pigs; 100 sheep.   E
The value was and is £3.

3   William holds ALLER from the Earl. Ednoth held it before 1066;
it paid tax for ½ hide. Land for 2 ploughs, with 1 slave and   L
    1 smallholder and 1 villager.
    Meadow, 1 acre; pasture, 36 acres; woodland, 6 acres.   286
The value was 20s; now 15s.   b 3

4   St. Severus' Church holds HENSTRIDGE from the Earl.   E
Ednoth held it before 1066; it paid tax for 4 hides.
Land for 3 ploughs, of which 3½ hides are in lordship;
2 ploughs there; 4 slaves;   286
    6 smallholders with 1 plough & ½ hide.   b 4
    Meadow, 30 acres; pasture, 30 acres; woodland 4 furlongs   E
      long and 1 furlong wide. 8 cattle; 5 pigs.
Value £4 10s; when the Count acquired it, £5.

19   LAND OF THE COUNT OF MORTAIN

1   The Count of Mortain holds CRICKET (St. Thomas) from the King,
and Thurstan from him. Sheerwold held it before 1066; it paid
tax for 6 hides. Land for 5 ploughs, of which 4 hides are in
lordship; 3 ploughs there; 2 slaves;   265
    6 villagers and 5 smallholders with 3 ploughs & 2 hides.   a 1
    A mill which pays 12s; meadow, 1½ acres; woodland 7 furlongs
      long and 2 furlongs wide. 14 cattle; 14 pigs; 124 sheep; 24 goats.
The value was £4; now 100s.

2   Mauger holds SEAVINGTON from the Count. Alfward held it before
1066; it paid tax for 7 hides. Land for 7 ploughs, of which 5½
hides are in lordship; 3 ploughs there; 6 slaves;   265
    8 villagers and 7 smallholders with 3 ploughs & 1½ hides.   b 1
    A mill which pays 5s; meadow, 40 acres. 4 cows; 9 pigs; 116 sheep.
The value was £8; now 100s.

De hoc M̄ st̄ ablatæ x.ac̄ filuæ 7 xxv.ac̄ moræ 7 p̄ti .7 funt in Sudperet M̄ regis.

Malger ten de Co.CONTVNE.Godric tenuit T.R.E.7 geldb̄ p̄.III. hid̄.Tra.ē.III.car̄.In dn̄io.ē.I.car̄.7 VI.uilti cū.VI.bord hn̄t.I.car̄.

Anfger ten STANTVNE.de com.Aluuard tenuit ⌐Valet.LX.folid. T.R.E.7 geldb̄ p̄.III.hid̄.Tra.ē.VIII.car̄.In dn̄io.ē.I.car 7 dim.7 VI. ferui.7 xVIII.uilti 7 IIII.bord cū.III.car̄ 7 dim.Ibi molin̄ fine cenfu. 7 CCLx.ac̄ filuæ.7 L.ac̄ pafturæ redd.IIII.blomas ferri.Val.Lx.fot.

Ipfe Comes ten SCEPTONE.Algar tenuit T.R.E.7 geldb̄ p̄.VI.hid̄. Tra.ē.IIII.car̄.De ea st̄ in dn̄io.IIII.hidæ dim virg min.7 ibi.I.car̄ 7 dim.7 III.ferui.7 Ix.uilti 7 III.bord   7 xv.ac̄ p̄ti. Valuit.c.folid.Modo.IIII.lib̄.

Gerard ten de.co.LOPENE.Aluuard tenuit T.R.E.7 geldb̄ p̄.I.hida. ✠ Tra.ē.I.car̄.Ibi.ē.I.bord cū.I.feruo.7 x.ac̄ p̄ti.Valet.xx.folid.

Rob̄tus ten de Co.CRAWECVBE.Æccla S Suuithuni Winton̄ tenuit T.R.E.Ibi st̄.x.hidæ.fed n̄ geld nifi p̄.IIII.hid̄.Tra.ē xII.car̄.De ea.ē in dn̄io.I.hida.7 ibi.III.car̄.7 VI.ferui.7 xxxI.uilt 7 x.bord cū.x.car̄.Ibi.xI.ac̄ p̄ti.7 xx.ac̄ filuæ.Paftura.I.leū lḡ. 7 dimid̄ leū lat̄.Valuit 7 ual.VIII.lib̄.

Anfger ten de.Co.ISLE.Vlnod tenuit T.R.E.7 geldb̄ p̄.VI.hid̄. Tra.ē.VI.car̄.In dn̄io st̄.II.car̄.7 v.ferui.7 v.uilti 7 IIII.bord cū

From this manor have been taken away 10 acres of woodland E
and 25 acres of moor and meadow; they are in South Petherton,
a manor of the King's.

3 Mauger holds COMPTON (Durville) from the Count. Godric held it
before 1066; it paid tax for 3 hides. Land for 3 ploughs.
In lordship 1 plough; 2 hides.   265
  6 villagers with 6 smallholders have 1 plough & 1 hide.   b 2
  14 cattle; 42 sheep.
Value 60s; when the Count acquired it, 40s.

4 Ansger the Breton holds WHITESTAUNTON from the Count. Alfward
held it before 1066; it paid tax for 3 hides. Land for 8
ploughs. In lordship 1½ ploughs; 6 slaves; 1 hide & 1 virgate.   265
  18 villagers and 4 smallholders with 3½ ploughs & 1 hide & 3 virgates.   b 3
  A mill without dues; woodland, 260 acres; pasture, 50
  acres, which pays 4 blooms of iron. 1 cob; 7 cattle;
    16 pigs; 59 sheep; 13 goats.
Value 60s; when the Count acquired it, 30s.

5 The Count holds SHEPTON (Beauchamp) himself. Algar held it
before 1066; it paid tax for 6 hides. Land for 4 ploughs,
of which 4 hides, less ½ virgate, are in lordship; 1½ ploughs
there; 3 slaves;   266
  9 villagers and 3 smallholders (with) 2 hides & 1 virgate.   a 1
  Meadow, 15 acres. 1 cob; 4 cattle; 7 pigs; 64 sheep.
The value was 100s; now £4.

6 Gerard holds LOPEN from the Count. Alfward held it before
1066; it paid tax for 1 hide. Land for 1 plough.
  1 smallholder with 1 slave.   266
  Meadow, 10 acres. 3 cattle; 3 pigs; 61 sheep.   a 2
Value 20s; when the Count acquired it, 10(s).

7 Robert the Constable holds CROWCOMBE from the Count. St. Swithun's E
† Church, Winchester, held it before 1066. 10 hides, but they
did not pay tax, except for 4 hides. Land for 12 ploughs,
of which 1 hide is in lordship; 3 ploughs there; 6 slaves;   266
  31 villagers and 10 smallholders with 10 ploughs & 9 hides.   a 3
  Meadow, 11 acres; woodland, 20 acres; pasture 1 league
    long and ½ league wide. 26 cattle; 26 pigs; 70 sheep; 28 goats.
The value was and is £8.   E

8 Ansger the Breton holds ISLE (Brewers) from the Count. Wulfnoth
held it before 1066; it paid tax for 6 hides. Land for 6 ploughs.
In lordship 2 ploughs; 5 slaves; 4½ hides.   266
  5 villagers and 4 smallholders with 2 ploughs & 1½ hides.   a 4

.ii.caŕ.Ibi moliñ redđ.xiiii.ſoliđ.7 xvii.ãc p̃ti.Silua.iii.q̃ʒ
✠ 7 dimiđ lḡ.7 ii.q̃ʒ lat.Valet.c.ſoliđ.

Ipſe cõm ten *TINTEHALLE*.Æccƚa glaſtingƀiæ tenuit T.R.E.Ibi ſt
vii.hidæ 7 una v̔ træ.ſed p.v.hiđ geldƀ.Tra.ē.x.caŕ.De ea ſt
in dñio.iiii.hidæ.7 ibi.ii.caŕ.7 v.ſerui.7 xix.uiƚƚi 7 ix.borđ cũ.viii.
caŕ.Ibi moliñ redđ.xxx.denaŕ.7 lx.ãc p̃ti.7 cc.ãc paſturæ.7 lvii.
ãc ſiluæ.Valet.xvi.liƀ.Drogo teñ de̜ Co.unã v̔ de ipſa tra.7 uaƚ.i.

92 a   ⨍ marƙ arḡti,

Huƀtus teñ de.co.*CHINGESTONE*.Æccƚa glaſtingƀie tenuit ✠
T.R.E.7 geldƀ p.viii.hiđ.Tra.ē.viii.caŕ.De ea ſt in dñio.i͡iii.hidæ.
7 ibi.ii.caŕ.7 iii.ſerui.7 xi.uiƚƚi.7 xiii.borđ cũ.v.caŕ.Ibi.xl.7.i.
ãc p̃ti.Silua.vi.q̃ʒ lḡ.7 iii.q̃ʒ lat.Valuit 7 uaƚ.ix.liƀ.Æccƚa ſer
Malgeri teñ de.co.*STOCHET*.Aluuiñ tenuit ⨍uitiũ non habet.
T.R.E.7 geldƀ p.ii.hiđ 7 una v̔ tre 7 dim.Tra.ē.iii.caŕ.In dñio
ſt.ii.caŕ.7 vii.ſerui cũ.i.uiƚƚo 7 i.borđ.Ibi moliñ redđ.xl.deñ.
7 x.ãc p̃ti,Vaƚ.xl.ſoliđ.
Witts teñ de Co.*DRAICOTE*.Vluui tenuit T.R.E.7 geldƀ
p.ii.hiđ.Tra.ē.iii.caŕ.In dñio eſt una caŕ 7 dim.7 ix.borđ
cũ.i.caŕ 7 dim.Ibi moliñ redđ.xv.ſoliđ.7 xxvi.ãc p̃ti 7 dim.
7 xxx.i.ãc paſturæ.7 tñtđ ſiluæ minutæ.Vaƚ.xl.ſoliđ.
Roƀt teñ de.Co.*STOCHE*.Quinq̃ taini tenueŕ T.R.E.
7 geldƀ p.v.hiđ 7 dim.Supeſt ibi una virg træ q̃ ñ geldƀ

A mill which pays 14s; meadow, 17 acres; woodland 3½ furlongs long and 2 furlongs wide. 6 cobs; 27 cattle; 15 pigs; 90 sheep; 60 goats.
Value 100s; when the Count acquired it, 60s.

† 9 The Count holds TINTINHULL himself. Glastonbury Church held   E
it before 1066. 7 hides and 1 virgate of land, but it paid
tax for 5 hides. Land for 10 ploughs, of which 4 hides are
in lordship; 2 ploughs there; 5 slaves;   266
    19 villagers and 9 smallholders with 8 ploughs & the rest of the land.   b 1
  A mill which pays 30d; meadow, 60 acres; pasture, 200 acres;
    woodland, 57 acres. 2 cobs; 5 cows; 30 pigs; 100 sheep, less 6.
Value £16; when the Count acquired it, £10.   E
  Drogo holds 1 virgate of this land from the Count; value 1 silver   E
mark.

10 Hubert of Saint-Clair holds KINGSTONE from the Count. Glastonbury   E   92 a
Church held it before 1066; it paid tax for 8 hides. Land for 8   †
ploughs, of which 4 hides are in lordship; 2 ploughs there;
3 slaves;   266
    11 villagers and 13 smallholders with 5 ploughs & 3 hides & 1 virgate.   b 2
  Meadow, 41 acres; woodland 6 furlongs long and 3 furlongs
    wide. 38 pigs; 61 sheep.
The value was and is £9.
The church does not have service.

11 Mauger holds STOKE (sub Hamdon) from the Count. Alwin held
it before 1066; it paid tax for 2 hides and 1½ virgates of land.
Land for 3 ploughs. In lordship 2 ploughs & 1 hide & 3 virgates;   7
slaves, with   267
    1 villager and 1 smallholder (who have) the rest of the land.   a 1
  A mill which pays 40d; meadow, 10 acres. 2 cattle; 20 sheep.
Value 40s; when he acquired it, 60s.

12 William of Courseulles holds DRAYCOTT from the Count. Wulfwy
held it before 1066; it paid tax for 2 hides. Land for 3 ploughs.
In lordship 1½ ploughs; 1 hide & 3 virgates.
    9 smallholders with 1½ ploughs & 1 virgate.   267
  A mill which pays 15s; meadow, 26½ acres; pasture, 31   a 2
    acres; underwood, as much. 11 pigs; 83 sheep.
Value 40s; when he acquired it, 20s.

13 Robert son of Ivo holds STOKE (sub Hamdon) from the Count.   E
Five thanes held it before 1066; it paid tax for 5½ hides.   E
In addition, 1 virgate of land which did not pay tax before   267
                                             b 1

T.R.E.Tra̅.e̅.vɪɪɪ.car̅. In dn̅io s̅t.ɪɪ.car̅.7 v.ſerui 7 ɪɪ.uilłi.

7 xɪɪɪɪ.borđ cū.ɪɪɪ.car̅.Ibi.ɪɪ.molini redđ.ɪx.ſoliđ.7 xxv.

ac̅ p̅ti.7 ɪɪ.q̅ʒ.paſturæ.7 ɪɪɪ.ac̅ ſiluæ.Valuit 7 uał.vɪɪ.liƀ.

R̅obt̅ ten̅ de Co.Sтocheт.Tres taini tenuer̅ T.R.E.7 gelđƀ

p.ɪɪ.hiđ.dimiđ v̅ træ min̅.Tra.e̅.ɪɪ.car̅.Ibi s̅t.ɪɪɪɪ.borđ.

7 x.ac̅ p̅ti.7 xv.ac̅ paſturæ.7 ʟɪɪɪ.ac̅ ſiluæ.Valƀ 7 uał.xʟ.ſoł.

B̅retel ten̅ de Co.Sewelle.Aluuald tenuit T.R.E.7 gelđƀ

p.ɪɪɪ.hiđ.Tra.e̅.ɪɪɪɪ.car̅.In dn̅io.e̅.ɪ.car̅ cū.ɪ.ſeruo.7 vɪ.

uilłi 7 xɪɪ.borđ cū.ɪɪ.car̅.Ibi.xxxɪɪɪɪ.ac̅ p̅ti.Silua.v.q̅ʒ

7 x.p̅tic̅ l̅g.7 ɪɪ.q̅ʒ lat̅.Valet.ʟx.ſoliđ.

M̅alger ten̅ de.co.Brvcheford.Ordulf̅ tenuit T.R.E.

7 gelđƀ p.ɪɪ.hiđ.Tra.e̅.xɪɪ.car̅.In dn̅io e̅.ɪ.car̅.7 ɪɪ.ſerui.

7 x.uilłi 7 v.borđ cū.ɪɪ.car̅.Ibi molin̅ redđ.xɪɪ.ſoliđ.

7 vɪ.den̅.7 vɪ.ac̅ p̅ti.7 xvɪɪ.ac̅ ſiluæ.Paſtura dimiđ leū

l̅g.7 ɪɪɪ.q̅ʒ lat̅.Valet.ɪɪɪɪ.liƀ.

M̅alger ten̅ de co.Brede.Aluric tenuit T.R.E.7 gelđƀ

p una hida.Tra.e̅.ɪ.car̅.Ibi.e̅ un̅ borđ.Vał.x.ſoliđ.

Hoc M̅ debet p c̅ſuetuđ in Cvri M̅ regis unā oue̅ cū agno.

1066. Land for 8 ploughs. In lordship 2 ploughs; 5 slaves;
3 hides.
   2 villagers and 14 smallholders with 3 ploughs & 2½ hides & 1 virgate.   E
   2 mills which pay 9s; meadow, 25 acres; pasture, 2 furlongs;   E
      woodland, 3 acres. 2 cobs; 12 cattle; 10 pigs; 40 sheep.
The value was and is £7.

14 Robert son of Ivo holds STOKE (sub Hamdon) from the Count.   E
Three thanes held it before 1066; it paid tax for 2 hides, less ½   E
virgate of land. Land for 2 ploughs. In lordship 1½ hides.
   4 smallholders (have) the rest of the land.   267
   Meadow, 10 acres; pasture, 15 acres; woodland, 4 acres. 6 cows.   b 2
The value was and is 40s.

15 Bretel holds SWELL from the Count. Alfwold held it before   E
1066; it paid tax for 3 hides. Land for 4 ploughs.
In lordship 1 plough & 1½ hides, with 1 slave;   268
   6 villagers and 12 smallholders with 2 ploughs & 1½ hides.   a 1
   Meadow, 34 acres; woodland 5 furlongs and 10 perches long
      and 2 furlongs wide. 1 cob; 7 cattle; 8 pigs; 75 sheep.
 - Value 60s; when he acquired it, 40s.
    In 1066 1 virgate of this manor lay in Curry (Rivel), a manor of the King's. It   E
paid 10s 8d in the King's revenue, but since Bretel received the land from the Count
of Mortain, this customary due has not been paid to the King's manor.

Mauger holds from the Count

16 BRUSHFORD. Ordwulf held it before 1066; it paid tax for 2 hides.
Land for 12 ploughs. In lordship 1 plough; 2 slaves; 1 hide,
1 virgate & 1 furlong.   268
   10 villagers and 5 smallholders with 2 ploughs & ½ hide & 3 furlongs.   a 2
   A mill which pays 12s 6d; meadow, 6 acres; woodland, 17
      acres; pasture ½ league long and 3 furlongs wide.
    10 cattle; 2 pigs; 60 sheep; 20 goats.
Value £4; when the Count acquired it, £8.

17 BRADON. Aelfric held it before 1066; it paid tax for 1 hide.
Land for 1 plough.   268
   1 smallholder.   b 1
Value 10s; when the Count acquired it, 20s.
   This manor owes 1 sheep with a lamb in customary dues to   E
Curry (Rivel), a manor of the King's.

Malger ten de co. *AISELLE*. Duo taini tenuer̃ T.R.E.7 geldb
p̃ . v . hid . Tra̔ . e̅ . v . car̔ . In dñio st̃ . ii . car̃ . 7 iiii . uilli . 7 xvii.
bord cũ . ii . car̔ . Ibi . xl . ac̃ p̃ti . Silua . xl . q̃꜀ lḡ . 7 xx . q̃꜀ lat.
Hoc M̃ debet redde in *CVRI* M̃ regis . xxx . denar / Val . lx . fol.

Malger ten̔ de . Co *BRADEWEI* . Alnod tenuit T.R.E.7 geldb
p una hida . Tra̔ . e̅ . i . car̔ . Ibi st̃ . iii . uilli 7 iii . bord cũ . i . feruo.
Ibi . xii . ac̃ p̃ti . 7 iiii . ac̃ filuæ . Valuit 7 ual . x . folid.

Bretel ten̔ de . Co . *AISSE* . Wado tenuit T.R.E.7 geldb p . iiii.
hid . Ibi . e̅ addita . i . hida quã tenuer̃ . ii . taini . Tra̔ . e̅ . x . car̔
int totũ . In dñio st̃ . ii . car̃ . 7 viii . ferui . 7 xvi . uilli . 7 xxii.
bord cũ . iiii . car̔ . Ibi . ii . molini redd . xv . fol . 7 iiii . ac̃ p̃ti . 7 xl.
ac̃ paſturæ . 7 xxxviii . ac̃ filuæ . Valuit 7 ual . c . folid.

Bretel ten̔ de . Co . *GRINDEHAM* . Alric tenuit T.R.E.7 geldb
p una hida . Tra̔ . e̅ . ii . car̔ . In dñio . e̅ . i . car̃ . 7 ii . ferui . 7 iii . uilli
7 ii . bord cũ dim car̃ . Ibi molin redd . v . fol . 7 iii . ac̃ p̃ti.
7 iii . ac̃ paſturæ . 7 x . ac̃ filuæ . Valet . xv . folid.

Bretel ten̔ de . Co . *APPELIE* . Brifmar tenuit . T.R.E.7 geldb
p una hida . Tra̔ . e̅ . ii . car̔ . Ibi st̃ . ii . uilli cũ . i . car̃ . 7 ii . ac̃
p̃ti . 7 iii . ac̃ paſturæ . 7 . iii . ac̃ filuæ . Valet . x . folid.

Drogo ten̔ de . Co . *BREDDE* . Celred tenuit T.R.E.7 geldb
p una hida . Tra̔ . e̅ . i . car̃ . q̃ ibi . e̅ cũ . i . feruo . Ibi . vii . ac̃
p̃ti . 7 iii . ac̃ filuæ minutæ . Valet . xv . folid.
Hoc M̃ debet p cfuetud in *CVRI* M̃ regis unã ove cũ agno.

18 ASHILL. Two thanes held it before 1066; it paid tax for 5 hides.   E
    Land for 5 ploughs. In lordship 2 ploughs; 3 hides & 3½ virgates.   268
      4 villagers and 17 smallholders with 2 ploughs & 1 hide & ½ virgate.   b 2
      Meadow, 40 acres; woodland 40 furlongs long and 20 furlongs
        wide. 2 cattle; 70 pigs; 20 goats.
    Value 60s; when the Count acquired it, £4.
    This manor ought to pay 30d to Curry (Rivel), a manor of   E
the King's.

19 BROADWAY. Alnoth held it before 1066; it paid tax for 1 hide.
    Land for 1 plough. In lordship 2 virgates.   268
      3 villagers and 3 smallholders with 1 slave, 2 virgates & ½ plough.   b 3
      Meadow, 12 acres; woodland, 4 acres.
    The value was and is 10s.

20 Bretel holds ASHBRITTLE from the Count. Wado held it before 1066;   E
it paid tax for 4 hides. 1 hide has been added which two thanes   E
held. Land for 10 ploughs in total. In lordship 2 ploughs; 8 slaves;
2½ hides.   269
      16 villagers and 22 smallholders with 4 ploughs & 3 hides.   a 1
      2 mills which pay 15s; meadow, 4 acres; pasture, 40 acres;
        woodland, 38 acres. 7 cattle; 10 pigs; 80 sheep; 60 goats.
    The value was and is 100s.

21 Bretel holds GREENHAM from the Count. Alric held it before 1066;
it paid tax for 1 hide. Land for 2 ploughs. In lordship 1 plough;
2 slaves; 3 virgates.   269
      3 villagers and 2 smallholders with ½ plough & 1 virgate.   a 2
      A mill which pays 5s; meadow, 3 acres; pasture, 3 acres;
        woodland, 10 acres. 12 cattle; 7 pigs; 40 sheep.
    Value 15s; when the Count acquired it, 10s.

22 Bretel holds APPLEY from the Count. Brictmer held it before 1066;
it paid tax for 1 hide. Land for 2 ploughs. In lordship 2½ virgates.
    2 villagers and 1 plough & 1½ virgates.   269
      Meadow, 2 acres; pasture, 3 acres; woodland, 3 acres.   b 1
    Value 10s; when the Count acquired it, as much.

23 Drogo holds BRADON from the Count. Ceolred held it   E
before 1066; it paid tax for 1 hide. Land for 1 plough,
which is there, with 1 slave.   269
      Meadow, 7 acres; underwood, 3 acres.   b 3
    Value 15s; when the Count acquired it, as much.
    This manor owes 1 sheep with a lamb in customary dues to   E
Curry (Rivel), a manor of the King's.

Drogo ten̄ de . Co . DONIET . Adulfus Sauuin 7 Dunſtan
teneb̄ p̄ . III . M̄ T.R.E . 7 geldb̄ p̄ . v . hid̄ , 7 ra , ē . v , car̄ .

Drogo ten̄ de Co.BREDENE .Orde tenuit T.R.E . 7 geldb̄ p̄ . II . hid̄ .
Tra . ē . II . car̄ . q̄ ibi ſt in dn̄io cū . I . ſeruo 7 III . bord̄ . Ibi molin̄ redd̄ . XII . ſot̄ .
7 VI . den̄ . 7 XVIII . ac̄ p̄ti . 7 XX . ac̄ paſturæ , 7 XX . ac̄ ſiluæ . Val̄ . XL . ſolid̄ 7 ualuit .
Hoc M̄ redd̄e deb̄ p̄ c̄ſuetud̄ , II . oues cū agnis , in CVRI . M̄ regis.

In dn̄io eſt . I . car̄ . 7 III . ſerui . 7 VI . uitti . 7 IX . bord̄ . cū . II . car̄ . Ibi
molin̄ ſine cenſu . 7 XX . ac̄ p̄ti . 7 L . ac̄ p̄ti . 7 parcus . Valuit 7 ual̄
H̄ M̄ debeſ p̄ c̄ſuetud̄ in CVRI M̄ regis . v . oues cū agnis . ſ c . ſolid̄ .
Ipſe comes ten̄ STAPLE . Duo taini tenuer̄ T.R.E . 7 geldb̄
p̄ . x . hid̄ . Tra . ē . IX . car̄ . De ea ſt in dn̄io . VII . hidæ . 7 ibi . III .
car̄ . 7 VI . ſerui . 7 XX . uitti cū . VI . car̄ . Ibi molin̄ redd̄ . XXX . den̄ .
7 XXIIII . ac̄ p̄ti . Paſtura dimid̄ leū lḡ . 7 una q̄z lat̄ . Silua
una leū lḡ . 7 II . q̄z lat̄ . Valuit . x . lib̄ . Modo . XII . lib̄ .
Huic M̄ p̄tin̄ unus ortus in Langeport redd̄ . L . anguitt .
Witts ten̄ de co.BICHEHALLE . Aluric tenuit T.R.E . 7 geldb̄
p̄ . v . hid̄ . Tra . ē . v . car̄ . In dn̄io ſt . II . car̄ . 7 III . ſerui . 7 IX . uitti .
7 VII . bord̄ cū . III . car̄ . Ibi . XIIII . ac̄ p̄ti . Silua . I . leū lḡ . 7 una
q̄z lat̄ . Valuit . xx . ſolid̄ . Modo . LXX . ſolid̄ .
Hoc M̄ debet p̄ c̄ſuetud̄ in CVRI M̄ regis . v . oues cū totid̄ agnis . 7 q̄ſq̄z
lib̄ h̄ō unā blomā ferri .
Rainald̄ ten̄ de . Co . BERE . Algar tenuit T.R.E . 7 geldb̄ p̄ . v . hid̄ .
Tra . ē . IIII . car̄ . In dn̄io ſt . III . car̄ . 7 IIII . ſerui . 7 VI . uitti 7 VII . bord̄ .

24 Drogo holds DONYATT from the Count. Adolf, Saewin and Dunstan   E
held it as three manors before 1066; it paid tax for 5 hides.   270
Land for 5 ploughs.   a 1
(continued after 19,25).

Entered at the foot of col. 92a,b with no transposition signs. See Notes.

25 Drogo holds BRADON from the Count. Orde held it before 1066;
it paid tax for 2 hides. Land for 2 ploughs, which are there,
in lordship, & 1 hide & 3 virgates, with 1 slave;
    3 smallholders (who have) 1 virgate.   269
    A mill which pays 12s 6d; meadow, 18 acres; pasture,   b 2
        20 acres; woodland, 20 acres. 2 cobs; 16 cattle; 10 pigs.
The value is and was 40s.   E
    This manor ought to pay 2 sheep with lambs in customary dues   E
to Curry (Rivel), a manor of the King's.

(19,24 continued)   **92 b**
    In lordship 1 plough; 3 slaves; 4 hides.
      6 villagers and 9 smallholders with 2 ploughs & 1 hide.   270
      A mill without dues; meadow, 20 acres, [woodland], 50 acres.   a 1
        a park. 1 cob; 12 unbroken mares; 9 cattle; 70 sheep; 30 goats.
    The value was and is 100s.
    These manors owe 5 sheep with lambs in customary dues to   E
Curry (Rivel), a manor of the King's.

26 The Count holds STAPLE (Fitzpaine) himself. Two thanes held it   E
before 1066; it paid tax for 10 hides. Land for 9 ploughs, of
which 7 hides are in lordship; 3 ploughs there; 6 slaves;
    20 villagers with 6 ploughs & 3 hides.   270
    A mill which pays 30d; meadow, 24 acres; pasture ½ league   a 2
      long and 1 furlong wide; woodland 1 league long and
      2 furlongs wide. 1 cob; 10 unbroken mares; 10 cattle; 50 sheep; 100 goats.
The value was £10; now £12.
A garden in Langport belongs to this manor; it pays 50 eels.

27 William of Lestre holds BICKENHALL from the Count. Aelfric held it
before 1066; it paid tax for 5 hides. Land for 5 ploughs.
In lordship 2 ploughs; 3 slaves; 1 hide.   270
    9 villagers and 7 smallholders with 3 ploughs & the rest of the land.   b 1
    Meadow, 14 acres; woodland 1 league long and 1 furlong wide.
      1 cob; 14 cattle; 3 pigs; 7 goats.
The value was 20s; now 70s.
    This manor owes 5 sheep with as many lambs in customary dues   E
to Curry (Rivel), a manor of the King's, and each free man (owes)
1 bloom of iron.

28 Reginald of Vautortes holds BEERCROCOMBE from the Count. Algar
held it before 1066; it paid tax for 5 hides. Land for 4 ploughs.   271
In lordship 3 ploughs; 4 slaves; 4 hides.   E a 1
    6 villagers and 7 smallholders (have) 1 hide.   E

Ibi.xx.ac pti.7 xii.ac pasturæ.7 v.ac siluæ. Valuit.c.sol.m̃.lx.sol.

Robt ten de.Co.*HACHE*.Godríc 7 Goduin 7 Bollo tenuer T.R.E.
p.iii.Man.7 geldb p.v.hid.Tra.e.vi.car.In dñio st.ii.car.7 iii.
serui.7 xi.uilli.7 iiii.bord cu.iii.car.Ibi.viii.ac pti.7 lx.ac siluæ.
Valuit.viii.lib.Modo.iiii.lib.De una ex his hid quã bollo tenuit.
debet in *CVRI* M p csuetud una ouis cu agno.

Drogo ten de.Co.*TORLABERIE*.Vluiet tenuit T.R.E.7 geldb
p.iii.hid.Tra.e.ix.car.In dñio st.ii.car.7 v.serui.7 xxi.uills
cu.vii.car.Ibi.xv.ac pti.7 xx.ac siluæ.Valuit 7 ual.vi.lib.

Ansger ten de.Co.*TORNE*.Algar tenuit T.R.E.7 geldb p.vi.hid.
Tra.e.vi.car.In dñio st.ii.car.7 iii.serui.7 v.uilli 7 iiii.bord
cu.ii.car.Ibi.viii.ac pti.7 ii.ac siluæ minutæ.Valuit 7 ual.iii.lib.

Dodeman ten de.Co.*MERIET*.Leuuin 7 Bristuuard tenuer
T.R.E.7 geldb p vii.hid.Tra.e.vii.car.In dñio st.ii.car.
7 vi.serui.7 x.uilli 7 vi.bord cu.iiii.car.Ibi.iii.molini redd
xxx.solid.7 xxv.ac pti.7 dimid leu pasturæ in lg.7 lat.Valuit

Turstin ten de co.*ESTHAM*.Goduin tenuit ⌐iiii.lib.m̃.vii.lib.
ppofit regis cu *CRVCHE* M regis.7 ñ poterat a firma separari
T.R.E.7 geldb p.ii.hid.Tra.e.ii.car.quæ ibi st in dñio cu.x.
bord 7 uno seruo.Ibi moliñ redd.xii.solid.7 xii.ac pti.7 xx.
ac siluæ.Valuit 7 ual.l.solid.

Meadow, 20 acres; pasture, 12 acres; woodland, 5 acres.

8 cattle; 4 pigs; 21 sheep; 20 goats.

The value was 100s; now 60s.

29 Robert the Constable holds HATCH (Beauchamp) from the Count.   E
Godric, Godwin and Bolle held it before 1066 as three manors;
it paid tax for 5 hides. Land for 6 ploughs. In lordship 2 ploughs;
3 slaves; 4 hides & 3 virgates.   271

11 villagers and 4 smallholders with 3 ploughs & 1 hide & 1 virgate.   a 2
Meadow, 8 acres; woodland, 60 acres. 2 cobs; 16 cattle;
112 sheep; 58 goats.

The value was £8; now £4.

From one of these hides, which Bolle held, is owed 1 sheep with
a lamb in customary dues to the manor of Curry (Rivel).   E

30 Drogo holds THURLBEAR from the Count. Wulfgeat held it before
1066; it paid tax for 3 hides. Land for 9 ploughs.
In lordship 2 ploughs; 5 slaves; 1½ hides.   271

21 villagers with 7 ploughs & the rest of the land.   b 1
Meadow, 15 acres; woodland, 20 acres. 1 cob; 3 cattle; 12 pigs; 60 sheep.

The value was and is £6.

31 Ansger holds THORNFALCON from the Count. Algar held it before
1066; it paid tax for 6 hides. Land for 6 ploughs.
In lordship 2 ploughs; 3 slaves; 3½ hides.   271

5 villagers and 4 smallholders with 2 ploughs & the rest of the land.   b 2
Meadow, 8 acres; underwood, 2 acres. 8 cattle; 7 pigs; 130 sheep.

The value was and is £3.

32 Dodman holds MERRIOTT from the Count. Leofwin and Brictward   E
held it before 1066; it paid tax for 7 hides. Land for 7 ploughs.
In lordship 2 ploughs; 6 slaves; 3½ hides.   271

10 villagers and 6 smallholders with 4 ploughs & the rest of the land.   b 3
3 mills which pay 30s; meadow, 25 acres; pasture, ½ league in
length and width. 1 cob; 10 cattle; 15 pigs; 35 sheep.

The value was £4; now £7.

33 Thurstan holds EASTHAMS from the Count. Godwin, the King's   E
reeve, held it with Crewkerne, a manor of the King's; it could not
be separated from the revenue before 1066. It paid tax for 2 hides.
Land for 2 ploughs, which are there, in lordship, with
10 smallholders and 1 slave.   272

A mill which pays 12s; meadow, 12 acres; woodland, 20 acres.   a 1
6 cattle; 11 pigs; 45 sheep.

The value was and is 50s.

Drogo ten de.co.CRVCHET.Duo taini tenuer̄ T.R.E.7 geldb
p.III.hid.Tra.ē.IIII.car.In dn̄io.ē una car cū.I.feruo.7 v.uilli.
7 IIII.bord cū dimid car.Ibi.VIII.ac̄ p̄ti.7 q̄t xx.ac̄ filuæ.
Valuit.x.fot.Modo.xxx.fot.

Rob̄t ten de.Co.in PRESTITONE.I.hidā.Hanc tenuit Herald com̄
Tra.ē.IIII.car.In dn̄io.ē dimid car cū.I.feruo.7 vI.uilti.
7 II.bord cū.II.car.Ibi molin̄ redd.xII.den.7 v.ac̄ p̄ti.7 III.ac̄
pafturæ.7 xI.ac̄ filuæ.Valuit 7 uat.xxx.folid.

H̄ tra jacuit in BVRNETONE M regis.cū firma.

Anfger ten de.Co.in AISSE.I.hid.Briftuin tenuit T.R.E.
Tra.ē.I.car.quā hn̄t ibi.II.uilli.Ibi.I.ac̄ p̄ti.7 II.ac̄ filuæ mi
nutæ.Valuit 7 uat.x.folid.

Rob̄t ten de co.HARPETREV.Alduin tenuit T.R.E.7 geldb
p.v.hid.Tra.ē.v.car.In dn̄io ft.II.car.7 vI.uilti.7 vI.bord.
cū.II.car.Ibi molin̄ redd.v.folid.7 xL.ac̄ p̄ti.7 Lx.ac̄ filuæ.
Paftura.VIII.q̄z lḡ.7 v.q̄z lat.Valuit 7 uat.xL.folid.

Duo portarij de Montagud ten de.Co.ESTVRT.Brifnod te
nuit T.R.E.7 geldb p.II.hid.Tra.ē.III.car.In dn̄io ft.III.car
7 IIII.ferui.cū.I.bord.7 I.uitto hn̄t.I.car.Ibi.xvI.ac̄ p̄ti.
Valuit.xxx.folid.Modo.L.folid.

Alured ten de.Co.BRADEFORD.Eduin tenuit T.R.E.7 geldb
92 c
p.v.hid.Tra.ē.VIII.car.In dn̄io ft.II.car.7 v.ferui.7 xIx.
uilti.7 VII.bord cū.vI.car.Ibi molin̄ redd.x.folid.7 xxx.ac̄ p̄ti.
7 x.ac̄ pafturæ.7 LxxII.ac̄ filuæ.Valuit.VIII.lib.Modo.xI.lib.

34 Drogo holds CRICKET (Malherbie) from the Count. Two thanes E
held it before 1066; it paid tax for 3 hides. Land for 4 ploughs.
In lordship 1 plough & 2½ hides, with 1 slave;   272
    5 villagers and 4 smallholders with ½ plough & ½ hide.   a 2
    Meadow, 8 acres; woodland, 80 acres. 5 cattle; 11 pigs; 22 sheep.
The value was 10s; now 30s.

35 Robert son of Ivo holds 1 hide in PRESTON from the Count.
Earl Harold held it. Land for 4 ploughs. In lordship ½ plough
& ½ hide & ½ virgate, with 1 slave;   272
    6 villagers and 2 smallholders with 2 ploughs & the rest of the land.   a 3
    A mill which pays 12d; meadow, 5 acres; pasture, 3 acres;
      woodland, 11 acres. 6 cattle; 7 pigs; 27 sheep.
The value was and is 30s.
    This land lay in (the lands of) Brompton (Regis), a manor   E
of the King's, with the revenue.

36 Anser holds 1 hide in ?ASHBRITTLE from the Count. Brictwin
held it before 1066. Land for 1 plough, which   L
    2 villagers have there.
    Meadow, 1 acre; underwood, 2 acres.   272
The value was and is 10s.   b 1

37 Robert son of Walter holds (East) HARPTREE from the Count. Aldwin
held it before 1066; it paid tax for 5 hides. Land for 5 ploughs.
In lordship 2 ploughs; 3½ hides.   272
    6 villagers and 6 smallholders with 2 ploughs & 1½ hides.   b 2
    A mill which pays 5s; meadow, 40 acres; woodland, 60 acres;
      pasture 8 furlongs long and 5 furlongs wide. 4 cattle; 1 pig;
      10 goats.
The value was and is 40s.

38 Two porters from Montacute held STEART from the Count.
Brictnoth held it before 1066; it paid tax for 2 hides. Land for
3 ploughs. In lordship 3 ploughs; 5 virgates; 4 slaves, with
    1 smallholder and 1 villager have 1 plough & 3 virgates.   272
    Meadow, 16 acres. 1 cob; 3 cattle; 15 pigs; 30 sheep.   b 3
The value was 30s; now 50s.

39 Alfred the Butler holds BRADFORD (on Tone) from the Count. Edwin E
held it before 1066; it paid tax for 5 hides. Land for 8 ploughs.   92 c
In lordship 2 ploughs; 5 slaves; 2 hides.
    19 villagers and 7 smallholders with 6 ploughs & 3 hides.
    A mill which pays 10s; meadow, 30 acres; pasture, 10 acres;
      woodland, 72 acres. 2 cobs; 8 cattle; 14 pigs; 40 sheep.   273
The value was £8; now £11.   a 1

Alured ten de . Co . *HELE* . Eldred tenuit . T . R . E . 7 geld̄b ꝓ uṇa
hida . Tra . ē . III . car . In dn̄io . ē . I . car . 7 IIII . ſerui . 7 II . uitti . 7 VII .
bord cū . I . car . Ibi molin redd̄ . x . ſolid̄ . 7 x . ac̄ ꝓti . 7 xv . ac̄

✠ ſiluæ . Valuit . xL . ſolid̄ . Modo . IIII . lib̄ .

H̄ tra T . R . E . n̄ poterat ſeparari a Tantone ꝏ W̄alchelini epi̇ . ᴴ uuintonienſis

Alured ten de . Co . *NORTONE* . Oſmund tenuit T . R . E . 7 geld̄b
ꝓ . v . hid̄ . Tra . ē . x . car . In dn̄io ſt . III . car 7 VI . ſerui . 7 XIII . uitti
7 VIII . bord cū . VIII . car . Ibi . II . molini redd̄ . xI . ſolid̄ . 7 III . denạr .
7 xxv . ac̄ ꝓtl . 7 xL . ac̄ ſiluæ ; Valuit . VIII . lib̄ . Modo . xv . lib̄ .

Alured ten de . co . *EFORD* . Teodric tenuit T . R . E . 7 geld̄b ꝓ dimid̄
hida . Tra . ē . I . car . q̄ ibi . ē cū . II . bord . 7 ibi . II . ac̄ ꝓti . Valuit . xx . ſot .

Rainald ten de . co . *CERLETONE* . Tres taini cū uno ſ modo . xxx . ſot .
clerico tenuer̄ T . R . E . 7 geld̄b ꝓ . v . hid̄ . Tra . ē . VI . car . In dn̄io
ſt . III . car . 7 VI . ſerui . 7 v . uitti . 7 VI . bord cū una car 7 dimid̄ .
Ibi . L . ac̄ ꝓti . 7 xL . ac̄ paſturæ . 7 xx . ac̄ ſiluæ minutæ .

Iꝑſe comes ten *CINIOCH* . Edmer tenuit T . R . E . 7 geld̄b ꝓ . VII . hid̄ .
Tra . ē . VII . car . In dn̄io ſt . III . car . 7 IIII . ſerui . 7 x . uitti . 7 xII .
bord cū . IIII . car . Ibi molin redd̄ . xv . den̄ . 7 Lx . ac̄ ꝓti .
7 xx . ac̄ paſturæ . Valuit . c . ſolid̄ . Modo . xII . lib̄ .

Bretel ten de . co . *PERET* . Algar tenuit T . R . E . 7 geld̄b ꝓ . x . hid̄ . Tra . ē
VIII . car . In dn̄io . ē . I . car . 7 II . ſerui . 7 VIII . uitti 7 xII . bord cū . III . car .
Ibi . II . molini redd̄ . xIIII . ſot . 7 xVIII . ac̄ ꝓti . Silua . vI . q̄ʒ lḡ . 7 III . q̄ʒ
lat . Valuit 7 uat . VII . lib̄ .

40 Alfred holds HELE from the Count. Aldred held it before 1066;
it paid tax for 1 hide. Land for 3 ploughs. In lordship 1 plough;
4 slaves; 3 virgates.   273
    2 villagers and 7 smallholders with 1 plough & 1 virgate.   a 2
    A mill which pays 10s; meadow, 10 acres; woodland, 15 acres.
        1 cob; 5 pigs.
The value was 40s; now £4.

†   Before 1066 this land could not be separated from Taunton,   E
Bishop Walkelin of Winchester's manor.

41 Alfred holds NORTON (Fitzwarren) from the Count. Osmund held   E
it before 1066; it paid tax for 5 hides. Land for 10 ploughs.
In lordship 3 ploughs; 6 slaves; 1 hide.   273
    13 villagers and 8 smallholders with 8 ploughs & 4 hides.   b 1
    2 mills which pay 11s 3d; meadow, 25 acres; woodland, 40 acres.
        2 cobs; 7 pigs; 50 sheep.
The value was £8; now £15.

42 Alfred holds FORD from the Count. Theodoric held it before 1066; E
it paid tax for ½ hide. Land for 1 plough, which is there, with   E
    2 smallholders.   273
    Meadow, 2 acres.   b 2
The value was 20s; now 30s.

43 Reginald of Vautortes holds CHARLTON (Adam) from the Count.   E
Three thanes with a clerk held it before 1066; it paid   E
tax for 5 hides. Land for 6 ploughs. In lordship 3   E
ploughs; 6 slaves; 2 hides.   E
    5 villagers and 6 smallholders with 1½ ploughs & 2½ hides.   273
    Meadow, 50 acres; pasture, 40 acres; underwood, 20 acres.   b 3
        1 cob; 5 cattle; 30 pigs; 60 sheep.
Value of this manor £6 a year; when the Count acquired it, as much.

44 The Count holds CHINNOCK himself. Edmer Ator held it
before 1066; it paid tax for 7 hides. Land for 7 ploughs.
In lordship 3 ploughs; 4 slaves; 4½ hides.   274
    10 villagers and 12 smallholders with 4 ploughs & 2½ hides.   a 1
    A mill which pays 15d; meadow, 60 acres; pasture, 20 acres.
        1 cob; 14 cattle; 122 sheep.
The value was 100s; now £12.   E

45 Bretel holds (North) PERROTT from the Count. Algar held it
before 1066; it paid tax for 10 hides. Land for 8 ploughs.
In lordship 1 plough; 2 slaves; 6 hides.   274
    8 villagers and 12 smallholders with 3 ploughs & 4 hides.   a 2
    2 mills which pay 14s; meadow, 18 acres; woodland 6 furlongs
        long and 3 furlongs wide. 2 cattle; 10 pigs; 120 sheep.
The value was and is £7.

Anſger teñ de co.*VDECOME*.Edmer tenuit T.R.E.7 geldb̄ ꝑ.v.hid̄.
Tra.ē.v.car̄.In dñio ſt.ii.car̄.7 iiii.ſerui.7 x.uitti.7 xvi.bord̄ cū.iii.
car̄.Ibi moliñ redd̄.vii.ſolid̄.7 vi.den.Ibi.xx.ac̄ p̃ti.7 xii.ac̄ paſtæ.
7 una q̃ꝯ ſiluæ minutæ.Valuit 7 uat̄.c.ſolid̄.

Alured teñ *CEOLSEBERGE*.Duo taini tenueṙ T.R.E.7 geldb̄ ꝑ.v.
hid̄.Tra.ē.v.car̄.In dñio.ē una car̄.7 ii.ſerui.7 x.uitti.7 xii.bord̄
cū.iiii.car̄.Ibi moliñ redd̄.xv.ſolid̄.7 xxxviii.ac̄ p̃ti.7 iii.ac̄ ſiluæ
minutæ.Valuit.lx.ſolid̄.Modo.c.ſolid̄.

Malger teñ de.Co.*CINIOCH*.Vnus tain tenuit T.R.E.7 geldb̄ ꝑ.iii.
hid̄.Tra.ē.iii.car̄.In dñio.ē.i.car̄.7 iii.ſerui.7 ii.uitti 7 ix.bord̄
cū.i.car̄.Ibi.xxxvi.ac̄ p̃ti.Valuit.iiii.lib̄.Modo.iii.lib̄.

Alured teñ de.Co.*CINIOCH*.Vñ tain tenuit T.R.E.7 geldb̄
ꝑ.iiii.hid̄.Tra.ē.iiii.car̄.In dñio ſt.ii.car̄.7 v.ſerui.7 v.uitti.
7 x.bord̄ cū.ii.car̄.Ibi moliñ redd̄.x.ſolid̄.7 xl.ac̄ p̃ti.7 ii.ac̄

Æccl̄a ⁊ Mariæ de Greiſtan teñ de Co.ꝼ paſturæ.Vat̄.iiii.lib̄.
Nortone.Vñ tain tenuit T.R.E.7 geldb̄ ꝑ.v.hid̄.Tra.ē.v.car̄.
De ea ſt in dñio.ii.hidæ.7 ibi.i.car̄.7 v.ſerui.7 viii.uitti 7 vi.
bord̄ cū.iii.car̄.Ibi.ii.molini redd̄.xx.ſolid̄.7 xxv.ac̄ p̃ti.
Sil̄ua.ii.q̃ꝯ l̄g.7 una q̃ꝯ lat̄.Valuit 7 uat̄.c.ſolid̄.

Alured teñ de.Co.*PENNE*.Aluuard tenuit T.R.E.7 geldb̄
ꝑ.v.hid̄.Tra.ē.v.car̄.In dñio ſt.iii.car̄.7 ii.ſerui.7 v.uitti.7 x.
bord̄ cū.iiii.car̄.Ibi.x.ac̄ p̃ti.7 iiii.q̃ꝯ paſturæ in l̄g 7 lat̄.
Sil̄ua.vii.q̃ꝯ l̄g.7 iii.q̃ꝯ lat̄.Valuit.xl.ſot̄.Modo.lx.ſot̄.

46 Ansger the Breton holds ODCOMBE from the Count. Edmer Ator
held it before 1066; it paid tax for 5 hides. Land for 5 ploughs.
In lordship 2 ploughs; 4 slaves; 2 hides.   274
   10 villagers and 16 smallholders with 3 ploughs & 3 hides.   E a 3
   A mill which pays 7s 6d. Meadow, 20 acres; pasture, 12
      acres; underwood, 1 furlong. 36 pigs; 126 sheep.
The value was and is 100s.

47 Alfred holds CHISELBOROUGH. Two thanes held it before 1066;   E
it paid tax for 5 hides. Land for 5 ploughs. In lordship 1
plough; 2 slaves; 1½ hides.   274
   10 villagers and 12 smallholders with 4 ploughs & 3½ hides.   b 1
   A mill which pays 15s; meadow, 38 acres; underwood, 3 acres.
      2 cobs; 10 cattle; 4 pigs; 29 sheep.
The value was 60s; now 100s.

48 Mauger holds CHINNOCK from the Count. A thane held it   E
before 1066; it paid tax for 3 hides. Land for 3 ploughs.
In lordship 1 plough; 3 slaves; 2 hides.   274
   2 villagers and 9 smallholders with 1 plough & 1 hide.   b 2
   Meadow, 36 acres. 6 pigs.
The value was £4; now £3.

49 Alfred holds CHINNOCK from the Count. A thane held it   E
before 1066; it paid tax for 4 hides. Land for 4 ploughs.
In lordship 2 ploughs; 5 slaves; 2 hides.   274
   5 villagers and 10 smallholders with 2 ploughs & 2 hides.   b 3
   A mill which pays 10s; meadow, 40 acres; pasture, 2 acres.
      2 cobs; 4 cattle; 20 pigs; 67 sheep.
Value £4; when the Count acquired it, £3.

50 St. Mary's Church, Grestain, holds NORTON (sub Hamdon) from   E
the Count. A thane held it before 1066; it paid tax for 5
hides. Land for 5 ploughs, of which 2 hides are in lordship;
1 plough there; 5 slaves;   275
   8 villagers and 6 smallholders with 3 ploughs & 2 hides.   a 1
   2 mills which pay 20s; meadow, 25 acres; woodland 2 furlongs
      long and 1 furlong wide. 1 cob; 10 cattle; 17 pigs; 40 sheep.
The value was and is 100s.

51 Alfred holds PENDOMER from the Count. Alfward Hunter held it
before 1066; it paid tax for 5 hides. Land for 5 ploughs.
In lordship 3 ploughs; 2 slaves; 3 hides.   275
   5 villagers and 10 smallholders with 4 ploughs & 2 hides.   a 2
   Meadow, 10 acres; pasture, 4 furlongs in length and width;
      woodland 7 furlongs long and 3 furlongs wide. 2 cobs;
      4 unbroken mares; 12 cattle; 35 pigs; 250 sheep.
The value was 40s; now 60s.

Ipſe.Comes ten CLOVEWRDE . Vn tain tenuit T.R.E.7 geldb
p.VII.hid. Tra.e.VI.car.In dnio ſt.III.car.7 III.ſerui.7 x.uilti.
7 VII.bord cu.III.car.Ibi molin redd.xv.ſolid.7 XII.ac pti.
Silua.IIII.q̃ʒ lg.7 II.q̃ʒ lat.Valuit 7 ual.VII.lib.

Alured ten de.Co.CLAFORD.Quinq̃ taini tenuer T.R.E.7 geldb
p.x.hid.Tra.e.IX.car.In dnio ſt.III.car 7 II.ſerui.7 III.cotarij.
7 XII.uilti 7 XVII.bord cu.VII.car.Ibi molin redd.III.ſol.7 xx.ac
pti.7 ccc.ac paſturæ.7 cLx.ac ſiluæ.Valuit.VII.lib.Modo.x.lib.

Ipſe comes ten GERLINTVNE.Alnod tenuit T.R.E.7 geldb p.VII.
hid.Tra.e.VII.car.In dnio.e.I.car 7 VI.ſerui.7 VIII.uilti 7 VI.
bord cu.II.car.Ibi molin redd.VII.ſolid.Silua.VI.q̃ʒ lg.

92 d

7 III.q̃ʒ lat.Valuit.VII.lib.Valet.c.ſol.

Drogo ten de.Co.VFETONE.Tres taini tenuer T.R.E.7 geldb
p.III.hid 7 una v træ 7 dim.Tra.e.II.car 7 dim.In dnio.e.I.car
7 VIII.cotar.cu.I.uilto.7 v.bord.cu.I.car.Ibi molin redd.xxx.
denar.7 x.ac pti.Valuit.L.ſolid.Modo.xL.ſolid.

Drogo ten de.Co.SVTONE.Bundi tenuit T.R.E.7 geldb p.v.
hid.Tra.e.v.car.In dnio ſt.II.car.7 II.ſerui.7 III.uilti.
7 IX.bord cu.II.car.Ibi molin ſine cenſu.7 xvi.ac pti.7 VIII.
ac ſiluæ.Valuit 7 ual.c.ſolid.

Drogo ten de.Co.SCEPTONE.Toli tenuit T.R.E.7 geldb p.v.
hid.Tra.e.v.car.In dnio ſt.II.car.7 VIII.ſerui.7 VIII.uilti
7 v.bord cu.III.car.Ibi.II.molini.unu ſine cenſu.alteru
redd.VII.ſol.7 VI.den.Ibi.xxx.ac pti.Silua.x.q̃ʒ lg.

52 The Count holds CLOSWORTH himself. A thane held it before 1066; E
it paid tax for 7 hides. Land for 6 ploughs. In lordship 3
ploughs; 3 slaves; 4 hides.   275
   10 villagers and 7 smallholders with 3 ploughs & 3 hides.   a 3
   A mill which pays 15s; meadow, 12 acres; woodland 4 furlongs
      long and 2 furlongs wide. 1 cob; 9 cattle; 23 pigs; 100 sheep; 100 goats.
The value was and is £7.

53 Alfred holds CLOFORD from the Count. Five thanes held it before   E
1066; it paid tax for 10 hides. Land for 9 ploughs. In lordship 3
ploughs; 2 slaves; 5½ hides.
   3 cottagers, 12 villagers and 17 smallholders with
      7 ploughs & 4½ hides.   275
   A mill which pays 3s; meadow, 20 acres; pasture, 300 acres;   b 1
      woodland, 160 acres. 2 cobs; 38 unbroken mares; 10 cattle;
      50 pigs; 150 sheep; 30 goats.
The value was £7; now £10.

54 The Count holds YARLINGTON himself. Alnoth held it before 1066;
it paid tax for 7 hides. Land for 7 ploughs. In lordship 1
plough; 6 slaves; 4 hides.   275
   8 villagers and 6 smallholders with 2 ploughs & 3 hides.   b 2
   A mill which pays 7s; woodland 6 furlongs long
      and 3 furlongs wide. 6 cattle; 3 pigs; 60 sheep.   92 d
The value was £7; value 100s.

55 Drogo holds WOOLSTON from the Count. Three thanes held it   E
before 1066; it paid tax for 3 hides and 1½ virgates of land.
Land for 2½ ploughs. In lordship 1 plough; 2½ hides and 1½ virgates.
   8 cottagers with 1 villager and 5 smallholders with   275
      1 plough & ½ hide.   b 3
   A mill which pays 30d; meadow, 10 acres. 66 sheep.
The value was 50s; now 40s.

56 Drogo holds SUTTON (Montis) from the Count. Bondi held it
before 1066; it paid tax for 5 hides. Land for 5 ploughs.
In lordship 2 ploughs; 2 slaves; 3 hides & 1 virgate.   276
   3 villagers and 9 smallholders with 2 ploughs   a 1
      & 2 hides, less 1 virgate.
   A mill without dues; meadow, 16 acres; woodland, 8 acres.
      11 pigs; 106 sheep.
The value was and is 100s.

57 Drogo holds SHEPTON (Montague) from the Count. Toli held it
before 1066; it paid tax for 5 hides. Land for 5 ploughs.
In lordship 2 ploughs; 8 slaves; 3 hides.   276
   8 villagers and 5 smallholders with 3 ploughs & 2 hides.   a 2
   2 mills, one without dues, the other which pays 7s 6d.
      Meadow, 30 acres; woodland 10 furlongs long

7 IIII . q̃ʒ lat . Valuit . VII . lib . modo . c . ſolid.

Huic M̃ eſt addita *STOCHE* . Drogo ten de com . Roḃtus f. Wimarc
tenuit T.R.E. 7 geldb ꝑ . III . hid . Tra . ē . IIII . car . In dñio . ē
una car . 7 II . ſerui 7 v . uilli . 7 VIII . borđ cũ . II . car . Ibi . v . ãc
ꝑti . 7 II . ãc ſiluæ . Valet . III . lib.

Bretel ten de . co . *ROLIZ* . Aluric teneb T.R.E. 7 geldb
ꝑ . IIII . hid . Tra . ē . VI . car . In dñio . ē . I . car . 7 IIII . uilli
7 III . borđ 7 VII . cotar cũ . I . car . Ibi . xv . ãc ꝑti . Silua
II . q̃ʒ lḡ . 7 dim̃ q̃ʒ lat . Valet . XL . ſolid.

Malgerus ten de . co . *CHINTVNE* . Duo taini tenuer̃ T.R.E.
7 geldb ꝑ . v . hid . Tra . ē . v . car . In dñio ſt . III . car . 7 v .
ſerui . 7 II . uilli 7 IIII . borđ cũ . I . cotar hñt . I . car 7 dim̃.
Ibi . xxx . ãc ꝑti . Valet . IIII . lib.

Ricarđ ten de . Co . *CREDELINCOTE* . Godeman tenuit
T.R.E. 7 geldb ꝑ . III . hid 7 dim̃ . Tra . ē . III . car . In dñio
ſt . II . car cũ . I . ſeruo . 7 uno uillo . 7 III . borđ . Ibi moliñ
redđ . v . ſolid . 7 x . ãc ꝑti . Valet . L . ſolid.

Alured ten de . co . *ECEWICHE* . Aleſtan tenuit T.R.E.
7 geldb ꝑ una uirg træ . Ibi . I . uills . 7 I . ſeruus . Valuit

Bretel ten de . co . *BERROWENE* . Almær ↿7 ual . x . ſol.
tenuit T.R.E. 7 geldb ꝑ . v . hid . Tra . ē . v . car . In dñio . ē
una car . 7 II . ſerui . 7 x . uilli . 7 I . borđ 7 IIII . cotar . cũ . IIII.
car . Ibi . VIII . ãc ꝑti . 7 xx . ãc paſturæ . 7 XL . ãc ſiluæ.
Valuit 7 ualet . IIII . lib.

and 4 furlongs wide. 2 cobs; 4 cows; 23 pigs; 210 sheep.
The value was £7; now 100s.

(Stoney) STOKE has been added to this manor. Drogo holds
from the Count. Robert son of Wymarc held it before 1066;
it paid tax for 3 hides. Land for 4 ploughs. In lordship 1
plough; 2 slaves; 1 hide.

5 villagers and 8 smallholders with 2 ploughs & 2 hides.
Meadow, 5 acres; woodland, 2 acres. 7 cattle; 11 pigs; 50 sheep.
Value £3; when the Count acquired it, £4.

Drogo holds these two manors from the Count as one manor.

58 Bretel holds REDLYNCH from the Count. Aelfric held it
before 1066; it paid tax for 4 hides. Land for 6 ploughs.
In lordship 1 plough; 3 hides.

4 villagers, 3 smallholders and 7 cottagers with 1 plough & 1 hide.
Meadow, 15 acres; woodland 2 furlongs long and ½ furlong wide.
1 cob; 20 pigs; 20 sheep.

Value 40s; when the Count acquired it, £4.

59 Mauger holds KEINTON (Mandeville) from the Count. Two thanes
held it before 1066; it paid tax for 5 hides. Land for 5 ploughs.
In lordship 3 ploughs; 5 slaves; 4 hides & 1 virgate, less 5 acres.

2 villagers and 4 smallholders with 1 cottager have 1½ ploughs
& 3 virgates & 5 acres.
Meadow, 30 acres. 5 pigs; 85 sheep.
Value £4; when the Count acquired it, £5.

60 Richard holds CARLINGCOTT from the Count. Godman held it
before 1066; it paid tax for 3½ hides. Land for 3 ploughs.
In lordship 2 ploughs & 3 hides & 1 virgate, with 1 slave and
1 villager and 3 smallholders (who have) 1 virgate.
A mill which pays 5s; meadow, 10 acres. 3 cows; 12 pigs; 162 sheep.
Value 50s; when the Count acquired it, 60s.

61 Alfred holds ECKWEEK from the Count. Alstan of Boscombe held
it before 1066; it paid tax for 1 virgate of land. 1 plough can plough it.
1 villager and 1 slave.
The value was and is 10s.

62 Bretel holds BARROW from the Count. Aelmer held it
before 1066; it paid tax for 5 hides. Land for 5 ploughs.
In lordship 1 plough; 2 slaves; 3 hides & ½ virgate.

10 villagers, 1 smallholder and 4 cottagers with 4 ploughs
& 1 hide & 3½ virgates.
Meadow, 8 acres; pasture, 20 acres; woodland, 40 acres.
1 cob; 11 cattle; 15 pigs; 55 sheep.
The value was and is £4.

E

276
a 3

276
a 4

E

276
b 1

E

276
b 2

276
b 3

277
a 1

Bretel ten de. Co. *STOCHE* . Duo taini tenuer̄ T.R.E.7 geldb̄
⸝p . iii . hid̄ . Tra . v . car̄ . In dn̄io . ē . i . car̄ . 7 vii . ſerui.
7 iii . uilli 7 viii . bord̄ 7 v . coſcez cū . ii . car̄ . Ibi molinū
redd̄ . x . denar̄ . 7 xv āc p̄ti . Silua . i . leū lḡ . 7 una q̄ʒ lat̄.

Bretel ten de . co . *COCINTONE* . Leuing ⌐Valuit 7 ual . lx . ſol.
7 Suain tenuer̄ T.R.E . 7 geldb̄ ⸝p . vii . hid̄ . Tra . ē . vi . car̄.
In dn̄io . ē . i . car̄ cū . i . ſeruo . 7 xii . uilli 7 viii . bord̄ cū
. ii . car̄ . Ibi . xxii . āc p̄ti . Silua . xviii . q̄ʒ lḡ . 7 iiii . q̄ʒ lat̄.
Valuit . vii . lib̄ . Modo . c . ſolid̄.

Anſger ten de co . *ALDEDEFORD* . Godric tenuit . T.R.E.
7 geldb̄ ⸝p . v . hid̄ . Tra . ē . v . car̄ . In dn̄io . ē . i . car̄ . 7 iii . ſerui.
7 vii . uilli 7 iiii . bord̄ . 7 iiii . cot̄ . cū . ii . car̄ . Ibi molin̄ redd̄
vii . ſol . 7 l . āc p̄ti . 7 de uillis . viii . blomas ferri . Valuit . c . ſol.

Robt ten de . Co . *BABACHAN* . Godric ⌐Modo . iiii . lib̄.
tenuit T.R.E . 7 geldb̄ ⸝p . ii . hid̄ 7 dim̄ . Tra . ē . iii . car̄ . In dn̄io
st̄ . ii . car̄ . 7 iii . ſerui . 7 vi . uilli 7 iiii . bord̄ . cū . i . car̄ . Ibi . xiiii.
āc p̄ti . 7 viii . āc paſturæ . Valuit . l . ſol . Modo . lx . ſolid̄.

Hugo ten de . Co . *FEDINTONE* . Celred tenuit . T.R.E . 7 geldb̄
⸝p . i . hida . 7 una v̄ træ 7 dim̄ . Tra . ē . ii . car̄ . In dn̄io . ē . i . car̄
cū . i . uillo 7 i . bord̄ cū . i . car̄ . 7 iiii . āc p̄ti . Valuit . xxx . ſol.

Malger ten de . Co . *CLOPETONE* . Duo taini ⌐Modo . xx.
tenuer̄ . T.R.E . 7 geldb̄ ⸝p . iii . hid̄ . Tra . ē . iii . car̄ . In dn̄io . ē . i.
7 ii . ſerui . 7 ii . uilli . 7 iii . bord̄ . Val . xxx . ſolid̄.

63 Bretel holds STOKE (Trister) from the Count. Two thanes held it   E
before 1066; it paid tax for 3 hides. Land for 5 ploughs.
In lordship 1 plough; 7 slaves; 1½ hides.
    3 villagers, 8 smallholders and 5 Cottagers with   277
     2 ploughs & the rest (of the land).   a 2
    A mill which pays 10d; meadow, 15 acres; woodland 1 league   E
     long and 1 furlong wide. 1 cob; 11 cattle; 20 pigs; 70 goats;
     8 unbroken mares.
The value was and is 60s.

64 Bretel holds CUCKLINGTON from the Count. Leofing and Swein   E
held it before 1066; it paid tax for 7 hides. Land for 6 ploughs.
In lordship 1 plough & 3½ hides, with 1 slave;   E
    12 villagers and 8 smallholders with 2 ploughs & 3½ hides.   277
    Meadow, 22 acres; woodland 18 furlongs long and 4 furlongs   a 3
     wide. 12 cattle; 13 pigs; 129 sheep; 25 ᵣ ⁱs.
The value was £7; now 100s.

65 Ansger holds ALFORD from the Count. Godric held it before 1066;
it paid tax for 5 hides. Land for 5 ploughs. In lordship 1 plough;
3 slaves; 2½ hides & 1 virgate.   277
    7 villagers, 4 smallholders and 4 cottagers with 2 ploughs   b 1
     & 2 hides & 1 virgate.
    A mill which pays 7s; meadow, 50 acres; from the villagers,   E
     8 blooms of iron. 20 pigs.
The value was 100s; now £4.

66 Robert son of Ivo holds BABCARY from the Count. Godric held it
before 1066; it paid tax for 2½ hides. Land for 3 ploughs.
In lordship 2 ploughs; 3 slaves; 1 hide & 1 virgate.   277
    6 villagers and 4 smallholders with 1 plough & the rest of the land.   b 2
    Meadow, 14 acres; pasture, 8 acres. 1 cob; 10 cattle; 15 pigs.
The value was 50s; now 60s.

67 Hugh of Vautortes holds FODDINGTON from the Count. Ceolred
held it before 1066; it paid tax for 1 hide and 1½ virgates of land.
Land for 2 ploughs. In lordship 1 plough & 1 hide, with   278
    1 villager and 1 smallholder with 1 plough & the rest of the land.   a 1
    Meadow, 4 acres.
The value was 30s; now 20(s).

68 Mauger of Carteret holds CLAPTON from the Count. Two thanes   E
held it before 1066; it paid tax for 3 hides. Land for 3 ploughs.
In lordship 1; 2 slaves; 2 hides.   278
    2 villagers and 3 smallholders (have) 1 hide.   a 2
     Woodland 2 furlongs long & 1 wide. 2 cattle; 10 pigs; 4 unbroken mares;
       100 sheep; 22 goats.
Value 30s; when the Count acquired it, £3.

Alured ten de . co . *WESTONE* . Brictuid tenuit T.R.E.

7 geldb ꝓ.ɪ.hida.7 ɪɪ.virg 7 dim. Tra . ē . ɪ . caɼ . q̃ ibi ē cū . v . borđ.

Ibi dimiđ moliñ redđ . xxx . den. Valuit . xx . foliđ . M̊ . xxx . fot.

92 c, d

Hunfriđ ten de . Co . ɪ . hiđ in *GATELME* . Godric tenuit T.R.E . Tra . ē . ɪɪ . caɼ

q̃ ibi ſꞇ cū . ɪɪ . uiꞇꞇis 7 ɪɪɪ . borđ . Ibi moliñ redđ . x . fot . 7 xv . ac pti.

ᵴ7 xv . ac filuæ . Vat . xxx . fot.

93 a

Warmund ten de . Co . in *MELEBVRNE* . ɪ . hiđ . Tra . ē . ɪ . caɼ . q̃ ibi.ē

in dñio.cū.ɪɪ.borđ 7 ɪɪ.feruis.7 xɪ.ac pti ibi.7 moliñ redđ.xvɪ.denaɼ.

7 v.burgſes redđ . ɪɪɪ.foliđ. Toꞇ uat xx . foliđ.

Ipfe.co.ten *MERSTONE* . Quattuor taini tenueɼ T.R.E.7 geldb ꝓ.v.

hiđ.Tra.ē.v.caɼ.In dñio.ē.ɪ.caɼ.cū.ɪ.feruo.7 v.uiꞇꞇi.7 x.borđ.cū.ɪɪɪ.

caɼ.Ibi.xL.ac pti.7 xxx.ac filuæ.Valuit 7 uat.x.lib.

Robt ten de.Co. *MERSTONE* . Quinꝗ taini tenueɼ T.R.E.7 geldb

ꝓ.ɪɪ.hiđ.Tra.ē.ɪɪ.caɼ.Has hñt ibi.v.uiꞇꞇi ⁊ ɪɪ.borđ.7 xxɪɪɪɪ.acs pti.

Valuit.xL.fot.Modo.Lx.foliđ.

Drogo ten de.Co.in *ETESBERIE*.ɪɪɪ.virg træ. Aluui tenuit T.R.E.

Tra.ē.dimiđ caɼ.q̃ ibi.ē cū.ɪɪɪ.borđ.Ibi.vɪ.ac pti.7 x.ac filuæ

Anſger ten de.Co. *TRENTE* . Brifnod tenuit T.R.E. ᵴ Valuit 7 uat.x.fot.

7 geldb ꝓ.vɪɪ.hiđ.Tra.ē.v.caɼ.In dñio.ē.ɪ.caɼ.7 vɪ.ferui.7 vɪɪ.uiꞇꞇi

7 x.borđ.cū.ɪɪɪɪ.caɼ.Ibi.xxx.ac pti.7 Lx.ac pafturæ.7 xxx.ac filuæ.

Valuit 7 uat . vɪɪɪ . lib.

69 Alfred holds WESTON (Bampfylde) from the Count. Brictwy
   held it before 1066; it paid tax for 1 hide and 2½ virgates.
   Land for 1 plough, which is there, with   E
       5 smallholders; 2 slaves.
       ½ mill which pays 30d. Woodland, 4 acres; meadow, 8 acres.   278
         2 cobs; 8 cattle; 10 pigs.   a 3
   The value was 20s; now 30s.

Written across the bottom of cols. 92 c, d with no transposition sign. See Notes.

70 Humphrey holds 1 hide in GOATHILL from the Count. Godric held
   it before 1066. Land for 2 ploughs, which are there, with   L
       2 villagers and 3 smallholders.   278
       A mill which pays 10s; meadow, 15 acres; woodland, 15 acres.   E   b 1
         2 dwellings in Milborne (Port). 1 cob; 2 cows; 15 pigs; 50 sheep.
   Value 30s; when he acquired it, 20s.

71 Warmund holds 1 hide in MILBORNE (Port) from the Count.   E   93 a
   Land for 1 plough, which is there, in lordship, with
       2 smallholders and 2 slaves.   E
       Meadow, 11 acres; a mill which pays 16d. 1 cob; 1 cow; 20 pigs.   278
       5 burgesses who pay 3s.   E   b 2
   Value of the whole 20s; when he acquired it, 15s.

72 The Count holds MARSTON (Magna) himself. Four thanes held it   E
   before 1066; it paid tax for 5 hides. Land for 5 ploughs.
   In lordship 1 plough & 2 hides & 3 virgates, with 1 slave;   278
       5 villagers and 10 smallholders with 3 ploughs & 2 hides & 1 virgate.   b 3
       Meadow, 40 acres; woodland, 30 acres. 1 cob; 16 pigs.
   The value was and is £10.

73 Robert holds MARSTON (Magna) from the Count. Five thanes held it   E
   it before 1066; it paid tax for 2 hides. Land for 2 ploughs.   279
       5 villagers and 2 smallholders have them there & that land, and   a 1
       meadow, 24 acres.
   The value was 40s; now 60s.

74 Drogo holds 3 virgates of land in ADBER from the Count.
   Alfwy held them before 1066. Land for ½ plough, which is
   there, in lordship, & 2½ virgates, with   279
       3 smallholders (who have) ½ virgate.   a 2
       Meadow, 6 acres; woodland, 10 acres.
   The value was and is 10s.

75 Ansger holds TRENT from the Count. Brictnoth held it
   before 1066; it paid tax for 7 hides. Land for 5 ploughs.
   In lordship 1 plough; 6 slaves; 4 hides.   279
       7 villagers and 10 smallholders with 4 ploughs & 3 hides.   a 3
       Meadow, 30 acres; pasture, 60 acres; woodland, 30 acres.
         20 pigs; 115 sheep.
   The value was and is £8.

Wilts ten *PONDITONE*. Adulf tenuit T.R.E. 7 geldb ꝑ.II.hid 7 dim.

Tra.ē.III.car. In dnio.ē.I.car.7 IIII.uilli 7 VI.bord cu.II.car. Ibi molin

redd.xxxII.den.7 dim ac ꝑti.7 xx.ac pasturæ. Valet.XL.solid.

Drogo ten de.Co.*TORNE*. Cheneue tenuit T.R.E.7 geldb ꝑ una hida

7 una v̄.Tra.ē.II.car. In dnio.ē.I.car.7 III.serui.7 III.bord.7 x.ac

ꝑti. Valuit.x.sol. modo.xx.solid.

Radulf ten de.Co.*TORNE*. Duo taini tenuer̄ T.R.E.7 geldb ꝑ.II.hid.

7 Tra.ē.III.car. In dnio.ē.I.car.7 v.uilli 7 II.bord cu.I.car.7 XIIII.ac

ꝑti. Valuit.XL.sol. Modo.xxxII.solid.

Alured ten de.Co.*CILTERNE*. Brictuin tenuit T.R.E.7 geldb ꝑ.III.hid.

Tra.ē.III.car. In dnio st.II.car.7 II.serui.7 III.uilli 7 v.bord.cu.II.car.

Ibi.xv.ac ꝑti.7 xx.ac siluæ. Valuit 7 ual.LX.solid.

Alured ten de.Co.*CILTERNE*. Aluui tenuit T.R.E.7 geldb ꝑ.II.hid.

Tra.ē.III.car. In dnio st.II.car.7 v.serui.7 II.uilli.7 IIII.bord cu.II.

car.7 xxx.ac ꝑti. Valuit.xxx.sol. Modo.XL.solid.

Ansger ten de.Co.*HVNDESTONE*. Tres taini tenuer̄ T.R.E.7 geldb

ꝑ una hida. Tra.ē.I.car. q̄ ibi.ē in dnio.7 II.serui.7 II.uilli 7 III.bord.

7 III.ac ꝑti 7 dimid. Valuit.x.sol. modo.xx.solid.

Ansger ten de.Co.in *LOCHETONE*.I.hid. Aluuin tenuit T.R.E.Tra.ē

una car.q̄ ibi.ē in dnio.7 II.serui.7 III.bord.7 x.ac ꝑti.Valet.xx.solid.

76 William holds POYNTINGTON from the Count. Adolf held it before 1066; it paid tax for 2½ hides. Land for 3 ploughs.
In lordship 1 plough; 1 hide & 5 acres.
    4 villagers and 6 smallholders with 2 ploughs & the rest of the land.
    A mill which pays 32d; meadow, ½ acre; pasture, 20 acres.
        1 cob; 1 pig; 30 sheep.
Value 40s; when he acquired it, 30s.

279
a 4

77 Drogo holds THORNE from the Count. Cynwy held it before 1066; it paid tax for 1 hide and 1 virgate. Land for 2 ploughs.
In lordship 1 plough; 3 slaves; 1 hide.
    3 smallholders (have) 1 virgate.
    Meadow, 10 acres. 30 sheep.
The value was 10s; now 20s.

279
b 1

78 Ralph the priest holds THORNE from the Count. Two thanes held it E before 1066; it paid tax for 2 hides. Land for 3 ploughs.
In lordship 1 plough; 1½ hides.
    5 villagers and 2 smallholders with 1 plough & the rest of the land.
    Meadow, 14 acres. 4 pigs.
The value was 40s; now 32s.

279
b 2

79 Alfred holds CHILTHORNE from the Count. Brictwin held it before 1066; it paid tax for 3 hides. Land for 3 ploughs.
In lordship 2 ploughs; 2 slaves; 2 hides.
    3 villagers and 5 smallholders with 2 ploughs & 1 hide.
    Meadow, 15 acres; woodland, 20 acres. 1 cob; 7 cattle; 24 pigs; 64 sheep.
The value was and is 60s.

279
b 3

80 Alfred the Butler holds CHILTHORNE from the Count. Alfwy held it before 1066; it paid tax for 2 hides. Land for 3 ploughs.
In lordship 2 ploughs; 5 slaves; 1 hide.
    2 villagers and 4 smallholders with 2 ploughs & 1 hide.
    Meadow, 30 acres. 1 cob; 11 cattle; 24 pigs; 115 sheep.
The value was 30s; now 40s.

280
a 1

81 Ansger holds HOUNDSTONE from the Count. Three thanes held it E before 1066; it paid tax for 1 hide. Land for 1 plough, which is there, in lordship, & ½ hide & ½ virgate; 2 slaves;
    2 villagers and 3 smallholders (who have) the rest of the land & ½ plough.
    Meadow, 3½ acres. 3 cattle; 50 sheep.
The value was 10s; now 20s.

280
b 1

82 Ansger holds 1 hide in LUFTON from the Count. Alwin held it before 1066. Land for 1 plough, which is there, in lordship; 2 slaves;
    3 smallholders.
    Meadow, 10 acres. 1 cob; 1 cow; 60 sheep.
Value 20s; when he acquired it, 12s.

280
b 2

Ipſe.Co.teń in *GIVELE*.i.hiđ.Tra.ē.ii.caŕ.Ibi ſt.ii.borđ.Valet.iii.ſoł.

In eađ uilla teń Amund de.co.i.hiđ.Tra.ē.i.caŕ.q̄ ibi.ē cū.ii.borđ.

Ibi moliń redđ.v.ſoliđ.Toŧ ualet.xx.ſoliđ.Quattuor taini tenueŕ

has.ii.hiđ T.R.E.7 ꝑ tanto geldb̄.

Roḃtus teń de.Co.*SOCHE*.Septē taini tenueŕ T.R.E.7 geldb̄ ꝑ.iii.

hiđ 7 dim.Tra.ē.v.caŕ.In dn̄io ſt.ii.caŕ.cū.i.ſeruo.7 viii.uiłłi

7 ii.borđ cū.ii.caŕ.Ibi.lxx.ac̄ ṗti.Valuit 7 uał.lxv.ſoliđ.

Ipſe comes teń iń dn̄io *BISCOPESTONE*.7 ibi.ē caſtellū ej̄ qđ uocat̄

MONTAGVD.Hoc m̄ geldb̄ T.R.E.ꝑ.ix.hiđ.7 erat de abbatia de

Adelingi.7 ꝑ eo deđ comes eiđ æcclæ m̄ qđ *CANDEL* uocatur.

In hoc m̄ Biſcopeſton.ē tra.vii.caŕ.De ea ſt in dn̄io.ii.hidæ 7 dim.

7 ibi.ii.caŕ.7 iiii.ſerui.7 iiii.uiłłi 7 iii.borđ cū.ii.caŕ.Ibi moliń

redđ.l.denaŕ.7 xv.ac̄ ṗti.

De his.ix.hiđ teń de comite Alured.i.hiđ 7 dim.Drogo.i.hidā.

Bretel.i.hiđ.Donecan,i.hiđ.Ibi ſt.v.caŕ.cū.i.ſeruo.7 xix.borđ

Valet comiti hoc m̄.vi.liḃ.Milîtibʒ.iii.liḃ 7 iii.ſoliđ.

.XX. TERRA BALDVINI DE EXECESTRE.

Baldvinvs teń *HAMITONE* de rege.Siuuarđ tenuit T.R.E.7 geldb̄

ꝑ.xxi.hiđ.Tra.ē.xx.caŕ.De ea ſt in dn̄io.viii.hidæ.7 ibi.iiii.caŕ.7 xi.

ſerui.7 xxvi.uiłłi 7 viii.borđ cū.xii.caŕ.Ibi.xii.ac̄ ṗti.7 l.ac̄ ſiluæ

minutæ.Paſtura dimiđ leū l̄g.7 dim leū lat̄.Valuit 7 uał.xix.liḃ.

De hac tra.i.hida.ē in cōmuni paſtura in Hardintone m̄ eṗi c̄ſtant̄.

83 The Count holds 1 hide in YEOVIL himself. Land for 2 ploughs. E

In lordship 1 hide.   281
   2 smallholders.   a 1
Value 3s; when he acquired it, 20s.

84 In the same village Amund holds 1 hide from the Count. E
Land for 1 plough, which is there, with
   2 smallholders.   281
   A mill which pays 5s. 5 cattle; 5 pigs; 100 sheep, less 5.   a 1
Value of the whole 20s; when he acquired it, 10s.
Four thanes held these 2 hides before 1066; they paid tax E
for as much.

85 Robert son of Ivo holds SOCK (Dennis) from the Count. Seven thanes E
held it before 1066; it paid tax for 3½ hides. Land for 5 ploughs.
In lordship 2 ploughs & 2½ hides, with 1 slave;   281
   8 villagers and 2 smallholders with 2 ploughs & the rest of the land.   a 2
   Meadow, 70 acres. 5 cattle; 35 pigs; 25 sheep.
The value was and is 65s.

86 The Count holds 'BISHOPSTONE' himself, in lordship. His castle, E
called Montacute, is there. This manor paid tax for 9 hides
before 1066; it was (part) of Athelney Abbey and for it the Count
gave that church the manor called (Purse) Caundle.   280
In this manor (of) 'Bishopstone', land for 7 ploughs, of which 2½   a 3
hides are in lordship; 2 ploughs there; 4 slaves;
   4 villagers and 3 smallholders with 2 ploughs & 1 hide.
   A mill which pays 50d; meadow, 15 acres. 1 cob; 100 sheep.
Of these 9 hides Alfred the Butler holds 1½ hides from the D
Count, Drogo 1 hide, Bretel 1 hide, Duncan 1 hide.
5 ploughs there, with 1 slave;
     19 smallholders.
Value of this manor to the Count £6; to the men-at-arms £3 3s.

19,87 written at the bottom of col. 93 a after ch. 20. See Notes.

20   LAND OF BALDWIN OF EXETER

1 Baldwin the Sheriff holds HEMINGTON from the King. Siward held
it before 1066; it paid tax for 21 hides. Land for 20 ploughs,
of which 8 hides are in lordship; 4 ploughs there; 11 slaves;
   26 villagers and 8 smallholders with 12 ploughs & 12 hides.   315
   Meadow, 12 acres; underwood, 50 acres; pasture ½ league   a 4
     long and ½ league wide. 2 cobs; 19 cattle; 23 pigs; 245 sheep; 58 goats.
The value was and is £19.   E
   1 hide of this land is in the common pasture in Hardington,   E
a manor of the Bishop of Coutances'.

Drogo ten de Bald *APELIE*.Norman tenuit T.R.E.7 geldb ,p.III.v̇ træ.
Tra.ē.II.caŕ.Ibi sŧ.IIII.uilli 7 III.borđ.7 v.ac̄ p̄ti.7 x.ac̄ pasturæ.Valet
Idem ten de Bald *PORTLOC*.Algar tenuit T.R.E.7 geldb ,p.III.⌐xv.ſoliđ.
hiđ.Tra.ē.XII.caŕ.Ibi sŧ.VI.uilli 7 III.borđ.7 VI.ſerui.7 ccc.ac̄ ſiluæ.
7 đngentæ ac̄ pasturæ.Valuit.IIII.liƀ qdo recep̄.Modo.XXV.ſoliđ.

Dodeman ten de.co.*MVNDIFORD*.Wnulf teneƀ T.R.E.7 geldb ,p.IIII.hiđ 7 dimiđ.
★ Tra.ē.IIII.caŕ.In dn̄io sŧ.II.caŕ.7 VII.ſerui.7 un uilłs 7 VII.borđ cū.I.caŕ.
Ibi moliñ redd.xx.ſol.7 xv.ac̄ p̄ti.7 xl.ac̄ pasturæ.Valuit 7 ual.IIII.liƀ.

.XXI.   ## TERRA ROGERIJ DE CORCELLE.

Rogerivs de Cvrcelle ten de rege *CVRI*.Briĉtric
tenuit T.R.E.7 geldb ,p.III.hiđ 7 dim.Tra.ē.IIII.caŕ.
De ea.ē in dn̄io.I.hida.7 ibi.II.caŕ.7 II.ſerui.7 xI.uilli
7 VII.borđ cū.III.caŕ 7 dimiđ.Ibi.XII.ac̄ p̄ti.7 v.ac̄ pasturæ.
7 dimiđ leū ſiluæ inŧ lḡ 7 lat.Valuit.IIII.liƀ.Modo.c.ſol.
Ipſe Rog.ten *CVRI*.Celric tenuit T.R.E.7 geldb ,p.III.
hiđ 7 dim.Tra.ē.IIII.caŕ.De ea.ē in dn̄io.I.hida.7 ibi
una caŕ.cū.I.ſeruo.7 x.uilli 7 VII.borđ cū.III.caŕ 7 dim.
Ibi.x.ac̄ p̄ti.7 v.ac̄ pasturæ 7 dimiđ leū ſiluæ in lḡ 7 lat.
Valuit.IIII.liƀ.Modo.c.ſoliđ.
Has.II.tras ten Rog ,p uno ꝏ.
Roƀt ten de.Ro.*NIWETONE*.Eilaf tenuit T.R.E.
7 geldb ,p.III.virg træ.Tra.ē.I.caŕ.q̃ ibi.ē cū.I.uilło
7 v.borđ 7 II.ſeruis.Ibi.VI.ac̄ ſiluæ.Valet.xx.ſoliđ.

2 Drogo holds APPLEY from Baldwin. Norman held it before 1066; E
it paid tax for 3 virgates of land. Land for 2 ploughs.
In lordship 2 virgates & ½ plough. 315
    4 villagers and 3 smallholders (have) 1 virgate & 1½ ploughs. b 1
    Meadow, 5 acres; pasture, 10 acres.
Value 15s; when Baldwin acquired it, 5s.

3 He also holds PORLOCK from Baldwin. Algar held it before 1066; E
it paid tax for 3 hides. Land for 12 ploughs. In lordship 1½ hides. 315
    6 villagers, 3 smallholders and 6 slaves (have) the rest of the land. a 3
    Woodland, 300 acres; pasture, 500 acres.
Value £4 when he acquired it; now 25s.

Written at the bottom of col. 93 a, with no corresponding transposition sign. See Notes.
19,87 Dodman holds MUDFORD from the Count. Winulf held it before
Ψ 1066; it paid tax for 4½ hides. Land for 4 ploughs. In lordship
2 ploughs; 7 slaves; 3 hides & 3 virgates. 280
    1 villager and 7 smallholders with 1 plough & the rest of the land. a 2
    A mill which pays 20s; meadow, 15 acres; pasture, 40 acres.
      1 cob; 6 cattle; 15 pigs.
The value was and is £4.

21   **LAND OF ROGER OF COURSEULLES** 93 b

1 Roger of Courseulles holds CURRY (Mallet) from the King.
Brictric held it before 1066; it paid tax for 3½ hides.
Land for 4 ploughs, of which 1 hide is in lordship; 2 ploughs E
there; 2 slaves; 429
    11 villagers and 7 smallholders with 3½ ploughs & 2½ hides. a 4
    Meadow, 12 acres; pasture, 5 acres; woodland, ½ league
      in both length and width. 1 cob; 9 pigs; 23 sheep.
The value was £4; now 100s.

2 Roger holds CURRY (Mallet) himself. Ceolric held it before 1066;
it paid tax for 3½ hides. Land for 4 ploughs, of which 1 hide
is in lordship; 1 plough there, with 1 slave; 429
    10 villagers and 7 smallholders with 3½ ploughs & 2½ hides. a 5
    Meadow, 10 acres; pasture, 5 acres; woodland, ½ league
      in length and width. 8 pigs; 22 sheep.
The value was £4; now 100s.
Roger holds these two lands as one manor. E

3 Robert holds NEWTON from Roger. Elaf held it before 1066; E
it paid tax for 3 virgates of land. Land for 1 plough, E
which is there, with 422
    1 villager, 5 smallholders and 2 slaves. a 1
    Woodland, 6 acres. 21 cattle; 20 pigs; 50 sheep.
Value 20s; when Roger acquired it, 10s. E

Rob̄t ten de . Ro . *HATEWARE* . Algar tenuit . T.R.E.

7 geldb̄ ꝑ . I . hida . Tra . ē . I . car̄ 7 dim̄ . Ibi st̄ . II . feruĩ.

7 I . uilts 7 IX . borđ . 7 IIII . ac̄ p̄ti . 7 VII . ac̄ filuæ . 7 XXXVI.

ac̄ pafturæ . Valuit . XV . fol . Modo . XX . foliđ.

De hac hida ht̄ . W . de douai unā v̄ træ.

Goisfrid ten de . Ro . *PERI* . Quattuor taini tenuer̄ T.R.E.

7 geldb̄ ꝑ . I . hida 7 uno ferling . Tra . ē . II . car̄ . In dn̄io

ē una car̄ . 7 II . uilti 7 v . borđ cū . I . car̄ . Ibi . XXXIII . ac̄

p̄ti . 7 XLIII . ac̄ pafturæ . 7 XXXVII . ac̄ filuæ . Val̄ . XXX . fol.

Wilts ten de . Ro . *VLVERONETONE* . Aluui tenuit T.R.E.

7 geldb̄ ꝑ . I . hida 7 uno ferling . Tra . ē . II . car̄ . In dn̄io

ē una car̄ . cū . I . feruo . 7 III . uilti . 7 III . borđ . cū . I . car̄.

Ibi . XI . ac̄ p̄ti . 7 VII . ac̄ pafturæ . 7 XIII . ac̄ filuæ.

Valuit 7 ual̄ XXII . foliđ.

Huic m̄ addita . ē . I . hida in *PERI* . Aluuard tenuit

T.R.E . 7 ꝑ . I . hida geldb̄ . Tra . ē . II . car̄ . In dn̄io . ē . I . car̄.

7 II . uilti 7 III . borđ cū . I . car̄ . Ibi . X . ac̄ p̄ti . 7 VII . ac̄

pafturæ . 7 XIII . ac̄ filuæ . Valuit 7 ual̄ . XX . foliđ.

Anfchitil ten de . Ro . *CLAIHELLE* . Ordgar tenuit T.R.E.

7 geldb̄ ꝑ . I . hida . Tra . ē . III . car̄ . In dn̄io . ē . I . car̄ . 7 II.

uilti 7 VII . borđ cū . II . car̄ . Ibi . III . ac̄ p̄ti . 7 VIII . ac̄ paf

turæ . 7 XII . ac̄ filuæ . Valuit 7 ual̄ . XX . foliđ.

Rob̄t ten de . Ro . *SIREDESTONE* . Sired tenuit T.R.E.

7 geldb̄ ꝑ dim̄ hida . Tra . ē . I . car̄ . q̄ ibi . ē in dn̄io . cū . I . feruo.

7 II . uilti 7 v . borđ cū . I . car̄ . Valuit . X . fol . Modo . XV . fol.

4 Robert holds HADWORTHY from Roger. Algar held it before 1066;
it paid tax for 1 hide. Land for 1½ ploughs. 2 slaves.
In lordship 2 virgates & 1 plough.
  1 villager and 9 smallholders (have) the rest of the land & ½ plough.
  Meadow, 4 acres; woodland, 7 acres; pasture, 36 acres.
    1 cob; 15 cattle.
The value was 15s; now 20s.
Of this hide W(alter) of Douai has 1 virgate of land.

422
a 2

5 Geoffrey of Vautortes holds PERRY from Roger. Four thanes held it
before 1066; it paid tax for 1 hide and 1 furlong. Land for
2 ploughs. In lordship 1 plough; 3 virgates.
  2 villagers and 5 smallholders with 1 plough & 1 virgate & 1 furlong.
  Meadow, 33 acres; pasture, 43 acres; woodland, 37 acres.
    1 cow; 2 pigs; 12 sheep.
Value 30s; when Roger acquired it, as much.

E

422
a 3
E

6 William holds WALDRON from Roger. Alfwy held it before 1066;
it paid tax for 1 hide and 1 furlong. Land for 2 ploughs.
In lordship 1 plough & ½ hide, with 1 slave;
  3 villagers and 3 smallholders with 1 plough & ½ hide & 1 furlong.
  Meadow, 11 acres; pasture, 7 acres; woodland, 13 acres.
    26 sheep; 3 pigs.
Value was and is 22s.
  1 hide in PERRY has been added to this manor. Alfward held
it before 1066; it paid tax for 1 hide. Land for 2 ploughs.
In lordship 1 plough; ½ hide.
  2 villagers and 3 smallholders with 1 plough & ½ hide.
  Meadow, 10 acres; pasture, 7 acres; woodland, 13 acres.
    3 pigs; 26 sheep.
The value was and is 20s.

422
a 4

E

E

7 Ansketel holds CLAYHILL from Roger. Ordgar held it before 1066;
it paid tax for 1 hide. Land for 3 ploughs. In lordship 1 plough;
½ hide.
  2 villagers and 7 smallholders with 2 ploughs & ½ hide.
  Meadow, 3 acres; pasture, 8 acres; woodland, 12 acres.
    4 cattle; 7 pigs; 12 sheep.
The value was and is 20s.

422
b 1

8 Robert *Herecom* holds SHEARSTON from Roger. Sired held it
before 1066; it paid tax for ½ hide. Land for 1 plough,
which is there, in lordship, & 1 virgate, with 1 slave;
  2 villagers and 5 smallholders with 1 plough & 1 virgate.
  6 cattle; 7 pigs; 30 sheep.
The value was 10s; now 15s.

422
b 2

Anſchitil teñ de.Ro. *RIME*. Aluui tenuit T.R.E.⁊ geldɓ
ꝓ dim v̇ træ.Tra.ē.II.boū.Ibi.ē uñ borđ ⁊ II.āc p̄ti.

Anſchitil teñ de.Ro.*CILLETONE*.　　�ⓕVał xxx.deñ.
Godric tenuit T.R.E.⁊ geldɓ ꝓ una v̇ træ.Tra.ē.I.caᷤ.
Ibi.ē.I.borđ.Valuit ⁊ uał.xx.ſoliđ.

Roɓt teñ de.Ro.*RACHEDEWORDE*.Godric tenuit T.R.E.
⁊ geldɓ ꝓ una v̇ træ.Tra.ē dimiđ caᷓ.Ibi ſt.II.borđ.⁊ VI.
a̅c ſiluæ.Valuit ⁊ uał.IIII.ſoliđ.

Ipſe Rog.teñ *CERDESLING*.Aluui tenuit T.R.E.⁊ geldɓ
ꝓ una hida ⁊ diṁ.Tra.ē.III.caᷓ.In dñio ſt.II.caᷓ.⁊ IIII.
ſerui.⁊ III.uilti ⁊ III.borđ cū.II.caᷓ.Ibi moliñ redđ.VI.deñ.
⁊ III.a̅c p̄ti.⁊ XIIII.a̅c paſturæ.⁊ II.a̅c ſiluæ.Valuit ⁊ uał

Ipſe Rog teñ *CVRIEPOL*.Aluui tenuit T.R.E.　⌐XL.ſoł.
⁊ geldɓ ꝓ.I.hida.Tra.ē.IIII.caᷓ.In dñio.ē dimiđ caᷓ.⁊ VI.
uilti ⁊ v.borđ hñt.III.caᷓ.Ibi.VII.a̅c p̄ti.⁊ c.a̅c paſturæ.
⁊ VI.a̅c ſiluæ.Valuit ⁊ uał.XL.ſoliđ.

Goisfrid teñ de.Ro.*PVCHELEGE*.Almaᷧ tenuit T.R.E.⁊ geldɓ
ꝓ.I.hida.Tra.ē.IIII.caᷓ.In dñio ſt.II.caᷓ.⁊ v.ſerui.⁊ II.
uilti ⁊ IIII.borđ cū.II.caᷓ.Ibi.VI.a̅c p̄ti.⁊ VI.a̅c paſturæ.
Valuit ⁊ uał.XL.ſoliđ.

Goisfrid teñ de.Ro.*GODELEGE*.Aluuard tenuit T.R.E.
⁊ geldɓ ꝓ dim hida.Tra.ē.II.caᷓ.In dñio.ē una.caᷓ.⁊ v.
uilti ⁊ v.coſcez cū.I.caᷓ.⁊ I.ſeruo.Ibi dimiđ moliñ redđ
x.denaᷓ.⁊ xx.a̅c paſturæ.Valet.xx.ſoł.Valuit.xxx.ſoł.

9 Ansketel holds *RIME* from Roger. Alfwy held it before 1066; it paid tax for ½ virgate of land. Land for 2 oxen.
    1 smallholder.
    Meadow, 2 acres.
Value 30d; when Roger acquired it, as much.

423
a 1

10 Ansketel holds CHILTON (Trinity) from Roger. Godric held it before 1066; it paid tax for 1 virgate of land. Land for 1 plough.
In lordship 1 virgate & 3 furlongs.
    1 smallholder has 1 furlong.
The value was and is 20s.

423
a 2
E

11 Robert holds REXWORTHY from Roger. Godric held it before 1066; it paid tax for 1 virgate of land. Land for ½ plough.
    2 smallholders.
    Woodland, 6 acres.
The value was and is 4s.

423
a 3

12 Roger holds CHARLINCH himself. Alfwy held it before 1066; it paid tax for 1½ hides. Land for 3 ploughs.
In lordship 2 ploughs; 4 slaves; 1 hide.
    3 villagers and 3 smallholders with 2 ploughs & ½ hide.
    A mill which pays 6d; meadow, 3 acres; pasture, 14 acres;
        woodland, 2 acres. 1 cob; 1 cow; 11 pigs; 80 sheep; 30 goats.
The value was and is 40s.

423
a 4

13 Roger holds CURRYPOOL himself. Alfwy held it before 1066; it paid tax for 1 hide. Land for 4 ploughs. In lordship ½ plough; ½ hide.
    6 villagers and 5 smallholders have 3 ploughs & ½ hide.
    Meadow, 7 acres; pasture, 100 acres; woodland, 6 acres.
The value was and is 40s.

423
a 5

14 Geoffrey of Vautortes holds PIGHTLEY from Roger. Aelmer held it before 1066; it paid tax for 1 hide. Land for 4 ploughs.
In lordship 2 ploughs; 5 slaves; 1 virgate.
    2 villagers and 4 smallholders with 2 ploughs & 3 virgates.
    Meadow, 6 acres; pasture, 6 acres. 4 cattle; 39 sheep; 20 goats.
The value was and is 40s.

423
b 1

15 Geoffrey holds GOTHELNEY from Roger. Alfward held it before 1066; it paid tax for ½ hide. Land for 2 ploughs. In lordship 1 plough; 1 virgate.
    5 villagers and 5 Cottagers with 1 plough & 1 virgate and 1 slave.
    ½ mill which pays 10d; pasture, 20 acres. 3 pigs.
Value 20s; the value was 30s.

423
b 2

Goisfrid ten de . Ro . *TERRACOLGRIN* . Colgrin tenuit T . R . E.
7 geldb p dimid virg træ . Tra . ē . II . boū . Ibi sī . III . borđ.
Robt ten de . Ro . *OTRAMESTONE* . Eduin ⁊ Valet . IIII . sol.
tenuit T . R . E . 7 geldb p dim hida . Tra . ē . I . car 7 dim . Ibi sī
IIII . uilli 7 I . borđ . 7 un seruus . Ibi . II . ac pti 7 dim . 7 XII . ac pastæ.
7 VII . ac siluæ minutæ . Valuit 7 ual . XVIII . solid.

93 c

Robt ten de . Ro . *VLWARDESTONE* . Vlf tenuit T . R . E.
7 geldb p dim hida . Tra . ē dim car . Ibi . ē un uilts . 7 XVII.
ac pti . 7 XLII . ac pasturæ . Valuit . x . sol . Modo . xv . sol.
Aluuard ten de . Ro . *HOLECVBE* . Ipse tenuit T . R . E.
7 geldb p una v træ . Tra . ē . II . car . In dnio . ē . I . car.
7 II . serui . 7 un uilts 7 v . borđ cū dim car . Ibi molin
redđ . VI . den . 7 LXXV . ac pasturæ 7 XV . ac siluæ.
Valuit 7 ual . x . solid.
Anschitil ten de Ro . *DVDESHĀ* . Tres taini tenuer T . R . E.
7 geldb p . III . uirg (7 dim' 7 . v . acr') træ . Tra . ē . II . car . q̄ ibi sī cū . VI . borđ.
Ibi . v . ac pti . 7 XII . ac pasturæ . Valuit 7 ual . XX . solid.
Anschitil ten de Ro . *PERREDEHĀ* . Goduin tenuit
T . R . E . 7 geldb p dimid v træ . Tra . ē . I . car . Hanc hnt
ibi . IIII . borđ . Ibi . I . ac pti . Valuit 7 ual . x . solid.
Anschitil ten de . Ro . terrā Aluuini . Aluuin tenuit
T . R . E . 7 geldb p una v træ 7 uno ferling . Tra . ē . I . car.
q̄ ibi . ē in dnio cū . I . borđ . Ibi . ē molin redđ . XII . den.
7 II . ac pti . 7 II . ac pasturæ . Valuit 7 ual . x . solid.

16 Geoffrey holds 'COLGRIM'S LAND' from Roger. Colgrim held it before 1066; it paid tax for ½ virgate of land. Land for 2 oxen.
3 smallholders.
Value 4s; when Roger acquired it, 7s.

423
b 3

17 Robert holds OTTERHAMPTON from Roger. Edwin held it before 1066; it paid tax for ½ hide. Land for 1½ ploughs. In lordship ½ virgate & 1 plough.
4 villagers, 1 smallholder and 1 slave (have) the rest of the land & ½ plough.
Meadow, 2½ acres; pasture, 12 acres; underwood, 7 acres. Cattle, 1.
The value was and is 18s.

424
a 1

18 Robert holds WOOLSTON from Roger. Ulf held it before 1066; it paid tax for ½ hide. Land for ½ plough.
1 villager.
Meadow, 17 acres; pasture, 42 acres.
The value was 10s; now 15s.

93 c

424
a 2

19 Alfward holds 'HOLCOMBE' from Roger. He held it himself before 1066; it paid tax for 1 virgate of land. Land for 2 ploughs.
In lordship 1 plough; 2 slaves; ½ virgate.
1 villager and 5 smallholders with ½ plough & ½ virgate.
A mill which pays 6d; pasture, 75 acres; woodland, 15 acres.
12 cattle; 3 pigs; 4 sheep; 12 goats.
The value was and is 10s.

424
a 3

Ansketel holds from Roger

20 'DODISHAM'. Three thanes held it before 1066; it paid tax for 3½ virgates and 5 acres of land. Land for 2 ploughs, which are there, with
6 smallholders.
Meadow, 5 acres; pasture, 12 acres.
The value was and is 20s.

E

424
E b 1

21 'PETHERHAM'. Godwin held it before 1066; it paid tax for ½ virgate of land. Land for 1 plough.
4 smallholders have it there & the whole of the land.
Meadow, 1 acre.
The value was and is 10s.

424
b 2

22 'ALWIN'S LAND'. Alwin held it before 1066; it paid tax for 1 virgate of land and 1 furlong. Land for 1 plough, which is there, in lordship, & the whole (of the land) except for 5 acres, with
1 smallholder who holds the said 5 acres.
A mill which pays 12d; meadow, 2 acres; pasture, 2 acres.
10 cattle; 9 pigs; 10 sheep.
The value was and is 10s.

424
b 3

Anſchitil teñ de Ro.*CILDETONE*.Leuegar tenuit
T.R.E.7 geldƀ ꝑ dim̃ hida.Tra.ē.ɪɪ.car̃.In dñio.ē
una car̃.cū.ɪ.ſeruo.7 ɪɪ.uiłłi 7 v.borđ cũ.ɪɪ.car̃.
Ibi.vɪ.ãc p̃ti.7 vɪɪɪ.ãc paſturæ.7 xvɪ.ãc ſiluæ.
Valuit.xx.ſoliđ.Modo.xʟ.ſoliđ.

Anſchitil teñ de Ro.*CILDETONE*.Mereſuuet tenuit
T.R.E.7 gᵉldƀ ꝑ dim̃ hida.Tra.ē.ɪɪ.car̃.Has hñt
ibi.ɪɪɪɪ.uiłłi 7 vɪ.borđ.7 in dñio.ē dimiđ car̃.7 dimiđ
moliñ redđ.xx.ſoliđ.Ibi.vɪ.ãc p̃ti.7 vɪɪɪ.ãc paſ
turæ.7 xvɪ.ãc ſiluæ.Valuit 7 uał.xʟ.ſoliđ.

Anſchitil teñ de.Ro.*PILLOCH*.Godric tenuit T.R.E.
7 geldƀ ꝑ dimiđ ferling.Tra.ē dim̃ car̃.In dñio tam̃
ē una car̃.7 ɪɪ.borđ.7 ɪɪɪ.ãc p̃ti.7 vɪɪ.ãc paſturæ.Valuit

Anſchitil teñ de.Ro.*STOCHELAND*. Ⱶ 7 uał.vɪ.ſoł.
Duo taini tenueᵣ̃ T.R.E.7 geldƀ ꝑ.ɪ.hida 7 dim̃.Tra
ē.ɪɪ.car̃.q̄ ibi ſt̃ in dñio.7 ɪɪ.ſerui.7 ɪɪɪ.uiłłi 7 ɪɪ.borđ
cū.ɪ.car̃.Ibi.xxɪɪɪɪ.ãc p̃ti.7 xɪɪ.ãc ſiluæ.

Valƀ.xxx.ſoliđ qdo receꝑ.modo.ʟxv.ſoliđ.

Anſchitil teñ de.Ro.*EDEVESTONE*.Aluuiñ tenuit
T.R.E.7 geldƀ ꝑ.ɪɪ.hiđ 7 dim̃.Tra.ē.ɪɪɪɪ.car̃.In dñio
ſt̃.ɪɪ.car̃.7 vɪɪ.ſerui.7 vɪɪ.uiłłi cū.ɪ.borđ hñt.ɪɪɪ.car̃.
Ibi.xʟ.ãc p̃ti.7 v.ãc ſiluæ.Valuit 7 uał.c.ſoliđ.

Roƀt teñ de.Ro.*RADEFLOTE*.Godric tenuit T.R.E.
7 geldƀ ꝑ dim̃ hida.Tra.ē.ɪɪ.car̃.Ibi.uiłł 7 ɪɪ.borđ.
7 moliñ redđ.vɪ.deñ.7 v.ãc p̃ti.7 xxɪɪɪɪ.ãc paſturæ.
7 una ãc ſiluæ.Valuit.xx.ſoliđ.Modo.xv.ſoliđ.

Rannulf teñ de.Ro.*SVINDVNE*.Aluuarđ tenuit T.R.E.
7 geldƀ ꝑ una v træ.Tra.ē.ɪ.car̃.q̄ ibi.ē in dñio.7 ɪɪ.ſerui.
7 v.borđ.7 moliñ redđ.ɪɪɪ.deñ.7 una ãc p̃ti.7 ɪɪɪ.ãc
paſturæ.7 vɪɪ.ãc ſiluæ.Valuit.xv.ſoliđ.Modo.xx.ſoł.

23 CHILTON (Trivett). Leofgar held it before 1066; it paid tax
for ½ hide. Land for 2 ploughs. In lordship 1 plough & ½ virgate,
with 1 slave; **424**
    2 villagers and 5 smallholders with 2 ploughs & 1½ virgates. **b 4**
    Meadow, 6 acres; pasture, 8 acres; woodland, 16 acres.
        6 unbroken mares; 8 cattle; 12 pigs.
The value was 20s; now 40s.

24 CHILTON (Trivett). Mereswith held it before 1066; it paid
tax for ½ hide. Land for 2 ploughs.
    4 villagers and 6 smallholders have them there, & the rest of the land.
    In lordship ½ plough & ½ virgate. **425**
    ½ mill which pays 20s. Meadow, 6 acres; pasture, 8 acres; E a 1
      woodland, 16 acres. 8 cattle; 12 pigs.
The value was and is 40s.

25 'PILLOCKS (Orchard)'. Godric held it before 1066; it paid tax
for ½ furlong. Land for ½ plough. In lordship, however, 1 plough
& the whole (of the land) except for 10 acres. **425**
    2 smallholders who hold the said 10 acres. **a 2**
    Meadow, 3 acres; pasture, 7 acres. 2 cattle; 7 pigs; 16 sheep.
The value was and is 6s.

26 STOCKLAND. Two thanes held it before 1066; it paid E
tax for 1½ hides. Land for 2 ploughs, which are there, in
lordship, & 3½ virgates; 2 slaves; **425**
    3 villagers and 2 smallholders with 1 plough & the rest of the land. **a 3**
    Meadow, 24 acres; woodland, 12 acres.
Value when he acquired it, 30s; now 65s.

27 IDSON. Alwin held it before 1066; it paid tax for 2½ hides.
Land for 4 ploughs. In lordship 2 ploughs; 7 slaves; 1 hide & 3 virgates.
    7 villagers with 1 smallholder have 3 ploughs & 3 virgates. **425**
    Meadow, 40 acres; woodland, 5 acres. 1 cob; 10 cattle; 80 sheep. **a 4**
The value was and is 100s.

28 Robert holds RADLET from Roger. Godric held it before 1066;
it paid tax for ½ hide. Land for 2 ploughs. In lordship 1½ virgates.
    [1] villager and 2 smallholders (have) ½ virgate. **425**
    A mill which pays 6d; meadow, 5 acres; pasture, 24 acres; **b 1**
      woodland, 1 acre.
The value was 20s; now 15s.

29 Ranulf holds ?SWANG from Roger. Alfward held it before 1066;
it paid tax for 1 virgate of land. Land for 1 plough, which
is there, in lordship, & the whole (of the land) except for 15 acres; 2 slaves;
    5 smallholders. **425**
    A mill which pays 3d; meadow, 1 acre; pasture, 3 acres; **b 2**
      woodland, 7 acres. 10 cattle; 8 pigs; 50 sheep; 24 goats.
The value was 15s; now 20s.

Herбtus ten de.Ro.terrā Teodrici.Tedric tenuit T.R.E.
7 geldƀ ꝑ una v̾ træ.Tra.ē.ı.car.Ibi una ac̄ p̄ti 7 dim̄.
Roƀt ten de.Ro.terrā Olta.Aluuard⁹   ſVal.x.ſoł.
tenuit T.R.E.7 geldƀ ꝑ una v̾ træ.Tra.ē.ı.car.Ibi s̄t
ıı.borđ 7 una ac̄ p̄ti 7 dimiđ.Valuit 7 uał.x.ſoliđ.
Joħs ten de.Ro.ICHETOCHE.Vlf tenuit T.R.E.7 geldƀ
ꝑ una v̾ træ.Tra.ē dimiđ car.q̄ ibi.ē in dn̄io.cū.vıı.
borđ.7 xx.ac̄ p̄ti.7 vıı.ac̄ ſiluæ minutæ.Valet.xıı.ſoł.
Wilłs ten de.Ro.WIDIETE.Edric tenuit T.R.E.7 geldƀ
ꝑ.ııı.v̾ træ.Tra.ē.ı.car 7 dim̄.Ibi s̄t.ıı.uiłłi 7 v.borđ
cū car̾.   7 molin̄ redđ.vı.den̾.Valuit 7 ual.xv.
Wilłs ten de Ro.STRENGESTVNE.Siuuard   ſſoliđ.
tenuit T.R.E.7 geldƀ ꝑ una v̾ træ 7 dim̄.Tra.ē dim̄ car̾.
q̄ ibi.ē in dn̄io cū.ı.borđ.7 una ac̄ p̄ti.7 vı.ac̄ paſturæ.
Anſchitil ten de Ro.BLACHEMORE.ſValuit 7 uał.vııı.ſoł.
Aluric tenuit T.R.E.7 geldƀ ꝑ una v̾ træ.Tra.ē dim̄ car̾.
Huic m̄ addita.ē una ac̄ træ̾.quā teneƀ un̄ tain⁹ T.R.E.
Ibi s̄t.ıı.borđ.Tot ualuit 7 uał.vııı.ſoliđ.
93 d
Wilłs ten de.Ro.WORDE.Duo taini tenueꝛ T.R.E.7 geldƀ ꝑ.ı.
hida 7 dim̄.Tra.ē.ııı.car̾.Ibi s̄t.x.uiłłi cū.ıı.car 7 dimiđ.7 ıııı.
ac̄ p̄ti.7 ıııı.q̄ꝛ ſiluæ in lḡ.7 ıı.q̄ꝛ in lat̾.Valuit 7 uał.Lx.ſoliđ.

30 Herbert holds 'THEODORIC'S LAND' from Roger. Theodoric held
it before 1066; it paid tax for 1 virgate of land.
Land for 1 plough. Herbert...has 2 oxen there.
  Meadow, 1½ acres.
Value 10s; when he acquired it, 20s.

425
b 3

31 Robert holds ?AISHOLT from Roger. Alfward held it before 1066;
it paid tax for 1 virgate of land. Land for 1 plough.
In lordship the whole (of the land) except for 10 acres.
  2 smallholders who hold the said 10 acres.
  Meadow, 1½ acres.
The value was and is 10s.

426
a 1

32 John holds 'EDSTOCK' from Roger. Ulf held it before 1066;
it paid tax for 1 virgate of land. Land for ½ plough, which
is there, in lordship, & ½ virgate, with
  7 smallholders (who have) ½ virgate.
  Meadow, 20 acres; underwood, 7 acres. 3 cattle; 20 sheep.
Value 12s; when he acquired it, 10s.

426
a 2

33 William holds WITHIEL from Roger. Edric held it before 1066;
it paid tax for 3 virgates of land. Land for 1½ ploughs.
In lordship 1½ virgates & ½ plough.
  2 villagers and 5 smallholders with a plough &1½ virgates.
  A mill which pays 6d. 3 cattle; 3 pigs; 3 goats.
The value was and is 15s.

426
a 3

34 William holds STRINGSTON from Roger. Siward held it before 1066;
it paid tax for 1½ virgates of land. Land for ½ plough, which
is there, in lordship, with
  1 smallholder.
  Meadow, 1 acre; pasture, 6 acres.
The value was and is 8s.

E

426
a 4

35 Ansketel holds BLACKMORE from Roger. Aelfric held it
before 1066; it paid tax for 1 virgate of land.
Land for ½ plough.
  To this manor has been added 1 acre of land which a
thane held before 1066.
    2 smallholders.
The value of the whole was and is 8s.

426
E a 5

E

36 William of Daumeray holds 'WORTH' from Roger. Two thanes held it
before 1066; it paid tax for 1½ hides. Land for 3 ploughs.
  10 villagers with 2½ ploughs.
  Meadow, 4 acres; woodland, 4 furlongs in length and 2
    furlongs in width.
The value was and is 60s.

E 93 d

426
b 1

Idē tē͞n de.Ro.*CHENOLLE*.Godric 7 Aluric tenuer̄ T.R.E.7 geldb̄
‚p.ı.hida 7 una v̄ træ.Tra.ē.ıı.car̄.In dñio.ē.ı.car̄.7 v.uiłłi.7 ıııı.
borđ cū dimiđ car̄.Ibi.ıııı.q̄ꝫ filuæ in łḡ.7 ıı.q̄ꝫ in łat̄.Valet.xxv.

Huic m̄ eſt addita *ILLEGE*.Bruning tenuit ‚p m̄ T.R.E.   Γ̄ ſoliđ.
7 geldb̄ ‚p.ııı.uirg træ.Tra.ē.ıı.car̄.Ibi.ē una car̄ cū.ı.uiłło.
7 ı.borđ 7 uno ſeruo.Valuit 7 uat̄.xv.ſoliđ.

Girard tē͞n de Ro.*LOPTONE* Leuuiñ tenuit T.R.E.7 geldb̄ ‚p una hida.
Tra.ē.ı.car̄.q̄ ibi.ē in dñio.cū.ı.borđ.7 x.ãc p̄ti.Valet.xx.ſot̄.

Eldred tē͞n de.Ro.*SELVE*.Ipſe tenuit Ŧ.R.E.7 geldb̄ ‚p dim̄ hida.
Tra.ē.ı.car̄ 7 dim̄.Ibi.ı.uiłłs 7 ıı.borđ cū.ı.ſeruo hñt.ı.car̄.
Ibi.ııı.ãc p̄ti.7 LXıı.ãc paſturæ.Valuit 7 uat̄.xx.ſoliđ.

Alric tē͞n de.Ro.*SELVE*.Briſmar tenuit T.R.E.7 geldb̄ ‚p dimiđ
hida.Tra.ē.ı.car̄ 7 dim̄.Ibi.ıııı.uiłłi cū.ı.borđ hñt.ı.car̄.
Ibi.vı.ãc p̄ti.7 xvı.ãc paſturæ.7 xvı.ãc filuæ minutæ.Valuit

Alric tē͞n de Ro.*HALSVVEIE*.Ipſe tenuit T.R.E.7 geldb̄ Γ 7 u̅at̄.xx.ſoliđ.
‚p.ııı.virg træ.Tra.ē.ııı.car̄.In dñio.ē car̄ 7 dim̄.7 ııı.ſerui.7 ıııı.
uiłłi cū.ı.borđ hñt car̄ 7 dim̄.Ibi.ııı.ãc p̄ti.7 cccc.ãc paſturæ.

Alric tē͞n de Ro.*COLFORDE*.Ipſe tenuit T.R.E.7 geldb̄ Γ Valet.xx.ſot̄.
‚p.ııı.ferlings træ.Tra.ē.dimiđ car̄.In dñio tam̄.ē.ı.car̄.Vat̄.ı̋ı.ſot̄.

37 He also holds KNOWLE (St. Giles) from Roger. Godric and Aelfric   E
   held it before 1066; it paid tax for 1 hide and 1 virgate of land.
   Land for 2 ploughs. In lordship 1 plough; ½ hide & 1 virgate.   426
      5 villagers and 4 smallholders with ½ plough & ½ hide.   b 2
      Woodland, 4 furlongs in length and 2 furlongs in width.
         6 cattle; 48 sheep.
   Value 25s; when Roger acquired it, 10s.
     ELEIGH has been added to this manor. Browning held it as   E
   a manor before 1066; it paid tax for 3 virgates of land.
   Land for 2 ploughs. 1 plough there, with   E
      1 villager, 1 smallholder and 1 slave.   426
   The value was and is 15s.   E b 3

38 Gerard Ditcher holds LOPEN from Roger. Leofwin held it before
   1066; it paid tax for 1 hide. Land for 1 plough, which is there,
   in lordship, & the hide, with   427
      1 smallholder.   a 1
      Meadow, 10 acres. 66 sheep.
   Value 20s; when Roger acquired it, 10s.

39 Aldred holds MONKSILVER from Roger. He held it himself
   before 1066; it paid tax for ½ hide. Land for 1½ ploughs.
   In lordship 1 virgate.   427
      1 villager and 2 smallholders with 1 slave have 1 plough   a 2
        & 1 virgate.
      Meadow, 3 acres; pasture, 62 acres.
   The value was and is 20s.

40 Alric holds MONKSILVER from Roger. Brictmer held it before
   1066; it paid tax for ½ hide. Land for 1½ ploughs.
   In lordship 1 furlong & 2 oxen.   427
      4 villagers with 1 smallholder have 1 plough & 1 virgate & 3 furlongs.   a 3
      Meadow, 6 acres; pasture, 16 acres; underwood, 16 acres.
   The value was and is 20s.

41 Alric holds HALSWAY from Roger. He held it himself before 1066;
   it paid tax for 3 virgates of land. Land for 3 ploughs.
   In lordship 1½ ploughs; 3 slaves; 1½ virgates.   427
      4 villagers with 1 smallholder have 1½ ploughs & 1½ virgates.   a 4
      Meadow, 3 acres; pasture, 400 acres. 50 sheep.
   Value 20s; when Roger acquired it, as much.

42 Alric holds COLEFORD from Roger. He held it himself before 1066;
   it paid tax for 3 furlongs of land. Land for ½ plough.
   In lordship, however, 1 plough.   427
      40 sheep.   a 5
   Value 4s; when Roger acquired it, as much.

Bertran ten de Ro.*Hewis*.Vlgar tenuit T.R.E.7 geldb ꝓ.III.

uirg træ.Tra.ē.II.caꞃ.In dnio.ē una.cū.I.feruo.7 III.uilti.7 II.

borđ hn̄t.I.caꞃ.Ibi.III.aꞔ p̄ti.7 xxx.aꞔ pafturæ.Valet.xx.foliđ.

Alric ten de Ro.*Fescheforde*.Domne tenuit T.R.E.7 geldb

ꝓ dim hida.Tra.ē.I.caꞃ.Hanc hn̄t ibi.II.uilti cū.I.borđ.

7 in dnio.ē dim caꞃ.Ibi.IIII.aꞔ p̄ti.7 III.aꞔ pafturæ.7 xI.aꞔ filuæ.

Robt ten de.Ro.*Fescheforde*.Brifmar ⌐Valet.x.foliđ.

tenuit T.R.E.7 geldb ꝓ dim hida.Tra.ē.II.caꞃ.In dnio.ē.I.caꞃ.

7 un uilts 7 III.borđ hn̄t.I.caꞃ.Ibi.II.aꞔ p̄ti.7 xx.aꞔ pafturæ.

7 xL.aꞔ filuæ.Valuit 7 ual.xvII.foliđ.

Alric ten de.Ro.*Imele*.Vlgar tenuit T.R.E.7 geldb ꝓ dim hida.

Tra.ē.II.caꞃ.In dnio.ē dimiđ caꞃ.7 una aꞔ p̄ti 7 dim.7 IIII.aꞔ paftæ.

Ipfe Rog ten *Clive*.Brictric tenuit T.R.E.7 geldb ⌐Val.v.foliđ.

ꝓ.II.hiđ 7 dim.Tra.ē.IIII.caꞃ.In dnio ſt.II.caꞃ.cū.I.feruo.7 v.uilti.

7 v.borđ cū.II.caꞃ.Ibi molin redđ.vI.foliđ.7 xIII.aꞔ p̄ti.7 xII.aꞔ

filuæ.Paftura.I.leū 7 dim lḡ.7 dim lcū laꞇ.Valuit 7 ual.IIII.lib.

Huic m̄ eft addita *Hille*.Eduuald tenuit ꝓ m̄ T.R.E.7 geldb ꝓ.II.hiđ.

Tra.ē.II.caꞃ.Ibi un uilts 7 v.borđ 7 II.ferui hn̄t dim caꞃ.Ibi molin

redđ.xII.den.7 vII.aꞔ p̄ti.7 xx.aꞔ filuæ.Valuit 7 ual.xxx.foliđ.

Eiđ m̄ addita.ē *Plestone*.Perlo tenuit T.R.E.7 geldb ꝓ dim hida.

Tra.ē.I.caꞃ.q̄ ibi.ē in dnio.7 II.uilti 7 IIII.borđ cū dim caꞃ.Ibi III.

aꞔ p̄ti.7 xII.aꞔ pafturæ.7 vI.aꞔ filuæ.Valuit 7 ual.x.fol.Norman ten.

43 Bertram holds HUISH from Roger. Wulfgar held it before 1066;
it paid tax for 3 virgates of land. Land for 2 ploughs.
In lordship 1 (plough) & 2 virgates, with 1 slave.
   3 villagers and 2 smallholders have 1 plough & 1 virgate.
   Meadow, 3 acres; pasture, 30 acres.
Value 20s; when Roger acquired it, as much.

427
b 1

44 Alric holds VEXFORD from Roger. Dunn held it before 1066;
it paid tax for ½ hide. Land for 1 plough.
   2 villagers with 1 smallholder have it there & ½ virgate.
In lordship ½ plough & 1½ virgates.
Meadow, 4 acres; pasture, 3 acres; woodland, 11 acres.
     2 cattle; 3 pigs; 10 sheep; 8 goats.
Value 10s; when Roger acquired it, as much.

E

427
b 2

45 Robert holds VEXFORD from Roger. Brictmer held it before 1066;
it paid tax for ½ hide. Land for 2 ploughs. In lordship 1 plough;
[1] virgate & 1 furlong.
   1 villager and 3 smallholders have 1 plough & the rest of the land.
   Meadow, 2 acres; pasture, 20 acres; woodland, 40 acres.
     2 pigs; 15 sheep.
The value was and is 17s.

E

427
b 3

46 Alric holds EMBELLE from Roger. Wulfgar held it before 1066;
it paid tax for ½ hide. Land for 2 ploughs. In lordship ½ plough.
   Meadow, 1½ acres; pasture, 4 acres.
Value 5s; when Roger acquired it, as much.

428
a 1

47 Roger holds KILVE himself. Brictric held it before 1066;
it paid tax for 2½ hides. Land for 4 ploughs.
In lordship 2 ploughs & 2 hides & 3 furlongs, with 1 slave;
   5 villagers and 5 smallholders with 2 ploughs & 1 virgate & 1 furlong.
   A mill which pays 6s; meadow, 13 acres; woodland, 12 acres;
     pasture 1½ leagues long and ½ league wide. 2 cobs; 9 cattle;
     7 pigs; 40 sheep; 50 goats.
The value was and is £4.

428
a 2

   HILL has been added to this manor. Edwald held it as a
manor before 1066; it paid tax for 2 hides. Land for 2 ploughs.
   1 villager, 5 smallholders and 2 slaves have ½ plough.
   A mill which pays 12d; meadow, 7 acres; woodland, 20 acres.
The value was and is 30s.

E

428
a 3

   PARDLESTONE has also been added to this manor. Perlo held
it before 1066; it paid tax for ½ hide. Land for 1 plough,
which is there, in lordship, & 1½ virgates.
   2 villagers and 4 smallholders with ½ plough.
   Meadow, 3 acres; pasture, 12 acres; woodland, 6 acres.
     13 sheep; 24 goats.
The value was and is 10s.
   Norman holds it.

E

E 428
a 4

E

Goisfrid 7 Wilts teñ de Ro.*WAICOME*.Tres taini tenueř T.R.E.

7 geldb̄ p̱.ı.hida.Tra.ē.ı.cař 7 dim̄.Ibi.ē uñ bord̄.Toť ual.xxxıı.ſol.

Wilts teñ de Ro.*WESTOV*.Edeluuald tenuit T.R.E.7 geldb̄ p̱ una

hida.Tra.ē.ıı.cař.In dñio.ē una cař.7 ııı.ſerui.7 ıı.uilti 7 ııı.bord̄

cū dim̄ cař.Ibi.ıııı.ắc p̄ti.7 vııı.ắc paſturæ.7 xv.ắc ſiluæ.Valuit

Hugo teñ de.Ro.*ASCWEI*.Aluric tenuit T.R.E. ┌7 ual.xl.ſol.

7 geldb̄ p̱ dimid̄ hida 7 uno ferling.Tra.ē.vı.cař.In dñio

eſt.ı.cař.7 ıı.ſerui.7 xı.uilti 7 ııı.bord̄ cū.ıı.cař.Ibi.ı.ắc p̄ti.

7 lx.ắc ſiluæ.Paſtura.ı.leū lḡ.7 dim̄ leū lať.Valet.xxv.ſolid̄.

Wilts teñ de Ro.*BROFORD*.Vluuiñ tenuit T.R.E.7 geldb̄ p̱ una v́

træ.Tra.ē.ıı.cař.In dñio.ē una.7 ıııı.uilti hñt aliã.Ibi.v.ắc ſiluæ.

Wilts teñ de Ro.*BROFORD*.Almar tenuit T.R.E.┌Val.vıı.ſolid̄.

7 geldb̄ p̱ uno ferling.Tra.ē dim̄ cař.Ibi ſť.ıı.bord̄ 7 ıııı.ắc ſiluæ.

Ip̄ſe Rog teñ *POTESDONE*.Brictric tenuit ┌Val xxvı.denař.

T.R.E.7 geldb̄ p̱ una v́ træ.Tra.ē.ıı.cař.Ibi.xx.ắc paſturæ.

7 ııı.ắc ſiluæ.Valuit 7 ual.xxx.denař.

Wilts teñ de Ro.*POCHINTVNE*.Leuing tenuit T.R.E.7 geldb̄

p̱.ı.hida 7 dim̄.Tra.ē.ı.cař 7 dim̄.Ibi ſť.ııı.uilti 7 ııı.bord̄ 7 ıı.

ſerui cū.ı.cař.7 xı.ắc p̄ti 7 dim̄.7 vı.ắc paſturæ.7 lxvı.ắc ſiluæ.

Huic m̄ addita.ē *POCHINTVNE*.Aluuard tenuit T.R.E.p̱ m̄.

7 geldb̄ p̱ una hida 7 dim̄.Tra.ē.ı.cař 7 dim̄.Ibi ſť.ıııı.bord̄

cū.ı.uilto 7 ı.ſeruo.7 ıı.ắc p̄ti.7 vı.ắc paſturæ.7 lxvı.ắc ſiluæ.

48 Geoffrey and William hold WEACOMBE from Roger. Three thanes   E
held it before 1066; it paid tax for 1 hide. Land for 1½ ploughs.
    1 smallholder.   428
Value of the whole 32s.   b 1

49 William holds WESTOWE from Roger. Aethelwold held it
before 1066; it paid tax for 1 hide. Land for 2 ploughs.
In lordship 1 plough; 3 slaves; 3½ virgates.   428
    2 villagers and 3 smallholders with ½ plough & ½ virgate.   b 2
    Meadow, 4 acres; pasture, 8 acres; woodland, 15 acres.   26 sheep.
The value was and is 40s.

50 Hugh holds ASHWAY from Roger. Aelfric held it before 1066;
it paid tax for ½ hide and 1 furlong. Land for 6 ploughs.
In lordship 1 plough; 2 slaves; 1 virgate.   428
    11 villagers and 3 smallholders with 2 ploughs & 1 virgate & 1 furlong.   b 3
    Meadow, 1 acre; woodland, 60 acres; pasture 1 league long
       and ½ league wide. 3 cattle; 12 pigs; 26, both sheep & goats.
Value 25s; when Roger acquired it, 20s.

51 William holds BROFORD from Roger. Wulfwin held it before 1066;
it paid tax for 1 virgate of land. Land for 2 ploughs.
In lordship 1 (plough) & ½ virgate & 1 furlong.   429
    4 villagers have the other (plough) & 1 furlong.   a 1
    Woodland, 5 acres.
Value 7s; when Roger acquired it, 5s.

52 William holds BROFORD from Roger. Aelmer held it before 1066;
it paid tax for 1 furlong. Land for ½ plough.
    2 smallholders.   429
    Woodland, 4 acres.   a 2
Value 26d; when Roger acquired it, as much.   E

53 Roger holds PIXTON himself. Brictric held it before 1066;
it paid tax for 1 virgate of land. Land for 2 ploughs.   429
    Pasture, 20 acres; woodland, 3 acres.   a 3
The value was and is 30d.

54 William holds PUCKINGTON from Roger. Leofing held it before
1066; it paid tax for 1½ hides. Land for 1½ ploughs.   429
In lordship 1 hide & ½ virgate & ½ plough.   b 1
    3 villagers, 3 smallholders and 2 slaves with 1 plough & 1½ virgates.   E
    Meadow, 11½ acres; pasture, 6 acres; woodland, 66 acres.
       3 pigs; 2 goats.
PUCKINGTON has been added to this manor. Alfward held it
before 1066 as a manor; it paid tax for 1½ hides.
Land for 1½ ploughs. In lordship 1 hide & ½ virgate & ½ plough.
    4 smallholders with 1 villager and 1 slave (have) 1½ virgates
       & 2 oxen.
    Meadow, 2 acres; pasture, 6 acres; woodland, 66 acres. 3 pigs.

Has.ıı.tras teneb Leuing 7 Aluuard de æccła S Petri.nec ab ea
poterant fepari.T.R.E.Valeb.L.folid.Modo.LX.folid.

Ogifus ten de Rog LAMORE.Suetth tenuit T.R.E.de æccła
Mucelenie.nec poterat ab ea fepari.7 geldb ꝑ.ı.hida 7 dim v træ.
7 eſt de.xx.hid de DRAITVNE.7 eſt Tainlande.Tra.ē.ı.caꝛ.ꝗ ibi
ē in dñio.7 vı.ſerui.7 x.ac ꝑti.7 vıı.ac filuæ.Valuit 7 ual.xx.fol.

Ipſe Rog ten EDMVNDESWORDE.Edric tenuit T.R.E.7 geldb
ꝑ una v træ.Tra.ē.vı.caꝛ.In dñio.ē.ı.caꝛ.7 ıı.ſerui.7 vı.uiłłi
7 ıx.bord cū.ııı.caꝛ.Ibi.vııı.ac ꝑti.7 xxx.ac filuæ minutæ.
Paſtura.ıı.leu lg.7 ıı.lat.Valet.xxv.folid.

Eileua ten de Ro.DONESCVBE.Lefmer tenuit T.R.E.7 geldb
ꝑ uno ferling.Tra.ē.ı.caꝛ.Ibi.ē.ı.bord cū dimid caꝛ.7 vı.ac
ꝑti.7 ııı.ac filuæ.7 vı.ac paſturæ.Valet.ıı.folid.

Ipſe Rog ten AISSEFORD.Aiulf tenuit T.R.E.7 geldb ꝑ dim
uirg.Tra.ē.ıı.caꝛ.Ibi.ı.bord 7 ı.ſeruus cū dim caꝛ.7 x.ac ꝑti.
7 x.ac paſturæ.7 xıı.ac filuæ minutæ.Valet.ııı.folid.

Ednod ten de Ro.AISSEFORDE.Edric tenuit T.R.E.7 geldb
ꝑ uno ferling.Tra.ē.ı.caꝛ.Ibi.ē.ı.bord cū dim caꝛ.7 ıı.ac
filuæ.7 ııı.ac ꝑti.7 x.ac paſturæ.Valet.xxx.denaꝛ.

Ipſe Ro.ten STOCHE.Ailhalle tenuit T.R.E.7 geldb ꝑ dim v træ.
Tra ē.ıı.caꝛ.Ibi.ē.ı.caꝛ cū.ı.ſeruo.7 ıı.bord.7 L.ac paſturæ.
7 LX.ac filuæ.Valuit 7 ual.v.folid.

Leofing and Alfward held these two lands from St. Peter's †
Church; they could not be separated from it before 1066. E 94 a
Now Roger holds from the King.
The value was 50s; now 60s.

55 Ogis holds MOORTOWN from Roger. Sweet held it before 1066 †
from Muchelney Church; he could not be separated from it.
It paid tax for 1 hide and ½ virgate of land. It is (part)
of the 20 hides of Drayton; it is thaneland. Land for 1 plough,
which is there, in lordship, & 3½ virgates.
    6 slaves who hold 1 virgate. 429
    Meadow, 10 acres; woodland, 7 acres. 1 cob; 7 pigs. b 2
    Roger holds from the King.
The value was and is 20s.

56 Roger holds 'ALMSWORTHY' himself. Edric held it before 1066;
it paid tax for 1 virgate of land. Land for 6 ploughs.
In lordship 1 plough; 2 slaves; ½ virgate. 430
    6 villagers and 9 smallholders with 3 ploughs & ½ virgate. a 1
    Meadow, 8 acres; underwood, 30 acres; pasture 2 leagues
      long and 2 wide. 1 cob; 6 cattle; 47 sheep; 27 goats.
Value 25s; when he acquired it, it was completely waste.

57 Aeleva holds DOWNSCOMBE from Roger. Leofmer held it before
1066; it paid tax for 1 furlong. Land for 1 plough.
    1 smallholder with ½ plough. E
    Meadow, 6 acres; woodland, 3 acres; pasture, 6 acres. 430
Value 2s; when he acquired it, it was waste. a 2

58 Roger holds EXFORD himself. Aiulf held it before 1066;
it paid tax for ½ virgate. Land for 2 ploughs. E 430
    1 smallholder and 1 slave with ½ plough. E a 3
    Meadow, 10 acres; pasture, 10 acres; underwood, 12 acres. 5 sheep.
Value 3s; when he acquired it, it was completely waste.

59 Ednoth holds EXFORD from Roger. Edric held it before 1066;
it paid tax for 1 furlong. Land for 1 plough. 430
    1 smallholder with ½ plough. E a 4
    Woodland, 2 acres; meadow, 3 acres; pasture, 10 acres. E
      4 cattle; 3 pigs; 40 sheep; 10 goats.
Value 30d; when he acquired it, 2s.

60 Roger holds STOKE (Pero) himself. Ailhilla(?) held it before 1066;
it paid tax for ½ virgate of land. Land for 2 ploughs. 1 plough L
there, with 1 slave; 430
    2 smallholders. b 1
    Pasture, 50 acres; woodland, 60 acres. 5 cattle; 7 pigs; 20 sheep; E
      20 goats.
The value was and is 5s.

Caſlo ten de Ro.*BAGELIE*.Ipſe tenuit T.R.E.7 geldb ℈p dim v̈ træ.
In dñio.ē.ɪ.car̃.7 ɪɪ.borđ hñt dim car̃.Ibi.ʟ.ãc paſturæ.7 xɪɪ.ãc
ſiluæ.Valuit.xɪɪ.den̄.Modo.xʟ.denar̃.

Ipſe Rog ten *CV̄BE*.Alric tenuit T.R.E.7 geldb ℈p una v̈ træ.Tra
ē.ɪ.car̃.Ibi.ē dim car̃ cū.ɪ.borđ.7 xvɪ.ãc paſturæ.7 xvɪɪɪ.ãc ſiluæ.

Ogiſus ten de Rog *ALRE*.Briſmar 7 Edmar tenuer̃ ∫ Valet.v.ſoɫ.
T.R.E.7 geldb ℈p dim hida.Tra.ē.ɪ.car̃ 7 dim.In dñio.ē.ɪ.car̃.cū.ɪ.
ſeruo.7 ɪ.uitto.7 ɪ.borđ q̃ hñt dim car̃.Ibi.ʟx.ãc paſturæ.Valet

Alric ten de Ro.*GILDENECOTE*.Eduin tenuit T.R.E. ∫ vɪɪɪ.ſoliđ.
7 geldb ℈p dim hida.Tra.ē.ɪ.car̃ 7 dim.Ibi.ē.ɪ.car̃ cū.ɪɪɪ.borđ.
7 vɪ.ãc p̃ti.7 ʟ.ãc paſturæ.7 xv.ãc ſiluæ.Valet.x.ſoliđ.

Witts ten de Ro.*HVNECOTE*.Aluric 7 Brictuin tenuer̃ T.R.E.
7 geldb ℈p dim hida 7 dim v̈ træ.Tra.ē.ɪɪ.car̃ 7 dim.Ibi ſt.ɪɪɪɪ.uitti
cū.ɪ.borđ 7 hñt.ɪɪ.car̃.Ibi.xvɪ.ãc paſturæ.Valet.xxɪɪ.ſoliđ.

Alric ten de Ro.*DOVRI*.Eddeue tenuit T.R.E.7 geldb ℈p una v̈ træ.
Tra.ē.ɪ.car̃.Ibi.ɪɪ.uitti cū.ɪ.borđ.Valet.vɪɪɪ.ſoliđ.

Witts ten de Ro.*HOLME*.Godric tenuit T.R.E.7 geldb ℈p una v̈ træ.
Tra.ē.ɪɪ.car̃ 7 dim.Ibi.ɪɪɪ.uitti 7 ɪɪɪɪ.borđ cū.ɪ.car̃ 7 dimiđ.7 dim
ãc p̃ti.7 xxx.ãc paſturæ.7 xɪɪɪɪ.ãc ſiluæ minutæ.Valet.vɪ.ſoliđ.

61 Kafli holds 'BAGLEY' from Roger. He held it himself before 1066; it paid tax for ½ virgate of land. In lordship 1 plough; 1 furlong.   E
     2 smallholders have ½ plough & 1 furlong.   430
     Pasture, 50 acres; woodland, 12 acres.   b 2
The value was 12d; now 40d.

62 Roger holds COMBE himself. Alric held it before 1066; it paid
tax for 1 virgate of land. Land for 1 plough. ½ plough there,   430
in lordship, & ½ virgate, with   b 3
     1 smallholder (who has) ½ virgate.   E
     Pasture, 16 acres; woodland, 18 acres. 1 pig; 8 sheep; 4 goats.
Value 5s; when he acquired it, as much.

63 Ogis holds ALLER from Roger. Brictmer and Edmer held it   E
before 1066; it paid tax for ½ hide. Land for 1½ ploughs.
In lordship 1 plough & 1½ virgates, with 1 slave and   430
     1 villager and 1 smallholder who have ½ plough & the rest of the land.   b 4
     Pasture, 60 acres. 1 cob.
Value 8s; when Roger acquired it, 5s.   E

64 Alric holds 'GILCOTT' from Roger. Edwin held it before 1066; it paid tax for ½ hide. Land for 1½ ploughs. 1 plough there, with   L
     3 smallholders.   431
     Meadow, 6 acres; pasture, 50 acres; woodland, 15 acres.   a 1
         2 cattle; 1 pig; 11 sheep; 11 goats.
Value 10s; when he acquired it, 3s.

65 William holds HOLNICOTE from Roger. Aelfric and Brictwin   E
held it before 1066; it paid tax for ½ hide and for ½ virgate
of land. Land for 2½ ploughs.   E
     4 villagers with 1 smallholder; they have 2 ploughs & hold the
       land from William.   431
     Pasture, 16 acres.   a 2
Value 22s; when Roger acquired it, as much.
    From the manor called Holnicote, which Roger of Courseulles holds, has been taken
away 1 furlong of land, which Odo son of Gamelin holds. Roger pays tax on it wrongly.

66 Alric holds DOVERHAY from Roger. Edeva held it before 1066; it paid tax for 1 virgate of land. Land for 1 plough.   431
     2 villagers with 1 smallholder.   a 3
Value 8s; when Roger acquired it, 10s (?).   E

67 William holds 'HOLNE' from Roger. Godric held it before 1066; it paid tax for 1 virgate of land. Land for 2½ ploughs.
In lordship ½ virgate.   431
     3 villagers and 4 smallholders with 1½ ploughs.   a 4
     Meadow, ½ acre; pasture, 30 acres; underwood, 14 acres.
Value 6s; when Roger acquired it, 30d.

Wilts teñ de Ro. *AISSEFORD* . Vluuiñ tenuit T.R.E.7 geldɓ ꝑ uno

ferling . Tra . ē . ı . car̃ . Ibi . ıı . borð cū dim car̃ . 7 ııı . ãc p̃ti . 7 x .

ãc pastur̃æ . Valuit 7 ual . xxx . denar̃ .

Ipfe Rog teñ *ESTONE* . Brictric tenuit T.R.E. Ibi . ē dim v̄ træ

Tra . ē . ıı . car̃ . fed uafta . ē .

Bertran teñ de Ro . *FIFHIDE* . Aldred tenuit T.R.E.7 geldɓ ꝑ . ı .

hida 7 dim . Tra . ē . ıı . car̃ . In dñio . ē . ı . car̃ . 7 ıı . ferui . 7 ıııı . borð .

Ibi . xv . ãc p̃ti . 7 xx . ãc filuæ . Valuit . xxx . fot . Modo . xl . folið .

Vluuard teñ de Ro . *ERNESHELE* . Liuing tenuit T.R.E.7 geldɓ

ꝑ dim hida . Tra . ē . ı . car̃ 7 dim . In dñio . ē . ı . car̃ . cū . ı . feruo . 7 ııı .

borð . Ibi . vııı . ãc p̃ti . 7 vııı . ãc pafturæ . Valet . xıı . folið .

Ogifus teñ de Ro . *SANFORD* . Aluuiñ tenuit T.R.E.7 geldɓ ꝑ . ıı .

hið . Tra . ē . vıı . car̃ . In dñio st . ıı . car̃ . 7 v . ferui . 7 xı . uilti 7 vı .

borð cū . ııı . car̃ . Ibi moliñ redð . vııı . den . 7 v . ãc p̃ti . 7 cc . ãc pa

fturæ . 7 xlvıı . ãc filuæ . Valuit . xx . fot . Modo . l . folið .

Alric teñ de Ro . *TORNE* . Tres taini tenuer̃ T.R.E.7 geldɓ ꝑ una

hida 7 ııı . v̄ træ . Tra . ē . v . car̃ . In dñio . ē . ı . car̃ . 7 ııı . ferui . 7 ıx .

uilti 7 v . borð cū . ııı . car̃ . Ibi moliñ redð . x . folið . 7 ıııı . ãc p̃ti .

7 xxx . ãc pafturæ . 7 vııı . ãc filuæ . Valuit . xx . folið . Modo . xl . fot .

Goisfrid teñ de . Ro . *ANIMERE* . Algar tenuit T.R.E.7 geldɓ pro

una hida . Tra . ē . ıııı . car̃ . In dñio . ē . ı . car̃ . 7 ıı . ferui . 7 ııı . uilti .

7 ııı . borð cū . ııı . car̃ . Ibi . lx . vııı . ãc filuæ . Valuit 7 ual . xl . fot .

68 William holds EXFORD from Roger. Wulfwin held it before 1066; it paid tax for 1 furlong. Land for 1 plough. In lordship 1 furlong (?).   E
    2 smallholders with ½ plough.   431
    Meadow, 3 acres; pasture, 10 acres.   b 1
The value was and is 30d.

69 Roger holds STONE himself. Brictric held it before 1066;   431
½ virgate of land. Land for 2 ploughs, but it is waste.   E b 2

70 Bertram holds FIVEHEAD from Roger. Aldred held it before 1066; it paid tax for 1½ hides. Land for 2 ploughs. In lordship 1 plough; 2 slaves; 1 hide & 1 virgate.   431
    4 smallholders who have 1 virgate.   b 3
    Meadow, 15 acres; woodland, 20 acres. 2 cattle; 15 pigs;
        40 sheep; 30 goats.
The value was 30s; now 40s.

71 Wulfward holds EARNSHILL from Roger. Leofing held it before 1066; it paid tax for ½ hide. Land for 1½ ploughs. In lordship 1 plough & 1½ virgates, with 1 slave;   E
    3 smallholders who hold ½ virgate.   431
    Meadow, 8 acres; pasture, 8 acres. 5 cows; 3 pigs; 10 sheep.   b 4
Value 12s; when Roger acquired it, 20s.

72 Ogis holds SAMPFORD (Arundel) from Roger. Alwin held it before 1066; it paid tax for 2 hides. Land for 7 ploughs. In lordship 2 ploughs; 5 slaves; 1 hide.   431
    11 villagers and 6 smallholders with 3 ploughs & 1 hide.   b 5
    A mill which pays 8d; meadow, 5 acres; pasture, 200 acres;
        woodland, 47 acres. 2 cobs; 11 cattle; 9 pigs; 120 sheep.
The value was 20s; now 50s.

73 Alric holds THORNE (St. Margaret) from Roger. Three thanes held   E
it before 1066; it paid tax for 1 hide and 3 virgates of land.   432
Land for 5 ploughs. In lordship 1 plough; 3 slaves; 3 virgates.   a 1
    9 villagers and 5 smallholders with 3 ploughs & 1 hide.
    A mill which pays 10s; meadow, 4 acres; pasture, 30 acres;
        woodland, 8 acres. 1 cob; 5 cattle; 7 pigs.
The value was 20s; now 40s.

  Geoffrey holds from Roger
74 ENMORE. Algar held it before 1066; it paid tax for 1 hide.
Land for 4 ploughs. In lordship 1 plough; 2 slaves; 1 virgate.   E
    3 villagers and 3 smallholders with 3 ploughs & 3 virgates.   432
    Woodland, 68 acres.   a 2
The value was and is 40s.

Goisfrid ten de Ro.*LECHESWRDE*.Orgar tenuit T.R.E.7 geldb
ꝓ una v̄ træ.Tra.ē.I.car̄.Hanc hn̄t ibi.II.uilti 7 II.borđ.Ibi molin̄
redđ.II.plūbas ferri.7 IIII.ac̄ filuæ ibi.Valuit 7 ual.XV.foliđ.

94 b

Goisfrid ten de Ro.*LECHESWFDE*.Adeſtan tenuit T.R.E.7 geldb
ꝓ una v̄ træ.Tra.ē.III.car̄.Ibi.IIII.uilti 7 IIII.borđ 7 II.ſerui hn̄t
II.car̄.Ibi molin̄ redđ.II.plūbas ferri.7 v.ac̄ p̄ti.7 xx.ac̄ filuæ.
Valuit 7 ual.XL.foliđ.

Goisfrid ten de Ro.*BLACHESHALE*.Leuric tenuit T.R.E.7 geldb
ꝓ una v̄ træ.Tra.ē.III.car̄.Ibi.III.uilti 7 III.borđ cū.I.ſeruo hn̄t
.II.car̄.Ibi.LX.ac̄ filuæ.Valuit.xx.fot.Modo.xxx.foliđ.

Robt ten de Ro.*CEDER*.Adulf tenuit T.R.E.7 geldb ꝓ.II.hiđ
7 una v̄ træ.Tra.ē.IIII.car̄.In dnīo ſt.II.car̄.cū.v.uilłis 7 v.borđ.
Ibi.xv.ac̄ p̄ti.Valuit.XL.foliđ.Modo.xxx.foliđ.

Robt ten de Ro.*SIPEHAM*.Alduin tenuit T.R.E.7 geldb ꝓ.IIII.
hiđ.Tra.ē.VI.car̄.In dnīo ſt.II.car̄.7 II.uilłi 7 VII.borđ cū.I.
car̄.Ibi.III.ac̄ p̄ti.7 cc.ac̄ paſturæ.7 x.ac̄ filuæ minutæ.
Valuit.XL.foliđ.Modo.xxx.foliđ.

Ipfe Rog ten dim hidā in *PANTESHEDE*.7 ibi hт dim car̄.cū
uno feruo.Ibi dim ac̄ p̄ti.Valuit 7 ual.x.foliđ.

Goisfrid ten de Ro.*ACHE*.Dòmno tenuit T.R.E.7 geldb ꝓ.III.hiđ.
7 dimiđ.Tra.ē.VI.car̄.In dnīo ſt.II.car̄.7 IIII.ſerui.7 XIIII.uilłi.
7 XIIII.borđ hn̄t.III.car̄ 7 dim.Ibi molin̄ redđ.IIII.fot.7 XVII.
ac̄ p̄ti.7 xv.ac̄ paſturæ.7 x.ac̄ filuæ.In Miluertone una dom
redđ.xi.denar̄.Totū ual.IIII.lib.Q̄do recep̄.L.fot ualb.

75 LEXWORTHY.   Ordgar held it before 1066; it paid tax for 1
virgate of land. Land for 1 plough. In lordship ½ virgate.

    2 villagers and 2 smallholders have it (plough) there & ½ virgate.
A mill which pays 2 blooms of iron; woodland, 4 acres.
The value was and is 15s.

432

a 3

76 LEXWORTHY.   Athelstan held it before 1066; it paid tax for 1
virgate of land. Land for 3 ploughs. In lordship ½ virgate.

    4 villagers, 4 smallholders and 2 slaves have 2 ploughs
       & ½ virgate.
A mill which pays 2 blooms of iron; meadow, 5 acres;
    woodland, 20 acres.
The value was and is 40s.

94 b

432

b 1

77 BLAXHOLD.   Leofric held it before 1066; it paid tax for 1 virgate
of land. Land for 3 ploughs. In lordship ½ virgate.

    3 villagers and 3 smallholders with 1 slave have 2 ploughs
      & ½ virgate.
Woodland, 60 acres.
The value was 20s; now 30s;

432

b 2

78 Robert holds CHEDDAR from Roger. Adolf held it before 1066;
it paid tax for 2 hides and 1 virgate of land. Land for 4 ploughs.
In lordship 2 ploughs, with

    5 villagers and 5 smallholders.
    Meadow, 15 acres. 1 cow; 16 pigs; 20 sheep.
The value was 40s; now 30s.

E

432

b 3

79 Robert holds SHIPHAM from Roger. Aldwin held it before 1066;
it paid tax for 4 hides. Land for 6 ploughs. In lordship 2 ploughs;
3 hides & 3 virgates.

    2 villagers and 7 smallholders with 1 plough & 1 virgate.
    Meadow, 3 acres; pasture, 200 acres; underwood, 10 acres.
      1 cow; 36 sheep.
The value was 40s; now 30s.

433

a 1

80 Roger holds ½ hide in 'PONTESIDE' himself; he has ½ plough,
with 1 slave.

    Meadow, ½ acre.
The value was and is 10s.
      Godric held it in 1066.

433

a 2

81 Geoffrey of Vautortes holds OAKE from Roger. Dunn held it before
1066; it paid tax for 3½ hides. Land for 6 ploughs. In lordship
2 ploughs; 4 slaves; 1 hide.

    14 villagers and 14 smallholders have 3½ ploughs & 2½ hides.
    A mill which pays 4s; meadow, 17 acres; pasture, 15 acres;
      woodland, 10 acres. In Milverton 1 house which pays 11d.
      14 pigs; 62 sheep.
Value of the whole £4; when he acquired it the value was 50s.

433

a 3

Wiłłs teñ de . Ro . *TALHAM* . Vluuin tenuit T.R.E.7 geldb ᵽ.ıı.
hiđ . Tra . ē . vı . cař . In dñio sī . ıı . cař . cū . ı . feruo.7 xı . uiłłi
7 ıııı . borđ hñt . ıııı . cař . Ibi . x . ač p̃ti .7 xv . ač filuæ .7 lx . ač
paftur æ . Valuit 7 uał . l . foliđ .

Wiłłs teñ de Ro . *HOLEFORD* . Adeluualđ tenuit T.R.E.7 geldb
ᵽ dimiđ hida . Tra . ē . ı . cař . Ibi . ıı ; borđ . 7 ıı . ferui .7 una ač
p̃ti .7 x . ač pafturæ .7 una ač filuæ . Valet . xvııı . foliđ .

Alric teñ de Ro . *HOLEFORDE* . Aluuard tenuit T.R.E.7 geldb
ᵽ dimiđ v træ . Tra . ē dimiđ cař . q̃ ibi . ē cū . ı . uiłło .7 redđ . ııı . foliđ .

Norman teñ de . Ro . *LITELTONE* . Almar 7 Osbñ 7 Godricus
ᵽ . ııı . maneř tenueř T.R.E.7 geldb ᵽ . ııı . hiđ . Tra . ē . ıııı . cař .
In dñio sī . ıı . cař .7 ııı . ferui .7 ıııı . uiłłi .7 ııı . borđ cū . ı . cař .
Ibi . xl . ač p̃ti .7 totiđ ač filuæ minutæ . Valuit 7 uał . xl . foliđ .

Robt teñ de . Ro . *STALREWICHE* . Smeuuin tenuit T.R.E.7 geldb
ᵽ . ı . hida 7 dim . Tra . ē . ııı . cař . In dñio . ē . ı . cař .7 ıı . uiłłi 7 vıı .
borđ . Ibi . vı . ač p̃ti .7 ıııı . ač filuæ . Valuit . l . fot . Modo . xx . fot .

Almar teñ de Ro . *ECFERDINTONE* . Aluric tenuit T.R.E.7 geldb ′
ᵽ . ı . hida . Tra . ē . ıııı . cař . Ibi . vı . uiłłi 7 ııı . borđ cū . ııı . cař .7 xııı .
cofcez . Ibi . vı . ač p̃ti .7 lx . ač filuæ . Valuit . lx . fot . Modo . xl . fot .

Almar teñ de Ro . *FERLEGE* . Smeuuin tenuit T.R.E.7 geldb
ᵽ dim hida . Ibi . ı . uiłłs 7 ııı , borđ 7 ıı . cotař hñt . ı . cař . Ibi . ııı .
ač p̃ti .7 vı . ač filuæ . Valuit . xx . fot . Modo . x . foliđ .

82 William son of Robert holds TOLLAND from Roger. Wulfwin held it before 1066; it paid tax for 2 hides. Land for 6 ploughs. In lordship 2 ploughs & ½ hide and 1 furlong, with 1 slave.
    11 villagers and 4 smallholders have 4 ploughs & 1½ hides, less 1 furlong.
    Meadow, 10 acres; woodland, 15 acres; pasture, 60 acres.
    2 cows; 14 pigs; 50 sheep.
The value was and is 50s.

433
a 4

83 William holds HOLFORD from Roger. Aethelwold held it before 1066; it paid tax for ½ hide. Land for 1 plough.
    2 smallholders and 2 slaves.
    Meadow, 1 acre; pasture, 10 acres; woodland, 1 acre.
Value 18s; when Roger acquired it, 10s.

433
b 1
E

84 Alric holds HOLFORD from Roger. Alfward held it before 1066; it paid tax for ½ virgate of land. Land for ½ plough, which is there, with
    1 villager.
It pays 3s; when Roger acquired it, as much.

433
b 2

85 Norman holds LITTLETON from Roger. Aelmer, Osbern and Godric D held it as 3 manors before 1066; it paid tax for 3 hides.
Land for 4 ploughs. In lordship 2 ploughs; 3 slaves;
    4 villagers and 3 smallholders with 1 plough.
    Meadow, 40 acres; underwood, as many acres.
The value was and is 40s.

433
b 3
E

86 Robert holds STANDERWICK from Roger. Smewin held it before 1066; it paid tax for 1½ hides. Land for 3 ploughs. In lordship 1 plough; 1 hide.
    2 villagers and 7 smallholders (have) ½ hide.
    Meadow, 6 acres; woodland, 4 acres.
The value was 50s; now 20s.

434
a 1

87 Aelmer holds FAIROAK from Roger. Aelfric held it before 1066; it paid tax for 1 hide. Land for 4 ploughs. In lordship 1 virgate.
    6 villagers and 3 smallholders with 3 ploughs & 3 virgates.
    13 Cottagers.
    Meadow, 6 acres; woodland, 60 acres.
The value was 60s; now 40s.

434
E a 2

88 Aelmer holds FARLEIGH (Hungerford) from Roger. Smewin held it before 1066; it paid tax for ½ hide. In lordship 1½ virgates.
    1 villager, 3 smallholders and 2 cottagers have 1 plough & ½ virgate.
    Meadow, 3 acres; woodland, 6 acres. 3 pigs.
The value was 20s; now 10s.

434
a 3

Rob̃ ten de Ro.*WITOCHESMEDE*.Duo taini tenuer̃ T.R.E.
7 geldb̃ ꝑ.i.hida.T̃ra.ẽ.ii.car̃.q̃ ibi st̃ in dñio.cū.i.feruo.7 vi.
bord̃.Ibi.iii.ãc p̃ti.7 xxx.ãc filuæ.Valuit 7 ual.iii.lib̃.

Wilts ten̄ de.Ro.*WITEHA*.Erlebald tenuit T.R.E.7 geldb̃
ꝑ.ii.hid̃.T̃ra.ẽ.iii.car̃.In dñio.ẽ.i.car̃.7,ii.ferui.7 iiii.uilti
7 iii.bord̃ 7 iiii.cofcez cū.ii.car̃.Ibi.xx.ãc p̃ti.7 xxx.ãc pafturæ.
Silua.i.q̂ɀ lg̃.7 dim q̂ɀ lat.Valuit.xx.folid.Modo.xxx.fol.
H̃ t̃ra T.R.E.jaceb̃ in *BRIWEHA* maner̃ Wilti de moion.nec
poterat inde feparari.

Erneis ten̄ de Ro.*BRIWETONE*.Goduin tenuit T.R.E.7 geldb̃
ꝑ.i.hida 7 una v̄ t̃ræ.T̃ra.ẽ.ii.car̃.Ibi.ẽ.i.car̃ cū.iii.bord̃.
7 molin̄ redd̃.xxx.den.Valuit 7 ual.xxx.folid.

Norman ten̄ de Ro.*BERTONE*.Aleftan tenuit T.R.E.7 geldb̃
ꝑ.i.hida 7 dim.T̃ra.ẽ.ii.car̃.In dñio.ẽ.i.car̃.7 ii.uilti 7 iiii.
bord̃ cū.i.car̃.Ibi molin̄ redd̃.v.folid̃.7 xxiiii.ãc p̃ti.7 totid̃
ãc pafturæ.Valuit.xl.folid̃.Modo.xxx.folid̃.   V̄ tenet.
In hoc ⓜ jacuit *CHINTONE* T.R.E.Ibi.ẽ.i.hida.Comes morit̃

Ipfe Rog̃ ten̄ *LIMINTONE*.Saulf tenuit T.R.E.7 geldb̃ ꝑ.vii.
hid̃.T̃ra.ẽ.viii.car̃.In dñio st̃.iii.car̃.7 iii.ferui.7 un̄ uilts
7 xiii.bord̃ cū.i.car̃.Ibi molin̄ redd̃.xx.folid̃.7 lx.ãc p̃ti.
Paftura.xii.q̂ɀ lg̃.7 ii.q̂ɀ lat.Valuit 7 ual.vii.lib̃.

Vitalis ten̄ de Ro.*ESSENTONE*.Goduin tenuit T.R.E.7 geldb̃
ꝑ.iii.hid̃.T̃ra.ẽ.iii.car̃.In dñio.ẽ.i.car̃.cū.i.feruo.7 ii.uilti
7 iiii.bord̃ cū.i.car̃.Ibi.xliii.ãc p̃ti.7 xx.ãc pafturæ.
Valuit 7 ual.xl.folid̃.

89 Robert Gernon holds WHITE OX MEAD from Roger. Two thanes   E
held it before 1066; it paid tax for 1 hide. Land for 2 ploughs,
which are there, in lordship, & ½ hide & ½ virgate, with 1 slave;   434
   6 smallholders (who have) 1½ virgates.   a 4
   Meadow, 3 acres; woodland, 30 acres. 1 cob; 1 ass; 12 pigs; 120 sheep.
The value was and is £3.

90 William holds WITHAM (Friary) from Roger. Erlebald held it
before 1066; it paid tax for 2 hides. Land for 3 ploughs.   434
In lordship 1 plough; 2 slaves; 6 virgates.   b 1
   4 villagers, 3 smallholders and 4 Cottagers with 2 ploughs
     & 1 hide.
   Meadow, 20 acres; pasture, 30 acres; woodland 1 furlong
     long and ½ furlong wide. 5 cattle.
The value was 20s; now 30s.
   Before 1066 this land lay in (the lands of) Brewham, a manor
of William of Mohun's; it could not be separated from it.   E

91 Erneis holds BRUTON from Roger. Godwin held it before 1066;
it paid tax for 1 hide and 1 virgate of land. Land for 2 ploughs.
1 plough there, with   E
   3 smallholders.   434
   A mill which pays 30d.   b 2
The value was and is 30s.

92 Norman holds BARTON (St. David) from Roger. Alstan held it
before 1066; it paid tax for 1½ hides. Land for 2 ploughs.
In lordship 1 plough; 1 hide.   434
   2 villagers and 4 smallholders with 1 plough & ½ hide.   b 3
   A mill which pays 5s; meadow, 24 acres; pasture, as many
     acres. 18 pigs.
The value was 40s; now 30s.
   Keinton (Mandeville) lay in this manor before 1066. 1 hide.   E
The Count of Mortain holds it.

93 Roger holds LIMINGTON himself. Saewulf held it before 1066;
it paid tax for 7 hides. Land for 8 ploughs. In lordship 3 ploughs;
3 slaves; 4 hides & 1 virgate.   435
   1 villager and 13 smallholders with 1 plough & 3 hides, less 1 virgate.   a 1
   A mill which pays 20s; meadow, 60 acres; pasture 12 furlongs
     long and 2 furlongs wide. 1 cob; 3 cows, 20 pigs; 80 sheep.
The value was and is £7.

94 Vitalis holds ASHINGTON from Roger. Godwin held it before 1066;
it paid tax for 3 hides. Land for 3 ploughs. In lordship 1 plough,
with 1 slave;   435
   2 villagers and 4 smallholders with 1 plough.   a 2
   Meadow, 43 acres; pasture, 20 acres. 5 pigs; 20 sheep.
The value was and is 40s.

Vitalis ten de.Ro.*Soche*.Tochi tenuit T.R.E.7 geldb ꝑ hida
7 dim.Tra.ē.II.car.In dnio.ē.I.car.7 III.bord.7 x.ac p̄ti.
7 xv.ac paſturæ.Valuit 7 ual.xv.ſolid.

Herbt ten de Ro.*Brunetone*.Seulf tenuit T.R.E.7 geldb
ꝑ.III.hid.Tra.ē.IIII.car.In dnio ſt.II.car.7 II.ſerui.7 II.uitti
7 VIII.bord cū.II.car.Ibi.xIII.ac p̄ti.7 IIII.ac ſiluæ minutæ.
Valuit.xL.ſolid.Modo.Lx.ſolid.

Ipſe Rog ten dimid hidā q̄ ual.x.ſolid.h̄ ꝑtineb T.R.E
in Barintone c͡o regis.

✠ Dodeman 7 Warmund ten de Ro.*Sytone*.Duo taini te
nuer T.R.E.de æccła Adelingi.7 n̄ poteraꝑ ab ea ſeparari.
7 geldb ꝑ.II.hid.Tra.III.car.In dnio ſt.III.car.cū.I.ſeruo.
7 IIII.uitti 7 III.bord hn̄t.I.car.Ibi.vIII.ac p̄ti.Val.L.ſolid.

.XXII.   TERRA ROGERIJ ARVNDEL.

Rogerivs Arundel ten de rege *Halse*.Ailmar tenuit
T.R.E.7 geldb ꝑ.IIII.hid.Tra.ē.vII.car.In dnio ſt.II.car.
7 III.ſerui.7 xvI.uitti 7 vII.bord cū.III.car 7 dim.Ibi moliñ
redd.x.ſolid.7 vIII.ac p̄ti.7 xII.ac ſiluæ.7 xx.ac paſturæ.
Q̄do recep ualb ; c.ſolid.modo.vI.lib.

Ipſe Rog ten *Hiwis*.Ailric tenuit T.R.E.7 geldb ꝑ.II.hid
7 III.v̄ træ.Tra.ē.xII.car.In dnio ſt.II.car.7 v.ſerui.7 xx.
uitti 7 vI.bord cū.vI.car.Ibi moliñ redd.xII.denar.7 xx.
ac p̄ti.7 Lx.ac ſiluæ.Paſtura.I.leū lḡ.7 dim leū lat.
Valb qdo recep.vI.lib.Modo.vII.lib.

Ipſe Rog ten *Wislagetone*.Almar tenuit T.R.E.7 geldb
ꝑ.x.hid.Tra.ē.x.car.In dnio.ē.I.car.7 vII.ſerui.7 Ix.uitti
7 xxx.bord cū.vII.car.7 vII.porcarij.redd.xL.porcos.

95 Vitalis holds (Mudford) SOCK from Roger. Toki held it before
1066; it paid tax for 1½ hides. Land for 2 ploughs.
In lordship 1 plough; [1] hide.
   3 smallholders (have) the rest of the land.
     Meadow, 10 acres; pasture, 15 acres. 15 sheep; 4 pigs.
The value was and is 15s.

E 94 c

E

435

a 3

96 Herbert holds BRYMPTON from Roger. Saewulf held it before 1066;
it paid tax for 3 hides. Land for 4 ploughs. In lordship 2 ploughs;
2 slaves; 1½ hides.
   2 villagers and 8 smallholders with 2 ploughs & 1½ hides.
     Meadow, 13 acres; underwood, 4 acres. 1 cob; 6 pigs; 60 sheep.
The value was 40s; now 60s.

435

a 4

97 Roger holds ½ hide himself; value 10s. Before 1066 it belonged
to Barrington, a manor of the King's.

435

E b 1

†98 Dodman and Warmund hold (Long) SUTTON from Roger. Two
thanes held it before 1066 from Athelney Church; they could
not be separated from it. It paid tax for 2 hides. Land for 3
ploughs. In lordship 3 ploughs, with 1 slave.
   4 villagers and 3 smallholders have 1 plough.
     Meadow, 8 acres.
Value 50s.

D

435

E b 2

E

22   LAND OF ROGER ARUNDEL

1 Roger Arundel holds HALSE from the King. Aelmer held it
before 1066; it paid tax for 4 hides. Land for 7 ploughs.
In lordship 2 ploughs; 3 slaves; 1 hide.
   16 villagers and 7 smallholders with 3½ ploughs & 3 hides.
   A mill which pays 10s; meadow, 8 acres; woodland, 12 acres;
     pasture, 20 acres. 1 cow; 7 pigs; 40 sheep.
Value when he acquired it, 100s; now £6.
   This land is (part) of Taunton Hundred.

442

b 2

E

2 Roger holds HUISH (Champflower) himself. Alric held it before
1066; it paid tax for 2 hides and 3 virgates of land. Land for
12 ploughs. In lordship 2 ploughs; 5 slaves; ½ hide & 1 furlong.
   20 villagers and 6 smallholders with 6 ploughs & 2 hides & 1 furlong.
   A mill which pays 12d; meadow, 20 acres; woodland, 60 acres;
     pasture 1 league long and ½ league wide. 3 cattle; 100 sheep.
Value when he acquired it, £6; now £7.

442

b 3

3 Roger holds WHITELACKINGTON himself. Aelmer held it before
1066; it paid tax for 10 hides. Land for 10 ploughs. In lordship
1 plough; 7 slaves; 5 hides & 1 virgate.
   9 villagers and 30 smallholders with 7 ploughs & 4 hides & 3 virgates.
     7 pigmen who pay 40 pigs.

443

E a 1

E

Ibi moliñ redđ.xv. ſoliđ.7 L.aͨ p̃ti.7 LXI.aͨ paſturæ.7 cc.7 XL.

aͨ ſiluæ.Valƀ qdo recep̃.xii.liƀ.Modo.ix.liƀ.

Ricard⁹ teñ de.Ro. DESTONE. Aluui tenuit T.R.E.7 geldƀ ,p.ii.

hiđ 7.iiii.v̕ træ.Tra.ē.iiii.caͬ.In dñio.ē.i.caͬ.7 iiii.ſerui.7 iiii.

uilli.7 v.borđ 7 iiii.cotar.cū.iii.caͬ.Ibi.xv.aͨ p̃ti.7 xx.aͨ

paſturæ.7 xx.aͨ ſiluæ.Valuit 7 ual.XL.ſoliđ.

Radulf⁹ teñ de Rog̕ SANFORD. Ailuuard tenuit T.R.E.7 geldƀ

,p.i.hida.7 dim̕ v̕ træ.7 uno ferling.Tra.ē.iii.caͬ.In dñio

ē una caͬ.7 iii.ſerui.7 ii.uilli 7 iiii.borđ cū.i.caͬ.7 xii.aͨ p̃ti.

Valuit 7 ual.xxx.ſoliđ.

Radulf⁹ teñ de.Ro.PERI. Vluric tenuit T.R.E.7 geldƀ ,p dim̕

hida.Tra.ē.i.caͬ.q̄ ibi.ē in dñio.7 viii.aͨ p̃ti.Valuit 7 ual.x.ſol.

Radulf⁹ teñ de Ro.unā v̕ træ in NEWETONE.Briſtuuold

tenuit T.R.E.Tra.ē dim̕ caͬ.Ibi.i.aͨ p̃ti.7 ii.aͨ ſiluæ.Val

Hugo teñ de Ro.FITINTONE. Ailuuard tenuit T.R.E.ſ̷ v.ſol.

7 geldƀ ,p.iiii.hiđ.Tra.ē.vi.caͬ.In dñio ſt.ii.caͬ.7 ii.ſerui.

7 vi.uilli.7 v.borđ cū.iii.çaͬ.Ibi.ii.molini redđ.ii.ſol.7 xxi.

aͨ p̃ti.7 q̃t xx.aͨ paſturæ.7 XLiii.aͨ moræ.7 XL.ii.aͨ ſiluæ.

Valuit 7 ual.iiii.liƀ.

Hugo teñ de Ro.TOCHESWELLE. Eſtan tenuit T.R.E.7 geldƀ

,p una v̕ træ.Tra.ē dim̕ caͬ.Ibi.ii.uilli 7 iii.borđ hñt.i.caͬ.

Ibi.cXL.aͨ ſiluæ.7 XL.i.aͨ moræ.7 XL.aͨ paſturæ.

Valƀ qdo recep̃.xx.ſoliđ.Modo.xii.ſoliđ 7 vi.denaͬ.

A mill which pays 15s; meadow, 50 acres; pasture, 61 acres;
woodland, 240 acres. 4 cattle; 9 pigs; 44 sheep.
Value when he acquired it, £12; now £9.

4 Richard holds DURSTON from Roger. Alfwy held it before 1066;
it paid tax for 2 hides and 3 virgates of land. Land for 4 ploughs.
In lordship 1 plough; 4 slaves; 1 hide & 1½ virgates.
    4 villagers, 5 smallholders and 4 cottagers with 3 ploughs &
    the rest of the land.
    Meadow, 15 acres; pasture, 20 acres; woodland, 20 acres. 7 cattle.
The value was and is 40s.

441
a 1

5 Ralph holds SANDFORD from Roger. Alfward held it before 1066;
it paid tax for 1 hide, ½ virgate of land and 1 furlong.
Land for 3 ploughs. In lordship 1 plough; 3 slaves; 3 virgates.
    2 villagers and 4 smallholders with 1 plough & the rest of the land.
    Meadow, 12 acres. 11 cattle; 23 pigs.
The value was and is 30s.
    Two thanes held ½ virgate of this manor; they could not be separated from
the said manor.

441
a 2

6 Ralph holds PERRY from Roger. Wulfric held it before 1066;
it paid tax for ½ hide. Land for 1 plough, which is there,
in lordship.
    Meadow, 8 acres. 20 sheep.
The value was and is 10s.

441
a 3

7 Ralph holds 1 virgate of land in NEWTON from Roger. Brictwold
held it before 1066. Land for ½ plough.
    Meadow, 1 acre; woodland, 2 acres.
Value 5s; when he acquired it, as much.

441
a 4

8 Hugh holds FIDDINGTON from Roger. Alfward held it before 1066;
it paid tax for 4 hides. Land for 6 ploughs. In lordship 2 ploughs;
2 slaves; 3 hides.
    6 villagers and 5 smallholders with 3 ploughs & 1 hide.
    2 mills which pay 2s; meadow, 21 acres; pasture, 80 acres;
    moor, 43 acres; woodland, 42 acres. 12 cattle; 11 pigs; 60 sheep;
    14 goats.
The value was and is £4.

441
b 1

E

9 Hugh holds TUXWELL from Roger. Estan held it before 1066;
it paid tax for 1 virgate of land. Land for ½ plough.
In lordship 1 furlong.
    2 villagers and 3 smallholders have 1 plough & the rest of the land.
    Woodland, 140 acres; moor, 41 acres; pasture, 40 acres.
Value when he acquired it, 20s; now 12s 6d.

441
b 2

Odo ten de Ro. *CVDEWORDE*. Tres taini tenuer T.R.E.7 geldb
p.III.hid 7 dim.Tra.e.IIII.car.In dnio.e.I.car.7 II.ferui.
7 IIII.uilli 7 II.bord cu dimid car.Ibi.IIII.ac pti.Paftura
VIII.qz lg.7 II.qz lat.Valuit.XL.fol.Modo.XXX.folid.

Robt ten de.Ro.*SCHELIGATE*.Goda tenuit T.R.E.7 geldb p.I.hida
7 una v træ.Tra.e.IIII.car.In dnio st.II.car.7 v.ferui.7 v.uilli
7 II.bord cu dimid car.Ibi molin redd.x.den.7 II.ac pti.7 LX.
ac filuæ.Paftura.IIII.qz lg.7 una qz lat.Valet.XXX.folid.

Ide ten de Ro.*MILDETVNE*.Dunno tenuit T.R.E.7 geldb p.I.hida.
uno ferling min.Tra.e.III.car.In dnio.e.I.car.7 II.ferui.7 III.
uilli 7 I.bord cu.I.car.Ibi.II.ac pti.7 v.ac filuæ.Paftura.III.qz
lg.7 una qz lat.Valuit.XXX.folid.Modo.xx.folid.

Robt ten de Ro.*RADINGETVNE*.Duo taini teneb T.R.E.7 geldb

94 d

p.II.hid.Tra.e.VIII.car.In dnio st.II.car.7 III ferui.7 v.uilli.7 v.bord
cu.IIII.car.Ibi molin ad aula moleS.7 III.ac pti.7 VI.ac filuæ.
Paftura.IIII.qz lg.7 III.qz lat.Valuit 7 ual.XXX.folid.

Drogo ten de Ro.*TIMBRECVBE*.Aluerd tenuit T.R.E.7 geldb
p una hida 7 dim.Tra.e.VIII.car.In dnio.e.I.car.7 II.ferui.7 III.
uilli 7 VIII.bord cu.I.car.Ibi.XI.ac pti.7 CL.ac pafturæ.7 LXI.
ac filuæ.Valb qdo recep.c.folid.Modo.XL.folid.

Huic M addit.e un ferling.Algar tenuit T.R.E.Tra.e.I.car.Ibi
e dim car cu.II.bord.7 VIII.ac pafturæ.7 IIII.ac filuæ.Val.v.folid.

10 Odo holds CUDWORTH from Roger. Three thanes held it before   E
1066; it paid tax for 3½ hides. Land for 4 ploughs. In lordship 1
plough; 2 slaves; 2½ hides.   441
    4 villagers and 2 smallholders with ½ plough & 1 hide.   b 3
    Meadow, 4 acres; pasture 8 furlongs long and 2 furlongs wide.
        2 cattle; 12 pigs; 60 sheep.
The value was 40s; now 30s.

11 Robert of *Gatemore* holds SKILGATE from Roger. Goda held
it before 1066; it paid tax for 1 hide and 1 virgate of land.   442
Land for 4 ploughs. In lordship 2 ploughs; 5 slaves; 3 virgates. a 1
    5 villagers and 2 smallholders with ½ plough & ½ hide.   E
    A mill which pays 10d; meadow, 2 acres; woodland, 60 acres;
        pasture 4 furlongs long and 1 furlong wide. 10 cattle; 150 sheep.
Value 30s; when Roger acquired it, 40s.

12 He also holds MILTON from Roger. Dunn held it before 1066;
it paid tax for 1 hide, less 1 furlong. Land for 3 ploughs.
In lordship 1 plough; 2 slaves; 3 virgates, less 1 furlong.   442
    3 villagers and 1 smallholder with 1 plough & 1 virgate.   a 2
    Meadow, 2 acres; woodland, 5 acres; pasture 3 furlongs
        long and 1 furlong wide. 3 cattle; 3 pigs; 30 sheep; 20 goats.
The value was 30s; now 20s.

13 Robert holds RADDINGTON from Roger. Two thanes held it   E
before 1066; it paid tax for 2 hides. Land for 8 ploughs.   94 d
In lordship 2 ploughs; 3 slaves; 1½ hides & ½ virgate.   E
    5 villagers and 5 smallholders with 4 ploughs & ½ hide & ½ virgate. 442
    A mill which grinds for the hall; meadow, 3 acres; woodland,   a 3
        6 acres; pasture 4 furlongs long and 3 furlongs wide.
        4 cattle; 9 pigs; 48 sheep; 5 goats.
The value was and is 30s.

14 Drogo holds TIMBERSCOMBE from Roger. Alfward held it before
1066; it paid tax for 1½ hides. Land for 8 ploughs. In lordship 1
plough; 2 slaves; 3 virgates.   442
    3 villagers and 8 smallholders with 1 plough & 3 virgates.   b 1
    Meadow, 11 acres; pasture, 150 acres; woodland, 61 acres.
        30 sheep; 10 goats.
Value when he acquired it, 100s; now 40s.
    1 furlong has been added to this manor. Algar held it   E
before 1066. Land for 1 plough. ½ plough there, in lordship, with
    2 smallholders.
    Pasture, 8 acres; woodland, 4 acres.
Value 5s; when he acquired it, 6s.

Witts ten de Ro. *CHEDESFORD*. Ofmund Stramun tenuit T.R.E.
7 geldb p. II. hid. Tra. e. VII. car. In dnio st. II. car. 7 III. ferui. 7 v.
uitti. 7 VI. bord cu. III. car 7 dim. Ibi molin redd. VII. fot. 7 III. ac
pti. 7 x. ac pafturæ. 7 XII. ac filuæ. Valuit. XL. fot. Modo. LX. fot.

Witts ten de Ro. una v træ in *SIDEHA*. Cheping tenuit T.R.E.
Tra. e. I. car. Ibi. XV. ac pafturæ. Valet. XV. denar.

Wido ten de Ro. *HASEWELLE*. Aluuard tenuit T.R.E. 7 geldb
p. I. hida. Tra. e. II. car. In dnio. e. I. car. 7 II. ferui. 7 II. uitti. 7 III. bord
cu. I. car. Ibi. XIIII. ac filuæ. Valet. XXV. folid.

Robt ten de Ro. *CARI*. Duo taini tenuer T.R.E. 7 geldb p. I. hida.
uno ferling min. Tra. e. I. car. q ibi. e in dnio. cu. IIII. cotar. Ibi
xx. ac pti. Valuit 7 uat. xx. folid.

Ipfe Rog ten *CERLETVNE*. Aluerd tenuit T.R.E. 7 geldb p. III. hid.
Tra. e. VI. car. In dnio. e. I. car. 7 IIII. ferui. 7 III. uitti 7 IX. bord. cu. III.
car. Ibi. XXX. ac pti. 7 II. ac filuæ. Valuit. VI. lib. Modo. c. folid.

Ipfe Rog ten *AIXE*. Ailric tenuit T.R.E. 7 geldb p. II. hid. Tra. e. IIII.
car. In dnio. e. I. car. 7 III. ferui. 7 v. uitti. 7 v. bord cu. II. car. Ibi. VIII.
ac pti. 7 x. ac filuæ. Paftura. II. q̄ʒ lḡ. 7 una q̄ʒ lat. Valet. xx. fot.

15 William holds KITTISFORD from Roger. Osmund Stramin held it
before 1066; it paid tax for 2 hides. Land for 7 ploughs.
In lordship 2 ploughs; 3 slaves; 1 hide.   443
    5 villagers and 6 smallholders with 3½ ploughs & 1 hide.   a 2
A mill which pays 7s; meadow, 3 acres; pasture, 10 acres;
    woodland, 12 acres. 1 cob; 16 pigs; 50 sheep.
The value was 40s; now 60s.

16 William holds 1 virgate of land in SYDENHAM from Roger.
Cheping held it before 1066. Land for 1 plough.   443
    Pasture, 15 acres.   a 3
Value 15d; when he acquired it, 5d.

17 Guy holds HALSWELL from Roger. Alfward held it before 1066;
it paid tax for 1 hide. Land for 2 ploughs. In lordship 1
plough; 2 slaves; ½ hide & ½ virgate.   443
    2 villagers and 3 smallholders with 1 plough & the rest of the land. a 4
    Woodland, 14 acres. 2 cattle; 10 sheep.   E
Value 25s; when he acquired it, 17s 6d.

18 Robert holds CARY (Fitzpaine) from Roger. Two thanes held it   E
before 1066; it paid tax for 1 hide, less 1 furlong.
Land for 1 plough, which is there, in lordship, with   443
    4 cottagers.   b 1
Meadow, 20 acres. 10 cattle; 9 pigs.
The value was and is 20s.

  Roger himself holds
19 CHARLTON (Mackrell). Alfward held it before 1066; it paid
tax for 3 hides. Land for 6 ploughs. In lordship 1 plough;
4 slaves; ½ hide.   443
    3 villagers and 9 smallholders with 3 ploughs & 2½ hides.   b 2
    Meadow, 30 acres; woodland, 2 acres. 1 cob; 14 pigs; 15 sheep. E
The value was £6; now 100s.

    ½ hide of land has been added to Roger Arundel's manor called Charlton   516
(Mackrell), which a thane held jointly in 1066. Warmund held it from Roger and   b 4
still vouches him to warranty, but Roger has failed him entirely in this, from the   E
day on which King William made him put Warmund in possession again of this land.

20 ASH (Priors). Alric held it before 1066; it paid tax for 2
hides. Land for 4 ploughs. In lordship 1 plough; 3 slaves;
1½ hides, less 1 furlong.   443
    5 villagers and 5 smallholders with 2 ploughs & ½ hide & 1 furlong. b 3
    Meadow, 8 acres; woodland, 10 acres; pasture 2 furlongs
    long and 1 furlong wide.
Value 20s; when he acquired it, as much.

✠ Huic m̄ additą. ē *AIXA* . Sauuin⁹ tenuit de ep̄o Wellenſi.7 n̄ poterat
ab eo ſepari T.R.E.7 geldɓ ꝓ.ı.hida 7 una v́ træ. Tra. ē.ııı.caŕ. In
dn̄io. ē.ı.caŕ.7 uilłi hn̄t.ıı.caŕ 7 dimiđ . Valuit 7 uał.xxx.ſoliđ.
Rog ten de rege 7 Giuold de eo.

Iꝓſe Ro. ten *OPECEDRE* . Domno tenuit T.R.E.7 geldɓ ꝓ.ııı.hiđ
7 dim. Tra. ē.v.caŕ. In dn̄io. ē.ı.caŕ.7 ıı.ſerui.7 vı.uilłi 7 vı.borđ
hn̄t.ııı.caŕ. Ibi.xxııı.ac̄ p̄ti.7 xv.ac̄ paſturæ 7 ıı.ac̄ ſiluæ.
Valuit. L.ſoliđ.modo. Lx.ſoliđ.

De hac ꞇra huj⁹ m̄ ten Roɓt.ı.hiđ.7 ibi.ı.caŕ ht̄.cū.ı.ſeruo.
7 v.borđ.7 molin̄ redđ.ııı.ſoł. Ibi.ııı.ac̄ p̄ti.7 v.ac̄ paſturæ.7 ıııı.
ac̄ ſiluæ. Valuit.xv.ſoł. Modo.xx.ſoliđ.

Iꝓſe Rog ten *CEDRE* . Vluuin⁹ tenuit T.R.E.7 geldɓ ꝓ.ıı.hiđ 7 dim
Tra. ē.ıııı.caŕ. In dn̄io. ē.ı.caŕ.7 ııı.ſerui.7 vı.uilłi 7 vı.borđ cū
ııı.caŕ. Ibi.xxıııı.ac̄ p̄ti.7 xv.ac̄ paſturæ. Valet.Lx.ſoliđ.

Roger ten de.Ro. *SYTONE* . Vluuard tenuit T.R.E.7 geldɓ ꝓ.v.
hiđ. Tra. ē.v.caŕ. Ibi ſt̄.vı.borđ 7 ıııı.cotaŕ.7 molin̄ redđ.xvı.ſoliđ.
Ibi.xıı.ac̄ p̄ti. Paſtura.ııı.q̄ꝝ łg.7 ıı.q̄ꝝ lat̄. Valuit.c.ſoł.m̄.xxx.ſoł.

Iꝓſe Rog ten *BECHINTONE* . Ailuert tenuit T.R.E.7 geldɓ ꝓ x.hiđ.
Tra. ē.x.caŕ. In dn̄io ſt̄.ıı.caŕ.7 ıx.uilłi 7 vıı.borđ hn̄t.vı.caŕ.
Ibi molin̄ redđ.xx.ſoliđ.7 xıı.ac̄ p̄ti.7 vııı.ac̄ paſturæ.7 c.ac̄
ſiluæ. Valɓ qdo recep̄.x.liɓ. Modo.vı.liɓ.

Roɓt⁹ ten de.Ro. *BERCHELEI* . Toui tenuit T.R.E.7 geldɓ ꝓ.ıı.hiđ
7 dimiđ. Tra. ē.ııı.caŕ. In dn̄io ſt̄.ıı.caŕ.cū.ı.ſeruo.7 ııı.uilłi

†   ASH (Priors) has been added to this manor. Saewin held it   E
from the Bishop of Wells; he could not be separated from him   E
before 1066. It paid tax for 1 hide and 1 virgate of land.
Land for 3 ploughs. In lordship 1 plough.
    The villagers have 2½ ploughs.
    The value was and is 30s.
    Roger holds from the King, and Givold from him.

21 UPPER CHEDDON. Dunn held it before 1066; it paid tax for 3½
hides. Land for 5 ploughs. In lordship 1 plough; 2 slaves;
1 hide & ½ virgate.   444
    6 villagers and 6 smallholders have 3 ploughs & 1 hide & 1½ virgates.   a 1
    Meadow, 23 acres; pasture, 15 acres; woodland, 2 acres.
    The value was 50s; now 60s.
    Robert holds 1 hide of this manor's land; he has 1 plough there, E
in lordship, & ½ hide, with 1 slave;
    5 smallholders (who have) ½ hide & 1 plough.
    A mill which pays 3s. Meadow, 3 acres; pasture, 5 acres;
        woodland, 4 acres. 2 cows; 15 sheep; 5 goats.
    The value was 15s; now 20s.

22 CHEDDON (Fitzpaine). Wulfwin held it before 1066; it paid tax
for 2½ hides. Land for 4 ploughs. In lordship 1 plough;
3 slaves; 1 hide & ½ virgate.   444
    6 villagers and 6 smallholders with 3 ploughs & the rest of the land.   a 2
    Meadow, 24 acres; pasture, 15 acres.
Value 60s; when Roger acquired it, 50s.

23 Roger Bushell holds SUTTON (Bingham) from Roger. Wulfward
held it before 1066; it paid tax for 5 hides. Land for 5 ploughs.
  In lordship 4½ hides & 1 furlong.   444
    6 smallholders and 4 cottagers (have) the rest of the land.   a 3
    A mill which pays 16s. Meadow, 12 acres; pasture 3 furlongs   E
        long and 2 furlongs wide.
    The value was 100s; now 30s.

24 Roger holds BECKINGTON himself. Aethelfrith held it before 1066;
it paid tax for 10 hides. Land for 10 ploughs. In lordship 2
ploughs; 5 hides & 3 virgates.   444
    9 villagers and 7 smallholders have 6 ploughs & 4 hides & 1 virgate.   b 1
    A mill which pays 20s; meadow, 12 acres; pasture, 8 acres;
        woodland, 100 acres. 24 pigs; 100 sheep; 50 goats.
Value when he acquired it, £10; now £6.

25 Robert holds BERKLEY from Roger. Tovi held it before 1066;
it paid tax for 2½ hides. Land for 3 ploughs. In lordship 2   E 444
ploughs & 2 hides, with 1 slave;   b 2

7 IIII.borđ.cū.I.cař.Ibi moliñ redđ.XII.foł 7 VI.den.7 VI.ac
p̃ti.7 LXX.ac filuæ.Valuit 7 uał.XL.foliđ.

Ipfe Rog̃ ten MERSITONE.Aeluert tenuit T.R.E.7 gelđb p.III.
hiđ 7 dim.Tra.ē.V.cař.In dñio.ē.I.cař.7 II.ferui.7 V.uiłłi.
7 XIIII.borđ hñt.V.cař.Ibi moliñ redđ.VI.foliđ.7 XVI.ac p̃ti.
7 C.ac pafturæ.Silua.I.leū lḡ.7 tntđ lat.Valet.VII.liḃ.

Wiłłs ten de Ro.PENNE.Britnod tenuit T.R.E.7 gelđb p.III.
hiđ.Tra.ē.III.cař.In dñio.ē.I.cař.7 IIII.uiłłi 7 VIII.borđ 7 IIII.
cotar cū.I.cař 7 dim.Ibi moliñ redđ.XL.denar.7 XII.ac p̃ti.
7 XX.ac pafturæ.Silua.XII.q̃ƺ lḡ.7 IIII.q̃ƺ 7 XII.p̃tic lat.
Valḃ qdo recep̃.VII.liḃ.Modo.III.liḃ.

Azelin ten de Ro.ESLIDE.Goduin 7 Seric tenuer T.R.E.7 gelđb
p.II.hiđ.Tra.ē.II.cař.q̃ ibi ſt in dñio.7 IIII.ferui cū.I.borđ.
Ibi.IIII.ac p̃ti.7 II.ac filuæ.Valuit 7 uał.XL.foliđ.

.XXIII   TERRA WALTERIJ GIFARD.

WALTERIVS Gifard ten de rege GERNEFELLE.7 Wiłłs
de eo.Ernebold tenuit T.R.E.7 gelđb p.II.hiđ.Tra.ē.III.
cař.In dñio ſt.II,cař.cū.I.feruo.7 V.borđ cū.I.cař.
Ibi.XX.ac pafturæ.7 LX.ac filuæ.Valuit.XL.foł.m̃.XXX.foł.

.XXIIII.   TERRA WALTERIJ DE DOWAI.

WALTERIVS DE DOWAI ten de rege WORLE.Efgar tenuit
T.R.E.7 gelđb p.VI.hiđ 7 dim.Tra.ē.XV.cař.In dñio ſt.IIII.
cař.7 V.ferui.7 XXII.uiłłi 7 III.borđ cū.IX.cař.Ibi.L.ac p̃ti.
Paftura.XIII.q̃ƺ lḡ.7 II.q̃ƺ lat.Valuit.X.liḃ.Modo.VII.liḃ.

3 villagers and 4 smallholders with 1 plough & 3 virgates.
A mill which pays 12s 6d; meadow, 6 acres; woodland, 70 acres.
15 cattle; 9 pigs.
The value was and is 40s.

26 Roger holds MARSTON (Bigot) himself. Aethelfrith held it before
1066; it paid tax for 3½ hides. Land for 5 ploughs. In lordship 1
plough; 2 slaves; 1½ hides.   444
    5 villagers and 14 smallholders have 5 ploughs & 2 hides.   b 3
    A mill which pays 6s; meadow, 16 acres; pasture, 100 acres;
      woodland 1 league long and as wide. 9 cattle; 14 pigs; 9 sheep.   E
Value £7; when Roger acquired it, £6.

27 William Gerald holds PENSELWOOD from Roger. Brictnoth held
it before 1066; it paid tax for 3 hides. Land for 3 ploughs.
In lordship 1 plough; 2 hides.   445
    4 villagers, 8 smallholders and 4 cottagers with   E   a 1
      1½ ploughs & 1 hide.
    A mill which pays 40d; meadow, 12 acres; pasture, 20 acres;
      woodland 12 furlongs long and 4 furlongs and 12 perches   E
      wide. 3 cattle; 13 pigs; 100 sheep.
Value when he acquired it, £7; now £3.

28 Azelin holds LYDE from Roger. Godwin and Saeric held it   E
before 1066; it paid tax for 2 hides. Land for 2 ploughs,   445
which are there, in lordship, & 1 hide & 3½ virgates; 4 slaves, with   a 2
    1 smallholder (who has) ½ virgate.
    Meadow, 4 acres; woodland, 2 acres. 4 pigs; 53 sheep.   E
The value was and is 40s.

23   LAND OF WALTER GIFFARD   95 a

1 Walter Giffard holds YARNFIELD from the King, and William
from him. Ernebald held it before 1066; it paid tax for 2 hides.
Land for 3 ploughs. In lordship 2 ploughs & 1 hide & 2½ virgates,   447
with 1 slave;   a 4
    5 smallholders with 1 plough & 1½ virgates.
    Pasture, 20 acres; woodland, 60 acres. 2 cows; 25 pigs; 124 sheep.
The value was 40s; now 30s.

24   LAND OF WALTER OF DOUAI

1 Walter of Douai holds WORLE from the King. Asgar held it
before 1066; it paid tax for 6½ hides. Land for 15 ploughs.
In lordship 4 ploughs; 5 slaves; 3 hides & 1½ virgates.   350
    22 villagers and 3 smallholders with 9 ploughs & 3 hides & ½ virgate. b 2
    Meadow, 50 acres; pasture 13 furlongs long and 2 furlongs wide.
      1 cob; 24 cattle; 18 pigs; 60 sheep.
The value was £10; now £7.

Walscinvs ten̄ *Stragelle* .7 Reneuuald̄ de eo. Leuegar
tenuit T.R.E.7 geldb̄ p̄ dimid̄ hida. Tra.ē.II.car̄. In dn̄io.ē
una car̄.cū.I.feruo.7 III.bord̄.7 x.ac̄ p̄ti. Valuit 7 ual.L.fol.

Reneuuald̄ ten̄ de.W.*Stragelle*. Eduuold̄ tenuit T.R.E.
7 geldb̄ p̄ dim̄ hida. Tra.ē.I.car̄. In dn̄io ft.II.car̄.7 II.ferui.
7 un uitts 7 II.bord̄ cū.I.car̄ 7 dim̄. Ibi.x.ac̄ p̄ti. Valet.L.fol.

Rademer̄ ten̄ de.W.*Wallepille*. Eduuard̄ tenuit T.R.E.
7 geldb̄ p̄.III.v trǣ. Tra.ē.I.car̄.q̄ ibi.ē in dn̄io.7 un uitts
7 III.bord̄ cū dimid̄ car̄. Valuit 7 ual.xx.folid̄.

Walteri ten̄ unā v trǣ q̄ uocat̄ Donehā. Algar tenuit T.R.E.
H̄ eft de illa tra quā rex ded̄ ei int.II.aq̄s. Valet.XII.den̄.

Rademer̄ ten̄ de.W.*Crvce*. Eduuard̄ tenuit T.R.E.7 geldb̄
p̄ una.v.Tra.ē.I.car̄.q̄ ibi.ē in dn̄io.cū.IIII.bord̄. Val.x.

Rademer̄ ten̄ de.W.*Bvre*. Saric tenuit T.R.E.   ╭ folid̄.
7 geldb̄ p̄ dim̄ hida. Tra.ē.III.car̄. In dn̄io.ē.I.car̄.cū.I.
feruo.7 III.uitti 7 II.bord̄ hn̄t.II.car̄. Valuit 7 ual.xL.folid̄
H̄ tra ptinuit T.R.E.ad Melecome q m̄ ten̄ Robt̄ de Odbor uile.

Walfcin ten̄ *Werre*. Æluuacre tenuit T.R.E.7 geldb̄ p̄.v.
hid̄. St̄ tam ibi.VI.hide. Tra.ē.VIII.car̄. De ea ft in dn̄io
III.hidæ 7 dim̄.7 ibi.II.car̄.7 II.ferui.7 v.uitti 7 VIII.bord̄
cū.II.car̄. Ibi.II.molini redd̄.xLII.folid̄.7 xxxII.ac̄ p̄ti.
Qdo recep̄ ualb̄.x.lib̄.Modo.c.folid̄.

24,2 written at bottom of col. 95 a, with no transposition signs. See Notes.

3 Walscin holds STRETCHOLT, and Rainward from him. Leofgar held
it before 1066; it paid tax for ½ hide. Land for 2 ploughs.
In lordship 1 plough & 1 virgate, with 1 slave;
 3 smallholders (who have) 1 virgate & ½ plough.
 Meadow, 10 acres. 8 cattle; 14 pigs; 32 sheep.
The value was and is 50s.

  350
  a 2

4 Rainward holds STRETCHOLT from W(alscin). Edwald held it
before 1066; it paid tax for ½ hide. Land for 1 plough.
In lordship 2 ploughs; 2 slaves; 1 virgate.
 1 villager and 2 smallholders with 1½ ploughs & 1 virgate.
 Meadow, 10 acres. 8 cattle; 43 pigs; 31 sheep.
Value 50s; when Walscin acquired it, 40s.

  350
  a 3

5 Rademar holds WALPOLE from W(alscin). Edward the Breton(?) held
it before 1066; it paid tax for 3 virgates of land. Land for
1 plough, which is there, in lordship, & 1½ virgates.
 1 villager and 3 smallholders with ½ plough & 1½ virgates.
The value was and is 20s.

  350
  a 4

6 Walter holds 1 virgate of land called ?DUNWEAR. Algar held it
before 1066. This is (part) of the land which the King gave
him between the two waters.
Value 12d.

  E
  350
  a 1

7 Rademar holds ?'CROOK' from W(alscin). Edward held it before
1066; it paid tax for 1 virgate. Land for 1 plough, which is there,
in lordship, & ½ virgate, with
 4 smallholders (who have) ½ virgate.
  3 cattle; 3 pigs.
Value 10s; when Walscin acquired it, as much.

  350
  a 5

8 Rademar holds BOWER from W(alscin). Saeric held it before
1066; it paid tax for ½ hide. Land for 3 ploughs.
In lordship 1 plough & 1 virgate, with 1 slave.
 3 villagers and 2 smallholders have 2 ploughs & 1 virgate.
  15 cattle; 21 pigs.
The value was and is 40s.
 Before 1066 this land belonged to Melcombe, which Robert
of Auberville now holds.

  350
  b 1

  E

9 Walscin holds WEARE. Alwaker held it before 1066; it paid
tax for 5 hides; however, there are 6 hides there.
Land for 8 ploughs, of which 3½ hides are in lordship; 2
ploughs there; 2 slaves;
 5 villagers and 8 smallholders with 2 ploughs & 2½ hides.
 2 mills which pay 42s; meadow, 32 acres. 18 cattle; 5 pigs.
Value when he acquired it, £10; now 100s.

  350
  b 4

Fulcuin ten de.W. *Bagewerre*. Duo taini tenuer̄ T.R.E. ^{p.II.Man'}

7 geldb̄ p̄.II.hid̄.Tr̄a.ē.II.car̄.In dn̄io.ē una car̄.7 II.uilti

7 VIII.bord̄ cū.I.car̄.Ibi.IX.ãc p̄ti.Valuit.XV.fot.m̄.XX.fot.

Radulf ten de.W. *Alwarditone*. Vlnod tenuit T.R.E.

7 geldb̄ p̄.V.hid̄.Ibi additæ st̄.VI.hidæ q̄s teneb̄.II.taini

T.R.E. p̄.II.maner̄.Int tot̄ Tr̄a.ē.VIII.car̄.De ea st̄ in

dn̄io.IX.hidæ dim uirḡ min.7 ibi.III.car̄.7 IIII.ferui.7 IX.uilti

7 IX.bord̄ cū.IIII.car̄.Ibi.XL.ãc p̄ti.7 CCC.ãc pafturæ

Q̄do recep̄ uatb̄.VIII.lib̄.Modo.c.folid̄.

Ludo ten de.W. *Ternoc*. Aluuard tenuit T.R.E.7 geldb̄

p̄.I.hida.Tr̄a.ē.II.car̄|q̄ ibi st̄ in dn̄io.7 II.ferui.7 IIII.bord̄. ^{7 dimid}

Ibi.XX.ãc p̄ti.7 V.q̄z̄ pafturæ in lḡ.7 tn̄td in lat̄.Vat.XX.

Ricard ten de.W. *Ternoc*. Leuuin tenuit.T.R.E. ∠folid̄.

7 geldb̄ p̄.I.hida.Tr̄a.ē.II.car̄ 7 dim.In dn̄io tam̄ st̄.III.car̄.

7 II.ferui.7 I.uilt 7 II.bord̄.Ibi.XXX.ãc p̄ti.7 VI.q̄z̄ paft̄æ

in lḡ.7 tn̄td in lat̄.Valuit.XV.fot.Modo.XXV.folid̄.

Hub̄t ten de.W. *Alnodestone*. Duo taini tenuer̄ T.R.E.

7 geldb̄ p̄.IIII.hid̄ 7 dim.Tr̄a.ē.VI.car̄.In dn̄io st̄.III.car̄.

cū.I.feruo.7 VI.uilti 7 III.bord̄,cū.II.car̄.Ibi.XV.ãc p̄ti.

7 XX.ãc filuæ.Valuit 7 uat̄.LX.folid̄.

Gerard ten de.W. *Broctvne*. Elfi tenuit T.R.E.7 geldb̄

p̄.IIII.hid̄.Tr̄a.ē.VIII.car̄.In dn̄io st̄.II.car̄.7 VI.ferui.7 VII.

uilti cū.IIII.car̄.Ibi.IIII.ãc p̄ti,7 VI.q̄z̄ filuæ in lḡ 7 lat̄.

Valuit.VII.lib̄.q̄do recep̄.Modo.IIII.lib̄.

10 Fulcwin holds BADGWORTH from W(alscin). Two thanes held it as   E
two manors before 1066; it paid tax for 2 hides.
Land for 2 ploughs. In lordship 1 plough; 1 hide & 3 virgates.   351
  2 villagers and 8 smallholders with 1 plough & 1 virgate.   a 1
  Meadow, 9 acres. 10 cattle; 18 pigs; 34 sheep.
The value was 15s; now 20s.

11 Ralph of Conteville holds ALLERTON from W(alter). Wulfnoth
held it before 1066; it paid tax for 5 hides. 6 hides have been
added there, which two thanes held before 1066 as two manors.   E
In total, land for 8 ploughs, of which 9 hides, less ½ virgate,
are in lordship; 3 ploughs there; 4 slaves;   351
  9 villagers and 9 smallholders with 4 ploughs & 2 hides & ½ virgate.   a 2
  Meadow, 40 acres; pasture, 300 acres. 4 cattle; 13 pigs.
Value when he acquired it, £8; now 100s.   E

12 Ludo holds TARNOCK from W(alter). Alfward held it before 1066;   E
it paid tax for 1 hide. Land for 2½ ploughs, which are there,
in lordship; 2 slaves;
  4 smallholders.   351
  Meadow, 20 acres; pasture, 5 furlongs in length and as   b 1
    much in width. 8 unbroken mares; 13 cattle.
Value 20s; when Walter acquired it, 15s.

13 Richard holds TARNOCK from W(alter). Leofwin held it before   E
1066; it paid tax for 1 hide. Land for 2½ ploughs. In lordship,
however, 3 ploughs; 2 slaves; 3½ virgates.   351
  1 villager and 2 smallholders (have) ½ virgate & 1 plough.   b 2
  Meadow, 30 acres; pasture, 6 furlongs in length and as much
    in width. 1 cob; 9 unbroken mares; 16 cattle; 14 pigs; 45 sheep.
The value was 15s; now 25s.

14 Hubert holds ALSTON (Sutton) from W(alter). Two thanes held it   E
before 1066; it paid tax for 4½ hides. Land for 6 ploughs.
In lordship 3 ploughs & 4 hides, less 1 virgate, with 1 slave;   351
  6 villagers and 3 smallholders with 2 ploughs & 3 virgates.   b 3
  Meadow, 15 acres; woodland, 20 acres. 23 cattle; 7 pigs.
The value was and is 60s.

15 Gerard holds BRATTON (Seymour) from W(alscin). Alfsi held it
before 1066; it paid tax for 4 hides. Land for 8 ploughs.
In lordship 2 ploughs; 6 slaves; 2 hides & 1 virgate.   352
  7 villagers with 4 ploughs & 2 hides, less 1 virgate. 8 smallholders.   a 1
  . Meadow, 4 acres; woodland, 6 furlongs in length and width.
    10 cattle; 11 pigs; 37 sheep; 23 goats.
Value when he acquired it, £7; now £4.

Ricard ten de.W.*MIDDELTONE*.Eluuacre teneb T.R.E.7 geldb ꝑ hida 7 dim̄.
T̃ra.ē.ıı.caꝝ.Ibi,ııı,uilli hn̄t.ı.caꝝ.Val 7 ualuit.xxv.folıd.

Reneuuarus ten de.W.*WINCALETONE*.Elfi tenuit T.R.E.7 geldb
ꝑ.ııı.hid 7 dim̄.Tra.ē.vıı.caꝝ.In dn̄io.ē.ı.caꝝ.7 ıı.ferui.7 xvı.
uilli 7 vı.bord 7 v.cotar cū.vıı.caꝝ.Ibi.l.āc p̄ti.7 totid filuæ.
Valuit 7 ual.lxx.folid.

Huic ꝏ addita.ē dim̄ hida.q̄ Brifmar teneb ꝑ ꝏ T.R.E.7 ꝑ dim̄ hida
Tra.ē.v.caꝝ.Ibi hт̃ Reneuu.ı.caꝝ.7 ıı.feru.7 vıı.uilli 7 ıx.bord ⌐ geldb.
7·ıı·cotar' cū.ııı.caꝝ.Ibi molin̄ redd.xxx.den.7 lx.āc p̄ti.7 xxx.āc
pafturæ.7 c.āc filuæ.Valuit 7 ual.xl.folid.

Walter ten *CARI*.Elfi tenuit T.R.E.7 geldb ꝑ.xv.hid.
Tra.ē.xx.caꝝ.De ea ſt in dn̄io.vııı.hidæ.7 ibi.vı.caꝝ.7 vı.
ferui.7 xxıı.uilli 7 xx.bord cū.xvıı.caꝝ.Ibi.ııı.molini
redd.xxxııı.fol.7 c.āc p̄ti.Silua.ı.leu lḡ.7 dim̄ leu laꝝ.
7 un̄ burḡfis in Giueleceftre 7 alt in Briuueton reddt.xvı.den
Q̄do receꝑ ualb.xvı.lib.Modo.xv.lib.   ⌐ 7 obolū.

Fulcuin ten de.W.*SPCHEFORDE*.Eluuacre tenuit T.R.E.
7 geldb ꝑ.v.hid 7 una v̄ træ.Tra .ē.v.caꝝ.In dn̄io ſt.ıı.caꝝ
7 dimid.7 vı.ferui.7 ıx.uilli 7 vıı.bord cū.ıııı.caꝝ Ibi molin̄
redd.vıı.fol 7 dim̄.7 xl.āc p̄ti.7 c.āc pafturæ.7 una q̄rent
filuæ in lḡ 7 laꝝ.Valuit.ıııı.lib.Modo.c.folid.

Vluric ten de.W.*ALMVNDESFORD*.Chetel tenuit T.R.E.
7 geldb ꝑ.v.hid.Tra.ē.vı.caꝝ.In dn̄io ſt.ıı.caꝝ.7 ııı.ferui.
7 v.uilli 7 ıııı.bord cū.v.caꝝ.Ibi molin̄ redd.vıı.fol 7 dim̄.
7 xx.āc p̄ti.7 xx.āc pafturæ.Silua.ıııı.q̄ꝫ lḡ.7 ı.7 dim̄ lat.
Q̄do receꝑ ualb.ıııı.lib.Modo.ııı.lib.

24

Written at the bottom of col. 95 a, with no transposition signs. See Notes.

24,2 Richard holds MILTON from W(alscin). Alwaker held it before
1066; it paid tax for 1½ hides. Land for 2 ploughs.   350
   3 villagers have 1 plough there.   b 3
The value is and was 25s.

16 Rainward holds WINCANTON from W(alscin). Alfsi held it before   95 b
1066; it paid tax for 3½ hides. Land for 7 ploughs.
In lordship 1 plough; 2 slaves; 1 virgate.   352
   16 villagers, 6 smallholders and 5 cottagers with 7 ploughs   a 2
    & 3 hides & 1 virgate.
   Meadow, 50 acres; woodland, as many. 1 cob; 14 cattle; 15 pigs; 32 sheep.
The value was and is 70s.
   To this manor has been added ½ hide which Brictmer the   E
priest held as a manor before 1066; it paid tax for ½ hide. Land E
for 5 ploughs. Rainward has 1 plough there, in lordship, & 1 virgate;
2 slaves;
   7 villagers, 9 smallholders and 2 cottagers with 3 ploughs
    & 1 virgate.
   A mill which pays 30d; meadow, 60 acres; pasture, 30 acres;
   woodland, 100 acres.
The value was and is 40s.
   The above 4 hides paid tax for 3 hides before 1066.

17 Walter holds (Castle) CARY. Alfsi held it before 1066; it paid
tax for 15 hides. Land for 20 ploughs, of which 8 hides are
in lordship; 6 ploughs there; 6 slaves;   352
   23 villagers and 20 smallholders with 17 ploughs & 7 hides.   b 1
   3 mills which pay 34s; meadow, 100 acres; woodland 1 league
   long and ½ league wide. 2 cobs; 16 cattle; 20 pigs.
    8 pigmen who pay 50 pigs. 117 sheep.
   A burgess in Ilchester and another in Bruton pay 16½d to this manor.
Value when he acquired it, £16; now £15.

18 Fulcwin holds SPARKFORD from W(alter). Alwaker held it before
1066; it paid tax for 5 hides and 1 virgate of land. Land for
5 ploughs. In lordship 2½ ploughs; 6 slaves; 2½ hides & 1 virgate.   352
   9 villagers and 7 smallholders with 4 ploughs & 2½ hides.   b 2
   A mill which pays 7½s; meadow, 40 acres; pasture, 100 acres;
   woodland, 1 furlong in length and width. 16 cattle; 19 pigs; 72 sheep.
The value was £4; now 100s.

19 Wulfric holds ANSFORD from W(alter). Ketel held it before 1066;
it paid tax for 5 hides. Land for 6 ploughs. In lordship 2 ploughs;
3 slaves; 3 hides.   352
   5 villagers and 4 smallholders with 5 ploughs & 2 hides.   b 3
   A mill which pays 7½s; meadow, 20 acres; pasture, 20 acres;
   woodland 4 furlongs long and 1½ wide. 1 cob; 9 cattle; 11 pigs;
   60 sheep.
Value when he acquired it, £4; now £3.

Radulf⁹ ten de . W . *BERVE* . Elfi tenuit T.R.E. 7 geldb p . v .
hid . Tra . e̅ . v . car̅ . In dñio st̅ . ii . car̅ . 7 iii . serui . 7 vii . uitti
7 v . bord cu̅ . iii . car̅ . Ibi . xxv . a̅c p̅ti . 7 iii . q̅z siluæ in lg̅ . 7 i . q̅z
lat . Q̷do recep̅ . ualb . c . sot . Modo . lx . solid .

Walscin⁹ ten *BRVGIE* . Merlesuain tenuit T.R.E. 7 geldb
p . v . hid . Tra . e̅ . x . car̅ . In dñio st̅ . iii . car̅ . 7 v . serui . 7 xiii .
uitti 7 ix . bord 7 v . cotar cu̅ . viii . car̅ . Ibi molin̅ redd . v . sot .

★ 7 x . a̅c p̅ti . 7 c . A̅c siluæ minutæ . 7 xxx . a̅c pasturæ .

Q̷do recep̅ . ualb . c . sot . Modo . vii . lib .

Ludo ten de . W . *WADMENDVNE* . Merlesuain̅ tenuit T.R.E.
7 geldb p . ii . hid . Tra . e̅ . vi . car̅ . In dñio st̅ . ii . car̅ . cu̅ . i . seruo .
7 v . uitti 7 vi . bord cu̅ . iiii . car̅ . Ibi . x . a̅c p̅ti . 7 xiii . a̅c pasturæ ,
7 v . a̅c siluæ . Q̷do recep̅ . ualb . iii . lib . Modo . iiii . lib .

Reneuuald⁹ ten de . W . *BAGETREPE* . Merlesuain tenuit T.R.E.
7 geldb p . ii . hid . Tra . e̅ . viii . car̅ . In dñio . e̅ . i . car̅ . 7 vi . serui .
7 xi . uitti 7 vii . bord|cu̅ . v . car̅ . Ibi molin̅ redd . iiii . sot . 7 c . a̅c
7.iii.cotarij.
p̅ti . 7 xl . a̅c pasturæ . Valb . l . solid . Modo . lx . solid .

Reneuuald⁹ ten de . W . *BREDENIE* . Alnod tenuit T.R.E. 7 geldb
p una hida . Tra . e̅ . i . car̅ 7 dim . Ibi . e̅ un⁹ uiits 7 v . bord . 7 i . cotar
7 i . seruus cu̅ car̅ 7 dim . Ibi . xxv . a̅c p̅ti . Valet . xx . solid .

Rademer ten de . W . *HVRSI* . Eluuard teneb T.R.E. 7 geldb
p . ii . hid . Tra . e̅ . vii . car̅ . In dñio st̅ . ii . car̅ . 7 ii . serui . 7 viii . uitti
7 vi . bord 7 iii . cotar cu̅ . v . car̅ . 7 xxiiii . a̅c pasturæ . Valet . iiii . lib .

20 Ralph holds BARROW from W(alter). Alfsi held it before 1066; it paid tax for 5 hides. Land for 5 ploughs. In lordship 2 ploughs; 3 slaves; 3½ hides & ½ virgate.

    353 a 1

    7 villagers and 5 smallholders with 3 ploughs & 1½ hides, less ½ virgate. Meadow, 25 acres; woodland, 3 furlongs in length and 1 furlong wide. 10 cattle; 24 pigs; 73 sheep.

Value when he acquired it, 100s; now 60s.

21 Walscin holds BRIDGWATER. Merleswein held it before 1066; it paid tax for 5 hides. Land for 10 ploughs. In lordship 3 ploughs; 5 slaves; 2 hides.

    353 E a 2

    13 villagers, 9 smallholders and 5 cottagers with 8 ploughs & 3 hides.

A mill which pays 5s; meadow, 10 acres; underwood, 100 acres; pasture, 30 acres. 13 cattle; 7 pigs; 61 sheep.

Value when he acquired it, 100s; now £7.

22 Ludo holds WEMBDON from W(alter). Merleswein held it before 1066; it paid tax for 2 hides. Land for 6 ploughs. In lordship 2 ploughs & 1 hide, with 1 slave;

    353 E a 3

    5 villagers and 6 smallholders with 4 ploughs & 1 hide. Meadow, 10 acres; pasture, 13 acres; woodland, 5 acres. 1 cob; 18 cattle; 20 pigs; 30 sheep; 17 goats.

Value when he acquired it, £3; now £4.

23 Rainward holds BAWDRIP from W(alter). Merleswein held it before 1066; it paid tax for 2 hides. Land for 8 ploughs. In lordship 1 plough; 6 slaves; 1 hide.

    353 a 4

    11 villagers, 7 smallholders and 3 cottagers with 5 ploughs & 1 hide.

A mill which pays 4s; meadow, 100 acres; pasture, 40 acres. 1 cob; 7 cattle; 20 pigs.

The value was 50s; now 60s.

24 Rainward holds BRADNEY from W(alter). Alnoth the reeve held it before 1066; it paid tax for 1 hide. Land for 1½ ploughs. In lordship 3 virgates & 1 plough.

    E E 353 b 1

    1 villager, 5 smallholders, 1 cottager and 1 slave with 1½ ploughs & 1 virgate. Meadow, 25 acres.

    E

Value 20s; when he acquired it, 15s.

25 Rademar holds HORSEY from W(alter). Alfward Glebard held it before 1066; it paid tax for 2 hides. Land for 7 ploughs. In lordship 2 ploughs; 2 slaves; 3 virgates.

    353 b 2

    8 villagers, 6 smallholders and 3 cottagers with 5 ploughs & 1 hide & 1 virgate. Pasture, 24 acres. 1 cob; 10 cattle; 20 pigs; 50 sheep.

Value £4; when Walter acquired it, 60s.

Rademer ten̄ de.W.*PAVELET*.Semar tenuit T.R.E.⁊ geldb̄
ꝓ una v̄ træ.Tra.ē.ı.car̄.q̄ ibi.ē in dn̄io cū.ı.feruo.⁊ ıı.bord̄
⁊ ııı.cotar̄.⁊ v.ac̄ p̄ti.Valuit ⁊ ual̄.x.folid.

Ipfe.W.ten̄ *BVRNEHĀ*.Brixi tenuit T.R.E.⁊ geldb̄ ꝓ.ıııı.hid.
Tra.ē.xıı.car̄.In dn̄io.ē.ı.car̄.⁊ ııı.ferui.⁊ vıı.uilli.⁊ vııı.bord̄
cū.v.car̄.Ibi.cl.ac̄ p̄ti.⁊ xx.ac̄ pafturæ.Valet.ıııı.lib̄.

De hac t̄ra ten̄ Rademer de Walt.ıı.hid.⁊ ibi ht̄.ı.car̄.⁊ ııı.
feruos.⁊ vıı.uill̄ ⁊ vııı.bord|cū.v.car̄.⁊ cl.ac̄s p̄ti.⁊ xx ac̄s pafte.
(⁊ ııı.cotar̄.)

Ipfe.W.ten̄ *HONSPIL*.Eluuacre tenuit T.R.E. ⌠Valet.ıııı.lib̄.
⁊ geldb̄ ꝓ.ı.hida.Tra.ē.xııı.car̄.In dn̄io ſt̄.ıı.car̄.⁊ v.ferni.
⁊ xxı.uill̄ ⁊ v.bord̄ ⁊ vıı.cotar̄ cū.xı.car̄.Ibi.c.ac̄ p̄ti.⁊ ꝭc.ac̄
pafturæ Valuit ⁊ ual̄.vııı.lib̄.

Ipfe.W.ten̄ *BRIEN*.Merlefuain tenuit T.R.E.⁊ geldb̄ ꝓ.ıı.hid.
Tra.ē.vııı.car̄.In dn̄io ſt̄.ııı.car̄.cū.ı.feruo,⁊ ıx.uilli ⁊ vıı.bord̄

95 c

⁊ vııı.cotar̄ cū.ııı.car̄ ⁊ dim̄.Ibi.xxx.ac̄ pafturæ.Valet c.folid.

Radulf⁹ ten̄ de.W.*CONTVNE*.Eluuacre tenuit T.R.E.⁊ geldb̄
ꝓ.ıııı.hid.Tra.ē.ııı.car̄.In dn̄io ſt̄.ıı.car̄.⁊ ıııı.bord̄ ⁊ vıı.
cotar̄.⁊ ı.uills̄ cū dim̄ car̄.Ibi molin̄ redd̄.vı.den̄.⁊ xıı.ac̄
p̄ti.⁊ x.q̄ꝫ pafturæ in lḡ.⁊ ıı.q̄ꝫ lat̄.⁊ ı,ıı.q̄ꝫ filuæ in lḡ.
⁊ ıı.q̄ꝫ in lat̄.Valuit ⁊ ual̄.l.folid.

26 Rademar holds PAWLETT from W(alter). Saemer held it before 1066; it paid tax for 1 virgate of land. Land for 1 plough, which is there, in lordship, with 1 slave; 353
    2 smallholders and 3 cottagers. b 3
    Meadow, 5 acres. 8 cattle; 10 pigs; 20 sheep.
The value was and is 10s.

27 W(alter) holds BURNHAM (on Sea) himself. Brictsi held it before 1066; it paid tax for 4 hides. Land for 12 ploughs. In lordship 1 plough; 3 slaves; ½ hide. 354
    7 villagers and 8 smallholders with 5 ploughs & 1½ hides. a 1
    Meadow, 150 acres; pasture, 20 acres. 1 cob; 6 mares; 6 cattle;
       7 pigs; 50 sheep.
Value £4.
    Rademar holds 2 hides of this land from Walter; he has 1 E
plough there, and 3 slaves & ½ hide.
    7 villagers, 8 smallholders and 3 cottagers with 5 ploughs & 1½ hides. E
    Meadow, 150 acres; pasture, 20 acres. 6 mares; 5 cattle; 6 pigs; 50 sheep.
Value £4; when Walter acquired it, £6.

28 W(alter) holds HUNTSPILL himself. Alwaker held it before 1066; E
it paid tax for 1 hide. Land for 13 ploughs.
In lordship 2 ploughs; 5 slaves; ½ hide. 354
    21 villagers, 5 smallholders and 7 cottagers with 11 ploughs a 2
     & ½ hide.
    Meadow, 100 acres; pasture, 200 acres. 14 mares; 8 cattle; 20 pigs;
     28 sheep.
The value was and is £8.

29 W(alter) holds BREAN himself. Merleswein held it before 1066; it paid tax for 2 hides. Land for 8 ploughs. In lordship 3 354
ploughs & 1 hide, with 1 slave; a 3
    9 villagers, 7 smallholders and 8 cottagers with 3½ ploughs 95 c
     & 1 hide.
    Pasture, 30 acres. 10 cattle; 4 pigs; 53 sheep.
Value 100s; when Walter acquired it, £8.

30 Ralph holds CHILCOMPTON from W(alter). Alwaker held it before E
1066; it paid tax for 4 hides. Land for 3 ploughs. In lordship 2 ploughs; 3½ hides & ½ virgate. 354
    4 smallholders, 7 cottagers and 1 villager with ½ plough b 1
     & 1½ virgates.
    A mill which pays 6d; meadow, 12 acres; pasture, 10 furlongs
     in length and 2 furlongs wide; woodland, 3 furlongs in
     length and 2 furlongs in width. 2 cattle; 2 pigs; 120 sheep; 70 goats.
The value was and is 50s.

Huic m̄ addita.ē.ɪ.hida CONTVNE uocata.Alric teneꞇ ꝑ m̄
T.R.E.⁊ ꝑ tanto geldꞇ.Tra.ē.ɪ.car̄.Ibi.ē dim̄ car̄ cū ⁊ɪ.uillo
⁊ ɪɪ.borđ.⁊ ɪɪ.ac̄ p̄ti.⁊ ɪɪɪɪ.ac̄ pafturæ.⁊ ɪɪɪɪ.ac̄ filuæ minutæ.
Valuit ⁊ ual.x.foliđ.

Radulf⁹ ten̄ de.W.HARPETREV.Eluuacre tenuit T.R.E.
⁊ geldꞇ ꝑ.v.hid.Tra.ē.ɪɪɪɪ.car̄.In dn̄io.ē.ɪ.car̄.⁊ ɪɪ.ferui.
⁊ v.uilli ⁊ ɪɪ.borđ cū.ɪɪ.car̄.Ibi molin̄ redđ.v.fot.⁊ ʟvɪɪɪ.ac̄
p̄ti.⁊ ʟxɪɪ.ac̄ filuæ.Pafturæ.ɪ.leu in lḡ ⁊ lat̄.Valuit ⁊ ual.xʟ.fot.

Radulf⁹ ten̄ de.W.ECEWICHE.Eluuacre tenuit T.R.E.⁊ geldꞇ
ꝑ una v̄ træ ⁊ dim̄ ⁊ vɪɪɪ.acris.Tra.ē.ɪ.car̄.Ibi.ē.ɪ.borđ.Valet

Rademer ten̄ de W.ALSISTVNE.Aluuold tenuit   ⌈x.foliđ.
T.R.E.⁊ geldꞇ ꝑ.ɪ.hida.Tra.ē.ɪɪɪ.car̄.In dn̄io.ē.ɪ.car̄.cū.ɪ.
feruo.⁊ ɪ.uillo.⁊ ɪɪɪɪ.borđ ⁊ ɪɪɪ.cotar̄ hn̄tib⁹.ɪ.car̄.⁊ xʟ.ac̄
pafturæ.Valuit ⁊ ual.xx.foliđ.

Ipfe.W.ten̄ HVNESPIL.Aluuin⁹ tenuit T.R.E.⁊ geldꞇ ꝑ.ɪɪɪ.
uirg træ.Tra.ē.ɪɪ.car̄.In dn̄io.ē.ɪ.car̄.⁊ ɪɪɪɪ.ferui.⁊ ɪɪ.uilli.
⁊ v.borđ ⁊ ɪɪɪɪ.cotar̄ cū.ɪ.car̄.Ibi.xx.ac̄ p̄ti.Valuit ⁊ ual.xx.

Raimar ten̄ de.W.HIWIS.Chinefi tenuit T.R.E.   ⌈foliđ.
⁊ geldꞇ ꝑ una v̄ træ.Tra.ē.ɪ.car̄.q̄ ibi.ē cū.ɪ.feruo ⁊ ɪ.cotar̄ ⁊ ɪɪɪ.
borđ.Valuit ⁊ ual.x.foliđ.

Radulf⁹ ten̄ de.W.HIWIS.Aluui tenuit T.R.E.⁊ geldꞇ ꝑ
una v̄ træ.Tra.ē.ɪ.car̄.q̄ ibi.ē cū.v.borđ.Valuit ⁊ ual.x.fot.

1 hide called CHILCOMPTON has been added to this manor. E
Alric held it as a manor before 1066; it paid tax for as much. E
Land for 1 plough. ½ plough there, with L
  1 villager and 2 smallholders.
  Meadow, 2 acres; pasture, 4 acres; underwood, 4 acres.
The value was and is 10s.

31 Ralph holds (West)HARPTREE from W(alter). Alwaker held it
before 1066; it paid tax for 5 hides. Land for 4 ploughs.
In lordship 1 plough; 2 slaves; 4 hides. 354
  5 villagers and 2 smallholders with 2 ploughs & 1 hide. b 2
  A mill which pays 5s; meadow, 58 acres; woodland, 62 acres;
    pasture, 1 league in length and width. 2 cattle.
The value was and is 40s.

32 Ralph holds ECKWEEK from W(alter). Alwaker held it before 1066;
it paid tax for 1½ virgates of land and 8 acres. Land for 1 plough. 354
He has the whole in lordship. b 3
  1 smallholder.
Value 10s; when Walter acquired it, as much.

33 Rademar holds ALSTONE from W(alter). Alfwold held it before
1066; it paid tax for 1 hide. Land for 3 ploughs. In lordship 1
plough & 3 virgates, with 1 slave and 355
  1 villager, 4 smallholders and 3 cottagers who have 1 plough a 1
    & 1 virgate.
  Pasture, 40 acres. 10 cattle; 19 pigs; 45 sheep.
The value was and is 20s.

34 W(alter) holds HUNTSPILL himself. Alwin son of Goda held it before
1066; it paid tax for 3 virgates of land. Land for 2 ploughs.
In lordship 1 plough; 4 slaves; ½ hide. 355
  2 villagers, 5 smallholders and 4 cottagers with 1 plough a 2
    & 1 virgate.
  Meadow, 20 acres. 6 wild mares; 12 cattle; 18 pigs; 80 sheep.
The value was and is 20s.

35 Raimer the clerk holds 'HUISH' from W(alscin), his brother. Kinsey
held it before 1066; it paid tax for 1 virgate of land. Land for 1
plough, which is there, with 1 slave; 355
  1 cottager and 3 smallholders. a 3
    5 cattle; 10 pigs.
The value was and is 10s.

36 Ralph of Conteville holds 'HUISH' from W(alscin). Alfwy held it
before 1066; it paid tax for 1 virgate of land. Land for 1 plough,
which is there, with 355
  5 smallholders. a 4
The value was and is 10s.

Idē Rad ten de.W.ATEBERIE . Elſi tenuit T.R.E.7 geldb ꝑ.1.
hida 7 una v træ.Tra.ē.1.car.q̄ ibi.ē cū.1.uitto 7 1.borđ.
Ibi.x.ac̄ p̃ti.7 xx.ac̄ ſiluæ.Valuit 7 uat.xv.ſolid.

.XXI. TERRA WILLELMI DE MOION.

WILLELM de MOIVN ten de rege STOCHELANDE . Algar
tenuit T.R.E.7 geldb ꝑ.IIII.hid 7 una v træ.Tra.ē.v.car.
In dñio ſt.III.car.7 vi.ſerui.7 v.uitti.7 IIII.borđ cū dim car.
Ibi moliñ.redđ.x.den.7 xLVᴸxI.ac̄ p̃ti.7 xII.ac̄ ſiluæ.
Q̣do recep̃.ualb.Lx.ſolid.Modo.IIII.lib 7 x.ſolid.
Huic m̃.ē addit̃ SEDTAM̃TONE . Aluric teneb T.R.E.ꝑ uno m̃.
7 geldb ꝑ.III.v træ.Tra.ē.1.car.Ibi ſt.xIII.ac̄ p̃ti.7 vI.ac̄
ſiluæ.Valuit 7 uat.x.ſolid.

Ipſe ten TORRE.7 ibi.ē caſtellū ej.Aluric tenuit T.R.E.7 geldb
ꝑ dim hida.Tra.ē.1.car.Ibi.II.molini redđ.x.ſot.7 xv.borđ.
7 v.ac̄ p̃ti.7 xxx.ac̄ paſturæ.Valb oli.v.ſot.Modo.xv.ſolid.

Hugo ten de.W.TETESBERGE.Sex taini tenb T.R.E.7 geldb
ꝑ.II.hiđ.Tra.ē.IIII.car.In dñio.ē.1.car.7 III.ſerui.7 vi.uitti
7 xII.borđ cū.III.car 7 dim.Ibi.vI.ac̄ p̃ti.7 c.ac̄ paſturæ.
7 x.ac̄ moræ.7 II.ac̄ ſiluæ.Valuit 7 uat xL.ſolid.

Garmund ten de.W.AILGI.Algar tenuit T.R.E,7 geldb ꝑ dim
hida.Tra.ē.II.car.In dñio.ē una.cū.1.ſeruo.7 vi.borđ cū.1.
car.Ibi.x.ac̄ ſiluæ.Valuit 7 uat.xx.ſolid.

Robt ten de.W.LEGE.Sireuuald tenuit T.R.E.7 geldb
ꝑ.III.hiđ.Tra.ē.IIII.car.In dñio.ē.1.car.cū.1.ſeruo.

37 Ralph of Conteville also holds ADBER from W(alter). Alfsi held it
before 1066; it paid tax for 1 hide and 1 virgate of land. L
Land for 1 plough, which is there, with 355
   1 villager and 1 smallholder. b 1
   Meadow, 10 acres; woodland, 20 acres.
The value was and is 15s.

[25]   LAND OF WILLIAM OF MOHUN

1 William of Mohun holds STOCKLAND from the King. E
Algar held it before 1066; it paid tax for 4 hides and 1 virgate
of land. Land for 5 ploughs. In lordship 3 ploughs; 6 slaves;
3½ hides & 1 virgate. 356
   5 villagers and 4 smallholders with ½ plough & ½ hide. a 3
   A mill which pays 10d; meadow, 48 acres; woodland, 12 acres.
      3 cobs; 5 cattle; 15 pigs; 74 sheep.
Value when he acquired it, 60s.; now £4 10s.
   'SEABERTON' has been added to this manor. Aelfric held it E
before 1066 as one manor; it paid tax for 3 virgates of land.
Land for 1 plough. William holds it in lordship. E
   Meadow, 13 acres; woodland, 6 acres.
The value was and is 10s.

2 He holds DUNSTER himself; his castle is there. Aelfric held it
before 1066 ; it paid tax for ½ hide. Land for 1 plough.
   2 mills which pay 10s. 359
   15 smallholders. a 1
   Meadow, 5 acres; pasture, 30 acres.
Value formerly 5s; now 15s.

3 Hugh holds ADSBOROUGH from William. Six thanes held it before E
1066; it paid tax for 2 hides. Land for 4 ploughs. In lordship 1
plough; 3 slaves; 3 virgates. 356
   6 villagers and 12 smallholders with 3½ ploughs & 1 hide & 1 virgate. a 2
   Meadow, 6 acres; pasture, 100 acres; moor, 10 acres;
      woodland, 2 acres. 3 cattle; 1 pig.
The value was and is 40s.

4 Warmund holds ALEY from William. Algar held it before 1066;
it paid tax for ½ hide. Land for 2 ploughs. In lordship 1,
& 1 virgate, less ½ furlong, with 1 slave; 356
   6 smallholders with 1 plough & the rest of the land. b 1
   Woodland, 10 acres. 1 cob.
The value was and is 20s.

5 Robert holds LEIGH from William. Sheerwold held it before 1066;
it paid tax for 3 hides. Land for 4 ploughs. In lordship 1 356
plough & 2 hides & 2½ virgates, with 1 slave; b 2

7 v . uilli 7 ii . borđ .7 . viii . ac p̃ti . Silua . ii . q̃ʒ lg̃ .7 una q̃ʒ lat̃.
Valuit oli̐ . xxx . fol . Modo . xx . foliđ.

R̃ogeri ten de . W . *STRATE* . Hufcarl 7 Almar T.R.R.
7 geldb̃ p̃ . i . hida 7 dịm . Tra . e̐ . ii . car̃ . Ibi fſ . iii . uilli 7 i . borđ
cū . i . car̃ .7 una ac p̃ti 7 dimiđ . Paftura . v . q̃ʒ lg̃ .7 ii . q̃ʒ lat̃.

T̃urgis ten de . W . *BERNETONE* . Briftric ⌐ Valb̃ 7 ual . xv . fol.
tenb̃ T.R.E .7 geldb̃ p̃ . iii . hiđ 7 dimiđ . Tra . e̐ . xii . car̃ . In dn̄io
ſt . ii . car̃ .7 vii . ferui .7 xvi . uilli 7 ii . borđ cū . viii . car̃,

95 d

Ibi molin̄ redđ . xxx . den̄ .7 vi . ac p̃ti .7 xx . ac filuæ .7 i . leu
pafturæ . Q̃do recep̃ . ualb̃ . xl . fol . Modo . iiii . lib̃.

✠ H̃ tra fuit de æccla Glaftingbie . nec poterat inde fepari T.R.E.

O̐gifus ten de . W . *CLATEVRDE* . Aluiet teneb̃ T.R.E .7 geldb̃
p̃ . i . hida 7 dịm . Tra . e̐ . vii . car̃ . In dn̄io ſt . ii . car̃ .7 ii . ferui.
7 xvi . uilli 7 v . borđ cū . v . car̃ . Ibi molin̄ redđ . vi . den̄.
7 v . ac p̃ti .7 xxv . ac filuæ . Paftura dimiđ leū lg̃ .7 iiii . q̃ʒ
lat̃ . Valuit oli̐ . xx . fol . Modo . xl . foliđ.   ⌐ lande T.R.E.

✠ H̃ tra n̄ poterat fepari ab æccla Glaftingbie . fed erat ibi tain

Ipfe . W . ten *VDECOME* . Ælmer teneb̃ T.R.E .7 geldb̃ p̃ . iii.
hiđ . Tra . e̐ . xv . car̃ . In dn̄io ſt . iiii . car̃ .7 vi . ferui .7 xviii.
uilli 7 v . borđ cū . v . car̃ . Ibi . vi . porcarij redđ . xxxi . porc̃.
7 molin̄ redđ . v . fol .7 vi . ac p̃ti . Paftura . ii . leū lg̃ .7 i . leu lat̃.
Silua . i . leū lg̃ .7 dim leū lat̃ . Valb̃ oli̐ . iii . lib̃ . Modo . vi . lib̃.
De hac tra huj M̃ ten . iii . milites de . W . unā hiđ 7 dimiđ
virg træ .7 ibi hn̄t . ii . car̃ .7 iiii . uill 7 vi . borđ cū . i . car̃.
Ibi . ii . ac p̃ti .7 xiiii . ac filuæ . Paftura dimiđ leū lg̃ .7 v . q̃ʒ
lat̃ . Valb̃ 7 ual . xxxv . foliđ 7 vi . denar̃.

5 villagers and 2 smallholders.
Meadow, 8 acres; woodland 2 furlongs long and 1 furlong wide.
1 cob; 6 cattle; 24 sheep.
Value formerly 30s; now 20s.

6 Roger holds STREET from William. Guard and Aelmer held it E
[before 1066]; it paid tax for 1½ hides. Land for 2 ploughs.
In lordship 1 hide & 1 virgate & 4 oxen. 357
 3 villagers and 1 smallholder with 1 plough & 1 virgate. E a 1
 Meadow, 1½ acres; pasture 5 furlongs long and 2 furlongs wide.
The value was and is 15s.

7 Thorgils holds BROMPTON (Ralph) from William. Brictric held
it before 1066; it paid tax for 3½ hides. Land for 12 ploughs.
In lordship 2 ploughs; 7 slaves; 1 virgate. 357
 16 villagers and 2 smallholders with 8 ploughs & 3 hides & 1 virgate. a 2
 A mill which pays 30d; meadow, 6 acres; woodland, 20 acres; 95 d
  pasture, 1 league. 1 cob; 8 cattle; 5 pigs; 107 sheep; 12 goats.
Value when he acquired it, 40s; now £4.
† This land was (part of the lands) of Glastonbury Church; E
it could not be separated from it before 1066.

8 Ogis holds CLATWORTHY from William. Alfgeat, a woman, held it
before 1066; it paid tax for 1½ hides. Land for 7 ploughs.
In lordship 2 ploughs; 2 slaves; 3 virgates. 357
 16 villagers and 5 smallholders with 5 ploughs & 3 virgates. a 3
 A mill which pays 6d; meadow, 5 acres; woodland, 25 acres;
  pasture ½ league long and 4 furlongs wide. 1 cob; 8 cattle;
  20 pigs; 100 sheep; 30 goats.
Value formerly 20s; now 40s.
† This land could not be separated from Glastonbury Church; E
but it was thaneland there before 1066.

9 William holds CUTCOMBE himself. Aelmer held it before 1066;
it paid tax for 3 hides. Land for 15 ploughs. In lordship 4
ploughs; 6 slaves; 3 virgates. 357
 18 villagers and 5 smallholders with 5 ploughs & 1 hide & ½ virgate. b 1
 6 pigmen who pay 31 pigs.
 A mill which pays 5s; meadow, 6 acres; pasture 2 leagues long
  and 1 league wide; woodland 1 league long and ½ league
  wide. 36 unbroken mares; 2 cobs; 5 cattle; 3 pigs; 250 sheep; 47 goats.
Value formerly £3; now £6. E
 Of this manor's land three men-at-arms hold 1 hide and ½ E
virgate of land from William; they have 2 ploughs there, & 3
virgates, in lordship.
 4 villagers and 6 smallholders with 1 plough & 1½ virgates.
 Meadow, 2 acres; woodland, 14 acres; pasture ½ league long
  and 5 furlongs wide. 3 wild mares; 50 sheep.
The value was and is 35s 6d.

Ipſe.W.ten̄ MANEHEVE.Algar teneƀ T.R.E.7 geldƀ ᵽ.v.
hiđ.Tra.ē.xii.car̄.In dn̄io ſt.iii.car̄.7 xii.ſerui.7 xxvii.
uiłłi.7 xxii.borđ cū.x.car̄.Ibi molin̄ redđ.iii.ſoliđ.7 xii.
ac̄ ᵽti.7 xxiiii.ac̄ ſiluæ.Paſtura.iiii.leū łḡ.7 ii.leū lat̄.
Q̣do recep.ʼ ualƀ.c.ſoliđ.Modo.ʼvi.liƀ.

Ipſe.W.ten̄ AVCOME.Algar tenuit T.R.E.7 geldƀ ᵽ una hida.
Tra.ē.iii.car̄.In dn̄io.ē.i.car̄.7 iiii.ſerui.7 iii.uiłłi 7 iiii.borđ.
cū.ii.car̄.Ibi.viii.ac̄ ᵽti.7 iii.q̣ƺ paſturæ.Valuit 7 ual̄.xx.ſol.

Durand ten̄ de.W.BRVNE.Eduuold tenuit T.R.E.7 geldƀ
ᵽ.i.hida.Tra.ē.vi.car̄.In dn̄io ſt.ii.car̄ 7 dim.7 ii.ſerui.
7 xiii.uiłłi 7 iii.borđ cū.iiii.car̄.Ibi.i.ac̄ ᵽti.7 q̣t xx.ac̄
paſturæ.7 xii.ac̄ ſiluæ.Valƀ oł.xx.ſol.Modo.xl.ſoliđ.

Tres milites ten̄ de.W.LANGEHA.Tres taini teneƀ T.R.E.
7 geldƀ ᵽ.i.hida.Tra.ē.vi.car̄.In dn̄io ſt.iii.car̄.cū.i.ſeruo.
7 v.uiłłi 7 viii.borđ cū.iii.car̄ 7 dim.Ibi molin̄ redđ.iii.
ſoliđ.7 iiii.ac̄ ᵽti.7 lx.ac̄ paſturæ|Valuit 7 ual̄.xxx.ſol.
7 xxxvi. acræ ſiluæ,

Mainfrid ten̄ de.W.COARME.Ailuuard tenuit T.R.E.
7 geldƀ ᵽ dim hida.Tra.ē.iiii.car̄.In dn̄io.ē.i.car̄.cū uno
ſeruo.7 v.uiłłi 7 iiii.borđ cū.i.car̄.Ibi.i.ac̄ ᵽti.7 x.ac̄ ſiluæ.
Paſtura.v.q̣ƺ łḡ.7 v.lat̄.Valƀ oł.vii.ſol.Modo.xv.ſoliđ.

Ricarđ ten̄ de.W.BICHECOME.Duo taini teneƀ T.R.E.
7 geldƀ ᵽ una v̄ træ.Tra.ē.ii.car̄.In dn̄io.ē.i.car̄.7 iii.uiłłi
7 vi.borđ cū dim car̄.Ibi.iii.ac̄ ᵽti.7 xl.ac̄ paſturæ
Valƀ oł.vi.ſol.Modo.xv.ſoliđ.

10 William holds MINEHEAD himself. Algar held it before 1066;
it paid tax for 5 hides. Land for 12 ploughs. In lordship 3
ploughs; 12 slaves; 2½ hides.   358
    27 villagers and 22 smallholders with 10 ploughs & 2½ hides.   a 1
    A mill which pays 3s; meadow, 12 acres; woodland, 24 acres;
        pasture 4 leagues long and 2 leagues wide. 1 cob; 16 cattle;
        10 pigs; 300 sheep.
Value when he acquired it, 100s; now £6.

11 William holds ALCOMBE himself. Algar held it before 1066;
it paid tax for 1 hide. Land for 3 ploughs. In lordship 1
plough; 4 slaves; 3 virgates.   358
    3 villagers and 4 smallholders with 2 ploughs & 1 virgate.   a 2
    Meadow, 8 acres; pasture, 3 furlongs. 1 cob; 5 cattle; 200 sheep.
The value was and is 20s.

12 Durand holds 'BROWN' from William. Edwald held it before 1066;
it paid tax for 1 hide. Land for 6 ploughs. In lordship 2½
ploughs; 2 slaves; ½ hide.   358
    13 villagers and 3 smallholders with 4 ploughs & ½ hide.   a 3
    Meadow, 1 acre; pasture, 80 acres; woodland, 12 acres.
        2 cobs; 15 cattle; 23 pigs; 200 sheep, less 10; 44 goats.
Value formerly 20s; now 40s.

13 Three men-at-arms hold LANGHAM from William. Three thanes held E
it before 1066; it paid tax for 1 hide. Land for 6 ploughs.
In lordship 3 ploughs & ½ hide & 1 furlong, with 1 slave;   358
    5 villagers and 8 smallholders with 3½ ploughs & the rest of the land. a 4
    A mill which pays 3s; meadow, 4 acres; pasture, 60 acres;
        woodland, 36 acres. 8 cattle; 3 pigs; 75 sheep; 34 goats.
The value was and is 30s.
      William holds it as one manor.

14 Manfred holds QUARME from William. Alfward held it before 1066;
it paid tax for ½ hide. Land for 4 ploughs. In lordship 1
plough & 1 virgate, with 1 slave;   358
    5 villagers and 4 smallholders with 1 plough & 1 virgate.   b 1
    Meadow, 1 acre; woodland, 10 acres; pasture 5 furlongs long
        and 5 wide. 2 unbroken mares; 15 cattle; 42 wethers; 20 goats.
Value formerly 7s; now 15s.   E

15 Richard holds BICKHAM from William. Two thanes held it before   E
1066; it paid tax for 1 virgate of land. Land for 2 ploughs.
In lordship 1 plough; ½ virgate.   358
    3 villagers and 6 smallholders with ½ plough & ½ virgate.   b 2
    Meadow, 3 acres; pasture, 40 acres.
Value formerly 6s; now 15s.

Ipſe.W.teñ BRADEWRDE.Alric teneð T.R.E.7 geldð ꝓ diṁ
hida.Tra.ē.ɪ.car̄.q̄ ibi.ē in dñio.7 ɪɪ.ſerui.7 ɪɪɪ.uiłłi 7 ɪɪ.
borð cū.ɪ.car̄.Ibi.v.ac̄ p̄ti,Paſtura.ɪ.leū lḡ.7 diṁ leū lat̄.
Silua.ɪ.leū lḡ.7 ɪɪɪɪ.q̄ lat̄.Valð oli.x.ſot.Modo.xv.ſot.

Radulf⁹teñ de.W.AVENA.Aluric teneð T.R.E.7 geldð pro
diṁ hida.Tra.ē.ɪɪ.caŕ.In dñio.ē.ɪ.caŕ.7 ɪ.uiłłs 7 v.borð
cū diṁ car̄.Ibi moliñ redð.xx.deñ.7 ɪɪɪɪ.ac̄ p̄ti.7 ɪɪ.ac̄ ſiluæ.
7 ʟ.ac̄ paſturæ.Valuit 7 uat.x.ſolið.

Ipſe.W.teñ STANTVNE.Walle teneð T.R.E.7 geldð pro
ɪɪɪ.virḡ træ.Tra.ē.ɪɪ.car̄.Ibi.ɪɪ.uiłłi 7 ɪɪ.ſerui.7 ɪɪ.borð
cū.ɪ.car̄.7 v.ac̄ p̄ti.7 xʟ.ac̄ paſturæ.Valet.xv.ſolið.
Huic m̄ addita una v træ.quã tenuit uñ tain⁹ T.R.E.ꝓ uno m̄.
Tra.ē.ɪ.car̄.Ibi.ē uñ borð 7 ɪɪɪ.ac̄ p̄ti.7 ʟ.ac̄ paſturæ.

Ipſe.W.teñ AISSEFORDE.Domno tenuit T.R.E ╱Valet.ɪɪɪ.ſot.
7 geldð ꝓ uno ferling.Tra.ē.ɪɪ.boū.Ibi.ē uñ uiłłs 7 xv.ac̄
paſturæ.Valuit 7 uat.xv.denar.

Ipſe.W.teñ AISSEFORDE.Sarpo teneð T.R.E.7 geldð ꝓ.ɪ.ferling
7 dimið.Tra.ē diṁ car̄,Sed jaçet in paſtura.7 redð.xɪɪ.denar.

96 a
Durand⁹ teñ de.W.STAWEIT.Leuing tenuit T.R.E.7 geldð
ꝓ una v træ.Tra.ē.ɪ.car̄.q̄ ibi.ē in dñio.cū.ɪ.uiłło 7 ɪ.borð.
Ibi.xɪɪɪɪ.ac̄ ſiluæ.Valð.ɪɪɪ.ſot.Modo.x.ſolið.

16 William holds BROADWOOD himself. Alric held it before 1066;
it paid tax for ½ hide. Land for 1 plough, which is there,   E
in lordship, & 1½ virgates; 2 slaves;   358
   3 villagers and 2 smallholders with 1 plough & ½ virgate.   b 3
  Meadow, 5 acres; pasture 1 league long and ½ league wide;
    woodland 1 league long and 4 furlongs wide. 2 cobs; 4 cattle;
    60 sheep.
Value formerly 10s; now 15s.

17 Ralph holds AVILL from William. Aelfric held it before 1066;
it paid tax for ½ hide. Land for 2 ploughs. In lordship 1 plough;
the whole (of the land), except for 12 acres of land.   E
   1 villager and 5 smallholders with ½ plough & the said 12 acres.   359
   A mill which pays 20d; meadow, 4 acres; woodland, 2 acres;   a 2
    pasture, 50 acres. 1 (head of) cattle.
The value was and is 10s.

18 William holds STAUNTON himself. Wallo held it before 1066;
it paid tax for 3 virgates of land. Land for 2 ploughs.
In lordship 2½ virgates.   359
   2 villagers, 2 slaves and 2 smallholders with 1 plough   a 3
     & ½ virgate.
  Meadow, 5 acres; pasture, 40 acres.
Value 15s; when he acquired it, 7s 6d.
   To this manor has been added 1 virgate of land which a thane   E
held as one manor before 1066. Land for 1 plough.
   1 smallholder.
   Meadow, 3 acres; pasture, 50 acres.   E
Value 3s; when he acquired it, as much.

19 William holds EXFORD himself. Dunn held it before 1066;
it paid tax for 1 furlong. Land for 2 oxen.   359
   1 villager.   b 1
   Pasture, 15 acres.
The value was and is 15d.

20 William holds EXFORD himself. Sharp held it before 1066;
it paid tax for 1½ furlongs. Land for ½ plough; but it lies   359
in the pasture.   b 2
It pays 12d; when he acquired it, as much.

21 Durand holds (Old) STOWEY from William. Leofing held it   96 a
before 1066; it paid tax for 1 virgate of land.
Land for 1 plough, which is there, in lordship, & 3½ furlongs, with
   1 villager and 1 smallholder (who have) ½ furlong.   359
   Woodland, 14 acres. 4 cattle; 20 sheep.   b 3
The value was 3s; now 10s.

Durand ten̄ de.W.*WOCHETREV*.Manno tenuit T.R.E.
7 geldb̄ p̄ dim̄ uirḡ træ.Tra.ē.ɪ.car̄.Ibi sꝼ,ɪɪ.uiꝉꝉi cū dim̄ car̄.
7 ɪɪɪɪ.ac̄ filuæ.Valuit,ɪɪɪɪ.folid̄.Modo.vɪ.folid̄.

Durand ten̄ de.W.*ALVRENECOTE*.Leuuin tenuit T.R.E.7 geld̄
p̄ dim̄ virḡ.Tra.ē.ɪɪ.car̄.Ibi.ē.ɪ.car̄ cū.ɪɪ.uiꝉꝉis 7 ɪɪ.bord̄
7 vɪɪɪ.ac̄ pafturæ.7 ɪɪ.ac̄ filuæ.Valuit 7 uaꝉ.vɪ.folid̄.

Goisfrid ten̄ de.W.*MENE*.Leuuin tenuit T.R.E.7 geldb̄
p̄ dim̄ hida.Tra.ē.ɪɪ.car̄.q̄ ibi sꝼ in dn̄io.7 ɪɪɪɪ.ferui cū.ɪ.bord̄
Ibi.ɪ.ac̄ p̄ti.7 ɪɪɪɪ.ac̄ filuæ.7 ʟ.ac̄ pafturæ.Valuit,xv.foꝉ.

Roger ten̄ de.W.*BRATONE*.Aluric teneb̄ T.R.E.7 geldb̄
p̄.ɪɪɪ.virḡ træ.Tra.ē.ɪɪɪɪ.car̄.In dn̄io sꝼ.ɪɪ.car̄.cū.ɪ.feruo.
7 ɪɪ.uiꝉꝉi,7 ɪɪɪɪ.bord̄ cū.ɪɪ.car̄.Ibi.ɪɪ.ac̄ p̄ti.7 c.ac̄ pafturæ.
Valuit oꝉi.v.folid̄.Modo.xxx.folid̄.

Rogeri ten̄ de.W.*ERNOLE*.Paulin teneb̄ T.R.E.7 geldb̄ p̄
una hida.Tra.ē.ɪɪɪ.car̄.In dn̄io.ē car̄ 7 dim̄.7 ɪ.feruus.7 ɪ.bord̄
7 ɪɪɪɪ.uiꝉꝉi cū.ɪ.car̄.Ibi.ɪ.leū filuæ minutæ in lḡ,7 dim̄ leū laꝼ
Valb̄ oꝉi.v.folid̄.Modo.xxv.folid̄.

Rannulf ten̄ *LOLOCHESBERIE*.Duo taini tenuer̄ T.R.E.7 geldb̄
p̄.ɪ.hida.Tra.ē.ɪɪɪɪ.car̄.In dn̄io.ē una car̄.7 ɪɪɪ.ferui.7 vɪ.uiꝉꝉi
7 ɪɪɪ.bord̄ cū.ɪɪɪ.car̄.Ibi.c.ac̄ pafturæ.7 xxx.ac̄ filuæ.Valet

Nigel ten̄ de.W.*LOLOCHESBERIE*.Brifmar ⌠xx.folid̄.
tenuit T.R.E.7 geldb̄ p̄.ɪ.hida.Tra.ē.ɪɪɪ.car̄.Ibi.ɪɪ.ac̄ p̄ti.
7 c.ac̄ pafturæ.7 xxx.ac̄ filuæ.Valuit 7 uaꝉ.xv.folid̄.

22 Durand holds OAKTROW from William. Manni held it before 1066; it paid tax for ½ virgate of land. Land for 1 plough. In lordship 1 furlong & ½ plough.

   2 villagers with ½ plough & 1 furlong.

   Woodland, 4 acres. 6 cattle; 50 sheep; 20 goats; 8 pigs.

The value was 4s; now 6s.

359
b 4

23 Durand holds ALLERCOTT from William. Leofwin held it before 1066; it paid tax for ½ virgate. Land for 2 ploughs. 1 plough there, with

   2 villagers and 2 smallholders.

   Pasture, 8 acres; woodland, 2 acres. 4 cattle.

The value was and is 6s.

L
360
a 1

24 Geoffrey holds MYNE from William. Leofwin held it before 1066; it paid tax for ½ hide. Land for 2 ploughs, which are there, in lordship; 4 slaves with

   1 smallholder.

   Meadow, 1 acre; woodland, 4 acres; pasture, 50 acres.

     107 sheep; 50 goats.

The value was (is) 15s; when he acquired it, 10s.

360
a 2

25 Roger holds BRATTON from William. Aelfric held it before 1066; it paid tax for 3 virgates of land. Land for 4 ploughs. In lordship 2 ploughs & 2 virgates, with 1 slave;

   2 villagers and 4 smallholders with 2 ploughs & 1 virgate.

   Meadow, 2 acres; pasture, 100 acres. 12 cattle; 60 goats.

Value formerly 5s; now 30s.

360
a 3

26 Roger holds KNOWLE from William. Paulinus held it before 1066; it paid tax for 1 hide. Land for 3 ploughs. In lordship 1½ ploughs; 1 slave; 3 virgates.

   1 smallholder and 4 villagers with 1 plough & 1 virgate.

   Underwood, 1 league in length and ½ league wide.

     7 wild mares; 20 cattle; 16 pigs; 120 sheep.

Value formerly 5s; now 25s.

360
a 4

27 Ranulf holds LUXBOROUGH. Two thanes held it before 1066; it paid tax for 1 hide. Land for 4 ploughs. In lordship 1 plough; 3 slaves; 1 virgate.

   6 villagers and 3 smallholders with 3 ploughs & 3 virgates.

   Pasture, 100 acres; woodland, 30 acres. 6 cattle; 12 pigs; 100 sheep.

Value 20s; when he acquired it, 15s.

E
360
b 1

28 Nigel holds LUXBOROUGH from William. Brictmer held it before 1066; it paid tax for 1 hide. Land for 3 ploughs. In lordship 1 virgate & 1 plough.

   6 villagers & 3 smallholders (have) 3 virgates & 1 plough.

   Meadow, 2 acres; pasture, 100 acres; woodland, 30 acres.

The value was and is 15s.

360
b 2

Ipſe.W.ten̄ CANTOCHEVE.Elnod teneꝶ T.R.E.7 geldꝶ ꝓ.III.hiꝺ
7 dim̄.Tra.ē.VIII.caꝛ.In dn̄io ſt.III.caꝛ.7 VII.ſerui.7 X.uiꝉꝉi
7 IIII.borꝺ cū.VI.caꝛ.Ibi.XVI.ac̄ p̄ti.7 L.ac̄ ſiluæ.Paſtura
una leū lḡ.7 una leū laꝶ.Valuit,III.liꝧ.Modo.IIII.liꝧ.

Ipſe.W.ten̄ GHILVETVNE.Aluuarꝺ 7 Leuric teneꝶ ꝓ.II.m̄ T.R.E,
7 geldꝶ ꝓ.X.hiꝺ 7 dim̄.Tra,ē.X.caꝛ.In dn̄io ſt.IIII.caꝛ.7 VII,
ſerui.7 XVI.uiꝉꝉi 7 VI.borꝺ cū.V.caꝛ.Ibi.LX.ac̄ p̄ti.7 LX.ac̄ pa
ſturæ.7 c.ac̄ ſiluæ.Valuit oli.c.ſoꝉ,Modo.VII.liꝧ,

De eaꝺ ꞇra ten̄ Radulf̄ de,W.una hiꝺ.7 ibi hꝶ,I.caꝛ.7 II.uiꝉꝉos
cū.I.caꝛ,Ibi.V.ac̄ p̄ti.7 una uirḡ paſturæ.Valet,XX,ſoliꝺ.

Ipſe.W.ten̄ NIWETVNE.Aluiet tenuit T.R.E,7 geldꝶ ꝓ.IIII.
hiꝺ 7 dim̄.Tra,ē.VII.caꝛ,In dn̄io ſt.II.caꝛ.7 IIII.ſerui.7 XIII,uiꝉꝉi
7 IIII.borꝺ cū.V.caꝛ.Ibi molin̄ redꝺ.XL,denaꝛ.7 XVIII.ac̄ p̄ti.
7 L.ac̄ ſiluæ.7 una leū paſturæ in lḡ 7 laꝶ,Valꝧ.LX.ſoꝉ.m̄.c.ſoꝉ.

Ipſe.W.ten̄ VLVRETVNE.Britmar tenuit T.R.E.7 geldꝶ ꝓ dim̄
hida.Tra.ē.I.caꝛ,Ibi.II.uiꝉꝉi 7 II.borꝺ hn̄t.II.caꝛ.Ibi.VII.ac̄ p̄ti.
7 X.ac̄ paſturæ,7 VII.ac̄ ſiluæ.Valꝧ oli.X.ſoꝉ.Modo.XX.ſoliꝺ.

Dudeman ten̄ ELWRDE.de.W.Dunne teneꝶ T.R.E.7 geldꝶ ꝓ.IIII.
virg.Tra.ē.V.caꝛ.In dn̄io ſt.II.caꝛ.7 II.ſerui.7 IX,uiꝉꝉi 7 VIII,
borꝺ cū.III.caꝛ.Ibi molin̄ redꝺ,IIII.ſoꝉ.7 una ac̄ p̄ti 7 dimiꝺ,
7 cXX.ac̄ paſturæ.7 L.ac̄ ſiluæ.Valꝧ oli.XX.ſoꝉ.Modo.XL,ſoliꝺ.
De hac hida ten̄ rex una v꞉ ꞇræ ad maneꝛ de Welletune.

William himself holds

29 (West) QUANTOXHEAD. Alnoth the reeve held it before 1066;
it paid tax for 3½ hides. Land for 8 ploughs.
   In lordship 3 ploughs; 7 slaves; 2 hides & 1 virgate.
      10 villagers and 4 smallholders with 6 ploughs & 1 hide & 1 virgate.
      Meadow, 16 acres; woodland, 50 acres; pasture 1 league
         long and 1 league wide. 2 cobs; 6 cattle; 8 pigs; 200 sheep.
   The value was £3; now £4.

360
b 3

30 KILTON. Alfward and Leofric held it as two manors before 1066;
it paid tax for 10½ hides. Land for 10 ploughs. In lordship 4
ploughs; 7 slaves; 7½ hides & ½ virgate.
      16 villagers and 6 smallholders with 5 ploughs & 2 hides,
         less ½ virgate.
      Meadow, 60 acres; pasture, 60 acres; woodland, 100 acres.
         4 cobs; 4 cattle; 10 pigs; 130 sheep.
   Value formerly 100s; now £7.
      Ralph holds 1 hide of this land from William; he has 1 plough
   & 3 virgates & 1 furlong in lordship, and
      2 villagers with 1 plough & 3 furlongs.
      Meadow, 5 acres; pasture, 1 virgate. 4 cattle; 2 pigs; 22 sheep; 5 goats.
   Value 20s.

E

360
b 4

E
E

E

31 NEWTON. Alfgeat held it before 1066; it paid tax for 4½ hides.
Land for 7 ploughs. In lordship 2 ploughs; 4 slaves;
3 hides, less 1 virgate & 1 furlong.
      13 villagers and 4 smallholders with 5 ploughs & 1 hide, 3 virgates
         & 1 furlong.
      A mill which pays 40d; meadow, 18 acres; woodland, 50 acres;
         pasture, 1 league in length and width. 2 cobs; 4 cattle;
         6 pigs; 80 sheep.
   The value was 60s; now 100s.

361
a 1

32 WOOLSTON. Brictmer held it before 1066; it paid tax for ½ hide.
Land for 1 plough. In lordship 5 acres.
      2 villagers and 2 smallholders have 2 ploughs.
      Meadow, 7 acres; pasture, 10 acres; woodland, 7 acres.
   Value formerly 10s; now 20s.

361
a 2

E

33 Dodman holds ELWORTHY from William. Dunn held it before 1066;
it paid tax for 4 virgates. Land for 5 ploughs. In lordship 2
ploughs; 2 slaves; 1 virgate.
      9 villagers and 8 smallholders with 3 ploughs & 2 virgates.
      A mill which pays 4s; meadow, 1½ acres; pasture, 120 acres;
         woodland, 50 acres. 1 cob; 12 pigs; 72 sheep.
   Value formerly 20s; now 40s.
      Of this hide the King holds 1 virgate of land as (part of) the
   manor of Williton.

361
a 3

Dudeman teñ de . W , *WILLET* . Dunne teneб T.R.E .7 geldб ᵽ
dim̃ hida . T̃ra . ē , IIII . car̃ . In dñio . ē . I . car̃ . cū . I . ſeruo .7 IX . uiłłi
7 VI . borđ cū , III . car̃ . Ibi moliñ ſine cenſu ,7 III . ac̃ p̃ti ,7 L . ac̃ pa
ſturæ .7 XL , ac̃ ſiluæ . Valb oł̃ . X . ſoliđ . Modo . XX . ſoliđ .

Idē teñ de , W , *COLEFORD* . Brictuin teneб T.R.E .7 geldб ᵽ dim̃
hida . uno ferling miñ . T̃ra . ē . II , car̃ , Ibi , II . uiłłi hñt . I , car̃ .

Idē . D . teñ de , W . *WACET* . Aluuold teneб   ⌐Valet . VI . ſoliđ ,
T.R.E .7 geldб ᵽ una v̄ tr̃æ , T̃ra . ē dim̃ car̃ . Ibi tam̃ , ē . I , car̃ ,
cū . I . ſeruo .7 I , borđ . Ibi moliñ redđ , X . ſoliđ , Valet . XV , ſoł .

Hugo teñ de , W ; *TVRVESTONE* . Lefſin teneб T.R̃.E .7 geldб
ᵽ . I . hida 7 dim̃ , T̃ra . ē . III . car̃ . In dñio ſt . II . car̃ .7 v . uiłłi 7 VI .
borđ cū . II . car̃ . Ibi moliñ ſine cenſu .7 XV . ac̃ p̃ti 7 dim̃ .7 XI . ac̃
paſturæ .7 XLVI , ac̃ ſilu꙰ . Valb oł̃ , XXX , ſoliđ . Modo , L , ſoliđ ,

96 b
Hugo teñ de , W . *HOLEFORD* . Aluuold teneб T.R.E ,7 geldб ᵽ , I .
hida , T̃ra . ē . II , car̃ . q̃ ibi ſt in dñio . cū , I . ſeruo .7 I . uiłło ,
7 v . borđ cū . I , car̃ . Ibi moliñ redđ , X . den̄ ,7 III , ac̃ p̃ti ,7 LX ,
ac̃ paſturæ .7 IIII . ac̃ ſiluæ . Valb oł̃ . X . ſoliđ . Modo , XX . ſoliđ ,

Rogeri teñ de , W . *HARETREV* . Vluuold teneб T.R.E .7 geldб
ᵽ , I . hida . T̃ra . ē . IIII , car̃ . In dñio . ē . I . car̃ . cū . I . ſeruo .7 II . uiłłi
7 VI . borđ cū . I . car̃ . Ibi moliñ redđ . VI . den̄ .7 v . ac̃ p̃ti .7 C , ac̃
paſturæ ,7 VI . ac̃ ſiluæ . Valb oł̃ . X . ſoł . Modo . XX . ſoliđ ,

Meinfrid 7 Roбt teñ de . W . *CIBEWRDE* . Duo taini teneб T.R.E .
7 geldб ᵽ . I . hida , T̃ra . ē . III , car̃ . In dñio . ē . I . car̃ .7 uñ uiłłs 7 IIII .

34 Dodman holds WILLETT from William. Dunn held it before 1066; it paid tax for ½ hide. Land for 4 ploughs. In lordship 1 plough & 1 virgate, with 1 slave;   361
    9 villagers and 6 smallholders with 3 ploughs & 1½ virgates.   b 1
    A mill without dues; meadow, 3 acres; pasture, 50 acres; woodland, 40 acres. 1 cob; 4 cattle; 3 pigs; 100 sheep.
Value formerly 10s; now 20s.

35 He also holds COLEFORD from William. Brictwin held it before 1066; it paid tax for ½ hide, less 1 furlong. Land for 2 ploughs.
In lordship 1½ virgates.   361
    2 villagers have 1 plough & 2 furlongs.   b 2
Value 6s; when William acquired it, 3s.

36 Dodman(?) also holds WATCHET from William. Alfwold held it   E
before 1066; it paid tax for 1 virgate of land. Land for ½ plough.
1 plough there, however, with 1 slave;   E
    1 smallholder.   361
    A mill which pays 10s. 1 cob.   b 3
Value 15s; when William acquired it, 5s.

37 Hugh holds TORWESTON from William. Leofsi held it before 1066; it paid tax for 1½ hides. Land for 3 ploughs. In lordship 2 ploughs; 1 hide, less ½ virgate.   361
    5 villagers and 6 smallholders with 2 ploughs & ½ hide & ½ virgate.   b 4
    A mill without dues; meadow, 15½ acres; pasture, 11 acres; woodland, 46 acres. 14 cattle; 2 pigs; 88 sheep.
Value formerly 30s; now 50s.

38 Hugh holds HOLFORD (St. Mary) from William. Alfwold held it   E 96 b
before 1066; it paid tax for 1 hide. Land for 2 ploughs,
which are there, in lordship, & 3 virgates, with 1 slave and   362
    1 villager and 5 smallholders with 1 plough & 1 virgate.   a 1
    A mill which pays 10d; meadow, 3 acres; pasture, 60 acres; woodland, 4 acres. 9 pigs; 4 sheep; 64 goats.   E
Value formerly 10s; now 20s.

39 Roger holds HARTROW from William. Wulfwold held it before 1066; it paid tax for 1 hide. Land for 4 ploughs. In lordship 1 plough & 1 hide, less 1 furlong, with 1 slave;   362
    2 villagers and 6 smallholders with 1 plough & 1 furlong.   a 2
    A mill which pays 6d; meadow, 5 acres; pasture, 100 acres; woodland, 6 acres. 5 cattle; 3 pigs; 20 sheep; 20 goats.
Value formerly 10s; now 20s.

40 Manfred and Robert hold CHUBWORTHY from William. Two thanes   E
held it before 1066; it paid tax for 1 hide. Land for 3 ploughs.
In lordship 1 plough;   362
    1 villager and 4 smallholders with ½ plough.   a 3

borđ cũ dim car̃ . Ibi . IIII . ac̃ p̃ti . 7 L . ac̃ pasturæ . 7 v . ac̃ filuæ.

Valb oli . x . fol . Modo . xII . foliđ.

Turgis ten de . W . COME , Ailmer teneb T.R.E . 7 geldb p . I . hida.
Tra . ē . III . car̃ , In dñio . ē . I . car̃ . cũ . I . feruo . 7 vI . borđ cũ dim
car̃ . Ibi moliñ fine cenfu . 7 IIII . ac̃ p̃ti . 7 L . ac̃ pasturæ . 7 IIII .
q̃ƺ filuæ in lg̃ . 7 II . q̃ƺ in lat̃ , Valb oli . xv . fol , Modo . xx . fol,

Brictric ten de , W . SORDEMANEFORD . Brictric tenb T.R.E.
7 geldb p una v træ . Tra . ē dim car̃ , Hanc hr̃ ibi . I . borđ . 7 vII .
ac̃s filuæ . Valuit 7 ual̃ , vI . foliđ.

Nigel ten de , W . BADEHELTONE . Duo taini teneb T.R.E .
7 geldb p . II . hiđ . Tra . ē . v . car̃ , In dñio . ē . I . car̃ . 7 III . ferui,
7 xII . uilti 7 I . borđ 7 v . cotar̃ . cũ . IIII . car̃ . Ibi moliñ redđ
vII . fol 7 vI . den . 7 vI . ac̃ p̃ti . 7 xL . ac̃ pasture , 7 xII . ac̃ filuæ,

Valb oli . xx . fol . Modo . L . foliđ.

Rannulf ten de , W . MANEWORDE , Ulf teneb p . I . hida , Tra . ē
III . car̃ . In dñio . ē . I , car̃ . cũ . I . feruo , 7 III . uilti 7 II . borđ cũ dim
car̃ . Ibi . vII . ac̃ p̃ti , 7 xII . ac̃ filuæ , 7 xII . ac̃ pasturæ,

Valb oli . x . fol . Modo . xx . foliđ.

Dodeman ten de . W . RVNETONE , Duo taini teneb T.R.E ,
7 geldb p . II . hiđ , Tra . ē . II . car̃ . In dñio . ē . I . car̃ . 7 IIII . ferui.
7 un uilts 7 vIII . borđ cũ . I . car̃ . Ibi moliñ redđ . v . foliđ , 7 vIII .
ac̃ p̃ti . 7 x . ac̃ filuæ . Valb oli . xx . foliđ , Modo . L . foliđ,

Dodeman ten de . W . POVSELLE . Vluric̃ teneb T.R.E . 7 geldb
p dim hida . Tra . e . II . car̃ . Ibi . ē un feruus . 7 III . ac̃ p̃ti | 7 , xx . ac̃ filuæ. Val̃ . x . fol,
Huic M̃ addita , ē una hida quã teneb T.R.E , un tain libe,
Tra . ē . I . car̃ , Valuit 7 ual̃ . xxx . denar,

Meadow, 4 acres; pasture, 50 acres; woodland, 5 acres.
9 cattle; 80 sheep; 32 goats.
Value formerly 10s; now 12s.

41 Thorgils holds COMBE (Sydenham) from William. Aelmer held it
before 1066; it paid tax for 1 hide. Land for 3 ploughs.
In lordship 1 plough & ½ hide, with 1 slave;
1 villager and 6 smallholders with ½ plough & 1 furlong.
A mill without dues; meadow, 4 acres; pasture, 50 acres;
woodland, 4 furlongs in length and 2 furlongs in width.
3 pigs; 30 sheep.
Value formerly 15s; now 20s.

362
b 1
E

42 Brictric holds 'SHORTMANSFORD' from William. Brictric also held it
before 1066; it paid tax for 1 virgate of land. Land for ½ plough. E
1 smallholder has it there, and
woodland, 7 acres. 11 goats.
The value was and is 6s.

E 362
b 2

43 Nigel holds BATHEALTON from William. Two thanes held it before E
1066; it paid tax for 2 hides. Land for 5 ploughs. In lordship
1 plough; 3 slaves; 1 hide.
12 villagers, 1 smallholder and 5 cottagers with 4 ploughs & 1 hide.
A mill which pays 7s 6d; meadow, 6 acres; pasture, 40 acres;
woodland, 12 acres. 3 cattle; 3 pigs; 50 sheep; 50 goats.
Value formerly 20s; now 50s.

362
b 3

44 Ranulf holds MANWORTHY from William. Ulf held it (. . . .) for
1 hide. Land for 3 ploughs. In lordship 1 plough & 3 virgates & 1 furlong,
with 1 slave;
3 villagers and 2 smallholders with ½ plough & 3 furlongs.
Meadow, 7 acres; wooodland, 12 acres; pasture, 12 acres.
1 cob; 2 cattle.
Value formerly 10s; now 20s.

362
b 4

45 Dodman holds RUNNINGTON from William. Two thanes held it E
before 1066; it paid tax for 2 hides. Land for 2 ploughs.
In lordship 1 plough; 4 slaves; 1 hide & 3 virgates.
1 villager and 8 smallholders with 1 plough & 1 virgate.
A mill which pays 5s; meadow, 8 acres; woodland, 10 acres.
1 cob; 4 cattle; 23 pigs.
Value formerly 20s; now 50s.

363
a 1

46 Dodman holds POLESHILL from William. Wulfric held it before
1066; it paid tax for ½ hide. Land for 2 ploughs. 1 slave there.
Meadow, 3 acres; woodland, 20 acres. 1 cow.
Value 10s; when he acquired it, as much.
To this manor has been added 1 hide which a thane held freely E
before 1066. Land for 1 plough.
The value was and is 30d.

363
a 2

Mainfrid ten de . W . LEGE . Cheping teneb T.R.E. 7 geldb
p dim hida . Tam ibi . ē . I . hida . Tra , II . car . In dnio , ē , I . car .
7 II . ſerui , 7 II . uilti , 7 III . bord cū dim car , Ibi . I . ac pti , 7 XII .
ac paſturæ . 7 xx . ac ſilue , Valb oli . v . ſot , Modo . XII . ſolid .

Rogeri ten de . W. STOCHE . Eddida tenb T,R,E, 7 geldb p . II .
hid , Tra . ē , II . car . q̄ ibi ſt in dnio , cū . VIII . bord . Ibi , VIII .
ac pti . 7 IIII . ac ſiluæ minutæ . Valuit 7 ual . xxx . ſolid .

Ipſe . W , ten BRVNFELLE , Alnod teneb T.R.E. 7 geldb p . III . hid . Tra . ē , x , car .
In dnio . ē . I . car . 7 VIII . ſerui . 7 XII . uilti 7 II . bord . cū . IIII . car .
Ibi . x . ac pti . 7 una leū paſturæ , 7 una leū ſiluæ in lḡ 7 lat .
Qdo recep . ualb . XL . ſot , Modo . LX , ſolid .

Ipſe . W . ten LIDIARD , Alric teneb T,R,E, 7 geldb p . II , hid ,
Tra , ē , VI . car , In dnio , ē , I , car , 7 IIII . ſerui . 7 x , uilti 7 VI . bord
cū , I . car . Ibi moliñ redd . VIII . ſolid , 7 xv , ac pti , 7 x , ac paſtæ .
7 xx , ac ſiluæ , Valuit 7 ual . VII , lib .

Ipſe , W . ten BAGEBERGE . Leuric teneb T,R.E, 7 geldb p , III .
hid . Tra . ē . x . car . In dnio ſt . III . car . 7 VII . ſerui . 7 XXI , uilt .
7 II . bord cū . IIII . car , Ibi . XI . ac pti , 7 cc . ac paſturæ . 7 x , ac
ſiluæ , Valb 7 ual . c . ſolid .

Ipſe . W . ten STOCHE , Aluuard teneb T,R,E. 7 geldb p , II , hid .
Tra . ē , VI . car . Ibi VI , uilti 7 II . bord cū . I . ſeruo hñt . II . car .
Ibi . I . ac pti , 7 cc . ac paſturæ . 7 VI . ac ſiluæ . Valb 7 ual . xxx . ſot ,

Radulf ten de . W . HERFELD . Eluuin teneb T,R.E. 7 geldb
p . III . hid 7 dim . Tra . ē . VI . car , In dnio . ē , I . car , 7 v . ſerui .

47 Manfred holds LEIGH from William. Cheping held it before 1066; it paid tax for ½ hide. 1 hide there, however. Land for 2 ploughs. In lordship 1 plough; 2 slaves; 3 virgates & 1 furlong.   363
    2 villagers and 3 smallholders with ½ plough & 3 furlongs.   a 3
    Meadow, 1 acre; pasture, 12 acres; woodland, 20 acres.
Value formerly 5s; now 12s.

48 Roger holds STOCKLINCH from William. Edith held it before 1066; it paid tax for 2 hides. Land for 2 ploughs, which are there, in lordship & 1½ hides & 3 furlongs, with   363
    8 smallholders (who have) 1 virgate & 1 furlong.   b 1
    Meadow, 8 acres; underwood, 4 acres. 14 sheep.   E
The value was and is 30s.

  William himself holds

49 BROOMFIELD. Alnoth held it before 1066; it paid tax for 3 hides. Land for 10 ploughs. In lordship 1 plough; 8 slaves; 1 hide & 3 virgates.   363
    12 villagers and 2 smallholders with 4 ploughs & 1 hide & 1 virgate.   b 2
    Meadow, 10 acres; pasture, 1 league; woodland, 1 league
      in length and width. 1 cob; 13 cattle; 17 pigs; 155 sheep; 16 goats.
Value when he acquired it, 40s; now 60s.

50 (East) LYDEARD. Alric held it before 1066; it paid tax for 2 hides. Land for 6 ploughs. In lordship 1 plough; 4 slaves; 1½ virgates.   363
    10 villagers and 6 smallholders with 1 plough & 6½ virgates.   b 3
    A mill which pays 8s; meadow, 15 acres; pasture, 10 acres;
      woodland, 20 acres. 1 cob; 5 cattle; 115 sheep.
The value was and is £7.

51 BAGBOROUGH. Leofric held it before 1066; it paid tax for 3 hides. Land for 10 ploughs. In lordship 3 ploughs; 7 slaves; 3 virgates.   364
    21 villagers and 2 smallholders with 4 ploughs & 2 hides & 1 virgate.   a 1
    Meadow, 11 acres; pasture, 200 acres; woodland, 10 acres.
      2 cobs; 4 cattle; 6 pigs; 150 sheep; 45 goats.
The value was and is 100s.

52 STOKE (St. Mary). Alfwold held it before 1066; it paid tax for 2 hides. Land for 6 ploughs. In lordship 1 hide & 1 virgate.   364
    6 villagers and 2 smallholders with 1 slave have 2 ploughs   a 2
      & 3 virgates.
    Meadow, 1 acre; pasture, 200 acres; woodland, 6 acres.
The value was and is 30s.

53 Ralph holds HEATHFIELD from William. Alwin held it before 1066; it paid tax for 3½ hides. Land for 6 ploughs. In lordship 1 plough; 5 slaves; 2½ hides.   364
    a 3

7 VII . uilli . 7 v . borđ cū . I . car . Ibi moliñ redđ . xxx . denar . 7 xviiI,
āc p̃ti . 7 L . āc pasturæ , 7 xxx , āc siluæ , Valb , xxx . sol . Modo.

 $\big\Gamma$ IIII . lib,

Turgis teñ de . W. NOIVN . Colo teneb T . R . E . 7 geldb p . v . hid.
Tra . ē . III . car . In dñio . ē . I . car . 7 IIII . serui . 7 III . uilli 7 VIII.
borđ cū . I . car . Ibi dimiđ moliñ redđ . xxx . denar . 7 xx . āc
p̃ti . 7 totiđ pasturæ . 7 c . āc siluæ . Valb oli . xL . sol . m̃ . Lx . sol.
Ipse . W . teñ BRIWEHA . Robt . F . Wimarc teneb T . R . E.
7 geldb p . xII . hid . Tra . ē . xv . car . In dñio st . IIII . car . 7 II.
serui . 7 xxII . uilli . 7 xxvIII . borđ cū . xIII . car . Ibi . II . molini
redđ . IX . sol 7 II . deñ . 7 Lx . āc p̃ti . 7 cc . āc silue.
Qdo recep̃ ualb . xII . lib . Modo . xIIII . lib 7 xII . soliđ.
Huic M̃ st additæ . III . v træ . Almar teneb T . R . E.
Tra . ē dim car . Ibi st . III . cotarij . Valb 7 ual . v . soliđ.
De hoc Mañ st ablate . III . hidæ . q̃s teneb Erlebold T . R . E
de Robto . nec poterat separi a Maner . Roger de Corcelle teñ
Warmund teñ de . W . EIRETONE . Ernui teneb T . R . E.
7 geldb p . III . hid . Tra . ē . III . car . In dñio . ē . I . car 7 dimiđ.
7 uñ uilts 7 IIII . borđ cū dim car . Ibi . x . āc p̃ti . 7 totiđ pas
turæ . 7 xII . āc siluæ . Valuit 7 ual . xL . soliđ.

.XXII. TERRA WILLELMI DE OW.
WILLELM de Ow . teñ de rege WATELEGE . T . R . E . geldb pro
una hida . Tra . ē . I . car . Ibi st . II . uilli . 7 vI . q̃ siluæ in lg . 7 IIII . in lat.
Ipse . W . teñ HANTONE . T . R . E . geldb p . xIII . hid . $\big\Gamma$ Val . x . sol.
Tra . ē . xII . car . De ea st in dñio . v . hidæ . 7 ibi . IIII . car . 7 v . serui.

7 villagers and 5 smallholders with 1 plough & 1 hide.
A mill which pays 30d; meadow, 18 acres; pasture, 50 acres;
woodland, 30 acres. 5 cattle; 71 sheep.
The value was 30s; now £4.

54 Thorgils holds NUNNEY from William. Cola held it before 1066;
it paid tax for 5 hides. Land for 3 ploughs. In lordship 1 plough;
4 slaves; 4 hides & 1 virgate.
   3 villagers and 8 smallholders with 1 plough & 3 virgates.
   ½ mill which pays 30d; meadow, 20 acres; pasture, as many;
      woodland, 100 acres. 1 cob; 8 cattle; 20 pigs; 100 sheep.
Value formerly 40s; now 60s.

96 c

364
a 4

55 William holds BREWHAM himself. Robert son of Wymarc held it
before 1066; it paid tax for 12 hides. Land for 15 ploughs.
In lordship 4 ploughs; 2 slaves; 6 hides.
   22 villagers and 28 smallholders with 13 ploughs & 6 hides.
   2 mills which pay 9s 2d; meadow, 60 acres; woodland, 200
      acres. 3 cobs; 22 wild mares; 17 cattle; 60 pigs; 300 sheep.
Value when he acquired it £12; now £14 12s.
   3 virgates of land have been added to this manor. Aelmer
held them before 1066. Land for ½ plough.
   3 cottagers.
The value was and is 5s.
   From this manor have been taken away 3 hides which Erlebald
held from Robert before 1066; he could not be separated from
the manor. Roger of Courseulles holds them now.
Value 30s; when Roger acquired them, 20s.

364
E b 1

E

56 Warmund holds CHERITON from William. Ernwy held it before
1066; it paid tax for 3 hides. Land for 3 ploughs. In lordship
1½ ploughs; 2 hides & 1 virgate.
   1 villager and 4 smallholders with ½ plough & 3 virgates.
   Meadow, 10 acres; pasture, as many; woodland, 12 acres.
      1 cow; 50 sheep; 15 pigs.
The value was and is 40s.

364
b 2

E

[26]   LAND OF WILLIAM OF EU

1 William of Eu holds WHATLEY from the King. Before 1066 it paid
tax for 1 hide. Land for 1 plough.
   2 villagers.
   Woodland, 6 furlongs in length and 4 in width.
Value 10s; when William acquired it, as much.

438
a 1

2 William holds HINTON (St. George) himself. Before 1066 it paid
tax for 13 hides. Land for 12 ploughs, of which 5 hides are
in lordship; 4 ploughs there; 5 slaves;

438
a 2

7 XVI.uilli 7 XXIIII.bord cũ.X.caɾ.Ibi.II.molini redđ.VII.fol

7 VI.den.7 LX.ac̃ p̃ti.Siluæ.I.leũ in lg̃.7 dim̃ leũ laɾ.

Q̃do recep̃:ualb.XII.lib.Modo.XV.lib.

Radulf' teñ de.W.GEVELTONE.T.R.E.geldb ꝑ.VIII.hiđ.

Tra.ẽ.VIII.caɾ.In dñio st̃.III.caɾ.7 IIII.ſerui.7 VI.uilli 7 IIII.

bord cũ.V.caɾ.Ibi.II.molini redđ.XXX.fol.7 q̃t XX 7 X.ac̃

p̃ti.7 XL.ac̃ pafturæ.Q̃do recep̃ ualb.IX.lib.Modo tantđ.

Huic m̃ st̃ additæ.II.hidæ.q̃s teneb.V.taini T.R.E.in paragio.

Tra.ẽ.II.caɾ.Val.XXX.foliđ.

Herbt teñ de W.LAVRETONE.T.R.E.geldb ꝑ.X.hiđ.Tra.ẽ

X.caɾ.In dñio st̃.III.caɾ.7 II.ſerui.7 VI.uilli 7 VIII.bord cũ

IIII.caɾ.Ibi.XII.ac̃ p̃ti.7 LX.ac̃ pafturæ.7 LX.ac̃ filuæ.

Q̃do recep̃:ualb.VII.lib.Modo.VIII.lib.

Radulf' teñ de.W.HANTONE.T.R.E.geldb ꝑ.VIII.hiđ.

Tra.ẽ.VI.caɾ 7 dim̃.In dñio st̃.II.caɾ 7 dim̃.7 IIII.ſerui.7 VII.

uilli 7 III.bord.7 IIII.cotar cũ.III.caɾ.Ibi moliñ redđ.IIII.foliđ.

7 LX.ac̃ p̃ti.Silua.I.leũ lg̃.7 una q̃ɋ laɾ.Valb.VI.lib.m̃.c.foliđ.

De hac tra teñ Hugo de.W.dim̃ hidã.Sẽp ual.III.fol.

Hugo teñ de.W.IVLE.T.R.E.geldb ꝑ.VI.hiđ.Tra.ẽ.VI.caɾ.

In dñio.ẽ.I.caɾ.7 III.ſerui.7 XI.uilli 7 XIIII.bord cũ.VI.caɾ.

Ibi moliñ redđ.X.foliđ.7 XXXIII.ac̃ p̃ti.7 XXX.ac̃ pafturæ.

Huic m̃ additæ st̃.XXII.maſuræ.quas ꝼ Sẽp ual.VIII.lib.

teneb.XXII.hoẽs in paragio T.R.E.Redđt.XII.foliđ.

Warneri' teñ de.W.CITERNE.T.R.E.geldb ꝑ.I.hida.Tra.ẽ.I.

caɾ.Val.X.foliđ.Has tras p̃dictas teneb Aleftan boſcõme T.R.E.

16 villagers and 24 smallholders with 10 ploughs & **8** hides.
2 mills which pay 7s 6d; meadow, 60 acres; woodland, 1 league
in length and ½ league wide. 36 cattle; 44 pigs; 200 sheep, less 10.
Value when he acquired it, £12; now £15.

3 Ralph Blewitt holds YEOVILTON from William. Before 1066 it paid
tax for 8 hides. Land for 8 ploughs. In lordship 3 ploughs;
4 slaves; 4 hides.

      438

6 villagers and 4 smallholders with 5 ploughs & 4 hides.

      a 3

2 mills which pay 30s; meadow, 90 acres; pasture, 40 acres.
2 cobs; 2 unbroken mares; 12 cattle; 16 pigs; 100 sheep.
Value when he acquired it, £9; now as much.
To this manor have been added 2 hides which five thanes held   E
jointly before 1066. Land for 2 ploughs.
Value 30s.

4 Herbert holds LAVERTON from William. Before 1066 it paid tax
for 10 hides. Land for 10 ploughs. In lordship 3 ploughs; 2
slaves; 6 hides & 3 virgates.

      438

6 villagers and 8 smallholders with 4 ploughs & 3 hides & 1 virgate.

      b 2

Meadow, 12 acres; pasture, 60 acres; woodland, 60 acres.
1 cob; 3 cattle; 7 pigs; 68 sheep; 15 goats.
Value when he acquired it, £7; now £8.

      E

5 Ralph Blewitt holds HINTON (Blewitt) from William. Before 1066
it paid tax for 8 hides. Land for 6½ ploughs. In lordship 2½   E
ploughs; 4 slaves; 5 hides.

      438

7 villagers, 3 smallholders and 4 cottagers with 3 ploughs

      b 3

& 1½ hides.
A mill which pays 4s; meadow, 60 acres; woodland 1 league
long and 1 furlong wide. 1 cob; 5 cattle; 17 pigs; 25 goats.
The value was £6; now 100s.
Hugh Maltravers holds ½ hide of this land from William; value
always 3s.

6 Hugh holds YEOVIL from William. Before 1066 it paid tax for 6
hides. Land for 6 ploughs. In lordship 1 plough; 3 slaves; 1½ hides.
11 villagers and 14 smallholders with 6 ploughs & 4½ [hides].   E
A mill which pays 10s; meadow, 33 acres; pasture, 30 acres.

      439

3 cattle; 5 pigs; 32 sheep.

      a 1

Value always £8.
To this manor have been added 22 plots of land which 22 men   E
held jointly before 1066; they pay 12s.

7 Warner holds CHILTON (?Cantelo) from William. Before 1066 it
paid tax for 1 hide. Land for 1 plough.

      439

Value 10s.

      a 2

Alstan Boscombe held the said lands before 1066.

      E

Ipſe.W.teñ *TICHEHĀ*.Saulf 7 Teolf tenꝥ T.R.E..p.ii.maneꝛ.
7 geld�ب .p.viii.hid 7 dim.Tra.ē.ix.caꝛ.In dñio ſt.iii.caꝛ.7 iiii.
ſerui.7 xii.uitti 7 v.borđ cū.vi.caꝛ.Ibi.xxx.ac̄ p̄ti.7 lx.ac̄
paſturæ.7 cx.ac̄ ſiluæ.Valꝺ.c.ſot qđo recep̄.Modo.vi.liꝺ.

.XXIII. ## TERRA WILLI DE FALEISE.

WILLſ de FALEISE teñ *STOCHE*. Brixi teneꝺ T.R.E.7 geldꝺ
.p.iiii.hiđ 7 7 dim.Tra.ē.xiiii.caꝛ.In dñio ſt.iiii.caꝛ.7 v.ſerui.
7 xxxviii.uitti 7 iii.borđ 7 iii.colibti cū.x.caꝛ.Ibi moliñ redđ
xvi.deñ.7 cl.ac̄ p̄ti.7 xix.ac̄ paſturæ.7 c.ac̄ ſiluæ.
Qꝺo recep̄.ualꝺ.xxv.liꝺ.Modo.xx.liꝺ.
Huic c̄m̄ addita.ē dimiđ hida.quā teneꝺ T.R.E. uñ taiñ in
paragio 7 poterat ire quo uoleꝺ.Tra.ē.i.caꝛ.q̄ ibi.ē cū.i.borđ
7 ii.ſeruis.Vat ſep̄.x.ſoliđ.

96 d

Ipſe.W.teñ *OTONE*.Algar teneꝺ T.R.E.7 geldꝺ .p.iii.hiđ.Tra.ē
x.caꝛ.In dñio ſt.iii.caꝛ.7 vi.ſerui.7 x.uitti 7 viii.borđ cū.iii.caꝛ.
Ibi moliñ redđ.x.deñ.7 iiii.ac̄ p̄ti.Paſtura.i.leū lḡ.7 dim lat
7 tāntđ ſiluæ.Valuit 7 uat.c.ſoliđ.
Ipſe.W.teñ *WORSPRINC*.c̄ceſſu regis.W.Serlo deđ ei cū ſua
filia.Euroac teneꝺ T.R.E.7 geldꝺ .p.vi.hiđ.7 una v tra.Tra.ē
xii.caꝛ.In dñio   Ibi.xiii.uitti 7 vi.borđ hñt
vi.caꝛ.Ibi.x.ac̄ paſturæ 7 x.ac̄ ſiluæ minutæ.Sēp uat.c.ſot.
Huic c̄m̄.ſt additæ.iii.hidæ q̄s teneꝺ T.R.E.Aluuard 7 Colo .p.ii.
maneꝛ.7 .p.iii.hiđ geldꝺ.Tra.ē.viii.caꝛ.In dñio ſt.iii.caꝛ.
7 iiii.ſerui.7 vii.uitti 7 iiii.borđ cū.iii.caꝛ.7 viii.ac̄ paſturæ.
Sēp uat.iiii.liꝺ.

8 William holds TICKENHAM himself. Saewulf and Theodulf held it   E
before 1066 as two manors; they paid tax for 8½ hides.
Land for 9 ploughs. In lordship 3 ploughs; 4 slaves;

5 hides, less 1 furlong.   438
     12 villagers and 5 smallholders with 6 ploughs & 3½ hides & 1 furlong.   b 1
     Meadow, 30 acres; pasture, 60 acres; woodland, 110 acres.

         1 cob; 7 cattle; 7 pigs; 47 sheep.
Value when he acquired it, 100s; now £6.

[27]   LAND OF WILLIAM OF FALAISE

1 William of Falaise holds STOGURSEY from the King. Brictsi held   E
it before 1066; it paid tax for 4½ hides. Land for 14 ploughs.
In lordship 4 ploughs; 5 slaves; 2 hides.   369
     38 villagers, 3 smallholders and 3 freedmen with 10 ploughs   a 1

         & the rest of the land.
     A mill which pays 16d; meadow, 150 acres; pasture, 19 acres;
         woodland, 100 acres. 3 cobs; 29 cattle; 10 pigs; 250 sheep.
Value when he acquired it, £25; now £20.
     To this manor has been added ½ hide which a thane held   E
jointly before 1066; he could go where he would. Land for 1   E
plough, which is there, with
     1 smallholder and 2 slaves.
Value always 10s.

2 William holds WOOTTON (Courtenay) himself. Algar held it   96 d
before 1066; it paid tax for 3 hides. Land for 10 ploughs.
In lordship 3 ploughs; 6 slaves; 1 hide & 1 virgate.   369
     10 villagers and 8 smallholders with 3 ploughs & 2 hides.   a 2
     A mill which pays 10d; meadow, 4 acres; pasture 1 league
         long and ½ wide; woodland, as much. 1 cob; 13 cattle; 7 pigs;
         150 sheep; 18 goats.
The value was and is 100s.

3 William holds WOODSPRING himself, with King William's assent.   E
Serlo of Burcy gave it to him with his daughter. Everwacer held it
before 1066; it paid tax for 6 hides and 1 virgate [of] land.   369
Land for 12 ploughs. In lordship 4 hides & 3 virgates.   b 1
     13 villagers and 6 smallholders have 6 ploughs & 1½ hides.
     Pasture, 10 acres; underwood, 10 acres. 16 cattle; 92 sheep.
Value always 100s.
     To this manor have been added 3 hides which Alfward and Cola   E
held before 1066 as two manors; they paid tax for 3 hides.
Land for 8 ploughs. In lordship 3 ploughs; 4 slaves; 2½ hides.
     7 villagers and 4 smallholders with 3 ploughs & ½ hide.
     Pasture, 8 acres. 2 pigs.
Value always £4.

TERRA WILLELMI FILIJ WIDONIS.

Wiłłs filius Widon ten de rege *HORSTENETONE*. Sauard
7 Eldeua teneb T.R.E. p. 11. ꝏ. 7 quo uoleb ire poteraꝼ. 7 geldb
p. xi. hid. Tra. e̅. x. car̅. In dn̅io. e̅. 1. car̅. 7 1111. ſerui. 7 xii. uiłłi.
7 x. bord. 7 xii. cotar cu̅. vii. car̅ 7 dim̅. Ibi moliñ redd̅. xlii.
denar̅. 7 c. ac̅ p̃ti. Paſtura. vi. q̃ẓ lg̅. 7 v. q̃ẓ lat̅. Silua. vii. q̃ẓ
lg̅. 7 vi. q̃ẓ lat̅. Qdo recep̅. ualb. viii. lib 7 xv. ſol. Modo tn̅td.
De hac tra ten Radulf de. W. 1. hid 7 dim̅. 7 ibi ht̅. 1. car̅
7 dimid̅. Se̅p ual. xxv. ſolid̅.

Bernard ten de. W. *CHERINTONE*. Aluuold teneb T.R.E. 7
7 geldb p. vi. hid. Tra. e̅. vi. car̅. In dn̅io ſt̅. 11. car̅. 7 vi. ſerui.
7 v. uiłłi 7 1111. bord 7 11. cotar cu̅. 111. car̅. Ibi. cxxv. ac̅ p̃ti.
Paſtura. v. q̃ẓ lg̅. 7 111. q̃ẓ lat̅. Silua. vii. q̃ẓ lg̅. 7 tn̅td lat̅.
Qdo recep̅. ualb. c. ſolid̅. Modo. vi. lib.
De hac ead̅ tra. v. hid emit Aluuold de abbatia Cernel. in
uita ſua tantm̅. 7 poſt morte̅ ej tra debeb redire ad æccłam.

TERRA RADVLFI DE MORTEMER.

Radvlfvs de Mortemer ten de rege *WALTONE*. 7 Ricard
de eo. Gunni teneb T.R.E. 7 geldb p. 111. hid 7 dim̅. Tra. e̅
1111. car̅. In dn̅io. e̅. 1. car̅. 7 vii. uiłłi 7 v. bord cu̅. 111. car̅.
Ibi. xx. ac̅ p̃ti. 7 c. ac̅ paſturæ. 7 l. ac̅ filuæ.
Qdo recep̅. ualb. l. ſolid̅. Modo plus. xx. ſolid̅. h̅. e̅. lxx.

TERRA RADVLFI DE POMEREI.

Radvlfvs De Pomerei ten *STAWEI*. 7 Beatrix de eo. Almer
teneb T.R.E. 7 geldb p una v træ. Tra. e̅. 111. car̅. In dn̅io ſt̅. 11. car̅.
7 111. ſerui. 7 un uiłłs 7 1111. bord. Ibi. 11. ac̅ p̃ti. 7 vi. ac̅ filuæ. 7 Pa
ſtura dim̅ leu̅ lg̅. 7 1111. q̃ẓ lat̅. Valuit 7 ual. xx. ſolid̅.

[28]   LAND OF WILLIAM SON OF GUY

1 William son of Guy holds HORSINGTON from the King. Saeward and   E
   Aldeva held it before 1066 as two manors; they could go where
   they would. They paid tax for 11 hides. Land for 10 ploughs.
   In lordship 1 plough; 4 slaves; 4½ hides, less 5 acres.   386
      12 villagers, 10 smallholders and 12 cottagers with 7½ ploughs   a 1
      & 5 hides & 5 acres.
      A mill which pays 42d; meadow, 100 acres; pasture 6 furlongs
      long and 5 furlongs wide; woodland 7 furlongs long and
      6 furlongs wide. 1 (head of) cattle; 16 pigs; 5 sheep.
   Value when he acquired it, £8 15s; now as much.
      Ralph holds 1½ hides of this land from William; he has 1½   E
      ploughs. 2 cobs; 6 cattle; 12 pigs; 60 sheep.   386
   Value always 25s.   a 2

2 Bernard holds CHERITON from William. Alfwold held it before
   1066; it paid tax for 6 hides. Land for 6 ploughs.
   In lordship 2 ploughs; 6 slaves; 4 hides, less 1 virgate.   386
      5 villagers, 4 smallholders and 2 cottagers with 3 ploughs   a 3
      & 2 hides & ½ virgate.
      Meadow, 125 acres; pasture 5 furlongs long and 3 furlongs
      wide; woodland 7 furlongs long and as wide. 1 cob; 22 cattle;   E
      28 pigs; 3 sheep.
   Value when he acquired it, 100s; now £6.
      Alfwold bought 5 hides of this land from Cerne Abbey for   E
   his life-time only; after his death the land had to return
   to the church.

[29]   LAND OF RALPH OF MORTIMER
1 Ralph of Mortimer holds WALTON (in Gordano) from the King,
   and Richard of Barre from him. Gunni the Dane held it before
   1066; it paid tax for 3½ hides. Land for 4 ploughs.   447
   In lordship 1 plough; 2 hides & 1 virgate.   b 2
      7 villagers and 5 smallholders with 3 ploughs & 1 hide & 1 virgate.
      Meadow, 20 acres; pasture, 100 acres; woodland, 50 acres.
      1 (head of) cattle; 5 pigs; 43 sheep; 25 goats.
   Value when he acquired it, 50s; now 20s more, that is 70(s).

[30]   LAND OF RALPH OF POMEROY
1 Ralph of Pomeroy holds 'STOWEY', and Beatrix, his sister, from him.
   Aelmer held it before 1066; it paid tax for 1 virgate of land.
   Land for 3 ploughs. In lordship 2 ploughs; 3 slaves; 3½ furlongs.
      1 villager and 4 smallholders (have) ½ furlong.   344
      Meadow, 2 acres; woodland, 6 acres; pasture ½ league long   a 2
      and 4 furlongs wide. 6 cattle; 60 sheep; 30 goats.
   The value was and is 20s.

Ipſe Rað . teñ _ARE_ . Edric teneƀ T.R.E.7 geldƀ ꝑ . I . hida . Tra . ē
vi . caŕ . In dñio ſt . ii . caŕ . 7 iiii . ſerui . 7 vii . uitti 7 v . borð cū . iiii .
caŕ . Ibi . ii . ac̄ ꝑti . 7 xv . ac̄ ſiluæ . Paſtura . ii . leū lḡ . 7 una laŕ . Vaɫ . xxx . ſoɫ .
Hoc ᛘ redð ꝑ c̄ſuetuð . xii . oues in Carentone ᛘ regis ꝑ anñ .
Radulf⁹ retinet hanc c̄ſuetuð .

.XXVII.   TERRA RADVLFI PAGENEL.

Radvlfvs Pagenel teñ de rege _STOCHELAND_ . 7 Radulf⁹ de eo.
T.R.E. geldƀ ꝑ . iii . hið . Tra . ē . v . caŕ . In dñio ſt . ii . caŕ . 7 iiii . ſerui .
7 vii . uitti 7 iiii . borð cū . iii . caŕ . Ibi . l . ac̄ ꝑti . 7 q̄t xx . ac̄ paſturæ .
Idē Rað teñ de Rað _CANTOCHEHEVE_.   ⨍ Sēp uaɫ . c . ſoliđ .
T.R.E. geldƀ ꝑ . vii . hið . Tra . ē . xx . caŕ . In dñio ſt . ii . caŕ . 7 v .
ſerui . 7 xiii . uitti 7 vii . borð cū . vii . caŕ . Ibi moliñ redð . vii .
ſoliđ 7 vi . denaŕ . 7 xx . ac̄ ꝑti , 7 l . ac̄ ſiluæ . Paſtura . ii . leū lḡ .
7 una leū laŕ . Valuit . xi . liƀ . q̄do recep̄ . Modo . viii . liƀ.
Idē Rað teñ de Rað _HEWIS_ . T.R.E. geldƀ ꝑ . i . hida 7 dim . Tra
ē . vi . caŕ . In dñio ſt . ii . caŕ . 7 v . ſerui . 7 ix . uitti 7 vi . borð cū . iii .
caŕ . Ibi moliñ redð . iii . ſoɫ . 7 xii . ac̄ ꝑti . 7 c . ac̄ paſturæ . Sēp uaɫ
Idē . R . teñ de Rað _BAGEBERGE_ . T.R.E. geldƀ ꝑ . i . hida ⨍ . iii . liƀ .
Tra . ē . iiii . caŕ . In dñio . ē dim caŕ . 7 iii . ſerui . 7 v . uitti 7 v . borð
cū . ii . caŕ 7 dim . Ibi . iii . ac̄ ꝑti . 7 lx ac̄ paſturæ . Sēp uaɫ . l . ſoɫ .
Robt⁹ teñ de Rað _NEVHALLE_ . T.R.E. geldƀ ꝑ una v̄ træ .
Tra . ē . ii . caŕ . Ibi ſt . ii . borð . 7 dimiđ leū ſiluæ . Sēp uaɫ . x . ſoɫ.
Has tras p̄dictas teneƀ Merleſuain T.R.E.

96 d

2 Ralph holds OARE himself. Edric held it before 1066; it paid
tax for 1 hide. Land for 6 ploughs. In lordship 2 ploughs; 4
slaves; ½ hide.   344
   7 villagers and 5 smallholders with 4 ploughs & ½ hide.   a 3
   Meadow, 2 acres; woodland, 15 acres; pasture 2 leagues long
     and 1 wide. 20 cattle; 100 sheep.
Value 30s; when he acquired it, 20s.
   This manor paid 12 sheep a year in customary dues to   E
Carhampton, a manor of the King's. Ralph keeps back this
customary due.

[31]   LAND OF RALPH PAGNELL   E

1 Ralph Pagnell holds STOCKLAND from the King, and Ralph of Reuilly
from him. Before 1066 it paid tax for 3 hides. Land for 5 ploughs.
In lordship 2 ploughs; 4 slaves; 2½ hides.   462
   7 villagers and 4 smallholders with 3 ploughs & ½ hide.   b 2
   Meadow, 50 acres; pasture, 80 acres. 6 cattle; 20 pigs; 40 sheep.
Value always 100s.

2 Ralph of Reuilly also holds (East) QUANTOXHEAD from Ralph.
Before 1066 it paid tax for 7 hides. Land for 20 ploughs.
In lordship 2 ploughs; 5 slaves; 5 hides & 1 furlong.   463
   13 villagers and 7 smallholders with 7 ploughs & 2 hides, less 1 furlong. b 3
   A mill which pays 7s 6d; meadow, 20 acres; woodland, 50 acres;
     pasture 2 leagues long and 1 league wide. 4 pigs.
Value when he acquired it, £11; now £8.

3 Ralph of Reuilly also holds HUISH from Ralph. Before 1066 it paid
tax for 1½ hides. Land for 6 ploughs. In lordship 2 ploughs; 5
slaves; 3 virgates.   464
   9 villagers and 6 smallholders with 3 ploughs & 3 virgates.   a 1
   A mill which pays 3s; meadow, 12 acres; pasture, 100 acres.   E
     2 cattle; 1 cob; 1 pig; 30 sheep.
Value always £3.

4 Ralph also holds BAGBOROUGH from Ralph. Before 1066 it paid
tax for 1 hide. Land for 4 ploughs. In lordship ½ plough; 3 slaves;
½ hide.   464
   5 villagers and 5 smallholders with 2½ ploughs & ½ hide.   a 3
   Meadow, 3 acres; pasture, 60 acres.
Value always 50s.

5 Robert son of Rozelin holds NEWHALL from Ralph. Before 1066
it paid tax for 1 virgate of land. Land for 2 ploughs.
   2 smallholders.   464
   Woodland, ½ league.   a 2
Value always 10s.

  Merlesom held the said lands before 1066.

TERRA RADVLFI DE LIMESI.

.XXVI. RADVLFVS DE LIMESI tenet de rege COMICH .7 Walter
de eo. Liuuara teneb T.R.E.7 geldb ꝑ.1.hida 7 dim.Tra.ē
vi,car̃. In dñio.ē,1.car̃.cū.1.feruo.7 1111.uitti 7 v.bord cū,11.
car̃.Ibi.xxv111.ac̃ pti.7 v.ac̃ pafturæ.7 11.ac̃ filuæ.Sēp uat

Ipfe Radulf ten LOCVBE .Eddida regina teneb T.R.E.ƒxl.fot.
7 geldb ꝑ.11.hid.Tra.ē.v111.car̃.In dñio.ſt.111.car̃.7 11.ferui.
7 xv111.uitti 7 vi.bord cū.1111.car̃.Ibi.v.ac̃ pti.7 l.ac̃ filuæ.
Paftura.1.leū lg.7 dim leū lat̃.Valeb.111.lib.Modo.1111.lib.

Ipfe.Rad ten SELEVRDE .Eddid regina teneb T.R.E.7 geldb
ꝑ una hida.Tra.ē.v.car̃.In dñio ſt.11.car̃.7 11.ferui.7 v11.
uitti 7 v.bord cū.111.car̃,Ibi molin redd.xx.denar̃.7 v.ac̃
pti.7 lx.ac̃ pafturæ.7 xl.ac̃ filuæ.Valb xx.folid.m̃.xxv.fot.

Ipfe Rad ten ALRESFORD .Edric teneb T.R.E.7 geldb ꝑ.1.
hida.Tra.ē.v.car̃.In dñio ſt.11.car̃.7 11.ferui.7 vi.uitti 7 11.
bord cū.1.car̃.Ibi molin redd.xv.den.7 vi.ac̃ pti.7 xx.ac̃
pafturæ.7 una ac̃ filuæ.Valuit.xv.fot.modo.xx.folid.
Hoc ⊙ redd p c̃fuetud xii.oues p ann̄ in Carentone ⊙ regis.
Radulf hanc c̃fuetudinē ufꝗ m̃ detinuit.

★ Ipfe Rad ten BOSINTVNE .Æccta de Adelingi tenuit T.R.E.
7 de uictu monacho₎ fuit.7 geldb ꝑ.1.hida.Tra.ē.v.car̃.
In dñio.ē.1.car̃.cū.1.feruo.7 v.uitti 7 11.bord cū.1.car̃.
Paftura.1.leū in lg.7 dim leū lat̃.Valuit 7 uat.xx.folid.
Qdo rex ded tr̃a fuā Radulfo.erat æccta faifita de hoc ⊙.

Ipfe Rad ten TRABERGE .Edric teneb T.R.E.7 geldb ꝑ dim
hida.Tra.ē.v.car̃.In dñio.ē.1.car̃.Ibi.ē un̄ uitts.7 xxx.ac̃
filuæ.Paftura.1.leū lg.7 tntd lat̃.Vat.v11.fot.Nā uaftata.ē.

1 Ralph of Limesy holds COMBWICH from the King, and Walter Bowman
  from him. Leofwara held it before 1066; it paid tax for
  1½ hides. Land for 6 ploughs. In lordship 1 plough & 1 hide,
  with 1 slave;   462
    4 villagers and 5 smallholders with 2 ploughs & ½ (hide).   b 3
    Meadow, 28 acres; pasture, 5 acres; woodland, 2 acres.
      5 cattle; 50 sheep.
  Value always 40s.
   Ralph himself holds
2 LUCCOMBE. Queen Edith held it before 1066; it paid tax for 2
  hides. Land for 8 ploughs. In lordship 3 ploughs; 2 slaves; 1 hide.
    18 villagers and 6 smallholders with 4 ploughs & 1 hide.   463
    Meadow, 5 acres; woodland, 50 acres; pasture 1 league long   a 1
      and ½ league wide. 1 cob; 6 cattle; 6 pigs; 100 sheep; 50 goats.
  The value was £3; now £4.
3 SELWORTHY. Queen Edith held it before 1066; it paid tax for 1
  hide. Land for 5 ploughs. In lordship 2 ploughs; 2 slaves; ½ hide.
    7 villagers and 5 smallholders with 3 ploughs & ½ hide.   463
    A mill which pays 20d; meadow, 5 acres; pasture, 60 acres;   a 2
      woodland, 40 acres. 1 cob; 2 cattle; 4 pigs; 60 sheep.
  The value was 20s; now 25s.
4 ALLERFORD. Edric held it before 1066; it paid tax for 1 hide.
  Land for 5 ploughs. In lordship 2 ploughs; 2 slaves; ½ hide.
    6 villagers and 2 smallholders with 1 plough & ½ hide.   463
    A mill which pays 15d; meadow, 6 acres; pasture, 20 acres;   a 3
      woodland, 1 acre. 1 cob; 1 pig; 60 sheep.
  The value was 15s; now 20s.
    This manor paid 12 sheep a year in customary dues to   E
  Carhampton, a manor of the King's. Ralph has withheld this
  customary due until now.
5 BOSSINGTON. Athelney Church held it before 1066; it was for   E
  the monks' supplies. It paid tax for 1 hide. Land for 5 ploughs. †
  In lordship 1 plough & ½ hide, with 1 slave;   463
    5 villagers and 2 smallholders with 1 plough & ½ hide.   b 1
    Pasture 1 league in length and ½ league wide.
  The value was and is 20s.   E
    When the King gave his land to Ralph, the church was in
  possession of this manor.
6 TREBOROUGH. Edric held it before 1066; it paid tax for ½ hide.
  Land for 5 ploughs. In lordship 1 plough & the whole (of the land),
  except for 10 acres.   463
    1 villager who holds the said 10 acres.   b 2
    Woodland, 30 acres; pasture 1 league long and as wide.
  Value 7s, for it has been laid waste; when he acquired it, as much.   E

Ipſe Rađ teñ *EPSE*. Vluuard tenuit T.R.E.7 geldb ꝑ dim
hida.Tra.ē.ɪ.car̄.Ibi.ē uñ uiłłs 7 xvɪ.ac̄ p̄ti.Val.ɪɪɪ.ſoliđ.

Ipſe Rađ teñ *ALRE*. Vluuard teneb̄ T.R.E.7 geldb ꝑ.ɪɪ.hiđ.
Tra.ē.ɪɪɪɪ.car̄.In dñio ſt.ɪɪ.car̄.7 ɪɪ.ſerui.7 v.uiłłi.7 xɪɪ.borđ
cū.ɪɪ.car̄.Ibi.xv.ac̄ p̄ti.7 cc.ac̄ paſturæ.7 x.ac̄ ſiluæ.
Qdo recep̄.ualb̄.c.ſoliđ.Modo.vɪ.lib̄.

.XXIX   TERRA ROBERTI FILIJ GEROLDI.

Robertvs filius Girold teñ de rege *CERLETONE*.7 God
zelin de eo.Godman teneb̄ T.R.E.7 geldb ꝑ.v.hiđ.Tra.ē.xɪɪ.
car̄.In dñio ſt.ɪɪɪ.car̄.7 vɪɪ.ſerui.7 ɪɪɪɪ.uiłłi 7 xv.borđ 7 ɪɪɪ.
coſcez cū.vɪɪɪ.car̄.Ibi moliñ redđ.v.ſoł.7 ʟ.ac̄ p̄ti.Paſtura
ɪɪɪɪ.q̄ʒ lḡ.7 ɪɪɪ.q̄ʒ lat̄.Silua dimiđ leū lḡ.7 tñtđ lat̄.
Valuit.x.lib̄.Modo.vɪ.lib̄.

Ipſe Robt teñ   Vitel teneb̄ T.R.E.7 geldb ꝑ.x.
hiđ.Tra.ē.x.car̄.In dñio ſt.ɪɪɪ.car̄.7 vɪɪɪ.ſerui.7 ɪɪɪɪ.colibti.
7 xɪ.uiłłi 7 xvɪɪ.borđ cū.v.car̄.Ibi.xxx.ac̄ p̄ti.7 c.ac̄ paſ
turæ.Silua.ɪɪɪ.q̄ʒ lḡ.7 ɪɪ.q̄ʒ lat̄.
Qdo recep̄.ualb̄.xvɪɪɪ.lib̄.Modo redđ.c.caſeb̄.7 x̄.bacons.

.XXX.   TERRA ALVREDI DE MERLEBERGE.

Alvredvs de Merleberge teñ de rege *CELLEWERT*.
7 Nicolaus de eo.Carle teneb̄ T.R.E.7 geldb ꝑ.v.hiđ.Tra.ē
v.car̄.In dñio.ē.ɪ.car̄.7 ɪɪɪɪ.ſerui.7 ɪɪɪ.uiłłi.7 ɪɪɪɪ.coſcez
cū.ɪ.car̄.Ibi.vɪɪ.ac̄ p̄ti.7 xxx.ac̄ ſiluæ.Valuit 7 ual.c.ſoliđ.

.XXX.   TERRA ALVREDI DE ISPANIA.

Alvredvs De Iſpania teñ de rege *VLMERESTONE*.7 Walter
de eo.Aluui teneb̄ T.R.E.7 geldb ꝑ dimiđ hida.Tra.ē.ɪɪɪ.
car̄.In dñio.ē.ɪ.car̄.cū.ɪ.ſeruo.7 ɪɪɪɪ.uiłłi.7 xɪɪɪ.borđ.cū.ɪ.
car̄.Ibi.x.ac̄ p̄ti.7 xx.ac̄ ſiluæ.Valuit 7 ual.xxx.ſoliđ.

7 ?RAPPS. Wulfward held it before 1066; it paid tax for ½ hide.   E
   Land for 1 plough.
   1 villager.   464
   Meadow, 16 acres.   a 4
   Value 3s.

8 ALLER. Wulfward held it before 1066; it paid tax for 2 hides.
   Land for 4 ploughs. In lordship 2 ploughs; 2 slaves; 3 virgates.   464
   5 villagers and 12 smallholders with 2 ploughs & 1 hide & 1 virgate.   b 1
   Meadow, 15 acres; pasture, 200 acres; woodland, 10 acres.
      12 cattle; 6 pigs; 16 sheep.
   Value when he acquired it, 100s; now £6.

[33]   LAND OF ROBERT SON OF GERALD   E

1 Robert son of Gerald holds CHARLTON (?Musgrove) from the King,
   and Jocelyn from him. Godman held it before 1066; it paid
   tax for 5 hides. Land for 12 ploughs. In lordship 3 ploughs; 7
   slaves; 2 hides.   436
   4 villagers, 15 smallholders and 3 Cottagers with 8 ploughs.   b 1
   A mill which pays 5s; meadow, 50 acres; pasture 4 furlongs
      long and 3 furlongs wide; woodland ½ league long and as wide.
   The value was £10; now £6.

2 Robert holds . . . . . . himself. Vitalis held it before 1066; it
   paid tax for 10 hides. Land for 10 ploughs. In lordship 3 ploughs;
   4 hides; 8 slaves; 4 freedmen;   436
   11 villagers and 17 smallholders with 5 ploughs.   b 2
   Meadow, 30 acres; pasture, 100 acres; woodland 3 furlongs
      long and 2 furlongs wide.
   Value when he acquired it, £18; now it pays 100 cheeses and
   10 bacon-pigs.

[34]   LAND OF ALFRED OF MARLBOROUGH

1 Alfred of Marlborough holds CHELWOOD from the King, and Nicholas
   from him. Karl held it before 1066; it paid tax for 5 hides.
   Land for 5 ploughs. In lordship 1 plough; 4 slaves; 3 hides.   447
   3 villagers and 4 Cottagers with 1 plough & 2 hides.   b 1
   Meadow, 7 acres; woodland, 30 acres. 2 cobs; 12 pigs; 100 sheep; 30 goats.
   The value was and is 100s.

[35]   LAND OF ALFRED OF 'SPAIN'

1 Alfred of 'Spain' holds WOOLMERSDON from the King, and Walter   E
   from him. Alfwy held it before 1066; it paid tax for ½ hide.   371
   Land for 3 ploughs. In lordship 1 plough & 1 virgate, with 1 slave;   b 1
   4 villagers and 13 smallholders with 1 plough & 1 virgate.
   Meadow, 10 acres; woodland, 20 acres. 4 pigs.
   The value was and is 30s.

Huic M̄.ē addita . una v̄ trǽ 7 dim . H̄ tra fuit de Peret M̄ regis.

p̄pofit prǽftit̄ Aluui T.R.E . Valuit 7 ual . x . folid.

Ipfe Alu . ten̄ *BVR* . Aluui teneb̄ T.R.E . 7 geldb̄ p̄ dim̄ hida.

Tra . ē . v . car̄ . Ibi ſt . vIII . uilti 7 vI . borđ . 7 III . ſerui . Sēp ual . c.

Huic M̄ eſt addita una v̄ trǽ . q̄ fuit de firma regis in Peret . ꟊ folid.

ꟊ Tra . ē . I . car̄ . Val . x . folid.

Ricarđ ten̄ de Alu *HVNTEWORDE* . Aluui teneb̄ T.R.E . 7 geldb̄

p̄ . I . hida . Tra . ē . II . car̄ . q̄ ibi ſt cū . II . ſeruis 7 vII . borđ . Ibi . IIII.

ac p̄ti . 7 x . ac morǽ . Q̄do recep̄ . ualb̄ . v . fol . Modo . xx . folid.

Rannulf ten̄ de Alu . *STRENEGESTONE* . Aluui teneb̄ T.R.E.

7 geldb̄ p̄ . I . hida . Tra . ē . III . car̄ . In dn̄io ſt . II . car̄ . 7 IIII . ſerui.

7 III . uilti cu . I . car̄ . Ibi . IIII . ac p̄ti . 7 L . ac paſturǽ . Val . L . fol.

Huic M̄ ē addita dimiđ v̄ trǽ . quā teneb̄ Briſtiue libe

T.R.E . Tra . ē dim̄ car̄ . Hanc h̄t ibi . I . uilts . Sēp ual . v . fol.

Ipfe Alu ten̄ *SPACHESTONE* . Aluui teneb̄ T.R.E . 7 geldb̄

p̄ . II . hiđ 7 dim̄ . Tra . ē . vIII . car̄ . In dn̄io . ē . I . car̄ . 7 II . ſerui.

7 III . uilti . 7 II . borđ cū . I . car̄ . Ibi . xxvI . ac p̄ti . 7 Ix . ac filuǽ.

Q̄do recep̄ ualb̄ . L . fol . Modo fimilit̄.

De hac eađ tra ten̄ un̄ miles de Alu . I . hiđ 7 dim̄ . 7 ibi h̄t . II.

car̄ . 7 III . ſeruos 7 III . cotar̄ . 7 vI . uilt 7 v . borđ . Ibi . IIII . ac p̄ti.

7 xx . ac filuǽ . Valb̄ . III . lib̄ . modo tntđ.

Herbert ten̄ de Alu *OTREMETONE* . Eſtan teneb̄ T.R.E . 7 geldb̄

p̄ . I . hida 7 II . v̄ trǽ 7 dimiđ . Tra . ē . III . car̄ . In dn̄io ſt . II . car̄.

cū . I . ſeruo . 7 v . uilti 7 III . borđ 7 III . cotar̄ cū . II . car̄ 7 dimiđ.

1½ virgates of land have been added to this manor. This land E
was (part) of (North) Petherton, a manor of the King's. Alfwy
the reeve leased it before 1066.
The value was and is 10s.

2 Alfred holds BOWER himself. Alfwy held it before 1066; it paid
tax for ½ hide. Land for 5 ploughs. In lordship 1 virgate. 371
    8 villagers, 6 smallholders and 3 slaves (have) the other virgate. b 2
    1 cow; 2 pigs.
Value always 100s.
    To this manor has been added 1 virgate of land which was (part) E
of the King's revenue in (North) Petherton. Land for 1 plough.
Value 10s.

3 Richard of Merri holds HUNTWORTH from Alfred. Alfwy held it 97 b
before 1066; it paid tax for 1 hide. Land for 2 ploughs, which E
are there, with 2 slaves; 371
    7 smallholders. b 3
    Meadow, 4 acres; moor, 10 acres. 8 cattle; 60 sheep.
Value when he acquired it, 5s; now 20s.

4 Ranulf holds STRINGSTON from Alfred. Alfwy held it before 1066;
it paid tax for 1 hide. Land for 3 ploughs. In lordship 2 ploughs;
4 slaves; 3 virgates. 372
    3 villagers with 1 plough & 1 virgate. a 1
    Meadow, 4 acres; pasture, 50 acres. 8 cattle; 15 pigs; 200 sheep, less 7.
Value 50s; when he acquired it, 40s.
    To this manor has been added ½ virgate of land which Bricteva E
held freely before 1066. Land for ½ plough.
    1 villager has it there.
Value always 5s.

5 Alfred holds SPAXTON himself. Alfwy held it before 1066; it
paid tax for 2½ hides. Land for 8 ploughs. In lordship 1 plough;
2 slaves; ½ hide.
    3 villagers and 2 smallholders with 1 plough & ½ hide. 372
    Meadow, 26 acres; woodland, 9 acres. 17 sheep. a 2
Value when he acquired it, 50s; now the same.
    A man-at-arms holds 1½ hides of this land from Alfred; he has
2 ploughs & 1 hide in lordship, and 3 slaves;
    3 cottagers, 6 villagers and 5 smallholders (who have) ½ hide & 2 ploughs.
    Meadow, 4 acres; woodland, 120 acres. 16 pigs; 37 sheep; 14 goats.
The value was £3; now as much.

6 Herbert holds OTTERHAMPTON from Alfred. Estan held it before 1066;
it paid tax for 1 hide and 2½ virgates of land. Land for 3 ploughs.
In lordship 2 ploughs & 1 hide & ½ virgate, with 1 slave; 372
    5 villagers, 3 smallholders and 3 cottagers with 2½ ploughs & ½ hide. b 1

Ibi . v . aͨ p̃ti .7 iii . aͨ paſturæ .7 iii . aͨ ſiluæ . Sẽp ual . xl . ſol.

Herbͭ teñ de Alu RADEFLOT . Eſtan teneͫ T.R.E.7 geldͫ ᵱ dim hida
uno ferding min . Tra . ē . i . caͬ 7 dim . Ibi ſͭ . ii . uilli cũ . i . bord 7 v . aͨ
p̃ti .7 xxi . aͨ paſturæ .7 iii aͨ ſiluæ . Valuit 7 ual . xv . ſolid.

Hugo teñ de Alu PLANESFELLE . Edred teneͫ T.R.E.7 geldͫ
ᵱ una hida . Tra . ē . ii . caͬ . Ibi ſͭ . iii . bord 7 i . ſeruus .7 ii . aͨ p̃ti.
7 xv . aͨ ſiluæ . Q̃do recep̃ . ualͫ . xx . ſol . Modo . x . ſolid.

Hugo teñ de Alu MVLSELLE . Aluuin teneͫ T.R.E.7 geldͫ ᵱ . i.
hida . Tra . ē . i . caͬ . Ibi . ē . i . bord cũ . i . ſeruo .7 xv . aͨ p̃ti . Sẽp ual

Ricard teñ de Alu SELVRE . Aluui teneͫ T.R.E.   ⌐ xv . ſol.
7 geldͫ ᵱ . i . hida 7 dim . Tra . ē . ix . caͬ . In dñio ſͭ . ii . caͬ .7 iiii . ſerui.
7 xi . uilli 7 v . bord cũ . vii . caͬ . Ibi molin redd . iii . ſol .7 ii . aͨ
p̃ti .7 clx . aͨ paſturæ . Silua . iii . q̃ꝝ lͬg .7 ii . q̃ꝝ laͬt . Valuit . iii . liͫ.

Ipſe Alu teñ STALVVEI . Herald teneͫ T.R.E.   ⌐ Modo . iiii . liͫ.
7 geldͫ ᵱ . iii . hid . Tra . ē . v . caͬ . In dñio . ē . i . caͬ .7 v . ſerui.
7 viii . uilli 7 iiii . bord cũ . ii . caͬ . Ibi molin redd . iiii . denaͬ.
7 vii . aͨ p̃ti .7 c . aͨ paſturæ . Siluæ . i . leu 7 dim int lͬg 7 laͬt.

Oſuuard 7 Ailuuard teñ de Alu STALVVEI . Ipſi teneͫ T.R.E.
7 geldͫ ᵱ . ii . hid . Tra . ē . iiii . caͬ . In dñio . ē . i . caͬ 7 dim . cũ . i.
ſeruo .7 iiii . uilli 7 iii . bord cũ . i . caͬ . Ibi . iii . aͨ p̃ti . Sẽp ual . xx.
H̃ tra . ē addita ꞇris Aluui q̃s Alured tenet.   ⌐ ſolid.

Meadow, 5 acres; pasture, 3 acres; woodland, 3 acres.
4 cattle; 11 pigs; 45 sheep.
Value always 40s.

7 Herbert holds RADLET from Alfred. Estan held it before 1066;
it paid tax for ½ hide, less 1 furlong. Land for 1½ ploughs.
In lordship 3 furlongs.
   2 villagers with 1 smallholder (have) 1 virgate & 1 plough.
   Meadow, 5 acres; pasture, 21 acres; woodland, 3 acres.
The value was and is 15s.

                                                    372
                                                  b 2

8 Hugh holds PLAINSFIELD from Alfred. Edred held it before 1066;
it paid tax for 1 hide. Land for 2 ploughs.
   3 smallholders and 1 slave.
   Meadow, 2 acres; woodland, 15 acres.
Value when he acquired it, 20s; now 10s.

(372, b 3)

9 Hugh holds(Marsh)MILLS from Alfred. Alwin held it before 1066;
it paid tax for 1 hide. Land for 1 plough.
   1 smallholder with 1 slave.
   Meadow, 15 acres.
Value always 15s.

(372, b 4)

10 Richard holds MONKSILVER from Alfred. Alfwy held it before
1066; it paid tax for 1½ hides. Land for 9 ploughs. In lordship
2 ploughs; 4 slaves; ½ hide & 3 furlongs.
   11 villagers and 5 smallholders with 7 ploughs & the rest of the land.
   A mill which pays 3s; meadow, 2 acres; pasture, 160 acres;
      woodland 3 furlongs long and 2 furlongs wide. 1 cob; 1 cow;
      12 pigs; 30 sheep.
The value was £3; now £4.

(373, a 1)

11 Alfred holds (Nether) STOWEY himself. Earl Harold held it before
1066; it paid tax for 3 hides. Land for 5 ploughs. In lordship 1
plough; 5 slaves; 2 hides.
   8 villagers and 4 smallholders with 2 ploughs.
   A mill which pays 4d; meadow, 7 acres; pasture, 100 acres;
      woodland, 1½ leagues in both length and width. 9 cattle; 7 pigs;
      100 sheep, less 10.
Value £10; when he acquired it, £8.

(373, a 2)

12 Osward and Alfward hold (Nether) STOWEY from Alfred. They held   E
it themselves before 1066; it paid tax for 2 hides. Land for 4
ploughs. In lordship 1½ ploughs & the whole of that land, with 1 slave;
   4 villagers and 3 smallholders with 1 plough & ½ virgate.
   Meadow, 3 acres; woodland, 1 league. 8 pigs; 20 sheep.
Value always 20s.
   This land has been added to Alfwy's lands which Alfred holds.   E

(373, a 3)

Rannulf⁹ ten de Alu ALFAGESTONE 7 LEDING . Aluui teneð
T.R.E.7 geldð ꝑ.ɪɪ.hið . Tra .ē.ɪɪɪ . caꝛ. In dñio .ē.ɪ. caꝛ. cū.ɪ. ſeruo.
7 ɪɪɪɪ.uiłłi.7 ɪɪ.borð cū.ɪɪ.caꝛ.Ibi.vɪɪɪ.ač p̄ti.7 xxx.ač paſturæ.7 xxxv.ač ſiluæ.

Hugo ten de Alu LEGE . Domno teneð ⌐Valuit 7 uał xx.ſoł.
T.R.E.7 geldð ꝑ dim hida. Tra .ē.ɪ. caꝛ 7 dim . Ibi ſt.ɪɪ.borð.
7 ɪɪ.ač p̄ti. Silua .ɪɪɪ.q̃ʒ łḡ.7 dim q̃ʒ łat . Valuit 7 uał. xvɪɪ . ſoł.
Ħ tra addita .ē tris Aluui q̃s ten Alured.

Hugo ten de Alu RADEHEWIS . Aluui teneð T.R.E.7 geldð
ꝑ una v træ. Tra .ē.ɪ. caꝛ. q̃ ibi.ē in dñio. cū.ɪ.borð.7 ɪ.ač p̄ti.
7 xɪɪ.ač paſturæ. Q̃do recep̄. ualð.ɪɪ.ſoł. Modo.vɪ.ſolið.

Roƀt⁹ 7 Herƀt⁹ ten de Alu STAWEI . Aluui teneð T.R.E.7 geldð
ꝑ.ɪɪɪ.hið. Tra.ē   In dñio ſt.ɪɪ.caꝛ.cū.ɪ.ſeruo.7 ɪɪ.
uiłłi 7 ɪɪɪɪ.borð.   Ibi.ɪɪɪɪ.ač p̄ti.7 xx.ač ſiluæ.
Q̃do recep̄. ualð.c.ſolið. Modo.ʟx.ſolið.

Ricard ten de Alu ILE . Aluui teneð T.R.E.7 geldð ꝑ.ɪɪ.hið.
Tra.ē.ɪɪ.caꝛ. In dñio.ē.ɪ.caꝛ.cū.ɪ.ſeruo.7 vɪɪɪ.uiłłi 7 ɪɪ.borð
cū.ɪ.caꝛ.Ibi molin redd.xx.den.7 x.ač p̄ti.7 x.ač paſturæ.
7 xxx.ač ſiluæ. Q̃do recep̄. ualð.xx.ſoł. Modo.xʟ.ſolið.

Hugo ten de Alu PRESTETONE . Aluui teneð T.R.E.7 geldð
ꝑ.ɪɪɪ.hið.una v min. Tra .ē.v.caꝛ. In dñio .ē.ɪ.caꝛ.7 ɪɪ.ſerui.
7 xɪɪɪɪ.uiłłi cū.ɪ.caꝛ. Ibi molin redd.xx.den.7 vɪɪɪ.ač p̄ti.
7 xv.ač ſiluæ. Q̃do recep̄. ualð.xxx.ſoł. Modo.ʟx.ſolið.

97 c
Walteri 7 Aniger ten de Alu GAHERS . Aluui teneð T.R.E.
7 geldð ꝑ.ɪ.hida 7 ɪɪɪ.virg træ. Tra .ē.vɪ.caꝛ. In dñio ſt.ɪɪ.caꝛ.

13 Ranulf holds ALFOXTON and DYCHE from Alfred. Alfwy son of Banna
held them before 1066; they paid tax for 2 hides. Land for 3
ploughs. In lordship 1 plough & 1½ hides, with 1 slave;
    4 villagers and 2 smallholders with 2 ploughs & ½ hide.   373
    Meadow, 8 acres; pasture, 30 acres; woodland, 35 acres.   b 1
The value was and is 20s.

14 Hugh holds ?LEIGH from Alfred. Dunn held it before 1066;
it paid tax for ½ hide. Land for 1½ ploughs.
    2 smallholders.   373
    Meadow, 2 acres; woodland 3 furlongs long and ½ furlong wide.   b 2
The value was and is 17s.
    This land has been added to the lands of Alfwy son of Banna   E
which Alfred holds.

15 Hugh holds RODHUISH from Alfred. Alfwy held it before 1066;
it paid tax for 1 virgate of land. Land for 1 plough, which
is there, in lordship, with   373
    1 smallholder.   b 3
    Meadow, 1 acre; pasture, 12 acres.
Value when he acquired it, 2s; now 6s.

16 Robert and Herbert hold STAWLEY from Alfred. Alfwy son of Banna
held it before 1066; it paid tax for 3 hides. Land for . . . . . .
In lordship 2 ploughs & 2 hides & 3 virgates, with 1 slave;   373
    2 villagers and 4 smallholders (who have) 1 virgate.   b 4
    Meadow, 4 acres; woodland, 20 acres. 8 pigs; 24 sheep.
Value when he acquired it, 100s; now 60s.

17 Richard of Merri holds ISLE (Brewers) from Alfred. Alfwy held it
before 1066; it paid tax for 2 hides. Land for 2 ploughs.
In lordship 1 plough & 1 hide, with 1 slave;   374
    8 villagers and 2 smallholders with 1 plough & 1 hide.   a 1
    A mill which pays 20d; meadow, 10 acres; pasture, 10 acres;
       woodland, 30 acres. 1 cob; 1 cow; 60 sheep.
Value when he acquired it, 20s; now 40s.

18 Hugh holds PRESTON from Alfred. Alfwy held it before 1066;
it paid tax for 3 hides, less 1 virgate. Land for 5 ploughs.
In lordship 1 plough; 2 slaves; 1½ hides & ½ virgate.   374
    14 villagers with 1 plough & the rest of the land.   a 2
    A mill which pays 20d; meadow, 8 acres; woodland, 15 acres.
       7 cattle; 5 pigs; 48 sheep.
Value when he acquired it, 30s; now 60s.

19 His brother Walter, 5 virgates, and Ansger Fower, 2 virgates of land,   97 c
hold GOATHURST from Alfred. Alfwy held it before 1066; it paid   D
tax for 1 hide and 3 virgates of land. Land for 6 ploughs.   374
In lordship 2 ploughs; 4 slaves;   a 3

7 IIII.ſerui.7 XIII.uiłłi.7 v.borđ cū.ɪɪɪɪ.caſ.Ibi.ɪx.ɪɪ.ac ſiluæ

Q̇do recep̄ꞏualb.ɪxx.ſoliđ.Modo ſimiliter.

Rannulf ten de Alu MALRIGE Aluui teneb T.R.E.7 geldb
p dim hida.Tra.ē.ɪɪ.caſ 7 dim.Jn dnĩo.ē.ɪ.caſ.7 ɪɪ.ſerui.7 ɪɪɪɪ.
uiłłi 7 ɪ.borđ cū.ɪ.caſ 7 dim.Ibi molin redđ.vɪ.den.7 xxx.ac
paſturæ.7 xx.ac ſiluæ.Valuit 7 ual.xx.ſoliđ.

Robt ten de Alu CANTOCHE.Aluui teneb T.R.E.7 geldb p una
virg træ.Tra.ē.ɪ.caſ 7 dim.Has hnt ibi.ɪɪɪ.uiłłi.7 vɪɪɪ.ac ſiluæ
minute.Q̇do recep̄.ualb.xx.ſoł.Modo.xxv.ſoliđ.

Walter ten de Alu HILLE.Aluui teneb T.R.E.7 geldb p.ɪɪɪ.
hiđ.Tra.ē.vɪ.caſ.In dnĩo.ē.ɪ.caſ.7 ɪɪɪɪ.ſerui.7 xɪ.uiłłi 7 ɪɪɪɪ.
borđ 7 ɪ.cotar cū.ɪ.caſ.Ibi molin redđ.xxx.denaſ.7 xvɪɪ.
ac p̄ti.7 x.ac paſturæ.7 xvɪɪ.ac ſiluæ.Valuit.ɪɪɪ.lib.Modo.ɪɪ.lib.

Ipſe Alu ten LOCHINTONE.Aluui teneb T.R.E.7 geldb p.v.
hiđ.Tra.ē.v.caſ.In dnĩo ſt.ɪɪ.caſ.7 ɪɪɪ.ſerui.7 vɪɪɪ.borđ cū
una caſ.Ibi molin redđ.x.ſoł.7 xɪɪ.ac p̄ti.Silua dim leu
lḡ.7 ɪɪɪ.q̇̃ lat.Q̇do recep̄ꞏualb.vɪ.lib.Modo.ɪɪɪ.lib.

Ipſe Alu habuit ACHELAI.Aluui tenuit T.R.E.H addita.ē in
Mertoch ꝋ regis.7 ual.ɪ.ſoliđ p annũ.

<h2>.XXXII. TERRA TVRSTINI FILIJ ROLF.</h2>

Tvrstinvs filius Rolf ten de rege PIDECOME.Aluuold teneb
T.R.E.7 geldb p.v.hiđ.Tra.ē.v.caſ.In dnĩo ſt.ɪɪ.caſ.7 v.
uiłłi 7 xɪx.borđ.cū.ɪɪɪ.caſ.Ibi.ɪɪ.molini redđ.xv.ſoł.7 xxɪɪ.
ac p̄ti.7 v.ac ſilue.In Briuuetone.xɪ.burḡſes redđ.xxɪɪɪ.ſoł.
Tot ualet.vɪɪ.lib.Q̇do recep̄ꞏualb.vɪɪɪ.lib.

13 villagers and 5 smallholders with 4 ploughs.
Woodland, 62 acres.
Value when he acquired it, 70s; now the same.

20 Ranulf holds MERRIDGE from Alfred. Alfwy held it before 1066;
it paid tax for ½ hide. Land for 2½ ploughs. In lordship 1 plough;
2 slaves; 1 virgate.
    4 villagers and 1 smallholder with 1½ ploughs & 1 virgate.   374
    A mill which pays 6d; pasture, 30 acres; woodland, 20 acres.   b 1
        4 cattle; 31 sheep; 12 goats.
The value was and is 20s.

21 Robert holds QUANTOCK from Alfred. Alfwy held it before 1066;
it paid tax for 1 virgate of land. Land for 1½ ploughs.
    3 villagers have them there.   374
    Underwood, 8 acres.   b 2
Value when he acquired it, 20s; now 25s.

22 Walter holds HILLFARRANCE from Alfred. Alfwy held it before
1066; it paid tax for 3 hides. Land for 6 ploughs. In lordship 1
plough; 4 slaves; ½ hide.   374
    11 villagers, 4 smallholders and 1 cottager with 1 plough   b 4
       & 2½ hides.
    A mill which pays 30d; meadow, 17 acres; pasture, 10 acres;
        woodland, 17 acres. 6 cattle; 14 pigs.
The value was £3; now £4.

23 Alfred holds LUCKINGTON himself. Alfwy held it before 1066;
it paid tax for 5 hides. Land for 5 ploughs. In lordship 2
ploughs; 3 slaves; 4 hides & 3 virgates.   375
    8 smallholders with 1 plough & 1 virgate.   a 1
    A mill which pays 10s; meadow, 12 acres; woodland ½ league
        long and 3 furlongs wide. 1 cob; 8 cattle; 108 sheep; 31 goats.
Value when he acquired it £6; now £3.

24 Alfred had OAKLEY himself. Alfwy (? Alwin) son of Banna held it   E
before 1066. This has been added to Martock, a manor of the   374
King's.   b 3
Value 50s a year.   E

[36]   LAND OF THURSTAN SON OF ROLF

1 Thurstan son of Rolf holds PITCOMBE from the King. Alfwold
held it before 1066; it paid tax for 5 hides. Land for 5 ploughs.
In lordship 2 ploughs; 4 hides.   382
    5 villagers and 19 smallholders with 3 ploughs & 1 hide.   b 1
    2 mills which pay 15s; meadow, 22 acres; woodland, 5 acres.
        1 cob; 6 unbroken mares; 12 cattle; 60 pigs; 104 sheep.
    In Bruton 11 burgesses who pay 23s.
Value of the whole £7; value when he acquired it, £8.

Butolf ten de Turſt *WITEHA*. Chetel teneĐ T.R.E.7 geldĐ
ꝓ una hida. Tra.ē.II.caꝛ. In dñio.ē.I.caꝛ.7 VI.cotaꝛ cū.I.
caꝛ. Qdo recep. ualĐ. xv. ſol. Modo. xx. ſolid.

Huic ⋒ addita.ē una hida in Wltune. quā Chetel teneĐ
ꝓ uno Man T.R.E. Tra.ē.I.caꝛ.q̄ ibi.ē cū.I.ſeruo.7 VI.cotaꝛ.
Ibi.II.āc p̃ti. Valet.x.ſol. Qdo recep. ualĐ.xxx. ſolid.
Ħ tra.ē addita tris Aluuoldi. quas ten Turſtin.

Rippe ten de. T. *STORPE*. Æluuin teneĐ T.R.E.7 geldĐ ꝓ una
hida. Tra.ē.I.caꝛ.q̄ ibi.ē cū.III.cotaꝛ. Silua.I.q̃⅄ lḡ.7 laꝛ.

Hugo ten de. T. *SINDERCOME*. Cerric teneĐ ∫ Sēp ual.xx.ſol.
T.R.E.7 geldĐ ꝓ.I.hidᵒ caꝛ. Tra.ē.v.caꝛ. In dñio.ē.I.caꝛ.7 VII.
uilti 7 VII.borđ cū.III.caꝛ.Ibi.xvII.āc p̃ti.7 una leū paſturæ
in lḡ 7 laꝛ. ⁷ᴸ·ᵃᶜʳᵉ ᶠⁱˡᵘᵉ· Valuit 7 ual.xx.ſolid.

Ipſe. Turſt ten *CADEBERIE*. Aluuold teneĐ T.R.E.7 geldĐ
ꝓ.xII.hidᵒ. Tra.ē.xII.caꝛ.In dñio ſt.III.caꝛ.7 VI.ſerui.7 xvI.
uilti 7 xx.borđ cū.vIII.caꝛ.7 un porcari redđ.xII.porcos ꝓ anñ.
Ibi.II. molini redđ.xxII.ſolid.7 L.āc p̃ti.7 Lxx.āc paſturæ.
Silua. IIII.q̃⅄ lḡ.7 una q̃⅄ laꝛ.Valuit.xx.liĐ.Modo.xII.liĐ.

Huic ⋒ eſt addita *WESTONE*. Aluui teneĐ T.R.E.ꝓ man.
7 poterat ire quo uoleĐ.7 gelđĐ ꝓ.II.hidᵒ.7 II.virḡ træ 7 dim.
In dñio.ē.I.caꝛ 7 dim.7 II.ſerui.7 vI.borđ cū.I.caꝛ.Ibi
dimiđ moliñ redđ.xLv.deñ.7 xxIIII.āc p̃ti.Silua.II.q̃⅄
lḡ.7 una q̃⅄ laꝛ.Valuit 7 ual.xL.ſolid.Ricard ten de Turſt.

2 Botolph holds WITHAM (Friary) from Thurstan. Ketel held it
before 1066; it paid tax for 1 hide. Land for 2 ploughs.
In lordship 1 plough; 2½ virgates.   382
 3 villagers & 6 cottagers with 1 plough & 1½ virgates.   b 2
 12 cattle; 10 pigs; 35 sheep.
Value when he acquired it, 15s; now 20s.
 To this manor has been added 1 hide in *WLTUNE* which Ketel   E
held as one manor before 1066. Land for 1 plough, which is
there, with 1 slave.   382
 6 cottagers.   b 3
 Meadow, 2 acres.
Value 10s; value when he acquired it, 30s.
 This land has been added to Alfwold's lands which Thurstan holds. E

3 Ripe holds 'EASTRIP' from Thurstan. Alwin held it before 1066;
it paid tax for 1 hide. Land for 1 plough, which is there, with   E
 3 cottagers.   382
 Woodland 1 furlong long and wide. 3 cows; 12 pigs; 30 sheep.   b 4
Value always 20s.

4 Hugh holds SYNDERCOMBE from Thurstan. Ceolric held it before
1066; it paid tax for 1 hide. Land for 5 ploughs. In lordship
1 plough; 1 virgate.   383
 7 villagers and 7 smallholders with 3 ploughs & 3 virgates.   a 1
 Meadow, 17 acres; pasture, 1 league in length and width;
  woodland, 50 acres.
The value was and is 20s.

5 Thurstan holds (North) CADBURY himself. Alfwold held it
before 1066; it paid tax for 12 hides. Land for 12 ploughs.
In lordship 3 ploughs; 6 slaves; 4 hides.   383
 16 villagers and 20 smallholders with 8 ploughs & 8 hides.   a 2
  A pigman who pays 12 pigs a year.
 2 mills which pay 22s; meadow, 50 acres; pasture, 70 acres;
  woodland 4 furlongs long and 1 furlong wide. 1 cob; 31 cattle;
  60 pigs; 42 sheep.
The value was £20; now £12.
 WESTON (Bampfylde) has been added to this manor. Alfwy held   E
it before 1066 as a manor; he could go where he would. It paid   E
tax for 2 hides and 2½ virgates of land. In lordship 1½ ploughs;
2 slaves; 1½ hides.   383
 6 smallholders with 1 plough & the rest of the land.   a 3
 ½ mill which pays 45d; meadow, 24 acres; woodland 2 furlongs
  long and 1 furlong wide. 1 cob; 9 pigs.
The value was and is 40s.
 Richard holds from Thurstan.

Aluuin̉ ten̉ de.T.*WESTONE*.Ipſe teneb T.R.E.7 geldb
ᵽ dim̉ hida.Tra.ē dim̉ car̃.Ibi tam̃.ē.ı.car̃ cũ.ı.uiłło.Valet

Bernard̉ ten̉ de.T.*SVDCADEBERIE*.Aluuold̉ teneb ⨍x.ſolid.
T.R.E.7 geldb ᵽ.ııı.virg̉ træ.Ibi additæ ſt.ıı.hidæ 7 una v̛
træ.q̉s teneb libe.ıııı.taini T.R.E.Inł toł Tra.ē.ııı.car̃.

Bernard̉ hł.ıı.hid.Vn̉ cleric dimid hid.Vn̉ anglic̉ dim̉ hid.
Valb 7 uał.ııı.lib.Hæ om̃s træ ſt addite tris Aluuoldi
quas tenet Turſtinus.

⨍Adhuc.ē addita.ı.hida In *VLTONE*.qua teneb Alnod̉
libe T.R.E.Tra.ē.ı.car̃.Leuiet ten̉ de Turſt.7 ibi hł.ı.ſerũ.
7 ııı.coſcez.7 ıııı.ac̃s ᵽti.7 ııı.ac̃s ſiluæ minutæ.Valet.x.ſoł.

⨍Adhuc.ē addita *CLOPTONE*.Alnod̉ libe teneb T.R.E.7 geldb
ᵽ.ıı.hid.Tra.ē.ııı.car̃.Radulf̉ ten̉ de Turſt.7 ibi hł.ı.car̃.
cũ.ı.uiłło.7 ıııı.bord.7 ıı.ſeruis.Ibi.x.ac̃ ᵽti.7 ıııı.q̉ꝝ ſiluæ
in lg̃.7 ıı.q̉ꝝ lat̃.Qdo recep̉᷄ uałb.xɫ.ſoł.Modo.xx.ſolid.

Aluuard̉ ten̉ de.T.*BLACHEFORD*.Idē tenuit T.R.E.7 geldb
ᵽ una hida Tra.ē.ı.car̃.g̃ ibi.ē cũ.ııı.bord.Valet.xv.ſoł.

Goisfrid̉ ten̉ de.T.*CVNTONE*.Aluuard̉ teneb T.R.E.7 geldb
ᵽ.vı.hid.Tra.ē.vı.car̃.In dn̄io.ē dim̉ car̃.7 ıııı.ſerui.
7 ıx.uiłłi 7 xı.bord cũ.v.car̃.Ibi molin̄ redd.vııı.ſolid.
7 xv.ac̃ ᵽti.Silua.ıııı.q̉ꝝ lg̃.7 una q̉ꝝ lat̃.Valet.c.ſoł.

Goisfrid̉ ten̉ de.T.*MALPERTONE*.Aluuold̉⨍Olim.vı.lib.
teneb T.R.E.7 geldb ᵽ.v.hid.Tra.ē.vı.car̃.In dn̄io ſt
ıı.car̃.7 x.ſerui.7 ııı.uiłłi.7 ıx.coſcez cũ.ııı.car̃.Ibi.ıı.mo
lini redd.v.ſolid.7 v.den̉.7 v.ac̃ ᵽti.7 x.ac̃ paſturæ.

6 Alwin holds WESTON (Bampfylde) from Thurstan. He held it himself before 1066; it paid tax for ½ hide. Land for ½ plough. 1 plough there, however, with   383
    1 villager.   a 4
Value 10s.

7 Bernard holds SOUTH CADBURY from Thurstan. Alfwold the Bald   E
held it before 1066; it paid tax for 3 virgates of land. 2 hides   E
and 1 virgate of land have been added to it, which four thanes   E
held freely before 1066. In total, land for 3 ploughs. Bernard
Pancevolt has 2 hides, a clerk ½ hide, an Englishman ½ hide.   383
The value was and is £3.   b 1

    All these lands have been added to Alfwold's lands which Thurstan holds.

    A further hide in WOOLSTON has been added, which Alnoth held   E 97 d
freely before 1066. Land for 1 plough. Leofgeat holds from Thurstan and has 1 slave there, and
    3 Cottagers and   383
    meadow, 4 acres; underwood, 3 acres. 50 sheep.   b 2
Value 10s; when Thurstan acquired it, 15s.

    Further, CLAPTON has been added. Alnoth held it freely   E
before 1066; it paid tax for 2 hides. Land for 3 ploughs.   383
Ralph Trenchard holds from Thurstan; he has 1 plough there, with   b 3
    1 villager, 4 smallholders and 2 slaves.
    Meadow, 10 acres; woodland, 4 furlongs in length and 2   E
        furlongs wide.
Value when he acquired it, 40s; now 20s.

8 Alfward holds BLACKFORD from Thurstan. He also held it
before 1066; it paid tax for 1 hide. Land for 1 plough,   E
which is there, with   383
    3 smallholders.   b 4
    3 cattle; 8 pigs; 40 sheep.
Value 15s; when Thurstan acquired it, 20s.

9 Geoffrey holds COMPTON (Pauncefoot) from Thurstan. Alfward held it before 1066; it paid tax for 6 hides. Land for 6 ploughs.
In lordship ½ plough; 4 slaves; 3 hides.   E
    9 villagers and 11 smallholders with 5 ploughs & 3 hides.   383
    A mill which pays 8s; meadow, 15 acres; woodland 4 furlongs   b 5
        long and 1 furlong wide. 4 cattle; 20 pigs; 80 sheep.
Value 100s; formerly £6.

10 Geoffrey holds MAPERTON from Thurstan. Alfwold held it before 1066; it paid tax for 5 hides. Land for 6 ploughs.
In lordship 2 ploughs; 10 slaves; 2 hides.   384
    3 villagers and 9 Cottagers with 3 ploughs & the rest of the land.   a 1
    2 mills which pay 5s 5d; meadow, 5 acres; pasture, 10 acres;

Silua.v.q̴ lḡ.⁊ iii.q̴ laṫ.Valuit olĩ.viii.liḃ.Modo.vi.liḃ.

Norman teñ de.T.*WANDESTREV*. Aluuold teneḃ T.R.E.
⁊ geldḃ ꝓ.v.hiḋ.Trã.ē.v.caṙ.In dñio sṫ.ii.caṙ.⁊ iiii.ſerui.
⁊ iiii.uiⱦi ⁊ iiii.borḋ cũ.i.caṙ.Ibi.xxxvi.aͨ p̃ti.⁊ xxx.
aͨ paſturæ.Silua.i.leũ lḡ.⁊ dim leũ laṫ.Valet.iii. liḃ.

Norman teñ dè.*CHAIVERT*.Leuedai   ſOlim.vi.liḃ.
teneḃ T.R.E.⁊ geldḃ ꝓ dim hida.Trã.ē dim caṙ.q̄ ibi.ē
in dñio cũ.iiii.cotaṙ.Ibi.iiii.aͨ p̃ti.⁊ iiii.aͨ paſturæ.Valet

Bernard teñ de.T.*DVNGRETONE*.Aluuoldus ſ vii.ſoⱦ.
teneḃ T.R.E.⁊ geldḃ ꝓ.iii.hiḋ.Trã.ē.viii.caṙ.In dñio
sṫ.iiii.caṙ.⁊ viii.ſerui.⁊ x.uiⱦi ⁊ vi.borḋ cũ.iiii.caṙ.
Ibi moliñ redḋ.vii.ſoⱦ.⁊ vi.deñ.⁊ vi.aͨ p̃ti.Paſtura.
iiii.q̴ lḡ.⁊ ii.q̴ laṫ.Valet.vi.liḃ.Olim ualḃ.c.ſoliḋ.
Huic ꝏ eſt addita.una v tr̃æ ⁊ ualet.v.ſoliḋ.Eduui teneḃ
libere T.R.E.

Roḃtus teñ de.T.*CIRETVNE*.Aluuold teneḃ T.R.E.⁊ geldḃ
ꝓ.ii.hiḋ.Trã.ē.ii.caṙ.In dñio.ē.i.caṙ.cũ.i.uiⱦo ⁊ iiii.borḋ.
Ibi.vi.aͨ p̃ti.⁊ una q̴ ſiluæ in lḡ ⁊ in laṫ.Valet xxx.ſoⱦ.

                                        ſOlĩ ualḃ.xl.ſoⱦ.

.XXXIII.   TERRA SERLONIS DE BVRCI.

Serlo de Bvrci teñ de rege *BLACHEDONE*.Almar tenḃ
T.R.E.⁊ geldḃ ꝓ.x.hiḋ.Trã.ē.x.caṙ.In dñio sṫ.ii.caṙ.cũ.i.
ſeruo.⁊ v.uiⱦi ⁊ viii.borḋ cũ.v.caṙ.Ibi.ii.molini redḋ.v.ſoⱦ.
⁊ x.aͨ p̃ti.⁊ cc.aͨ ſiluæ.Paſtura.i.leug in lḡ ⁊ laṫ.
Q̊do receᵖ.ualḃ.x.liḃ.Modo.vii.liḃ.   ſValet.xx.ſoⱦ.
De hac tra teñ Lanḃt.i.hiḋ de.Serⱦ.⁊ ibi hṫ.ii.caṙ cũ.ii.uiⱦo.

woodland 5 furlongs long and 3 furlongs wide. 17 cattle; 20 pigs; 80 sheep.
Value formerly £8; now £6.

11 Norman holds WANSTROW from Thurstan. Alfwold held it before 1066; it paid tax for 5 hides. Land for 5 ploughs. In lordship 2 ploughs; 4 slaves; 4 hides.
    4 villagers and 4 smallholders with 1 plough & the rest of the land.
Meadow, 36 acres; pasture, 30 acres; woodland 1 league long and ½ league wide. 5 cobs; 6 cattle; 27 pigs; 86 sheep.
Value £3; formerly £6.

384
a 2

E

12 Norman holds KEYFORD from Thurstan. Leofday held it before 1066; it paid tax for ½ hide. Land for ½ plough, which is there, in lordship, with
    4 cottagers.
Meadow, 4 acres; pasture, 4 acres. 7 cattle; 8 pigs; 14 sheep.
Value 7s; when the Count acquired it, 5s.

384
a 3

13 Bernard Pancevolt holds DUNKERTON from Thurstan. Alfwold held it before 1066; it paid tax for 3 hides. Land for 8 ploughs. In lordship 4 ploughs; 8 slaves; 1½ hides.
    10 villagers and 6 smallholders with 4 ploughs & 1½ hides.
A mill which pays 7s 6d; meadow, 6 acres; pasture 4 furlongs long and 2 furlongs wide. 1 cob; 11 cattle; 36 pigs; 212 sheep.
Value £6; value formerly 100s.
    1 virgate of land has been added to this manor. Value 5s; when Thurstan acquired it, as much. Edwy held it freely before 1066.

384
b 1

E
E

14 Robert holds CHERITON from Thurstan. Alfwold held it before 1066; it paid tax for 2 hides. Land for 2 ploughs. In lordship 1 plough & 1½ hides, with
    1 villager and 4 smallholders (who have) ½ hide.
Meadow, 6 acres; woodland, 1 furlong in length and in width.
Value 30s; value formerly 40s.

384
b 2

[37]   LAND OF SERLO OF BURCY

1 Serlo of Burcy holds BLAGDON from the King. Aelmer held it before 1066; it paid tax for 10 hides. Land for 10 ploughs. In lordship 2 ploughs & 7½ hides, with 1 slave;
    5 villagers and 8 smallholders with 5 ploughs & 1½ hides.
2 mills which pay 5s; meadow, 10 acres; woodland, 220 acres; pasture 1 league in length and width. 3 cattle; 13 pigs; 50 sheep; 60 goats.
Value when he acquired it, £10; now £7.
    Lambert holds 1 hide of this land from Serlo; he has 2 ploughs there, with
    2 villagers.
Value 20s.

452
a 1

E
L

Quattuor milites teñ de . S . *Opopille* . Euuacre teneƀ
T . R . E .7 geldƀ ꝓ . vi . hiđ 7 dim . Tra . ē . x . car̄ . In dñio s̄t . iiii
car̄ . cū . i . feruo . 7 vii . uilti 7 iiii . borđ cū . iii . car̄ . Ibi . Lxx .
ac̄ p̃ti . 7 c . ac̄ paſturæ . ualuit 7 uat̄ . vi . liƀ .

Ipfe . S . teñ *Stoche* . Euuacre teneƀ T . R . E . 7 geldƀ ꝓ dimiđ
hida . Tra . ē . i . car̄ . cū . i . feruo ibi . ē in dñio . 7 i . ac̄ p̃ti 7 dim .
Silua . iiii . q̃ƶ lḡ . 7 una q̃ƶ lat̄ . Valet . x . foliđ .

Ipfe . S . teñ *Cilele* . Euuacre teneƀ T . R . E . 7 geldƀ ꝓ . iii . v
træ . Tra . ē . ii . car̄ . g̃ ibi s̄t cū . i . uitto 7 i . borđ . 7 i . feruo .
Ibi . i . ac̄ p̃ti 7 dim . Valet . xv . foliđ .

Huic addita . ē *Stoche* . Aluric tenuit ꝓ m̄ T . R . E . 7 geldƀ
ꝓ dim hida . Tra . ē . i . car̄ . g̃ ibi . ē cū . ii . borđ . 7 dim ac̄ p̃ti .

Walter teñ de S . *Aldvic* . Almar teneƀ ⌐ Vat̄ . x . fot .
T . R . E . 7 geldƀ ꝓ . ii . hiđ . Tra . ē . v . car̄ . In dñio . ē . i . car̄ .
7 ii . ferui . 7 iiii . uilti 7 i . borđ   Ibi moliñ redđ . iii . fot .
7 xv . ac̄ p̃ti . 7 xlix . ac̄ filuæ . Olim 7 modo . uat̄ . xl . foliđ .

Guntard teñ de . S . *Ragiol* . Quattuor taini teneƀ T . R . E .
7 geldƀ ꝓ . ii . hiđ . Tra . ē . ii . car̄ . In dñio . ē . i . car̄ . cū . i . feruo .
7 i . uitto . Ibi . v . ac̄ p̃ti . 7 v . ac̄ filuæ minutæ . Valet . xxx . foliđ .
Huic addita . ē una hida 7 una v træ . Vn tain teneƀ liƀe T . R . E .
Tra . ē . iii . car̄ . Walter teñ de Serlone . 7 ibi h̄t . i . car̄ . 7 iiii .
ferui . cū . i . uitto 7 i . borđ . Ibi . iii . ac̄ p̃ti . 7 iii . q̃ƶ filuæ in lḡ 7 lat̄ .

2 Four men-at-arms hold UPHILL from Serlo. Everwacer held it
before 1066; it paid tax for 6½ hides. Land for 10 ploughs.
In lordship 4 ploughs & 5 hides & 3 virgates, with 1 slave;   452
   7 villagers and 4 smallholders with 3 ploughs & 3 virgates of land.   a 2
   Meadow, 70 acres; pasture, 100 acres. 8 cattle; 25 pigs; 100 sheep.
The value was and is £6.

3 Serlo holds (Chew) STOKE himself. Everwacer held it before 1066;
it paid tax for ½ hide. Land for 1 plough; with 1 slave, it   E
is there, in lordship.   452
   Meadow, 1½ acres; woodland 4 furlongs long and 1 furlong wide.   a 3
     13 cattle; 12 pigs; 27 sheep; 20 goats.
Value 10s.

4 Serlo holds CHILLYHILL himself. Everwacer held it before 1066;
it paid tax for 3 virgates of land. Land for 2 ploughs,   L
which are there, with   452
   1 villager, 1 smallholder and 1 slave.   b 1
   Meadow, 1½ acres.
Value 15s.
   (Chew) STOKE has been added to this (manor). Aelfric held it as   E
a manor before 1066; it paid tax for ½ hide. Land for 1 plough,   E
which is there, with   452
   2 smallholders & 1 villager.   b 2
   Meadow, 1½ acres.
Value 10s; when Serlo acquired it, 20s.

5 Walter holds ALDWICK from Serlo. Edmer Ator held it before 1066;   E
it paid tax for 2 hides. Land for 5 ploughs. In lordship 1
plough; 2 slaves; 3 virgates.   452
   4 villagers and 1 smallholder (have) 1 hide & 1 virgate.   b 3
   A mill which pays 3s; meadow, 15 acres; woodland, 49 acres.
     1 cob; 14 cattle; 11 pigs; 14 sheep.
Value formerly and now 40s.

6 Guntard holds RIDGEHILL from Serlo. Four thanes held it   E   98 a
before 1066; it paid tax for 2 hides. Land for 2 ploughs.
In lordship 1 plough, with 1 slave and   452
   1 villager.   b 4
   Meadow, 5 acres; underwood, 5 acres. 15 cattle; 6 pigs; 55 sheep.
Value 30s; when Serlo acquired it, 20s.
   1 hide and 1 virgate of land have been added to this (manor). A   E
thane held them freely before 1066. Land for 3 ploughs. Walter   E
holds from Serlo; he has 1 plough there, in lordship; 4 slaves with
   1 villager and 1 smallholder.
   Meadow, 3 acres; woodland, 3 furlongs in length and as much in
     width. 1 cob; 4 cattle; 10 pigs.

Olim.x.folid.Modo.xxx.folid. H̅ t̃ra n̅ ꝑtinuit ad Euuacre.

E̅ccla S̅ Edwardi ten̅ de.S.CHELMETONE.ꝑ filia ej a̅ ibi.e̅.
Alfi teneb̅ T.R.E. Ibi s̅t.v.hidæ.f; ꝑ una hida geld̅.T̃ra.e̅.v.
car̅.In dn̅io.e̅.1.car̅.7 IIII.uilti 7 III.bord̅ cu̅.IIII.car̅. Ibi una
leu̅ filuæ in l̅g.7 III.q̂ɀ lat̅.Oli.xxx.fot.Modo.xL.folid.

Iꝑfe.S.ten̅ LOVINTVNE.Tres taini teneb̅ T.R.E.ꝑ trib; maner'.|7 geld̅b ꝑ.vI.
hid̅.T̃ra.e̅.vIII.car̅.In dn̅io s̅t.II.car̅.7 II.ferui.7 vIII.uilti
7 IX.bord̅ cu̅.vI.car̅. Ibi molin̅ redd̅.x.folid.7 xL.ac̅ ꝑti.
Silua.IIII.q̂ɀ l̅g.7 II.q̂ɀ lat̅.Oli.vI.lib̅.Modo.c.folid.
De hac t̃ra ten̅ Lanbt̅.1.hid̅.7 ibi ht̅.1.car̅ cu̅.III.uilti s.
Ibi.xII.ac̅ ꝑti.Valet.xx.folid.

★ S̅ipfe erlo ten̅ WATEHELLE.Elmer teneb̅ T.R.E. de æccla glaf
tingb̅ie.nec poterat ab ea fepari.7 geld̅b ꝑ.III.hid̅.T̃ra.e̅.IIII.
car̅.In dn̅io.e̅.1.car̅.cu̅.1.feruo.7 1.bord̅.Oli.xL.fot.M̅.xL.fot.
De hac t̃ra ten̅ de.S.Goisfrid̅.1.hid̅.7 ual.x.folid.

Iꝑfe.S.ten̅ CONTONE.Euuacre teneb̅ T̅.R.E.7 geld̅b ꝑ.v.
hid̅.T̃ra.e̅.v.car̅.In dn̅io.s̅t.II.car̅.7 II.ferui.7 v.uilti.7 vI.cot̅.
7.v.bord̅.cu̅.IIII.car̅.Ibi.xv.ac̅ ꝑti.7 una leu̅ pafturæ in l̅g.
7 II.q̂ɀ lat̅.Silua.xI.q̂ɀ l̅g.7 IX.q̂ɀ lat̅.Oli.c.fot.Modo
De hac t̃ra ten̅ Ricard de.S.una̅ v̅ t̃ræ 7 1.fert̅.⌐ IIII.lib̅.
7 ibi ht̅.1.car̅.cu̅.II.bord̅.7 v.ac̅ ꝑti.Oli.v.fot.m̊.xv.fot.

[Value] formerly 10s; now 30s.
This land did not belong to Everwacer. E

7 St. Edward's Church holds KILMINGTON from Serlo for his daughter E
who is there. Alfsi held it before 1066. 5 hides, but it paid tax E
for 1 hide. Land for 5 ploughs. In lordship 1 plough;
4 hides & 1 virgate.
  4 villagers and 3 smallholders with 4 ploughs & 3 virgates.   453
  Woodland, 1 league in length and 3 furlongs wide.   a 1
   14 cattle; 15 pigs; 137 sheep.
[Value] formerly 30s; now 40s.

Serlo himself holds
8 LOVINGTON. Three thanes held it before 1066 as three manors; E
it paid tax for 6 hides. Land for 8 ploughs. In lordship 2 ploughs;
2 slaves; 3 hides, less 5 acres.
  8 villagers and 9 smallholders with 6 ploughs & 2 hides & 5 acres.   453
  A mill which pays 10s; meadow, 40 acres; woodland 4 furlongs   a 2
   long and 2 furlongs wide. 16 cattle; 1 cob; 11 pigs; 30 sheep.
[Value] formerly £6; now 100s.
  Lambert holds 1 hide of this land; he has 1 plough there, with L
  3 villagers.
  Meadow, 12 acres. 2 pigs.   453
Value 20s.   a 3

9 WHEATHILL. Aelmer held it before 1066 from Glastonbury Church; †
he could not be separated from it. It paid tax for 3 hides.
Land for 4 ploughs. In lordship 1 plough & 2 hides, with 1 slave;   453
1 smallholder.   a 4
[Value] formerly 40s; now 40s.
  Geoffrey holds 1 hide of this land from Serlo; value 10s. E

10 COMPTON (Martin). Everwacer held it before 1066; it paid tax
for 5 hides. Land for 5 ploughs. In lordship 2 ploughs; 2 slaves;
2 hides & 3 virgates.
  5 villagers, 6 cottagers and 5 smallholders with 4 ploughs   453
   & 1 hide & 3 virgates.   b 1
  Meadow, 15 acres; pasture, 1 league in length and 2 furlongs
   wide; woodland 11 furlongs long and 9 furlongs wide.
   6 cattle; 7 pigs; 17 sheep; 9 goats.
[Value] formerly 100s; now £4.
  Of this land Richard holds 1 virgate of land and 1 furlong E
from Serlo; he has 1 plough there, with
  2 smallholders (who have) 1 furlong.   453
  Meadow, 5 acres. 12 cattle; 10 pigs; 30 goats.   b 2
[Value] formerly 5s; now 15s.

Ipſe.S.ten *MORTONE*.Tres taini teneb̄ T.R.E. 7 geldb̄ ꝑ.v.
hid̄.Tra.ē.v.car̄.Godric ten de hac t̄ra.7 Elric.ıı.hid̄.
In dn̄io ſt̄.ıı.car̄.7 ıx.uilli.7 xı.bord̄.cū.ıı.car̄.Ibi moliñ
redd̄.v.ſolid̄.7 xl.ac̄ p̄ti.7 xv.ac̄ ſiluæ.Olı̄ 7 m̄ ual.ııı.lib̄.
De ead̄ t̄ra ten Ricard̄.ııı.v t̄ræ.7 Hunfrid̄.ı.virḡ t̄ræ.
Ibi.ē.ı.car̄.7 ıı.uilli 7 ııı.bord̄.7 xvııı.ac̄ p̄ti.7 ıııı.ac̄ ſiluæ.
7 ıı.ac̄ paſturæ.Olim 7 modo.ual.xv.ſolid̄.

Rainald ten de.S.*MVDIFORD*.Elmar teneb̄ T.R.E.7 geldb̄
ꝑ.ııı.hid̄.Tra.ē.ııı.car̄.In dn̄io.ē car̄ 7 dim̄.7 ııı.uilli 7 ıııı.
bord̄ cū.ıı.car̄.Olim 7 m̄ ual.ııı.lib̄.
Huic m̄.ē addita *STANE*.Sared teneb̄ ꝑ man libere T.R.E.7 geldb̄
ꝑ.ıı.hid̄.Tra.ē.ı.car̄ 7 dim̄.Olim 7 m̄ ualet.x.ſolid̄.

.XXXII. TERRA ODONIS FILIJ GAMELIN.

Odo filius Gamelini ten de rege *LOCVBE*.7 Vitalis de eo.
Fitel teneb̄ T.R.E.7 geldb̄ ꝑ.ı.hida.Tra.ē.vı.car̄.In dn̄io
ē.ı.car̄.7 ıı.ſerui.7 vııı.uilli 7 ı.bord̄ cū.ıı.car̄ 7 dim̄.Ibi
ıı.ac̄ p̄ti.7 xıı.ac̄ ſiluæ.7 l.ac̄ paſturæ.Olı̄ 7 m̄ ual.xl.ſol.

.XXXV. TERRA OSBERNI GIFARD.

Osbernvs Gifard ten de rege *CANOLE*.Alnod teneb̄ T.R.E.7 geldb̄
ꝑ.ıı.hid̄.Tra.ē.ııı.car̄.In dn̄io.ē.ı.car̄.7 v.uilli 7 vı.bord̄
cū.ıı.car̄.Ibi.xvı.ac̄ p̄ti.7 xx.ac̄ paſturæ.Silua.ıı.q̄ᷝ 7 dim̄
lḡ. 7 dimid̄ q̄ᷝ lat̄.Olim.xxx.ſol.Modo ual.xl.ſolid̄.
Ipſe.O.ten *TELVVE*.Dōno teneb̄ T.R.E.7 geldb̄ ꝑ.v.hid̄.
Tra.ē.ıııı.car̄.In dn̄io.ē.ı.car̄.7 ıı.ſerui.7 ııı.uilli 7 ıııı.bord̄
cū.ııı.car̄.Ibi.ıı.molini redd̄.c.denar̄.7 xıııı.ac̄ p̄ti.7 xvı.
ac̄ ſiluæ minutæ.7 xıııı.ac̄ paſturæ.Olim.ııı.lib̄.Modo.ıııı.lib̄.

11 MORETON. Three thanes held it as three manors before 1066; it paid   E
tax for 5 hides. Land for 5 ploughs. Godric holds 2 hides of   D
this land and Alric 2 hides. In lordship 2 ploughs;   453
> 9 villagers and 11 smallholders with 2 ploughs.   E b 3-4
>> A mill which pays 5s; meadow, 40 acres; woodland, 15 acres.   E

Value formerly and now £3.
> Of this land Richard holds 3 virgates of land and Humphrey 1   D
virgate of land. 1 plough there.
>> 2 villagers and 3 smallholders.   454
>>> Meadow, 18 acres; woodland, 4 acres; pasture, 2 acres.   a 1-2

Value formerly and now 15s.

12 Reginald holds MUDFORD from Serlo. Edmer Ator held it before
1066; it paid tax for 3 hides. Land for 3 ploughs. In lordship
1½ ploughs; 1½ hides.   454
> 3 villagers and 4 smallholders with 2 ploughs & 1½ hides.   a 3
> 3 cattle; 8 pigs; 26 sheep.

Value formerly and now £3.
> STONE has been added to this manor. Saered held it freely as a   E
manor before 1066; it paid tax for 2 hides. Land for 1½ ploughs.
Reginald holds it from Serlo; he has ½ plough there, & 10 sheep.
Value formerly and now 10s.

[38]   LAND OF ODO SON OF GAMELIN

1 Odo son of Gamelin holds LUCCOMBE from the King, and Vitalis
from him. Vitalis held it before 1066; it paid tax for 1 hide.
Land for 6 ploughs. In lordship 1 plough; 2 slaves; ½ hide.   380
> 8 villagers and 1 smallholder with 2½ ploughs & ½ hide.   a 1
>> Meadow, 2 acres; woodland, 12 acres; pasture, 50 acres.

Value formerly and now 40s.

[39]   LAND OF OSBERN GIFFARD

1 Osbern Giffard holds KNOWLE from the King. Alnoth the Constable
held it before 1066; it paid tax for 2 hides. Land for 3 ploughs.
In lordship 1 plough; 1 hide.
> 5 villagers and 6 smallholders with 2 ploughs & 1 hide.   447
>> Meadow, 16 acres; pasture, 20 acres; woodland 2½ furlongs   a 1
>> long and 1½ furlongs wide. 1 cob; 8 cattle; 25 pigs.

Formerly 30s; value now 40s.

2 Osbern holds ELM himself. Dunn held it before 1066;
it paid tax for 5 hides. Land for 4 ploughs. In lordship 1
plough; 2 slaves; 4 hides & 1 virgate.   447
> 3 villagers and 4 smallholders with 3 ploughs & 3 virgates.   a 2
>> 2 mills which pay 100d; meadow, 14 acres; underwood, 16 acres;
>> pasture, 14 acres. 1 cob; 15 cattle; 16 pigs; 250 sheep; 30 goats.

[Value] formerly £3; now £4.

Ipſe.O.ten�add̄ *VDEBERGE*.Dōno teneð T.R.E.7 geldð ꝑ una
hida.Ṫra.ē.ıı.caꝛ.In dn̄io.ē.ı.caꝛ.7 vı.borð cū.ı.ſeruo.
7 vıııı.ac̄ ꝑti.Olim.xxx.ſolid.Modo ual.xL.ſolid.

.XXXVI.   TERRA EDWARDI SARISBER̃.

Edward Sarisber̃ ten de rege *HANTONE*.Vluuen teneð
T.R.E.7 geldð ꝑ.x.hiđ.Ṫra.ē.x.caꝛ.In dn̄io ſt.ııı.caꝛ.7 ıx.
ſerui.7 xıı.uilli 7 xv.borð cū.vı.caꝛ.Ibi.ıı.molini redð
xxxıııı.ſol.7 xıı.ac̄ ꝑti.Silua.ı.leū lḡ.7 dım̄ leū lat̃.
In *BADE*.ıı.dom.una redð.vıı.den 7 obolū.Oli.x.lið.m̄ ual.xıı.lið:
Ipſe.E.ten *NORTVNE*.Iuing teneð T.R.E.7 geldð ꝑ.x.hiđ.
Tra.ē.x.caꝛ.In dn̄io ſt.ııı.caꝛ.7 ııı.ſerui.7 ııı.uilli 7 xııı.
borð cū.ııı.caꝛ.Ibi molin̄ redð.v.ſolid.7 xx.ac̄ ꝑti.7 totid
paſturæ.Silua.ı.leū lḡ.7 tn̄tđ lat̃.Oli.vı.lið.Modo.vıı.lið.
De his.x.hiđ deđ rex.E.ꝑdicto Iuing.ıı.caruc̃ træ.

.XXXVI.   TERRA ERNVLFI DE HESDING.

Ernvlfvs De Heſding ten de rege *WESTONE*.Edric teneð
T.R.E.7 geldð ꝑ.v.hiđ.Ṫra.ē.vıı.caꝛ.In dn̄io ſt.ıı.caꝛ.7 x.
ſerui.7 vı.uilli 7 ı.borð cū.ııı.caꝛ.Ibi molin̄ redð.xx.ſolid.
7 xııı.ac̄ ꝑti.7 Lx.ac̄ paſturæ.7 xxx.ac̄ ſiluæ.In *BADE*.ııı.don̄
redð xxvıı.den.Totū oli 7 modo ual.vııı.lið.
Engeler ten de Ern *TICHEHA*.Edric teneð T.R.E.7 geldð
ꝑ.ı.hida 7 ııı.v træ.Tra.ē.ııı.caꝛ.Ibi ſt.ıı.uilli.7 ı.borð
7 ı.ſeruus.7 vı.ac̄ ꝑti.Silua.ııı.q̃ꝛ lḡ.7 una q̃ꝛ lat̃.Val.xL.ſol.

3 Osbern holds WOODBOROUGH himself. Dunn held it before 1066;
   it paid tax for 1 hide. Land for 2 ploughs. In lordship 1 plough;
      6 smallholders with 1 slave who have ½ virgate.   447
         Meadow, 8 acres. 1 cow; 150 sheep.   a 3
   Formerly 30s; value now 40s.

[40]   LAND OF EDWARD OF SALISBURY   E 98 b

1 Edward of Salisbury holds HINTON (Charterhouse) from the King.
   Wulfwen held it before 1066; it paid tax for 10 hides.
   Land for 10 ploughs. In lordship 3 ploughs; 9 slaves; 5 hides.
      12 villagers and 15 smallholders with 6 ploughs & 5 hides.   437
      2 mills which pay 34s; meadow, 12 acres; woodland 1   ague   a 1
         long and ½ league wide; in Bath 2 houses, one which pays 7½d E
         & the other dwelling empty. 3 cobs; 40 cattle; 200 sheep; 90 pigs; 60 goats. E
   Formerly £10; value now £12.

2 Edward holds NORTON (St. Philip) himself. Ifing held it before 1066;
   it paid tax for 10 hides. Land for 10 ploughs. In lordship 3 ploughs;
      3 slaves; 5 hides & ½ virgate.   437
      3 villagers and 13 smallholders with 3 ploughs & 5 hides, less ½ virgate. a 2
      A mill which pays 5s; meadow, 20 acres; pasture, as many;
         woodland 1 league long and as wide. 2 cobs; 20 cattle; 28 pigs;
         240 sheep.   E
   [Value] formerly £6; now £7.
      Of these 10 hides King Edward gave 2 carucates of land to   E
   the said Ifing.

[41]   LAND OF ARNULF OF HESDIN

1 Arnulf of Hesdin holds WESTON from the King. Edric held it
   before 1066; it paid tax for 5 hides. Land for 7 ploughs.
   In lordship 2 ploughs; 10 slaves; 4 hides, less ½ virgate & 3 acres. 448
      6 villagers and 1 smallholder with 3 ploughs & 1 hide, ½ virgate & b 1
      3 acres.
      A mill which pays 20s; meadow, 13 acres; pasture, 60 acres;
         woodland, 30 acres; in Bath 3 houses which pay 27d.   E
         6 cobs; 8 cattle; 16 pigs; 250 sheep.
   Value of the whole formerly and now £8.

2 Engelhere holds TICKENHAM from Arnulf. Edric held it before
   1066; it paid tax for 1 hide and 3 virgates of land. Land for 3
   ploughs. In lordship 5 virgates.   448
      3 villagers, 1 smallholder and 1 slave (have) ½ hide.   b 2
      Meadow, 6 acres; woodland 3 furlongs long and 1 furlong wide.
         2 cattle; 1 pig; 3 sheep.
   Value 40s; when he acquired it, 60s.

Ingelramn teñ de . Er . *REDDENE* . Edric teneb̃ T.R.E. 7 geldb̃
ꝑ una hida . Tra . III . car̃ . q̄ ibi s̃t in dñio . 7 III . ſerui . 7 XXVIII.
bord . Ibi . II . molini redd . XV . ſolid . 7 XX . ac̃ pti . 7 XXX . ac̃
paſtûræ . Silua . I . leū lg̃ . 7 tntd laf . Olim 7 m̃ ual . IIII . lib̃ .

.XXXVIII. ## TERRA GISLEBERTI FILIJ TVROLDI.

GISLEBERTVS filius Turoldi teñ de rege *CHIWESTOCH.*
7 Osbñ de eo . Edric teneb̃ T.R.E. 7 geldb̃ ꝑ una hida 7 dim.
Tra . ē . II . car̃ . q̄ ibi s̃t in dñio . 7 II . ſerui . 7 II . bord . 7 XX . ac̃ pti .
7 X . ac̃ ſiluæ minutæ . Olim . XX . ſot . Modo ual . XXX . ſolid.

Walter̃ teñ de . G . *TVMBELI* . Edric teneb̃ T.R.E. 7 geldb̃
ꝑ . V . hid . Tra . ē . V . car̃ . In dñio . ē . I . car̃ . 7 II . ſerui . 7 V . uitti .
7 IIII . bord 7 IIII . coſcez cū . III . car̃ . Ibi moliñ redd . XXX . deñ .
7 XXXV . ac̃ pti . Paſtura . I . leū lg̃ . 7 dim leū laf . 7 tantd ſiluæ
Q̃do recep̃ . ualb̃ . c . ſot . Modo tñtd .

Idē teñ *ESTONE* . Edric teneb̃ T.R.E. 7 geldb̃ ꝑ . I . hida . Tra . ē . I .
car̃ . q̄ ibi . ē cū . III . bord . Redd . XXX . ſolid .

.XXXIX. ## TERRA GODEBOLDI.

GODEBOLD teñ de rege *CARME* . Albric̃t teneb̃ T.R.E. 7 geldb̃
ꝑ . III . virg træ . Tra . ē . III . car̃ . In dñio . ē . I . car̃ . cū . I . ſeruo.
7 III . uitti cū . I . bord . Ibi . III . ac̃ pti . 7 L . ac̃ paſturæ .
Olim . XX . ſot . Modo ual X . ſolid .

.XL. ## TERRA MATHIV DE MORETANIA.

MATHIV teñ de rege *CLIVEDONE* . 7 Ildeb̃t de eo . Johs teneb̃
T.R.E. 7 geldb̃ ꝑ . V . hid 7 dimid . 7 II . ferlings . Tra . ē . VI . car̃ .
In dñio s̃t . II . car̃ . cū . I . ſeruo . 7 VIII . uitti . 7 X . bord cū . IIII . car̃ .

3 Ingelrann holds RODDEN from Arnulf. Edric held it before 1066;
it paid tax for 1 hide. Land for 3 ploughs, which are there,
in lordship, & ½ hide; 3 slaves.   448
    28 smallholders (have) ½ hide.   b 3
    2 mills which pay 15s; meadow, 20 acres; pasture, 30 acres;
        woodland 1 league long and as wide. 1 cob; 20 cattle; 50 pigs;
        300 sheep.
Value formerly and now £4.

[42] LAND OF GILBERT SON OF THOROLD

1 Gilbert son of Thorold holds KEWSTOKE from the King, and
Osbern from him. Edric held it before 1066; it paid tax
for 1½ hides. Land for 2 ploughs, which are there, in lordship;
2 slaves;   446
    2 smallholders.   a 1
    Meadow, 20 acres; underwood, 10 acres. 5 unbroken mares; 18 cattle;
        30 pigs; 18 sheep; 15 goats.
Formerly 20s; value now 30s.

2 Walter holds UBLEY from Gilbert. Edric held it before 1066;
it paid tax for 5 hides. Land for 5 ploughs. In lordship 1 plough;
2 slaves; 3 hides & 1 virgate.   446
    5 villagers, 4 smallholders and 4 Cottagers with 3 ploughs   a 2
        & the rest of the land.
    A mill which pays 30d; meadow, 35 acres; pasture 1 league
        long and ½ league wide; woodland, as much . 5 cattle; 14 pigs.
Value when he acquired it, 100s; now as much.

3 He also holds (Ston) EASTON. Edric held it before 1066; it   E
paid tax for 1 hide. Land for 1 plough, which is there, with   E
    3 smallholders.   446
It pays 30s.   a 3

[43] LAND OF GODBOLD

1 Godbold holds QUARME from the King. Albrict held it before 1066;
it paid tax for 3 virgates of land. Land for 3 ploughs.
In lordship 1 plough & 2 virgates, with 1 slave;   473
    3 villagers with 1 smallholder (have) 1 virgate.   b 1
    Meadow, 3 acres; pasture, 50 acres.
Formerly 20s; value now 10s.

[44] LAND OF MATTHEW OF MORTAGNE

1 Matthew holds CLEVEDON from the King, and Hildebert from him.
John the Dane held it before 1066; it paid tax for 5½ hides and   450
2 furlongs. Land for 6 ploughs. In lordship 2 ploughs & 2 hides, a 1
with 1 slave;
    8 villagers and 10 smallholders with 4 ploughs & 3½ hides & 2 furlongs.

Ibi.xLVI.ac p̃ti.Paſtura.1.leũ 7 dim̃ lg̃.7 tn̄td̃ lat̃.Silua.11.
q̃rent lg̃.7 dim q̃ʒ lat̃.Olim.xL.ſolid.Modo ual̃.1111.lib̃.

Rumald̃ ten de.M.*CALVICHE*.Torchil ten̄ T.R.E.7 geld̃b
p̃ una hida.Tra.ẽ.111.car̃.In dñio.ẽ.1.car̃.7 11.ſerui.7 111.uilti
7 1111.bord̃ cũ.11.car̃.Ibi.v1.ac filuæ minutæ.Oli 7 m̃.xL.ſot.
De hoc m̃.ẽ ablata una v̄ træ.quã ten̄b Turchil cũ p̃dicta
tra.Ep̃s c̃ſtantienſis ten̄.

Ildeb̃tus ten de.M.*MIDELTVNE*.Vluuard ten̄b T.R.E.7 geld̃b
p̃ x.hid̃.Tra.ẽ.v1.car̃.In dñio ſt.11.car̃.7 1111.ſerui.7 1x.uilti
7 1x.bord̃ cũ.111.car̃.Ibi molin̄ redd̃.v.ſolid.7 xx1111.ac p̃ti.
Silua.x.q̃ʒ in lg̃ 7 lat̃.Qdo recep̃.ualb̃.c.ſot.Modo.v1.lib̃.

98 c

XLV. TERRA HVNFRIDI.

Hcamer᷑ vNFRID ten de rege *CVRI*.Ordric 7 Liuing ten̄b
T.R.E.7 geld̃b p̃.1.hida 7 uno ferling.Tra.ẽ.1.car̃.g̃ ibi.ẽ
in dñio.cũ.1.bord̃ 7 11.cotar̃.Ibi.xx.ac p̃ti.Oli.xx.ſolid.
modo ual̃.xL.ſolid.H̄ tra addita.ẽ tris Brictric.ſed ii
q̃ ten̄b T.R.E.quo uoleb̃ ire poterant.

Idem.H.ten̄ *CVRI*.Leuing ten̄b T.R.E.7 geld̃b p̃.11.hid̃.
Tra.ẽ.111.car̃.In dñio ſt.11.car̃.7 111.uilti 7 111.bord̃ cũ.1.
car̃.Ibi.xx1111.ac p̃ti.Olim.xxx.ſot.Modo ual̃.xL.ſolid.
☞ 7 H̄ eſt juncta tris Brictric.ſ; q̃ ten̄b T.R.E.q̃ uolb̃ ire poter̃.

Meadow, 46 acres; pasture 1½ leagues long and as wide;
woodland 2 furlongs long and ½ furlong wide.   7 unbroken mares;
1 cob; 22 cattle; 25 pigs; 115 sheep.
Formerly 40s; value now £4.

2 Rumold holds CHELVEY from Matthew. Thorkell the Dane held it   E
before 1066; it paid tax for 1 hide. Land for 3 ploughs.
In lordship 1 plough; 2 slaves; 1 virgate.   450
    3 villagers and 4 smallholders with 2 ploughs & 3 virgates.   a 2
    Underwood, 6 acres. 6 pigs.
[Value] formerly and now 40s.
    From this manor has been taken away 1 virgate of land which   E
Thorkell held with the said land. The Bishop of Coutances
holds it now. Value 5s.   E

3 Hildebert holds MILTON (Clevedon) from Matthew. Wulfward Tumbi
held it before 1066; it paid tax for 10 hides. Land for 6 ploughs.
In lordship 2 ploughs; 4 slaves; 5 hides.   450
    9 villagers and 9 smallholders with 3 ploughs & 5 hides.   a 3
    A mill which pays 5s; meadow, 24 acres; woodland 10 furlongs
        in length and width. 1 cob; 10 cattle; 18 pigs; 160 sheep; 40 goats.
Value when he acquired it, 100s; now £6.

45   LAND OF HUMPHREY [THE CHAMBERLAIN]   E 98 c

1 Humphrey the Chamberlain holds (Lytes) CARY from the King.
Ordric and Leofing held it before 1066; it paid tax for 1 hide   E
and 1 furlong. Land for 1 plough, which is there, in lordship,
with   479
    1 smallholder and 2 cottagers; they have 7 acres of land.   b 1
    Meadow, 20 acres. 12 cattle; 100 sheep.
Formerly 20s; value now 40s.
    This land has been added to Brictric's lands, but the holders   E
before 1066 could go where they would.

2 Humphrey also holds (Lytes) CARY. Leofing held it before 1066; it E
paid tax for 2 hides. Land for 3 ploughs. In lordship 2 ploughs;
1 hide & 1 virgate.   479
    3 villagers and 3 smallholders with 1 plough & the rest of the land.   b 2
    Meadow, 24 acres.
Formerly 30s; value now 40s.
    This (land) has been joined to Brictric's lands, but the holder   E
before 1066 could go where he would.

Transposition signs indicate that this chapter is continued on col. 99 b after 47,25.

.XLVI. marginal notes:

Hic Robt habuit un virg tre . quã tenuit Dodo libe T.R.E.
H addita fuit DOLVERTONE Maner regis. Modo dijudicata . ē ee . tainland. Val . x . fol.

ROTBERTVS de Odburuile ten de rege in WARNE.
.II . virg træ 7 dim q̃ nunq̃ geldau . Tra . ē dim car . Ibi . ē
un bord cu . I . feruo . Val . xv . folid . Vafta acceṗ.

Idē . R . ten dimid hid in WIDEPOLLE . Tres foreftarij te
neb T.R.E . Tra . ē . IIII . car . De hac reddeb Robt . xx . folid
in firma regis ad WINESFORD . Modo diratiocinata . ē in tainland.

Idē . R . ten WILESFORDE . Duo taini teneb T.R.E. 7 geld
ṗ una hida . Tra . ē . II . car . In dnio . ē . I . car . 7 II . ferui . 7 VIII.
bord hnt . I . car . Ibi . IIII . ac pti . 7 x . ac pafturæ . 7 III . ac
filuæ minutæ . Olim . x . folid . Modo ual . xv . folid.
De hac hida ten Com morit una v . 7 Bretel de eo.

Idē . R . ten MELECOME . Saric teneb T.R.E. 7 geldb pro
una v træ 7 dimid . Tra . ē . I . car 7 dim . 7 ibi st cu . x . bord.
Ibi molin redd . XII . den . 7 x . ac filuæ minutæ . Oli 7 modo
De hoc M̃ . ē ablata dimid hida . quæ T.R.E. ibi fuat . xv . fot
ptineb . Hanc ten Walfcin de Douuai cu BVR maner fuo.

JoHs Hoftiari ten de rege PEGENS . Briftric teneb T.R.E.
7 geldb ṗ una hida 7 una v træ . Tra . ē . II . car . In dnio . ē . I . car.
7 II . uitti cu . I . bord . Ibi pbr cu . I . car 7 II . bord . Ibi . v . ac pti.
Olim . XL . folid . Modo . xxx . folid ualet.

Idē JoHs ten PERI . Orgar teneb T.R.E. 7 geldb ṗ dim hida
7 dim v træ . 7 dimid ferling . Tra . ē . I . car . q̃ ibi . ē cu . II . uitt
7 II . bord . Ibi . v . ac pti . Oli . x . fot . Modo ual . xv . folid.

46 [LAND OF ROBERT OF AUBERVILLE AND OTHERS OF THE KING'S SERVANTS]

E

1 Robert of Auberville holds from the King in WEARNE 2½ virgates
of land which have never paid tax. Land for ½ plough.　　　　479
　　1 smallholder with 1 slave. 4 cattle; 15 sheep.　　　　　　　b 3
Value 15s; it was waste when he received it.

2 Robert of Auberville also had 1 virgate of land which Doda held　　E
freely before 1066. It had been added to DULVERTON, a manor　　478
of the King's; now it has been judged to be thaneland.　　　E b 3
Value 10s.

3 Robert of Auberville also holds ½ hide in WITHYPOOL. Three foresters E
held it before 1066. Land for 4 ploughs. Robert paid 20s from　　E
it into the King's revenue in Winsford. Now it has been proved　　479
(to be) thaneland.　　　　　　　　　　　　　　　　　　a 2

4 Robert of Auberville also holds WELLISFORD. Two thanes held it　　E
before 1066; it paid tax for 1 hide. Land for 2 ploughs.
In lordship 1 plough; 2 slaves; ½ hide.　　　　　　　　　　478
　　8 smallholders have 1 plough & 1 virgate.　　　　　　　b 4
Meadow, 4 acres; pasture, 10 acres; underwood, 3 acres.
　　　1 cob; 18 cattle; 3 pigs; 17 sheep.
Formerly 10s; value now 15s.
　　The Count of Mortain holds 1 virgate of this hide, and
Bretel from him.

5 Robert of Auberville holds MELCOMBE. Saeric held it before 1066;
it paid tax for 1½ virgates of land. Land for 1½ ploughs;　　　E
they are there, with　　　　　　　　　　　　　　　　477
　　10 smallholders.　　　　　　　　　　　　　　　　b 4
　　A mill which pays 12d; underwood, 10 acres. 3 cows; 40 sheep.
Value formerly and now 15s.
　　From this manor ½ hide has been taken away which belonged
there before 1066. Walscin of Douai holds it with his manor
(of) Bower. Value 40s; when he acquired it, as much.　　　　E

6 John the Usher holds 'PIGNES' from the King. Brictric held　　D
it before 1066; it paid tax for 1 hide and 1 virgate of land.
Land for 2 ploughs. In lordship 1 plough;　　　　　　　477
　　2 villagers with 1 smallholder. A priest with 1 plough;　　E a 1
　　　2 smallholders.
　　Meadow, 5 acres.
Formerly 40s; value now 30s.

7 John also holds PERRY. Ordgar held it before 1066; it paid
tax for ½ hide, ½ virgate of land and ½ furlong.　　　　　477
Land for 1 plough, which is there, with　　　　　　　L a 2
　　2 villagers and 2 smallholders.
　　Meadow, 5 acres.
Formerly 10s; value now 15s.
　　Robert holds it from John.

Stable ten de Johe *NEWETVNE* . Samar teneb T.R.E .7

geldb ᵽ dim hida . Tra . ē . ɪ . caɍ . ᵹ̃ ibi . ē cū . ɪɪ . uiłłis .7 ɪɪ . bord

7 ɪɪɪ . feruis . Ibi . v . ac̄ ᵽti .7 v . ac̄ filuæ . Olim . x . foł . M̄ uał xv .

Robt ten de Johe *CANDETONE* . Semar teneb T.R.E. ſ ſolid .

7 geldb ᵽ dim hida . Tra . ē . ɪ . caɍ . ᵹ̃ ibi . ē in dñio . cū . ɪ . uiłło

7 ɪɪɪɪ . bord . Ibi moliñ redd . v . folid .7 xxɪɪɪ . ac̄ ᵽti .7 vɪ . ac̄ pa

fturæ . Olim . xv . folid . Modo uał . xx . folid .

Ipſe Johs ten *WINCHEBERIE* . Aluuard teneb T.R.E .7 geldb

ᵽ . ɪɪ . hid . Tra . ē . ɪ . caɍ 7 dim .7 ibi ſt cū . ɪɪ . uiłłis 7 ɪɪɪ . bord .

Ibi . vɪɪɪ . ac̄ ᵽti . Olim . xx . folid . Modo . xxx . folid .

Ipſe Johs ten *HUSTILLE* . Aluuard teneb T.R.E .7 geldb ᵽ una

virg træ . Tra . ē . ɪɪ . caɍ . ᵹ̃ ibi ſt cū . ɪɪɪ . uiłłis 7 ɪɪɪɪ . bord .

Ibi . x . ac̄ paſturæ . Olim . x . fol . Modo uał . xx . folid .

De hac tra dimid virg 7 uñ ferling T.R.E . ᵽtineb ad *SVMER*

Ansger ten de rege *CILDETONE* . Aluuin ſ *TONE* . Vał . v . fol .

teneb T.R.E .7 geldb ᵽ una v̄ træ . Tra . ē . ɪ . caɍ . ᵹ̃ ibi . ē cū . ɪ .

uiłło 7 ɪ . feruo . Ibi . xɪɪɪɪ . ac̄ ᵽti .7 v . ac̄ paſturæ . Oli . v . fol . m̄

Idē . A . ten *MICHAELISCERCE* . Aluui teneb T.R.E . ſ uał . xv , fol .

7 geldb ᵽ dim hida . Tra . ē . ɪ . caɍ . Olim 7 modo . uał . v . folid .

Idē . A . ten *SIWOLDESTONE* . Duo taini libe teneb T.R.E .7 geldb

ᵽ una v̄ træ . Tra . ē dim caɍ . Oli 7 modo uał . ɪɪɪɪ . folid .

Idē ten *DERLEGE* . Alſi teneb T.R.E .7 geldb ᵽ . ɪɪ . v̄ træ 7 dimid .

7 uno ferling . Tra . ē . ɪɪɪ . caɍ . ᵹ̃ ibi ſt cū . ɪɪɪɪ . uiłłis 7 ɪɪ . bord .7 ɪɪɪ . feruis .

8 Stable holds NEWTON from John. Saemer held it before 1066;
it paid tax for ½ hide. Land for 1 plough, which is there, with
    2 villagers, 2 smallholders and 3 slaves.
    Meadow, 5 acres; woodland, 5 acres. 10 sheep; 10 goats.
Formerly 10s; value now 15s.

L
477
a 3

9 Robert holds CANNINGTON from John the Usher. Saemer held it
before 1066; it paid tax for ½ hide. Land for 1 plough, which
is there, in lordship, & 1½ virgates, with
    1 villager and 4 smallholders (who have) ½ virgate & 2 oxen in a plough.
A mill which pays 5s; meadow, 23 acres; pasture, 6 acres.
      4 cattle; 1 pig; 40 sheep; 24 goats.
Formerly 15s; value now 20s.

478
a 2

10 John the Usher holds WIGBOROUGH himself. Alfward held it
before 1066; it paid tax for 2 hides. Land for 1½ ploughs; they
are there, with
    2 villagers and 3 smallholders.
    Meadow, 8 acres. 2 cows.
[Value] formerly 20s; now 30s.

L
478
a 3

11 John the Usher holds HUNTSTILE himself. Alfward held it before
1066; it paid tax for 1 virgate of land. Land for 2 ploughs,
which are there, with
    3 villagers and 4 smallholders.
    Pasture, 10 acres. 4 pigs.
Formerly 10s; value now 20s.
    ½ virgate and 1 furlong of this land belonged to Somerton
before 1066; value 5s.

L
479
a 3

E

12 Ansger Fower holds CHILTON (Trinity) from the King. Alwin
held it before 1066; it paid tax for 1 virgate of land.
Land for 1 plough, which is there, with
    1 villager and 1 slave.
    Meadow, 14 acres; pasture, 5 acres. 3 cows.
Formerly 5s; value now 15s.

L
477
b 1

13 Ansger also holds (St.) MICHAEL CHURCH. Alfwy held it before
1066; it paid tax for ½ hide. Land for 1 plough.
Value formerly and now 5s.

477
b 2

14 Ansger also holds SHOVEL. Two thanes held it freely before
1066; it paid tax for 1 virgate of land. Land for ½ plough.
Value formerly and now 4s.

E
477
b 3

15 He also holds DURLEIGH. Alfsi held it before 1066; it paid
tax for 2½ virgates of land and 1 furlong. Land for 3 ploughs,
which are there, with
    4 villagers, 2 smallholders and 3 slaves.

E
L
479
a 1

Ibi.xx.ac̄ siluæ. Olim 7 modo. ualet. xx. solid̄.

ANSGER coquus ten̄ de rege *LVLESTOCH*. Bricsic teneb̄ T.R.E. 7 geldb̄ p. v. hid̄. Tra. ē In dn̄io st̄. III. car̄. 7 II. serui. 7 XI. uitti 7 VII. bord̄. 7 xx. ac̄ siluæ in uno loco. 7 in alio Silua. I. leū lḡ. 7 dimid̄ leū lat̄. Olim 7 modo. uat. c. solid̄.

98 d

ANSCHITIL Parcher ten̄ de rege *NEWETVNE*. Osuard̄ teneb̄ T. R. E. 7 geldb̄ p. I. hida 7 una v̄ træ. Tra. ē. III. car̄. q̄ ibi st̄ cū. VIII. bord̄. Ibi. xv. ac̄ p̄ti. 7 xx. ac̄ moræ. 7 x. ac̄ siluæ. Olī. XL. sol̄.

Idē. A. ten̄ *HERDENEBERIE*. Aluric teneb̄ T.R.E 7 modo uat. xxx. 7 geldb̄ p una hida. Tra. ē. II. car̄. Ibi st̄. III. bord̄. cū. I. seruo. 7 LX. ac̄ pasturæ. Olim. xx. sol̄. Modo uat. v. solid̄.

Idē. A. ten̄ *MIDELTONE*. Osuuard̄ tenb̄ T.R.E. 7 geldb̄ p. I. hida. Tra. ē. I. car̄. q̄ ibi. ē cū. I. uitto 7 II. seruis. Ibi. VI. ac̄ p̄ti. 7 II. ac̄ siluæ minutæ. 7 xx. ac̄ pasturæ. Olim 7 m̄ uat. xv. sol̄.

Girard̄ ten̄ *ERNESEL*. Leuing teneb̄ T.R.E. 7 geldb̄ p. I. hida træ. Tra. ē. I. car̄. Ibi. ē. I. bord̄ 7 II. serui. 7 VI. ac̄ p̄ti. 7 x. ac̄ siluæ. Olim 7 modo uat. xxx. solid̄.

EDMVND filius Pagen ten̄ *BERTVNE* de rege. Iadulfus tenb̄ T.R.E. 7 geldb̄ p. III. hid̄ 7 dim̄. Tra. ē. VI. car̄. In dn̄io. ē. I. car̄. cū. I. seruo. 7 II. uitti 7 IIII. bord̄ 7 VI. cotar̄. Ibi molin̄ redd̄. x. solid̄. 7 L. ac̄ p̄ti. 7 LX. ac̄ pasturæ. Olī. VI. lib̄. Modo. III. lib̄. De hoc M̄. ē ablata. I. hida. q̄ ten̄ Malger de Cartrai.

Woodland, 20 acres.
Value formerly and now 20s.

16 Ansger Cook holds LILSTOCK from the King. Brictsi held it before 1066; it paid tax for 5 hides. Land for . . . . .
In lordship 3 ploughs; 2 slaves; 2½ hides. 478
11 villagers and 7 smallholders (have) 1 hide & 3 furlongs. b 1
Woodland, 20 acres in one place; in another, woodland 1 league long and ½ league wide. 1 cow; 25 pigs; 10 sheep.
Value formerly and now 100s.

17 Ansketel Parker holds NEWTON from the King. Osward held it before 1066; it paid tax for 1 hide and 1 virgate of land. L 98 d
Land for 3 ploughs, which are there, with E
8 smallholders. 477
Meadow, 15 acres; moor, 20 acres; woodland, 10 acres. b 5
Formerly 40s; value now 30(s).

18 Ansketel also holds HONIBERE. Aelfric held it before 1066; it paid tax for 1 hide. Land for 2 ploughs.
3 smallholders with 1 slave. 478
Pasture, 60 acres. a 1
Formerly 20s; value now 5s.

19 Ansketel also holds MILTON. Osward held it before 1066; it paid tax for 1 hide. Land for 1 plough, which is there, with L
1 villager and 2 slaves. 479
Meadow, 6 acres; underwood, 2 acres; pasture, 20 acres. a 4
Value formerly and now 15s.
Alfward holds it from Ansketel.

20 Gerard holds EARNSHILL. Leofing held it before 1066; it paid tax for 1 hide of land. Land for 1 plough.
1 smallholder and 2 slaves. 478
Meadow, 6 acres; woodland, 10 acres. b 2
Value formerly and now 30s.

21 Edmund son of Payne holds BARTON (St. David) from the King. Edwulf held it before 1066; it paid tax for 3½ hides.
Land for 6 ploughs. In lordship 1 plough & 3 hides & 1 virgate, with 1 slave; 480
2 villagers, 4 smallholders and 6 cottagers (who have) 1 virgate. a 1
A mill which pays 10s; meadow, 50 acres; pasture, 60 acres. 5 cattle; 4 pigs.
[Value] formerly £6; now £3.
From this manor 1 hide has been taken away which Mauger of Carteret holds.

Idem ten *PICOTE*. Iadulf teneb T.R.E. 7 geldb p. III. hid 7 dim.

Tra.e.IIII.car. In dnio st.II.car.7 II.ferui.7 III.uitti 7 VIII.bord

cu.II.car. Ibi molin redd.L.den. Ibi.VIII.ac pti.7 XII.ac

pafturæ.7 L.ac filuæ. Olim 7 modo ual.IIII.lib.

Idem.E.ten *WALTVNE*. Elmar teneb T.R.E.7 geldb p.III.hid

Tra.e.IIII.car. Ibi in dnio.I.car.7 un uitts 7 VI.bord cu.I.car

7 dimid. Ibi.VI.ac pti.7 XL.ac pafturæ. Siluæ minutæ.I.qz

in lg 7 lat. Olim.IIII.lib.modo.XL.folid.

Vxor Manaffes ten *HAIA*. Edric teneb T.R.E.7 geldb p.II.hid.

Tra.e.II.car. Ibi st.II.bord cu.I.cotar.7 VI.ac pti.7 XII.

ac pafturæ. Olim.XX.folid. Modo.ual.XV.folid.

Ead ten *ESTONE*. Alduin teneb T.R.E.7 geldb p una hida

7 una v træ. Tra.e.II.car. q ibi st in dnio.cu.I.uitto.7 III.bord

7 uno cotar. Ibi.VIII.ac pti.7 VI.ac pafturæ. Oli 7 m ual.XX.fot.

.XLVII. TERRÆ TAINOZ REGIS.

Brictric 7 Vluuard ten de rege *BOCHELANDE*. Ide ipfi

teneb T.R.E.7 geldb p.I.hida 7 dim. Tra.e.III.car. In dnio

st.II.car.7 II.uitti 7 IIII.bord. Valet.XX.folid.

Hanc tra teneb ifti de Petro epo du uix.7 reddeb ei.X.fot.

Modo ten de rege.f; p morte epi rex inde nil habuit.

De hac tra teneb uxor Bolle.III.virg T.R.E.

Siward ten *SEVENEMETONE*. T.R.E. geldb p.III.hid.

Tra.e.III.car. In dnio.e.I.car.7 II.uitti.7 III.bord.7 II.ferui.

7 VIII.ac pti. Valet.III.lib.

22 Edmund also holds PITCOTE. Edwulf held it before 1066;
it paid tax for 3½ hides. Land for 4 ploughs.
In lordship 2 ploughs; 2 slaves; 2½ hides.
   3 villagers and 8 smallholders with 2 ploughs.
   A mill which pays 50d. Meadow, 8 acres; pasture, 12 acres;
     woodland, 50 acres. 1 cob; 9 cattle; 45 sheep.
Value formerly and now £4.

480
a 2

23 Edmund also holds WALTON. Aelmer held it before 1066; it paid
tax for 3 hides. Land for 4 ploughs. In lordship 1 plough;
the whole (of the land), except for 1 virgate.
   1 villager and 6 smallholders with 1½ ploughs & 1 virgate.
   Meadow, 6 acres; pasture, 40 acres; underwood, 1 furlong
     in length and width. 15 sheep.
[Value] formerly £4; now 40s.

480
a 3

24 Manasseh Cook's wife holds HAY (Street). Edric held it
before 1066; it paid tax for 2 hides. Land for 2 ploughs.
   2 smallholders with 1 cottager.
   Meadow, 6 acres; pasture, 12 acres.
Formerly 20s; value now 15s.

480
a 4

25 She also holds (Ston) EASTON. Aldwin held it before 1066;
it paid tax for 1 hide and 1 virgate of land. Land for 2
ploughs, which are there, in lordship, & 1 hide, with
   1 villager, 3 smallholders and 1 cottager (who have) 1 virgate.
   Meadow, 8 acres; pasture, 6 acres.
Value formerly and now 20s.

480
b 1

47   LAND OF THE KING'S THANES   E

1 Brictric and Wulfward hold BUCKLAND (St. Mary) from the King.
They also held it themselves before 1066; it paid tax for 1½   E
hides. Land for 3 ploughs. In lordship 2 ploughs;   E
   2 villagers and 4 smallholders.
Value 20s.
   They held this land from Bishop Peter while he lived;
they paid him 10s from it in revenue. Now they hold from
the King, but since the Bishop's death the King has had nothing E
from it.
   Bolle's wife held 3 virgates of this land before 1066.   E

490
a 4

2 Siward holds SEAVINGTON. Before 1066 it paid tax for 3 hides.
Land for 3 ploughs. In lordship 1 plough; 2 hides & 3 virgates.
   2 villagers, 3 smallholders and 2 slaves (have) the rest of the land.
   Meadow, 8 acres. 1 cob; 2 cattle; 10 pigs; 120 sheep.
Value £3.

490
b 1

Hf.Alnod
ARDING teñ *LOPEN*. Toui teneb T.R.E.7 geldb ꝑ.ıı.hiđ.
Tra.e̅.ıı.car̅.In dn̅io.e̅.ı.car̅.7 ıı.ſerui.7 ıı.uiłłi 7 v.borđ
7 xx.ac̅ ꝑti.Olim.xx.ſoliđ.Modo uał.xl.ſoliđ.

Harding teñ *BRADE*.Toui teneb T.R.E.7 geldb ꝑ.ı.hida.
Tra.e̅.ıı.car̅.In dn̅io.e̅.ı.car̅.cu̅.ı.uiłło.Oli̅.xx.ſoł.m̅.x.ſoł.

Idē teñ *CAPILANDE*.Toui teneb T.R.E.7 geldb ꝑ.ı.hida.
Tra.e̅.ıı.car̅.In dn̅io.e̅.ı.car̅ cu̅.ı.borđ 7 ı.ſeruo.7 vı.ac̅
ꝑti.7 xxx.ac̅ ſiluæ.Olim.v.ſoł.Modo uał.xx.ſoliđ.

Huic m̅).e̅ addita dimiđ hida.ꝗ fuit de *CVRI* maner̅ regis.

Idem teñ *MERIET*.Goduin̊ teneb T.R.E.   ꝼ Vał.v.ſoliđ.
7 geldb ꝑ.v.hiđ.Tra.e̅.vı.car̅.In dn̅io ſt.ıı.car̅.7 ıı.ſerui
7 ıx.uiłłi 7 vı.borđ cu̅.ıı.car̅.Ibi moli̅n redđ.v.ſoliđ
7 x.ac̅ ꝑti.7 ııı.ꝗrent paſturæ.Olı̅.c.ſoł.Modo uał.ıııı.lib.

Harding teñ *BOCHELAND*.Toui teneb T.R.E.7 geldb ꝑ una
hida.Tra.e̅.ıııı.car̅.Ibi.ıɪı.ac̅ ꝑti.7 x.ꝗ℈ paſtæ in łg.7 ıııı.łat̅.

99 a
Silua.ıı.ꝗ℈ łg.7 una łat̅.Olim.xl.ſoł.Modo.x.ſoliđ.

Harding teñ *DINESCOVE*.Toui teneb T.R.E.7 geldb ꝑ.ı.hida.
Tra.e̅.ııı.car̅.In dn̅io ſt.ıı.car̅.cu̅.ııı.uiłłis.Ibi.vııı.ac̅ ꝑti.
7 ııı.ꝗ℈ paſturæ in łg 7 łat̅.Olim 7 modo.uał.xl.ſoliđ..

3 Harding son of Alnoth holds LOPEN. Tovi the Sheriff held it
before 1066; it paid tax for 2 hides. Land for 2 ploughs.
In lordship 1 plough; 2 slaves; 1½ hides & 3 furlongs.   490
   2 villagers and 5 smallholders (have) 1 virgate & 1 furlong.   b 2
   Meadow, 20 acres. 1 cob; 7 cattle; 10 pigs; 150 sheep.
Formerly 20s; value now 40s.

4 Harding holds BRADON. Tovi held it before 1066; it paid
tax for 1 hide. Land for 2 ploughs. In lordship 1 plough
& 3 virgates, with   491
   1 villager (who has) 1 virgate.   b 1
   50 sheep.
[Value] formerly 20s; now 10s.
   Ceolric holds it from Harding.

5 He also holds CAPLAND. Tovi held it before 1066; it paid tax
for 1 hide. Land for 2 ploughs. In lordship 1 plough, with
   1 smallholder and 1 slave.   491
   Meadow, 6 acres; woodland, 30 acres. 3 cattle; 1 pig.   b 2
Formerly 5s; value now 20s.
   To this manor has been added ½ hide which was (part) of   E
Curry (Rivel), a manor of the King's. Value 5s; when Harding
acquired it, it had been laid waste.

6 He also holds MERRIOTT. Godwin held it before 1066; it paid tax
for 5 hides. Land for 6 ploughs. In lordship 2 ploughs; 2 slaves;
2½ hides.   491
   9 villagers and 6 smallholders with 2 ploughs & the rest of the land.   b 3
   A mill which pays 5s; meadow, 10 acres; pasture, 3 furlongs.
   1 cob.
Formerly 100s; value now £4.

7 Harding holds BUCKLAND (St. Mary). Tovi held it before 1066;
it paid tax for 1 hide. Land for 4 ploughs. Godwin holds it
from Harding. In lordship ½ hide.   492
   His villagers (have) ½ hide.   a 1
   Meadow, 3 acres; pasture, 10 furlongs in length and 4 wide;   E
      woodland 2 furlongs long and 1 wide. 6 cattle; 10 sheep;   99 a
      20 goats.
[Value] formerly 40s; now 10s.

8 Harding holds DISCOVE. Tovi held it before 1066; it paid tax
for 1 hide. Land for 3 ploughs. In lordship 2 ploughs
& 1½ virgates, with   493
   3 villagers (who) have 2½ virgates & ½ plough.   a 2
   Meadow, 8 acres; pasture, 3 furlongs in length and width.
   1 cob; 28 pigs; 71 sheep.
Value formerly and now 40s.

Briſtric ten TOCHESWELLE. Goduin teneƀ T.R.E. Ibi.ē dim

uirg træ.7 ñ geldƀ T.R.E. Tra.ē.1.caƀ. Ibi ſƀ.iiii.borđ cū.i.

ſeruo. Olim 7 modo.ualƀ xii.ſolid.7 vi.denaƀ.

Siuuard ten DVNINTONE. Edmar teneƀ T.R.E.7 geldƀ

ꝑ.iii.hiđ.Tra.ē.iii.caƀ.g̃ ibi ſƀ cū.vi.uiſtis 7 iii.borđ.

Ibi moliñ redđ.viii.denaƀ.7 viii.aͨ ꝑti.Paſtura.iii.q̃ʒ

lḡ.7 ii.q̃ʒ laƀ.Silua.iii.q̃ʒ lḡ.7 ii.q̃ʒ laƀ.Oli.xx.ſoliđ.

Siuuard ten ETTEBERE. Idem ipſe teneƀ ⸗Modo⸗ual.xL.

T.R.E.7 geldƀ ꝑ.i.hida.Tra.ē.i.caƀ 7 dim.7 ibi ſƀ cū.ii.

uiſtis 7 iii.borđ.Ibi.vi.aͨ ꝑti.7 una q̃ʒ ſiluæ in lḡ 7 laƀ.

Olim 7 modo.ual..xx.ſoliđ.

Dodo ten STAWE.Siuuold teneƀ T.R.E.7 geldƀ ꝑ.iii.v træ.

Tra.ē.iii.caƀ. In dñio.ē.i.caƀ.7 iii.ſerui.7 vi.uiſti.7 ii.borđ.

7 moliñ ſine cenſu.7 v.aͨ ꝑti.7 xxx.aͨ paſturæ.7 iii.aͨ ſiluæ.

Olim 7 modo ual.xx.ſoliđ.

VLF ten HAVECHEWELLE.Idē ipſe teneƀ T.R.E.7 geldƀ

ꝑ una v træ.7 uno ferling 7 iiii.parte uni ferling.Tra.ē

iii.caƀ.Ibi ſƀ.iii.caƀ cū.i.ſeruo.7 iii.uiſti 7 iiii.borđ.

Valet.xxv.ſoliđ.

ALWARD 7 frs ej ten STOCHE.Pat eoʒ teneƀ T.R.E.7 geldƀ

ꝑ.iii.hiđ.Tra.ē.ii.caƀ.g̃ ibi ſƀ cū.i.uiſto 7 i.ſeruo 7 xiii.borđ.

Ibi.xv.aͨ ꝑti.7 viii.aͨ paſturæ.Olim.Lx.ſol.ṁ ual.L.ſol.

9 Brictric holds TUXWELL. Godwin held it before 1066. ½ virgate
of land; it did not pay tax before 1066. Land for 1 plough.
In lordship ½ plough.

    4 smallholders with 1 slave.

    Woodland, 4 acres; pasture, 7 acres.

Value formerly and now 12s 6d.

490
b 3

10 Siward Falconer holds DINNINGTON. Edmer Ator held it
before 1066; it paid tax for 3 hides. Land for 3 ploughs,
which are there, with

    6 villagers and 3 smallholders.

    A mill which pays 8d; meadow, 8 acres; pasture 3 furlongs
    long and 2 furlongs wide; woodland 3 furlongs long and
    2 furlongs wide.

Formerly 20s; value now 40(s).

L

490
b 4

11 Siward Guntram holds ADBER. He also held it himself before
1066; it paid tax for 1 hide. Land for 1½ ploughs; they are
there, with

    2 villagers and 3 smallholders.

    Meadow, 6 acres; woodland, 1 furlong in length and width.

      7 cattle; 13 pigs; 62 sheep.

Value formerly and now 20s.

L

493
b 2

12 Doda holds DODINGTON. Siwold held it before 1066; it paid
tax for 3 virgates of land. Land for 3 ploughs. In lordship 1
plough; 3 slaves; 1 virgate.

    6 villagers and 2 smallholders.

    A mill without dues; meadow, 5 acres; pasture, 30 acres;
    woodland, 3 acres.

Value formerly and now 20s.

E

491
a 1

13 Ulf holds HAWKWELL. He also held it himself before 1066;
it paid tax for 1 virgate of land, 1 furlong and the fourth
part of 1 furlong. Land for 3 ploughs. 3 ploughs there,
with 1 slave. An Englishman, Wulfmer, holds 1 furlong &
a quarter of a furlong jointly. Ulf has 1 furlong.

    3 villagers and 4 smallholders (have) 3 furlongs.

    4 cattle; 30 sheep; 40 goats.

Value 25s.

E

491
a 2

E

14 Alfward and his brothers hold ?STOCKLINCH. Their father held it
before 1066; it paid tax for 3 hides. Land for 2 ploughs, which
are there, in lordship, & 2½ hides & ½ virgate, with

    1 villager, 1 slave and 13 smallholders (who have) the rest of
    the land & ½ plough.

    Meadow, 15 acres; pasture, 8 acres. 1 cob; 6 cattle; 5 pigs;
    17 sheep.

Formerly 60s; value now 50s.

491
a 3

Godvin ten DRAICOTE . Ipſe 7 mat ej teneƀ T.R.E .7 defdƀ ſe
p una v træ.Tra . ē diṁ caƀ . Redđ . ii . ſoł p anñ.

Aldvi ten STOCHE . Idem ipſe teneƀ T.R.E .7 geldƀ p . i . hida.
7 iii . v træ.Tra.ē . ii . caƀ.Ibi ſt . iii . borđ 7 ii.ſerui.cū . i . caƀ.
Ibi moliñ redđ . vi . ſolid 7 viii . den .7 vi . ac p̃ti . Paſtura . v.
q̃ʒ lḡ.7 ii . q̃ʒ laƀ.Silua . iii.q̃ʒ lḡ.7 ii . q̃ʒ laƀ.

Brismar ten HALBERGE . Idē ipſe teneƀ T.R.E .7 geldƀ p . x.
hiđ.Tra.ē.viii.caƀ.In dñio.ē . i . caƀ .7 ii .ſerui.7 viii.uitti 7 xvi.
borđ cū . v . caƀ.Ibi moliñ redđ . v . ſolid .7 xiii . ac p̃ti 7 diṁ.
7 dimiđ leu paſturæ in lḡ 7 laƀ .7 tñtđ ſiluæ.Valet . viii . liƀ.

Alverd ten WICHE . Idē ipſe teneƀ T.R.E .7 geldƀ p . ii . hiđ.
Tra.ē.iii.caƀ.q̃ ibi ſt cū . ii . uittis 7 vi . borđ 7 iii . ſeruis.
Ibi moliñ redđ . v . ſolid .7 v . ac p̃ti .7 x . ac ſpineti . Vał . xl.

Donno ten BOCHELANDE . Idē ipſe teneƀ T.R.E . ſolid.
7 geldƀ p . xii . hiđ.Tra.ē.vii.caƀ.Ibi ſt . v . caƀ .7 xi.uitti
7 v . borđ.7 vii.ſerui.7 xl.ac p̃ti .7 xxx.ac ſiluæ minutæ.7 diṁ
leu paſturæ in lḡ.7 una q̃ʒ 7 dim in laƀ.7 moliñ redđ.vii . ſoł.
Olim . viii . liƀ . modo uał.c.ſolid.

Agelric ten CVME . Eddid regina teneƀ T.R.E .7 geldƀ p . ii.
hiđ.Tra.ē . v . caƀ.q̃ ibi ſt.7 vi . uitti 7 v . borđ.7 iii . ſerui.
Ibi moliñ redđ . l . deñ.7 viii . ac p̃ti .7 xx . ac ſiluæ.Olĩ.xx . ſoł.

Alvric ten LIDEFORD . Brictric teneƀ T.R.E . Modo.iiii . liƀ.
7 geldƀ p . ix . hiđ.Tra.ē.viii . caƀ.Ibi ſt . vii . caƀ .7 vi . uitti

15 Godwin the Englishman holds DRAYCOTT. He himself and his mother
   held it before 1066; it answered for 1 virgate of land.   492
   Land for ½ plough. Godwin has 2 oxen.   a 2
   It pays 2s a year.

16 Aldwin holds (Chew) STOKE. He also held it himself
   before 1066; it paid tax for 1 hide and 3 virgates of land.
   Land for 2 ploughs. In lordship 1 hide & 1 virgate.   492
     3 smallholders and 2 slaves with 1 plough & 3 virgates.   a 3
     A mill which pays 6s 8d; meadow, 6 acres; pasture 5 furlongs   E
        long and 2 furlongs wide; woodland 3 furlongs long and
        2 furlongs wide. 2 cattle; 2 pigs; 8 sheep.
   Value 25s.

17 Brictmer the Englishman holds HASELBURY (Plucknett). He also
   held it himself before 1066; it paid tax for 10 hides. Land for
   8 ploughs. In lordship 1 plough; 2 slaves; 5 hides.   492
     8 villagers and 16 smallholders with 5 ploughs & 5 hides.   a 4
     A mill which pays 5s; meadow, 13½ acres; pasture, ½ league
        in length and width; woodland, as much. 1 cob; 8 cattle; 7 pigs.
   Value £8.

18 Alfred holds SWAINSWICK. He also held it himself before 1066;
   it paid tax for 2 hides. Land for 3 ploughs, which are there, with   L
     2 villagers, 6 smallholders and 3 slaves.   492
     A mill which pays 5s; meadow, 5 acres; spinney, 10 acres.   b 1
        1 cob; 8 pigs; 60 sheep.
   Value 40s.

19 Dunn holds BUCKLAND (Dinham). He also held it himself
   before 1066; it paid tax for 12 hides. Land for 7 ploughs.   L
   5 ploughs there.
     11 villagers, 5 smallholders and 7 slaves.   492
     Meadow, 40 acres; underwood, 30 acres; pasture, ½ league in   b 2
        length and 1½ furlongs in width; a mill which pays 7s.
        2 cattle; 8 pigs; 12 sheep.
   Formerly £8; value now 100s.
   Now Dunn holds from the King.

20 Agelric holds COMBE (?Hay). Queen Edith held it before 1066;
   it paid tax for 2 hides. Land for 5 ploughs, which are there.   L
     6 villagers, 5 smallholders and 3 slaves.   492
     A mill which pays 50d; meadow, 8 acres; woodland, 20 acres.   b 3
        1 cob; 3 cattle; 7 pigs; 126 sheep.
   [Value] formerly 20s; now £4.

21 Aelfric holds (West) LYDFORD. Brictric, his father, held it
   before 1066; it paid tax for 9 hides. Land for 8 ploughs.   L 493
   7 ploughs there.   a 1

7 IX . borđ 7 II . cotar .7 VIII . ſerui . Ibi moliñ redđ . XV . ſoliđ.

7 LX . ac̅ p̊ti .7 XXX . ac̅ paſturæ .7 una leu̅ ſiluæ in l̅g̅ 7 lat̅ .7 porca

rius redđ . X . porcos . Olim 7 modo ual̅ . VIII . lib̅.

Alvric ten̅ SCEPEWORDE . Brictric teneb̅ T.R.E .7 geldb̅

p dimiđ hida . Tra . e̅ dimiđ car̅ . Valet . V . ſoliđ.

Brictoward ten̅ WRITELINCTONE . Brictuuold teneb̅ T.R.E.

7 geldb̅ p . VI . hiđ . Tra . e̅ . V . car̅ .7 tot ibi ſt̅ cu̅ . VIII . uilłis .7 III.

cotar . Ibi . XII . ac̅ p̊ti .7 XXIIII . ac̅ paſturæ .7 XII . ac̅ ſiluæ minutæ.

Olim . C . ſoliđ . Modo ual̅ . IIII . lib̅.

Huſcarle ten̅ una̅ v̅ træ qua̅ ipſemet teneb̅ T.R.E . In ESTROPE.

Ibi h̅t̅ dimiđ car̅ . Valet . XL . denar̅.

Osmer ten̅ una̅ v̅ træ in OTREMETONE . Pat̅ ej̅ teneb̅ T.R.E.

De ea ſt̅ . II . partes ablatæ .7 in CANDETONE Maner̅ regis poſitæ.

ITEM HVNFRIDI TERRA .7 QVORVNDA̅ ALIOꝫ.

Hvnfrid̅ ten̅ BABECARI . Bruno libe teneb̅ T.R.E .7 geldb̅

p . II . hiđ 7 dimiđ . Tra . e̅ . III . car̅ . In dñio ſt̅ tam̅ . II . car̅ .7 II . ſerui.

7 VI . uilłi 7 III . borđ cu̅ . III . car̅ . Ibi . XIIII . ac̅ p̊ti .7 VIII . ac̅ paſturæ.

Olim . XL . ſol̅ . Modo ual̅ . L . ſoliđ . H̅ eſt addita tris Brictric.

Hunfrid̅ ten̅ ALTONE . Alnod teneb̅ T.R.E .7 geldb̅ p . II . hiđ . Tra

e̅ . II . car̅ . In dñio . e̅ . I . car̅ .7 un̅ uilłs 7 IIII . borđ cu̅ dimiđ car̅.

7 I . ſeruo . Ibi . VI . ac̅ p̊ti .7 VI . ac̅ ſiluæ . Olim . XX . ſol̅ . m̅ ual̅ . XXX . ſol̅.

Hunfrid̅ ten̅ SANFORD . Tres taini teneb̅ libe T.R.E .7 geldb̅

p . VI . hiđ . Tra . e̅ . VI . car̅ .7 tot ibi ſt̅ .7 IIII . uilłi .7 XV . borđ.

6 villagers, 9 smallholders, 2 cottagers and 8 slaves.
A mill which pays 15s; meadow, 60 acres; pasture, 30 acres; woodland, 1 league in length and width; a pigman who pays 10 pigs. 2 cobs; 20 cattle; 25 pigs; 60 sheep; 25 goats.
Value formerly and now £8.

Aelfric holds it from the King.

22 Aelfric holds SCEPEWORDE. Brictric held it before 1066; it paid tax for ½ hide. Land for ½ plough. Rahere holds it from Aelfric; he has 10 sheep.
Value 5s.

23 Brictward holds WRITHLINGTON. Brictwold held it before 1066; it paid tax for 6 hides. Land for 5 ploughs; as many there, with 8 villagers and 3 cottagers.
Meadow, 12 acres; pasture, 24 acres; underwood, 12 acres. 24 sheep.
Formerly 100s; value now £4.

24 In 'EASTRIP' Guard holds 1 virgate of land which he held himself before 1066. He has ½ plough there.
4 cattle; 7 pigs; 20 sheep.
Value 40d.

25 Osmer holds 1 virgate of land in OTTERHAMPTON. His father held it before 1066. 2 parts of it have been taken away and placed in Cannington, a manor of the King's.

ch. 45 continued from col. 98c, before ch. 46, indicated by transposition signs.

[45] MORE LAND OF HUMPHREY AND OF CERTAIN OTHERS

3 Humphrey the Chamberlain holds BABCARY. Brown held it freely before 1066; it paid tax for 2½ hides. Land for 3 ploughs.
In lordship, however, 2 ploughs; 2 slaves; 1 hide.
6 villagers and 3 smallholders with 3 ploughs & 1½ hides.
Meadow, 14 acres; pasture, 8 acres. 2 cobs.
Formerly 40s; value now 50s.
This (land) has been added to Brictric's lands.

4 Humphrey holds HOLTON. Alnoth held it before 1066; it paid tax for 2 hides. Land for 2 ploughs. In lordship 1 plough; 1½ hides.
1 villager and 4 smallholders with ½ plough & ½ hide and 1 slave.
Meadow, 6 acres; woodland, 6 acres. 1 cob; 2 cows; 12 pigs; 12 sheep.
Formerly 20s; value now 30s.

Aelfric holds it from Humphrey.

5 Humphrey the Chamberlain holds SANDFORD (Orcas). Three thanes held it freely before 1066; it paid tax for 6 hides. Land for 6 ploughs; as many there.
4 villagers, 15 smallholders and 4 slaves.

Marginal references (right column):
493 a 3
L E
493 a 4
99 b
E
493 b 1
E 493 b 3
E
466 a 2
466 a 3
E L
466 b 4

7 IIII.ſerui.7 VIII.ac̄ p̄ti.Paſtura.II.q̃ɀ lḡ.7 una q̃ɀ lat̄.Silua

IIII.q̃ɀ lḡ.7 una q̃ɀ lat̄.Olim.VIII.lib̄.Modo ual̄.IX.lib̄.

Odo Flandr̄.ten̄ TIMESBERIE.Gonuerd tenet̄ T.R.E.7 geldb̄

ꝑ.v.hid̄.Tra.e̅.IIII.car̄.Ibi ſt̄.II.car̄.7 v.uitti 7 III.bord̄

7 moliñ redd̄.XL.denar̄.7 XL.ac̄ p̄ti.I.min.7 XXX.IX.ac̄ paſturæ.

Wilts ten̄ TATEWICHE.Tres taini tenet̄ ⨍ Valet.III.lib̄.

T.R.E.7 geldb̄ ꝑ.I.hida 7 dimid̄.Tra.e̅.I.car̄.q̃ ibi.e̅ in dñio.

7 III.ſerui.7 II.bord̄.7 dimid̄ ac̄ p̄ti.7 x.ac̄ ſiluæ minutæ.

Olim.x.ſolid̄.Modo ual̄.XXX.ſolid̄.

R^{de berchelai}ADVLFVS ten̄ TATEWICHE.Godric tenet̄ T.R.E.7 geldb̄

ꝑ dimid̄ hida.Tra.e̅.I.car̄.q̃ ibi.e̅ cū.III.ſeruis.Ibi.I.ac̄ ſiluæ.

Olim.x.ſolid̄.modo ual̄.xv.ſolid̄.

H^{inſpres}UGOLIN ten̄ de rege HERLEI.Azor tenet̄ T.R.E.7 geldb̄

ꝑ.I.hida.Tra.e̅.III.car̄.7 tot ibi ſt̄ cū.I.uitto 7 v.bord̄.7 II.ſeruis.

Ibi dimid̄ ac̄ p̄ti.7 ſiluæ minutæ.III.q̃ɀ int lḡ 7 lat̄.Oli 7 m̄

Idem ten̄ ESTONE.Ingulf tenet̄ T.R.E.7 geldb̄ ꝑ.III.⨍ ual̄.L.ſot.

hid̄.Tra.e̅.v.car̄.Ibi ſt̄.III.car̄.7 III.uitti 7 vi.bord̄.7 II.ſerui.

7 moliñ redd̄.v.ſolid̄.Olim.XL.ſolid̄.modo ual̄.LX.ſolid̄.

Idē ten̄ CLAFTERTONE.Suain tenet̄ T.R.E.7 geldb̄ ꝑ.v.hid̄.

Tra.e̅.vi.car̄.7 tot ibi ſt̄.7 IIII.uitti.7 vii.bord̄.7 IIII.ſerui.

7 moliñ redd̄.vii.ſot 7 vi.denar̄.7 xx.ac̄ p̄ti.7 XII.q̃ɀ paſt̄

in lḡ 7 lat̄.Olim 7 modo.ual̄.vii.lib̄.

Meadow, 8 acres; pasture 2 furlongs long and 1 furlong wide; woodland 4 furlongs long and 1 furlong wide. 2 cobs; 2 cows; 13 pigs; 150 sheep.
Formerly £8; value now £9.
The whole of this land has been added to Brictric's lands, to which it did not belong.

6 Odo of Flanders holds TIMSBURY. Gunfrid held it before 1066; it paid tax for 5 hides. Land for 4 ploughs. 2 ploughs there.   L
  5 villagers and 3 smallholders.   464
  A mill which pays 40d; meadow, 40 acres, less 1; pasture,   b 2
    39 acres. 56 sheep; 4 pigs.
Value £3.
Odo holds it from the King.

7 William Hussey holds TADWICK. Three thanes held it before 1066;   E
it paid tax for 1½ hides. Land for 1 plough, which is there,   464
in lordship, & 1 hide & 1 virgate; 3 slaves;   E b 3
  2 smallholders have ½ virgate.
  Meadow, ½ acre; underwood, 10 acres. 1 cob; 100 sheep.
Formerly 10s; value now 30s.   E

8 Ralph of Berkeley holds TADWICK. Godric held it before 1066;   E
it paid tax for ½ hide. Land for 1 plough, which is there,   E
with 3 slaves.   465
  Woodland, 1 acre. 89 sheep.   a 1
Formerly 10s; value now 15s.

9 Hugolin the Interpreter holds WARLEIGH from the King. Azor held it before 1066; it paid tax for 1 hide. Land for 3 ploughs; as   L
many there, with   465
  1 villager, 5 smallholders and 2 slaves.   a 2
  Meadow, ½ acre; underwood, 3 furlongs in both length and width.
    100 sheep.
Value formerly and now 50s.

10 He also holds BATHEASTON. Ingulf held it before 1066;   E
it paid tax for 3 hides. Land for 5 ploughs. 3 ploughs there.   L
  3 villagers, 6 smallholders and 2 slaves.   465
  A mill which pays 5s.   a 3
Formerly 40s; value now 60s.

11 He also holds CLAVERTON. Swein held it before 1066; it paid   E
tax for 5 hides. Land for 6 ploughs; as many there.   L
  4 villagers, 7 smallholders and 4 slaves.   465
  A mill which pays 7s 6d; meadow, 20 acres; pasture, 12   a 4
    furlongs in length and width. 1 cob; 4 cattle; 29 pigs;
    120 sheep; 20 goats.
Value formerly and now £7.

D^{de Montagud}ᵏROGO ten CHENOLLE. Alnod teneb̄ T.R.E.⁊ geldb̄ ᵽ.ı.hida

⁊ dimiđ.Tra.ē.ııı.caŕ.⁊ tot ibi st̄.⁊ vı.uiłłi.⁊ ıııı.ſerui.cū

uno cotaŕ.Ibi.xv.ac̄ p̄ti.Silua.ıııı.q̃ᵹ in lḡ.⁊ ııı.q̃ᵹ in lar̄.

Olim.xl.ſoł.Modo uał.ıııı.lib̄.   ⨍Valet.xxˢ.ſoł.

De hac tra.ē ablata.ı.hida træ.quæ T.R.E.ibi erat.ᶠ·ᴿᵒˡᶠTurſtin ten

HUGO ten FODINDONE. Aluuarđ teneb̄ T.R.E.⁊ geldb̄ ᵽ.ıı.hiđ.

⁊ una v træ.Tra.ē.ııı.caŕ.⁊ tot ibi st̄.⁊ ıı.uiłłi ⁊ ı.cot ⁊ vı.ſerui.

⁊ xıııı.ac̄ p̄ti.Olim.xxx.ſoł.Modo uał.xl.ſoliđ.

Ricard ten in RODE.ı.hiđ.quā ipſe tenuit de Rainboldo.ᵖᵇʳᵒ

licentia regis ut dicit.Reinbold ū tenuit T.R.E.Tra.ē dim caŕ.

Ibi.ē un borđ.Olim ⁊ modo uał.x.ſoliđ.

SCHELIN ten FODINDONE. Bricſtouuard teneb̄ T.R.E.⁊ geldb̄

ᵽ.ı.hida ⁊ una v træ ⁊ dim.Tra.ē.ıı.caŕ.q̃ ibi st̄ cū.ı.ſeruo.

⁊ uno borđ.Ibi.vı.ac̄ p̄ti.Olim ⁊ modo uał.xx.ſoliđ.

ELDRED ten BROCHELIE.Idem ipſe teneb̄ T.R.E.⁊ geldb̄

ᵽ.ıııı.hiđ.Tra.ē.ıııı.caŕ.⁊ tot ibi st̄.⁊ vı.uiłłi ⁊ vıı.borđ

⁊ xvı.ac̄ p̄ti.Valet.xxx.ſoliđ.

ELDRED ten GRENEDONE.Idē ipſe teneb̄ T.R.E.⁊ geldb̄ pro

dimiđ hida.Tra.ē dim caŕ.Ibi st̄.ıııı.borđ cū.ı.ſeruo.

⁊ moliñ redđ.xxx.denar.⁊ ııı.ac̄ p̄ti.⁊ ıı.ac̄ ſiluæ minutæ.

A^{de Montagud}NSGERvs ten de rege PRESTETONE.   ⨍Valet.v.ſoliđ.

Aluuard teneb̄ T.R.E.⁊ geldb̄ ᵽ.ıı.hiđ.Tra.ē.ı.caŕ.q̃ ibi.ē

in dñio.cū.ı.ſeruo ⁊ vııı.borđ.Ibi.x.ac̄ p̄ti.Oli.xv.ſoł.M̄ uał

⨍xl.ſoł.

12 Drogo of Montacute holds KNOWLE (Park). Alnoth held it before
1066; it paid tax for 1½ hides. Land for 3 ploughs; as many there.   L
   6 villagers and 4 slaves with 1 cottager.   465
   Meadow, 15 acres; woodland 4 furlongs in length and 3 furlongs   b 2
     in width. 26 pigs.
Formerly 40s; value now £4.   E
   Drogo holds it from the King.
   From this land 1 hide of land has been taken away which was   E
there before 1066. Thurstan son of Rolf holds it, & an Englishman
from him. Value 20s.

13 Hugh of Vautortes holds FODDINGTON. Alfward held it before
1066; it paid tax for 2 hides and 1 virgate of land. Land for   L
3 ploughs; as many there.   466
   2 villagers, 1 cottager and 6 slaves.   a 1
   Meadow, 14 acres. 2 cobs; 20 cattle; 15 pigs; 28 sheep.
Formerly 30s; value now 40s.

14 Richard the Interpreter holds in RODE 1 hide which he held   E
himself from Reinbald the priest, by permission of the King, as he
states. Reinbald indeed held it before 1066. Land for ½ plough.
   1 smallholder.   466
Value formerly and now 10s.   b 3

15 Azelin holds FODDINGTON. Brictward held it before 1066;
it paid tax for 1 hide and 1½ virgates of land.   466
Land for 2 ploughs, which are there, with 1 slave and   E b 2
   1 smallholder.
   Meadow, 6 acres. 1 cob.
Value formerly and now 20s.   E

16 Aldred holds BROCKLEY. He also held it himself before 1066; it
paid tax for 4 hides. Land for 4 ploughs; as many there.   L
   6 villagers and 7 smallholders.   466
   Meadow, 16 acres. 2 cattle; 2 pigs.   b 1
Value 30s.

17 Aldred holds CRANDON. He also held it himself before 1066; it
paid tax for ½ hide. Land for ½ plough. He has the whole in lordship.
   4 smallholders with 1 slave.   465
   A mill which pays 30d; meadow, 3 acres; underwood, 2 acres. 1 pig.   b 1
Value 5s.

18 Ansger of Montacute holds PRESTON (Plucknett) from the King.
Alfward held it before 1066; it paid tax for 2 hides.   467
Land for 1 plough, which is there, in lordship, with 1 slave;   a 2
   8 smallholders.
   Meadow, 10 acres. 1 cob; 5 cattle; 80 sheep.
Formerly 15s; value now 40s.

The Latin text of these entries is given in the county volumes concerned.
Exon. references and additions are given in small type.

In BEDFORDSHIRE

| | 3 | LAND OF THE BISHOP OF COUTANCES | 209 |

EBe 8 In BOLNHURST the Bishop also has 3 virgates of land in   210
1   exchange for Bleadon...

EBe   In the Hundred of WILLEY
2   10 M. Geoffrey of Trelly holds 4 hides from the Bishop...
         The Bishop holds this land in exchange for Bleadon,
         as his men state.

EBe 11 M. In TURVEY the Bishop also holds 4 hides... The Bishop
3   has this land in exchange for Bleadon, as his men state.

In BUCKINGHAMSHIRE

| | 5 | LAND OF THE BISHOP OF COUTANCES | 145 |

EBu 10 In TYRINGHAM Ansketel holds 2½ hides and 3 parts of 1
1   virgate from the Bishop as one manor... This land is in
         exchange for Bleadon.

EBu   In MOULSOE Hundred   145
2   18 In CLIFTON (Reynes) Morcar holds 1½ hides from the Bishop...
         This land is in exchange for Bleadon, as the Bishop's men state.

In DEVON

| | 37 | LAND OF THURSTAN SON OF ROLF | 115 |

EDe 1 Thurstan son of Rolf holds CHURCHSTANTON from the King,
1   and Geron from him. Aelfeva* held it before 1066; it paid
         tax for 3 hides. Land for 20 ploughs. In lordship 1 plough;
         4 slaves; 1 hide.
             24 villagers and 8 smallholders with 9½ ploughs & 2 hides.   38,
             Meadow, 7 acres; pasture 1½ leagues long and 1 league   a
                wide; woodland 5 furlongs long and 4 furlongs wide.
                 7 cattle; 27 pigs; 130 sheep; 23 goats.
         Formerly £10; value now 100s.

         * *Alwena* (Aelfwen) in Exon; possibly a scribal error.

2   LAND OF THE BISHOP OF SALISBURY

Do 1
1
The Bishop holds SHERBORNE himself. Queen Edith held it,
and before her Bishop Alfwold. Before 1066 it paid tax for
43 hides. Land for 46 ploughs. The Bishop holds 12 hides
of this land; he has
25 villagers and 14 smallholders with 12 ploughs.
Meadow, 130 acres, of which 3 acres are in Somerset
near Milborne (Port); ...

In WILTSHIRE

B (WILTSHIRE CUSTOMS)

W 4
1
From the third penny of SALISBURY the King has £6; from
the third penny of MARLBOROUGH, £4; from the third penny
of CRICKLADE, £5; from the third penny of BATH, £11; from
the third penny of MALMESBURY, £6. From the increase, £60
by weight. Edward the Sheriff pays this.

Finn ... R. Welldon Finn *An Introduction to Domesday Book,* London 1963.

Finn LE ... R. Welldon Finn *Domesday Studies: The Liber Exoniensis,* London 1964.

Forssner ... Thorvald Forssner *Continental-Germanic Personal Names in England in Old and Middle English Times,* Uppsala 1916.

Förstemann ... E. Förstemann *Altdeutsches Namenbuch,* Band 1, *Personennamen* (2nd edn. Bonn 1900).

Freeman ... E.A. Freeman *The History of the Norman Conquest of England* 6 vols. Oxford 1867-79.

Galbraith ... V.H. Galbraith *Domesday Book: its Place in Administrative History,* Oxford 1974.

GC ... Dom Aelred Watkin *The Great Chartulary of Glastonbury* vols. i-iii SRS 59; 63-64 (1944,1948, 1949-50). References are to vol. ii.

GF ... F.W. Weaver *A Feodary of Glastonbury Abbey* SRS 26 (1910).

HD ... Sir H.C. Maxwell-Lyte *Documents and Extracts Illustrating the History of the Honour of Dunster,* SRS 33 (1917-18).

Hill ... J.S. Hill *The Place Names of Somerset,* Bristol 1914.

Humphreys ... A.L. Humphreys *Somersetshire Parishes,* London 1906, 2 vols.

James ... M.R. James *A Descriptive Catalogue of Manuscripts in the Library of Corpus Christi College Cambridge,* Cambridge 1912, 2 vols.

KCD ... J.M. Kemble *Codex Diplomaticus Aevi Saxonici,* London 1839-48, 6 vols.

KQ ... F. Dickinson (ed.) *Kirby's Quest for Somerset,* SRS 3 (1889). See FA above.

Lennard ... R. Lennard *A Neglected Domesday Satellite* in EHR lviii (1943) pp. 32-41.

Lordship and Villagers' Table ... Table of Lordship and Villagers' Land and Ploughs, pp. 46-47 of this edition.

LSR (1327) ... F. Dickinson (ed.) *Exchequer Lay Subsidies* in SRS 3 (1889) pp. 79-281.

LSR (1334) ... R.E. Glasscock (ed.) *The Lay Subsidy of 1334,* British Academy Records of Social and Economic History, New Series II, London 1975.

MAC ... E.H. Bates (ed.) *Two Cartularies of the Benedictine Abbeys of Muchelney and Athelney,* SRS 14 (1899).

Maitland DBB ... F.W. Maitland *Domesday Book and Beyond,* Cambridge 1897.

MC ... *Cartulary of the Cluniac Priory of Montacute* in H.C. Maxwell-Lyte and T.S. Holmes *Bruton and Montacute Cartularies,* SRS 8 (1894).

MCGB ... G.R.C. Davis *Medieval Cartularies of Great Britain,* London 1958.

ME ... Middle English.

Mon. Ang. ... W. Dugdale *Monasticon Anglicanum,* London 1846, 6 vols.

Morland I ... S.C. Morland *Some Somerset Manors,* PSANHS 99-100 (1954-55) pp. 38-48.

Morland II ... S.C. Morland *Further Notes on Somerset Domesday,* PSANHS 108 (1963-64) pp. 94-98.

MS ... Manuscript.

NV ... F.H. Dickinson (ed.) *Nomina Villarum for Somerset,* in SRS 3 (1889) pp. 53-78. See FA above.

OD ... Old Danish.

OE ... Old English.

OEB ... G. Tengvik *Old English Bynames,* Uppsala 1938 (Nomina Germanica 4).

OED ... Oxford English Dictionary.

OFr ... Old French.

OG ... Old German.

ON ... Old Norse.

OS ... Ordnance Survey First Edition 1" maps (early 19th century) ed. J.B. Harley, reprinted Newton Abbot 1969.

PNDB ... O. von Feilitzen *Pre-Conquest Personal Names of Domesday Book,* Uppsala 1937 (Nomina Germanica 3).

PSANHS ... *Proceedings of the Somerset Archaeological and Natural History Society,* Taunton.

Reaney ... P.H. Reaney *Dictionary of British Surnames,* 2nd edn. London 1976.

Rectitudines ... *Rectitudines Singularum Personarum* in F. Liebermann *Die Gesetze der Angelsachsen* 1, Halle 1903, translated in part in D.C. Douglas (ed.) *English Historical Documents* vol. 2 no. 172 (London 1968).

Regesta ... H.W.C. Davies (ed.) *Regesta Regum Anglo-Normannorum* vol. i (1913).

RH ... *Rotuli Hundredorum,* Record Commission 1812-18, 2 vols.

Robertson ... A.J. Robertson *Anglo-Saxon Charters,* Cambridge 1939, 2nd edn. 1956.

Round FE ... J.H. Round *Feudal England,* London 1909.

Sawyer ... P.H. Sawyer *Anglo-Saxon Charters: An Annotated List and Bibliography,* Royal Historical Society 1968.

SC ... T.D. Tremlett and N. Blakiston *Stogursey Charters* SRS 61 (1946).

Searle ... W.G. Searle *Onomasticon Anglo-Saxonum,* Cambridge 1897.

SM ... Sir H.C. Maxwell-Lyte *Historical Notes on Some Somerset Manors formerly connected with the Honour of Dunster,* SRS (Extra Series) 1931.

SRS ... Somerset Record Society.

Stenton ... F. M. Stenton *Anglo-Saxon England,* Oxford 1947.

Stephenson ... C. Stephenson *The 'Firma Unius Noctis' and the Customs of the Hundred* in EHR xxxix (1924) pp. 161-174.

TA ... *Tithe Award Records* (c.1840) in Somerset County Record Office, Taunton.

Tax Return ... Tax Returns for Somerset Hundreds, Exon. folios 75a - 82b; 526b - 527a. See List on p. 21.

Terrae Occupatae ...*Terrae Occupatae: in Sumerseta,* folios 508b - 525a of Exon. Book.

VCH ... *The Victoria History of the Counties of England:* Somerset vol. i (1906); Domesday Survey p. 383 ff., introduction by J. H. Round, translation by E.H. Bates. References are to vol.i, unless otherwise stated.

Vinogradoff ... P. Vinogradoff *English Society in the Eleventh Century,* Oxford 1908.

Whale, *Analysis* ... T.W. Whale *Analysis of the Somerset Domesday.*

Whale, *Principles* ... T.W. Whale *Principles of the Somerset Domesday.* These two were published together in Bath in 1902 and the latter printed also in the Proceedings of the Bath Natural History and Antiquarian Field Club vol. x (1902-05) pp. 38-86.

Zachrisson ... R.E. Zachrisson *A Contribution to the Study of Anglo-Norman Influence on English Place-Names,* Lund 1909.

The Editors are deeply grateful to the following:

Dr. R.W. Dunning, General Editor of the Somerset Victoria County History, for some material contained in the Places Notes at 5,3. 6,5. 8,38. 16,13. 17,8. 21,36. 24,8. 26,7. 36,14.

Miss Celia Parker of the County Records Office for information incorporated in the Places Notes at 19,85. 21,56; 64. 24,35 - 36.

The Staff of the County Records Office for their unfailing helpfulness.

The Librarian and Staff of the Parker Library, Corpus Christi College, Cambridge.

Miss Margaret Condon and Dr. David Crook of the Public Records Office for help in making available the Exchequer DB MS and with various palaeographical questions.

Mr. J.D. Foy for checking and proof-reading.

Mr. John McN. Dodgson for advice on numerous personal names.

Miss Frances Sheppard for help with the Somerset Hundreds.

These notes do not mention gaps in the MS caused by erasures or imperfections in the parchment, when they are not reproduced by Farley. Likewise occasions when a number has been corrected in the MS, except where it is important or there is a similar correction in the Exon. MS which is noteworthy.

References to other DB counties are to the Chapter and Sections of the editions in this series. A concordance to the chief editions of charters cited in the notes is given on p. 369 at the end of the Places Notes.

The manuscript is written on leaves, or folios, of parchment (sheepskin), measuring about 15 by 11 inches (38 by 28 cms.), on both sides. On each side, or page, are two columns, making four to each folio. The folios were numbered in the 17th century, and the four columns of each are here lettered a, b, c, d. The manuscript emphasises words and usually distinguishes chapters and sections by the use of red ink. Underlining in the MS indicates deletion.

SOMERSET. *Sūmersete* written in red above cols. 86 a, b; 88 c, d; 89 a, b; 90 a, b; 91 a, b. *Sumersete* written in red above the remaining cols. *Summersete* written at the head of the List of Landholders.

The MS, followed by Farley, does not give numbers to chs. 1 - 5. The scribe numbers William of Mohun's land (25 in the List of Landholders) as ch. 21, and perpetuates his mistake up to ch. 40 (44 in the Landholders' list). The translation and indices here follow the numbering of the List of Landholders.

L 24   WALTER, OR WALSCIN, OF DOUAI. He is sometimes referred to by his name Walter (OG *Walt(h)er*, Forssner 243) and sometimes by the nickname variant of it (not discussed by PNDB, OEB or Ellis; Searle is misleading). This *Walscin* appears to be the Norman French version of an OG **Walzin* (*sc* etc. for *z*, see Zachrisson 37-8; PNDB 110-11; Forssner 39 and compare his spellings for *Azelin*) which would be a double-diminutive pet-form of *Walter* (an *-in* suffix derivative - see Forssner 278-9 - of the recorded *-z* suffix form *Walz(e)*, see Bach 1,i, para. 97.1; 100.2).

He is known as *Walter* in DB Surrey; as *Walscin* and *W.* in DB Dorset and in DB Wiltshire; as *Walter*, *W.* and *Walscin* (*Walscin'*, *Valscin'*, *Walcin'*) in DB Devon and DB Somerset. Comparison of the usage of DB and Exon. for Somerset shows that the DB Landholders' list has both forms; the chapter heading has *Walter* in DB, *Walscin* in Exon; that where DB cites the name in full (*Walter* 8, 7;11. 24, 1; 6; 17; 27. and *Walscin* 8, 34. 24, 3; 9; 21. 46, 5) Exon. agrees, but DB often cites only the initial *W.* where Exon. has either *Walter* (24, 11-14; 18-20; 22-34; 37) or *Walscin* (24, 2; 4-5; 7-8; 10; 15-16; 36) or both (24, 35) or *W.* too (see 21, 4 note below). Comparison in Devon shows that he is *Walter* in the Landholders' list; the chapter heading has *Walter* in DB, *Walscin* in Exon; DB 23, 1 matches Exon. *Walter*; DB *W.*, *Walter* and *Walscin* in 23, 5 are all represented as *Walscin* in Exon; DB *Walscin* in 23, 6 is matched by Exon; DB *W.* is represented in Exon. as *Walscin* for 23, 2; 4; 6-27 and as both *Walter* and *Walscin* for 23,3. For both Devon and Somerset, the *Terrae Occupatae* refer to him as *Walscin*.

The DB clerk appears to know that Walter and Walscin are the same man, so that *W.* will suffice as there is no need to distinguish between them. The Exon. clerk seems to be recording the use of the alternative personal name forms as they appeared in different returns before him.

In this translation DB *W.* is expanded to the form used in Exon. Thus W(alter) or W(alscin) indicate that DB's *W.* is represented by *Walter* or *Walscin* respectively in Exon.

Douai (*dowai, douai* in DB; *duaco* in Exon.) is in the département of Nord in France; OEB 87.

L 25   *WILLELMUS DE MOION*. Rendered as William of Mohun in deference to the more popular 13th century spelling of the English form of the surname; but the place of origin was Moyon in the département of Manche, France. The DB spelling is *Moiun, Moion* etc.; Exon. *Moione, Mouin*; see OEB 98.

1,1   THE KING HOLDS. Repeated at the beginning of 1, 1-34.
HIDES ARE THERE. *sint*, subjunctive, here and in 1, 2 ; *st* in 1, 3-10, which could abbreviate either *sint* or *sunt*; *habentur*, indicative, in 1,20. Exon. has *sunt* or *s* for all entries except for 1, 9 (*sint*). *Sint* occurs in the same phrase in the first chapter of Wilts., Dorset and Devon. The subjunctive and indicative are interchangeable in indirect questions in Medieval Latin. But see Round FE p.109.

LAND FOR ... An estimate of the arable land, probably earlier than 1066.

ACRES, FURLONG. *Acra* (Exon. *agra, ager*) is used in DB both as a linear measure (as in Wilts. 26,4) and as a square measure, as here. *Quarentina* (Exon. *quadragenaria*) 'furlong' is commonly used in DB for measurements of length, but also as a measurement of area, each side being 1 furlong, as in 19,13 and 25,11. See DB Oxfordshire 18,1 note.

COBS. *Roncini*, probably pack-horses.

£79 10s 7d. DB uses the old English currency system which lasted for a thousand years until 1971. The pound contained 20 shillings, each of 12 pence, abbreviated as £(ibrae), s(olidi) and d(enarii). DB often expresses sums above a shilling in pence (e.g. 100d in 1,4) and above a pound in shillings (e.g. 116s in 1,6).

ORA. Literally an ounce; a unit of currency still in use in Scandinavia. It was reckoned at either 16d or 20d. 16d was normal, the 20d payment being regarded as the equivalent of 16d in blanched or assayed coin. See S. Harvey *Royal Revenue and Domesday Terminology* in EcHR (2nd series) xx (1967) p.221 ff.

5½ HIDES. The hide is a unit of land measurement, either of productivity, of extent or of tax liability, and contained 4 virgates. Administrators attempted to standardize the hide at 120 acres, but incomplete revision and special local reductions left hides of widely differing extents in different areas. See Dr. J. Morris in DB Sussex Appendix.

VALUE 10s. *Valet, (valebat, valuit* past tense) normally means the sums due to lords from their lands; Exon.'s use of *reddit, reddidit* supports this view (see introduction to Exon. Notes p. 310).

1,2 FREEDMAN. *colibertus*. A former slave. A continental term, not otherwise found in England; used in DB to render a native term, stated on two occasions to be (*ge*)*bur*. The *coliberti* are found mainly in the counties in Wessex and Western Mercia, particularly in Wiltshire and Somerset. In DB they are generally listed between the slaves and villagers, though occasionally (e.g. 12,1) they are included with the villagers and smallholders. Some of them at least seem to have held land and ploughs (e,g, 2,1) and paid various dues (see DB Herefordshire 1,6, col. 179 d).

PEOPLE WHO PAY ... IN TRIBUTE. *Gablatores* (Exon. *gabulatores*). This is the only occurrence in DB of this word; they were probably the same as *censores* 'tributaries', (see the Exon. Notes for DB Dorset 16,1 and DB Notts. 10,3 note).

CATTLE. Exon. *animalia;* commonly called *animalia otiosa* 'idle animals' elsewhere, i.e. beef, dairy cattle, in contrast to ploughing oxen; see VCH p. 424, but see also Exon. Notes to 25,41

WILLIAM THE SHERIFF. William of Mohun, Sheriff of Somerset from c.1068. See L 25 note above.

ONE NIGHT'S REVENUE. Many royal manors, especially in the south-west, had to pay this revenue which took the place of the normal tax payment, the manors not being assessed in hides. Originally this meant the amount of food needed to support the King and his household for one night, though by the 11th century these food rents were generally commuted. £80 is a probable figure before 1066, and £100 after, for one night's revenue; see R.L. Poole *The Exchequer in the Twelfth Century* p. 29. Sometimes a manor combined with one or more others to provide this rent, as for example North and South Petherton and Curry Rivel in 1,5, and Frome and Bruton in 1,9. See also 1,10 note below. Latin *firma* here = OE *feorm* 'a food rent'; see OED *farm* sb. i.

1,3 LAND FOR 30 PLOUGHS. The detail amounts to 26 ploughs. Unlike in some other counties in DB, the lordship and villagers' ploughs in Somerset do not always add up to the number of ploughs in the assessment; often, as here, they fall short, sometimes, as in 1,10, they exceed the estimate. On the frequent artificiality of the numbers in the plough assessment see R. Welldon Finn p. 97 ff. of *The Teamland of the Domesday Inquest* in EHR lxxxiii (1968).

6 SLAVES. Written above the '20 pigmen' with no indication as to its correct position. Slaves are normally listed after the lordship ploughs, but in this case there was no room for the interlineation there.

1,4 MERLESWEIN. Sheriff of Lincolnshire. All the entries of this name in Somerset refer to the same man.

THANELAND. Land reserved by a lord, commonly a church, for the maintenance of a thane, armed and mounted; it was usually inalienable and not automatically heritable. See Finn pp. 28-9; 138-9.

CUSTOMARY DUE...SHEEP. According to C. Stephenson in EHR xxxix (1924) p. 173, these were pasture rents.

BLOOM OF IRON. *Bloma* or, as in 17,3 *plumba*. A dish used as a measure for ore; afterwards the due payable on the measure; see Eyton i 41.

COUNT OF MORTAIN. See 19,1 for details of the rest of his holding at Cricket St. Thomas.

1,5   1 VIRGATE. It is at Swell, 19,15.

1,6   3 LEAGUES. In the MS there is a gap of about 6 letters, due to an erasure. Farley reproduces the gap, although he does not always do so when there are erasures in the MS (e.g. in the last line of 1,12 after *detiñ*).

[PAYS]. *redd'it* (=*reddidit*, perfect tense) in the MS in error for the present *reddit*, or *reddunt* (to agree with the plural *geldaverunt*). Exon. has the correct present tense.

ALFRED'S MANOR. Alfred of 'Spain'; see 35,10.

1,8   31 VILLAGERS. *villanus*, singular, for *villani*, plural, as frequently occurs with 21, 31, etc. in DB.

ST. JOHN'S CHURCH, FROME. See 16,1.

8 CARUCATES. *Carucata* here and elsewhere in the south-west counties in DB is not the carucate of the former Danish areas, but the equivalent of 'land for *x* ploughs'. The fact that on many occasions (e.g. 525 a 2; see Exon. Notes for 1,7 and 2,1) Exon. uses the term *carucatae terrae* where DB has *terra est ... car̄* proves that the two terms were synonymous.

REINBALD. The first chancellor of England, also called Reinbald of Cirencester (DB Berks. ch.61 col. 63 b). He held land in Berks., Dorset, Herefords. and Bucks. See Round FE p. 421 ff; *Regesta* pp. xiii; xv; W.H. Stevenson in EHR xi (1896) p. 731 n.

1,9   GOATS. *caprae*, she-goats, important for their milk.

9 ACRES. *agri* instead of the usual DB word *acrae; agri* is one of the regular Exon. words for 'acres'. The 9 acres are at Redlynch (see Exon. Notes to 1,9); see 19,58 for other details of Bretel's holding there.

IT WAS (PART) OF. Or 'they were (part) of', referring to the 9 acres as well as the ½ hide.

JOCELYN OF RIVERS. Exon.*Goselinus deriuaria, (Godscelinus deriuuaria* in the *Terrae Occupatae); see* OEB 109 - 110.

1,10   MOOR. Or 'marsh'; see DGSW p. 187.

56 BURGESSES. In the MS *sunt lvi burgenses;* Farley abbreviates the *sunt* to *s̄t.* See also in 3,1. The reverse happens in DB Wilts. 2,10.

MARKET WITH ITS DEPENDENCIES. *append',* perhaps meaning 'appurtenances' (market tolls, stallage rents etc.).

£80 OF WHITE SILVER. Or 'blanched', *albas, candidas* or *blancas* in DB. A sample of coin was melted as a test for the presence of alloy or baser metal. Money could also be said to be blanched when, without a test by fire, a standard deduction was made to allow for alloying or clipping. See *Dialogus de Scaccario* (ed. C. Johnson 1950) p. 125 and 1,1 note above on *ora*.

½ AND ¼ NIGHT'S REVENUE. See 1,2 note above. Bedminster (1,7), which is the only unhidated manor not stated to have paid a night's revenue, was perhaps linked with Milborne Port in the payment of the night's revenue. It is interesting that the total of the 1086 payments of Bedminster and Milborne Port is £100 10s 9½d, the same as that of the linked manors of Somerton and Cheddar (1,1-2). See DGSW p. 170.

1,11   GYTHA. Countess Gytha, wife of Earl Godwin. See Exon. Notes for 1,11.

3 HIDES...LORDSHIP. The MS has .*iiii. hidae*, but the first *i* has been partially erased. It is interesting that in Exon. too *iiii hidas* was originally written and the first *i* badly, but definitely, erased to make *iii.*

PIGMEN...32s. An example of a rent being commuted: pigmen usually paid so many pigs (e.g. 1,9;23). Also occurs in 2,1.

WOODLAND, AS MUCH IN LENGTH AND WIDTH. Exon. indicates that as much woodland as pasture is meant (i.e. 3 leagues by 1 league), not that the length and width of the woodland were the same, a frequent meaning of *tantundem* with length and width in DB (e.g. in the pasture in 1,18).

PRIEST HOLDS 1...IN ALMS. There is a gap of one letter in the MS between *i* and *elemosina;* the normal phrase is *in elemosina.*

MEADOW, 3 ACRES. *acras*, accusative after *habet.*

COUNT...1 HIDE. See 19,35; the differences in TRE and 1086 holders, value etc. may be due to a separate return perhaps being made for the King's land; see VCH p.427.

HUGH OF VAUTORTES. Exon. *Hugo de ualle torta* here and for 19,67; *de uale torta* for 45,13. Vautortes in the département of Mayenne, France; OEB 117.

THIRD PENNY. A third of a Borough's total revenues, to which the King was entitled; see J.H. Round *The 'Tertius Denarius' of the Borough* in EHR xxxiv (1919) pp. 62-4.

1,12   OF WHICH...IN LORDSHIP.   *de ea* (literally 'of it ') refers to *terra*, 'land', not *car(ucas),* 'ploughs'.

MEADOW...PASTURE. In the MS *$ti 7 Pastura;* the *7* is squashed in and possibly written later - Farley omits it.

THIRTEEN THANES. *Duodeci̅ taini* with *Tre* written above the *Duo* in darker ink and probably later, to correct the number. Exon. has 13 thanes.

MAUGER. The Count of Mortain's tenant in a number of his manors. For Brushford see 19,16.

THROUGH THE COUNT. *per comitem,* perhaps 'on behalf of'; presumably he withheld the due with the Count's knowledge. He was responsible for the non-payment of other customary dues, e.g. in 19,17-18 (see Exon. Notes for those sections).

1,13 WETHERS. *berbices,* male sheep.

'BOROUGH-RIGHT'. *Burgherist.* Probably a corruption of *burhgerihta,* 'burh-rights, borough-dues', or perhaps, but less likely on formal grounds, of *burhgrith,* 'the peace of the burh' (Maitland DBB p. 88 n.). See 2,2 note below.

(OF) CARHAMPTON. In the MS *7* for *de* in error.

1,14 IT PAYS £... A gap of about 4 letters in the MS, with *r̃q* for *require* ('enquire' as to the amount) in the left margin level with it. Exon. omits the number of £'s as well, but leaves no gap.

WILLIAM. *W.* here and for 1,15-16; 18-19. Probably William of Mohun, as in 1,13;17 as *W. de Moione,* and in 1,21-25 as *W. vicecomes.* He acquired the collection of various manors' revenues for the King, *accepit/recepit* having a rather different meaning from when, for example, the Count of Mortain 'acquired' a manor or land.

1,17 EARL TOSTI. Earl Harold's brother, Earl of Northumbria till his expulsion in 1065; killed in 1066.

11 SMALLHOLDERS. Written, perhaps later, in darker ink above the *xiii car̃* with a line extending down between *cum* and *xiii car̃* to show where it was intended to go; the line, however, should have been before the *cum xiii car̃.*

1,18 GUNHILDA. Almost certainly Earl Godwin's daughter, as in 1,24.

1,19 100 VILLAGERS, LESS 5. This edition keeps to the exact translation here and elsewhere with *minus,* rather than translating as 95, because sometimes the reason for the subtraction is noted (e.g. in DB Wilts. 2,1 col. 65c, '100 hides, less 3' where the removal of the 3 hides is explained). Exon. has the same phrase.

BISHOP MAURICE. Bishop of London 1085 - 1107.

IT PAYS. Or pehaps 'they pay', referring to the 3 hides. *Redd'* can abbreviate both *reddit* or *reddunt,* (and see 1,24 note below). Exon. has *reddit* here in the main entry, but the plural *valent* in the *Terrae Occupatae.*

1,20 EDEVA. Possibly Edeva (OE *Eadgifu*) the Fair, Earl Harold's mistress, although she could not be classed as one of Earl Godwin's children (see Exon. Notes to 1,11). Or perhaps *Eddeua* (DB and Exon. form) is a scribal error for *Eddida* (OE *Fadgyð*) 'Edith', and Queen Edith, daughter of Earl Godwin and wife of King Edward, is meant, although manors held by her are detailed below. In 32,2-3, however, Exon. has *Edeua regina* where DB has *Eddid(a) regina,* which suggests that the pronunciation of the two personal names, *Eadgifu* and *Eadgyð* was similar in all but the last consonant [*v,* ð] and even there very close.

EASTHAMS. See 19,33.

1,21 3 HIDES AND 3 VIRGATES. The details, as given in Exon., total 3 hides, which also add up with the other hides to the 20 hides tax. The error may have come from Ordwulf's holding of 3 virgates. _

LORD. The MS has *dno;* Farley misprints a capital *D.*

1,24 10 HIDES. In the MS *Ibi s̅t x hidae;* Farley misprints *ibi.*

IT PAID TAX. *geld'* which, though it is usually the abbreviation for the present *geldat,* can also be the contraction for *geldabat.* In Exon. *reddidit gildum. Geld'* also occurs in 5,37 and some 8 other times where the past tense is expected. Likewise *redd'* is sometimes the abbreviation for *reddebat* (e.g. 30,2. 32,4); and *ten'* for *tenuerunt* (as in 9,3).

1,26 IN QUEEN EDITH'S TIME. Wife of King Edward and daughter of Earl Godwin; she died in 1075.

1,27 £70. *Septuag̃ (septuaginta)* written in the left margin of the MS, with *lxx* below it.

1,28 WILLIAM HUSSEY. Exon. *Willelmus hosatus* here and for 5,43 and 7,8; *hosed* for 37,6 (main entry only). OFr *hosed* 'provided with hose; wearing hose'; OEB 370. William Hussey' may possibly be a mistake for 'William of Mohun' as he had the collection of the revenues from most of the other royal manors in Somerset.

COUNT EUSTACE...4 HIDES. His holding is repeated in 17,6. It is interesting that *libere* appears to take the place there of *pro uno manerio* in describing how Tovi held the 4 hides before 1066; see the introduction to the Exon Notes p. 310.

TOVI. William of Mohun's predecessor as Sheriff of Somerset c. 1061-68 (PNDB 384 n.4).
ROGER. Probably Roger *de stantone* (Stanton Drew) of the Tax Return for Keynsham Hundred; (see p. 21 for a list of Hundreds with their references in the Exon. Tax Returns; the King had no tax from 3 hides he held.
WULFWARD HELD... Almost certainly Wulfward White; in the next statement 'the same Wulfward' is called in Exon. 'Wulfward White'. His wife was called Edeva (DB Bucks.5,1 col. 145 b and 14,14 col. 147 b).
AELFRIC. Aelfric of Keynsham according to the Tax Return for Keynsham Hundred.

1,30 IT PAID. *geld'*; or perhaps 'it pays'; see 1,24 note above.

1,31 1 GOLD MARK. £6.
EDWARD...BOROUGH. Edward of Salisbury, Sheriff of Wiltshire. See DB Wilts. B 4 col. 64 c.
HUGH THE INTERPRETER. The same person as Hugolin the Interpreter who held 3 other manors in the Bath area; OEB p. 258 n.l. Probably the same person as the Hugolin *legatus* of the Tax Return for Bath Hundred, from whom the King had no tax on 13 hides he held (12 hides holding and 6 hides in lordship only, however, in DB).

1,32 WULFWARD WHITE. *Ulwardus albus* in DB, *Wite* in Exon. here and *uuyte* for 1,28.

1,35 WARMUND. Exon. has *G(u)armundus* here and regularly for DB's *Warmund* (exceptions are in 516 b 4 and in 364 b 2). DB has *Garmundus* for 25,4. See PNDB § 55 on *g, gu* substitution for OE *W.*

2,1   BISHOP OF WINCHESTER. Walkelin, Bishop from 1070 to 1098. The privileges he enjoyed in the Hundreds of Taunton and Pitminster are similar to those of the Bishop of Worcester in his 300-hide Hundred of Oswaldslow in Worcs.: DB Worcs. 2,1 col. 172 c.
ARCHBISHOP STIGAND. Consecrated Bishop of Winchester in 1047, he held that See with the Archbishopric of Canterbury from 1052 until he was deposed in 1070.

2,2-5 THE APPEARANCE of these sections dealing with the customary dues is different from that of the rest of ch.2. A gap of about 2 lines after 2,5, not shown by Farley, suggests that the scribe originally left space after 2,1 for the dues to be entered later.

2,2   THESE CUSTOMARY DUES. See Robertson, Appendix 4 (= ECW no. 544) for an Anglo-Saxon record of the dues pertaining to Taunton in 1066.
'BOROUGH-RIGHT'. *Burgheristh.* See, 1,13 note above. According to Ballard p. 100 it may be merely *burh-bot* and that the specified rural manors had to repair the walls of Taunton.
THIEVES; BREACH OF THE PEACE; HOUSE-BREAKING. The King normally received the fines from these.
HUNDRED PENCE. Perhaps only the ordinary revenue of Taunton Hundred; see C. Stephenson in EHR xxxix (1924) p.161 ff.
CHURCH TAXES. *Ciricieti*; OE *ciric-sceat*, an obscure tax, see Maitland DBB p. 321 ff. They were due in kind and payable at Martinmas (Ballard p.101). See DB Worcs. 9,7 (col. 175 c) and also the duties and rights of the *cotsetla* in the note at 8,30 below on 'Cottagers'.

2,3   THESE TWO LANDS. Shopnoller and Stoke St. Mary.

2,6   HUGH *DE VILLANA*. See end of notes, page 21.

2,8   THESE THREE LANDS. *Terrae;* used throughout the south-west counties, and probably elsewhere in DB, as a synonym of *manerium, mansio*, as comparison between DB and Exon. plainly shows (see Exon. Notes to 1,1). According to J. Morris in DB Surrey 19,22, however, *terra* there was land not classified as a manor.

2,9   A THANE HELD JOINTLY. *Pariter;* see the introduction to the Exon. Notes. p. 310.
CUSTOMARY DUES AND SERVICE. Those detailed in 2,2; see Exon. Notes to 2,3.
KING WILLIAM GRANTED. See *Regesta* i no. 386 a for the confirmation of this grant by William II.
ST. PETER'S. Old Minster, now Winchester Cathedral.
BISHOP OF DURHAM. William of St. Carilef, or Calais, bishop from 1081 to 1096.

2,10 THIS ENTRY is written, probably a little later, in paler ink and slightly into the left margin at the bottom of col. 87 c.
14 PLOUGHS. *xii* with the superscript *ii* to correct it to *xiiii.*

2,11 BLEADON. See 19,7 note below.
MONKS' SUPPLIES. The monks of the Benedictine monastery which was connected with Winchester Cathedral were provided from the manor's revenue with a certain amount of food.
MEADOW, 16 ACRES. Accusative after *habet;* likewise the 1 acre of underwood.

2,12 BISHOP STIGAND. See 2,1 note above.

3,1   BISHOP OF SALISBURY. Osmund, bishop from 1078 to 1099.
TWO LANDS ARE NOT. The MS has *sunt;* Farley abbreviates to *st;* see also 1,10 and note.

3,2   WALTER TIRRELL. Exon. *Walterus tirellus.*

PASTURE, 1 LEAGUE: 'League' is used here as a square measure.

4,1   BISHOP OF BAYEUX. Odo, half-brother of King William and elder brother of the Count of Mortain. Earl of Kent 1066-7 to 1082, then 1087 to 1088. He was 'regent' during some of King William's absences abroad.
SAMSON THE CHAPLAIN. Chaplain to King William, later Bishop of Worcester 1096-1112. Probably the compiler of DB, and possibly, though less likely, its scribe; see V.H. Galbraith *Notes on the career of Samson bishop of Worcester (1096 - 1112)* in EHR lxxxii (1967) pp. 86-101 and in his *Domesday Book* p.50 ff.
EARL LEOFWIN. Brother of Earl Harold; Earl of Kent and the Home Counties.

5,1   BISHOP OF COUTANCES. Geoffrey of Mowbray, one of King William's chief justices. He was also Bishop of St. Lô, near Coutances.
WILLIAM OF MONCEAUX. Exon. *Willelmus de moncels* here and for 5,25, *de moncellis* for 5,3;63, *de muntcellis* for 5,42-43; Monceaux in the département of Calvados, France; OEB 99.

5,2   THE BISHOP ALSO HOLDS. Repeated at the beginning of 5,2-6.

5,4   ALFGEAT PUTTOCK. Exon, *aluiedus pottoch;* see OEB 365.
IT PAID. *geld';* see 1,24;30 notes above. Exon. has the past *reddiderunt.*
PASTURE... 2s IN ADDITION. In addition, as much pasture as would pay 2s a year.
ROGER WHITING. Exon. *Rogerus Witen (Wytent* in the Tax Return for Cheddar Hundred); the same person as Roger of Courseulles according to OEB 11. Cf. 5,47.

5,7   OSMUND STRAMIN. Exon. *Osmundus estramin;* OEB 217.

5,15   MILL...MILL. Probably parts of the same mill despite the parts not paying at a proportionate rate.
SIBBI. *Sibe* in DB, *Sibus* in Exon; perhaps 'Sibba'; see PNDB 358.

5,16   WULFEVA ... 4 HIDES. The Tax Return for Chew Hundred states that the King had no tax from 4 hides she held in that Hundred.

5,18   5 HIDES, 5 PLOUGHS. In the MS originally *ii* in both cases, but corrected to *v;* see Exon. Notes to 5,18.

5,30   NIGEL. Possibly Nigel of Gournai. In the Tax Return for Hartcliffe Hundred Nigel *de gornaio* had not paid tax on ½ hide he held and Fulcran on 1½ hides he held from the Bishop of St. Lô (Coutances).
THEM. *has;* the 14 ploughs, as made clear in Exon.

5,32   NIGEL OF GOURNAI. Exon. *Nigellus de gurnai (de gurnaio* for 5,44-45); Gournai-en-Brai in the département of Seine-Maritime, France; OEB 90. Hence the English surname Gurney; see Places Notes to 5,32.

5,34   ROGER ... 7 HIDES. The lordship and villagers' land total 7 hides, less 1 virgate. There may be a scribal error here, or the missing virgate is that belonging to the church.
BISHOP ... THREE MANORS. The three manors are the main holding and those of Roger and Guy.

5,35   TOVI. The Sheriff; see 1,28 note above.
½ MILL. See Places Notes.

5,37   BISHOP ... TWO MANORS. Bathwick and the hide in Woolley; added land is often called 'a manor' in Exon.

5,42   3 VILLAGERS AND 6 SMALLHOLDERS. In the MS it was originally *iii bord',* but the scribe corrected it to *vi bord'* and at the same time began to change the *iii* in *iii vill'* to *vi* in error. Exon. agrees with DB.

5,43   THE MS has †'s beside this entry and 5,50, for which Farley prints 'hands', although elsewhere he reproduces the † sign. The 'hands' mislead the reader into thinking that the Stratton entry belongs after the Babington one. 5,43 must succeed 5,42 as William of Monceaux holds both manors according to Exon, and DB's *Idem W.* would only make sense here. These crosses, of which there are 14 in Somerset, are written next to entries in which land was held in 1066 by or from a church (most often Glastonbury) or could not be separated from one, but by 1086 had become alienated. However, by no means all entries recording land taken from a church have these crosses beside them.
HE COULD GO WHERE HE WOULD. He was not bound to the Bishop of Coutances: he could choose any lord he liked as his patron and protecter.
WILLIAM, WILLIAM. The surnames in Exon. show that this is an example of added land being held in 1086 by a different person to the main manor. See also 5,53.

5,44   TAX FOR 10 HIDES. The details of the lordship and villagers' land total 11 hides. There is no obvious reason for the discrepancy and similar discrepancies occur in some 40 entries in Somerset.

5,46   GEOFFREY MALREGARD. Exon. *Gosfridus Malruuardus;* OEB 322. Norton Malreward (5,16) is probably named after one of his descendants.

5,47	ROGER. Probably Roger Wythent; see VCH p. 452 n.1. Cf. 5,4.
5,48	1 HIDE ... HEMINGTON. See 20,1. It is Baldwin the Sheriff.
5,50	MARGINAL CROSS. See 5,43 note above.
5,52	LORDSHIP 3 PLOUGHS. So MS and Exon; Farley misprints '4 ploughs'.
5,53	½ MILL ... 9s. The original returns may possibly have read 90d for this ½ mill, which would then have paid the same as the other half (DGSW p.191 n.1), but there are several instances in DB of ½ mills not paying equal amounts e.g. at Weston Bampfylde (19,69 and 36,5).
	ROGER HOLDS. See 5,43 note above.
5,54	RICHARD ... 1 HIDE. The Exon. Details Table (p.338) shows that this is not the same hide as that held by Richard in Rode in 45,14.
5,63	LAND FOR 1 PLOUGH. In the MS *trã;* Farley misprints capital T.
5,66	BURGESS. Misplaced: burgesses are normally listed with the villagers. It is interesting that in Exon. the burgess is added as an afterthought.
6,1	BISHOP OF WELLS. Giso, bishop from 1060 to 1088.
	FOR THE BISHOP'S USE. *ad opus episcopi*; perhaps 'for the Bishop's work' which meant, according to Dr. Morris, that the villagers worked for the Bishop. Exon. sometimes has e.g. 'value to the Bishop' where DB has 'value for the Bishop's use'(in 6,14) and vice versa (in 8,2). For DB Dorset 11,1 Exon. has "This manor pays ... for the Church's use", where DB has "Value of the Church's lordship".
	MANASSEH'S WIFE ... 2 HIDES. This is Manasseh Cook's wife. It would seem from the Tax Return for Bishop Giso's Hundred that she had not paid tax in 1084 on these 2 hides; likewise on the 3 hides 1 virgate she held in 46,24-25 (Tax Return for Chewton Hundred). However, it is possible that the 2 hides in 6,1 are the same as those in 46,24; see Places Notes to 6,1.
	ALFWARD CROC. Exon. *Ailuuardus crocco*.
6,2	THE BISHOP ALSO HOLDS. Repeated at the beginning of 6,2-11.
6,6	THIS LAND. That is, the 9 hides.
6,9	PASTURE. *pasturae*, genitive singular, not nominative plural, as Exon. makes clear; the latter is the usual case in this formula.
	RALPH CROOKED HANDS. Exon. has *Radulfus tortes manus* here; *tortes mans.* (8,2); *tortasmanus* (8,20); *tortae manus* (8,30); see OEB 339.
	BOFA. DB *Bono*, Exon. *Bouo*, the DB form probably being a misreading of the Exon, which is from a Latinised form *(Bovus)* of the OE *Bofa*. A possible alternative is that the DB form is correct and is from a Latinised form *(Bonus)* of the OE *Goda*.
	ALFWY SON OF BANNA(?). *Eluui Haussonna* in Exon; probably a scribal error in Exon. (*H* for *B*, *u* for *n*), of which there are many in this entry in Exon. See Exon Notes. to 35,24.
	ORDWULF. Oddly, there is nothing more about him, even in Exon; he occurs there at the end of the entry after the details of the holding of Alfwy son of Banna(?).
6,10	MAGHERE. *Macharius* in DB and Exon, from OG *Maghari, Magher; see* Forssner 180 s.v. *Macharius.*
6,12	OSMUND. Probably Bishop Giso's nephew; see the Tax Return for the Bishop's Hundred where the King had no tax from 3 hides Osmund held; also the Tax Return for Abdick Hundred where the King had no tax from 10 hides Osmund held. See Places Notes.
6,13	AELFRIC OF STOWEY. Exon. *Aluricus de stauue;* OEB 50.
6,14	BENZELIN. *Benthelm'* in the MS, probably in error; Exon. has *Benthelinus.*
6,16	ST. ANDREW'S. The cathedral church of Wells.
6,18	THE KING HOLDS ... There is an ink blot in the MS between *ten* and *M̄,* under which *un* (= *unum*, 'a'.) is just visible.
6,19	ASH (PRIORS). See 22,20; the value of the two manors there is 50s, however.
7,1	CHURCH OF ST. PETER. Bath Abbey.
7,3	2 HIDES. Probably a scribal error in Exon: Bath A (see App. II no.6) has *ii (hidas) et dimidiam,* which then adds up with the ½ hide lordship to the 3 hides tax. A similar error occurs in 7,9.
7,4	WALTER HUSSEY. Exon. *Walterus hosatus.* See 1,28 note above on the surname.
7,9	2 HIDES. Probably a scribal error in Exon. for '3 hides'; see 7,3 note above and App. II no.4.
7,11	HUGH THE INTERPRETER. See 1,31 note above.
7,15	WHOLE OF THIS LAND. All Ch.7.
8,1	ST. MARY'S OF GLASTONBURY. Glastonbury Abbey.
	ARPENTS. A French measure of uncertain and probably variable size, usually applied in DB to vineyards, but occasionally to meadow and woodland; see DB Wilts. 12,4 note.
8,8	LORDSHIP. The lordship detail is misplaced; it is in its usual place in Exon. Also occurs in 21,24;44.

8,9   115 ACRES. In the MS *xv ac* with *c* written above and to the left of the *xv*, with a mark to show *cxv* was intended. Farley omits the mark, though he includes the similar one in 8,11.

8,11   27 VILLAGERS. In the MS *xvii vill'i*, with another *x* interlined with a line extending down after the ₇ to show its position. Farley misprints the interlineation as *cc* (200). Exon. has *xxvii*.

8,15   GERARD DITCHER. Exon. has *Girardus fosarius* here and for 8,17; *Gerardus fossor* for 21,38; OEB 251.

8,16   THANELAND; HOWEVER... The *tamen* is unusual because normally thaneland could not be separated from the church (see 8,20 and Exon. Notes to 25,8; DB 25,8 puts it differently).

8,17   ROBERT OF AUBERVILLE. The Tax Return for High Ham Manor states that Robert of Auberville had not paid the King tax on 5 virgates he held from the Abbot of Glastonbury; likewise Serlo of Burcy had not paid tax on 2 hides ½ virgate he held.

8,18   ALSTAN HOLDS ½ HIDE. *dimid'* interlined after the erasure of the original figure, probably *i*, which had been written between the two full stops.

8,19   HUMPHREY THE CHAMBERLAIN. The Tax Return for Ringoldsway Hundred states that the King had no tax on 2 hides that Humphrey the Chamberlain held; Lattiford is a detached part of Ringoldsway Hundred.

8,30   3 COTTAGERS. *Coscet* singular, *coscez, cozets* plural, represent Anglo-Norman versions of OE *cot-seta* sing., *cot-seta(n)* pl., 'a cottage-dweller; cottage-holder' (OE *cot, saeta*, see *English Place-name Elements* s.v. *cot-saeta;* OED s.v. *cotset*): the Anglo-Norman letter *z* represents the sound *ts* and the spelling *sc* a miscopied *st* representing metathesis of *ts* so *coscet* = *cotset, coscez* and *cozets* = *cotsets*. The plural in -*s* represented by *cozets* (= *cotsets*, is the result of either a French adaptation or an OE change of inflexion.

      'Cottagers' are almost entirely confined to the south-west counties in DB, Wiltshire providing about 80% of the total entries. In Somerset there are only about 20 occurrences of the 'Cottager' and with one exception (21,15, Gothelney) they are in manors on the eastern side of the county. It is interesting that in Bath A (see App. II) *coceti* are replaced in the corresponding Exon. and DB entries by *bordarii*, 'smallholders'.

      Not much is known about the status and economic position of *coscez*, though as can be seen from this entry they did have at least part of a plough. However, a class of person called in OE *cotsetla*, 'cottage-dweller', which seems equivalent, has its obligations spelt out in the 10th-11th century *Rectitudines Singularum Personarum* pp. 445-6. His rights varied according to local custom: in some places he had to work for his lord every Monday throughout the year or* 3 days a week at harvest; in some places every day at harvest, reaping 1 acre of oats or ½ acre of other corn; he was to be allowed his sheaf by the steward; he was not to pay land-tax; he was to have 5 acres of his own, more where customary, but less would be too little because his duty-labour was frequently called for; he was to pay his hearth-penny at Holy Thursday like every free man, to relieve his lord's demesne, if required, of its obligations to sea-defences, royal deer parks and such things, according to his condition, and pay his church-dues at Martinmas. *So Anglo Saxon version; 'and' in the Latin.

8,31   EDMER ATOR. See 37,5 note below. In the MS a word of about 4 letters has been erased after *Edmer*.
      TINTINHULL. See 19,9 and Ch.19 note.

8,32   HARDING. Perhaps the Harding of Wilton *(de uiltona)* in the Tax Return for Frome Hundred; his lordship there is said to have been 9 hides; see Places Notes.

8,33   RALPH OF CONTEVILLE. Exon. *Radulfus decunteuill'* here; *de contiuilla* (main entry), *de cunteuilla (Terrae Occupatae)* for 24,11; *de conteuilla* for 24,36-37. Conteville is in the département of Eure, France; OEB 83.
      AELFRIC SON OF EVERWACER. Exon. *Alfricus filius Eueruuacre;* see PNDB 249 and 27,3 note below.

8,34   WALSCIN OF DOUAI. Walter of Douai, see L 24 note above.

8,36   SIWARD. Probably Siward Falconer; see 47,10.

8,36   THESE HOLDINGS are included in the *Terrae Occupatae* (see Exon. Notes for references),
41   which suggests that there was some doubt as to whether they had been rightfully taken from Glastonbury. Most of them are repeated elsewhere in DB (see Places Notes). Cf. the last two entries for Ch. 6 and 10,6, which also deal with land that belonged to the church in 1066.

8,38   VALUE 100s AND MORE. 100s is the present value of the first two places named (see 5,10-11); the value of the other two (see 5,3;43) adds £5 - or £6 if the added Pitcote is included with Stratton's value. See Exon. Notes for different values.

8,41   HIS FATHER. Possibly William of Courseulles, who holds the adjacent Draycott under the Count of Mortain (19,12); see Eyton i 60.

9,1   ST. PETER'S CHURCH. Muchelney Abbey.

4 CARUCATES. See 1,8 note above.

ARPENT. See 8,1 note above.

9,2 THE CHURCH ITSELF HOLDS. Repeated at the beginning of 9,2-8.

9,4-5 GODRIC^A; EDWIN^B. See 9,8 note below.

9,5 ANOTHER ONE IN LORDSHIP. *alia (hida);* see Exon. Notes to 9,5.

9,6 TAX FOR 20 HIDES. The lordship and villagers' land and the 2 hides held by Ceolric and Wulfward total only 18 hides 2½ virgates. The 1 hide ½ virgate at Moortown (21,55) may account for part of the deficiency.

9,7 MEADOW, 2 ACRES. Accusative after *habet.*

9,8 GODRIC^A, EDWIN^B AND WADDELL^C. The A,B,C written above these names correspond with those written over the names in 9,4-5;8.

10,1 ST. PETER'S CHURCH. Athelney Abbey.

10,2 ROGER ... 2 HIDES. See 21,98; the details are not identical, however. See Exon. Notes to 10,2 and 21,98.

10,3 VILLAGERS. According to the Tax Return for South Petherton Hundred the King had no tax in 1084 from 1 hide held by villagers of the Abbot of Athelney (see Lordship and Villagers' Table p. 334).

10,6 A SUMMARY of lands taken away, probably wrongfully, from Athelney and for that reason included in the *Terrae Occupatae.*
THE WORDS IN ITALICS are underlined for deletion in the MS. The *in* before *Aisselle* is written into the left margin, and the second *in* is written above both *de* and $\overline{M}$: Farley does not make this clear. It is likely that the scribe intended to underline the *de* $\overline{M}$ before *Sutone* and interline *in* as correction, as he did for *de* $\overline{M}$ *Bosintone.*

11,1 THIS ENTRY is written entirely over an erasure, apart from *Eccl'a* at the beginning.
PURITON. The only holding of the Church of Rome in DB. The Pope encouraged William to conquer England and this was his reward.
DID NOT PAY. *non geld' ;* perhaps 'do not pay', although Exon. has *non reddidit.* See 1,24 note above.

12,1 ST. STEPHEN'S CHURCH, CAEN. *Cadom* written above *Stefani* in the MS; the chapter headings were written in red ink after the main body of the text and had to avoid the interlineation here. Farley prints the *cadom* in bigger type than is usual for interlineations. The heading and the first line of this entry are written over an erasure.

13,1 THIS ENTRY is written entirely over an erasure, apart from *Eccl'a* at the beginning.
MONTEBOURG. In the diocese of Coutances, in the département of Manche, France. NIGEL THE DOCTOR. St. Mary's of Montebourg held another manor from him in DB Wilts. 56,4 col. 73 b. Spirtes the priest was Nigel's predecessor there, as in many of his manors; he was a wealthy churchman who held a total of nearly 80 hides in Somerset, Hampshire, Wiltshire, Herefordshire and Shropshire.

14,1 ST. EDWARD'S CHURCH. At Shaftesbury.

16,1 REINBALD. Reinbald the priest; see 1,8.

16,2 RICHERE OF LES ANDELYS. Exon. *Richerus de andeleio;* Les Andelys in the département of Eure, France; OEB 68. He is also called Richere of Stogumber *(de stochas);* see the Tax Return for Williton Hundred where he holds 2 hides in alms.
VALUE £3 AND 4 COWS. The same in Exon, the *iiii vaccas* being written in the line below their normal position (i.e. after slaves).

16,6 WHEN THE BISHOP DIED. Peter, Bishop of Lichfield and Chester from 1072 to 1085; he transferred his see to Chester in 1075.

16,10 GODWIN. Probably Godwin the Englishman from the Tax Return for Hartcliffe Hundred; the King had no tax from ½ hide he held.

16,14 NOW IT IS IN THE KING'S HANDS. The Tax Return for Frome Hundred states that the King had no tax from ½ hide held in alms in Kilmersdon.

17,1 COUNT EUSTACE. Of Boulogne; he was married first to Goda, King Edward's sister (died c. 1056), and then to Ida of Lorraine. He was father of Godfrey of Boulogne and of King Baldwin of Jerusalem.
(HOLDS). In the MS *tenuit,* in error for *tenet:* present tense in Exon.

17,5 ANOTHER (PLOUGH). The *alia* refers to *car;* the Exon. addition makes this unclear.

17,6 BELLUTON. See 1,28 note above.

17,7 COUNTESS IDA OF BOULOGNE. Wife of Count Eustace. The *boloniens'* is written in large red letters above *Ida,* probably later because it is omitted in Exon: it is very unusual for the Exchequer text to have information not in Exon, when there is a corresponding entry. The gloss may have been written when it was not generally known who Countess Ida was. It is interesting that she holds directly from the King, not as a sub-tenant of her husband.

17,8	10 SMALLHOLDERS. The gap printed by Farley is due to a hole in the parchment. Farley does not always indicate defects in the parchment (e.g. in 5,24-25 and 5,37 where there is an oblique cut of 4 lines depth in the MS).
18,1	EARL HUGH. Hugh of Avranches, nephew of King William and Earl of Chester 1071/77 to 1101.
18,1; 3-4	EDNOTH. Ednoth (Alnoth) the Constable, who was Earl Hugh's predecessor in other counties as well. See 39,1 note below. For some reason his son Harding did not inherit his numerous estates.
18,4	ST. SEVERUS' CHURCH. In Coutances. Founded by Earl Hugh c.1085 (Mon. Ang. vi,110) VALUE £4 10s. The MS has *valet iiii lib' 7 ix sól'*, but the *i* is written very close to the *x*. There is some evidence that the scribe wrote *ii sol'* first and changed the second *i* to an *x*, giving it a long 'tail' (as is often done to emphasise corrections), and omitting to erase the first *i*. Exon has *iiii lib' 7 dim'* for the present value.
19,1	THE COUNT OF MORTAIN. Robert, half-brother of King William and younger brother of Bishop Odo of Bayeux. He held more land in England than any other follower of King William (see Freeman iv 762), especially in Cornwall and other south-west counties - 623 manors in Dorset, Devon, Cornwall and Wilts., according to a summary in Exon. 531 a 2. He was responsible for the 'removal' of numerous parts of manors, illegally in many cases, and for the cessation of payment of various customary dues owed to royal manors in Somerset and Devon. In the 'exchanges' he made of manors he invariably got the better bargain (e.g. Tintinhull for Camerton which has less than half the value; 8,32 and 19,9). Mortain is the département of Manche, France. CRICKET (ST. THOMAS). See 1,4 for the customary due payable by this manor to South Petherton.
19,5	3 SMALLHOLDERS. In the MS there is a gap of about 8 letters after this, perhaps for the later inclusion of the villagers' ploughs; Exon. gives no villagers' ploughs, however.
19,7	ROBERT THE CONSTABLE. Exon. *Robertus constabulo*. The same person as Robert son of Wymarc, Sheriff of Essex. He died before 1086 and was succeeded by his son Swein in some of his manors; see Freeman iv Appendix Note D. ST. SWITHUN'S. The Old Minster. St. Swithun was bishop 852-62 and his name was added to the original dedication to Holy Trinity and St. Peter and St. Paul. Countess Gytha had given it Crowcombe and Bleadon (2,11); see *Annales Monastici* ii 26 (ECW no. 532). DID NOT PAY. *non geld'*; possibly 'do not pay', but Exon. has *non reddidit* and 19,9 has *geldabat* in a similar formula. See 1,24 note above.
19,7; 9-10	THE MARGINAL CROSSES are for alienated church land; see 5,43 note above.
19,9	TINTINHULL. See 8,31 and the note to 19,1 above. 1 SILVER MARK. 13s 4d.
19,10	HUBERT OF SAINT-CLAIR. Exon. *Hubertus de sancto claro*; see OEB 112. DOES NOT HAVE SERVICE. VCH p.474 translates as 'receives no due'.
19,13	ROBERT SON OF IVO. The Count of Mortain's constable, possibly of Montacute Castle; VCH p.427 and Eyton i 97.
19,15	1 VIRGATE. See 1,5.
19,16	MAUGER HOLDS FROM THE COUNT. Repeated at the beginning of 19,16-19. Mauger is Mauger of Carteret for 19,16 (see Places Notes) and probably for the other entries (he had not paid tax on 3 hides held in Abdick Hundred, and the places in 19,17-19 are all in that Hundred).
19,17	1 SHEEP... IN CUSTOMARY DUES. It would seem from this entry and 19,23-25; 27;29 that 1 sheep with a lamb per hide of land was a regular payment in customary dues. However, Brushford (19,16) paid tax for only 2 hides, while 1,12 says that it paid 24 sheep a year to Dulverton before 1066; likewise Oare (30,2) and Allerford (32,4) paid 12 sheep each for their 1 hide taxed, and 18 sheep were payable by the 1½ hide Monksilver to Williton (1,6 and 35,10). There may thus have been another rate consisting of 12 sheep per hide.
19,18	30d. In customary dues; see Exon. Notes.
19,24	[WOODLAND]. In the MS *prati* repeated in error; Exon. has *nemoris*.
19,25	THIS ENTRY is written across the bottom of cols. 92a,b below the bottom marginal rulings, indicating that it was written after the folio was completed. It is written in 2 lines, the second of which is exdented here in the Latin text. There are no signs to show its correct position in the chapter, but it obviously belongs with Drogo's other manors; in Exon. it is placed between the manors of Appley and Bradon (19,22 and 19,23).
19,26	A GARDEN. Latin *(h)ortus* is probably rendering OE *geard*, 'garden, enclosure, etc.', in the sense seen in *fisc-geard*, 'fishery, fish pound'. Perhaps here an inland river fishery; DGSW p.18

19,27	WILLIAM OF LESTRE. Exon. *Willelmus de lestra;* Lestre in the département of Eure, France; OEB 94-5.

19,27 WILLIAM OF LESTRE. Exon. *Willelmus de lestra;* Lestre in the département of Eure, France; OEB 94-5.

19,28 REGINALD OF VAUTORTES. Exon. *Raginaldus de valle torta;* Vautortes in the département of Mayenne, France; OEB 117.

19,33 EASTHAMS. See 1,20.

19,35 1 HIDE IN PRESTON. See 1,11 and note.

19,38 LORDSHIP ... SLAVES, WITH ... HAVE. Perhaps *habent* is a mistake for *habentibus* ('who have'), to avoid two main verbs (*sunt* and *habent*) in one sentence.

19,39 ALFRED THE BUTLER. He was the Count's butler and held a considerable amount of land from him in many other counties.

19,40 THE MARGINAL CROSS refers to alienated church land; see 5,43 note above. For Taunton see 2,5.

19,47 ALFRED HOLDS. Probably *de Co.* (*de Comite*, 'from the Count') omitted in error in the MS; it is in Exon.

19,50 ST. MARY'S CHURCH, GRESTAIN. Grestain in the département of Eure, France.

19,59 KEINTON (MANDEVILLE). See 21,92 and, probably, 46,21 for land added to this manor from Barton (St. David). It is not clear whether the same, or separate, hides are intended; the *Terrae Occupatae* details for 19,59 (Exon. 519 b 6) tend to support the latter. Mauger here is probably Mauger of Carteret, one of the Count's chief sub-tenants and the holder of the hide in 46,21.

19,61 ALSTAN OF BOSCOMBE. Exon. *Alestanus deboscoina;* OEB 38. See 26,7 note below. 1 PLOUGH ... IT. The Exon. equivalent of DB's 'Land for 1 plough'.

19,68 MAUGER OF CARTERET. Exon. *Malgerus de cartrai* here and for 10,1 (see Exon. Notes); *Maelgerus de chartreia* for 46,21. Carteret in the département of Manche, France; OEB 81.

19,70 THIS ENTRY is written in 1¼ lines across the foot of cols. 92c,d below the bottom marginal rulings, indicating that it was probably written after the rest of the folio. There are no signs to show its correct position in the chapter, but Exon. places it between Weston Bampfylde and Milborne Port (19,69 and 19,71).

19,73 THEM. The 2 ploughs, as also in 21,24. 'That land' presumably means the 2 hides, although Exon. normally gives either the number of hides etc. or says 'the rest of the land' or 'the whole of the land'. The meadow is, unusually, also the object of the villagers and smallholders.

19,86 PURSE (CAUNDLE). See DB Dorset 15,1 col.78c. Another example of the Count getting the better of the bargain: Purse Caundle paid tax for 4 hides and 1½ virgates and its value was 67s 6d. Alfred the Butler held land in both manors.
DROGO. Probably Drogo of Montacute, one of the Count's chief sub-tenants; VCH p.412.
DUNCAN. *Donecan* in DB, *Donecannus* in Exon., from Old Irish *Donnchad, Dunchad,* 'brown warrior'; Reaney s.v. Duncan.

19,87 THIS ENTRY is written at the foot of col. 93a, two spaces into the left margin. In the MS there is a very faint Ψ sign in the left margin, partly hidden by the binding and not reproduced in the facsimile or by Farley. There is no corresponding sign in ch.19; in Exon. this manor comes between Chilthorne and 'Bishopstone' (19,80 and 19,86).

20,1 BALDWIN OF EXETER. Baldwin of Moeles, (now Meulles) and of Sap in Normandy; son of Count Gilbert of Brionne, and younger brother of Richard, (a landholder in Wilts.); he was married to a cousin of King William. He was Sheriff of Devon and a very large landholder there. 1 HIDE. See 5,48.

21,1 ROGER OF COURSEULLES. Courseulles-sur-Mer, in the département of Calvados, France. Also known as Roger Whiting; see 5,4 note above.

21,4 W(ALTER) OF DOUAI. *W.* in DB and, unusually, in Exon. too; see L 24 note above.

21,5 GEOFFREY OF VAUTORTES. Exon. *Goffridus deualle;* Vautortes in the département of Mayenne, France; OEB 117 (Tengvik gives *Godefridus* - Godfrey - but he only occurs in the Devon Tax Returns; Somerset Exon. has *Goffridus* for 21,5; 14 and *Gosfridus* for 21,81).

21,8 ROBERT *HERECOM*. Exon. *Herecom,* probably 'of Heathcombe'; see Places Notes.

21,15 ½ MILL. See 21,24 note below.

21,24 THEM. See 19,73 note above. The lordship detail is misplaced, as also in 8,8 and 21,44. ½ MILL AT 20s. Possibly *xx solid'* is a mistake for *xx den'*. The other half of the mill is probably at the adjacent Gothelney (21,15) and pays 10d. As Exon. gives '1 mill' it may be that the scribe gave the payment of the whole mill rather than of ½ mill (assuming that the *solid'* is an error); see DB Wilts. 67,43 note. 20d is a common payment for a mill (e.g. in 25,17. 35,17-18).

21,28 [1] VILLAGER. Number supplied from Exon. Farley has *vill',* but in the MS it looks as though the scribe tried to insert a *.i.* at the beginning of *vill'*.

21,29 EXCEPT FOR 15 ACRES. Normally, as in 21,22; 25; 31 etc., one would expect the 15 acres to be held by the smallholders. It is likely that the scribe of this entry in Exon.

omitted this information in error: the entry contains several other mistakes.

21,33 A PLOUGH. In the MS there is a gap of about 4 letters, due to an erasure, possibly of 7 *dim'*. Exon. gives 1 villagers' plough.

21,36 WILLIAM OF DAUMERAY. Exon. *Willelmus de Almereio;* Daumeray in the département of Maine-et-Loire, France; OEB 85.

21,37 HE ALSO. William of Daumeray, as in Exon.

21,44 IT. The plough.
LORDSHIP. See 21,24 note above.

21,54-5 THE MARGINAL CROSSES indicate alientated church land; see 5,43 note above.

21,55 SLAVES WHO HOLD 1 VIRGATE. It is unusual for slaves to hold land in DB; cf. 47,16.

21,60 AILHILLA(?). *Ailhalle* in DB, *Ailhailla* in Exon; see PNDB 141.

21,61 KAFLI. *Caflo* in DB and Exon: ON *Kafli;* PNDB 301.

21,65 TAX FOR ... ½ VIRGATE. In the MS *geldb' p'* ... *7 p' dim b;* Farley omits the second *p' (pro)* in error.

21,74 GEOFFREY HOLDS FROM ROGER. Repeated at the beginning of 21,74-77.

21,89 ROBERT GERNON. Exon.*Robertus Greno* (main entry), *Gernon (Terrae Occupatae),* from OFr *grenon, gernon* 'moustache'; OEB 314-5.

21,90 BREWHAM. See 25,55 and note.

21,92 KEINTON (MANDEVILLE). See 19,59 note above.

21,98 (LONG) SUTTON. See 10,2 and note. The marginal cross indicates alienated church land; see 5,43 note above.

22,1 ROGER ARUNDEL. From OFr *arondel,* 'little swallow' (OEB 359), no connection with the Sussex place-name or the Earls of Arundel.

22,11- ROBERT OF *GATEMORE.* Exon. *Robertus de Gatemore,* unidentified (OEB 43); he
12 may be named after a part of one of his holdings, such as Skilgate. He is also given in Exon. as the holder of 22,12. A *Galfridus Gatemar* is found in LSR (1327) p.140 in Currypool, and a Robert *Gatemore* in Aisholt *(ibidem* p.142).

22,13 8 PLOUGHS. In the MS it was originally *iiii car,* but corrected to *viii* and *to* for *octo* written in above to emphasise the change; the last 2 letters of a number are often interlined when a correction has been made.

22,19 ROGER HIMSELF HOLDS. Repeated at the beginning of 22,19-22.
WARMUND HELD IT. After 1066, but presumably not in 1086, unless *tenuit* is a scribal error for *tenet.*
VOUCHES HIM TO WARRANTY. Calls on Roger to support his claim on the ½ hide. A tenant could call on his lord to defend him against any claim on his land made in the lord's court by some other person. If the lord thought that the claimant had more right to the land, he might not uphold his tenant's claim and the matter might then be brought before the King for decision. The wording and tenses of this part of the entry (see Exon. Notes to 22,19) suggest that there may have been two claims on the added land, e.g. someone claimed against Warmund who vouched Roger; Roger failed to vouch and the case went to the King who gave Warmund possession; later another person claimed against Warmund who again vouched Roger; Roger failed and the outcome was unknown. The fact that there is no mention of Warmund in DB may suggest that he had lost his case and Roger had possession of the land, or the DB scribe may not have seen the *Terrae Occupatae* entry (there is no mention of the added land in the main Exon. entry).

22,20 ASH (PRIORS). See 6,19 and note. The marginal cross indicates alienated church land; see 5,43 note above.
THE VILLAGERS. No number is given in Exon. either.

22,23 ROGER BUSHELL. In DB *buissel,* in Exon. *bissellus;* OEB 373-4.

22,24;26 AETHELFRITH. *Ailuert, Aeluert* in DB; *Aelueru', Aeluer'* in Exon.

22,25 TOVI. The Sheriff; see 1,28 note above.

22,27 WILLIAM GERALD. *Wilelmus geral;* OEB 219.
PERCHES. A measure of length, usually reckoned as 5½ yards, though a 20 foot perch was in use for measuring woodland until last century. See Ellis i 158.

23,1 WALTER GIFFARD. Created Earl of Buckingham in 1100/1101.

24,2 THIS ENTRY is written in a slightly smaller hand at the foot of col. 95 a, extending 4 letters' space into the left and right margins. There is no sign to show its correct position in the chapter, but there is a gap of about 2 lines after 24,1, not shown by Farley. In Exon. this entry succeeds the one for Worle (24,1): they are adjacent villages now in Weston super Mare.

24,3	RAINWARD. In DB the forms of this name are *Reneuuald'* (24,3-4; 23-24); *Reneuuarus* and *Reneuu'* (24,16). In Exon. the forms are *Renewalus* (for 24, 3-4; 16); *Regval* (in the *Terrae Occupatae* for 24,16, the *v* probably being a mistake for *n*); *Reineuualus* (for 24,33); *Reineuual'* (for 24,24). The variation of form is the result of Norman French *l/r* interchange and the confusion of the OE personal-name themes *-ward, -wald* (see PNDB § 60); cf. Alfwold in the Exon. Notes to 19,15. See also Exon. Notes for 24,27.
24,4	W(ALSCIN). See L 24 note above.
24,5	EDWARD THE BRETON (?). Exon. *Edwardus brit*;'the Breton' or, less likely, 'the Briton'; see OEB 130.
24,8	MELCOMBE. See 46,5.
24,17	WALTER. Probably Walter *de badentona* (Bainton; OEB 37) from the Tax Return for Bruton Hundred, although his lordship holding is 7 hides 3½ virgates there.
24,21	UNDERWOOD, 100 ACRES. In the MS, small *a* in *ac'*; Farley misprints a capital.
24,25	ALFWARD GLEBARD. Exon. *Eluuardus Glebard;* see OEB 220.
24,27	MEADOW ... PASTURE ... ACRES. Accusative after 'he has'.
24,30	VILLAGER. In an unusual place; it is interesting that in Exon. the villager is separated from the smallholders and cottagers (see Exon. Notes 5,21), and may have been overlooked at first by the DB scribe (assuming that he copied from Exon.).
25	IN THE MS and Farley *xxi* (not *xxv*, as VCH p. 507 n.5 seems to believe); see Introduction to these notes p. 293.
25,1	WILLIAM OF MOHUN. Sheriff of Somerset. See L 25 note above.
25,2	DUNSTER. The seat of William of Mohun's barony; he founded the Priory there c. 1095.
25,5	ROBERT. Possibly the Robert son of Gilbert who had not paid tax in 1084 on 2 hides he held from William of Mohun in South Petherton Hundred (see the Tax Return for that Hundred).
25,6	GUARD AND AELMER HELD IT [BEFORE 1066]. Farley omits *teneb'* after *Almar,* in error. *TRR* in the MS and Farley in error for *TRE.*
25,7;8	THE MARGINAL CROSSES indicate alienated church land; see 5,43 note above.
25,8	ALFGEAT, A WOMAN. *Aluiet* in DB and Exon. See PNDB 173-4.
25,20	IT LIES IN THE PASTURE. This may mean that the ploughland was situated in the middle of the pasture (cf. 'woodland, pasture in places', DB Rutland R 5 etc.), or that though there was sufficient land for ½ plough to till, it was not actually ploughed as it was pastureland. VCH p.503 has 'but it has been laid down to grass'. Exon has *hanc terram potest arare dimidia carruca & haec iacet in pastura;* the *haec* could refer to the plough or the land.
25,24	THE VALUE WAS (IS). In the MS *valuit,* most probably a mistake for the present *valet,* as Exon. gives both values - the 1086 one being 15s.
25,27	RANULF HOLDS. Probably *de W.,* 'from William', omitted in error; it is in Exon. Also occurs in 19,47.
25,29	WILLIAM HIMSELF HOLDS. Repeated at the beginning of 25,29-32 and 25,49-52.
25,33	4 VIRGATES. The scribe wrote *iii virg'* originally, but added another *i* to make *iiii virg'* and interlined *hid'* to make the correction clear. The confusion may have been caused by the King's holding of a virgate. Exon. has '4 virgates', probably also corrected from '3 virgates'.
25,36	DODMAN(?). See Exon. Notes to 25,36.
25,42	SMALLHOLDER HAS IT. Grammatically *hanc* could refer to the land or the ½ plough, but most probably refers to the latter, as DB does not normally give the villagers' land holding. But see Exon. Notes to 25,42. WOODLAND, 7 ACRES. Accusative after '1 smallholder has', probably in error, as in Exon. Brictric has the woodland, as is usual in both DB and Exon.
25,44	ULF HELD IT (...) FOR 1 HIDE. *Ulf tenebat pro i hida;* probably *TRE 7 geldabat* omitted in error after *tenebat,* making the translation 'Ulf held it before 1066 and it paid tax for 1 hide', the usual formula and the one Exon. has here.
25,49	WILLIAM HIMSELF HOLDS. See 25,29 note above.
25,55	3 HIDES ... ROGER OF COURSEULLES. See Witham (Friary), 21,90. '3 hides' is probably a scribal error for '2 hides'; see Exon. Notes for this entry.
26,1	WILLIAM OF EU. Eu in the département of Seine-Maritime, France. He was married to the sister of Earl Hugh (see ch.18). Executed for treason against William II in 1096.
26,3	RALPH BLEWITT. Exon. *Radulfus blouuet* here; *bloet* for 26,5; OEB 294.
26,5	HUGH MALTRAVERS. Exon. *Hugo maltravers;* see OEB 351.
26,6	HUGH. Probably Hugh Maltravers because his land in Yeovil later became Henford Matravers; see Places Notes. PLOTS OF LAND. *Mansiones.* The Exon. words *mansure terrae* here suggest that these are probably not 'dwellings' (as, for example, in DB Wilts. M 1,' 'In Malmesbury ... the King has 26 occupied dwellings'), but pieces of land suitable for dwellings to be built on them.

Mansiones may include both land and a dwelling on it, but see DB Berks. B2 where a distinction seems to be made between *hagae*, 'sites', and *mansiones*, the 'dwellings' on them. See also Ellis i 244-5 n.2 and Exon. Notes to 40,1.

26,7   ALSTAN BOSCOMBE. 'Of Boscombe' *(deboscoina, deboscoma)* in Exon. and in DB Herts., Glos., and Beds. In Wilts. 71 c,d he occurs once as Alstan Boscombe (32,2) and once as Alstan of Boscombe (32,14). Undoubtedly the same person, he was a frequent sub-tenant of William of Eu and 'a thane of King Edward's', (see DB Herts. 28,1 note).

27,1   WILLIAM OF FALAISE. Falaise in the département of Calvados, France. He was married to the daughter of Serlo of Burcy (see 27,3 and Exon. Notes).
4½ HIDES. In the MS *iiii hid'* 7 7 *dih* in error.

27,3   EVERWACER. In DB the forms of this OG name are *Euroac* (27,3) and *Euuacre* (37,2-4; 6;10) and in Exon. *Euroacus* (for 27,3. 37,2), *Euroacro* (for 37,10), *Eueruuacrer* (for 37,3) *Eueruuacher* (for 37,4) and *Aluuacre* (for 37,6). *Aluuacre* is probably a scribal error; see Exon. Notes to 24,28.
[OF] LAND. In the MS and Farley *tra (terra)*, a mistake for the normal *tre (terrae)*, genitiv
IN LORDSHIP. In the MS there is a gap of about 15 letters for the lordship details to be filled in when available. The scribe may have been waiting for the lordship ploughs, not given in Exon.

28,1   THEY PAID TAX. The two manors.
28,2   IT PAID TAX. In the MS 7 7 *geldb'* in error.
29,1   RALPH OF MORTIMER. Exon. *Radulfus de mortuomari;* Mortemer in the département of Seine-Maritime, France; OEB 101-2. He was the son of Roger of Mortimer.
RICHARD OF BARRE. Exon. *Ricardus de barra;* Barre-en-Ouche in the département of Eure, France; see OEB 70.
THAT IS 70(s). In the MS *h e̅ lxx* is written in much paler ink., probably later.

30,1   RALPH OF POMEROY. *Radulfus de Pomeria/Pomaria* in Exon.; see OEB 107.
30,2   THIS MANOR PAID. *redd';* see note 1,24 above.
31,1   RALPH OF REUILLY. Exon. *Radulfus de roileio;* Reuilly in the département of Eure, France; OEB 111.
31,4   RALPH ALSO. The *Idem R.* implies Ralph of Reuilly, though Exon. has only *Raulf'* with no byname.
31,5   ROBERT ... 1 VIRGATE. He had not paid his tax in 1084; see the Tax Return for Williton Hundred.
32   RALPH OF LIMESY. Limésy in the département of Seine-Maritime, France.
32,1   WALTER BOWMAN. Exon. *Walterus harbalistarius,* 'crossbowman'; OEB 234-5.
32,2   RALPH HIMSELF HOLDS. Repeated at the beginning of 32,2-8.
32,2-3 QUEEN EDITH. *Edeua regina,* but in Exon. *Eddid(a) regina;* see 1,20 note above.
32,4   THIS MANOR PAID. See 1,24 note above.
32,5   THE MARGINAL CROSS is omitted by Farley in error and indicates alienated church land; see 5,43 note above.
THE CHURCH WAS IN POSSESSION. i.e. Athelney Church.
33,2   ROBERT HOLDS ... In the MS there is a gap of about 10 letters, and a similar sized one in the Exon.MS. See Places Notes.
100 CHEESES AND 10 BACON-PIGS. Cf. DB Wilts. ch.24p where 100 cheeses and 32 bacon-pigs are among the renders Edward the Sheriff receives from his Shire.
35,1   ALFRED OF 'SPAIN'. Epaignes in the département of Eure, France; OEB 92. The Latin *Hispania* is a kind of word play. He held land in Dorset, Devon, Somerset, Wiltshire, Gloucestershire and Herefordshire.
WALTER. Probably Walter of 'Spain' *(de ispania)* from the Tax Return for North Petherton Hundred; the King had no tax on ½ virgate he held.
ALFWY ... 1066. Or possibly 'The reeve leased it to Alfwy' (so VCH p. 426). The case of *Aluui* is not made clear in either DB or Exon. The 'it' refers in fact to only 1 virgate (see Exon. Notes here), but DB implies all 1½ virgates were leased. Alfwy was Alfred of 'Spain's' predecessor in a great many of his holdings. According to Eyton i 65 Alfwy the reeve was the same as Alfwy son of Banna (this is supported by the last lines of 35,12; 14).
LEASED. The MS has *prestit* with *li* interlined and a hair line to show it belongs between the *i* and *t*, making *praestitit;* Farley omits the hair line.
35,3   RICHARD OF MERRI. Exon.*Ricardus demeri;* Merri in the département of Orne, France; see OEB 98.
35,4   RANULF. Probably Ranulf of Stringston because in the Tax Return for Williton Hundred *Rannulfus de Strangestona* pays no tax on 1 virgate; see Places Notes.
35,8   HUGH. Probably Hugh of 'Spain' *(de hispania)* from the Tax Return for Cannington Hundred.

35,9   HUGH. Probably Hugh of Teversham (*de teuera;* OEB 52) from the Tax Return for Cannington Hundred.

35,10   MONKSILVER. See 1,6 for a customary due added to Williton from this manor.

35,12   LORDSHIP ...WHOLE OF THAT LAND ... VILLAGERS ...½ VIRGATE. An error on the part of the Exon. scribe or confusion in the original returns probably accounts for the villagers' having ½ virgate when all the land is said to be in lordship.

35,13   ALFOXTON AND DYCHE. Described in Exon. as one manor.

35,16   LAND FOR ... In the MS there is a gap of about 8 letters. Exon. does not state how many ploughs could till the land, either.
4 SMALLHOLDERS. In the MS there is a gap after this of about 9 letters, probably intended for the villagers' ploughs; Exon. does not give any.

35,19   ANSGER FOWER. Exon. *Ansgerus focarius,* 'the hearth-keeper'; OEB 251.

35,24   OAKLEY. 2 hides there; see Exon. Notes to 1,27.
ALFWY (? ALWIN) SON OF BANNA. See Exon. Notes for this entry.

36,4   TAX FOR 1 HIDE. In the MS *hid'* written above *car'* ('plough') which is underlined for deletion.

36,6   HE HELD. Alwin (Exon).

36,7   ALFWOLD THE BALD. Exon. *Aluualdus caluus;* OEB 298.
BERNARD PANCEVOLT. Exon. *bernardus panceuuoldus* here and *panceuuolt* for 36,13; 'paunch-face' (OEB 324-5); places with the addition 'Pauncefoot' are named from his descendants.
RALPH TRENCHARD. Exon. *Radulfus trencart* (main entry), *trenchardus (Terrae Occupatae);* OEB 381.

36,12   NORMAN HOLDS ... FROM THURSTAN. *Norman teñ de T.* in the MS, the *T.* being written, possibly later, over an erasure of a word of about 3 letters; Farley omits the *T.* in error.
WHEN THE COUNT ... Probably an error for 'when Thurstan ...'

37   SERLO OF BURCY. Burcy in the département of Calvados, France.

37,1   HE HAS 2 PLOUGHS THERE. Exon. (Lordship and Villagers Table) shows that both these ploughs are not in lordship, as is usually meant by this phrase in DB, but that only one of them is.
WITH 2 VILLAGERS. In the MS *cum ii vill'o* was originally *cum i vill'o,* but when the scribe changed it to *ii* he omitted to change the *vill'o* to the plural *vill'is.*

37,5   EDMER ATOR. DB *Almar,* Exon. *Almarus atter;* also 37,12 DB *Elmar,* Exon. *A(i)lmarus at(t)er;* whereas at 8,31. 19,44;46. 47,10 DB *Edmer, -mar* matches Exon. *Edmerator-.* *Edmarator-.* The mistake *(A(i)lmar, Elmar,* for the name *Edmer, -mar)* also occurs at 21,63 (DB *Edmar,* Exon. *Elmarus* corrected to *e^dmarus*) and in the Exon. text for Devon *(Almerator-, Elmerator-).* It is likely that these are scribal errors : in the carolingian minuscule a badly made *ed-* might well look like *al-* (with parallel *el-, ail-,* the acceptable spelling for protothemes in *Æl-, Æpel-, Ægel-* and corresponding *El-, Epel-, Egel-),* hence the Exon. correction at 21,63 here. Certainly, OEB 341, PNDB 232 and VCH for Somerset, Devon and Herts. all agree that there is only one person, Edmer Ator. Full discussion of this surname in OEB 341. Cf. DB Middlesex 8,6 note.
1 SMALLHOLDER. In the MS there is a gap of about 5 letters after this, probably intended for the villagers' ploughs; Exon. does not give any.

37,7   ST. EDWARD'S CHURCH. At Shaftesbury.
IT PAID TAX. *geld';* see 1,24 note above. Exon. has *redd'it (reddidit).*

37,8   SERLO HIMSELF HOLDS. Repeated at the beginning of 37,8-11.
LAMBERT. Perhaps Lambert *de uuatileia* from the Tax Return for Bruton Hundred; *uuatileia* could be Wheathill, adjacent to Lovington, or, as OEB 52, Whatley near Frome. He did not have to pay tax on 1 hide *teñ* (Ellis *teñi) fegadrorum,* (see VCH p. 535 n.3).

37,9   THE MARGINAL CROSS is omitted by Farley in error and denotes land taken from Glastonbury Church; see 5,43 note above.
[VALUE] 40s; NOW 40s. In the MS *valet* possibly omitted in error, although there are a number of cases in DB where it is similarly omitted (e.g. 37,6-10). The present value is probably a mistake for '30s', (as in Exon.), as normally DB Somerset has 'Value was and is ...' or 'Value formerly and now ...' or 'Value always ...' if the two amounts are the same.

38,1   VITALIS HELD. *Fitel* in DB, *Fitellus* in Exon; probably the same person as the 1086 holder. See PNDB 405-6.

39,1   ALNOTH THE CONSTABLE. *Alnod* in DB, *Alnodus Stalro* in Exon. The same person as Ednoth the Constable, father of Harding (47,3-8), and probably as Ednoth the Steward *(dapifer).* See VCH p. 417 f. and Freeman iv p. 755ff.

40,1	EDWARD OF SALISBURY. Sheriff of Wiltshire.
41	ARNULF OF HESDIN. Hesdin in the département of Pas-de-Calais, France.
42,2-3	WALTER. Probably Walter of Maine *(cenomannensis;* OEB 133) from the Tax Return for Chewton Hundred.
42,3	HE ALSO. Walter, as in Exon.
43,1	GODBOLD. He holds some 14 manors in DB Devon (ch.48) and is styled *arbalestarius, archibalistarius* ('Bowman', 'Crossbowman') in the Exon. for Devon.
44,1	MATTHEW OF MORTAGNE. Mortagne in the département of Manche, France.
44,3	WULFWARD TUMBI. Exon. *Wluuardus Tŭbi;* OEB 226.
45,1	BRICTRIC. Brictric son of Algar, most of whose lands passed to Queen Matilda (see DB Cornwall 1,13 note). Humphrey was her chamberlain and she bestowed various manors on him (see DB Glos. 69,7 col. 170a).
45,4	HUMPHREY. Almost certainly Humphrey the Chamberlain, although he is plain *Hunfridus* in Exon. (but cf. plain *Hunfridus* in Exon. 466 b 4, DB 45,5, where the *Terrae Occupatae* entry, 521 b 4, gives his byname).
	AELFRIC. *Albric'* in Exon; see PNDB 176-180.
45,6	GUNFRID. *Gonuerd* in DB and Exon; ON *Gunnfrø̸ dr;* PNDB 277.
45,9-11	HUGOLIN THE INTERPRETER. See 1,31 note above.
45,14	RICHARD ... 1 HIDE. See 5,54 note above.
45,15	AZELIN. *Schelin* in DB; *Eschelin, Escelin* in Exon. See Forssner 38; Förstemann 221.
45,18	ANSGER OF MONTACUTE. Apparently the same person as Ansger the Breton; VCH p. 412.
46	[LAND ...SERVANTS]. Omitted in the MS; the chapter number is entered, however.
46,1	ROBERT OF AUBERVILLE. Exon. *Otboruilla, Odburuilla; Otburgi uilla* (for 1,2). Probably Auberville-la-Renault in the département of Seine-Maritime, France; OEB 104.
46,2	THIS ENTRY is written in the left margin of the MS beside 46,1; 3-4, with no sign as to where it belongs in the chapter. In Exon. it appears between Earnshill (46,20) and Wellisford (46,4).
	ROBERT ... ALSO. *Hic Robertus; hic* in place of the usual *idem,* rather than meaning 'here', i.e. in Wearne. (46,1).
46,3	PROVED (TO BE). Or 'adjudged in'; the main Exon. entry has *est deraciocinata ad teglandam* and the *Terrae Occupatae* has *est deraciocinata esse tenglanda.*
46,5	½ HIDE. See 24,8.
46,6	THE DETAILS of this entry are a combination of the holdings of John the Usher and the priest; see Details Table.
46,7	FORMERLY 10s. The MS has *xv* with the *v* mostly erased, though visible as *xι; x sol'* is no doubt the intended value, as in Exon.
46,8	JOHN. Despite being styled plain John in Exon, he is almost certainly John the Usher, as this DB chapter does not separate the holdings of each of the King's servants and Exon. gives John's byname in entries before and after this one.
46,16	LAND FOR ... In the MS there is a gap of about 7 letters; Exon. omits all mention of the plough estimate.
46,17	ANSKETEL PARKER. Exon. *Anschetillus parcarius;* 'a park-keeper'; OEB 263.
	VALUE NOW 30(s). In the MS *sol'* omitted, probably through lack of space; also occurs in 47,10.
46,21	1 HIDE. See 19,59 note above.
46,24-25	2 HIDES. 1 HIDE AND 1 VIRGATE. See 6,1 note above.
47,1	BISHOP'S DEATH. In 1085; see 16,6 note above.
47,3	HARDING SON OF ALNOTH. Called Harding of Merriott in the Tax Return for Crewkerne Hundred after his main holding (47,6). He was the founder of the Somerset house of Merriott. Alnoth is Alnoth (Ednoth) the Constable; see 18,1 and 39,1 notes above.
47,3-5; 7-8	TOVI. The Sheriff; see 1,28 note above.
47,4-8	HARDING. HE ALSO. HARDING. Almost certainly Harding son of Alnoth, although Exon. has only *Hardinc* for 47,4; 7-8 and *Idem Hardinc* for 47, 5-6.
47,7	GODWIN. Probably Godwin of Chittlehampton *(de cicemetona;* OEB 39) from the Tax Return for Abdick Hundred; the King had no tax from ½ hide he held there.
	HIS VILLAGERS. Despite their land holding being given in Exon., no villagers are mentioned there for this entry, probably in error.
47,10	SIWARD FALCONER. Exon. *Siuuardus accipitrarius;* OEB 234.
	EDMER ATOR. In the MS there is a gap of about 4 letters after *Edmar,* due to an erasure. Also occurs in 8,31.

40(s). See 46,17 note above.

47,11   SIWARD GUNTRAM. Exon. *Seuuardus hundrannus;* ME *Gundran*<OG *Gundram, Guntran* (Forssner 134). For initial *H* for *G* see PNDB § 128 on *ch* for *g*. VCH p.523 has 'the Hundred-man', hardly supportable by this material.

47,12   DODA. Probably Doda *de Cori* (one of the Curry's) from the Tax Return for Williton· Hundred.

47,15   IT ANSWERED FOR. The only instance of this formula in Somerset, though it is common in other DB counties. Exon. also has the formula, but for no other Somerset manor, which suggests direct copying by the Exchequer scribe (as do the numerous other instances of unusual words, phrasing etc. in the two books, e.g. see 5,66 and 24,30 notes above).

47,18   ALFRED. Possibly Alfred *de Wica* (OE *wic,* dative sing. *wice,* whence place names in *wich, wick, wike, week* etc.) of the Tax Return for Bath Hundred, though his lordship holding there is given as 1 hide ½ virgate.

47,23   BRICTWARD. Probably Brictward the priest from the Tax Return for Frome Hundred; his lordship holding is given as 5 hides there, as here.

EBe 2   GEOFFREY OF TRELLY. *de Tralgi;* probably Trelly in the département of Manche, France; OEB 116.

Addendum

2,6   HUGH *DE VILLANA.* Possibly 'of Velaine' or 'Villaines'. Of the several places of this name, derived from Lat. *villana,* from *villa,* 'farm', Villaines sous Lucé, département of Sarthe, or Villaines-la-Juhel, département of Mayenne, seem to be the most likely. See Dauzat, *Dictionnaire des noms de lieux de France,* Larousse, 1963, p. 703 s.v. Velaine.

TAX RETURNS

The 1084 Tax Returns are found in the following order in Exon:

Taunton and Pitminster Hundreds	75 a 1	Williton Hundred	79 b 2
Milverton Hundred	75 a 2	Winsford Hundred	80 a 1
Whitstone Hundred	75 a 3	Cannington Hundred	80 a 2
Keynsham Hundred	75 b 1	Milborne Port Hundred	80 a 3
Portbury Hundred	75 b 2	North Petherton Hundred	80 b 1
Bath Hundred	76 a 1	Chew Hundred	81 a 1
Cheddar Hundred	76 a 2	Andersfield Hundred	81 a 2
Cutcombe and Minehead Hundreds	76 b 1	South Petherton Hundred	81 a 3
Hartcliffe Hundred	76 b 2	Abdick Hundred	81 b 1
Bedminster Hundred	76 b 3	Bruton Hundred	81 b 2
Carhampton Hundred	76 b 4	Loxley Hundred	82 a 1
Winterstoke Hundred	77 a 1	Ringoldsway Hundred	82 b 1
Brompton Ralph Hundred	77 b 1	Manor of High Ham	82 b 2
Bempstone Hundred	77 b 2	West Monkton Hundred	82 b 3
Huntspill Hundred	78 a 1	Bulstone Hundred	526 b 1
Chewton Hundred	78 a 2	Manor of Thorn Falcon	526 b 2
Congresbury Hundred	78 a 3	Manor of Thurlbear	526 b 3
Land of Bishop Giso	78 b 1	Tax paid by Mauger of Carteret	526 b 4
Thurlbear Hundred	78 b 2	Tax total for Somerset	526 b 5
Yeovil Hundred	79 a 1	Frome Hundred	527 a 1
Crewkerne Hundred	79 b 1		

There is a translation and analysis of the Tax Returns in VCH pp. 527-37.

EXON. EXTRA INFORMATION AND DISCREPANCIES WITH DB

Information given in DB that is omitted in Exon. is mentioned in the notes below, but not information given in DB or corresponding Exon. entry that is omitted in the *Terrae Occupatae* entry. Additional information and discrepancies, however, are given for both Exon. entries.

Somerset has almost 200 entries in the *Terrae Occupatae*, filling folios 508b-525a. They fall into 2 main categories: 1) lands which were held in 1066 by 2 or more people and were combined in one manor in 1086; 2) lands added to or taken from a manor. Also included are manors, often held TRE by a church, whose transfer to another tenant, often lay, is questioned; and manors which have not paid their customary dues. For 1) the form of the entry in the *Terrae Occupatae* is usually: "A. has a manor called B. which a thane held jointly in 1066; x hides which 1-2 thane(s) held jointly in 106 (or "the lands of 1-2 thanes") have been added to it. C. holds from A. Value (of the added lands) £y when acquired £z." In the notes below the main part of this type of entry is given next to the manor name. The forms of the other types of *Terrae Occupatae* entry are self-evident and only additional information and discrepancies in them are given below.

There is a list of equivalent formulae for DB and Exon. in Ellis *DB3* xiii-xiv; see also the specimen a the front of this edition. Four formulae need more explanation.

(a) Exon. uses the word *pariter* a great deal when describing holdings; it has generally been translate 'in parage', this edition translates it as "jointly". Parage is a form of land tenure whereby the deceased's land is held jointly by his sons, or daughters. One son, or daughter, often the eldest, was usually responsible to the lord or King for the services due from the land, but the other heirs did no pay him, or her, homage. According to Vinogradoff p. 248 the phrase 'a thane held this land jointly' *(pariter)*, which occurs many times in the *Terrae Occupatae* and the main Exon. Domesday, meant either that the deceased had only one son, but tenure in parage would continue as the son would probably have more than one child, or that the heir held responsible for the whole holding was the only one mentioned. But see Finn *LE* p. 86-93. As can be seen from the notes below, Exon.'s *pariter* is regularly used where DB has *in paragio, libere, pro manerio, pro duobus maneriis* etc., as well as where DB does not distinguish the type of tenure. In many cases, especially in Devon, the abbreviation *par'* (for *pariter*) is written in the margin of DB, generally beside *libere* in an entry, where Exon. has *pariter* or *libere et pariter*. It may be that these phrases were included so that in the event of a succession being questioned, the type of 1066 tenure could be known; important information when so many lands were acquired unlawfully. In 46,2 land which had been held *libere* (DB), *pariter* (Exon.), in 1066, but had been subsequently added to one of the King's manors, was restored to its free status by 1086.

(b) In the 'Value' statement and also in the payments of mills etc. (e.g. 1,11), Exon. often has *reddit* for DB's *valet* or vice versa. To the scribes of Exon. there seems to have been no real difference between these two words. Although in 89 b 5 (DB 1,1) *reddunt* has been underlined for deletion an *valent* written above, and the reverse in 90 a 2 (1,1), yet in 467 a 1 (4,1) and 143 b 1 (5,33) *vel reddit* has been written above *valet*. (Ellis omits the underlining in the first two examples and misprints & *redd'* in the last one).

(c) Exon. regularly has *valet per annum* for DB's plain *valet*, and *valebat quando recep* for DB's *valebat (olim)*. Where DB has "Value always..." Exon. gives both the present value and the value when acquired.

(d) For DB's "mill without dues" *(molinus sine censu)* Exon. has "a mill which grinds his (lord's; or possibly "its") corn" *(molendinum qui molit annonam suam)*, implying that it did that instead of paying dues. (In DB Hants. the formula is "a mill which serves the hall/manor house", *aula*). In 22,13 the DB formula is "a mill which grinds for the hall".

Exon. uses the term *villani* generically in the statement "the villagers have x hides and y ploughs": often no villagers are mentioned in the holding, just smallholders and slaves. However, in 453 b 2 (DB 37,10), and on several other occasions in Somerset, Exon. has "the smallholders (have) 1 furlong where 2 smallholders are the only people in the village.

Exon. often omits nouns (as DB less often), as in "woodland, 2 furlongs in length and 1 in width" an "the King has 3 ploughs and the villagers 4", where "1 furlong" and "4 ploughs" are intended; where DB gives the expected noun no attention is drawn here to the omission in Exon. Likewise obvious mistakes made by the Exon. scribes are not mentioned.

Ellis' edition of Exon. is not as accurate as Farley's one of the Exchequer DB. Apart from his larger errors and omissions, there are numerous occasions when Ellis puts gaps where there are none in the MS and vice versa, omits underlining or puts it in wrongly, positions interlineations incorrectly, omits transposition signs etc. He is also inconsistent within entries, for example in 433 b 3 (DB 21,85) where he prints the erased, but visible, *i hid'* and last *x* in *xxx sol'*, but omits the similarly erased but visible *ii hidis* in the added lands' tax, printing the corrected *i hid'*. This edition can only mention the more important mistakes.

VCH Volume 1 translates the Exchequer DB text with additional information from the main Exon. entry (not the *Terrae Occupatae*) in inverted commas, and discrepancies in the footnotes; there are several omissions and mistakes in both additions and discrepancies, however.

The order of these notes follows the numerical order; that is, notes to Ch. 45 are given in one block rather than with those to Chs. 46 and 47 in the middle, as printed in the text.

Quotations are from, and references to, the Exon. folios given beside the translation, unless otherwise stated. When quoting from the text, the abbreviated forms of the Latin are extended only where there is no reasonable doubt.

1,1 34 BURGESSES. |So Exon. MS; Ellis misprints *xxiiii.*
WHO PAY 15s. "It pays 15s", referring to Langport.
TO THIS MANOR.. £7 15s. In Exon. this paragraph is separated from the rest of the Somerton entry by the Cheddar entry (DB 1,2); *b* is written in the margin next to the first line and corresponds with an *a* (omitted by Ellis) at the end of folio 89b after the paragraph on Deadmans Well.
3 LANDS WHICH THREE THANES.. HELD. "3 manors which three thanes held jointly"; so also 515 b 3 without "jointly".
AELFRIC. His 1 hide (see Details Table)is now held by Ogis. No present holder is given for Brictnoth's land.
SAEWIN. He still holds his ½ hide and pays his 30s "into the King's revenue".
£7 15s. "It (Somerton; or perhaps "they", the added manors) pays 30s a year into the King's revenue".. 515 b 3; an example of the *Terrae Occupatae* confusing the payment of one thane with the total payment of the added lands.
FROM THIS MANOR.. 10s. Also in 515 b 3.
1,2 OF THIS MANOR.. VALUE 15d. Also in 515 b 4.
GISO.. HELD.. WILLIAM.. ACCOUNTS. "William.. accounts.. but the Bishop held it from King Edward for a long time before King Edward's death". So also 515 b 4. See *Mon. Ang.* ii 287 (No. 6) for King Edward's grant to Giso.
1,3 NOR IS IT KNOWN.. "Because it is not known".
20 PIGMEN. "Who pay100s a year".
1,4 IT NOW PAYS.. REVENUE. "It now pays revenue into the said manor, namely 60s and 24 sheep". So also 508 b 2.
½ HIDE. "Which was (part) of the King's lordship revenue in 1066" .. 508 b 3.
CRICKET (ST. THOMAS). ".. a manor of the Count of Mortain's".
6 SHEEP WITH AS MANY LAMBS. "6 sheep with their lambs". So also in 265 a 1 and 509 b 4 (DB 19,1).
THURSTAN.. LAND. "But since Thurstan received the land from the Count this customary due has not been paid into the King's manor" .. 265 a 1. "Since the Count held this land, the King has not had the customary due from it; Thurstan holds from the Count".. 509 b 4.
1,5 IT HAS NEVER.. NOR.. THERE. "It is not known.. because it did not pay tax before 1066".
1,6 THEY HAVE NEVER PAID TAX. "They have never been hidated" follows this, before "nor is it known.. ".
£100 116s 16½d. "£100 116s 6½d".
½ HIDE.. ADDED.. TWO MANORS. "2 manors have been added which Saeric held jointly". So also 509 b 5.
½ HIDE.. ALWIN HELD. "Besides these 2 manors a third manor has been added which Alwin held jointly". So also 509 b 6.
FURTHER ½ HIDE.. "½ hide of land has been added to the above manor of Cannington and which is called.. it pays 7s into the King's revenue". This entry is written in the left margin of the Exon. MS and the gap of about 4 letters after "called" was no doubt for the later addition of the name. Ellis misprints *Cantoctonet* for the MS's *Cantoctonae*. Unusually this entry is not repeated in the *Terrae Occupatae*.
FROM ALFRED'S MANOR.. 1066. Also in 509 b 7.

1,7 IT HAS NEVER.. NOR.. THERE. "It is not known.. because it never..". This phrasing also occurs in 90 b 2 for 1,8 and in 91 a 4 for 1,10.
IT PAYS.. "It pays £21 2½d of silver..".
A PRIEST OF THIS MANOR. "A priest" only; so also 525 a 2.
LAND FOR 1 PLOUGH. So 90 b 1; "1 carucate of land" in 525 a 2. See General Notes to 1,8
OF THIS MANOR.. "From this manor have been taken away..". So also 525 a 2.

1,8 IT HAS NEVER.. NOR.. THERE. See 1,7 note above.
ST. JOHN.. HOLDS. "St. John.. has". Also in 198 a 3.
HELD SIMILARLY. "Held from King Edward in alms".
REINBALD IS A PRIEST THERE. Omitted; instead "Now Reinbald holds it; he held it before 1066".

1,9 ONE NIGHT'S REVENUE. ".. with their dependencies (apenditiis)".
9 ACRES. So in 91 a 1, but "20 acres" in 520 a 3. "in Redlynch" (Retlis, 91 a 1; Redlisc, 520 a 3).
FROM THE SAME MANOR.. REVENUE. Also in 520 a 4, written in the right margin of the FROM THIS MANOR.. 20s. Also in 523 a 2.
1 HIDE. ".. which lay there before 1066".

1,10 IT HAS NEVER.. NOR.. THERE. See 1,7 note above.
65 PLOUGHS. "65½ ploughs". Ellis misprints "55½ ploughs".
56 BURGESSES.. 60s. "56 burgesses and 1 market and between (them) the burgesses and market pay 60s a year into the King's revenue".
REINBALD.. 30s. "Of this manor the Church of St. John of Milborne (Port) has 1 hide which it held itself in alms from King Edward in 1066. Reinbald the priest holds it; he serves the church and has 1 plough there. Value 30s a year".

1,11-25 THESE ENTRIES occur in Exon. under the heading of "Lands of the King which Earl Godwin and his sons held in Somerset". "Sons", filii, although his daughter Gunhilda and wife Gytha were among the holders in 1066. At the top left of folio 107a (after the entry for Queen Camel, DB 1,22) appear the words mansiones de comitatu ("comital manors") written in a smaller, but contemporary, hand.

1,11 2 MILLS WHICH PAY... valaent per annum.
FROM THE KING. "2 ploughs can plough it" added after this.
OF THIS MANOR.. 40s. Also in 510 b 6.
1 HIDE IN PRESTON, WHICH.. "1 hide of land called Preston has been taken away, which..".
VALUE WAS. "Value when the Count received it", i.e. the Count of Mortain. According to VCH (p. 419 n. 10), however, Comes is apparently an error for vicecomes, referring to William of Mohun, the Sheriff; but the error, if there is one, appears also in the Terrae Occupatae.

1,12 TO THIS MANOR.. COUNT. Also in 510 b 8.
THIRTEEN THANES HELD THEM. ".. jointly"; so also 510 b 8.
MAUGER KEEPS IT BACK THROUGH THE COUNT. "Since Mauger acquired the land from the Count, this customary due has not been paid". So also 510 b 8 in different words.

1,17 TO THIS MANOR.. REVENUE. Also in 516 a 1.
THREE THANES HELD. ".. jointly"; so also 516 a 1.
SERVED THE REEVE. "Had to go into the service of the reeve", written in the left margin.

1,19 BISHOP.. LAND. "Of the above 20 hides Bishop Maurice holds 3 hides which are in (the lands of) this village's church". So also 515 b 5.
ANSGER.. 20s. Also in 515 b 5.

1,20 EASTHAMS. "1 manor called Easthams which Godwin, the King's reeve, held". See DB 19,33 for the other details of this manor, which are recorded here and in 514 b 3, as well as in 272 a 1

1,21 3 HIDES AND 3 VIRGATES. "3 hides of thaneland".
THEY COULD.. MANOR. "They could not be separated from the manor, nor can they".
SERLO OF BURCY AND GILBERT SON OF THOROLD. They each hold ½ hide and the values are 20s each; so also 517 a 3.

1,22 4 PLOUGHS. So Exon. MS; Ellis omits the number of ploughs, in error.

1,25 MILL.. 30d. "20d", written at the end of a line in the MS with no full-stop after, so xxx may have been intended.
HE COULD NOT .. MANOR. "But he could not be separated from the manor in 1066".

1,26-31 THESE ENTRIES occur in Exon. under the heading of "Land of Queen Edith in Somerset".

1,26 MILVERTON. Queen Edith held it " on the day on which she was alive and dead"; ipsa, instead of the usual ipse (= King Edward). This peculiarity does not occur again here.
IN LORDSHIP 1 PLOUGH. "The King has land for 1 plough, which is there, in lordship", this plough is in addition to the 16 ploughs in the estimate.
A SMALL WOOD. Nemusculi, the usual equivalent of DB's "underwood". Also occurs in 5,12; 17. According to DGSW p.177, however, silva modica ("a small wood") and silva minuta ("underwood") were interchangeable.

1,27   TO THIS MANOR..MARTOCK. "To this manor 4 hides have been added, 2 of which Alfwy (?Alwin) son of Banna held in 1066 and it is (*sic*) called Oakley; it pays 50s a year to the King's manor of Martock. Two thanes held the other 2 hides jointly in 1066, but they paid 40d in customary dues to Martock; now it pays 40s to the King's manor of Martock". Also in 516 b 1. *Aluuin' banesone; Ailuuin' banasunt;* see 35,24 note below and OEB 150 for this byname.
FROM THIS MANOR.. (? DURVILLE). "From this manor has been taken away 1 manor called Compton (? Durville) which lay in Martock in 1066.. 1 hide and 1 virgate there". Also in 516 b 3.
ALSO.. AS MUCH. Also in 516 b 3.

1,28   8 BURGESSES IN BATH. "7 burgesses in the Borough of Bath".
COUNT EUSTACE.. "Count Eustace has a manor called Belluton which Tovi held freely in 1066; it paid tax for 4 hides. 4 ploughs can plough them..".
IN STANTON. "In the manor called Stanton (Drew) which Wulfward White held freely in 1066. 10 ploughs can plough it".
BISHOP OF COUTANCES.. HAS ½ PLOUGH. "There is ½ plough".
WIFE.. WULFWARD.. "Of these 50 hides Wulward White's wife has a manor called Burnett which Wulfward held freely before 1066; it paid tax for 1 hide. 4 ploughs can plough it".
AELFRIC HOLDS 1 HIDE. "..1 hide of thaneland".
1 PLOUGH THERE. "This land can be ploughed with 1 plough. Aelfric has 1 plough."

1,29   ½ HIDE OF LAND. "3 ploughs can plough it" written after this.

1,31   THE SHIRE. *Vicecomitatus.*
OTHER MEN. "The King's barons".
PAY 60s THERE. "Pay 60s to this Borough".
THE MINT PAYS 100s. "The burgesses pay 100s from the mint".
£11. "£11 at 20 (pence) to the *ora*".
FROM THIS BOROUGH.. 2s. Also in 518 b 1.
OF BRUTON 20s. "Of Bruton 10s".

1,32-35   THESE ENTRIES occur in Exon. under the heading of "Land which was Wulfward White's in Somerset". He was a thane of Queen Edith's (see VCH p. 393;399 f.)

1,32   WULFWARD WHITE. For 1,32 *Uluuard' uuite*, underlined faintly but perhaps not for deletion, with *Alti* written above *Uluuard'*, presumably as a correction. *Alti* may be an error for *Alsi*, 'Alfsi', Wulfward White's son-in-law, or for the OD name *Auti* (see PNDB §61). In the value statement Wulfward is left uncorrected, however.

1,34   PITNEY. DB appears to condense two entries in Exon. which read: "Wulfward White had a manor called Pitney which he (held) himself in 1066; it paid tax for ½ hide. ½ plough can plough it. The King has it in his hand. Value 5s a year".. 116 a 4. And: "Humphrey holds a manor which he held from Wulfward White; ½ hide of land there. 1 plough can plough it. Humphrey has 1 plough; 1 cob, 12 cattle, 6 pigs, 45 sheep; 3 acres of woodland and 6 acres of meadow. Value 20s; value as much before" .. 116 a 5. Exon. does not actually state that Humphrey's manor is also in Pitney.

2,1   TAX FOR 54 HIDES AND 2½ VIRGATES. 54 hides only, in 517 a 1.
BESIDES.. LAND FOR 20 PLOUGHS. ".. 20 carucates of land". "20 carucates" is also the phrase used in the Tax Return for Taunton Hundred.
FROM THE MINT, 50s. Omitted.
PAYS £154 13d. "Pays to the Bishop £154 13d from the revenue".

2,3   THESE LANDS. *Lediart* and *Lega* (Lydeard St. Lawrence and Leigh) also included in this list.
NORTON.. HEATHFIELD. ".. have to go three times a year to the Bishop's pleas and pay St. Peter's pence in Taunton and the Hundred-pence (? *den' in hundreto)*". Ellis misprints *denarii sci petri* for the MS's *denariū (denarium)*. These lands are entered separately in Exon. and presumably these were the only dues they had to pay.

2,6-7   OF THE SAID 54½ HIDES.. "Of the.. thanes hold 17½ hides and ½ virgate from the Bishop, which 8 thanes held in 1066". In DB the total of the 9 holders in 1086 comes to 19½ hides ½ virgate. It would seem that Leofeva's holding is not included in the Exon. total, possibly because she was not a thane (but see 5,65. 19,72. 37,8. for instances of women being counted as thanes).

2,7   IN LORDSHIP 7 PLOUGHS. 7½ ploughs; see Details Table.
WOODLAND, 61 ACRES. 60 acres of woodland and 1 acre of underwood; see Details Table.

2,8   COUNT.. 1 HIDE. ".. and Alfred holds it from the Count". So also 517 a 1.
ALFRED OF 'SPAIN'. His holding is from the church's lordship.. 517 a 1.
JOHN THE USHER. He holds from the King.. 517 a 1.
WOODLAND, 20 ACRES. 15 acres; see Details Table.
THESE THREE LANDS.. 1066. ".. and they could not be separated from the church"; so also 517 a 1.

2,9   LYDEARD (ST. LAWRENCE) AND LEIGH. Described as two manors; so also 517 a 1.
FROM THE BISHOP WITH THE ASSENT OF KING WILLIAM. Omitted.
4 SLAVES. 7 slaves; see Details Table.

WOODLAND, 49 ACRES. 51 acres; see Details Table.

2,11   BLEADON. "Winchester Church held it in 1066."
IT WAS AND IS FOR THE MONKS' SUPPLIES. "It is for the monks' supplies", only.
8 SLAVES. " 7 slaves".
SAEWULF .. 1 HIDE. ".. Saswald *(Sawald')* held it in 1066; he could not be separated from the church."
1 PLOUGH THERE. "1½ ploughs in lordship".

2,12   60 SHEEP. *iii.xx* (3x20), in line with *iiii.xx* (= 80; cf. DB's *quattuor viginti;* it occurs in 113 b 1, DB 1,28). VCH translates as "23", however.
THE VALUE WAS.. £7. "Value when the Bishop acquired it, £6".

3,1   2 SLAVES. "1 slave", written in the right margin, rather cramped, so probably a mistake.
ANOTHER SEABOROUGH. "The manor of Seaborough"; "Another manor called Seaborough .. 513 a 5.
ALFHERE. *Aluer,* but *Alfred'* in 513 a 5.
THE HOLDERS. "The thanes who held them"; "2 thanes held these 2 manors".. 513 a 5.

4,1   THIS ENTRY, like 436 b 1-2 (33,1-2), is written in the formulae and script of the Exchequer DB, which suggests that officials from the *curia* may have been in Exeter; see R. Welldon Finn, EHR lxvi (1951) pp. 561-564 and V.H. Galbraith in EHR lxxxii pp. 89;91. The livestock and villagers' land are supplied from 467 a 1, where Samson's holding is repeated under "Lands of French Thanes in Somerset".

SAMSON. "Samson the Chaplain".. 467 a 1 only. Above the first line is written *de epō baiocen* in an uneven, but probably contemporary, hand. Ellis omits it.
ALFWARD.. AS ONE MANOR. "Alfward held jointly".. 467 a 1 and 523 a 1.
13s. "14s". So also 467 a 1 and 523 a 1.

5,1   24s. "23s", *iii* being written above *xx.*
TO THIS MANOR.. Also in 509 a 6, without details of holdings.
THREE THANES.. AS 3 MANORS. "Three thanes held jointly". So also 509 a 6.

5,2   CHAFFCOMBE. "Ralph holds these 4 manors as 1 manor from the Bishop", written at the end of this entry.
"3 manors have been added to it (Chaffcombe), which 3 thanes held jointly in 1066.. Value 40s a year; when acquired, as much".. 509 a 8.
RALPH RUFUS. *Rufus* is written above *Radulfus tenet,* but after, as usual, in 509 a 8.
TWO THANES HELD. ".. jointly", and instead of "as 2 manors" in the added manors.

5,3   'HISCOMBE'. "1 hide and 1 virgate have been added to it, which 3 thanes held jointly in 1066. Value 22s a year; value when the Bishop acquired them, 15s".. 510 b 7.
FOUR THANES HELD. "..jointly. Saeric held 1½ hides, Alwin ½ hide, Alwin ½ hide, Godric 1 virgate", written above and into right margin, probably later.

5,4   2s IN ADDITION. "As much pasture as pays 2s a year".

5,5   ALSO OF THIS LAND.. MUCH. Also in 510 b 2. The value does not occur in the main Exon. entry.

5,7   VILLAGERS.. 1 PLOUGH. In Exon. the plough is in lordship.

5,8   PASTURE, 550 ACRES. So Exon. MS; Ellis misprints *D. ag' ae L pascuę* for *D. ag' et L pascuę.*

5,9   (EAST) HARPTREE. ".. which a thane, Wulfwy, held jointly. 3 hides have been added to it; Alric held them jointly in 1066. Azelin holds these 2 manors from the Bishop as 1 manor. Value 24s a year; when *R.* acquired them, as much".. 515 a 4. *R.* probably an error for *eps* (the Bishop) or *A.* (Azelin); Roger Arundel was the holder in the previous entry in the *Terrae Occupatae.*
ALRIC AND WULFWY.. TWO MANORS. "2 thanes held jointly.. Alric held 3 hides and Wulfwy held 2 hides.. The Bishop holds these 2 lands as 1 manor."

5,10   HUTTON. ".. which a thane held jointly. 2½ hides of land have been added to it, which a thane held jointly in 1066. Azelin holds them (2½ hides) in 'Hutton itself; value 30s a year. The said thanes held this Hutton from Glastonbury Abbey in 1066".. 516 a 3.
TWO THANES.. AS TWO MANORS. "Two thanes held it jointly.. one held half, the other the other half. Now Azelin holds them as 1 manor".

5,11   ELBOROUGH. Also in 516 a 4, without details.

5,12   A SMALL WOOD. *Nemusculi,* see 1,26 note above.

5,15   ADDED 2 HIDES. "Added a manor called Timsbury.. William holds it from the Bishop.. The Bishop holds these 2 manors as 1 manor". So also 518 a 2.
SIBBI.. AS ONE MANOR. "Sibbi held jointly"; so also 518 a 2.

5,17   A SMALL WOOD. *Nemusculi,* see 1,26 note above.

5,18   TAX.. 5 HIDES. LAND.. 5 PLOUGHS. "2 hides" and "2 ploughs", but in both cases an attempt seems to have been made to make the *ii* into a *v*.

5 HIDES..ADDED."Added a manor called Farmborough"; so also 518 a 3. "The Bishop holds them (the 2 manors) as 1 manor".

AELFRIC.. AS ONE MANOR. "Aelfric held" only, but "Aelfric held jointly".. 518 a 3.

5,19 6 VILLAGERS. *7 uill' .i. virg ... Ibi hnt iiii uill' 7 x ag pti.* Either the interlined *ii* is a mis-placed correction of the villagers' holding, making 2 virgates, less 1 furlong, which would then add up with the lordship land to the amount taxed (so VCH p. 448 n. 2) but make a discrepancy in the number of villagers; or the meaning is "2 villagers (have) 1 virgate, less 1 furlong .. They (holders) have 4 villagers.." The separation of villagers into those who hold land and ploughs and those who presumably do not, is unusual in Exon. See 5,21 note below.

5,21 4 VILLAGERS, 4 SMALLHOLDERS. "Azelin.. has.. 3 villagers who have 2 ploughs; and 4 smallholders.." This separation of the villagers from the smallholders, cottagers etc. occurs in some 30 entries in Somerset Exon.

5,23 FOUR THANES HELD. ".. jointly.. Roger Whiting holds it as one manor". Unusually for a combined manor, there is no corresponding entry in the *Terrae Occupatae*.

5,26 LORDSHIP.. 1½ VIRGATES. *ii hid' 7 dim' 7 dim' virg'* with *7 i virg'* written above *7 dim' virg'*; possibly a later addition, as 1½ virgates do not add up with the other details to the 3 hides 1 virgate of tax, whereas ½ virgate does.

5,27 ALGAR HELD. "..jointly".

5,28 TIDWULF HELD. ".. jointly".

5,30 FULCRAN AND NIGEL. ".. have 2 hides"; *in dominio* perhaps omitted in error.

5,34 THREE THANES HELD. ".. jointly".

5,37 AELFRIC HELD. ".. jointly".. 518 b 4 only.

AELFRIC.. AS ONE MANOR. "The same Aelfric held jointly".. 518 b 4; "as one manor" omitted in main entry.

MILLS.. 2s. "Mills.. 10s".

5,40 2 PLOUGHS THERE. "He has 2 ploughs, between himself and his (villagers)", (*inter se et suos*).

A THANE HELD. ".. jointly". So also 518 b 5.

5,41 19 VILLAGERS. 17 villagers; see Details Table.

PASTURE. The 4 acres in Roger's holding are omitted; see Details Table.

TO THIS MANOR.. 25s. Also in 518 b 6.

AELFRIC HELD. ".. jointly". So also 518 b 6.

5,43 ALFWOLD. "Wulfwold the priest". So also 519 a 2, with "jointly".

WULFMER HELD. ".. jointly". "Another thane held jointly".. 519 a 2.

HE COULD GO WHERE HE WOULD. "He could go with his land to whichever lord he would".

WOODLAND. "1 furlong in both length and width".

PASTURE. "2 furlongs in both length and width".

WILLIAM HUSSEY. So 519 a 2; 145 b 2 has plain *Willelmus*.

5,44 A THANE HELD. ".. jointly".

5,45 THREE THANES HELD. ".. jointly".

5,46 A THANE HELD. ".. jointly".

5,47 RADSTOCK. ".. which a thane held. 1 hide and 3 virgates of land have been added to it, which 2 thanes held jointly in 1066.. Value 26s 9d a year. The Bishop holds these 3 thanelands as 1 manor".. 519 a 4.

ALFGEAT, ALWIN AND ALGAR. Named and described as "3 thanes" and they held "jointly". Alfgeat held 6 hides, Alwin held 1 hide and Algar held 3 virgates.

3 COTTAGERS. "4 cottagers", but it looks as though the *iii* was changed to *iiii* later.

MILL.. 13s. "Mill.. 12s"; *x*, then an erasure and *ii* written above; probably a scribal error.

5,48 HARDINGTON. ".. which a thane held. 2 hides of land have been added to it, which 2 thanes held jointly in 1066.. Value 10s a year; when the Bishop acquired them, as much. The Bishop holds these 3 manors as 1 manor".. 519 b 1.

THREE THANES HELD. ".. jointly".

HEMINGTON. Described as Baldwin's manor.

5,49 BABINGTON. ".. which a thane held jointly; it paid tax for 2½ hides. 2½ hides have been added to it, which a thane held jointly in 1066.. Value 30s a year; when the Bishop acquired them, as much".. 519 b 2.

TWO THANES HELD. ".. jointly".

2 SMALLHOLDERS. "3 cottagers" included after this.

5,50 'MIDDLECOTE' "The Bishop of Coutances has..'Middlecote' which he holds himself from the King.. It was thaneland of (Glastonbury) Church."

HELD FROM GLASTONBURY CHURCH. Omitted; also omitted in 519 b 3. The 2 thanes' holdings are not recorded separately in the *Terrae Occupatae*, as in 5,47-49; 52;54 etc., probably because the entry was included there not because it was a combined manor, but because Glastonbury may have questioned the transfer of the 5½ hides to the Bishop of Coutances. This also happens for 45,5.

5,52 ORCHARDLEIGH. ". which a thane held jointly. 2 manors have been added to it, which 2 thanes held jointly in 1066. Value 53s 4d a year; when the Bishop acquired them, as much" . 520 b 5.
THREE THANES HELD. ".. jointly".

5,53 3 HIDES..ADDED. ALFGEAT HELD. "Added a manor which Alfgeat held jointly"; so also 521 a 5.

5,54 RODE. "A village called Rode", instead of the usual "manor called..". "A village called Rode, which 3 thanes held jointly; it paid tax for 3 hides.. 6 hides of land have been added to them, which 4 thanes held jointly in 1066. Value £6 2s; when he acquired them, £5 2s".. 521 b 1.
SEVEN THANES HELD. ".. jointly".
LORDSHIP 7 PLOUGHS. 6½; see Details Table.
MILLS. Robert has ½ mill which pays 6s; Moses has the fourth part of a mill which pays 3s; Robert has the sixth part of a mill which pays 30d; Roger has 2 parts of 2 mills which pay 8s; Sheerwold has ½ mill which pays 7s 6d.
WOODLAND. The 12 acres of underwood *(nemusculi)* are included in DB with the other measurements of woodland.
VALUES. Then £7 13s; now £9 3s; see Details Table.

5,57 TWO THANES HELD. "9 thanes held jointly"; so also 521 b 2.
(IN LORDSHIP). *In dominio* probably omitted in error, as is often the case.

5,59 (STON) EASTON. ".. which a thane held jointly. 2½ hides of land have been added to it, whi˙ 2 thanes held jointly in 1066.. Value 33s 8d a year .".. 522 a 3.
THREE THANES HELD. "jointly.. Saewulf held 2 hides; Aelfric 2 hides; Wulfsi ½ hide".

5,61 EMBOROUGH. ".. which a thane held. 1 hide of land has been added to it, which Wulfric he˙ jointly in 1066.. Value 20s a year; when the Bishop acquired it, 6s 8d".. 522 a 6.
TWO THANES HELD. ".. jointly.. Alnoth held 2 hides and Wulfric 1 hide".
4 SMALLHOLDERS. "3 cottagers" included after them.

5,62 CAMELEY. ".. which Sheerwold held. 4½ hides have been added to it, which Ordwold held jointly in 1066. Value £4 10s a year; when the Bishop acquired them, £3.".. 522 b 1.
TWO THANES HELD. ".. jointly.. Sheerwold held 4½ hides and ½ virgate and Ordwold 4½ hides".

5,64 KINGSTON (SEYMOUR). ".. in which are 2 hides of land which Aelfric the priest held. 2½ hides of land have been added to it, which 3 thanes held jointly in 1066.. Value 34s a year; when the Bishop acquired them, as much".. 522 b 2.
FOUR THANES HELD. ".. jointly.. Aelfric the priest held 2 hides, Siward 1 hide, Saeric 1 hide, and Saewulf ½ hide.. William of Monceaux holds them as one manor".
BEFORE 1066.. 1 HIDE. "These 5½ hides did not pay tax except for 1 hide in 1066"; "5½ hides" probably in error for "4½ hides".

5,65 HALLATROW. ".. which a woman held. 3 hides and 3½ virgates have been added to it, which˙ 3 thanes held jointly in 1066. Value 23s; when the Bishop acquired them, 34s 6d".. 522 b 3. ˙ agree with the details of the 3 thanes' holdings given below, the added land should be 2 hides 3½ virgates; probably a scribal error.
FOUR THANES HELD. ".. jointly.. A woman held 2 hides; Sheerwold 1½ hides, Alfward ½ hide, and Forthred *(Fordret')* 3½ virgates".

5,66 ALFWOLD. "Alnoth" *(Ainod')*.

5,67 LEOFMER. "Ledmer" *(Letmer')*; probably a scribal error.

5,69 WEATHERGROVE. ".. which a thane held jointly. 1 hide of land has been added to it, which 2 other thanes held jointly in 1066.. Value 12s 6d; when the Bishop acquired them, 10s".. 522 b 4.
THREE THANES HELD. ".. jointly".

6,1 BISHOP OF WELLS. "Bishop Giso", and elsewhere.
FASTRAD, RICHARD, ERNEIS. 2 thanes held Fastrad's land, a thane held Richard's, and a thane held Erneis'; none of the thanes could be separated from the church.
17 VILLAGERS. 25 villagers; see Details Table. For Fastrad's 10 villagers Ellis misprints *x 7 vill'* for *x vill'*.
MANASSEH'S WIFE.. "Manasseh's wife holds 2 hides wrongfully; she does not hold from the Bishop".. 524 a 6.
BISHOP..2 HIDES. Alfward holds one, Edric the other.

6,4 MEADOW, 20 ACRES. "Meadow, 15 acres".

6,6   BISHOPRIC'S LORDSHIP.. BISHOP. "Church's lordship..church".
VALUE TO THE BISHOP. "It pays to the Bishop"; *reddit* is written above *valet*, possibly
to replace it, though *valet* is not underlined. See the introduction to these notes (p.310).

6,7   VALUE OF THE WHOLE £25. "Value for the Bishop's use £24 a year.. Value for (John the
Usher's) use 20s". *(ad opus episcopi/eius;* see General notes to 6,1).
TO THIS MANOR.. 30s. Also in 513 b 3.
AELFEVA HELD AS A MANOR. "Aelfeva held jointly"; so also 513 b 3.

6,8   WOODLAND.. "Woodland 1 league long and 2 furlongs wide".
VALUE OF THE WHOLE £13. "Total value for the Bishop's use £10, for the men-at-arms'
use £3."

6,9   24 VILLAGERS. "23 villagers".
25 VILLAGERS. 23 villagers; see Details Table. Serlo's 5 villagers are written above an erased,
but visible, *iii;* as there are several corrections in this entry a scribal error probably accounts for
the discrepancy.

6,10   A PRIEST AND 2 OTHER ENGLISHMEN HOLD. "3 Englishmen — 2 laymen and 1 priest —
hold".

6,13   VALUE TO THE BISHOP. "To the Bishop" omitted.
RICHARD.. 5 HIDES. ".. which a thane held in 1066; he could not be separated from the
Bishop". The same for Aelfric's 7 virgates.
ROGHARD 6 HIDES. ".. of the villagers' land". The same for Stephen's and Wulfric's holdings.
27 SMALLHOLDERS. 18 smallholders; see Details Table.
2 MILLS.. 10s. 2 mills.. 9s 4d; see Details Table.

6,14   VALUE TO THE BISHOP. "Value for the Bishop's use".
HILDEBERT 4 HIDES. After Hildebert's holding (see Details Table): "Of the 4 hides which
Hildebert holds, a woman, Aethelrun, had 1 hide jointly in 1066. With this hide, which Aethelrun held, lies a pasture called Wemberham.." In 518 a 1 "the Bishop has.. Yatton.. 1 hide of
land has been added to it, which a woman called Aethelrun held jointly in 1066. With this hide
lies a pasture.. Value of the hide and pasture 25s."
BENZELIN. "Benzelin.. holds 1 hide from the Bishop; it belongs to the church".

6,15   18 COTTAGERS. Not separated from the villagers and smallholders — the ploughs and land
were held by the 'villagers' as a class. Likewise for the smiths in 8,1; see also 21,87 note.

6,16   THEY HELD IT THEMSELVES. "(The Bishop) held it himself."

6,17   THEY HOLD. "The canons of St. Andrew's Church hold".
THEY HELD IT THEMSELVES. "(The Bishop) held it himself".
MILLS.. 10s. "Mills.. 10s 10d".

6,19   IT LAY. "It lies" *(iacet;* perhaps a mistake for *iacuit* or *iacebat).*
VALUE £3. So Exon. MS; Ellis misprints "£4".

7,1   THE CHURCH. "The Abbot has a manor called Bath, which is the head of the Abbey itself..".
"Abbot" for "Church" in all entries in this chapter.

7,7   6 HIDES.. LORDSHIP. "6 hides, less 1 virgate.."

7,11   6 SMALLHOLDERS. 9 smallholders; see Details Table.

7,15   THE WHOLE OF THIS LAND.. Abbot Saewold is given as the 1066 holder for 7,1;5-7;9;13.
Plain "Abbot" is given as the 1066 holder for 7,2-3; Abbot Wulfward is given as the 1066 holder
for 7,14-15.
COULD NOT BE SEPARATED. Mentioned for 7,4;8;12. In 186 a 3 (7,10) "This land cannot
be separated..".

8,1   SMITHS. See 6,15 note above.
'ANDERSEY'.. 2 HIDES. ".. which a thane held; he could not be separated from the church
in 1066".
1 PLOUGH THERE. "Godwin has 1 plough"; *in dominio* probably omitted in error.

8,2   THE CHURCH HOLDS. "The Abbot (of Glastonbury) has", as elsewhere for "church" in this
chapter.
WINSCOMBE. ".. which Glastonbury Church held in 1066".
5 PLOUGHS THERE. Roger has 3, Ralph 1, and Pipe 1. Also, 3 ploughs could plough Roger's
holding and 2 ploughs Pipe's one.
VALUE.. TO THE ABBOT. "Value for the Abbot's use..".
VALUE.. 55s. Roger 30s, Ralph 15s, Pipe 10s.
BISHOP.. 1 HIDE. ".. which Herlwin holds from him"; also in 515 b 2.

8,3   PODIMORE. ".. which the Abbot held in 1066".

8,5   SHAPWICK.".. which Abbot Alnoth held in 1066".
12 VILLAGERS' PLOUGHS THERE. "The villagers (have) 12 ploughs on that land which has
not paid tax".

FOURTEEN THANES. 5 thanes held the land in Sutton (Mallet), 3 thanes held in Edington, thanes in Chilton (Polden), and 4 thanes in Catcott.

MEADOW, 100 ACRES, LESS 1. 119 acres; see Details Table.

WOOLAVINGTON.".. which Alfwy son of Banna *(Alwi bannesona)* held in 1066".

13 HORSES. *caballos* ("riding horsés") with the more usual *roncinos* ("cobs") glossed above

WARMUND.. ½ HIDE. ".. ½ hide of thaneland".

VALUE.. TO THE ABBOT £12. "To the Abbot" omitted. "Value when Abbot Thurstan acquired it, £7".

(VALUE) TO ROGER £19. The details total £15 present value and £19 when acquired. An example of DB putting the past value in Exon. as the present; also occurs in 26,4 and 45,12.

(VALUE) TO ALFRED."Value £7; when he acquired it, as much".

8,6	MIDDLEZOY. ".. which Abbot Alnoth held in 1066".
8,7	VALUE.. £6. So Exon. MS; Ellis has "£5" in error, probably because the *v* is exceptionally large compared to the *i* after it.
8,8	OSWALD. *Osward';* see PNDB §60;68 on *l/r* interchange.
8,11	WALTON. ".. which Abbot Alnoth held in 1066".

WOODLAND.. ".. 4 furlongs wide".

THE HOLDERS. 2 monks held Roger's land, 2 thanes held Walter's land in Ashcott, and Algar held Walter's land in Pedwell. Only the 2 thanes are said not to have been able to be separated from the church; this statement is omitted for the monks and Algar.

VALUE BETWEEN THEM £8. £10; see Details table.

8,12	TAX.. 3 VIRGATES. So Exon. MS; Ellis interlines *i* above *virgis,* making it seem like a correction of *iii virgis* to *iiii virgis,* but the *i* is in fact only a faint mark in the MS with an oblique line through it.
8,15	GREINTON. "Gerard holds a manor called Greinton from the same manor" (i.e. Walton).
8,16	OVERLEIGH. ".. which Abbot Alnoth held in 1066".

THANELAND. ".. and a thane held it in 1066".

8,17	HAM. ".. which Abbot Alnoth held in 1066".

ROBERT. His 1 hide 1 virgate are described as "thaneland".

LEOFRIC, ALFWOLD AND AELMER. Leofric held Robert's land, Alfwold held Gerard's, and Aelmer held Serlo's.

14 SMALLHOLDERS. 15 smallholders; see Details Table.

8,18	BUTLEIGH. ".. which Abbot Alnoth held in 1066".

VALUE TO THE ABBOT. "To the Abbot" omitted.

TWO THANES. 3 thanes held Thurstan's land, and Sheerwold held Roger's land.

VALUE.. £7. £7 present value, but £6 10s when acquired; see Details Table.

ALSTAN. "Alfward holds ½ hide which Alstan held in 1066".

8,19	THIS ENTRY is written in the left margin of 165b and the first 2 letters of each line are missing, the edge of the parchment probably having been torn or cut off at some stage. This also occurs in 434 b 3 (21,92). The whole entry also appears in 522 a 5.

MANOR. That is, of Butleigh, "which always was (part) of the church".. 522 a 5 only.

VALUE 20s. So 165 b 1, but "Value 30s; when he acquired it, as much".. 522 a 5.

8,20	PILTON. "..which Abbot Alnoth held in 1066".

WOODLAND. ".. 1½ leagues long".

ROGER. "Roger of Courseulles" and 'The same Roger" for both his 'manors' of Shepton (Mallet) and Croscombe.

THE HOLDERS. Aelmer held Edred's and Serlo's lands and Sheerwold held Ralph's. Exon. does not mention that Sheerwold could not be separated from the church.

WOODLAND, 4 ACRES. "Woodland, 2 acres; and underwood, 2 acres"; see Details Table.

VALUE.. £7 10s. £8 10s; see Details Table and Addenda p. 332.

8,21	PENNARD. ".. which Abbot Alnoth held in 1066".

1 HIDE OF THIS MANOR'S LAND. "1 hide of thaneland".

8,22	BALTONSBOROUGH. ".. which Alnoth held in 1066"; probably Abbot Alnoth, but possibly a layman as in DB 8,9.
8,23	DOULTING. ".. which Abbot Alnoth held in 1066".

VALUE TO THE ABBOT. "To the Abbot" omitted ; also omitted in the value paragraphs for 8,24-25.

CHARLTON.. ELSEWHERE. Wulfmer held Charlton in 1066 and Alfward held the other land; neither could be separated from the church.

8,24	BATCOMBE. ".. which Abbot Alnoth held in 1066".

THE OTHER FIVE WERE THANELAND. "The others were (part) of the thaneland".

8,25	MELLS. ".. which Abbot Alnoth held in 1066"; so also 520 a 1.

BISHOP OF COUTANCES.. AS MUCH. Also in 520 a 1. The value occurs only here, not in the main Exon. entry; it disagrees with the much higher value given in 5,50 (DB and Exon.), which repeats this part of the entry.

8,26 WHATLEY. "It paid tax for 5 hides"; that is, Walter's 4 hides and John's 1 hide.
1 PLOUGH.. THERE. The villagers have it.

8,27 WRINGTON. ".. which the Abbey itself held in 1066".
VALUE TO THE ABBOT. "Value for the Abbot's use".
SAEWULF.. HELD. ".. he could not be separated from the Abbot".

8,28 (WEST) MONKTON. ".. which Abbot Alnoth held in 1066.. Bishop Walkelin holds it now from the Abbot; it was (part) of the Abbot's lordship; of these (15 hides) Bishop Walkelin has 5 hides 1 virgate in lordship.." The statements "Bishop.. Abbot's lordship" are interlined, probably later.
THE HOLDERS. 3 thanes held Roger's land; none is mentioned for Serlo's land.
VALUE. "For Roger's use.. for Serlo's use..".

8,29 MARKSBURY. ".. which Abbot Alnoth held in 1066".

8,30 DITCHEAT. ".. which Abbot Alnoth held in 1066"; so also 519 a 3.
VALUE TO THE ABBOT. "Value for the Abbot's use".
LAMYATT. In 519 a 3 Lamyatt is described as having been taken away from Ditcheat and as paying tax for 5½ hides. The other details agree with those in 170 a 2.
THE HOLDERS. 2 thanes held Serlo's land, 2 thanes held Ralph's land and Spirtes the priest held Nigel's land.
12 SMALLHOLDERS. 13 smallholders; see Details Table.
WOODLAND.. 12 furlongs long and 1½ furlongs wide; see Details Table.
VALUE.. £11. "Value for Serlo's use.. for Ralph's use..".
OF THESE.. AELFRIC.. 20s. Written in the right margin of 170a. Also in 522 a 4.
OF THESE.. COUNT.. £7. Also in 519 a 3, written in the right margin.

8,31 VILLAGERS.. 2 PLOUGHS. ".. 3 ploughs".
2 MILLS.. 5s. "1 mill.. 5s."
ROGER.. 1 HIDE. "Roger.. 1 hide of thaneland.. which Alwin held in 1066; he could not be separated from the manor."

8,33 BRENT. ".. which Abbot Alnoth held in 1066".
VALUE TO THE ABBOT. "To the Abbot" omitted.
THOSE WHO HELD. A thane held Roger's land; Aelfric the Abbot's reeve held Aelfric's land, and a thane held Godwin's land. No holder is mentioned for Ralph's land.
3 VILLAGERS. 4 villagers; see Details Table.
10 COTTAGERS. 13 cottagers; see Details Table.

8,35 WULFGAR. "He could not be separated from the church".
3 PLOUGHS THERE. The villagers have them; not in lordship as DB implies.

8,36 SIWARD. "He could not be separated from the church in 1066".

8,37 BISHOP MAURICE. "Bishop Maurice of London". This entry also occurs in 522 a 1.

8,38 HUTTON, ELBOROUGH. Not described as thaneland. They also occur in 524 a 2. No value is given for them in either of the entries.
'HISCOMBE'. "Value 40s"; so also 524 b 1.
STRATTON (ON THE FOSSE). "Value 40s"; so also 524 b 2.
THE CHURCH.. THEM. "The Bishop does not pay any service from these manors (Hutton and Elborough) to the Abbey"; so also 524 a 2.

8,39 ?KINGSTONE. "Value £9; when the Count acquired it, as much"; so also 524 a 3.
STOKE, STOKE. Described as 2 manors. The combined value is given as 40s. So also 524 a 4.
DRAYCOTT. "Value 40s"; so also 524 a 7.
THANELAND IN GLASTONBURY. "Thaneland of Glastonbury Church".

8,40 WOODLAND. "Underwood" *(nemusculi)*.

8,41 ROGER.. IT. So also 524 a 1.
SERVICE. "Every service".

9,1 4 CARUCATES. So Exon. MS; Ellis misprints "3 carucates".

9,3 MARKET WHICH PAYS 20s. "(?) in the above total (payment); *(in predicto pretio)*". This statement is written at the end of the entry (not with the other resources as in DB), hence, perhaps, the need to state that the market's payment formed part of the manor's revenue. VCH does not translate it at all.
TWO THANES. "2 thanes, Leofric the priest and Wulfward, now his son Edward holds ½ hide", interlined.

9,4 GODRIC HELD. ".. jointly"; so also 512 b 1.

5 HIDES. "..which did not belong to the church in 1066".. 512 b 1.

9,5 EDWIN HELD. ".. jointly"; so also 512 b 2.
1½ HIDES. "..they did not belong to the church in 1066".. 512 b 2.
15 ACRES; ANOTHER.. LORDSHIP. "St. Peter's has 1½ hides, less 15 acres, which 3 small-holders hold"; *in dominio* omitted, as is often the case.

9,6 VALUE.. £10. "Value for the church's use, £9; for the thanes' use, 20s".

9,7 VILLAGERS.. 1 PLOUGH. "Villagers.. 1½ ploughs".
VALUE.. £10 10s. Value of the Abbot's holding, £9; of Dodman's, 20s; when Dodman acquir his, 10s. An example of DB adding together the past and present values given in Exon.

9,8 CATHANGER. ".. which did not belong to the church in 1066".. 512 b 3.
WADDELL HELD. ".. jointly"; so also 512 b 3.

10,1 ST. PETER'S CHURCH, ATHELNEY, HOLDS. "The Abbot of Athelney holds"; likewise fo: 10,2; just "Abbot" for 10,3-5.
ILTON. ".. which was always (part) of the church".. 512 a 1.
THE COUNT.. 1066. "From this manor 2 hides of the said 8 hides have been taken away; the were (part) of this church in 1066. Mauger of Carteret holds them from the Count of Mortair So also 512 a 1.

10,2 (LONG) SUTTON. ".. which (the Abbot) himself held in 1066". In 515 a 5 "which was alwa (part) of the church's lordship".
VALUE TO THE ABBOT. "Value for the Abbot's use."
ROGER OF COURSEULLES.. 2 HIDES. "Roger .. 2 manors; they paid tax for 2 hides. Valu: 30s".. 525 a 1.
AGAINST THE ABBOT'S WILL. In 191 a 2 Ellis prints ī *uno abbate* ('in an Abbot'). ī *uno* and ī *uto (invito)* look very similar in this scribe's hand, but it is more likely he wrote the correct ī *uto* than the meaningless ī *uno*; 515 a 5 has *invito abbate* in full.
MEADOW.. SHEEP. Part of Dodman's holding; the other details refer to both the men..
VALUE 50s. "Value for Dodman's use, 20s; for Warmund's use, 30s"; so also 515 a 5.
TWO MEN. Warmund and Dodman; so also 515 a 5.

10,3-5 SEAVINGTON, HAMP, LYNG. ".. which the Abbot also held in 1066", for each manor.

10,6 THE COUNT.. FROM IT. Also in 524 b 3-5.

11-13) THESE CHAPTERS are entered in Exon. under the heading of "Land *(sic)* which have been
15-16) given to the Saints in alms in Somerset."

12,1 ST. STEPHEN'S CHURCH.. HOLDS. "The Abbot of St. Stephen's, Caen, has".
VALUE TO THE ABBOT. "To the Abbot" omitted.

13,1 ST. MARY'S CHURCH OF MONTEBOURG HOLDS.. "The Abbot of St. Mary's of Montebo: has.."
BY GIFT OF NIGEL THE DOCTOR. "Nigel the Doctor gave it to the Abbey of Montebourg by grant *(concessione)* of King William."
A MILL. "½ mill".

14,1 ST. EDWARD'S CHURCH HOLDS. "The Abbess has.. "
(ABBAS) COMBE. ".. which Abbess Leofeva held in 1066".

16,1 REINBALD HOLDS.. "St. John's Church, Frome, has 8 carucates of land. Reinbald who *(qui: Ellis misprints *qua*) holds it has.."

16,2 RICHERE.. HOLDS. "St. Mary's Church has 2 hides in Stogumber from the King's alms.. Aelfric held them in 1066.. Richere of Les Andelys has them now in alms from the King".

16,3 IN.. CANNINGTON CHURCH. ".. which Aelfric the priest held in 1066".

16,5 SOUTH PETHERTON. ".. a manor of the King's, which he (Alfgeat) held himself in alms from King Edward in 1066".

16,7 IN.. LAND. "St. Mary's Church, (North) Petherton, has 3 virgates of land which were in (the l of) the church in 1066.. Ranulf, Peter's nephew, had the payments from them after the Bishop's death; the Bishop had them before".
BISHOP PETER HELD. ".. in alms" for 16,6 only.
IN THE KING'S HANDS. So for 16,6, but for 16,7 Exon. has "The King holds them in his lordship".

16,10 HE HAD.. 1066. *Ille idem qui prius habuit totam mansionem ea die..* Probably either *est* omitted after *ille*, or *qui* ought not to be there.

16,13 IN ?HOLNICOTE. ".. which 2 thanes held jointly in 1066. King William grants *(concedit)* this land to the said nuns in alms".

16,14 IN KILMERSDON. "In (the lands of) Kilmersdon Church".

17,3 4 VILLAGERS AND 3 SMALLHOLDERS. "3 villagers and 4 smallholders".

17,6 WOODLAND 4 FURLONGS LONG. ".. 3 furlongs long", which agrees with the woodland in the repeated entry (1,28).

17,7 OF BOULOGNE. Omitted; see General Notes.

18,2 SAMPFORD (BRETT). ".. which Alnoth held in 1066".
VILLAGERS.. 1 PLOUGH. "Villagers.. 2 ploughs".
A MILL.. VALUE.. £3. *i molendinum qui valet per annum iii libras;* the *qui* is obviously a mistake for *et.* The whole of this entry is full of scribal errors.

18,4 ST. SEVERUS' CHURCH. "The Abbot of St. Severus' ".
WOODLAND 4 FURLONGS LONG. ".. 3 furlongs long".

19,2 10 ACRES.. KING'S. Also in 512 b 4; "underwood" *(nemusculi)* for "woodland" in both entries.

19,7 CROWCOMBE. ".. which was (part) of the lordship of St. Swithun's.. it has been taken away from the church".. 510 a 6.
VALUE.. £8. "Value.. £6".. 510 a 6. In 266 a 3 *vi libras* corrected to *viii libras.* This suggests either that the value had changed between the writing of the main entry and that of the *Terrae Occupatae* or that the latter was not corrected. See 21,47 note below.

19,9 GLASTONBURY CHURCH HELD. "Alnoth, Abbot of Glastonbury, held"; so also 512 b 5.
VALUE £16. So 266 b 1, but "Value £17" in 512 b 5.
DROGO.. 1 VIRGATE. "A thane held this virgate jointly in 1066. Drogo holds it"; so also 512 b 5.

19,10 GLASTONBURY CHURCH. "The Abbot of Glastonbury".

19,13 ROBERT SON OF IVO. So 513 a 1; plain "Robert " in the main entry.
STOKE (SUB HAMDON). ".. to which 4½ hides and 1 virgate have been added; they did not pay tax in 1066. Robert son of Ivo holds these 4 hides *(sic)* and 1 virgate in this Stoke which he holds himself from the Count. Value £5 12s; when he acquired them, as much".. 513 a 1.
FIVE THANES HELD. ".. jointly.. Edwy held 2½ hides and 1 virgate. 4 brothers held the said 3 hides; each of them had 3 virgates".
2 VILLAGERS. "9 villagers".
MILLS.. 9s. "Mills.. 9s 8d".

19,14 ROBERT SON OF IVO. So 513 a 2; plain "Robert" in the main entry.
STOKE (SUB HAMDON). ".. which a thane held. 1 hide and 1 virgate have been added to it, which 2 thanes held jointly in 1066.. Value 32s (?); when the Count acquired them, as much" .. 513 a 2. "32s (?)"— *xxvi 7 vi d' sol';* perhaps 26s 6d, as the *vi d'* is written into the right margin.
THREE THANES HELD. ".. jointly.. Alfgeat held ½ hide and ½ virgate, Sweet ½ hide, Alfred ½ hide". That makes 1 hide 2½ virgates, not the 1 hide and 3½ virgates of the joint holdings' tax.

19,15 ALFWOLD. *Ailuuard,* the *i* interlined between *A* and *L.* See PNDB §60 on *l/r* interchange.
1 VIRGATE.. PAID TO.. MANOR. Also in 513 a 3.

19,17 THIS MANOR.. KING'S. "In 1066 this manor paid 1 sheep.. Since Mauger acquired this land from the Count this customary due has not been paid". So also 513 a 4.

19,18 ASHILL. ".. to which 2½ hides have been added, which a thane held jointly in 1066. Mauger holds them from the Count with the said manor. Value 30s; when the Count acquired them, 40s".. 513 b 1.
TWO THANES HELD. ".. jointly".
THIS MANOR.. KING'S. "In 1066 this manor paid 30d a year in customary dues.. but since Mauger acquired the land from the Count, this customary due has not been paid".. So also 513 b 1.

19,20 BRETEL HOLDS ASHBRITTLE. ".. as one manor"; so also 513 b 4.
1 HIDE.. HELD. "The land of 2 thanes has been added to it; it paid tax for 1½ hides". So also 513 b 4, with "Value £3 6s 8d; when the Count acquired them, as much". The 1½ hides add up with the 4 hides to make the 2½ hides and 3 hides of lordship and villagers' land.

19,23 1 PLOUGH.. THERE. Drogo has it, probably in lordship, though *in dominio* is omitted.
THIS MANOR.. KING'S. "In 1066 this manor paid each year 1 sheep.. but since Drogo acquired the land from the Count, it has not been paid"; so also 514 a 2.

19,24 DONYATT. ".. which Adolf held in 1066; it paid tax for 2 hides. The lands of 2 thanes have been added to this manor, which they held jointly in 1066. Saewin held 1½ hides and Dunstan 1½ hides.. Now Drogo holds them from the Count as 1 manor". So also 514 a 3, with "Value of these 2 added (manors) £3 6s 8d; when the Count acquired them, as much".
THESE MANORS.. KING'S. "In 1066 these manors paid 5 sheep.. but since Drogo acquired the land from the Count this customary due has not been paid". So also 514 a 3.

19,25 VALUE. "Value 40s; when the Count acquired it, 20s".
THIS MANOR.. KING'S. "This manor paid each year 2 sheep.. but since Drogo acquired the land from the Count this customary due has not been paid". So also 514 a 1.

19,26 STAPLE (FITZPAINE). ".. which a thane held jointly. 5 hides have been added to it, which another thane held jointly in 1066. Value £6; when the Count acquired them, £5".. 514 a 4.
TWO THANES HELD. ".. jointly".

19,27 THIS MANOR.. IRON."In 1066 this manor paid 5 sheep.. but since William acquired the lar from the Count, this customary due has not been paid". So also 514 a 5.

19,28 LORDSHIP 3 PLOUGHS. "The villagers have.. 3 ploughs"; no lordship ploughs mentioned. 7 SMALLHOLDERS. "8 smallholders".

19,29 HATCH (BEAUCHAMP). ".. which Godric held in 1066; it paid tax for 2 hides. Two other manors have been added to it, which 2 thanes held jointly in 1066. Godwin had 2 hides and paid tax for 2 hides, and Bolle (had) 1 hide.. Robert the Constable now holds them from the Count as 1 manor". So also 514 b 1, with "They (2 added manors) paid tax for 3 hides and 1 virgate" and "Value of these 2 added manors 60s; when the Count acquired them, 100s'.
FROM..(RIVEL)."The hide which Bolle held paid 1 sheep.. but since Robert acquired the lar it has not been paid". So also 514 b 1.

19,32 MERRIOTT. ".. which a thane held jointly. The land of a thane has been added to it; he hel jointly in 1066; it paid tax for 5 hides. Dodman holds them from the Count with the said manor. Value 100s; when the Count acquired it, 60s".. 514 b 2.
LEOFWIN AND BRICTWARD HELD. "2 thanes held jointly.. Leofwin held 5 hides and Br ward 2 hides".

19,33 EASTHAMS.. 1066. "Easthams, which Godwin, the King's reeve, held from Crewkerne with manor's revenue and he could not withdraw from Crewkerne with that land". In 514 b 3 "Easthams, which Godwin, the King's reeve, held in the revenue of the King's manor called Crewkerne.." The whole entry is also in 105 b 1 (DB 1,20).

19,34 CRICKET (MALHERBIE). ".. which a thane held jointly. 1½ hides have been added to it, which a thane held in 1066...Value 15s; when the Count acquired them, 5s".. 515 a 1.
TWO THANES HELD. ".. jointly".

19,35 THIS LAND.. REVENUE. "In 1066 this land lay in the revenue of the King's manor called Brompton". So also 515 a 2.

19,39 EDWIN HELD. ".. jointly".

19,40 COULD NOT BE SEPARATED. So 273 a 2, with "In 1066 it was (part) of the Bishop of Winchester's manor called Taunton". So also 516 b 2.

19,41 OSMUND HELD. ".. jointly".

19,42 THEODORIC HELD. ".. jointly".
1 PLOUGH.. THERE. "Alfred has 1 plough"; in dominio omitted, probably in error.

19,43 CHARLTON (ADAM). "..which 1 thane held jointly. 3 manors have been added to it, which 3 thanes held jointly in 1066.. Value £3 10s; when the Count acquired them, as much".. 523 b 1.
THREE THANES.. HELD. "3 thanes and a clerk held jointly".
5 HIDES. "Reginald of Vautortes holds 4½ hides of these from the Count".
6 SLAVES.. "2 cottagers" included after them; usually their position in Exon. is after the smallholders; also happens in 19,64.

19,44 VALUE. "Value £12; when the Count acquired it, as much".

19,46 16 SMALLHOLDERS. "6 smallholders".

19,47 CHISELBOROUGH. ".. which a thane held jointly. 2½ hides of land have been added to it, which a thane held jointly in 1066.. Value 100s; when the Count acquired them, £3.".. 517 b 6.
TWO THANES HELD. ".. jointly".

19,48-50;52 A THANE HELD. ".. jointly", in all four sections.

19,53 CLOFORD. ".. The lands of 4 thanes have been added to it; they paid (redd'; perhaps "pay" but the perfect reddiderunt in the same formula in 519 b 6, DB 19,59. See 1,24 General Not tax for 3½ hides.. Value £9; when the Count acquired them, £6" .. 523 b 2.
FIVE THANES HELD. ".. jointly".

19,55 WOOLSTON. ".. 2 hides of land and 1½ virgates have been added to it, which 2 thanes held jointly in 1066.. Value 25s; when the Count acquired them, 30s".. 519 b 4.
THREE THANES HELD. ".. jointly".

19,57 ROBERT.. HELD. ".. jointly"; so also 519 b 5.

19,59 KEINTON (MANDEVILLE). "...The lands of 2 thanes have been added to it; they paid tax 3 hides, 1 virgate and 2 parts of ½ virgate.. Value 53s 4d; when the Count acquired them, 60 8d".. 519 b 6.
TWO THANES HELD. "3 thanes held jointly".

19,60 GODMAN. *Goderăna*, an understandable mistake for *Godemon* if the deletion mark below the *n* were intended for the final *a* (Ellis puts it under the first *a*) and the *r* (like an *n* in insular minuscule) represented a miswritten *m*. See Addenda p. 332.

19,63 STOKE (TRISTER). ".. 1½ hides have been added to it, which a thane held jointly in 1066.. Value 30s; when the Count acquired them, as much".. 521 a 1.
TWO THANES HELD. ".. jointly.. One of whom had 1½ hides and the other as much.. Bretel holds them from the Count as 1 manor".
MEADOW, 15 ACRES. "Meadow, 16 acres".

19,64 CUCKLINGTON. ".. which Leofing held. Another manor has been added to it, which a thane held jointly in 1066; it paid *(redd';* see 19,53 note above) tax for 3½ hides.. Value 50s; when the Count acquired it, £3 10s".. 521 a 2.
LEOFING AND SWEIN HELD. "2 thanes, Leofing and Swein, held jointly.. 1 thane had one half, the other the other one.. The Count holds it as 1 manor".

1 SLAVE. "4 cottagers" included after him; see 19,43 note above.

19,65 FROM THE VILLAGERS. "From one of the said villagers".

19,68 CLAPTON. ".. which Wulfa held. 1½ hides of land have been added to it, which a thane held jointly in 1066. Value 15s; when the Count acquired them, 30s".. 523 b 3.
TWO THANES HELD. "Wulfa and his brother Aelfric held jointly.. Mauger of Carteret holds it from the Count as 1 manor".

19,69 1 PLOUGH.. THERE. "Alfred has 1 plough"; *in dominio* omitted, probably in error.

19,70 WOODLAND, 15 ACRES. ".. 25 acres".

19,71 1 HIDE IN MILBORNE (PORT). ".. which Godwin held in 1066".
2 SLAVES. "4 slaves".
5 BURGESSES. "5 burgesses in Milborne (Port) who pay 3s 9d".

19,72 MARSTON (MAGNA). ".. which Leofrun held. 2 hides of land have been added to it, which 2 thanes held jointly in 1066. Value £4; when the Count acquired them, as much".. 523 a 5.
FOUR THANES HELD. ".. jointly.. Leofrun held 3 hides, Edred 1 hide, Saeward and his mother 1 hide".

19,73 MARSTON (MAGNA). ".. 1½ hides of land have been added to it, which 4 thanes held jointly in 1066.. Value 40s; when the Count acquired them, 30s".. 523 a 6.
FIVE THANES HELD. ".. jointly".

19,78 THORNE. ".. which a thane held. 1 hide of land has been added to it, which another thane held jointly in 1066.. Value 16s; when the Count acquired it, 20s".. 523 b 4.
TWO THANES HELD. ".. jointly".

19,81 HOUNDSTONE. ".. which a thane held. 3 virgates of land have been added to it, which 2 thanes held jointly in 1066.. Value 15s; when the Count acquired them, 3s 4d".. 523 b 5.
THREE THANES HELD.. ".. jointly".

19,83-4 YEOVIL. One entry in Exon, with the details of the Count's hide and Amund's hide entered one after the other. In 523 b 6 "The Count has ½ hide of land in Yeovil, which a thane held. 1½ hides of land have been added to it, which 3 thanes held jointly in 1066. Value 17s 6d; when the Count acquired them, 22s 8d".
FOUR THANES HELD. ".. jointly". "They paid tax for as much" omitted.

19,85 SOCK (DENNIS). ".. The lands of 6 thanes have been added to it.. Value 50s; when the Count acquired them, as much".. 523 b 7.
SEVEN THANES HELD. ".. jointly".

19,86 'BISHOPSTONE'. ".. which the Abbot of Athelney *(Aliennia)* held in 1066".

20,1 VALUE. "Value £18; when Baldwin acquired it, £19".
1 HIDE.. HARDINGTON. "Of these 21 hides he has 1 hide (of) common pasture in.. from King Edward's time". This is written in the left margin of the MS.

20,2-3 DROGO.. HE ALSO. "Roger son of Nigel"; *Rogo*, see OEB 191.

21,1 LORDSHIP; 2 PLOUGHS. "1 plough in lordship"; in the MS *ii* was originally written, but the final *i* was erased, though visible.

21,2 TWO LANDS.. Also in 511 b 5.

21,3 1 PLOUGH.. THERE. "Robert has 1 plough"; *in dominio* omitted, probably in error.
VALUE 20s. "Value 15s"; *xx* altered to *xv*, but possibly vice versa.

21,5 PERRY. ".. 3 virgates of land have been added to it, which 4 thanes held jointly in 1066.. Value 30s; when he acquired them, as much".. 509 a 9.
FOUR THANES HELD. ".. jointly".
MEADOW, 33 ACRES. ".. 23 acres".

21,6 VALUE.. 22s. "Value.. 20s 15d".
1 HIDE IN PERRY.. ADDED. ".. added a manor called Perry; it paid tax for 1 hide". So also 509 a 1, where Alfward is not named but called "a thane".

21,10 VALUE.. 20s. "Value.. 15s".
21,20 'DODISHAM'. ".. 2 virgates of land and 5 acres have been added to it, which 2 thanes held jointly in 1066. Value 15s; when he acquired them, as much".. 509 b 1.
THREE THANES HELD. ".. jointly".
6 SMALLHOLDERS. ".. have half the land and 2 ploughs". No lordship land or ploughs mentioned.
21,24 ½ MILL. "1 mill".
21,26 STOCKLAND. There is no corresponding entry in the *Terrae Occupatae*, which is unusual with 2 manors combined in 1086; it also happens in 24,10 and 45,7.
TWO THANES HELD. ".. jointly; one held ½ hide and the other 1 hide".
21,34 ½ PLOUGH.. IN LORDSHIP. "William.. has ½ plough"; *in dominio* omitted, probably in error.
21,35 A THANE HELD. ".. jointly"; so also 510 a 1.
VALUE.. 8s. Both values of the virgate, 5s. Present value of the added acre, 3s, (no past value given).
21,36 'WORTH'. ".. ½ hide and 1 virgate of land have been added to it, which a thane held jointly 1066.. Value 30s; when Roger acquired it, as much".. 509 b 10.
TWO THANES HELD. ".. jointly".
21,37 KNOWLE (ST. GILES). ".. ½ hide and ½ virgate have been added to it, which a thane held jointly in 1066.. Value 12s 6d".. 510 a 2.
GODRIC AND AELFRIC HELD. ".. jointly".
BROWNING HELD AS A MANOR. "Browning held jointly".. 510 a 3.
1 PLOUGH THERE. "1 villager who has 1 plough".
VALUE.. 15s. 510 a 3 has *xii sol'* changed to *xv sol'*; Ellis reads *xii sol'*.
21,44 LAND FOR 1 PLOUGH. "1½ ploughs".
21,45 [1] VIRGATE. *habet R. virgam;* see 21,95 note below.
21,47 EDWALD HELD. ".. jointly". Edwald is called a thane in 510 b 3.
PERLO HELD. ".. jointly"; so also 510 b 4.
4 SMALLHOLDERS. "3 smallholders".
VALUE.. 10s. "Value 20s; when Roger acquired it, 10(s)'.. 510 b 4. In 428 a 4 the scribe corrected the present value of *xx sol'* to *x sol'*. See 19,7 note above.
21,48 GEOFFREY AND WILLIAM. "Geoffrey holds 1 virgate and William 3 virgates.. Geoffrey has ..virgate and 1 smallholder who pays him 7s 6d. The 3 virgates William holds pay him 25s, and.. when Roger acquired them, as much".
WEACOMBE. ".. ½ hide has been added to it, which 2 thanes held jointly in 1066. Value 16.. when he acquired it, as much".. 510 b 5.
THREE THANES HELD. ".. jointly".
21,52 VALUE 26d. "Value 2s 6d".
21,54 VILLAGERS..1 PLOUGH. "Villagers have.. ½ plough".
LEOFING AND ALFWARD. Described as thanes; so also in 511 b 6.
21,57 SMALLHOLDER WITH ½ PLOUGH. "Aeleva.. has ½ plough in lordship"; no ½ plough is ascribed to the smallholder.
21,58 ½ VIRGATE. "Roger has 1 furlong.. and the villagers ½ furlong"; *in dominio* probably omitted in error after "1 furlong".
SMALLHOLDER.. ½ PLOUGH. "Roger has.. ½ plough between himself and his men" *(inter ipse et suos homines).*
21,59 SMALLHOLDER.. ½ PLOUGH. "Ednoth has.. ½ plough"; no ½ plough is ascribed to the smallholder.
WOODLAND.. MEADOW. So Exon. MS; Ellis misprints *ii ag' nemoris* & *d' iii agros prati,* the *d'* is the remains of a partly erased letter, something not normally printed.
21,60 5 CATTLE. So Exon. MS; Ellis omits the *v* in error.
21,61 LORDSHIP 1 PLOUGH. "Lordship ½ plough".
21,62 1 SMALLHOLDER.. ½ VIRGATE. "The villagers (have) ½ virgate", plural despite only one 'villager', the smallholder. Possibly the scribe expected to hear of more 'villagers', but it is more likely he used the set phrase inadvertently.
21,63 ALLER. ".. which Brictmer held jointly. 1½ virgates of land have been added to it, which Edmer held jointly in 1066.. Value 3s 9d; when Roger acquired them, 2s 6d".. 512 a 2.
BRICTMER AND EDMER HELD. "Brictmer and Edmer *(Elmarus,* a scribal error) held jointly in 1066. Edmer held 1½ virgates and Brictmer held ½ virgate".
VALUE 8s. "Value 7s 6d".
21,65 HOLNICOTE. ".. which a thane held jointly. ½ hide of land has been added to it, which Aelfric held jointly in 1066.. Value 11s; when Roger acquired it, as much".. 512 a 3.
AELFRIC AND BRICTWIN HELD. "2 thanes held jointly in 1066; Aelfric held ½ hide,

Brictwin held ½ virgate".

LAND FOR 2½ PLOUGHS. "2 ploughs can plough the ½ hide and ½ plough can plough the ½. virgate".

21,66 VALUE 8s. "Value 7s 6d". Ellis prints the past value as *x sol'*, but in the MS the figure has been changed to a *v*, or possibly a *v* was changed to an *x*.

21,68 IN LORDSHIP 1 FURLONG (?). "William has it *(hanc)* in lordship". *Hanc* ought to refer to the manor *(mansio)* as the nearest feminine word, which is very unusual; a plain mistake for *hunc* or *hoc*, referring to *fertinus/fertinum* is more likely.

21,69 BUT IT IS WASTE. "But it was always waste after Roger acquired it".

21,71 1 SLAVE; 3 SMALLHOLDERS.. VIRGATE. *Wluuardus.. habet.. iii bord' 7 i seruum qui tenet dim̄' virḡ'.* Probably a scribal error for *tenent,* or only the slave held the land; cf. 21,55.

21,73 THORNE (ST. MARGARET). "... 1 hide and the third part of 1 virgate have been added to it, which 2 thanes held jointly in 1066.. Value 25s; when Roger acquired them, 13s 4d".. 512 a 4. THREE THANES HELD. ".. jointly.. Aelmer held 1 hide and 2 brothers held 3 virgates".

21,74 2 SLAVES. Repeated, in error.

21,78 IN LORDSHIP 2 PLOUGHS. "Robert has 5 villagers and 5 smallholders and they have 2 ploughs on that land" *(ii carr' habent in ea terra).*

21,83 VALUE 18s. "It pays 17s 6d".

21,85 LITTLETON. Entered as Littleton held in 1066 by Aelmer, to which have been added 2 manors held by 2 thanes jointly, Osbern holding 1 hide and Godric ½ hide. See Details Table. So also 517 b 5.

VALUE.. 40s. 60s in total; see Details Table. 40s for both values of the added land in 517 b 5 too. It would seem that DB reproduced only the value of the added land.

21,87 COTTAGERS. They are not separated in Exon. from the villagers and smallholders and their land and ploughs.

21,89 ROBERT .. HOLDS. "..as one manor".

WHITE OX MEAD. ".. which a thane held jointly. ½ hide of land has been added to it, which another thane held jointly in 1066.. Value 30s; when.. ".. 520 a 5. The entry, the last on the folio, ends here with *qñ (quando)*. It is interesting that 520b (DB 5,52) also originally ended *qñ Eps̄ accep̄* and someone later wrote *val' tantūd'* and perhaps intended to finish 520a similarly.

TWO THANES HELD. ".. jointly".

21,90 IT COULD NOT.. FROM IT. "The thane who held it could not be separated from Brewham manor".

21,91 1 PLOUGH THERE. "Erneis has 1 plough"; *in dominio* omitted, probably in error.

21,92 KEINTON.. IT. "(The Count) has a manor called Keinton (Mandeville) which Aelmer held in 1066; it paid tax for 1 hide.. and lay before 1066 in Barton (St. David), which Roger holds. Mauger holds *(tenent;* a scribal error) it from the Count". This passage is written in the left margin of the MS and the first 3 or 4 letters are missing from the beginning of each line; see 8,19 note above. The missing letters can easily be restored, except for a possible word before "it lay.. ". Ellis misprints *ies* for *(Co)mes* at the beginning.

21,95 TOKI. *Tochi* in Exon. MS; Ellis misprints *S Tochi,* but the *S* in the MS is only half there and is obviously an error.

[1] HIDE. *habet V(italis) hid'. i* is omitted quite often before a measure. See 21,45.

21,97 TO BARRINGTON.. KING'S. "To the lordship manor *(dominicae mansioni)* of the King, called Barrington". So also 524 b 7.

21,98 (LONG) SUTTON. "Roger has from the King 2 manors in (Long) Sutton". So also 525 a 1. Other elements of this entry are repeated in 515 a 5 (for DB 10,2) and 524 b 4.

IN LORDSHIP 3 PLOUGHS. 2 ploughs; see Details Table and also DB 10,2, although other details (livestock and meadow) do not agree.

VALUE 50s. So 435 b 2 and 515 a 5, but 525 a 1 has "30s", which in 10,2 is the value of Warmund's holding.

22,1 THIS LAND.. HUNDRED. Written in the left margin, probably by the same scribe as the rest of the entry.

22,3 30 SMALLHOLDERS. "25 smallholders".
7 PIGMEN. "6 pigmen".

22,8 MEADOW, 21 ACRES. *xxi agrũ; prati* omitted in error.

22,10 CUDWORTH. "...The land of 1 thane ("2 hides" interlined) has been added to it, which he held himself jointly in 1066. Value 15s; when he acquired it, 20s".. 509 b 3. THREE THANES HELD. ".. jointly".

22,11 VILLAGERS.. ½ PLOUGH. "The villagers (have) 1 plough".

E

22,13 RADDINGTON. ".. 1 hide of land has been added to it, which a thane held jointly in 1066. Value 15s; when Roger acquired it, as much".. 510 b 1.
TWO THANES HELD. ".. jointly".
3 SLAVES. "2 slaves".

22,14 ALGAR HELD. ".. jointly".. 510 a 8, and possibly also 422 b 1 but the parchment is rough here: Ellis prints a gap.

22,17 WOODLAND. "Underwood" (nemusculi).

22,18 CARY (FITZPAINE). ".. which a thane held jointly. ½ hide of land, less ½ furlong, has been added to it, which a thane held jointly in 1066.. Value 7s 6d; when Roger acquired it, as much".. 515 a 3. Ellis misprints dimid^{s}ui for dimidiu^s in the "½ furlong".
TWO THANES HELD. ".. jointly.. Alling held one half of it and Leofing the other".

22,19 WOODLAND. "Underwood" (nemusculi).
STILL VOUCHES.. LAND. adhuc inuocat eū ad guarant. sed Roger' inde omnino deficit ab ı die quo rex W. hunc Warmund' de ipsa t̄ra resaisire fecit. The last clause could also be translat "from the day on which King William made this Warmund take possession again of this land" See General Notes to 22,19.

22,20 ASH (PRIORS) HAS BEEN ADDED. "A manor called Ash (Priors) has been added.." So also 520 b 3.
BISHOP OF WELLS. "Bishop Giso"; so also 520 b 3.
SEPARATED FROM HIM. "Separated from the Bishop with his land".

22,21 ROBERT HOLDS 1 HIDE. ".. which a widow held, who could not be separated from the manor in 1066".

22,23 PASTURE 3 FURLONGS. "Woodland 3 furlongs".

22,25 TAX.. 2½ HIDES. Originally 2 hides 3 virgates in the Exon. MS, but the final i in iii virgis was erased, to make 2 hides 2 virgates. 2 hides 3 virgates, however, would agree with the total of the lordship and villagers' land.

22,26 WOODLAND.. WIDE. After this measurement of woodland is added " 1 furlong of woodland length and as much in width".

22,27 4 VILLAGERS. "3 villagers".
12 PERCHES. "13 perches".

22,28 LYDE. ".. which Godwin held. 1 hide of land has been added to it, which Saeric held jointly in 1066. Value 15s; when he acquired it, as much".. 523 a 3.
GODWIN AND SAERIC HELD. "2 thanes, Godwin and Saeric, held jointly.. 1 thane had 1 hide and the other, the other".
WOODLAND. "Underwood" (nemusculi).

24,6 ?DUNWEAR. This entry is written in the right margin of the Exon. MS, hard up against and level with the first Stretcholt entry; there are no signs to show its correct position.

24,8 BEFORE 1066.. HOLDS. "In 1066 this manor belonged to Robert of Auberville's manor called Melcombe". So also 508 b 7.

24,10 TWO THANES..AS TWO MANORS. "2 thanes, Saewulf and Aelfric, held jointly.. one held 1 hide and the other, the other; now Walter has them as 1 manor".

24,11 TWO THANES. "2 thanes held jointly.. one of whom had a manor of 5 hides, the other anoth manor of 1 hide". So also 518 a 4.
100s. "105s." c sol' with 7 v interlined with a mark to show it was to go with the c sol'. In 518 a 4 c.v. sol' with 7 interlined.

24,12 2½ PLOUGHS.. THERE.. LORDSHIP. "In it (manor) Ludo has 2 ploughs"; in dominio perhaps omitted in error, as also any villagers' ploughs.

24,13 LEOFWIN. Letuuin', possibly a scribal error, but see PNDB 310.

24,14 ALSTON (SUTTON). ".. which a thane held jointly. 2 hides and 1 virgate have been added to it, which a thane held jointly in 1066.. Value 30s; when Walscin acquired them, as much. Hubert holds these 2 thanelands as 1 manor".. 518 a 5.
TWO THANES HELD. ".. jointly".

24,16 ADDED ½ HIDE. ".. which did not belong to the above manor..". So also 520 b 2.
BRICTMER..HELD AS A MANOR. "Brictmer the priest held jointly". In 520 b 2 "Brictmer the priest held it; he could go with his land to whichever lord he would in 1066".
IT PAID TAX FOR ½ HIDE. Omitted.

24,21 8 PLOUGHS AND 3 IIIDES̄. Inde habet ii hid' 7 iii carr' in dominio 7 iii hid' 7 viii carr'. Probably villani sui omitted in error before iii hid' 7 viii carr'.

24,22 6 SMALLHOLDERS. "6 cottagers" included after them.

24,24 LORDSHIP 3 VIRGATES. So Exon. MS; Ellis misprints "4 virgates".
1 VILLAGER.. 1½ PLOUGHS. "1 villager (vill' i.) who has.. ½ plough.. 5 smallholders". See 5,21 note above.

326

MEADOW, 25 ACRES. ".. 20 acres".

24,27 RADEMAR. *"Reineuualus,* "Rainward"; perhaps a scribal error.
8 SMALLHOLDERS. "3 cottagers" included after them.

24,28 ALWAKER. *Eureuuacre,* one of the forms of the OG name Everwacer; perhaps the original
return read *Eiluuacre* and the scribe misread the *l* for a contraction mark; see also in 24,30. The
reverse occurs in 37,6.

24,30 ALWAKER. *Eluuacrer;* but *Eueruuacre* in 522 a 2, for which see 24,28 note above.
1 HIDE.. ADDED. "A manor.. added"; so also 522 a 2.
ALRIC HELD IT AS A MANOR. "Alric held it jointly".

24,36 1 PLOUGH.. THERE. "(Ralph) has 1 plough there"; *in dominio* probably omitted in error.

25,1 WILLIAM OF MOHUN. Described several times in this chapter in Exon. (e.g. for 25,33-36;38
-39) as "William the Sheriff". He was Sheriff of Somerset.
'SEABERTON'.. AELFRIC.. ONE MANOR. "A manor called Seaberton which Aelfric held
jointly". So also 509 a 4, but "which a thane held..".
WILLIAM HOLDS IT. .. *hanc,* the plough.

25,3 ADSBOROUGH. ".. to which the lands of 5 thanes have been added; they held them jointly in
1066. Value 30s; when William acquired them, as much".. 508 b 6.
SIX THANES HELD. ".. jointly.. they could go to whichever lord they would".

25,6 STREET. ".. which Guard held. ½ hide and 1 virgate of land have been added to it, which
Aelmer held jointly in 1066. Value 7s 6d; when William acquired them, as much".. 524 b 8.
1 PLOUGH. "4 oxen"; which normally form half a plough team; see 25,56 note below.

25,7 THIS LAND.. 1066. "This manor was thaneland of Glastonbury Church in 1066; it could not
separate from the church". In 509 b 2 "Brictric held it from Glastonbury Church; he could
not be separated from the church in 1066".

25,8 THIS LAND.. 1066. "This manor was thaneland of Glastonbury Church, so it could not
separate from the church".

25,9 VALUE.. £6. "Value £6 10s".
1 HIDE AND ½ VIRGATE. ".. which 3 thanes held; they could not separate from the lord of
the manor".

25,13 LANGHAM. ".. The lands of 2 thanes have been added to it, which 2 thanes held jointly in
1066. 2 men-at-arms hold it *(sic)* from William. Value 20s; when he acquired them, as much"
.. 511 a 2.
THREE THANES HELD. ".. jointly".

25,14 VALUE FORMERLY 7s. ".. 7s 6d".

25,15 BICKHAM. ".. ½ virgate of land has been added to it, which a thane held jointly in 1066..
Value 7s 6d; when William acquired it, 3s".. 511 a 1.
TWO THANES HELD. ".. jointly".

25,16 LAND FOR 1 PLOUGH. "..1½ ploughs.. William has 1 plough in lordship". The & *dim'*, the
last words on the folio, are written squashed into the right margin and could easily have been
overlooked by someone copying the MS.

25,17 THE WHOLE (OF THE LAND). *Tota,* which could agree with *dimidia hida, mansio* or an
understood *terra.* 35,12 has *in dominio totam istam terram,* but 25,42 has *totam illam virgam*
referring to the 1 virgate taxed. *Cf. totum* in 24,32.

25,18 A THANE HELD AS ONE MANOR. "A thane held jointly"; so also 511 a 3.
MEADOW, 3 ACRES. ".. 2 acres", *ii* being written over an erased *vi.*

25,27 LUXBOROUGH. "..3 virgates of land have been added to it, which a thane held jointly in
1066. Value 15s; when he acquired them, 10s".. 511 a 4.
TWO THANES HELD. ".. jointly; one held 3 virgates, the other 1 virgate".

25,30 KILTON. ".. 5 hides of land have been added to it, which Alfward held jointly in 1066. Value
£3 10s; when William acquired them, 50s".. 511 a 5.
KILTON.. 2 MANORS. "William has 2 manors. Alfward and Leofric held them jointly in 1066.
Leofric held 5½ hides and Alfward 5 hides".
VALUE.. £7. "Value for William's use £7".
RALPH. "A man-at-arms", with *Radulfusus* (no doubt in error for *Radulfus*) interlined. So
also 511 a 5, but *Radulfus* as usual.
VALUE 20s. "Value for Ralph's use, 20s".

25,32 MEADOW, 7 ACRES. ".. 6 acres".

25,36 DODMAN (?). *Modo tenet hanc D. .. habet ibi durandus..* The *Idem* in DB implies that Dodman is the holder of this entry, as he is of 25,33-35. Normally in Exon. the holder's name is
given in full first, then his initial for the lordship holding etc. *Durandus* may be a scribal error
for *dudemanus.*
1 PLOUGH THERE. "Durand (?) has 1 plough there"; *in dominio* probably omitted in error.

25,38 ALFWOLD. *Aduuold*: either the *d* is a scribal error for *l*, or Edwold was the TRE holder according to Exon.
WOODLAND, 4 ACRES. ".. 104 acres".

25,40 MANFRED AND ROBERT HOLD. "Manfred has 3 virgates and 1 plough in lordship. Robert (has) 1 virgate and a villager who has ½ plough. Manfred (has) 4 smallholders". The livestock and meadow follow this, and Manfred may have had them in his holding as well.
CHUBWORTHY. ".. ½ hide of land has been added to it. Value 6s; when William acquired it, 5s".. 511 b 1.
TWO THANES HELD. "2 thanes, Saeric and Uhtred, held it jointly".

25,41 ½ PLOUGH. The villager has "4 cattle *(animalia)* in a plough".

25,42 TAX FOR 1 VIRGATE. "Brictric.. has the whole virgate in lordship".
SMALLHOLDER HAS IT. "Brictric.. has.. in lordship... ½ plough". No plough or land is ascribed to the smallholder.

25,43 BATHEALTON. "..1½ hides of land have been added to it, which a thane held jointly in 1066. Value 40s".. 511 b 2.
TWO THANES HELD. ".. jointly.. Aelfric held 1½ hides and Algar ½ hide".

25,45 RUNNINGTON. ".. 1 hide of land has been added to it, which a thane held jointly in 1066.. Value 25s; when William acquired it, 10s".. 511 b 3.
TWO THANES HELD. ".. jointly; one held 1 hide and the other, the other hide".

25,46 ADDED 1 HIDE WHICH A THANE HELD FREELY. ".. added ½ hide of land which a thane held jointly in 1066." So also 511 b 4.

25,48 MEADOW, 8 ACRES. ".. 9 acres".

25,55 28 SMALLHOLDERS. "25 cottagers" included after them.
3 VIRGATES.. 3 HIDES. NOW. Also in 520 a 2, but Roger holds "2 hides" there and in 364 b 1 (as also in DB 21,90; Exon. 434 b 1). The value of the 2 hides is given only in 520 a 2.
AELMER HELD. ".. jointly"; so also 520 a 2.

25,56 ½ PLOUGH. "3 oxen". Normally there were 8 oxen to a plough-team, but there is evidence for smaller teams in the south-west; see R. Lennard in EHR lx (1945) p. 217 ff. and in EHR lxxxi (1966) p. 770 ff. and H.P.R. Finberg in EHR lxvi (1951) p. 67 ff.

26,3 TO THIS MANOR.. 30s. Also in 516 a 2.

26,4 VALUE.. £8. "Value £7; when William acquired it, £8."

26,5 TAX.. 8 HIDES. Originally *vii hidis*, but a final *i* was added to make *viii*. 7 hides, however, agrees with the total of lordship, villagers' and Hugh's land.

26,6 4½ [HIDES]. *iiii carr' 7 dim'* in error for *iiii hid' 7 dim'*. The ploughs are entered after, as usual.
22 PLOTS OF LAND. *mansure terrae;* see General Notes to 26,6. There is no corresponding entry in the *Terrae Occupatae*, which one would expect with added land, nor is there one for the land taken away in 46,21.

26,7 ALSTAN BOSCOMBE. *Alestan' deboscoma* only for 26,6; elsewhere in this chapter he is called plain *Alestan', Alestann'*.

26,8 TICKENHAM. ".. which a thane held jointly. 4 hides and 1 virgate have been added to it, which another thane held jointly in 1066. Value £3; when William acquired it, 50s".. 518 b
SAEWULF AND THEODULF.. AS TWO MANORS. "2 thanes, Saewulf and Theodulf, held jointly.. One of these thanes had one half of these hides and the other, the other. Now William holds them as 1 manor".

27,1 BRICTSI HELD. "A thane called Brictsi held jointly"..509 a 7.
TO THIS MANOR.. 10s. Also in 509 a 7, in shortened form.
HE COULD GO WHERE HE WOULD. "He could go to whichever lord he would".

27,3 KING'S ASSENT.. SERLO.. DAUGHTER. "Serlo of Burcy gave this manor to William after he had married *(acepit)* his daughter; King William grants this".
TO THIS MANOR.. The 2 manors were added "in Serlo's time", and in 516 a 6 "in Serlo of Burcy's time".
ALFWARD AND COLA HELD.. AS TWO MANORS. " 2 (thanes) held jointly"; *tegni* omitted in error, but *ii tanni* in 516 a 6. "Alfward held 2½ hides and Cola ½ hide".. 369 b 1.

28,1 SAEWARD AND ALDEVA HELD.. AS TWO MANORS. "A thane , Saeward, and a woman, Aldeva, held jointly; they could go to whichever lord they would..Saeward had 1 virgate and Aldeva 10 hides and 3 virgates". *Saluuard'*; a scribal error, see PNDB §66.
1½ HIDES.. 1½ PLOUGHS. ".. in lordship".

28,2 WOODLAND. "Woodland 1 league and 7 furlongs in length and 7 furlongs in width".
ALFWOLD.. CHURCH. "Alfwold bought.. on the condition that *(tali pacto quod)* they should return..".

30,2 THIS MANOR.. DUE. "This manor paid to a lordship manor of the King's, called Carhampton

.. in 1066; since Ralph has had it, it (or "he") has not paid this customary due". Ellis misprints *ac die..* instead of the MS *ae die..*, a scribal error for the usual form *ea die..* So also 509 b 8, but ".. since Ralph has held it, the King has not had this customary due from it".

31 RALPH PAGNELL. His holding is given under the heading "Lands of French Thanes in Somerset", as are the holdings of Ralph of Limesy, Humphrey the Chamberlain (most) and others in ch. 45.

31,3 MILL.. 3s. "Mill.. 4s".

32,4 THIS MANOR.. NOW. "This manor paid to a lordship manor of the King's, called Carhampton.. in 1066; since Ralph has had it, it (or "he") has not paid this customary due".
"Ralph of Limesy has 2 manors called Bossington and Allerford, which paid in customary dues each year to the King's manor, called Carhampton, 24 sheep or 5s. Since Ralph has had this land the King has not had this customary due from it".. 510 a 4.

32,5 BOSSINGTON. See above note.
ATHELNEY CHURCH,.. CHURCH. "The Abbot of Athelney.. the Abbot".
VALUE.. 20s. "Value 20s; when he acquired it, 15s; the *xv* changed from *xx*, or possibly vice versa which would agree with DB.

32,6 VALUE.. WASTE. *eo quod devastata est non valet nisi vii sol'* ("because it is waste the value is only 7s"). Ellis misprints *de eo quod..;* the *de* is an erased & in the MS.

32,7 WULFWARD HELD. ".. jointly".

33. SEE 4,1 note above.

35,1 WOOLMERSDON. ".. 1½ virgates of land have been added to it. The virgate was (part) of the lordship manor of the King's, called (North) Petherton, and was leased *(accomodata)* to a thane in 1066; value 5s. The ½ virgate was thaneland in 1066; value 5s".. 508 b 4.
1½ VIRGATES.. 10s. "2 lands have been added to this manor; they paid tax for 1½ virgates. The virgate was (part) of (North) Petherton, a manor of the King's, in 1066. The King's reeve, Alfwy, leased *(prestuerat)* this virgate in King Edward's day (this sentence interlined). A thane held the ½ virgate jointly and now it has been added to the said manor. Value of this ½ virgate 5s; of the virgate, as much".

35,2 ADDED 1 VIRGATE.. PETHERTON. ".. which Saemer held in 1066 in the King's revenue in the manor called (North) Petherton". So also 508 b 5, but Saemer is not named, only described as a thane.

35,3 2 PLOUGHS.. THERE. "Richard has 2 ploughs"; *in dominio* probably omitted in error.

35,4 TO THIS MANOR.. 5s. So 372 a 1, with "Bricteva held jointly" for "freely". In 509 a 5 "½ virgate of land and 2 parts of ½ virgate have been added to it, which Brictmer held jointly in 1066. Value 5s; when Alfred acquired them, as much".

35,12 OSWARD AND ALFWARD. Described as thanes; they held jointly. *Ailu'd* with the *l* added later, half obliterating the *i*. In 510 a 5 "(Nether) Stowey which 2 (thanes) held jointly in 1066"; *tegni/tanni* ("thanes") omitted in error.
THIS LAND.. HOLDS. Also in 510 a 5.

35,14 THIS LAND.. HOLDS. So also 510 a 7.

35,24 ALFWY.. HELD. "Alfwy(?Alwin) son of Banna *(Aluuin' banesona)* held jointly". So also 517 a 2. It is hard to tell whether there are two people (Alwin and his brother Alfwy) or one. If one, it is difficult to know whether we have here *Aluui* (= Alwin from OE *Aelfwine*) in which the nunnation mark has been lost, or — more likely — *Aluui* (= Alfwy from OE *Aelfwig*) in which, in 4 cases (for DB 1,27 and 35,24) an unnecessary nunnation mark has been mistakenly added.
OAKLEY.. ADDED TO MARTOCK. ".. it did not belong to it in 1066".. 517 a 2.
VALUE. "It pays 50s a year into the King's revenue". So also 517 a 2.

36,2 WLTUNE WHICH KETEL HELD AS ONE MANOR. *"Wlftuna* which Ketel held jointly.. Botolph holds it from Thurstan and has 1 plough there,. Thurstan holds these 2 manors as 1 manor". Botolph is *Butor* here, with loss of *f* in *lf* (PNDB §94) and substitution of *r* for *l* (PNDB §60).
ADDED TO ALFWOLD'S LANDS. "Added to the Honour of Alfwold". So also 520 b 1.

36,3 1 PLOUGH THERE. "Ripe.. has 1 plough there"; *in dominio* probably omitted in error.

36,5 WESTON.. THURSTAN. Also in 520 b 4 in a shortened form.
WESTON.. ALFWY HELD.. AS A MANOR. "A manor called Weston (Bampfylde) which Alfwy held". So also 520 b 4, but ".. Alfwy held jointly".
HE COULD GO WHERE HE WOULD. "He could choose for himself with his land a lord according to his will".

36,7 BERNARD HOLDS.. Bernard (Pancevolt) is not mentioned in Exon. as the sub-tenant of the whole of South Cadbury, only of the 2 hides mentioned after the plough assessment.
2 HIDES AND 1 VIRGATE ADDED. "..Value 40s".. 521 a 4.
FOUR THANES HELD FREELY. "4 thanes held jointly"; so also 521 a 4.

E

A FURTHER HIDE. "Besides these added lands which I have mentioned *(comemoravi)*above has been added another hide.." A rare occurrence of the first person; see also 40,2 below, an entry written by the same scribe.

ALNOTH HELD FREELY. "Alnoth held jointly", both in the case of Woolston and of Clapton. So also 521 a 4.

CLAPTON. "Another manor, called Clapton"; so also 521 a 4.

WOODLAND.. ".. 4 furlongs in width and 2 in width "; first "width" in error.

36,8 1 PLOUGH.. THERE. "Alfward has 1 plough"; *in dominio* probably omitted in error.

36,9 ½ PLOUGH. "4 oxen".

36,11 86 SHEEP. *.iiii.xx. oues 7 vi 7 i leugā nemoris*..86 sheep are probably intended, as Exon. ofte writes numbers like this, especially with *c, cc, ccc* etc. (see 40,2 note below). However, *capras* "goats", could have been omitted after the *vi;* "6+1 leagues of woodland" are unlikely.

36,13 1 VIRGATE.. VALUE. "Value when Thurstan acquired it," only in 523 a 4.

EDWY HELD IT FREELY. "Edwy held jointly"; so also 523 a 4.

37,1 1 HIDE. "1 plough can plough it".

37,3 WITH 1 SLAVE, IT IS THERE, IN LORDSHIP. "1 (plough) is there and 1 slave"; *in dominic* perhaps omitted in error.

37,4 AELFRIC HELD IT AS A MANOR. "Aelfric held jointly"; so also 517 b 3.
1 PLOUGH.. THERE. The villager has it.

37,5-6 ALDWICK, RIDGEHILL. "Serlo holds these 2 manors as 1 manor". In 519 a 1 "Serlo.. has.. Aldwick.. Another manor, called Ridgehill, has been added to it.. Serlo holds these 2 manors as 1 manor".

37,6 FOUR THANES HELD. ".. jointly"; so also 519 a 1.
A THANE HELD THEM FREELY. "A thane held jointly"; so also 519 a 1.
WALTER. "William Hussey"; so also 519 a 1.
LAND DID NOT BELONG. "Land never belonged".. 519 a 1.
EVERWACER. *Aluuacer;* but *Eueruuacre* in 519 a 1. *Aluuacre* is probably a scribal error; see 24,28 note above. It is interesting that there are three 'mistakes' in Exon. for 37,5-6: *Almarus atter,* see 37,5 in General Notes; Walter/William Hussey for 37,6 (though this may no be a mistake); and *Aluuacre* here. The scribe is the same for all these entries.

37,7 ST. EDWARD'S .. THERE. "Serlo has a manor called Kilmington.. Serlo of Burcy gave it to St. Edward's Abbey with his daughter".
BUT IT PAID TAX FOR 1 HIDE. "But it did not pay tax, except for 1 hide".

37,8 LOVINGTON. ".. which Aelmer held. 2 hides of land have been added to it, which Sigeric and Alfhild held jointly in 1066. Value 33s 4d; when Serlo acquired|them, 40s. Serlo holds these lands of the 3 thanes as 1 manor".. 521 a 3.
THREE THANES.. AS THREE MANORS. "3 thanes, Aelmer, Sigeric, and a woman, Alfhild held jointly.. Aelmer had 4 hides, Sigeric 1 (hide) and Alfhild the other hide. Serlo holds the lands as 1 manor".

37,9 [VALUE] NOW 40s. "..30s".

37,10 1 VIRGATE, 1 FURLONG, 1 PLOUGH. They are all in lordship.

37,11 MORETON. ".. which Aelfric held jointly. 2 hides of land have been added to it, which 2 thanes held jointly in 1066. Value 45s; when Serlo acquired them, as much. Serlo holds thes 3 lands as 1 manor".. 521 b 5.
THREE THANES.. AS THREE MANORS. "3 thanes, Aelfric, Alric and Alfwy, held jointly.. Aelfric had 3 hides, Alric 1 hide, and Alfwy 1 hide . Serlo holds these 3 lands as 1 manor".
LAND FOR 5 PLOUGHS. 5½ ploughs; see Details Table.
9 VILLAGERS AND 11 SMALLHOLDERS. 7 villagers and 9 smallholders; see Details Table
WOODLAND, 15 ACRES. 30 acres; see Details Table.
AFTER THIS ENTRY in the *Terrae Occupatae* at the bottom of folio 521b appear the word *omīs omo primum bonum* (Ellis misprints *omu);* "every man (is) the first good/most impor-tant thing". This motto (?) seems to have been written by a contemporary scribe; it has nothing to do with the text.

37,12 SAERED HELD IT FREELY AS A MANOR. "Saered held jointly"; so also 522 b 5.

40 EDWARD OF SALISBURY. Called Edward the Sheriff in the heading and in both entries.

40,1 IN BATH 2 HOUSES. "1 house *(domum)* in Bath.. and another dwelling *(mansuram)* also in this Borough".
90 PIGS. *7 l 7 xl porcos;* possibly a word omitted after *l,* making "50.. and 40 pigs", though more likely a similar phrase to those often used in Exon. with *cc, ccc* etc. (see next note).

40,2 240 SHEEP. *cc oues 7 xl* This splitting of numbers with *c, cc, ccc* etc. is quite common in Exon., especially in the parts relating to Dorset. Occasionally, as in 36,11 and perhaps 40,1, occurs with other numbers. See Addenda, page 332.
OF THESE 10 HIDES. "..which we have spoken of above". See 36,7 note above.

41,1 IN BATH. "In the Borough of Bath".
42,3 EDRIC. "The said Edric"; i.e. of 42,2.
TAX FOR 1 HIDE. "Tax for 1½ hides".
1 PLOUGH.. THERE. "Walter.. has 1 plough"; *in dominio* probably omitted in error.
44,2 THORKELL THE DANE. So 518 b 3; plain *Torchillus* in the main entry.
1 VIRGATE.. HELD. ".. in 1066".
VALUE 5s. Only in 518 b 3.
45 HUMPHREY THE CHAMBERLAIN. In Exon.the first 2 entries of his holding are given under the heading "Lands of the King's Servants in Somerset", and the rest under "Lands of the French Thanes in Somerset", hence probably the separation in DB of the two parts of ch. 45.
45,1 ORDRIC AND LEOFING HELD. "2 brothers, Ordric and Leofing, held jointly". In 517 b 1 "2 brothers held jointly".
THIS LAND.. WOULD. "It has been joined with Brictric's Honour, but they (Ordric and Leofing) could go to whichever lord they would". In 517 b 1 "This (manor) has been added to Brictric's Honour".
45,2 LEOFING HELD. ".. jointly"; so also 517 b 2.
THIS.. WOULD. "This (manor) has been joined with Brictric's Honour"; in 517 b 2 "added to Brictric's Honour". The phrase about the holders is omitted in both Exon. entries.
45,3 THIS ENTRY also appears in 521 b 3 in shortened form.
FREELY. *Libere* also, interlined, though usually Exon. has *pariter*, "jointly", for DB's *libere* (as in 45,5 below).
45,5 HUMPHREY THE CHAMBERLAIN. So 521 b 4; plain *Hunfridus* in the main entry.
THREE THANES HELD FREELY. "3 thanes held jointly"; so also 521 b 4.
45,7 THREE THANES HELD. ".. jointly.. Sigeric had 1½ virgates, Cuthwulf ½ hide, and Waldin ½ hide."
3 SLAVES.. ½ VIRGATE. Unusually *ii bord' 7 iii serui habent dim' virgam.*
(VALUE) FORMERLY 10s. ".. 15s".
45,8 RALPH OF BERKELEY. "Ralph, brother of Roger of Berkeley".
GODRIC HELD. ".. from the King".
1 PLOUGH.. THERE. "Ralph has.. 1 plough"; *in dominio* probably omitted in error.
45,10 INGULF HELD. ".. jointly".
45,11 SWEIN HELD. ".. from the King".
45,12 VALUE.. £4. "Value 40s; when Drogo acquired it, £4".
FROM THIS LAND.. 20s. Also in 522 b 6.
45,14 1 HIDE WHICH HE HELD..FROM. "1 hide which he bought from" *(emit);* according to Round FE pp. 425-6 *emit* is the correct word and the Exchequer scribe slipped up in writing the more usual *tenuit.* Also, *emit* and *enuit* look very similar in the Carolingian minuscule script and the scribe may have added the *t* to make sense of what he thought was a miswritten word.
45,15 2 PLOUGHS.. THERE. "Azelin has 2 ploughs"; *in dominio* probably omitted in error.
VALUE. "It pays 20s; when Azelin acquired it at a revenue *(ad firmam)* from the King, the value was as much."
46. [LAND OF ROBERT.. SERVANTS]. In Exon. entered under the heading "Lands of the King's Servants in Somerset".
46,2-5 ROBERT ALSO. "Robert of Auberville" in each case.
46,2 DODA HELD FREELY. "Doda held jointly".
NOW IT HAS BEEN JUDGED. "Now it has again been judged" *(iterum diudicata).*
46,3 THREE FORESTERS HELD. "3 foresters, Doda, Aelmer, and Godric, held jointly". So also 513 b 2.
ROBERT PAID.. WINSFORD. "From this (manor) Robert used to pay 20s in revenue *(de firma)* to the King's reeve of Winsford". So also 513 b 2.
46,4 WELLISFORD. ".. which a thane held jointly. ½ hide of land has been added to it, which a thane held jointly in 1066. Value 7s 6d; when Robert acquired it, 5s".. 515 b 1.
TWO THANES HELD. ".. jointly.. Edric held ½ hide and Browning ½ hide".
46,5 1½ PLOUGHS.. THERE. "Robert has 1 plough in lordship"; the other ½ plough is not mentioned.
VALUE.. AS MUCH. Only in 509 a 3.
46,6 A PRIEST. "A priest of this village's church".
46,11 SOMERTON. "A manor of the King's, called Somerton"; so also 516 a 5.
46,14 SHOVEL. ".. ½ virgate has been added to it, which a thane held jointly in 1066. Value 2s; when he acquired it, as much".. 509 a 2.
TWO THANES HELD IT FREELY. "2 thanes held jointly".

46,15 HE ALSO. "Ansger Fower".
46,17 3 PLOUGHS.. THERE. 2 villagers' ploughs only there; see Lordship and Villagers Table.
46,19 1 PLOUGH.. THERE. ½ villagers' plough only there; see Lordship and Villagers Table.
47.   LAND OF THE KING'S THANES. In Exon. entered under the heading "Land of the English Thanes in Somerset".
47,1   THEY ALSO HELD IT. ".. jointly".
      IN LORDSHIP 2 PLOUGHS. "They have 2 ploughs there"; *in dominio* probably omitted in error.
      THE KING.. NOTHING FROM IT. "The King has not had this land's payments" *(redditus)*. 3 VIRGATES. "6? virgates"; *iii* changed to a *vi* in the MS, or perhaps vice versa.
47,5   ½ HIDE.. VALUE 5s. "..6s"; so also 517 b 4. It was "(part) of the King's revenue of Curry (Rivel) in 1066".
47,7   PASTURE. *7 x q^{a}drag^b i long^b 7*.. with *nemoris* ("woodland") written above *ī long*, in error for *pascuae*.
47,12 DODINGTON. "A manor in Wellington Hundred called Dodington". See Places Notes to 47,12.
47,13 3 PLOUGHS.. THERE. "Ulf has.. 1 plough and the villagers have 1 plough.. Wulfmer has 1 plough".
      VALUE 25s. "Value, for Ulf's use, 20s; Wulfmer.. value 5s".
47,16 PASTURE 5 FURLONGS. *pascuae* omitted in error after *v q^{a}drag'*.
47,23 8 VILLAGERS AND 3 COTTAGERS. "3 villagers.. 8 smallholders and 3 cottagers".
47,24 ½ PLOUGH. "4 oxen".
47,25 2 PARTS.. PLACED IN. "2 parts.. added to"; so also 524 b 6.

ADDENDA

8,20   The present value of Serlo's holding was originally written *iii lib'* with another, larger *i* (not *J* as Ellis prints) added at the front to make *iiii lib'*; the Exchequer DB scribe may not have seen this correction.
19,60 The spelling *Goderona* represents the Scandinavian woman's name *Guthrun*, PNDB 264, 279.
40,2   The splitting of numbers is the habit of one particular scribe.

Details of Lordship Table 'L'

Details of Holdings Table 'D'

DETAILS OF LORDSHIP AND VILLAGERS' LAND AND PLOUGHS OMITTED IN DB AND GIVEN IN EXON.

The details below are for the main holding at the place named, unless marked with an asterisk. Exon. folio references are given on the translation pages. Rest = rest of the la[...] *(aliam* or *aliam terram).* h.= hide, v.= virgate, f = furlong.

DB reference	Place	In Lordship land	In Lordship ploughs	The villagers have land	The villagers have ploughs
1,11	Preston*	3 v.	1	1 v.	1
1,28	Burnett*	½ h.	2	½ h.	2
1,29	Chewton Mendip*	½ v.	½	Rest	2
3,1	Seaborough	3 v.	1	3 v.	1
”	Seaborough*	3 v.	1	3 v.	1
5,1	Dowlish	—	1	—	½
5,7	Culbone	1 h.	1	1 v.	—
5,12	Winterhead	3 v.	1	1 v.	1
5,15	Timsbury*	1½ h.	1	½ h.	1
5,19	Clewer	1 v.	½	1 v. less 1 f. ‡	1½
5,21	Bishopsworth	2½ v.	—	—	2
5,68	Midgell	2 v.	—	2 v.	2
8,12	?Butleigh	1½ v.	1	Rest	½
10,3	Seavington	1 h.	1	1 h.	1
16,8	Beere	3 f.	½	1 f.	½
18,3	Aller	1 v. 3 f.	1	1 f.	—
19,36	?Ashbrittle	3 v. 3 f.	—	Rest	1
19,70	Goathill	3 v.	1½	1 v.	½
21,60	Stoke Pero	1 f.	½	1 f.	½
21,64	'Gilcott'	1½ v.	½	½ v.	½
†24,30	Chilcompton*	3 v. less 1 f.	—	1 v. 1 f.	½
24,37	Adber	1 h.	1	1 v.	—
25,23	Allercott	1 f.	½	1 f.	½
†37,1	Blagdon*	3 v.	1	1 v.	1
†37,4	Chillyhill	½ h.	1	—	1
37,8	Lovington*	½ h.	½	½ h.	½
45,5	Sandford Orcas	3½ h. less 1 f.	3	Rest	3
45,6	Timsbury	4 h. less 1 v.	1	5 v.	1
45,9	Warleigh	½ h.	2	½ h.	1
45,10	Batheaston	1½ h.	1	1½ h.	2
45,11	Claverton	2½ h.	2	2½ h.	4
45,12	Knowle Park	3 v. 1 f.	2	3 v. less 1 f.	1
45,13	Foddington	2 h. less 1 v.	2	½ h.	1
45,16	Brockley	2 h.	—	2 h.	4
46,7	Perry	1 v. 1 f.	½	Rest	½
†46,8	Newton	1 v.	1	1 v.	—
46,10	Wigborough	1½ h. 1 f.	1	1½ v. 1 f.	½
46,11	Huntstile	½ v.	1	½ v.	1
46,12	Chilton Trinity	3 f.	½	1 f.	½
46,15	Durleigh	½ h. less 1 f.	1	Rest	2

DB reference	Place	In Lordship		The villagers have	
		land	ploughs	land	ploughs
46,17	Newton	1 h.	—	1 v.	2
46,19	Milton	3½ v.	—	½ v.	½
47,10	Dinnington	2 h.	1	1 h.	2
47,11	Adber	½ h.	1	½ h.	½
47,18	Swainswick	1 h.	2	1 h.	1
47,19	Buckland Dinham	8½ h.	1	3½ h.	4
47,20	Combe ?Hay	1 h.	1	1 h.	4
47,21	West Lydford	5½ h. less ½ v.	3	3 h. 1½ v.	4
47,23	Writhlington	5 h.	2	1 h.	3

‡   See Exon. notes to 5,19

†   *In dominio* omitted, probably in error.

DETAILS OF HOLDINGS OMITTED IN DB AND GIVEN IN EXON.

ac. = acre   f. = furlong   lg. = league   v. = virgate   h. = hide

DB ref.	PLACE	Sub-tenant	Holding	Land for ploughs	LORDSHIP land	LORDSHIP ploughs	VILLAGERS HAVE land	VILLAGERS HAVE ploughs	Villagers	Small-holders	Cottagers (cotarii)	Slaves
1,1	Somerton	Brictnoth	4h.*	4	-	-	-	3	7	5	-	-
		Aelfric	1h.*	-	-	-	-	-	-	-	-	-
		Saewin	½h.*	-	-	1	-	-	-	-	-	-
1,21	Congresbury	Alfward	1h.	-	3v.	1	1v.	½	1	5	-	-
		Ordric	1h. 1v.	-	3v.	1	2v.	2	4	8	-	2
		Ordwulf	3v.	-	2½v.	1	½v.	1	1	4	-	2
2,6	Taunton	Geoffrey	4h. 1v.	-	3h.	4	1h. 1v.	3	8	13	-	-
		Robert	4½h.	-	3h.	4	1½h.	4	8	18	-	8
		Hugh *de uillana*	2½h.	-	1½h.	2	1h.	3	4	6	-	4
2,7	Taunton	Godwin	2h. less ½v.	-	1½h.	2	1½v.	1	4	5	-	2
		Leofeva	2h.	-	1½h.	2	½h.	1	4	5	-	3
		Alfward	1h. 1½v.	-	1h. 1v.	1	½v.	½	1	5	-	2
		Aelfric & Edmer	3h.	-	2½h.	2	½h.	1	4	5	-	6
		Leofwy	½v.	-	-	½	-	-	-	-	-	-
2,8	Taunton	John the Usher	2h. ½v.	-	1h. 1½v.	1	3v.	1½	6	10	-	2
		Alfred of 'Spain'	1h.	-	-	-	-	1	4	-	-	-
		Count of Mortain	1h.	-	3v.	1	1v.	1	2	7	-	4

* Amount tax paid on; amount of holding not stated, but probably the same.

DB ref.	PLACE	Sub-tenant	Cobs	Cattle	Cows	Pigs	Sheep	Goats	Un-broken mares	Mills	Wood	Under-wood	Meadow	Pasture	VALUE 1086	VALUE when acquired
											(length by width)					
1,1	Somerton	Brictnoth	-	-	-	-	-	-	-	-	-	-	-	-	100s.	-
		Aelfric	-	-	-	-	-	-	-	-	-	-	-	-	25s.	-
		Saewin	-	-	-	-	-	-	-	-	-	-	-	-	30s.	-
1,21	Congresbury	Alfward	-	-	-	-	-	-	-	-	15ac.	-	20 ac.	-	20s.	-
		Ordric	-	12	-	10	-	-	-	-	15ac.	-	-	-	25s.	-
		Ordwulf	-	-	-	-	-	-	-	-	-	-	-	-	15s.	-
2,6	Taunton	Geoffrey	2	38	-	30	220	-	-	-	22ac.	-	16 ac.	-	£10	-
		Robert	4	28	-	30	200	-	-	-	16ac.	-	16 ac.	-	£12	-
		Hugh de uillana	2	12	-	16	60	-	-	-	5ac.	-	5 ac.	-	100s.	-
2,7	Taunton	Godwin	1	8	-	10	100	-	-	1 paying 40d.	5ac.	-	6 ac.	4 ac.	40s.	20s.
		Leofeva	1	2	-	-	50	-	-	1 paying 40d.	3ac.	-	6 ac.	8 ac.	40s.	20s.
		Alfward	-	-	-	-	-	-	-	-	32ac.	-	13 ac.	-	20s.	5s.
		Aelfric & Edmer	2	16	-	20	40	-	-	-	20ac.	-	20 ac.	-	£3	20s.
		Leofwy	-	-	-	-	-	-	-	-	-	1 ac.	-	-	3s.	2s.
2,8	Taunton	John the Usher	1	-	-	-	-	-	-	1 paying 50d.	-	-	7 ac.	100ac.	30s.	20s.
		Alfred of 'Spain'	-	-	-	-	-	-	-	-	-	-	2 ac.	-	20s.	10s.
		Count of Mortain	1	-	-	5	-	-	-	1 paying 10s.	15ac.	-	10 ac.	-	£4	40s.

DB ref.	PLACE	Sub-tenant	Holding	Land for ploughs	LORDSHIP land	LORDSHIP ploughs	VILLAGERS HAVE land	VILLAGERS HAVE ploughs	Villagers	Smallholders	Cottagers (cotarii)	Slaves
2,9	Lydeard St Lawrence	Wulfward	2h.*	4	-	-	-	-	6	2	-	3
	Leigh	Alfward	½h.*	1	-	-	-	-	-	1	-	4
5,1	Dowlish	2 thanes (TRE)	4h.	-	-	1	-	2	6	6	-	-
		1 thane (TRE)	3h.	3	-	1	-	3	5	5	-	2
5,41	Winford	Roger Whiting	4h.	-	-	3	-	9	9	6	-	6
		Fulcran	5h.	-	-	1	-	4	8	6	-	1
		Colswein	1h.	2	-	1	-	1	-	-	-	-
5,54	Rode	Robert	1h.	-	3v.	1	1v.	-	-	3	-	1
		Moses	½h.	-	1v.	-	1v.	½	-	3	-	-
		Robert	1½h.	-	-	1	-	½	-	2	-	2
		Roger	2½h.	-	-	2	-	2	1	13	-	1
		Sheerwold	2½h.	-	-	1½	-	1	2	6	-	1
		Richard the Interpreter	1h.	-	-	1	-	½	-	2	-	1
6,1	Wells	Fastrad	6h.	-	4h.	3	2h.	4	10	8	-	6
		Richard	5h.	-	3h.	2	2h.	3	8	4	-	2
		Erneis	5h.	-	4h.	1	1h.	4	7	4	-	2
		Fastrad	2h.	-	-	1	-	-	1	2	-	1
		Ralph	2h.	-	1h.	1	1h.	1	4	3	-	2
6,9	Banwell	Serlo of Burcy	3h.	8	-	1	-	3	5	3	-	2
		Ralph Crooked Hands	5½h.	-	-	3	-	5	6	2	-	-

* Amount tax paid on; amount of holding not stated, but probably the same.

DB ref.	PLACE	Sub-tenant	Cobs	Cattle	Cows	Pigs	Sheep	Goats	Un-broken mares	Mills	Wood	Under-wood	Meadow	Pasture	VALUE 1086	VALUE when acquired
											(length by width)					
2,9	Lydeard St Lawrence	Wulfward	-	-	-	-	-	-	-	-	15 ac.	-	9 ac.	100 ac.	40s.	40s.
	Leigh	Alfward	-	-	-	-	-	-	-	-	34 ac. + 2ac.	-	2 ac.	-	5s.	5s.
5,1	Dowlish	2 thanes (TRE)	1	-	3	14	21	-	-	-	8f. x 3f.	-	29 ac.	4f. x 3f.	60s.	-
		1 thane (TRE)	-	-	3	5	-	-	-	-	20 ac.	-	15 ac.	20 ac.	70s.	-
5,41	Winford	Roger Whiting	1	-	5	10	60	-	-	1 paying 40d.	1lg. x 2f.	-	20 ac.	4 ac.	£6	£6
		Fulcran	1	-	15	6	200	-	3	-	-	-	-	2f. x 1f.	£3	40s.
		Colswein	-	-	-	-	-	-	-	-	-	-	-	-	25s.	25s.
5,54	Rode	Robert	1	-	-	-	30	-	-	See	2 ac.	-	3 ac.	-	20s.	10s.
		Moses	-	-	-	-	-	-	-	)	-	-	3 ac.	-	8s.	8s.
		Robert	-	4	-	7	150	-	-	) Exon.	6 ac.	-	5 ac.	4 ac.	30s.	20s.
		Roger	-	2	-	12	47	21	-	)	-	12 ac.	10 ac.	9 ac.	60s.	40s.
		Sheerwold	1	6	-	20	100	-	-	) Notes	13 ac.	-	8 ac.	10 ac.	40s.	60s.
		Richard the Interpreter	-	5	-	6	48	-	-	-	-	-	4 ac.	2 ac.	25s.	15s.
6,1	Wells	Fastrad	1	15	-	30	200	-	-	1 paying 5s.	-	-	-	-	100s.	-
		Richard	-	15	-	20	200	-	-	-	-	-	-	-	£4	-
		Erneis	1	10	-	12	100	-	-	1 paying 5s.	-	-	-	-	£4	-
		Fastrad	-	-	-	-	-	-	-	1 paying 7s 6d.	-	-	-	-	30s.	-
		Ralph	-	10	-	6	50	30	-	-	-	-	-	-	40s.	-
6,9	Banwell	Serlo of Burcy	-	-	-	-	-	-	-	-	-	-	-	-	60s.	£6
		Ralph	-	-	-	-	-	-	-	-	-	-	-	-	-	-
		Crooked Hands	-	-	-	-	-	-	-	-	-	-	-	-	100s.	-

DB ref.	PLACE	Sub-tenant	Holding	Land for ploughs	LORDSHIP land	ploughs	VILLAGERS HAVE land	ploughs	Villagers	Small-holders	Cottagers (cotarii)	Slaves
6,9	Banwell	Roghard	5½h.	-	2h.	2	3½h.	4	9	10	-	3
		Fastrad	1h.	-	-	1	-	-	1	-	-	-
		Bofa	1h.	-	-	1	-	-	1	-	-	-
		Alfwy son of Banna (?)	1h.	-	-	1	-	½	1	-	-	-
6,10	Evercreech	Erneis	7h.	-	4h.	2	3h.	2	5	4	-	4
		Maghere	1½h.	-	-	1	-	-	-	-	-	-
		Hildebert	1h.	-	-	1	-	-	-	-	-	-
6,13	Chew Magna	Richard	5h.	-	4h.	1	1h.	1	2	4	-	2
		Roghard	6h.	-	3h.	2	3h.	6	11	2	-	2
		Aelfric of Stowey	7v.	-	1½h.	2	1v.	1	2	2	-	2
		Stephen	5h.	-	4h.3v.	1	1v.	1	2	7	-	1
		Wulfric	2h.	-	2h.less 1v.	1	-	1	1	3	-	1
6,14	Yatton	Fastrad	5h.	-	2h.	1	3h.	4	5	10	-	-
		Hildebert	4h.	-	2h.	2	2h.	7	13	13	-	4
7,11	Bathampton	Hugh the Interpreter	3h.	-	1½h.	2	1½h.	3	3	6	-	3
		Colgrim	2h.	-	-	1	-	-	-	3	-	-
8,5	Sutton Mallett	Roger of Courseulles	5h.	-	4h.1v.	3	3v.	2	4	5	-	2
	Edington	,, ,,	5h.	-	4½h.	2	½h.	1	2	4	-	1
	Chilton Polden	,, ,,	5h.	-	4h.	2	1h.	2½	8	7	-	3
	Catcott	,, ,,	5h.	-	3½h.½v.	2	Rest	3	5	7	-	5
8,11	Compton Dundon	Roger of Courseulles	5h.	-	2h.1v.	1	Rest	6	9	8	-	2
	Ashcott	Walter of Douai	3h.	-	2h.1v.	1	3v.	1	3	2	-	1
	Pedwell	Walter of Douai	3h.	-	2h.1v.	1	3v.	1	3	2	-	3

DB ref.	PLACE	Sub-tenant	Cobs	Cattle Cows	Pigs	Sheep	Goats	Un-broken mares	Mills	Wood	Under-wood (length by width)	Meadow	Pasture	VALUE 1086	when acquired
6,9	Banwell	Roghard	1	20	30	100	-	6	2 paying 10s.	-	-	-	-	100s.	£4
		Fastrad	-	-	-	-	-	-	-	-	-	-	-	20s.	-
		Bofa	-	-	-	-	-	-	-	-	-	-	-	10s.	-
		Alfwy son of Banna (?)	-	-	-	-	-	-	-	-	-	-	-	10s.	-
6,10	Evercreech	Erneis	1	6	12	100	-	-	-	-	-	-	-	£4	£4
		Maghere	-	8	10	80	-	-	-	-	-	-	-	20s.	20s.
		Hildebert	-	-	-	-	-	-	-	-	-	-	-	10s.	10s.
6,13	Chew Magna	Richard	-	4	4	50	30	-	-	-	-	-	-	40s.	-
		Roghard	1	16	20	50	50	-	1 paying 40d.	-	-	-	-	£5	-
		Aelfric of Stowey	-	1	-	200	-	-	-	-	-	-	-	30s.	-
		Stephen	-	-	-	-	-	-	1 paying 6s.	-	-	-	-	60s.	-
		Wulfric	1	-	-	-	-	-	-	-	-	-	-	30s.	-
6,14	Yatton	Fastrad	-	8	12	-	-	-	-	-	-	-	-	£4	20s.
		Hildebert	-	8	18	-	-	-	-	-	-	-	-	100s.	£4
7,11	Bathampton	Hugh the Interpreter	1	14	-	80	-	-	-	-	10 f.	20 ac.	-	£4	£3
		Colgrim	-	-	20	100	-	-	-	-	-	8 ac.	6 f.	30s.	-
8,5	Sutton Mallett	Roger of Courseulles	5	-	2	-	-	-	-	-	-	34 ac.	-	£3	100s.
	Edington	" " "	-	8	20	70	-	-	-	-	15 ac.	24 ac.	-	60s.	100s.
	Chilton Polden	" " "	-	10	56	15	-	-	-	-	8 ac.	30 ac.	-	£4	£4
	Catcott	" "	-	-	22	100	-	-	-	-	8 ac.	31 ac.	-	100s	100s.
8,11	Compton Dundon	Roger of Courseulles	1	2	-	46	49	-	-	6f. x 1f.	-	20 ac.	-	100s.	£4
	Ashcott	Walter of Douai	-	4	23	55	-	-	-	-	-	-	-	40s.	40s.
	Pedwell	Walter of Douai	-	3	-	-	-	-	-	-	40 ac.	12 ac.	-	60s.	40s.

341

DB ref.	PLACE	Sub-tenant	Holding	Land for ploughs	LORDSHIP land	ploughs	VILLAGERS HAVE land	ploughs	Villagers	Small-holders	Cottagers (cotarii)	Slaves
8,17	Ham	Robert of Auberville	1h. 1v.	-	1h.	-	1v.	-	-	6	-	1
		Gerard Ditcher	3v.	-	3v.	-	-	-	-	1	-	-
		Serlo of Burcy	5h.	-	2½h.½v.	2	Rest	2	2	8	-	3
8,18	Butleigh	Thurstan son of Rolf	8h.	-	5½h.	3	Rest	2	9	5	-	6
		Roger of Courseulles	2h.	-	1½h.	1	Rest	1	2	1	-	-
8,20	Shepton Mallet	Roger of Courseulles	6½h.	-	4h.1½v.	2	Rest	3	7	14	-	6
	Croscombe	" "	3h.	-	2h.1v.	1	3v.	3	6	5	-	2
	North Wootton	Edred	5h.	-	3½h.	2	Rest	1	2	11	-	4
	Pylle	Serlo of Burcy	5h.	-	1h.3v.	1½	3h.1v.	2	6	6	11	2
	Pilton	Ralph Crooked Hands	2h.	-	-	1	-	-	-	1	-	2
8,23	Charlton	Roger of Courseulles	3h. 1v.	-	3h.less ½v.	-	1½v.	1	2	2	-	-
	‡ elsewhere (?)	" "	2h. 3v.	-	1h.3v.	1	1h.	1	6	4	-	1
8,28	West Monkton	Roger of Courseulles	4h. 3v.	-	-	3	-	-	4	8	-	2
		Serlo of Burcy	2½h.	-	-	1	-	1½	4	3	-	1
8,30	Hornblotton	Serlo of Burcy	5½h.	-	-	1	-	7	12	2	-	3
	Alhampton	Ralph Crooked Hands	6½h.	-	-	1	-	3	7	6	-	1
	Lamyatt	Nigel the Doctor	5½h.	-	3h.	2	2½h.	5	10	5	3*	-

* Cocetos, "Cottagers", as distinct from cotarii, "cottagers".

‡ alibi in DB, but inde "there" (that is, in Charlton) in Exon.

DB ref.	PLACE	Sub-tenant	Cobs	Cattle	Cows	Pigs	Sheep	Goats	Un-broken mares	Mills	Wood Under-wood (length by width)	Meadow	Pasture	VALUE 1086	VALUE when acquired
8,17	Ham	Robert of Auberville	1	7	-	13	21	-	3+	-	-	10 ac.	10 ac.	20s.	10s.
		Gerard Ditcher	1	5	-	-	40	-	-	-	-	-	-	10s.	5s.
		Serlo of Burcy	-	2	-	-	42	-	-	-	-	20 ac.	10 ac.	£4	100s.
8,18	Butleigh	Thurstan son of Rolf	1	3	-	22	180	32	-	-	12 ac.	8 ac.	-	£6	£6
		Roger of Courseulles	1	-	-	-	150	-	-	-	-	6 ac.	-	20s.	10s.
8,20	Shepton Mallett	Roger of Courseulles	1	5	-	37	500	-	-	1 paying 15d.	12 ac.	38 ac.	3f.x 1f.	£7	£7
	Croscombe	” ”	-	10	-	-	100	45	-	1 paying 5s.	30 ac.	12 ac.	-	40s.	30s.
	North Wootton	Edred	-	11	-	8	48	16	-	1 paying 2s.	2 ac.	30 ac.	20 ac.	60s.	40s.
	Pylle	Serlo of Burcy	1	8	-	13	-	-	-	1 paying 30d.	2ac.	2½ ac.	-	£4	£4
	Pilton	Ralph Crooked Hands	1	-	-	-	-	-	-	-	-	4 ac.	-	30s.	40s.
8,23	Charlton	Roger of Courseulles	-	-	-	-	-	-	-	-	-	11 ac.	-	20s.	20s.
	‡ elsewhere(?)	” ”	1	24	-	4	320	-	-	1 paying 9d.	30 ac.	12 ac.	10 ac.	£4	30s.
8,28	West Monkton	Roger of Courseulles	-	-	-	6	20	-	4	-	-	19 ac.	40 ac.	60s.	-
		Serlo of Burcy	-	-	-	-	-	-	-	-	-	-	-	30s.	-
8,30	Hornblotton	Serlo of Burcy	1	11	-	24	100	-	-	1 paying 5s.	4f. x 1f.	20 ac.	-	£5	£3
	Alhampton	Ralph Crooked Hands	-	-	1	7	18	-	-	1 paying 40d.	5 ac.	15 ac.	-	£4	40s.
	Lamyatt	Nigel the Doctor	-	2	-	6	20	-	-	1 paying 5s.	3f. x ½f.	20 ac.	20 ac.	£5 10s	£6

+ .iii. equas; indomitas, "unbroken", not mentioned.

‡ alibi in DB, but inde "there" (that is, in Charlton) in Exon.

DB ref.	PLACE	Sub-tenant	Holding	Land for ploughs	LORDSHIP		VILLAGERS HAVE		Villagers	Small-holders	Cottagers (cotarii)	Slaves
					land	ploughs	land	ploughs				
8,33	Brent	Roger of Courseulles	1h.	-	-	1	-	-	-	5	-	-
		Aelfric son of Everwacer	5v.	-	-	1	-	1	1	-	3	1
		Ralph of Conteville	5v.	-	-	1	-	1	1	-	3	-
		Godwin the priest	1½h.	-	-	1	-	1	2	-	7	-
9,6	Drayton	Ceolric	1h.	-	1h.less 10ac.	-	10ac.	-	-	2	-	-
		Wulfward	1h.	-	1h.less 10ac.	-	10ac.	-	-	2	-	-
19,86	'Bishopstone'	Alfred the Butler	1½h.	-	-	1½	-	-	-	6	-	1
		Drogo	1h.	-	-	1½	-	-	-	5	-	-
		Bretel	1h.	-	-	1	-	-	-	2	-	-
		Duncan	1h.	-	-	1	-	-	-	6	-	-
21,85	Littleton	Norman	1½h.*	2	3½v.	-	½h.½v.	2 oxen	2	1	-	2
		Norman	1½h.	2	1h.½v.	2	Rest	½	2	2	-	1
21,98	Long Sutton	Dodman	1h.	-	-	1	-	-	-	-	-	1
		Warmund	1h.	-	-	1	-	1	4	3	-	1
35,19	Goathurst	Walter	1h. 1v.	-	½v.	2	1h.½v.	3	9	5	-	4
		Ansger Fower	2v.	-	-	-	-	1	4	-	-	-
37,11	Moreton	Godric	2h.	2	1½h.1f.	1	1v.3f.	1	3	5	1	-
		Alric	2h.	2	1½h.1f. less 1f.	1	½h.1f.	1	4	4	1	-
		Richard	3v.	1	½h.	-	1v.	1	1	3	-	-
		Humphrey	1v.	½	½v.	-	½v.	-	1	-	-	-

* Amount tax paid on; amount of holding not stated, but probably the same.

D

DB ref.	PLACE	Sub-tenant	Cobs	Cattle	Cows	Pigs	Sheep	Goats	Un-broken mares	Mills	Wood	Under-wood (length by width)	Meadow	Pasture	VALUE 1086	when acquired
8,33	Brent	Roger of Courseulles	1	3	-	-	50	-	-	-	-	6 ac.	5 ac.	-	20s.	20s.
		Aelfric son of Everwacer	-	1	-	-	-	-	-	-	-	-	-	-	20s.	-
		Ralph of Conteville	-	-	-	-	-	-	-	-	-	-	-	-	20s.	-
		Godwin the priest	-	5	-	10	36	-	-	-	-	-	-	-	30s.	-
9,6	Drayton	Ceolric	-	-	-	-	-	-	-	-	1 ac.	-	3 ac.	30 ac.	20s.}	-
		Wulfward	-	-	-	-	-	-	-	-	6 ac.	-	-	5 ac.	}	-
19,86	'Bishopstone'	Alfred the Butler	-	-	-	-	80	-	-	-	-	-	-	-	28s.	-
		Drogo	-	-	-	-	-	-	-	-	-	-	-	-	10s.	-
		Bretel	-	-	-	-	-	-	-	-	-	-	-	-	10s.	-
		Duncan	-	-	-	-	-	-	-	-	-	-	-	-	15s.	-
21,85	Littleton	Norman	-	-	-	-	-	-	-	-	-	20 ac.	20 ac.	-	20s.	20s.
		Norman	-	-	-	-	120	-	-	-	-	20 ac.	20 ac.	-	40s.	40s.
21,98	Long Sutton	Dodman	-	-	1	4	50	-	-	-	-	-	8 ac.	-	20s.	20s.
		Warmund	-	-	-	5	164	-	-	-	-	-	-	-	30s.	-
35,19	Goathurst	Walter	-	9	-	10	60	16	-	-	62 ac.	-	-	-	60s.	60s.
		Ansger Fower	-	-	-	-	-	-	-	-	-	-	-	-	10s.	10s.
37,11	Moreton	Godric	-	15	-	-	-	-	-	½ paying 30d.	15 ac.	-	20 ac.	-	30s.	-
		Alric	-	4	-	-	40	-	-	½ paying 30d.	15 ac.	-	20 ac.	-	30s.	30s.
		Richard	-	-	-	-	-	-	-	-	2 ac.	-	10 ac.	-	10s.	10s.
		Humphrey	-	-	-	-	-	-	-	-	2 ac.	-	8 ac.	2 ac.	5s.	5s.

D

DB ref.	PLACE	Sub-tenant	Holding	Land for ploughs	LORDSHIP		VILLAGERS HAVE		Villagers	Small-holders	Cottagers (*cotarii*)	Slaves
					land	ploughs	land	ploughs				
46,6	'Pignes'	John the Usher	1h. 1v.*	2	½h.	1	½v.	-	2	1	-	-
		a priest of this village's church			½h.	1	-	-	-	2	-	-

* Amount tax paid on; amount of holding not stated, but probably the same.

DB ref.	PLACE	Sub-tenant	Cobs	Cattle Cows	Pigs	Sheep	Goats	Un-broken mares	Mills	Wood Under-wood (*l e n g t h b y w i d t h*)	Meadow	Pasture	VALUE when acquired 1086
46,6	'Pignes'	John the Usher	-	8 -	10	-	-	-	-	-	-	5 ac.	15s. ⎱ 40s.
		a priest of this village's church	-	6 -	6	33	-	-	-	-	-	-	15s. ⎰

346

NOTES ON THE PLACE NAME IDENTIFICATIONS

In the text of the five south-western Counties, contrary to its practice elsewhere, Domesday Book does not include the Hundred rubrication that is an invaluable aid to the identification of places. In Somerset moreover, the same DB form can represent places of divergent modern spelling: *Cruche* and *Sanford,* for example, representing Cricket, Crewkerne, 'Crook', or Sandford, Sampford and Saltford, while *Stantune, Chenolle, Contone, Cildetone, Cumbe* and *Stoche* may each be one of several places of the same modern name scattered over the County. This lack of Hundred headings can in part be made good by the evidence of the Exon. Tax Return (folios 75a-82b, 526b-527a), printed by Ellis in DB 3 and translated in VCH i pp. 527-537. The present editors hope to publish their analysis of it as a separate volume.

The Exon. Tax Return lists tax paid, owed or waived for the holdings of major landholders and some sub-tenants, Hundred by Hundred, and although place-names are rarely included, most entries can be identified and located with more or less certainty by comparison with DB. For tax purposes it groups the presumed DB Hundreds of Frome, Wellow and Kilmersdon as a single 300 hide Hundred named Frome; Bruton, Catsash and Norton Ferris Hundreds form the 232 hides of Bruton Hundred, and Yeovil Hundred at 157½ hides contains the Hundreds of Stone, Tintinhull, Houndsborough and probably Coker. Where the evidence from these Tax Hundreds is cited below, places are said to fall in the 'Frome or Bruton or Yeovil group of Hundreds'.

A second source of place-name identification is the order in which places are entered in the text of the Exchequer or Exon. Books. While the order of the Exchequer Domesday for Somerset is broadly similar to that of the Exon. Book and has not suffered the wholesale re-arrangement done for Cornwall, it has been altered in parts, especially in order to place the *caput* of a landholder's fief as the first entry in his schedule of lands (e.g. in chapters 6-9). In the Exon. Book places are entered in a specific order, Hundred by Hundred, under each major landholder, probably as the Hundred returns came to hand, and this order, with minor exceptions, is that of the second list of Somerset Hundreds given in the Exon. Book (folios 64a-64b, reproduced in Appendix I). No landholder holds in every Hundred, so it is impossible to find all 58 Hundreds in sequence, and many of these 'Hundreds' are really individual royal or ecclesiastical manors, included probably because they were the source of an individual return to the Domesday Commissioners. Moreover, the order can be dislocated by the late entry of additional information for a Hundred largely entered earlier. As a general rule, however, if an isolated place-name appears earlier than the correct place for its Hundred group, or is found in the middle of a group belonging to another Hundred, it is usually a sign of a doubtful identification, of a border land that has subsequently changed its Hundred, or of an outlier. A comparison of the second Exon. list of Hundreds with a long chapter such as 19 (the Count of Mortain) or 21 (Roger of Courseulles) will show how clearly the principle works.

In the notes below, where it is necessary to identify the probable 1086 Hundred of a place, its position in the order of the Exon. Domesday only is referred to even where Exchequer order is the same, since Exchequer order is sometimes distorted, as explained above. The evidence of the Tax Return is cited only where an identification is certain: no attempt has been made to reconstruct the detail of the whole Tax Return Hundred, in the way that Eyton and Whale have done, since guessing is involved. Total and secure identification of places depends on a study of early name-forms and later manorial history, both outside the scope of this edition. The EPNS volume for Somerset, when published, will document the evolution of names, and the fine VCH series, proceeding by Hundreds, will trace the descent of holdings. In the meantime, while the notes below do not aim to be exhaustive, they attempt to offer enough later information to support identifications which might otherwise be reasonably disputed.

Several adjacent modern villages in Somerset, now distinguished by affixes such as East and West, St. Mary and St. Peter *etc.,* share the same DB form. If they existed as separate villages in 1086, this is rarely evidenced, *(Opecedre, Succedene* (2,3) and *Sudcadeberie* (36,7) being exceptional), and they are not here distinguished in text and index. In these cases, the Grid Reference refers to the larger village. Sometimes the existence of separate villages can be inferred as in the case of the adjacent East and West Harptree which, although not distinguished in DB, fall in different Tax Return Hundreds. Where the modern separate villages can be traced from individual DB holdings, this is recorded in the notes. But it is possible to be over precise. Brent (20 hides, 8,33) and Coker (15 hides, 1,23) must have included more than one settlement and extended beyond one modern parish, and it is misleading to talk of East Brent (the modern Parish) as the DB site, especially when the existence of the Hundred name *Suðbrenta* in the second Exon. list suggests that the main settlement was elsewhere in DB times.

The pioneering work of Collinson (1791) on the identification of places still repays study, and this, together with the analyses of Eyton (1880) and Whale (1902) and the early volumes of the Somerset Record Series, made possible the generally sound identifications of E.H. Bates in VCH Volume i (1906). A few changes were made in the years following that publication and more recently S.C. Morland in two valuable articles has changed or sharpened a few identities and these have been adopted by the Domesday Gazetteer. Set out below are the important differences between VCH, DG and this edition, the VCH identifications cited being those that appear in the translation, not the notes. Differentiation of adjacent places of the same basic name is ignored, as are variant spellings ar alternative forms (Podymore for Podimore, King's Brompton for Brompton Regis). Places within inverted commas are identifiable but now lost; a dash indicates that the place is not identified.

CHAPTER+ SECTION	EXCH. FOLIO	DB FORM	VCH	DG	THIS EDITIOI
1,1	86b	Denesmodeswelle	-	Deadmans Well	as DG
1,16	86d	Langeford	Langford (in Burrington)	Langford Budville	as DG
2,3	87c	Scobindare	-	Shopnoller	as DG
2,9	87c	Lega	Angersleigh	Leigh (in Milverton)	as DG
5,9	88a	Harpetreu	West Harptree	East Harptree	as DG
5,38	88c	Wiche	Bathwick	Bathwick + Swainswick	Swainswick
5,50	88d	Millescote	Middlecote	-	as VCH
6,5	89b	Litelande	-	Litnes Field	as DG
7,12	89d	Vndewiche	Woodwick	-	as VCH
7,14	89d	Evestie	-	-	'Eversy'
8,1	90a	Ederesige	Edgarley	Andersey	as DG
8,9	90a	Blacheford	Blackford (in Wincanton)	Blackford (in Wedmore)	as VCH
8,12	90b	Bodelege	-	Bagley	? Butleigh
8,19	90b	Lodreford	? Butleigh Moor	Lattiford	as DG
8,38	91a	Hetsecombe	Ashcombe	Hiscombe	as DG
8,39	91a	Stane	? Stone (in East Pennard)	as VCH	? Kingstone
16,13	91c	Honecote	Huntscott	as VCH	? Holnicote
17,8	91d	Contitone	Compton Bishop	Compton Pauncefoot	Compton Durville
18,3	91d	Alre	-	Aller (Sampford Brett)	as DG
19,61	92d	Ecewiche	Wick (in Camerton)	Eckweek	as DG
19,86	93a	Biscopeston	Bishopston	-	as VCH
21,6	93b	Ulveronetone	-	Waldron	as DG
21,20	93c	Dudesham	-	-	'Dodisham'
21,23-4	93c	Cildetone	Chilton Trinity	Chilton Trivett	as DG
21,25	93c	Pilloch	-	Pillock's Orchard	as DG
21,29	93c	Suindune	-	Swang	? as DG
21,31	93c	Terram Olta	? Aisholt	-	as VCH
21,33	93c	Widiete	-	Withiel	as DG
21,36	93d	Worde	Pt of Knowle St. Giles	Wreath	'Worth'
21,55	94a	Lamore	Pt of Drayton	Moortown	as DG

CHAPTER+ SECTION	EXCH. FOLIO	DB FORM	VCH	DG	THIS EDITION
21,62	94a	*Cumbe*	(in Carhampton Hundred)	Combe (in Withycombe)	as DG
21,64	94a	*Gildenecote*	Gilcot (in Carhampton)	Golsoncott	as VCH
21,65	94a	*Hunecote*	Huntscott	Holnicote	as DG
21,67	94a	*Holme*	Hollam (in Dulverton)	Hone	'Holne'(in Holnicote)
21,80	94b	*Panteshede*	-	-	'Ponteside'
21,87	94b	*Ecferdintone*	Egford (in Frome)	Fairoak	as DG
21,95	94c	*Soche*	Sock Dennis	Sock Malherbie	as DG (Mudford Sock)
22,21	94d	*Opecedre*	Cheddon Fitzpaine	Upper Cheddon	as DG
24,6	95a	*Doneham*	Downhead or Dunball	Dunwear	as DG
24,7	95a	*Cruche*	-	Crosse	'Crook'
24,32	95c	*Ecewiche*	?Wick (in Brent Knoll)	as VCH	Eckweek
25,1	95c	*Sedtametone*	-	Seavington	as DG ('Seaberton')
25,12	95d	*Brune*	Brown	Broom	as VCH
25,42	96b	*Sordemaneford*	-	Stelford	'Shortmansford'
25,50	96b	*Lidiard*	Lydeard Punchardon	Lydeard St. Lawrence	as VCH (East Lydeard)
26,7	96c	*Citerne*	Chilthorne Domer	Chilton Cantelo	? as DG
30,1	96d	*Stawei*	Nether Stowey	Stowey (in Oare)	as DG
35,14	97b	*Lege*	Leigh (in Old Cleeve)	Woodcock's Ley	? as VCH
36,4	97c	*Sindercome*	Syndercombe (in Clatworthy)	Combe (in Bruton)	? as VCH
42,1	98b	*Chiwestoch*	Chewstoke	Kewstoke	as DG
47,12	99a	*Stawe*	Nether Stowey	Dodington	as DG
47,14	99a	*Stoche*	Chewstoke	Stocklinch	? as DG
47,18	99a	*Wiche*	Bathwick	Bathwick and Swainswick	Swainswick

Apart from the works cited at the head of the General Notes, readers interested in place-names will consult the other volumes of the Somerset Record Society, and the bibliography in DGSW pp. 220-222.

Some places that were in existence in 1086 are only evidenced in the personal names: Stowey and Sutton (6,13 note); Heathcombe (21,8 note) and possibly *Gatemore* (22,11 General Notes).

DB does not mention every place in the County in 1086. Subdivisions of large holdings are only occasionally named in the text (e.g. under 8,20 Pilton); in most cases, only the holder's name is given. Some names are found only in the Tax Return or the Exon. Book (? Woodadvent 1,6 note; *Ledforda* 25,33 note; *Pirtochesworda*, 25,33 note; Burnett 1,28 note). Nor is the schedule of holdings complete: royal land is mentioned at Cranmore and (Chew) Stoke in the Tax Returns, and an unnamed 3-hide holding of the Abbess of St. Edward of Shaftesbury in the Return for Bath Hundred. From later evidence, it is apparent that the last mentioned was at Kelston.

See p. 309 at the end of the General Notes for a list of Tax Return Hundreds and their references.

The order of the notes is the numbered order of the text, those for Ch. 45 being given in a single block, not interrupted by chapters 46-47.

References to the Exon. Book are to those in the right-hand margin of the translation unless otherwise stated. Works cited below are specified at the head of the general notes.

Chapter 1

1,1   DEADMANS WELL. Alfred's ½ hide is in Broomfield, Andersfield Hundred. He holds Goathurst and Quantock adjacent. The whole Hundred was originally a dependency of Somerton (Fees 261), and Huntstile (46,11) partly in this Hundred has ½ virgate and 1 furlong belonging to Somerton. See RH ii 129a/134b and Morland I, 46.

1,2   CHEDDAR. A separate Hundred in the Tax Return and later part of Winterstoke. Robert's ½ virgate is probably part of his holding at Cheddar 21,78.
WEDMORE. The text here regards Bishop Giso's Wedmore (6,15) as part of Cheddar. It is later in Bempstone Hundred, and so placed by the Tax Return.

1,4   SOUTH PETHERTON. The ½ hide held by Norman from Roger of Courseulles may be 21,97 Barrington, although the value is different, and Roger holds alone there.
(OVER) STRATTON. Required by the Tax Return for South Petherton Hundred. See KQ 1

1,6   WILLITON. The ½ hide held by Saeric before 1066 as two manors is probably the *Oda* and *Imela* mentioned in the Tax Return for Williton Hundred which together with Westowe constituted 1 hide on which tax had not been paid. *Imela* is probably Embelle adjacent to Westowe and *Oda* either a nearby 'Wood' now lost or Woodadvent later (in KQ 7) held by *Robertus Avenant* from the Barony of Dunden, into which some of Roger of Courseulles' holdings are later grouped. Roger holds other parts of Embelle and Westowe 21,46;49. The addition of the 1 virgate called *Ledforda* is probably the virgate of Elworthy mentioned in 25,33. The name occurs also in the Tax Return for Williton Hundred as *Letfort*. If the first element is 'Leat' meaning 'water channel', it is possibly represented by 'Waterleat' a field (no. 259, TA of 1840) in St. Decumans parish, north of Williton, approximate Grid Reference ST 076 417.

1,7   BEDMINSTER. The 112 acres of meadow and woodland held by the Bishop of Coutances could be adjacent to Long Ashton (5,34) or Bishopsworth (5,20-21).

1,9   BRUTON. The 9 acres held by Bretel are at Redlynch named in Exon; see 19,58.
KILMINGTON. Serlo holds another 5 hides there in 37,7 and in the Tax Return for the Bruton group of Hundreds is ½ hide at *Cillemetona* that has not paid tax, probably part of Serlo's land. Ellis prints the place-name as *...etona*. The one hide held by Jocelyn from Robert, son of Gerald is probably part of Charlton Musgrove (33,1).

1,10 MILBORNE (PORT). Holwell, detached in Dorset, a few miles south, was probably a part of the holding, as in later times.
ILCHESTER. Apparently considered an outlier of Milborne Port in Horethorne Hundred in 1086. See 19,85 note.

1,11 PRESTON. In Milverton, north of Hillfarrance Brook. Torrels Preston and Preston Bowyer were detached parts of Williton Hundred. See 19,35 and 35,18 notes, SRS 3 p.326 and Morland II p.96.

1,12 DULVERTON. A separate Hundred in the Exon. lists. Dulverton is also named in the Tax Return for Williton Hundred where it is later found. The added virgate is unnamed in 46,2.

1,14 NETTLECOMBE. Named in the Tax Return for Williton Hundred. 3 virgates taken away are at Exton 5,5.

1,16 LANGFORD (BUDVILLE). The order of the Exon. Book (104 a 3) is against this place being the Langford in Burrington (VCH), which is probably accounted for in the hidage of Wrington and Banwell. It is royal land in Fees 84. See Morland I p.43.

1,17 WINSFORD. The entry in the *Terrae Occupatae* 516 a 1 lists this as *Winescuma* in error. The added ½ hide is probably at Withypool (46,3). Winsford had a separate Tax Return, accounting for 2 hides and 1 furlong of the royal land. The rest was in Williton Hundred, where the place is also named in the Tax Return.

1,18 CREECH (ST. MICHAEL). A separate Hundred in the second Exon. List. It was later a detached part of Andersfield Hundred.

1,19 NORTH CURRY. Ansger's 1 hide is perhaps part of Thornfalcon (19,31) whose hidage is given as 6 in DB and 7 in the Tax Return for *Torne*. See also 19,36 note.

1,20 CREWKERNE. It no doubt included the later parishes of Wayford and Misterton.

1,21 CONGRESBURY. A separate Hundred in the Tax Return, where the 11 hides of the King's villagers are named. The hide of Bishop Giso is probably the pasture at Wemberham (6,14) although the value given in Exon. is different. The hide shared by Gilbert and Serlo is not mentioned elsewhere in DB.

1,22   (QUEEN) CAMEL. Called *Camel Reginae* after Eleanor Queen of Edward I, or *Camel Regis* FF i pp. 250;263. Exon.order 106 b 1 suggests that it was in Somerton Hundred in 1086, as West Camel. See RH ii 129 a; NV 58; VCH iii p.57. It is later in Bruton Hundred.

1,23   COKER. The holding was large enough to contain the modern villages of North, East and West Coker. It is part of, and perhaps co-extensive with, the ancient Hundred of *Licget, Liet* or *Cochre* (Exon. lists I and II); see Appendix I.

1,24   HARDINGTON (MANDEVILLE) is held from the King by *Rob'tus de Mandevill'* in *Cokr'* Hundred in Fees 85.

1,25   HENSTRIDGE. Named in the Tax Return for Milborne (Horethorne) Hundred.

1,26   MILVERTON. See 6,18.

1,27   MARTOCK. Two of the three ('four' in Exon) hides added are named Oakley in Exon. 113 a 2. Two hides at Oakley on which tax had not been paid are mentioned in the Tax Return for Yeovil Hundred. See 35,24 note. The lands taken away and held by Ansger and Aelfric do not seem to occur elsewhere in DB.
COMPTON (?DURVILLE). The nearest Compton to Martock is Compton Durville, but this place may have been an outlier at Compton in Sherborne Hundred, Dorset. In the Tax Return for Sherborne Hundred, Ansger Cook does not pay tax on 1 hide and 1 virgate held by gift of the King, a holding that does not occur elsewhere in Dorset DB. See VCH Dorset iii p 145.

1,28   KEYNSHAM. Land of the King's villagers is named here *(Cainesham)* in the Tax Return. Exon. names the 1 hide of Wulfward's wife as Burnett (114 a 1).

1,29   CHEWTON (MENDIP). The 11 hides not in lordship are said to be at *Ciuuētona* (Chewton) in the Tax Return. The MS is faint here and the second and third of the four minim strokes forming the double *u* are joined at their tops, leading Ellis to print *Cumētone;* he similarly misnames the Hundred.

1,30   BATHEASTON. Named *(Estona)* in the Tax Return for Bath Hundred.

1,31   BATH. The 1 house taken away by Hugh the Interpreter could be adjacent to Hugh's land at Bathampton (7,11), or to that of Hugolin the Interpreter's at Warleigh, Claverton and Batheaston (45,9-11), Hugolin and Hugh being the same person; Hugolin is the diminutive form of *Hugo* (Hugh).

1,35   MUDFORD. See 19,87 note.

Chapter 2

2,1   TAUNTON. The place-name is given in the Tax Return for Taunton Hundred (as *Tantona*). The hides of Taunton no doubt included the detachment of Withiel Florey near Brompton Regis, see ECW no. 383, and a number of later parishes, see Anderson p.69.

2,3   TAUNTON. The lands and dues belonging to Taunton are specified in detail in a Record printed in Robertson (appendix 4) and summarised in ECW no.544. The same estates are mentioned, including the two Cheddons, but specifying two Holfords (21,83-84note). The places listed in DB in this section appear because they had lay tenants-in-chief in an Ecclesiastical Hundred. They thus mostly recur elsewhere in the Somerset schedule or represent the names of adjacent places that are listed. They seem largely to be grouped by holder in chief. For TOLLAND see 21,82; OAKE 21,81; HOLFORD 21,83-84; UPPER CHEDDON 22,21; *Succedene* (CHEDDON FITZPAINE)22,22. FORD is 19.42; HILLFARRANCE is 35,22 and HELE 19,40 (both held by Alfred, see 2,5); NORTON (FITZWARREN) is 19,41; BRADFORD (ON TONE) is 19,39; HALSE 22,1; HEATHFIELD 25,53; STOKE (ST. MARY) 25,52. For MAIDENBROOKE see Morland II p.95; for NYNEHEAD (East Nynehead or Nynehead Monachorum) see RH ii 125b and Morland II p.95. For SHOPNOLLER see Morland I p.46. Maidenbrooke, Nynehead and Shopnoller are not named elsewhere in Domesday Book. Maidenbrooke probably is part of Cheddon (22,21-22), and Shopnoller probably stands for Bagborough (25,51). Nynehead Monachorum is held by Montacute Priory in RH ii 125 b of the fee of *Wyggeberwe* (Wigborough), an Honour into which the estates of John the Usher were later tormed. Nynehead is thus probably the 2 hides and ½ virgate held by Alfred in 2,8. The greater part of Nynehead (Nine Hides) continued in later times to be held by Winchester to which the whole was originally granted (ECW no. 419). This part of Nynehead is no doubt included in the hidage of Taunton.

2,9   LEIGH. Probably in Lydeard St. Lawrence with which it is mentioned. See VCH p.444 note 2.

2,10   BLEADON. Like Rimpton below, Exon. order suggests that Bleadon was returned as part of the Bishop's fief, as an outlier of Taunton Hundred, rather than as part of Winterstoke Hundred. It is however included in the Winterstoke Tax Return. Later it is a free manor, (RH ii 131b) then in Bempstone Hundred (NV 61). Its identification in Bucks. and Beds. DB is unlikely (EBe 1-3, EBu 1-2 note).

2,12   RIMPTON. Later a detachment of Taunton Hundred, but included in the Tax Return for Milborne (Horethorne) Hundred.

3,1 SEABOROUGH. 'Another Seaborough' is clearly part of the same village, the whole forming a double manor. There is no trace later of two villages. Examples of this use of *alia* are found elsewhere in DB, e.g. at Thistleton in Rutland, Courteenhall in Northants.

3,2 CHILCOMPTON. DB *Contone*. In KQ 40 half the village of *Childe Cumtone* is held from the Bishop of Salisbury and half from *Hugo Lovel*, thus accounting for the two DB holdings.

4,1 (TEMPLE) COMBE. The Abbess of Shaftesbury (see 14,1) holds half the village of *Cumbe* and the Templars the other half in KQ 26. It is still regarded as one parish.
'THORENT'. See LSR (1327) pp.218-9; Morland II p.94. The land – DB *Tornie*, Exon. *Turnie Turnie* – is represented by Thorent Hill and Thorent Field in the Henstridge Tithe Award, a western part of the parish now in Milborne Port.

Chapter 5
The lands of the Bishop of Coutances (also the Bishop of Saint Lô in the Tax Return) are later held by the barony of Trowbridge or the Earls of Lincoln and of Gloucester. The Gurnays and Johannis le Sor are among principal tenants.

5,1 DOWLISH. In Exon. 136 b 1 the land is entered among South Petherton places, but the holding may have extended into Bulstone Hundred. *And: Wak* holds *Westdouewyz* in Bulstone from the Earl of Lincoln in KQ 30, while *Radulphus Wake* holds *Estdunelitz* (Dowlish Wake) in South Petherton Hundred in KQ 18. See NV 72, VCH iv pp.152-153.

5,3 'HISCOMBE'. The order of the Exon. Book is uncertain at this point, and the next entry (Rodney Stoke) seems also to be out of sequence. The place is probably the *Etecumbe* of KQ 23 in Tintinhull Hundred and the *Hececumbe* of NV 67, held from the barony of Trowbridge. It is a detached tything of Tintinhull in West Coker parish, VCH p.446 note 1, Morland I p.47, now represented by the field-name 'Hiscombe Mead' (TA 1844). The place-name form is different from Ashcombe (5,3 *Aisecombe*) with which it was once identified (see 8,38 note). The detached position of 'Hiscombe' is emphasised by a note in the Tax Return for the Yeovil group of Hundreds which included Tintinhull. It records tax on 2 hides 3 virgates (the extent of 'Hiscombe'), held by Osbern from the Bishop of St. Lô, as paid in the Hundred of *Liet* (Coker). Although the tenant seems to have changed, the Bishop holds nothing else in the area. For *Liet* Hundred, see Appendix I. The DB spelling *Hetsecombe* (8,38 note) supports derivation form OE *hægtesse* and *Cumbe* 'Witch's Combe', as Hascombe in Surrey.

5,4 (RODNEY) STOKE. The uncertain Exon. order would make the identity of this *Stoches* dubious but for the Tax Return for Cheddar Hundred and for the fact that it is held of the Earl of Gloucester as *Stokgiffard* in Winterstoke Hundred in RH 130b.

5,5 NETTLECOMBE. The King's manor is 1,14.

5,7 CULBONE. Formerly Kitnor, DB *Chetnore*.

5,9-13 A GROUP of Winterstoke Hundred places.

5,9 (EAST) HARPTREE. Included in a Winterstoke Hundred group. It is held by Anselmus *de Gurnay* as *Estharpet'* in RH ii 130 a-b. West Harptree is in Chewton Hundred. See Morland I p.39 and 19,37 note.

5,10 HUTTON. See 8,38.

5,11 ELBOROUGH. See 8,38.

5,12 WINTERHEAD. See 8,2 Winscombe, note.

5,13 ASHCOMBE. In Exon. it is the last of a group of Winterstoke places. The holding, later in the hands of the Earl of Gloucester, probably included Weston-Super-Mare; see RH ii 130b; KQ (supp.) 50. See 5,3;38 notes.

5,14-16 PLACES in Chew Hundred.

5,16 NORTON (MALREWARD). This *Nortone* is required by the Tax Return for Chew Hundred. The Earl of Gloucester holds *Bichenestoke* (lost, see 37,3-4 note) and *Nortone Marleward* (a metathesis of *Malreward*) in RH ii 137a, and the heirs of *Johannis le Sor* in KQ (supp.) 51. Norton Hawkfield is later part of this parish, but it is held from the Bishop of Bath in KQ (supp.) 47, which suggests that it was part of the Bishop of Wells' holding of Chew (6,13) in 1086, the Wells see being transferred to Bath in 1090.

5,17 CLAVERHAM. Its position in Exon. (141 a 1) suggests that it was part of Yatton Hundred in 1086. This was later amalgamated with Winterstoke. See RH ii 126 b.

5,18-34 PLACES predominantly in a group of northern Hundreds, Portbury, Hartcliffe and Keynsham.

5,19 CLEWER. Exon. order might suggest a Portbury or Bedminster Hundred place, such as Cleeve or Clevedon. But the Earl of Gloucester holds *Clywar'* in Bempstone Hundred in RH 132a.

5,22 WESTON (IN GORDANO). The Earl of Gloucester holds *Weston'* in RH ii 130b, KQ (supp.) 43.

5,23 SALTFORD. DB *Sanford*. An isolated Keynsham entry in a mainly Portbury group in Exon., but the Earl of Gloucester holds in Saltford in RH ii 133b, KQ (supp.) 48.

5,24-27 EASTON (IN GORDANO). PORTISHEAD. WESTON (IN GORDANO). CLAPTON (IN GORDANO). The Earl of Gloucester holds *Clivedon', Clopton', Weston, Portesheved,* and *Eston'* in Portbury Hundred in RH ii 130b. *Clivedon'* is possibly holding at Kenn 5,29 below (KQ (supp.) 43). DB *Clotune* is probably an error for *Cloptune,* VCH p.449 note 2.

5,28 HAVYATT. It is later absorbed into Brent and Wrington Hundred, but from its position in Exon. it was probably in Hartcliffe Hundred in 1086.

5,29 KENN. Its position in Exon. suggests that it counted as a part of Portbury Hundred in 1086. The boundary of the Hundred may then have been the old course of the Kenn river and this land, perhaps lying north of the river, may have included Clevedon (5,24-27 note). The village of Kenn itself was later in Winterstoke Hundred and another part of it was probably attached to Yatton in 1086, see VCH p.97 and 6,14 note.

5,32 BARROW (GURNEY). This *Berve* is held by *Johannes de Gurnay* from the Earl of Gloucester in KQ 29 in Hartcliffe Hundred. See KQ (supp.) 42. John is clearly a descendant of Nigel of Gournai, the 1086 holder.

5,35-38 PLACES in Bath Hundred.

5,35 FRESHFORD. The other half of the mill is probably at 'Woodwick' 7,12. See VCH p.450 note 2.

5,37 BATHWICK. *Wyke* and *Wolleye* are also held together by the Abbess of Wherwell in KQ (supp.) 49. From NV 71 it is clear that the Abbess' Wick is Bathwick. See Morland I p. 42 and 5,38 note.

5,38 SWAINSWICK. DB *Wiche.* Probably the same place as 47,18, both held by Alfred in 1066; see Morland I p. 42. *Swaneswych* is a Lincoln holding in Fees 750, but this is probably Swanage in Dorset, EPNS (Dorset) pt.I p. 52.

5,39 COMPTON (DANDO). This *Contone* is required by the Tax Return for Keynsham Hundred.

5,42-57 PLACES in the Frome group of Hundreds.

5,43 STRATTON and PITCOTE. This Stratton is required in the Frome group of Hundreds by Exon. order. It probably included Holcombe, held by the Earl of Gloucester with *Radestoke, Hirdington', Middelcote* and *Babington'* in RH ii 135a. See 8,38; KQ 3; Morland I p. 43.

5,44 ENGLISHCOMBE. The 10 hides probably included at least a part of Combe Hay since *Cumbeshawaye* was held from the Earl of Lincoln in KQ 13.

5,47 RADSTOCK. DB *Stoche.* Held by the Earl of Gloucester in RH ii 135a, KQ 3 in Kilmersdon Hundred.

5,48 HARDINGTON. See RH ii 135a, KQ 2. For HEMINGTON see 20,1.

5,50 'MIDDLECOTE'. Held by the Earl of Gloucester in RH ii 135a, 136b in Kilmersdon Hundred. See 8,25 note and Morland I p.47. It was a known but deserted site in Collinson's time (ii 450); probably the north-west part of Mells parish, including Vobster and Branch Farm.

5,56 (STONY) LITTLETON. Among a group of Frome places in Exon. *Lyttleton* in Wellow Hundred is held from the heirs of *Johannis le Soor* in FA iv 313.

5,57 NEWTON (ST. LOE). The Bishop of Coutances is also Bishop of Saint-Lô in the Tax Return. Newton is held from the Earl of Gloucester by a descendant, *Johannes de Sancto Laudo,* in Wellow Hundred in KQ 12.

5,58-66 PLACES in Chewton Hundred.

5,59 (STON) EASTON. DB *Estone.* It is among Chewton Hundred places in Exon. and held as *Stonyeston'* in Chewton Hundred by the Earl of Gloucester in RH ii 137b; KQ 40. See 42,3; 46,25 notes.

5,60 (WEST) HARPTREE. Included in a Chewton Hundred group in Exon. and held as West Harptree (Tilly) from the Earl of Gloucester in Chewton Hundred in KQ 39; RH ii 137b. See Morland I p. 39. East Harptree is in Winterstoke Hundred. The other half of West Harptree is `24,31.

5,63-64 KINGSTON (SEYMOUR). Exon. order includes it among Chewton places. It is a detachment of Chewton Hundred in KQ 38, and later times.

5,66 (HIGH) LITTLETON. In the order of Exon. this Littleton falls among Chewton Places. The Earl of Gloucester holds *Lutletone* in Chewton Hundred in KQ 39. High Littleton or Hallatrow (5,65) included Paulton *(Haleton'* in error in RH ii 137b, *Paltone* in LSR (1327) p. 108) held by the Earl of Gloucester.

5,67 UPTON (NOBLE). Falls in the middle of a group of Chewton entries, but apparently a delayed Bruton entry since it is held there from the Earl of Gloucester in KQ 33.

5,68 MIDGELL. Possibly, like Brockley (45,16), it was in Chewton Hundred in 1086. It was a later detachment of Chewton.

5,69-70 PLACES in Horethorne Hundred.

5,69 WEATHERGROVE. In Sandford Orcas (now in Dorset). See VCH p. 455 note 2.

Chapter 6

Names of the hamlets comprised within the Bishop's large holdings in this chapter are in the confirmation charter of Edward the Confessor to Bishop Giso of 1065 (ECW no. 542 = KCD 816). The
majority of the holdings in this Chapter form the *Terra Gisonis*, an Episcopal Hundred, in the Tax
Return. As a scattered Hundred containing the lands of a single church it resembles the Worcester-
shire Hundreds of Oswaldslow, Westminster and Pershore which appear to have been re-organised
from a series of geographically compact Hundreds containing a variety of holders, church and lay.
Bishop Giso's Hundred was a recent creation (Appendix I) and to a certain extent seems only to ha
existed for tax purposes. In the second Exon. list, the Bishop's holdings are listed as a series of sma
Hundreds, Combe, Wiveliscombe, Wellington *etc.* In the Exon. order of this Chapter, holdings appe
to be listed in the order of the second Exon. list as follows:

EXON.	DB	PLACE NAME	HUNDRED OF EXON. LIST
156 a 1	6,2	Combe St. Nicholas	15	*Cumbe*
156 a 2	6,3	Kingsbury Episcopi	19	*Cingesberia*
156 a 3	6,4	Chard		"
156 a 1	6,5	'Litnes'		"
156 b 2	6,6	Wiveliscombe	20	*Wyuelescoma*
156 b 3	6,7	Wellington	23	*Walintona*
157 a 1	6,8	Bishops Lydeard	24	*Lidiart*
157 a 2	6,9	Banwell	25	*Wenestoc*
157 b 1	6,1	Wells	29	*Wella*
158 a 1	6,10	Evercreech		"
158 b 1	6,11	Westbury sub Mendip		"
158 b 2	6,12	Winsham	?	
159 a 1	6,13	Chew Magna	34	*Chiu*
159 b 1	6,14	Yatton	35	*Iatona*
159 b 2	6,15	Wedmore	46	*Bimastan*
160 a 1	6,16	Wanstrow	52	*Briuuetona*

The remaining places, Litton, Ash Priors and Milverton, are probably late additions, out of order as
often in other chapters. The last two are disputed lands. Winsham appears out of order in the list. I
is in the Tax Return both for Giso's Hundred and for Abdick.

6,1   WELLS. The 2 hides of Manasseh's wife not held from the Bishop are possibly 46,24 Hay
       Street in Chewton Hundred, although the 20s value is there the past one.

6,2   COMBE ST. NICHOLAS. The Tax Return for Abdick Hundred records that 20 hides pay ta:
       in another Hundred. This evidently records the removal of Combe from Abdick to Bishop
       Giso's Hundred. See 6,12 note.

6,5   'LITNES'. DB *Litelaneia* (Little Island), having the same termination as Muchelney, Middlen
       and Thorney. The land is confirmed in the charter of Edward the Confessor cited above (Ch
       note.) as *Lytlenige*. The Charter counts it as a member of *Cyncgesbyrig* (Kingsbury Episcopi
       although it is separated from it. In the Charter *Cyncgesbyrig* is alloted 38 'mansus' and inclu
       Combe St. Nicholas, Winsham, Chard and *Hiwisc* (Huish Episcopi), this last mentioned imme
       iately after *Lytlenige. Lytlenige* at 2 hides probably stands for Huish as well (VCH iii p. 4).
       'Litnes' survives as a field name, Morland I p. 47. From this grant of *Cyncgesbyrig* and me:
       grew the Hundred of Kingsbury (East). Chard, 'Litnes' and Kingsbury are so grouped in Exo
       order (Ch. 6 note, above).

6,9   BANWELL. Ralph's holding was probably at Churchill and Stock'in Churchill. Serlo's 3 hide
       were probably at Christon, KQ (supp.) 46-7; Morland II p.97.

6,12   WINSHAM. Included in the Tax Return for Bishop Giso's Hundred and also in that for Abdi
       no doubt its original Hundred.

6,13   CHEW (MAGNA). Also called Chew Bishops (Hill, p. 5). The holding included three Suttons
       Bishops Sutton, Sutton Wick and Knighton Sutton (also Sutton Court), as well as Stowey
       (ECW no. 542; KQ 47). In the Tax Return for Bishop Giso's Hundred, Richard of Sutton
       (Richard in Domesday) owes tax on 1 hide and in Exon 159 a 1 Aelfric is Aelfric of Stowey.
       In Exon. order Chew Magna is entered in the correct place for a Chew Hundred name (Ch. 6
       note) but in the Tax Return it is in Bishop Giso's Hundred. See 5,16 note.

6,14   YATTON. A separate Hundred in the second Exon. list, but included in the Tax Return for
       Chewton Hundred. The 4 hides of Hildebert were at Kenn, Wemberham and Hewish, KQ (su
       47; Morland II p. 97. The pasture at Wemberham may be one of the 2 hides taken from Con
       gresbury, 1,21, although the value (see Exon.) is quite different. See 5,29 note.

6,15 WEDMORE. See 1,2 note.
6,16 WANSTROW. The Wells holding was East Wanstrow in Bruton Hundred (NV 59). See 36,11 note. It is included in the Tax Return for Bishop Giso's Hundred, but in this chapter falls naturally in a Bruton group.
6,18 MILVERTON. The royal holding is 1,26.

Chapter 7
LAND OF THE CHURCH OF BATH. Surveys of the Church's holdings closely related to DB are transcribed in Appendix II.
7,5 WESTON. This *Westone* is in a Bath group of places in Exon. 185 b 1, and required by the Tax Return for Bath Hundred.
7,7 (MONKTON) COMBE. See BC i 57 note and i, 73 and *passim*. Of the other 'Combes' in the area of Bath DB distinguishes Lyncombe and Charlcombe (7,9-10) and Widcombe is counted as part of Bath itself (BC ii 11 *etc.*)
7,12 'WOODWICK'. Near Peipards Farm in Freshford, Morland I p. 47. The other half of the mill is probably Freshford 5,35.
7,14 'EVERSY'. See ECW 486; BC i, 21; ii 581-2. It is *Eversy iuxta Cumbehawey* (Combe Hay) in FF i 314.

Chapter 8
Some of the lands held from the Abbot by Roger of Courseulles are later found (like his own Ch. 21 holdings) in the hands of the Malet family.
8,1 'ANDERSEY'. Now Nyland, Anderson p. 68 note 1; Morland I p. 39. The 2 hides are included in the Tax Return for Bempstone Hundred (where Nyland falls geographically), held by *Letaoldus* (OE *Leodwald* or OG *Leudouald*), from the Abbot. The conical hill standing out of the marshes was long a detachment of Glaston Hundred. See ECW no. 354.
8,2 WINSCOMBE. Ralph's holding was at Sandford, GF 112; Morland II p. 96. The 1 hide held from the King by the Bishop of Coutances was 5,12 Winterhead.
8,3-4 PODIMORE,(EAST)LYDFORD. These two entries fall between a Winterstoke entry (Exon. list II no. 25) and a Loxley group 8,5-10 (Exon. list II no. 38). They could be in Somerton Hundred (Exon. list II no. 33) or detached parts of Loxley in 1086. Podimore was formerly Milton Podimore, long a detached part of Whitley Hundred, KQ 28; NV 53. East Lydford was a detached part of Somerton Hundred in the Middle Ages; KQ 21; VCH iii p. 122. See 47,21 note.
8,5-10 A GROUP of Loxley Hundred places, later part of Whitley Hundred.
8,5 SUTTON (MALLET). Named in the text as a dependency of Shapwick, this *Sutone* is later held by John *Malet* from the Abbot of Glastonbury (KQ 28).
CHILTON (POLDEN). DB *Ceptone* is probably an error, see VCH p. 461 note 3. It is held from the Abbot in KQ 27, RH ii 135b.
WOOLAVINGTON. See 11,1 note.
8,6 MIDDLEZOY. DB *Sowi.* The 12 hides probably included Othery and Westonzoyland; KQ 28; NV 53; ECW no. 379 (= BCS 143).
8,8 DURBOROUGH. Near Nether Stowey, locally in Cannington Hundred. In Exon. 163 a 1 it falls in a group of Loxley places and is clearly a detached part, as it was later, from Whitley Hundred, the successor of Loxley; KQ (supp.) 45; RH ii 135b.
8,9 BLACKFORD. Near Wincanton. Morland I p. 45 identifies Blackford in Wedmore on the ground that Blackford in Wincanton is accounted for in the 8 hides of Butleigh (8,18), held by Thurstan. But in GF 58/62 the 20 hides of Butleigh are distinguished from the 8 of Blackford. Moreover in the order of both the Exchequer and Exon. books, *Blacheford* is included among Loxley Hundred places. Loxley Hundred cannot have extended to include Wedmore in 1086 or later. The Blackford in Wincanton is a known outlier of Whitley Hundred which absorbed Loxley (e.g. KQ 28) and the 8 hides of which Blackford consists in GF are probably to be found in DB in the 4 hides of *Blacheford* here, the 1 hide of Blackford (36,8), the 2 hides of Holton (45,4) with 1 hide from Thurstan's adjacent holdings in Woolston, Maperton, Clapton, or North Cadbury. There was a detached part of Blackford in North Cadbury later (Morland I p. 41). Blackford and Holton are held by *Henricus de Novo Mercato* and Roger *de Moeles* the successors of Thurstan in his ch. 36 holdings. See KQ 28; FA iv 306; RH ii 135b.
8,11-19 A GROUP of Ringoldsway places, later part of Whitley Hundred.
8,11 WALTON. Near Glastonbury. Required by the Tax Return for Ringoldsway Hundred. See Exon. order 163 b 1; KQ 28; NV 53.
8,12 ?BUTLEIGH. Morland I p. 39 points out that the 20 hides of which Butleigh consisted (GF 62) are fully accounted for in the entry at 8,18, and suggests Bagley (in Wedmore) here. But in Exon. (164 a 1) *Bodeslege* falls in a group of Ringoldsway places and despite the divergent spelling, VCH is probably right in identifying a part of Butleigh. It is perhaps listed separately as having a different 1066 holder (Winegot), and may duplicate a part of the 20 hides. See Hill p.201.

8,14 WALTON. See 8,11 note.
8,16 OVERLEIGH. DB *Lega* is required by the Ringoldsway Hundred Tax Return and is among Ringoldsway places in Exon. 164 b 3.
8,17 HAM. Separately listed in the Tax Return, but included in a sequence of Ringoldsway places here and in Exon, 165 a 1. The estates of Serlo and of Robert were both at Low Ham (GF 86-7; Morland II p. 96.)
8,19 LATTIFORD. Detached near Wincanton. Humphrey's 2 hides, held from the King, were no doubt adjacent to his Holton 45,4. Blackford, Holton and Lattiford later formed a detachme of Whitley Hundred. In Exon. Lattiford is among Ringoldsway places, and has been separate from Butleigh, its parent manor (see also Exon. 522 a 5). From GF 59 it is clear that it has been joined to Blackford and Holton. See Morland I p. 45.
8,20 SHEPTON (MALLET). This *Sepetone* is located by its dependence on Pilton. Held from Gla tonbury Abbey in KQ 33.
8,21 PENNARD. The 20 hides would include both East and West Pennard, the summit of Pennar Hill being centre of the holding, ECW no. 360 = BCS 61. West Pennard is later in Glaston Hundred. Serlo's hide was West Bradley GF 114; Morland II p. 97.
8,20-24 A GROUP of Whitstone Hundred places.
8,22 BALTONSBOROUGH. Later in Glaston 12 hides Hundred, it is among Whitstone Hundred places in Exon. 167 a 1. See KQ 34.
8,24 BATCOMBE. Roger's holding was Spargrove GF 111; Morland II p. 96.
8,25 MELLS. The 5½ hides held by the Bishop of Coutances were at 'Middlecote' 5,50 although t value is different. Mells and 'Middlecote' were probably in Kilmersdon Hundred (RH ii 135a, 136b) in 1086; later a Liberty and more recently in Frome Hundred where they are mapped, see Anderson pp. 43-44.
8,26 WHATLEY. Entered with Mells in Exon. 167 b 2. It is held from Glastonbury in Frome Hun dred in KQ 9.
8,27 WRINGTON. Required by the Tax Return for Hartcliffe Hundred. It is later the northern pa of Brent and Wrington Hundred.
8,28 (WEST) MONKTON. A separate Hundred in the second Exon. list and Tax Return. East Mon ton is Monkton Deverill in Wilts. Serlo's holding was Overton and Roger's Gotton, Hawkridge and Hyde (GF 87-88); Morland II p. 96. The 5 hides and 1 virgate held by Bishop Walkelin w no doubt adjacent to his land at Taunton (2,1).
8,30 DITCHEAT. In Whitstone Hundred in 1086 but parts of this manor seem to have been re moved to other Hundreds at the time of the Tax Return. There the 5 hides held by Nigel the Doctor at Lamyatt pay tax in another Hundred, probably Bruton; similarly 1 hide held from the King by Aelfric and Everard in the Tax Return for Whitstone Hundred pays tax in another Hundred. The hide is perhaps part of West Lydford or *Scepeworde* (47,21-22) held b Aelfric alone in DB. The 7 hides of the Count of Mortain are perhaps the 7 hides of the same value at Yarlington (19,54) held by Alnoth before 1066. In the Tax Return for Whitstone, 7 hides held by Drogo from the Abbot pay tax in another Hundred. Drogo is a frequent tenant of the Count of Mortain and the 7 hides of Yarlington in DB may be these. The 30 hides of Ditcheat itself probably correspond to the grant of Aethelwulf to Eanulf of 25 *cassati* at Ditcheat and 5 at Lottisham, ECW no. 405.
8,32 CRANMORE. Exon. order suggests that the land was in Frome Hundred in 1086, and in the Tax Return for the Frome group, Harding of Wilton (probably the sub-tenant Harding of DB) has 9 hides in lordship. The lordship is smaller in DB, but Cranmore is the likely identification Some of the Glastonbury land was later lost to Wells (GF 107) and so became joined with Evercreech as a detached part of Wells Forum Hundred. The Domesday Cranmore probably corresponded to the area of both West Cranmore (later in Wells Forum Hundred) and East Cranmore (for a time attached to Bempstone Hundred, then a free manor, then returned to Frome Hundred; see Eyton i, 161; Morland I p. 46.) A royal holding of 5 hides is included in the Tax Return for Frome Hundred at *Crenemere*, probably part of the King's land at Frome (1,9) rather than an otherwise unrecorded royal holding, or a part of Glastonbury land temporarily alienated due to the difficulties of Abbot Thurstan (ASC p. 214).
8,33 BRENT. Later the southern part of Brent and Wrington Hundred, but a separate Hundred (*Suðbrenta*) in the Exon. list (II) no. 48, which probably included Edingworth below. The 20 hides no doubt included several settlements. In RH ii 135b the church holds *Sutbrente*, *Estbrente* and *Limpelesham*. Ralph's holding was at Battleborough (GF 95; Morland II p. 96). 'South Brent' on the first edition Ordnance Survey map of 1809 is on the south side of the Knoll, Grid Reference ST 3350.
8,34 EDINGWORTH. DB *Lŏdenwrde*. NV 54 *Yadenworth* offers an intermediate spelling. See VCH p. 467 note 3.

8,35 DOWNHEAD. Apparently a separate Hundred in the first Exon. List. It is later in Whitstone Hundred.

8,37 ST. ANDREW'S CHURCH, ILCHESTER. The entry is repeated at 15,1. Northover Church is dedicated to St. Andrew and the 3 hides and 3 acres of meadow in 1086 correspond to the parish which had 360 acres of meadow and pasture and 75 acres of meadow at the end of the eighteenth century. Ilchester itself was probably in 1086 an outlier of Milborne (1,10 note); Northover, across the river Yeo, was later a part of Somerton Hundred (in RH ii 134a). With Ilchester it is still later in Tintinhull Hundred. See VCH iii p. 176; 225; Morland I p. 46.

8,38 HUTTON, ELBOROUGH, 'HISCOMBE', STRATTON (ON THE FOSSE). See 5,10-11; 3; 43. 'Hiscombe', DB Hetsecombe or Hasecumbe is distinguished by its value (Exon. 172 b 7, 524 b 2) from Ashcombe 5,13 which is Aisecombe (5,3 note).

8,39 ?KINGSTONE. Stone in East Pennard (VCH and DG) was certainly Glastonbury land (KQ 34 and ECW no. 444), but the entry refers to land appropriated by the Count of Mortain. The only 'Stone' held by the Count is Kingstone (19,10) which is said to have been Glastonbury land and falls with Stoke sub Hamdon. Stoket and Draycott (19,11-14) which are similarly listed here.
STOKE(SUB HAMDON), STOKE (SUB HAMDON). Only one Stoca is mentioned in Chapter 19, (section 13). One of the two here is probably the Stoket (East Stoke) (19,14) held by three thanes before 1066.

8,40 BUTLEIGH. The wood 2 furlongs by 1 furlong held by the Count of Mortain corresponds to that at Clapton, 19,68, which is adjacent to the detached portion of Butleigh, 8,18.

8,41 LIMINGTON. See 21,93.

9,3 ILMINSTER. May have included part of Fivehead (Five Hides) only 1½ hides of which are accounted for in 21,70. See NV 71.

9,7 (WEST) CAMEL. Also Camel Abbatis, KQ 20; NV 58; VCH iii p. 73.

10,1 ILTON. The Count of Mortain's 2 hides were at Ashill (19,18; see 10,6 note) and included Merryfield, MAC p. 192; Morland II p. 97.

10,2 (LONG) SUTTON. This Sutton is held from the Abbot of Athelney in Fees 1265, KQ 21. Sutton Abbatis NV 58. See 10,6 note.

10,3 SEAVINGTON. The Athelney holding is Seavington Abbots, NV 72. See 19,2. 47,2 notes; VCH iv p. 201.

10,4 HAMP. DB Hame. Held by the Abbot in North Petherton Hundred in KQ 11; MAC passim.

10,5 LYNG. The island of Athelney lies in this parish.

10,6 ASHILL. Held by Mauger from the Count of Mortain in 19,18. The land held by Roger of Courseulles is at 21,98; that held by Ralph of Limesy at 32,5.

11,1 PURITON. A Loxley place in Exon. order (197 b 3), but the Tax Return for Huntspill Hundred records that tax on 3 hides of Loxley Hundred has been paid there. This probably coresponds to the 3 hides of the villagers' land at Puriton which is later the southern half Huntspill and Puriton Hundred. An alternative is the 3 hides held in lordship by Alfred of 'Spain' from Glastonbury Abbey at Woolavington, 8,5.

13,1 ONE MANOR. The Tax Return and Exon. 198 a 4 suggest a place in the Frome group of Hundreds. It is possibly Nunney, the ½ mill at 30d recorded in Exon. complementing another ½ mill at 30d in Nunney 25,54. See Eyton i 158-60.

14 LAND OF ST. EDWARD'S CHURCH. The Tax Return for Bath Hundred gives 3 hides of the Abbey's land in lordship there. This holding, omitted from DB, is at Kelston KQ (supp.) 49; NV 70.

14,1 (ABBAS) COMBE. See 4,1 note.

15,1 ST. ANDREW'S CHURCH. In Northover (Ilchester), 8,37 note.

16,2 STOGUMBER. DB Warverdinestoch. Richere is probably the Richer de Stoches who holds in the Williton Hundred Tax Return. A successor, Robertus de Andely holds in KQ 7. See FF i 182; SRS 11 p. 64; VCH p. 471 note 1.

16,7 (NORTH) PETHERTON. DB Peretune. North and South Petherton are usually distinguished in the text. In Exon. this entry is the first of the Somerset 'Land in Alms' (196 a 2), the correct position for a place in North Petherton Hundred.

16,9 (ABBOTS) LEIGH. Included in the Tax Return for Bedminster Hundred, although it is later in Portbury. Abbots from the Abbey of St. Augustine, Bristol; NV 62.

16,12 12 ACRES. Possibly the i fertinum, a 'ferling' or quarter virgate from OE feording ME ferthing 'a fourth or quarter', held by a nun in the Tax Return for Cannington Hundred, since in Exon. order (196 a 3) it falls before a Cannington Hundred place, Beere (DB 16,8). This is more likely than identification with the half virgate which Edith held at Hunecot (Fees 83). That Edith may be one of the nuns in the entry below.

16,13 HOLNICOTE. DB Honecote and Hunecot probably both represent Holnicote, rather than

Holnicote and Huntscott (in Wootton Courtenay). See Chadwyck-Healey p. 6; Hill p. 149; and 16,12. 21,65;67 notes.

16,14 KILMERSDON. The ½ hide is named in the Frome Hundred Tax Return, at *Cenemerresdun* OE *Cynemæres-dune*, the first element being a personal name.

17,1 NEWTON. West Newton or Newton Comitis in North Pertherton Hundred. John *Tregoz* who also holds Lexworthy (17,3), holds in KQ 10; Morland I, p. 42.

17,8 COMPTON (DURVILLE). Falls in Exon. order (283 a 2) after Kingweston in the same hand, suggesting Compton Pauncefoot in Catsash Hundred which Morland prefers (II p. 98; see I p. 45). Dr. R. W. Dunning, prefers Compton Durville in South Petherton Hundred, pointing t the close tenurial ties between Compton Durville and Loxton (17,4) which lasted to the fifte century (Cal. CR. 1300-1326, 482; 1419-22, 261; VCH iv p. 183 note).

Chapter 18

EARL HUGH. Hugh's successors like himself are the Earls of Chester.

18,2 SAMPFORD (BRETT). William *le Bret* holds from the Barony of Chester in Williton Hundre KQ 6.

18,3 ALLER. DB *Alre*. Probably in Sampford Brett (18,2).

Chapter 19

COUNT OF MORTAIN. When his fief escheated to the King many of his tenants became tenants in chief, their lands forming separate baronies. Later fees and holdings are described as of Morton, Montague or **Montacute**; principal later holders are the *Beauchamps* and Henry *de Urtiaco*. Robert t Constable's holdings later form the Beauchamp barony of Hatch; Mauger's lands later form the Bar of Ashill and are held by the Vaux and Albemarle families. Drogo's lands later form the Barony of Shepton (Montague) held by Simon of Montacute.

19,1-6 A GROUP of South Petherton Hundred places.

19,1 CRICKET (ST. THOMAS). DB *Cruche*. This holding can be identified in the Tax Return for South Petherton Hundred. See Exon. order 265 a 1 and 1,4 note, and VCH iv p. 134.

19,2 SEAVINGTON. Seavington *Vaus* or St. Mary, KQ 18. See VCH p. 473 note 7; VCH iv p. 199 10,3 and 47,2 notes.

19,3 COMPTON DURVILLE. In Exon. order this 'Compton' is in the correct position for a South Petherton place. Held from the Honour of Ashill as *Cuintone Dureville*, KQ 18.

19,4 WHITESTAUNTON. DB *Stantune*. Among South Petherton places in Exon. 265 b 3; a Morta Fee in KQ 19. See VCH iv p. 232.

19,5 SHEPTON (BEAUCHAMP). Among South Petherton places in Exon. 266 a 1; a Beauchamp holding in Fees 86; KQ 18.

19,8 ISLE (BREWERS). Richard *Briuer* holds *Ile*, a Mortain Fee in Fees 86.

19,9-14 A GROUP of Tintinhull Hundred places according to the order of the Exon. Book.

19,10 KINGSTONE. See 8,39 note. Locally situated in South Petherton but apparently a detachme of Tintinhull in 1086 as later; see Exon. order 266 b 2; VCH iii p. 204. For the grant to Glast bury Abbey, see ECW no. 442.

19,11;13;14 STOKE (SUB HAMDON). In Tintinhull Hundred. DB *Stoket* (19, 11;14) survives as Sto (East Stoke) a hamlet of Stoke sub Hamdon in KQ 22; NV 67; LSR (1327) 223; MC 224. Sto itself is a Morton or Beauchamp holding; Fees 85, 1468; RH ii 126a; KQ 22. See 8,39 note; VCH iii p. 238.

19,12 DRAYCOTT. In Limington. Held from the Barony of Dunden in KQ 23; but FA iv 286 adds that it is a Mortain Fee. Barony of Dunden holdings are normally found among lands held in DB by Roger of Courseulles, and later by the Abbey of Glastonbury. Draycott had been Glas tonbury land (8,39) and seems to have been treated later as part of the Dunden Barony. Dun don, the *caput* of the fief, is held by Glastonbury in 1086 (8,13). Draycott is treated as a Tin inhull place in Exon. 267 a 2; KQ 23 and in the later Middle Ages. It is finally in Stone Hun dred; VCH iii p. 176.

19,13-14 STOKE (SUB HAMDON). See 19,11 note.

19,15-29 A MIXED GROUP of places, mainly in Abdick and Bulstone and in Milverton Hundreds.

19,16 BRUSHFORD. The Tax Return for Williton Hundred states that Mauger of Carteret has paid for 2 hides, **presumably** these, in another Hundred. The Hundred is probably Brompton Regis for which no Tax Return exists, or possibly Dulverton which is closer and a Hundred in the second Exon. list. But in the Tax Return Dulverton seems to have been included in Williton Hundred. See 1,12 note and Appendix I.

19,17 BRADON. There are four entries for Bradon in DB: 19,17; 23;25 and 47,4. In later times the are three separate villages: North, South and Goose Bradon. Mauger's holding (19,17) is prob ably North Bradon later in the hands of Muchelney Abbey (MAC 52; NV 71). Drogo's 2 hide holding is 19,25, South Bradon (Cal. Inq. PM. 20 Ric II 35); his 1 hide (19,23) being in North

Bradon, held from Simon of Montacute FA iv 314. See NV 71; VCH p. 475 note 5; 47,4 note.

19,18 ASHILL. See 10,6 note.

19,20 ASHBRITTLE. Named after the 1086 holder Bretel and required in the Tax Return for Milverton Hundred. See Fees 735; KQ 14.

19,23;25 BRADON. See 19,17 note.

19,28 BEERCROCOMBE. DB *Bere*. Held from Henry *de Urtiaco* in Abdick Hundred; KQ 2.

19,30-31 THURLBEAR, THORNFALCON. These manors have separate Tax Returns (that for Thurlbear being duplicated) and are later in North Curry Hundred. Exon. order 271 b 1-2 appears to
suggest that they were counted as part of Abdick and Bulstone, or of North Curry in 1086.
Thornfalcon is later a Mohun holding; KQ (supp.) 51; SM 352. See 1,19 note.

19,34 CRICKET (MALHERBIE). Held from Simon *de Montacute* in KQ 30.

19,35 PRESTON. Torrels Preston in Milverton; see 1,11 and 35,18 notes.

19,36 ?ASHBRITTLE. The order of entries in Exon. is not certain at this point. Milverton Hundred
places have already been entered in Ch. 19, but this could be the delayed entry of another part
of Ashbrittle (19,20). In 1,19 it is said that Ansger holds a hide taken away from North Curry;
Whale (*Analysis* p. 31) suggested this entry as representing the hide and proposed West Hatch.
The values are different however, and DB *Aisse* is unlikely to have produced 'Hatch', Hatch
Beauchamp having evolved from DB *Hache*. Consistent with the order of Exon. would be an
entry for a part of Ash Priors; this entry like the previous one for Preston would then have been
returned with Bishop's Lydeard (no. 24 in the second Exon. List.)

19,37 (EAST) HARPTREE. Named in the Tax Return for Winterstoke Hundred as *Harpetruua*. See
5,9 note.

19,38 STEART. Later in Catsash Hundred (NV 56). In Exon. order it is too early for a Catsash place,
but could possibly be a delayed Tintinhull entry, as an outlier of Montacute. It is even later a
free manor; LSR (1327) 264.

19,39-42 A GROUP of Taunton Hundred places.

19,41 NORTON (FITZWARREN). This *Nortone* is among Taunton places in Exon. order (273 b 1)
and is held with Bradford (on Tone) in Fees 84, and from the Honour of *Mortayn* in KQ 20.

19,43 CHARLTON (ADAM). This *Cerletone* is later given to Bruton Priory; BrC 41. See KQ 21; NV
58; VCH iii p. 84.

19,44-50 A GROUP of Houndsborough Hundred Places.

19,44 CHINNOCK. The three holdings at Chinnock (also 19,48-49) occupied an area later divided
into East, West and Middle Chinnock. 19,44, held by the Count himself, was the land given by
his son to Montacute Priory, the *Kinnoc Monachorum* (East Chinnock) of MC 119; KQ 24;
NV 66; Mauger's holding (19,48) is *Midlecinnock* (KQ 25) held of the Honour of Ashill; 19,49
is probably the West Chinnock of KQ 25. The tenant, Alfred, also holds Chiselborough (19,47)
which is adjacent. See VCH p. 479 note 3.

19,45 (NORTH) PERROTT. DB *Peret* is also the DB form of North or South Petherton. This
holding is among Houndsborough Hundred places in Exon. order (274 a 2), and held from
Henry *de Urtiaco* in KQ 24. South Perrott is across the border in Dorset (DB, Dorset 27,9).

19,48-49 CHINNOCK. See 19,44 note.

19,50 NORTON (SUB HAMDON). This *Nortone* is in the Tax Return for the Yeovil Hundreds, and
in Houndsborough Hundred in Exon. order (275 a 1).

19,51 PENDOMER. DB *Penne*, which also stands for Penselwood. Exon. order suggests that this and
the following entry (Closworth) were either in Houndsborough or Coker Hundreds in 1086
(Exon. list II nos. 36-7).

19,53-69 PLACES in the six Frome-Bruton Hundreds.

19,55 WOOLSTON. In South Cadbury. It is included in the Bruton/Frome group of Hundreds in
Exon. 275 b 3, and is a Montacute holding, with Yarlington in Bruton Hundred in NV 59. See
Morland I p. 41.

19,56 SUTTON (MONTIS). *Montis Acuti*, or Montacute. See Exon. order 276 a 1; NV 56.

19,57 SHEPTON (MONTAGUE). See Fees 81; 262 and KQ 23.

19,58 REDLYNCH. See 1,9 note.

19,59 KEINTON (MANDEVILLE). Perhaps the 2 hides taken from Barton St. David, 21,92. 46,21.
See General notes.

19,61 ECKWEEK. Among Bruton/Frome places in Exon. 276 b 3. See NV 61; Morland I, p. 44.

19,62 BARROW. The division of Barrow between the Count of Mortain and Walscin of Douai
(24,20), seems not to correspond with the later North and South Barrow. Henry *de Urtiaco*
holds *Suthbarwe* and Richard *Lovel Northbarwe* in KQ (supp.) 44; but in Fees 752 both North
and South Barrow are Mortain holdings; whereas Richard *Lovel* Holds both in NV 56.

19,63 STOKE (TRISTER). Held with Cucklington (19,64) from Henry *de Urtiaco* in RH ii 135b and
138b, and a Mortain holding in Fees 81. Named after the descendents of William of Lestre (DEPN).

19,68 CLAPTON. Given by William of Durville (who also held Compton Durville 19,3) to Bruton Priory; BrC 64. See Morland I pp. 40-41.

19,69 WESTON (BAMPFYLDE). Among Bruton and Frome places in Exon. order. The ½ mill at 3(is probably complemented by the ½ mill at 36,5 although the value is different.

19,70-76 PLACES in Milborne (Horethorne) Hundred.

19,72-73 MARSTON (MAGNA). Required by the Tax Return for Milborne (Horethorne) Hundred, and among Horethorne places in Exon. 278 b 3. It is a Beauchamp holding in KQ 25; FA iv 298; NV 59, and included the manor of Little Marston; VCH iii p. 74.

19,74 ADBER. The Montacute holding was at Over Adber in Horethorne Hundred (FA iv. 299), where it is also found in Exon. order. Nether Adber was in Stone Hundred; see 24,37 and 47, notes; Morland II p. 95.

19,77-84 PLACES in Stone Hundred.

19,77-78 THORNE. Formerly Thorn Coffin parish. It is included by Exon. 279 b 1-2 in a group of Stone Hundred places although part is later in Stone and part in Tintinhull (1841 Census p. 3: 332; VCH iii p. 176). Ralph's estate was held with Mudford as Thorn Priors by Montacute Priory, VCH iii p. 250; RH ii 131a.

19,79-80 CHILTHORNE. The holdings probably included both the later Chilthorne Domer and Vag(see KQ 4. The Tax Return for the Yeovil Hundreds records tax not paid on two hides of a place whose name, partially illegible, ends -ilterna. It is probably Cilterna, one of the two hold ings in this chapter.

19,85 SOCK (DENNIS). A civil parish including Sock Dennis now represented by Manor Farm (Grid Reference 51 21) and Wyndhams Sock (50 20) now Stonecroft Manor. Bates in VCH has prob ably attempted to form a five-hide unit by identifying Mudford Sock in Stone Hundred with this 'Sock'. In Exon. order this 'Sock' falls at the end of a group of Stone places. But as the final entry in the Exon. order of the Chapter 'Sock' could be a belated Tintinhull or Horethor entry. Ilchester, of which Sock Dennis was later part, was an outlier of Milborne (1,10 note). There is no doubt that the Mortain Sock was Sock Dennis, (Cal. Inq. PM H III no. 592; E I nos 1/609; FF i pp. 179-180).

19,86 'BISHOPSTONE'. The name of the Count's castle, Montacute, has now displaced the earlier name, though 'Bishopstone' survived as a tithing of Montacute into the 19th century. The sam holding is already called Montacute in the Tax Return for the Yeovil Hundreds. See VCH iii p. 213.

19,87 MUDFORD. Later divisions are Mudford Monachorum (or West Mudford) given by the Mortains to Montacute Priory (MC 119 ff) and Mudford Terry (KQ 5; FA iv 320; NV 57).

Chapter 21

Many of Roger of Courseulles' holdings are held later by the Malet family or by Hugh *Poynz*. Some o his lands later form the barony of Dunden (now Dundon in Compton Dundon) held from the Abbot of Glastonbury by Cecilia de *Bello Campo* (Beauchamp). Matthew Furneaux and William Malherbe ar frequently named as tenants.

21,1-2 CURRY (MALLET). Placed in DB at the head of Roger's lands, as *caput* of his fief, whereas ir Exon. it falls after 21,53 (429 a 4-5). *Hugo Poynz* holds *Curi malet* in KQ 2.

21,3-10 A GROUP of North Petherton Hundred places.

21,3 NEWTON. Heads a list of North Petherton places in Exon. 422 a 1. It is perhaps Tuckerton (Grid Reference ST 2929), Morland I p. 42.

21,4 HADWORTHY. Walter's 1 virgate is perhaps at ?Dunwear 24,6.

21,8 ROBERT *HERECOM*. Probably from Heathcombe (Grid Reference ST 2333) now in Broom-field parish, Andersfield Hundred. In 1086 it was probably part of Enmore (21,74), also held by Roger of Courseulles, FA iv 293.
    SHEARSTON. DB *Siredestona*, named after the 1066 holder. Held by Cecilia *de Bello Campo* and the Abbot of Glastonbury in KQ 10. See Morland I p. 45.

21,9 *RIME*. Unidentified, but clearly in North Petherton Hundred (Exon. 423 a 1). Whale *(Principle* p. 38) draws attention to Parker's farm (Grid Reference ST 28 38) now seemingly Wembdon Farm, this Ansketel perhaps being the Ansketel Parker of 46, 15-17. Parker's is also a field nam in North Petherton (ST 29 33).

21,10 CHILTON (TRINITY). In North Petherton Hundred (Exon. 423 a 2). See 21,23-24; Morland I p. 40. It is to be distinguished from Chilton Trivett in Cannington.

21,15 GOTHELNEY. See 21, 23-24 note.

21,16-35 A GROUP of Cannington Hundred places (Exon. order 423 b 1 ff), among which are a number of lost places.

21,18 WOOLSTON. Perhaps named from Ulf the 1066 holder.

21,19 'HOLCOMBE'. A lost place in Aisholt adjoining Durborough Farm, Morland II p. 94.

21,20 'DODISHAM'. Perhaps now represented by Dods Field in Cannington, Grid Reference ST 252 409 (field 509 1839 TA). See VCH p. 486 note 1.

21,21 'PETHERHAM'. Now represented by Moxham's Farm in Otterhampton; Morland I p. 47.

21,23-24 CHILTON (TRIVETT). See Morland I p. 40. William *Trevet* holds from *Hugo Poinz* in KQ 16. The ½ mill may complement that at Gothelney (21,15) although the values are very different (see General Notes).

21,25 'PILLOCKS ORCHARD'. A field name in Cannington (field 957, 1839 TA). There is also a Pillocks Hayes in Stogursey (Field 519, 1841 TA). See Morland I p. 46.

21,26 STOCKLAND. DB *Stocheland* probably covered an area larger than Stockland Bristol. The Courseulles holding may be Steyning; Morland I p. 43. See 25,1. 31,1 notes.

21,29 ?SWANG. Clearly in Cannington Hundred (Exon. 425 b 2); possibly Swang, VCH p. 487 note 1.

21,31 ?AISHOLT. DB *Terra Olta*. *Olta* represents the OE locative-dative *Holte* of *Holt* 'wood, copse', meaning 'place at the wood'. If the identification with Aisholt (OE *Aesc-holt*, 'ash wood') is correct it must have been an early acquisition of the Mohun family; see KQ 16; SM 294; 307 ff.; Eyton i p. 124.

21,33 WITHIEL. Possibly Wyndeats in Stogursey, Morland II p. 98.

21,36 'WORTH'. Probably part of Cudworth, the 1½ hides here forming a five-hide unit with the 3½ at 22,10. The Furneaux family held Cudworth from Robert Fitz Payne to whom some Ch. 22 holdings descend and *Cnolle*, *Worthe* and *Slegham* from *Hugo Ponz* who is a later holder of some Ch. 21 lands; KQ 18-19, FA iv 283. A Philip *de Worth* holds from the Furneaux family in 1249. The property descended with the manor and in 1497 was held by the Speke family. It then included a unit called Stockmansplace (Cal. Cl. 1485-1500 291-2), the same property being described as at 'Upton alias Werth and Cudworth' in a 1588 sale (Somerset Record Office DD/X/JS). The name Upton is not found in the vicinity, but a field name Stockman's Hay is found on the 19th century tithe map at Weare which is now the main settlement in Cudworth parish, and probably part DB *Worde*, VCH iv p. 143. Morland (II p. 96) and DG identify Wreath which is near Chard (Grid Reference ST 3408).

21,37 KNOWLE (ST. GILES). Required by the Tax Return for South Petherton Hundred, and held there by *Hugo Poinz* in KQ 19.

ELEIGH is now represented by Eleigh Water and Eleigh Water Farm; Manor Farm (Grid Reference ST 3311) is the site of the DB manor.

21,39-53 A GROUP of Williton Hundred places.

21,43 HUISH. In Nettlecombe, falling in Williton Hundred in Exon. order 427 b 1. The village had two parts, Lodhuish and Beggearnhuish. *Lodehywys* is held from the Barony of Dunden in FA iv 303. See 31,3 note.

21,44-45 VEXFORD. DB *Fescheforde*, Not Freshford near Bath, but clearly in Williton Hundred.

21,46 EMBELLE. See 1,6 note.

21,47 PARDLESTONE. Named after the 1066 holder.

21,48 HILL. Added to Kilve, and held with Kilve by Matthew Furneaux in FA iv 303.

21,49 WESTOWE. Included in a Williton group of places in Exon. 428 b 2 and in the Tax Return, as well as later in the Middle Ages (LSR 1327, p. 166). More recently it is in Lydeard St. Lawrence, Taunton Hundred.

21,54 PUCKINGTON. St. Peter's Church is probably the Abbey of Muchelney. Leofing held part of Drayton from the Abbey in 9,6.

21,55 MOORTOWN. For Drayton, see 9,6. Moortown is required in the Tax Return for Bulstone Hundred. See Exon. order 429 b 2; Morland I p. 41.

21,56-69 A GROUP of Carhampton Hundred places.

21,56 'ALMSWORTHY'. The centre of the manor lay between Wellshead and Westermill farm, the name surviving a short distance away as Almsworthy Common. See Morland I p. 47.

21,60 STOKE (PERO). See Tax Return for Carhampton Hundred and Exon. order 430 b 1.

21,61 'BAGLEY'. Marked on the first edition OS map, but the site is now deserted; Everett p. 54.

21,62 COMBE. In Withycombe; among Carhampton Hundred places in Exon. 430 b 3.

21,63 ALLER. Clearly in Carhampton Hundred, Exon. 430 b 4. See SM 205.

21,64 'GILCOTT'. Exon. order suggests that the place lay in Carhampton Hundred in 1086. In Carhampton itself an *Alicia de Gildencote* is found in LSR (1327) p. 245. The place probably lay on the border of Withycombe parish in the area of Gupworthy, the name being now represented by Gilcotts Copse at ST 001 405 on the 6" OS map, just above Oak. For the etymology of the name, see EPNS (Worcs.) p. 125. DG identifies Golsoncott, which is in Williton Hundred though on the Carhampton border. Its earlier form *Goldsmithecote* cited by DEPN could not derive from DB *Gildenecote*.

21,65 HOLNICOTE. See 16,13 and 21,67 notes. The 1 furlong taken away by Odo son of Gamelin is probably part of his holding at Luccombe, 38,1.

21,67 'HOLNE'. OE *holegn* 'holly tree, holly wood'. VCH p. 490 identifies Hollam in Dulverton and Mo~
land I p. 40 Hone in Exton or Hollam in Winsford. *Holme* is included in a group of Carhampton
places in Exon. 431 a 4, and is probably the *Holne* of KQ 36 held by William *de Hollne* from
Matthew Furneaux. The same man holds *Hunecote* from Matthew Furneaux in FA iv 341, 390
and *Holne* is thus probably part of Holnicote or an alternative form of the name. See FF iv
p. 51; Chadwyck-Healey p. 191 ff.

21,69 STONE. In Exford, ending a group of Carhampton Hundred places in Exon 431 b 2.

21,70 FIVEHEAD. See 9,3 note.

21,72-3 SAMPFORD (ARUNDEL). THORNE (ST. MARGARET). Clearly in Milverton Hundred
(from Exon. order) and held together from the Barony of Dunden in KQ 15. See SM 205.

21,80 'PONTESIDE'. The village is found in FF ii p. 28 as *Ponteside juxta Bannewelle*, VCH p. 492
note 1; see BrC p. 31. An *Alicia Pontyessde* holds land in Banwell in LSR (1327) p. 267. The
first element of DB *Panteshede* is probably a river name, deriving from Welsh *pant*, 'a valley',
see DEPN s.v. *Pant;* the second element is OE *heafod* 'source of a river'. The likely location is
the valley near Towerhead and Sandford Batch, running to Shipham, where the Towerhead
Brook rises.

21,83-84 HOLFORD. Among Taunton Hundred places in Exon. 433 b 1-2. The two holdings probably form the later Rich's and Treble's Holford. Two villages were in existence here in the
late 11th century; see 2,3 note.

21,85 LITTLETON. In Exon. 433 b 3 it falls between a Taunton Hundred and a Frome Hundred
entry and is written in a different hand. It is in the correct order for an isolated Somerton or
Ringoldsway Hundred entry. Littleton is in Compton Dundon which is in Whitley Hundred,
(which absorbed Ringoldsway), but Littleton itself was regarded as a part of Somerton Hundred. *Litteltone* in Somerton Hundred is held from Cecilia *de Bello Campo* and Glastonbury in
KQ 21. See 1841 Census p. 334 note c; VCH iii pp. 57-58.

21,87 FAIROAK. DB *Ecferdintone*, later *Egforton alias Feyroak* in SRS 49 p. 31. See Morland I
p. 44.

21,92 BARTON ST. DAVID. See 19,59 note above.

21,93 LIMINGTON. See 8,41 note.

21,95 (MUDFORD) SOCK. Also Old Sock, held by William Malherbe in NV 57. Roger's holding
probably included Ashington *(Estinton)* KQ 5. See Morland I p. 41; 19,85 note.

21,97 BARRINGTON. See 1,4 note.

21,98 (LONG) SUTTON. A Beauchamp holding in Somerton Hundred FA iv 300. See 10,2;6. The
details are not identical however.

Chapter 22

Roger Arundel's holdings are later divided between the families of Newburgh and Fitzpayne.

22,1 HALSE. A detached part of Williton Hundred, it having become so probably by the intrusion
of Bishop Giso's Wiveliscombe and Bishops Lydeard, themselves originally no doubt part of
Williton Hundred. In Exon. 442 b 2 Halse seems to be in a Williton group, but a marginal note
says that it is in Taunton Hundred, and it seems to be required by the Taunton Hundred Tax
Return.

22,2 HUISH (CHAMPFLOWER). Held from the Barony of Newburgh in KQ 7, in Williton Hundred,
where it appears to be in Exon. 442 b 3.

22,5 SANDFORD. In Wembdon, held from Robert *Filius Pagani* in KQ 11. See VCH p. 494 note 3;
Exon. order 441 a 2.

22,7 NEWTON. At the end of a group of North Petherton places in Exon. 441 a 4. The land was at
Maunsel (Grid Reference ST 3030). See Morland I p. 42.

22,10 CUDWORTH. See 21,36 note.

22,12 MILTON. In Skilgate. It is in a Williton Hundred group in Exon. 442 a 2.

22,18 CARY (FITZPAINE). Or Little Cary. See KQ 21; VCH iii p. 99.

22,19 CHARLTON (MACKRELL). Robert *Filius Pagani* holds in Fees 1265; KQ 21; see VCH iii
p. 97.

22,20 ASH (PRIORS). Exon. 443 b 3 seems to include Roger's original portion of Ash in Taunton
Hundred. The Wells holding (6,19) which he has appropriated is later in Kingsbury West.

22,22 CHEDDON (FITZPAINE). In 2,3 *Ubcedene* (OE *Ufan cedene*, 'place above Cheddon') and
Succedene, '*Suð cedene*' 'South Cheddon' pay customary dues to Taunton. *Ubcedene* is
Opecedre 22,21; the *Cedre* here being South Cheddon, now Cheddon Fitzpaine which also
names the parish.

22,23 SUTTON (BINGHAM). William *de Bingham* holds from Robert *Filius Pagani* in Coker
Hundred in KQ 24.

22,26 MARSTON (BIGOT). Required by the Tax Return for the Frome group of Hundreds.

22,27 PENSELWOOD. DB *Penne*, which is also Pendomer (19,51). Held from Robert *Filius Pagani* in Norton Hundred in KQ 23.

Chapter 24

Walter's lands are later held by the Lovels of Castle Cary or the Paganells of Bampton.

24,2 MILTON. In Kewstoke, forming with Worle (24,1) part of Winterstoke Hundred.

24,3-4 STRETCHOLT. Probably the later villages of West and East Stretcholt. *Westsrecholte* is held from *Hugo Lovel* in KQ 10 and *Estcrecholte* from *Johannes Coggan* who also holds Allerton (24,11).

24,6 ?DUNWEAR. DB *Doneham* identified by Eyton i p. 186 and VCH p. 497 note 2 and PSANHS lxvi (1920) p. 66 ff with Downend or Dunball. These, however, were probably a part of Puriton in 1086, and thus in Loxley Hundred whereas *Doneham* is clearly in North Petherton Hundred, in Exon. 350 a 1. See Morland I p. 44.

If *Doneham* is Dunwear, 'the two waters' are probably the Rivers Parrett and Cary, the latter now re-aligned as the King's Sedgmoor Drain, rather than the rivers Parrett and Brue proposed in DGSW p. 213. See 24,4 note. Other parts of the 'land between the 2 waters' might be 'Crook' and Bower , 24,7-8 below.

24,7 ?'CROOK'. Clearly in North Petherton Hundred (Exon. 350 a 5). *Cruk* is held there in FA iv p.300 from William of Pawlett who also holds Pawlett (24,26) and by Thomas Trivett from John of Horsey (24,25). See NV 74; Cal. Inq. PM. 9 Ed I 1281 p. 238. The name is probably represented by field names Great and Little Crook in Bawdrip. See PSANHS lxvi (1920) p. 56 ff. Other possible identifications are 'Crosse' near Durston (VCH), or *Croyce* in Dunwear (Morland I p. 44).

24,8 BOWER. Several Bowers existed near Bridgwater in the Middle Ages, and East and West survive on modern maps. It has not proved possible to identify this holding nor that at 35,22. This holding was formerly part of Melcombe (see 46,5) to which West Bower is closer; East Bower is, however, closer to ?Dunwear and 'Crook', 24,6 note above.

24,10 BADGWORTH. Exon. 351 a 1 places this village in Bempstone Hundred. Badgworth is south of the River Axe, but is later in Winterstoke Hundred, having been at one time an outlier of Congresbury; Fees 82; RH ii 130 a.

24,11 ALLERTON. Both Stone and Chapel Allerton, VCH p. 497 note 4.

24,14 ALSTON (SUTTON). DB *Alnodestone,* see DEPN 8.

24,15 BRATTON (SEYMOUR). This Bratton is among Bruton Hundred places in Exon. 352 a 1, and was conferred on Bruton Abbey by Walter's tenant; BrC 92 p. 22.

24,17 (CASTLE) CARY. The head of the Douai Barony and of Walter's successors the House of Lovel; Fees 80; KQ (supp.) 45.

24,20 BARROW. See 19,62 note.

24,21 BRIDGWATER. DB *Brugie,* to which Walter's name has been attached.

24,28 HUNTSPILL. Roger holds another part of Huntspill, 3 virgates in 24,34. There is a separate Tax Return for Huntspill Hundred which is said to contain 1 hide and pay 6s tax (the usual payment for 1 hide). It is likely that this 1 hide holding formed the Hundred, the later entry being in Bempstone Hundred. In each of the DB entries ½ hide is held in lordship. Since lordship land is usually exempt, and Huntspill Hundred pays tax for a hide, it is probable that at the time of the Tax Return, the 1 hide was held by sub-tenants.

24,30 CHILCOMPTON. See 3,2 note.

24,31 (WEST) HARPTREE. Held from *Hugo Lovel* as West Harptree (Gurney) in Chewton Hundred in KQ 39. See 5,60 note.

24,32 ECKWEEK. DB *Ecewiche;* the spelling discounts identification with Wick in Brent Knoll (VCH p. 500 n. 2), although a Wellow Hundred place (where Eckweek lies) should have been entered before Chewton Hundred places (24,30-31). See Morland I p. 44.

24,33 ALSTONE. DB *Alsistune.* Formerly Alston Maris or Morris, it is included in a Bempstone Hundred group in Exon. order. Later it is partly in Huntspill and Puriton Hundred, partly in Bempstone, 1841 Census pp. 313,322.

24,34 HUNTSPILL. See 24,28 note.

24,35-36 'HUISH'. In a group of Bempstone Hundred places in Exon. 355 a 3-4. The place is marked on the 1st edition OS map and it is represented by Huish Rhyne on the 1904 OS 6" sheet, half a mile north-west of Highbridge, and by a tithing of Burnham parish. It is *Hewyssh juxta Highbrygge* in an inquisition of Edward I cited in Humphreys i p. 377; see LSR (1327) p. 114.

24,37 ADBER. Over Adber in Horethorne Hundred. Ralph of Conteville owes tax on 1 virgate in the Tax Return for Milborne Hundred. See 19,74. 47,11 notes and Morland II p. 95.

Chapter 25

William's successors, the Mohuns, continue to hold his lands as the Barony of Dunster. For the later history of the holdings, see H. Maxwell-Lyte *The Honour of Dunster* (HD) and *Some Somerset Manors* (SM), details above.

25,1 STOCKLAND. The holding is Shurton (Sheriff's *Tun*)`in Stogursey; KQ 16; SM 335; HD *passim;* Morland I p. 42.
 'SEABERTON'. Required by the Tax Return for Cannington Hundred. A field name in Stogursey, also Seavrington (*r* partly erased) in TA of 1841. See Morland II p. 94.
25,2 DUNSTER. DB *Torre,* to which the name of an early owner has been prefixed.
25,3 ADSBOROUGH. The holding is later called from the adjacent Thurloxton; HD *passim;* KQ 1C Morland I p. 43.
25,4 ALEY. See SM p. 305.
25,5-6 LEIGH, STREET. In Winsham. The holding at Leigh is required by the Tax Return for South Petherton Hundred. Later the two places are drawn into the ecclesiastical Kingsbury East Hundred.
25,7 BROMPTON (RALPH). Named from Ralph FitzWilliam who held after William of Mohun (SM 190). Brompton Ralph is counted as a separate Hundred.in the Tax Returns, and in the second Exon. List of Hundreds. It probably included Clatworthy (25,8).
25,8 CLATWORTHY. Later in Williton Hundred, it appears from Exon. order 357 a 3 and the Tax Return to have been in Brompton Ralph Hundred in 1086.
25,9-28 A LARGE GROUP of places in the 1086 Hundreds of Carhampton, Cutcombe and Minehead all later in Carhampton.
25,9-10 CUTCOMBE, MINEHEAD. The heads of small Hundreds for which there are separate Tax Returns. (See Appendix I).
25,12 'BROWN'. In Treborough marked on the first edition OS map; now represented by Court Farms (Grid Reference SS 9936); Morland I p. 48. See KQ 37; LSR (1334) p. 272 note 1.
25,14 QUARME. North Quarme, itself divided in the Middle Ages into *Quarm Picot* and *Quarm Sibyl* SM p. 94. See 43,1.
25,18 STAUNTON. DB *Stantune.* Required in the Minehead Hundred Tax Return. See FA iv 302.
25,21 (OLD) STOWEY. The *Holestowy* of FA iv 431 and HD *passim;* distinct from 'Stowey' in Oare also in Carhampton Hundred (30,1).
25,25 BRATTON. Held from *Johannes de Mohun* in KQ 36.
25,26 KNOWLE. DB *Ernole.* In the Middle Ages it is *Oule Knowle.* Among Carhampton Hundred places in Exon. 360 a 4. See HD *passim;* SM p. 77.
25,29-42 A GROUP of Williton Hundred places.
25,29 (WEST) QUANTOXHEAD. The Mohun holding is Quantoxhead *Minor* in KQ 6. See 31,2 note
25,31-32 NEWTON, WOOLSTON. In Bicknoller. From the Tax Return and Exon. 361 a 1 they appear to be in Williton Hundred, and probably represent the Mohun holding later called Bicknoller; HD *passim;* SM p. 162.
25,33 ELWORTHY. The 1 virgate added to Williton is probably *Ledforda* 1,6 note. Dodman also holds Willett, Coleford and Watchet in this Hundred (Williton), 25,34-36, and it is probable that at one of them he held the 1 virgate of *Pirtochesworda* mentioned in the Tax Return. This unidentified place-name possibly represents a word such as *Wistowes-worth,* the latter element being OE *worð* 'a private estate or curtilage' the former perhaps being the same as Westowe (21,49) to which Coleford is adjacent. See Appendix III.
25,38 HOLFORD (ST. MARY). Clearly in Williton Hundred in Exon. 362 a 1, this holding is later in Whitley Hundred. See KQ 28; SM 316.
25,41 COMBE (SYDENHAM). This Combe is clearly in Williton Hundred in Exon. 362 b 1. See HD p. 49,53.
25,42 'SHORTMANSFORD'. DB *Sordemaneford.* In Williton Hundred in Exon. 362 b 2, before a change of scribe. Morland II p. 94 suggests 'Stelfords' in Holford but the place found as late as 1520 as Shortmansford can hardly have evolved to Stelfords (see HD p. 271). It may have been near Durborough, FF i p. 178, referring to 'a messuage and 2 carucates of land in *Dereberg* and *Schortmanisford'.* From OE *Sceortamannaford,* 'ford of the short men.'
25,43-47 A GROUP of Milverton Hundred places.
25,47 LEIGH. In Milverton Hundred, KQ 15.
25,48 STOCKLINCH. DB *Stoche.* In Exon. 363 b 1 it falls at the end of a group of Milverton places and before a solitary Andersfield entry, and is probably an isolated entry for Abdick and Bulstone. The Mohuns hold Stocklinch St. Magdalen; HD *passim;* SM 357; VCH p. 506 note 2.
25,50 (EAST) LYDEARD. DG identifies Lydeard St. Lawrence, but the Mohun land is *Lydeiard Punchardon,* HD *passim;*KQ 19; now East Lydeard, a part of Bishops Lydeard not in Kingsbury West Hundred.
25,51 BAGBOROUGH. West Bagborough; see Morland II p. 95; SM 294. East Bagborough was part o Bishops Lydeard.
25,52 STOKE (ST. MARY). Among Taunton Hundred places in Exon. 364 a 2. See HD pp. ii, 3.
25,54 NUNNEY. See 13,1 note.

25,55 BREWHAM. The Mohun land no doubt included both North and South Brewham; in KQ 32, two parts of the village are both held from the Dunster fief. See SM 379, HD *passim.*
25,56 CHERITON. North Cheriton, see FA iv 299; SM 393. Other parts of the village are 28,2. 36,14.
26,1 WHATLEY. In South Petherton Hundred; see Exon. 438 a 1 and the Tax Return.
26,2 HINTON (ST. GEORGE). Like Hinton (Blewitt), 26,5, this Hinton is later held by the Earl Marshall; KQ (supp.) 52; VCH iv p. 41. The Crewkerne Hinton here would precede the one in Chewton Hundred in Exon. order. See Tax Return for Crewkerne Hundred, and next note.
26,5 HINTON (BLEWITT). Named from the 1086 holder, Exon. 438 b 3. In the Chewton Hundred Tax Return, Hugh *Malus Transitus,* William's sub-tenant here, has failed to pay tax on 1 virgate. See KQ 39; 26,2 note.
26,6 YEOVIL. Hugh's portion of Yeovil was later Henford Matravers; Morland I p. 41.
26,7 CHILTON (?CANTELO). DB *Citerne* might be Chilthorne adopted by VCH p. 508 and Batten. But Chilton Cantelo was held in the time of Edward III from the heir of the Earl of Pembroke who succeeded William of Eu at Yeovilton and Hinton St. George. Later a detached part of Horethorne Hundred, it was probably in Stone Hundred in 1086.

Chapter 27
Some of William of Falaise's lands are later held by the families of Courcy and Courtenay.
27,1 STOGURSEY. Formerly Stoke-Courcy. DB *Stoches.* The church of the manor is granted to St. Mary of Lonlay by William *de Faleisia* in SC p. 1. See FA iv p. 275 and PSANHS lxvi (1920) p. 98 ff.
27,2 WOOTTON (COURTENAY). Belongs to the Barony of Stogursey in Fees 83. Held from the de Courtenays in Carhampton Hundred in RH ii 125b, KQ 37.
28,2 CHERITON. Probably South Cheriton, adjacent to Horsington (28,1). Both have the same holder in Fees 79. See 25,56. 36,14.
29,1 WALTON (IN GORDANO). See KQ (supp.) 43.
30,1 'STOWEY'. See Morland II p. 94; 25,21 note.
30,2 OARE. See Chadwyck-Healey p. 397 ff. Required by the Tax Return for Carhampton Hundred.

Chapter 31
Ralph Pagnell's holdings are later held partly by the Gaunt family.
31,1 STOCKLAND. Probably Stockland Bristol itself which was a Gaunt holding, KQ 17; LSR (1327) 141. See 21,26. 25,1 notes and Morland I p. 42.
31,2 (EAST) QUANTOXHEAD. Held as *Major' Cantokeheved* by Henry of Gaunt, RH ii 125 a. See KQ 6; 25,29 note.
31,3 HUISH. In Nettlecombe. *Ludehywys* and *Beggerhywys* are Gaunt holdings in RH ii 125a. See FA iv 304 and 21,43 note. In Exon. order it falls between two places that are required by the Tax Return for Williton Hundred.
31,4 BAGBOROUGH. West Bagborough. See 25,51 note.
32,5 BOSSINGTON. See KQ 36. For the Athelney Abbey claim, see 10,6 note.
32,7 ?RAPPS. DB *Epse.* In Exon. it falls between a place in Taunton Hundred and one in Somerton and is out of sequence for one in Abdick and Bulstone. It is identified with Rapps (*Apse* in NV 72) in VCH p. 511 note 1. The derivation is possible however, from OE *æpse,* a metathesis of *æspe 'aspen tree'* to which an r has become affixed from a phrase such as *æt pære æpse.* The initial E of the DB form is a French spelling.
32,8 ALLER. In Langport. See VCH iii p. 62.
33,1 CHARLTON (?MUSGROVE). Jocelyn holds 1 hide taken away from Bruton (1,9) which is perhaps part of this land.
33,2 THE UNNAMED HOLDING is certainly in Milborne (Horethorne) Hundred, for Robert son of Gerald holds 4 hides in the Tax Return. Eyton (i p. 177) suggests Charlton Horethorne.

Chapter 35
Alfred of 'Spain's' holdings later form the Barony of (Nether) Stowey, in the hands of the Colombières family.
35,2 BOWER. See 24,8 note.
35,4 STRINGSTON. Among Cannington Hundred places in Exon. 372 a 1, but part was in Williton Hundred for in the Williton Tax Return Ranulf of *Strangestona* pays no tax on 1 virgate. This entry begins a group of Cannington places in Exon. with a change of handwriting.
35,11-12 (NETHER) STOWEY. From the list of Knight's fees in FF ii p. 224 (18 E III 31) which represent Chapter 35 holdings, it appears that Over Stowey in Cannington Hundred was a part of DB *Stalwei* here. See Exon. 373 a 2; RH ii 127b; KQ 5.
35,15 DYCHE. Later a part of Stringston in Cannington Hundred, but here it shares an entry with Alfoxton in Williton Hundred, Exon. 373 b 1.
35,14 ?LEIGH. DB *Lege* falls at the end of a group of Williton Hundred places in Exon. 373 b 2, and before Rodhuish in Carhampton which is written in a different hand. *Lege* is thus unlikely

to be Woodcocks Ley in Carhampton Hundred (Morland I p. 44). The descent of the manor i
unclear, but the text says "it has been added to Alfwy's lands which Alfred holds". This
formula normally means that land formerly held by Alfwy and now by Alfred is adjacent to
Lege. Alfwy held Alfoxton and Dyche in Williton Hundred as well as Rodhuish in Carhampto
Lege may thus be a lost 'Leigh' near Holford St. Mary, or Leigh in Old Cleeve, adjacent to Ro
huish. Leigh and Rodhuish are both later Mohun (Dunster) holdings; HD *passim.*

35,16 STAWLEY. A Milverton Hundred place is suggested by the order of Exon.

35,18 PRESTON. Preston Bowyer in Milverton, probably named from Hugh *de Bures* the sub-tenan
(Hill 254). It was given to Goldclyve Priory by a descendant of Alfred, Cal. Inq. M.
Morland II p. 96. In Exon. it falls between Isle Brewers (Bulstone) and Goathurst (Andersfiel
and is written in a different hand. It is out of order for a Milverton Hundred place or for a pa
of Brompton Regis (1,11). It may possibly have been returned with Bishop Lydeard (no. 24 i
the second Exon. List). See 19,35 note.

35,20 MERRIDGE. Later in Cannington Hundred, but it appears in an Andersfield group here and i
KQ 31.

35,21 QUANTOCK. Probably Little Quantock in Enmore, Morland II p. 95.

35,22 HILLFARRANCE. The Honour of Stowey holds *Illeferun* in Taunton Hundred in KQ 20. Se
2,5.

35,24 OAKLEY. Exon. order here suggests that it was returned as an outlier of Martock. It is name
(Achileia) in the Tax Return for the Yeovil group of Hundreds, and is in Stone in later times.

Chapter 36

Thurstan's holdings are later held by the Neufmarché and Russel families and by Roger *de Moeles* o
form the Barony of North Cadbury.

36,1 PITCOMBE. *Hugo Lovel,* who also has Dunkerton (36,13), holds in KQ 33. Cole and
Honeywick were a part of the land.

36,2 *WLTUNE.* Unidentified, from OE *ule-tūn* or *ula-tūn* 'owl's farm' or 'owls' farm', or from
OE *Wull-tūn,* 'wool enclosure' or 'shearing-pens'.

36,3 'EASTRIP'. Now a field name near Sheephouse Farm in Bruton, Morland I p. 48; see SM 389
It is possibly derived from Ripe, the 1086 holder.

36,4 SYNDERCOMBE. In Clatworthy, now drowned by the Clatworthy reservoir. It falls in a gro
of Bruton and Frome places in Exon., and is identified by DG as Combe in Bruton, no doub
for that reason. Although displaced in Exon., Syndercombe, like other of Thurstan's holding
is held later of the Barony of North Cadbury and by the Russel family (KQ 7). Thurstan's ot
holdings lie in the Bruton-Frome area, and this isolated Williton Hundred place was probably
missed at first in compiling the schedule of his lands. The single entry in Exon. is in a differe
hand.

36,5 (NORTH) CADBURY. At 12 hides this is clearly the major Cadbury holding, from which So
Cadbury is distinguished in the text (36,7). The modern parochial acreage is in the same pro
portion.
WESTON (BAMPFYLDE). See 19,69 note.

36,7 WOOLSTON. In South Cadbury. See Morland I p. 40.
CLAPTON. See Morland I p. 41.

36,8 BLACKFORD. Together with Holton (45,4) this was Glastonbury land and returned subse
quently to the church, forming with Lattiford (8,19) a detached part of Whitley Hundred. In
Exon. order, Blackford and Holton appear to be included in one of the Bruton or Frome Hu
dreds here.

36,9 COMPTON (PAUNCEFOOT). In Exon. order, the place falls in a Bruton group. *Comptone* is
held from *Johannes de Moelys* in KQ (supp.) 45. 'Pauncefoot', from the descendants of
Bernard, 36,7;13.

36,11 WANSTROW. Serlo's holding was West Wanstrow in Frome Hundred KQ 9, where it is held
from Roger *de Moles.* See 6,16 note.

36,14 CHERITON. Perhaps North Cheriton, adjacent to Thurstan's holding at Blackford. See 25,56
note; but see Morland I p. 40.

Chapter 37

Serlo's Holdings are later held by the Martin family and form the Barony of Blagdon.

37, 3-4 (CHEW) STOKE, CHILLYHILL. Probably included Stoke Villice (Grid Reference ST 55 60
earlier Stoke Militis, possibly the 47,16 holding, and the lost *Beechenstoke* held in 1326 as
Bytthgnestoke from William Fitzwilliam Martin, Cal. Inq. PM. 19 E II 100; VCH p. 516 note
Another part is held by the Earl of Gloucester 5,16 note. Chillyhill is part of Stoke Villice in
LSR (1327) p. 138. There appears also to have been royal land at Chew Stoke not mentioned
in DB (Tax Return, Chew Hundred); see Morland I p. 46.

37,7 KILMINGTON. See 1,9 note.

37,9   WHEATHILL. Subsequently returned to Glastonbury which held it in 1066, becoming a
       detached part of Whitley Hundred, FA iv 306.
37,10 COMPTON (MARTIN). See Fees 377; KQ 39.
37,11 MORETON. Now flooded by Chew Valley Resevoir. See KQ 39.
37,12 MUDFORD. See 19,87 note.
       STONE. The Hundred Stone that names the place still stands at grid reference ST 557 178,
       north of Yeovil.
Chapter 38
38,1   LUCCOMBE. See 21,65 note.
Chapter 39
39,1   KNOWLE. Required by the Tax Return for Bedminster Hundred; and held from the heirs of
       Johannis Geffard in KQ (supp.) 42.
Chapter 40
40,1-2 HINTON (CHARTERHOUSE), NORTON (ST. PHILIP). This Norton is required by the Tax
       Return for the Frome group of Hundreds. The Earls of Salisbury, successors of Edward, and
       their successors the Earls of Lincoln hold *Henton* and *Norton* in Wellow Hundred Fees 81; KQ 12.
Chapter 41
41,1   WESTON. In Bath, required by the Tax Return for Bath Hundred.
Chapter 42
42,1   KEWSTOKE. See Morland I p. 38, and the Tax Return for Winterstoke Hundred.
42,2   UBLEY. See VCH p. 519 note 1. It is required by the Tax Return for Chewton Hundred.
42,3   (STON) EASTON. Required by the Tax Return for Chewton Hundred.
Chapter 43
43,1   QUARME. South Quarme or Quarme Monceaux SM 94. See 25,14 note.
Chapter 44
44,2   CHELVEY. The 1 virgate held by the Bishop of Coutances is perhaps part of Backwell 5,30, or
       Midgell, 5,68.
44,3   MILTON (CLEVEDON). Held by *Johannis de Cilvedon* from *Hugo Lovel* in KQ 32. The same
       sub-tenant holds Clevedon 44,1 (KQ (supp.)43).
Chapter 45
45,1-2 (LYTES) CARY. In KQ 21 William *Le Lit* holds from *Anselmus de Gurnay,* who also holds
       Sandford Orcas (45,5), another of Humphrey's holdings. The larger holding is perhaps Lytes
       Cary, the smaller may be Cooks Cary or Lower Lytes Cary; see VCH iii p. 100.
45,4   HOLTON. See 8,9, 8,19 and 36,8 notes.
45,5   SANDFORD (ORCAS). See 45,1-2 note. Required by the Tax Return for Milborne
       (Horethorne) Hundred. In Exon. 466 b 4 it begins a group of Horethorne places.
45,9   WARLEIGH. See VCH p. 525 note 8.
45,12 KNOWLE (PARK). The 1 hide held by Thurstan is probably part of Woolston or Clapton (36,
       7) also held by Alnoth before 1086 although the values are different. This 'Knowle' is required
       by the Tax Return for the Bruton group of Hundreds.
45,16 BROCKLEY. Exon. includes it among Chewton Hundred places (466 b 1), as does the Tax
       Return. It survived as a detachment of Chewton until modern times.
45,17 CRANDON. Later in North Petherton Hundred, but Fees 262 records that it was originally
       part of Puriton and at Exon. 465 b 1 it might well be an entry for Loxley Hundred where
       Puriton was in 1086. See 11,1 note.
45,18 PRESTON (PLUCKNETT). This Preston, required by the Tax Return for Yeovil, is probably
       the part of the parish of Preston Plucknett called Preston Monachorum or Bemondsey; KQ 4;
       Collinson III p. 223; Morland I p. 41.
Chapter 46
46,1   WEARNE. Exon. 479 b 3 seems to include it in Somerton Hundred. It is later in Pitney.
46,2   THE UNNAMED VIRGATE added to Dulverton may be Hawkridge; Morland I p. 43; see
       Collinson III p. 529.
46,3   WITHYPOOL. The ½ hide is probably that entered under Winsford (1,17) held by 3 thanes.
46,4   WELLISFORD. The 1 virgate held by Bretel from the Count of Mortain is probably part of
       Appley, 19,22, or of Greenham, 19,21.
46,5   BOWER. See 24,8 note.
46,6   'PIGNES'. See Morland I p. 48.
46,8   NEWTON. This Newton (Exon. 477 a 3) and the other (46,17 = 477 b 5) fall in a group of
       North Petherton places. See Morland I p. 42.
46,11 HUNTSTILE. Later both in North Petherton and Andersfield Hundreds, the boundary bisect-
       ing the village; see 1841 Census p. 327. In 1086, it was partly an outlier of Somerton; like the
       adjacent Deadmans Well (1,1 note). Exon. order suggests that the rest was in Andersfield Hun-
       dred.

367

46,12 CHILTON (TRINITY). See Tax Return for North Petherton.

46,17 NEWTON. See 46,8 note.

46,18 HONIBERE. Required by the Tax Return for Cannington. It is a border place and later in Williton Hundred.

46,19 MILTON. In Kewstoke; required by the Tax Return for Winterstoke Hundred.

46,21 BARTON (ST.DAVID). Mauger's 1 hide is probably at Keinton Mandeville, 19,59; see General Notes to 19,59.

46,23 WALTON. In Kilmersdon; see Tax Return for the Frome Hundreds and Exon. 480 a 3;also KQ3.

46,24 HAY (STREET). See 6,1 note.

46,25 (STON) EASTON. In Chewton Hundred in the Tax Return and in Exon. order; 480 b 1. See 5,59. 42,3 notes.

Chapter 47

47,2 SEAVINGTON. Probably Seavington St. Michael (alias Seavington Dennis), VCH iv p. 205. See 10,3, 19,2 notes.

47,3 LOPEN. Later Great Lopen, VCH iv p. 164.

47,4 BRADON. Harding's Bradon was Goose Bradon, a Meriet Fee in FA iv p. 315. See VCH p. 475 note 5 and 19,17 note. 'Meriet' is from Harding's land at Merriott, 47,6.

47,10 DINNINGTON. See 8,36. This land appears to represent the remains of the Glastonbury holding of Kingstone, the rest being lost to the Count of Mortain (19,10). See VCH iv p.148.

47,11 ADBER. Included by the Tax Return in the Yeovil group of Hundreds, and probably in Stone in 1086. See FA iv p. 316; Morland II p. 95 and 19,74, 24,37 notes.

47,12 DODINGTON. DB *Stawe*, part of Nether Stowey. Doda's portion was later called after him. It is required by the Tax Return for Williton Hundred. In Exon. 491 a 1 it is in the Hundred of *Wellintuna*, no doubt an error.

47,14 ?STOCKLINCH. The 2½ hides and ½ virgate in lordship of Alfward and his brothers are probably the land of identical size held by *Sauard* (OE *Saeweard*) in the Tax Return for Abdick Hundred. See Morland I p. 38. *Stoke Ostriter* (Stocklinch Ottersay) is held in KQ 2 from Alan *Plukenet* who also holds other Ch. 47 lands.

47,15 DRAYCOTT. In Rodney Stoke, required by the Tax Return for Cheddar Hundred.

47,16 (CHEW) STOKE. Required by the Tax Return for Chew Hundred. See 37,3-4 note.

47,18 SWAINSWICK. See 5,38 note.

47,19 BUCKLAND (DINHAM). See the Tax Return for the Frome Hundreds. It is probably named from Dunn or his descendants, Hill p. 201. See ECW no. 466.

47,20 COMBE (?HAY). In a Bruton-Frome group of places in Exon. 492 b 3. Combe Hay is possible, but may have been part Englishcombe in 1086 (5,44 note).

47,21 (WEST) LYDFORD. See 8,4 note. Required by the Tax Return for the Bruton Hundreds.

47,22 *SCEPEWORDE*. In a group of Bruton and Frome places in Exon. 493 a 3. Whale ('Principles p. 43) suggests Sheephouse Farm in Bruton, adjacent to 'Eastrip' below, but it is possibly adjacent to Aelfric's 9 hides at West Lydford (47,21 above). It represents OE *Scĕpaworde* 'at the sheep farm' from OE *Scepa*, genitive plural of *Scep* 'a sheep', and *word* 'a private farm or est'

EBe 1-3; EBu 1-2 BLEADON. In Bedfordshire 3 places and in Buckinghamshire 2 are said to have been exchanged by the Bishop of Coutances for *Bledone*. The only place named in DB with the same or similar spelling (OE *bleo dun* 'blue' or 'coloured' hill) is Bleadon in Somerset with which the Beds. and Bucks. VCHs followed by DG have identified it. The references are here included for the sake of completeness, but the identification with Bleadon, Somerset, is not probable, unless the land had been alienated from its ecclesiastical owner for a time. Bleadon was held by the Bishop of Winchester both before and after 1066 (2,11) whereas all the lands received by the Bishop of Coutances had been held by men of the King, except Tyringham (Bucks. 5,10), held by two thanes, one of them a man of Earl Waltheof, whose lands fell to the King on his execution, the other without a named lord. *Bledone* should therefore be a manor formerly held by the King or his men. There are two main alternative possibilities: either a variant spelling of Blewbury or Blewburton *(Bleo byrig dune)* EPNS Berks. 151-2, a manor of King Edward's and King William's (DB Berks. 1,5), or a lost place. Since the lands which the Bishop received lay close together, about the junction of Beds. Bucks. and Northants., DB may have omitted a King's manor in this area. See DB Beds. 3,8, Bucks. 5,10 notes.

CONCORDANCE TO THE PRINCIPAL EDITIONS OF CHARTERS
CITED IN THE NOTES

ECW	Sawyer	BCS	KCD	Mon. Ang.	Robertson
354	-	-	-	-	-
360	236	61	20(+vi 225)	i. 48-9	-
379	251	143	74(+vi 226)	i. 49	-
383	254	158	1002	-	-
405	292	438	253(+ii 227)	i. 56	-
419	1819	-	-	-	-
442	-	-	-	-	-
444	475	770	1140	-	-
466	555	889	-	-	-
486	692	1074	484(+iii. 455)	-	-
542	1042	-	816	ii. 285-6	-
544	-	-	-	-	App. iv.

APPENDIX I

The Somerset Hundreds

This appendix attempts to describe the probable hundredal organisation of Somerset in 1086 and records the major differences between that pattern and the medieval Hundreds of the Feudal Aids or *Nomina Villarum* as they survived to the mid-nineteenth century. [1]

Neither the text of Exchequer Domesday nor of the Exon. Book provides Hundred headings, but some conception of the Somerset Hundreds can be formed from the Tax Return (Exon. folios 75a-82b; 526b-527a), which records tax remitted, due or paid, Hundred by Hundred but usually without place-names; [2] and from two lists of Somerset Hundreds (I = folios 63b-64a; II = folios 64a-64b), the first fragmentary, the second probably complete, which are bound up with the Exon. Domesday. The places which each Hundred contained can often be deduced from Tax Return entries, or the order of sections in the Exon. Book, where, under each major landholder, places tend to be entered in Hundred groups, though with dislocations. As is explained below, the order of entries within chapters of the Exon. Book is largely the order of the second list of Hundreds, which appears to have been intended as an index the hundredal Returns on which Exon. was based.

The Tax Return lists 35 Hundreds, and three manors *Hama, Torna* and *Torleberga* [3] of which Ham is later in Whitley Hundred and Thornfalcon and Thurlbear in North Curry. The second Exon. list contains 58 names, and the probable relation between these lists and the 36 mid-nineteenth century Hundreds indexed and mapped in this edition is set out below. The numbers beside the two Exon. lists and the Tax Return Hundreds indicate their order; the numbers beside the modern Hundreds are those of the map and index of this volume. In the second Exon. list, royal manors have been starred, and holdings of Bishop Giso of Wells marked with a cross. An M indicates that the 'Hundred' was probably only a manor with a few or no members. A question mark directs attention to a doubt expressed at the end of the table. Difficult names are given their modern equivalent in brackets. The names of places ending in -a appear in the original in the genitive case dependent on the word 'Hundred' they are here restored to the nominative:

EXON. LIST II	EXON. LIST I	TAX RETURN	'MODERN' HUNDRED
1 *Nortpetret**	1 *Nort Peretu'*	xxvi *Nortpedret*	18 North Petherton
M 2 *Vicecomitis Brunetona*	- - - - - -	xiii *Brunetona*	Pt. of 15 Williton
? 3 *Chori**	23 *Couri*	xxxvi *Bolestana*	Pt. of 28 Abdick and Bulston
M 4 *Cudecoma* (Cutcombe)	- - - - - -	Pt. of viii *Cudecoma* and *Manehefua*	Pt. of 14 Carhampton
5 *Cantetona**	4 *Cantetu'*	xxiv *Cantetona*	16 Cannington
6 *Manehefua* [4] (Minehead)	- - - - - -	Pt. of viii ·*Cudecoma* and *Manehefua*	Pt. of 14 Carhampton
7 *Sutpetret**	26 *Sud peretonna*	xxix *Sutperetona*	34 South Petherton
8 *Willetona**	7 *Vueltetu'* [5]	Pt. of xxii *Willetona*	Pt. of 15 Williton
M 9 *Regis Brunetona** [6]	- - - - - -	- - - - - -	Pt. of 15 Williton
10 *Carentona**	10 *Carentu*	xi *Carentona*	14 Carhampton
M11 *Duluertona*	13 *Doluertu*	- - - - - -	Pt. of 15 Williton
12 *Miluertona**	19 *Meluertona*	ii *Miluertona*	25 Milverton
13 *Tintenella*	11 *Tintehella*	Pt. of xx *Giuela*	31 Tintinhull
M14 *Cliua** (Old Cleeve)	16 *Cliui*	- - - - - -	Pt. of 15 Williton
M15 *Cumbaf* [7] (Combe St. Nicholas)	- - - - - -	Pt. of xviii *Terra Gisonis*	Pt. of 12 Kingsbury (East)
M16 *Winesforda**	- - - - - -	xxiii *Winesfort*	Pt. of 15 Williton

EXON. LIST II	EXON. LIST I	TAX RETURN	'MODERN' HUNDRED
M17 Nortchori*	- - - - - -	xix Tierleberga	27 North Curry
		xxxviii Torleberga	
		xxxvii Tornā	
M18 Crica* (Creech St.Michael)	- - - - -	- - - - - -	Pt. of 17 Andersfield
M19 Cingesberia†	- - - - -	Pt. of xviii Terra Gisonis	Pt. of 12 Kingsbury (East)
M20 Wyuelescoma†	- - - - -	Pt. of xviii Terra Gisonis	Pt. of 12 Kingsbury (West)
21 Crucha*	2 Crucha	xxi Crucha	35 Crewkerne
?22 Chori	22 Abedic	xxx Abediccha	Pt. of 28 Abdick and Bulstone
M23 Walintona†	- - - - -	Pt. of xviii Terra Gisonis	Pt. of 12 Kingsbury (West)
M24 Lidiart†	- - - - -	Pt. of xviii Terra Gisonis	Pt. of 12 Kingsbury (West)
25 Wenestoc	?28 Vuelstestoc(8)	xii Winestoc (9)	Pt. of 6 Winterstoke
26 Andretesfella	12 Andretsfelt(10)	xxviii Andretesfelt	17 Andersfield
M27 Axebruga* (11)	25 Aucsebrigesū	vii Cetdra	Pt. of 6 Winterstoke
M28 Mertocha*	5 Merthoc	- - - - -	30 Martock
M29 Wella†	- - - - -	xviii Terra Gisonis	12 Wells Forum
30 Tantona	- - - - -	Pt. of i Tantotona and Pipeministra	Pt. of 26 Taunton and Taunton Dean
M31 Pinpeministra (Pitminster)	- - - - -	Pt. of i Tantotona and Pipeministra	Pt. of 26 Taunton and Taunton Dean
M32 Congresberia*	- - - - -	xvii Cungresberia	Pt. of 6 Winterstoke
33 Sumbretona*	9 Sunmertona (12)	- - - - -	29 Somerton
34 Chiu	- - - - -	xxvii Cui	3 Chew
M35 Iatona†	- - - - -	Pt. of xvi Ciuuētona	Pt. of 6 Winterstoke
36 Hundesbera	14 Hundesberga	Pt. of xx Givela	Pt. of 36 Houndsborough, Barwick and Coker
37 Licget* (13)	8 Liet (14) (Cochre erased)	Pt. of xx Givela	Pt. of 36 Houndsborough, Barwick and Coker
38 Locheslega	- - - - -	xxxii Lochesleia	Pt. of 20 Whitley
?39 Betmenistra*	29 Hiruescliua	ix Harecliua	Pt. of 2 Hartcliffe and Bedminster
40 Ringandesuuel	- - - - -	xxxiii Ringoltdeswea	Pt. of 20 Whitley
M41 Monechetona	- - - - -	xxxv Monachetona	Pt. of 20 Whitley
42 Bada	- - - - -	vi Bada	5 Bath Forum
43 Porberia	- - - - -	v Porberia	1 Portbury
?44 Bedmynstra*	- - - - -	x Betministra	Pt. of 2 Hartcliffe and Bedminster
?45 Ascleia	- - - - -	- - - - -	- - - - -
46 Bimastan	- - - - -	xiv Bimastana	11 Bempstone
47 Huuitestan	- - - - -	iii Witestana	13 Whitstone
M48 Suðbrenta	- - - - -	- - - - -	Pt. of Brent and Wrington
49 Froma*	15 Froma	Pt. of xli Froma	10 Frome
50 Chinesmaredona	21 Chinrmaresdū	Pt. of xli Froma	9 Kilmersdon
51 Weleuue	18 Vueluua	Pt. of xli Froma	8 Wellow
52 Briuuetona*	27 Briytona	Pt. of xxxi Bruiuetona	23 Bruton
53 Wincauuetona	24 Vuelcautona	Pt. of xxxi Bruiuetona	24 Norton Ferris
54 Blachethorna	3 Blacheterna (15)	- - - - -	- - - - -

EXON. LIST II	EXON. LIST I	TAX RETURN	'MODERN' HUNDRED
55 *Ciuuetona**	? 30 *Ci...*	xvi *Ciuuētona*	7 Chewton
M56 *Hunespil*	- - - - - -	xv *Hunespilla*	Pt. of 19 Huntspill and Puriton
57 *Hareturna*	20 *Haretona*	xxv *Meleborna*	33 Horethorne
58 *Stana*	17 *At Stana*	Pt. of xx *Giuela*	32 Stone
- - - - - -	6 *Donehetua*	- - - - - -	Pt. of 13 Whitstone
- - - - - -	- - - - - -	Pt. of xxxi *Bruiuetona*	22 Catsash
- - - - - -	- - - - - -	xxxiv *Hama*	Pt. of 20 Whitley
- - - - - -	- - - - - -	iv *Cainesham*	4 Keynsham
- - - - - -	- - - - - -	- - - - - -	21 Glaston 12 Hides
- - - - - -	- - - - - -	- - - - - -	- Pitney
- - - - - -	- - - - - -	- - - - - -	- Brent and Wrington

Some of the identifications of the second Exon. list are tentative. The two *Chori* entries (nos 3 and 22) could be a simple duplication, might represent Curry Rivel and Curry Mallet, thus referring to Bulstone and Abdick Hundreds respectively, or one *Chori* might merely be the royal manor of Curry Rivel (1,5) and the other a return for the two Hundreds attached to it. Abdick and Bulstone are partially intermingled and sometimes later treated as a single joint Hundred. [16] The layout of Ellis' text of the Exon. Book does not make it clear that *Abedic* in the first list is written above *Couri* and in smaller letters, possibly as an explanation, though both are preceded by gallows signs [17]. In the same way, the two Bedminsters of the second list (nos. 39 and 44) might be an erroneous duplication, or represent Bedminster and Hartcliffe Hundreds, often counted as a single Hundred in later times.

Two names in the second list, *Ascleia* (no. 45) and *Blachethorna* (no. 54) remain unidentified. For *Ascleia*, the manors of Ashill (Abdick Hundred), Oakley (in Chilthorne Domer, Stone Hundred) or Ashway have been suggested [18], or the Hundred of Catsash [19]. For *Blachethorna*, Thornfalcon has been proposed. It is not obvious why Ashill or Ashway (both linguistically unlikely), should have enjoyed even temporary status as Hundreds in 1086. Oakley (DB *Achelai*) is closer and was certainly in an anomalous position in 1086, having been added to Martock [20], and apparently counted as an outlier of Martock Hundred in Exon. order, but included in the Tax Return for Stone [21]. Thornfalcon has its own Tax Return, but it has not been shown that *Blachethorna* is an alternative form of the name. It is possible that *Ascleia* and *Blachethorna* represent two of the Hundreds missing from the second Exon. List. If one discounts the untaxed areas of Muchelney, Midelney and Thorney (later in Pitney Hundred) and Glastonbury and its three islands (later Glaston 12 Hides Hundred), two Hundreds, Catsash and Keynsham, are not represented in the second list. Catsash is only evidenced in the next century and it is possible that *Briuuetona* (no. 52) extended westwards to include the area of the later Hundred. On the other hand, *Blachethorna* occurs in the list with Bruton and Wincanton (= Norton Ferris) Hundreds (nos. 52-54) and places later found in Catsash are always found grouped with those in Bruton and Norton Ferris in the order of Exon.[22]. It is thus just possible that *Blachethorna* is an earlier name for Catsash.

Keynsham Hundred should be found in the second Exon. List since it has its own Tax Return; the position of *Ascleia* in the list (no. 45) is not inconsistent with the position of Keynsham Hundred entries in the order of the Exon. Book. [23]

The sixth place in the first Exon List, *Donehetua* is probably Downhead [24], enjoying a short existence as a Hundred, either because it was an isolated Glastonbury holding then locally in the Hundred of Frome or because it was briefly in the hands of the King because of the difficulties faced by Abbot Thurstan at this period [25] Downhead appears among Glaston Hundred holdings in chapter 8 order.

Suthbrenta , the predecessor of Brent and Wrington Hundred is also entered separately in the second Exon. list (no. 48).

Of the Tax Return Hundreds, only *Hama* is not obviously accounted for in the second Exon. list: it was probably considered a part of Ringoldsway Hundred where the order of Exon. entries seems to include it [26].

It will be seen that the list of 58 Hundreds is swollen by a number that are no more than manors, such as Cutcombe, Wellington and the two Bromptons, probably claiming the status and privileges of Hundreds. These small Hundreds that tend to be swallowed after 1086 in larger amalgamations are usually either royal holdings or manors of Bishop Giso, isolated from their natural Hundreds and gathered together in a single Tax Return for the episcopal Hundred, or isolated Glastonbury holdings. The only manors listed as Hundreds and not held by the King, Wells or Glastonbury are Brompton Ralph, Cutcombe and Minehead, all held by William of Mohun [27].

These small Hundreds are unevenly distributed on the map. The pattern in the north, east and south of the County seems to have been of a number of large integrated Hundreds which have changed little since 1086. But in the central marshy area of the Somerset levels and on the borders of Exmoor, there is a pattern of small Hundreds. The influence of the County's geography is apparent here: the isolated manors which later formed Winterstoke are separated by bog and sea marsh or upland heath; those from which Williton and Freemanners grew, by waste and moor.

It is probable that neither the Exon. lists nor the Tax Return reflect the original hundredal organisation of the County. By 1086 the effects of feudalism had begun to break up the 30 or so large Hundreds of which the County probably consisted earlier in the Conqueror's reign. Manors held in chief by major landowners had been withdrawn from their Hundred, becoming small 'Hundreds' or 'Free Manors'; other holdings looked to the chief manor of their lord, often remote, rather than to their own Hundred. This is especially so with ecclesiastical holdings: Wiveliscombe and Bishops Lydeard had, by 1086, intruded as outliers of Wells to isolate Halse and Preston from Williton Hundred [28] and a portion of Taunton Hundred from Taunton [29]. Ash Priors was actually being absorbed into the episcopal Hundred in 1086. [30] Brent Hundred cut Brean off from the rest of Bempstone, and Lattiford, soon to be joined by Blackford and Holton, severed Maperton from Catsash Hundred. Combe St. Nicholas by being taken into Bishop Giso's Hundred separated Whitestaunton off from Abdick. That the process was recent is shown by the Abdick Tax Return which records the loss of Combe and enters Winsham as still in the Hundred, thus duplicating the entry for it in Bishop Giso's Hundred [31]. Chew Hundred was clearly named after Chew Magna[32], but Chew was included in Bishop Giso's Hundred in the Tax Return.

In considering the Hundreds of the second Exon. list and of the Tax Return, it is important to bear in mind the purposes for which the list and the Return were compiled: the differences between them arise from their different purposes and different methods of survey. The Tax Return does not record the Hundreds of Old Cleeve, Creech St. Michael, North Curry, Martock or Coker, all of them royal holdings, presumably because, being held in lordship, they were not liable to tax. The Tax Return also groups Hundreds that clearly had a separate existence according to the second Exon. list: that for Yeovil contains details that belong to Tintinhull, Stone, Houndsborough and probably Coker Hundreds, the places in which are entered in distinct and separate Hundred groups in the order of the Exon. Book. Similarly, the Tax Return for Frome accounts for Frome, Wellow and Kilmersdon Hundreds, and that for Bruton for those later in Bruton, Catsash and Norton

Ferris Hundreds. That other Hundreds existed at the time of the Tax Return is shown by the entry for Mauger's two hides in the return for Williton Hundred. The tax on them, clearly Brushford, he had paid in another Hundred, probably the adjacent Dulverton or Brompton Regis, for neither of which is there a Tax Return. [33].

Dulverton and Brompton Regis were probably not included as being royal lordship land. But probably more than one Tax Return has failed to survive, since the total tax levied in the County exceeds the total of the individual returns. At least Somerton appears to be missing [34]

The purpose of the Exon. list of 58 Hundreds, on the other hand, seems to have been to serve as an index to the returns from which the Exon. Domesday was compiled. [35]. With a few exceptions, places are entered in the Exon. Book under each landholder in Hundred groups and in the order of the second Exon. list. No landholder holds in every Hundred, so that it is impossible to state that the order is precisely followed. Moreover, there are unexplained dislocations such as Draycott and 'Hiscombe' [36] and material accidentally omitted from a Hundred group is often entered later. But a study of a major fief such as that of the Count of Mortain (Ch.19) or of Roger of Courseulles (Ch.21) shows how remarkably the order of Hundreds in the text of the Exon. Book corresponds with the second Exon. list. Changes of Hundred frequently correspond with changes of scribe [37].

There are some exceptions. Whether the *Chori* entries (3 and 22) refer to Abdick and Bulstone Hundreds, or to Curry Rivel itself and to the combined Hundred of Abdick and Bulstone, places belonging to these Hundreds do not seem to be entered in separate groups, but to be intermingled in the text of Exon. Such groups, moreover, tend to fall about twelfth in the sequence of Hundreds. [38]. Minehead falls in the correct position in Chapter 25 for *Manehefua* Hundred (sixth), but the other members of this small Hundred are intermingled thereafter with Carhampton Hundred places (no.10). Places in Williton Hundred (no.8) fall after those for Carhampton (no. 10) in Chapters 16, 31 and 32, but before them in Chapters 21, 22 and 35. On the other hand, places belonging to Loxley Hundred (no.38) and to Ringoldsway (no.40), although later combined in Whitley Hundred, are clearly in separate groups in Chapter 8. Loxley begins with Shapwick [39] and Ringoldsway with Walton. [40] The exact identity of no.39 *Betminstra* and no.44 *Bedmynstra*, as has been seen, is hard to determine. In Chapter 5 [41] which has a large number of entries for the Hundreds of Portbury, Hartcliffe, Bedminster and Keynsham, places for the four Hundreds seem to be mixed together. In Chapter 7 however, Keynsham places precede the Bedminster group [42]. The six Hundreds of the Frome and Bruton group (nos.49-54) seem to be intermingled in all chapters.

Such groupings of Hundreds, different from those of the Tax Return, suggest that material for the Exon. Book was collected in separate circuits, some of them embracing more than one Hundred. They also impose caution on any attempt to identify places solely from the order of the Exon. Book, as do places such as Tuxwell [43], Clewer [44] Milton [45] and Huntstile [46], which, although out of order, are securely identified from other evidence. Nonetheless, if not used mechanically, the reconstructed order of the Hundreds in Exon. is evidence for place-name identification if it is accepted that while a place cannot usually be entered earlier than the normal position for its Hundred, it may well be entered later as an afterthought. This evidence is used in the Places Notes and the present editors hope to set out the Exon. order and probable 1086 Hundreds in a supplementary volume for the South West Counties.

The major difference between the 1086 Hundreds and the later arrangement was the tendency of small Hundreds to be swallowed or amalgamated in larger units, and for border manors to change Hundreds. The evidence of the Exon. order and of the Tax Return is set out below (figures in square brackets refer to the numbers of the modern Hundreds in the index and map of this edition).

The Hundred of HARTCLIFFE AND BEDMINSTER [2] grew from separate 1086 Hundreds of the same names. The 6½ hides of the Tax Return for Bedminster Hundred show that it contained Knowle, Bishopsworth, Bedminster and Abbots Leigh (later in Portbury [47]); Hartcliffe included the southern half of the later combined Hundred and contained Havyatt and Wrington [48], later in Brent and Wrington Hundreds.

WINTERSTOKE Hundred [6] later expanded to include the royal holdings of Axbridge and Cheddar, south of the Mendips, and Congresbury, isolated by the salt marshes of the river Yeo. In 1086, Cheddar Hundred had recently lost Wedmore to Bempstone Hundred [49], and the 7 hides 3 virgates allotted to it by the Tax Return are accounted for by Draycott, Rodney Stoke and Roger of Courseulles' holding at Cheddar [50]. Congresbury Hundred appears to have contained no other place named in Domesday, the 19 hides of the Tax Return corresponding to the 20 hides of the royal holding less the pasture at Wemberham [51]. Kenn was later in Winterstoke Hundred [52], but in 1086 would have been isolated by Congresbury, Yatton and Kingston Seymour (a detached part of Chewton). The northern boundary of the 1086 Hundred was probably the Yeo. Yatton, which in 1086 included the pasture of Wemberham (formerly in Congresbury) and probably Claverham [53], was later in Winterstoke. It is a separate Hundred in the first Exon. list, and is clearly a part of Chewton Hundred [7] in Exon. order and the Tax Return [54].

In addition to Yatton, CHEWTON [7] also included, but as detachments, Brockley (Tax Return) and Midgell and Kingston Seymour (Exon. order) as in later times. With Yatton they would have formed a large single detachment.

KILMERSDON Hundred [9] probably included 'Middlecote' and Mells [55], which are found in this Hundred in the twelfth century. They later became a free manor, or Liberty, and were subsequently absorbed by Frome Hundred. FROME Hundred [10] probably contained the whole of Cranmore [56].

The northern boundary of BEMPSTONE Hundred [11] was probably the river Axe at the time of Domesday, for it included Badgworth, which, being later attached to Congresbury, became part of Winterstoke Hundred.

The *caput* of the holding of Bishop Giso, WELLS FORUM [12] is entered in the Exon. list as *Wella*. Most of his other holdings in the County appear as a series of separate Hundreds in the same list: *Cingesberia, Wyuelescoma, Cumba, Walintona, Lidiart, Iatona*, whereas in the Tax Return they form a single Hundred. In the Exon. Book itself, the individual places are entered largely in the order of the second Exon. list of Hundreds, except that Chard and 'Litnes', the Domesday representative of Huish Episcopi, are included in Kingsbury Episcopi (*Cingesberia*). Winsham is out of order, and is also required in the Tax Return for Abdick [57].

Not all the Bishop's holdings are included in the Tax Return for the Episcopal Hundred: Banwell is counted in Winterstoke, Yatton is in Chewton, and Wedmore in Bempstone. Conversely, the Tax Return clearly includes Chew Magna and Wanstrow in the total of the Bishop's Hundred, whereas they are later in Chew and Frome Hundreds respectively.

Many of the scattered Wells holdings are in later times amalgamated into three distinct Hundreds. Wells Forum contained Wells, Westbury and Litton [58], as well as Evercreech (detached) and Cranmore acquired from Glastonbury. Kingsbury East contained Combe St.Nicholas, Chard, Winsham, Kingsbury Episcopi and Huish Episcopi ('Litnes'), while Kingsbury West contained Ash Priors, Bishops Lydeard, Wiveliscombe and Wellington. Whatley, Leigh and Street, not Wells holdings in Domesday, were later attracted into Kingsbury East, and Wearne in Langport, which was not church land in 1086, was later part of Huish Episcopi. The division of Kingsbury Hundred into East and West dates from the sixteenth century [59].

WHITSTONE Hundred [13] seems to have included both East and West Pennard, Baltonsborough, and North Wootton later in Glaston 12 Hides [60].

CARHAMPTON Hundred [14] later absorbed the small Hundreds of Cutcombe and Minehead, the 10 hides and 1 virgate of which in the Tax Return are probably accounted for by Cutcombe, Minehead, Alcombe, Dunster and Staunton [61].

WILLITON AND FREEMANNERS Hundred [15] grew from Williton and the royal holdings of Winsford, Dulverton [62], Old Cleeve as well as Brompton Ralph and Brompton Regis, from the last of which Preston had recently been separated [63]. The five hides of the Tax Return for Brompton Ralph must have included Clatworthy, while the separate Tax Return for Winsford accounts for only 2 hides and 1 furlong of the 3½ hides. The rest of Winsford is needed by the Return for Williton Hundred. The Tax Return for Williton and the order of the Exon. Book suggest that Westowe was in this Hundred, as later in the Middle Ages [64]. Exon. order also includes Holford St Mary, Dyche, part of Stringston and Halse here [65]. Torrels Preston and Preston Bowyer in Milverton are both Williton detachments in later times.

CANNINGTON Hundred [16] probably included Honibere and Lexworthy, both border places, and ANDERSFIELD [17] had Merridge. Creech St.Michael, later a detachment of Andersfield, is a separate Hundred in the second Exon. list.

HUNTSPILL Hundred [19] consisted of only one hide according to the Tax Return and thus contained only one holding of Walter of Douai [66]. Puriton, later the southern half of this Hundred, was in Loxley in 1086 [67].

WHITLEY Hundred [20] was a later 12th century amalgamation of Loxley and Ringoldsway, together with Ham and West Monkton which have their own Tax Returns. Loxley, named from a wood in Shapwick [68], was the western part of the Hundred, and included Middlezoy, Shapwick and places south-west, stretching to Puriton, later in Huntspill Hundred and possibly Crandon [69]. Ringoldsway, named from Reynalds Way near Butleigh wood [70], was the eastern half and contained Greinton, Ashcott and Pedwell and places south-east. Later detachments, Lattiford, Blackford and Durborough are evidenced as part of this Hundred by Exon. order. Another part of Blackford, and all of Holton, not church holdings, seem to have been in the Bruton group of Hundreds.

'Andersey' (Nyland) was a later detachment of GLASTON 12 HIDES [21], falling locally in Bempstone Hundred. In 1086 communication within Glaston 'Hundred' [71] was probably by boat, and 'Andersey' would naturally be reached across the marsh from the island of Panborough, along the river Axe.

The Hundred of NORTH CURRY [27] later included Thurlbear and Thornfalcon, for which there are separate Tax Returns [72].

SOMERTON Hundred [29] seems to have included Queen Camel [73] and Langport and Pitney, both the latter in Pitney Hundred, as well as Wearne (later in Huish Episcopi). Land in Andersfield Hundred, including Huntstile and Deadmans Well was attached to Somerton, and East Lydford may have been a detached part, as later [74].

Exon. order suggests that TINTINHULL Hundred [31] included Draycott, 'Hiscombe' and Kingstone, all later detachments, in addition to Montacute, 'Bishopstone' and Stoke sub Hamdon. Ilminster (probably including Northover and Sock Dennis) was later in this Hundred, but was a detachment of Milborne Port in Horethorne Hundred in 1086 [75].

STONE Hundred [32] includes Thorne according to Exon. order, although this is later partly in Tintinhull also [76].

In SOUTH PETHERTON Hundred [34] is found Whatley, according to the Tax Return. Street and Leigh were also probably in this Hundred in 1086, though later, with Whatley, they were absorbed into Kingsbury East [77]. West Dowlish was probably here in 1086, though later in Bulstone Hundred [78].

The later Hundred of HOUNDSBOROUGH, BARWICK and COKER [36] grew from *Hundesbera* and *Licget* Hundreds. *Licget*, also called Coker Hundred, later included Coker, Hardington, Pendomer, Sutton Bingham and Closworth [79]. The 1086 composition is unclear as both Hundreds are in the Tax Return for Yeovil, and *Hundesbera* places are difficult to distinguish from those in *Licget* since these Hundreds are entered next to one another in the second Exon. list [80].

The modern map of Somerset includes two Hundreds not evidenced in 1086. Brent cum Wrington was a later grouping of two Wells holdings which in 1086 were respectively a separate Hundred and in Hartcliffe Hundred. Havyatt was later absorbed into this Hundred. [81]. Pitney Hundred was a later 14th Century grouping of the unhidated Muchelney, Midelney and Thorney with Pitney and Langport, the latter two being probably in Somerton Hundred in 1086 [82].

With these exceptions, the 1086 boundaries seem to have been largely undisturbed, but since the evidence of both Domesday books and of the Tax Return, though suggestive, is insufficient to show the 1086 location of every place, places in this edition are mapped and indexed in their mid-nineteeenth century Hundreds [83], but ignoring Brent cum Wrington and Pitney. Bishop Giso's scattered holdings are mapped as Kingsbury East and West and Wells Forum Hundreds, but not including Street, Leigh and Whatley which were not church land in 1086. Abdick and Bulstone as well as Hartcliffe cum Bedminster are shown as single Hundreds. Most geographical detachments, apart from Bishop Giso's, are ignored in drawing the Hundred boundaries, even when evidenced in the two Domesday Books. Places that were detached in the mid-nineteenth century are given below, stars indicating that Domesday or the Tax Return give evidence that they were so detached in 1086.

7	CHEWTON	Brockley*, Kingston Seymour*, Midgell*.
11	BEMPSTONE	Brean [84].
12	WELLS FORUM	Cranmore, Evercreech*.
15	WILLITON	Halse*, Preston*.
17	ANDERSFIELD	Lyng, Athelney, Creech St. Michael.
20	WHITLEY	Blackford*, Holton, West Monkton, Wheathill, Lattiford*, Podimore, Durborough*, Holford St. Mary.
21	GLASTON 12 HIDES	'Andersey' (Nyland)*.
26	TAUNTON	Rimpton
29	SOMERTON	East Lydford
31	TINTINHULL	Draycott*, Kingstone*, 'Hiscombe'*.
36	HOUNDSBOROUGH	Chilton Cantelo

Also not mapped are the later Liberties of Hampton and Claverton in Bath, of Mells and Leigh near Frome, and of Witham Friary with its Mendip detachment, which included Charterhouse and separated East Harptree from Winterstoke Hundred.

Boundaries

Hundred boundaries sometimes divided parishes in later times and may have done so in 1086. Thorney was partly in Kingsbury Episcopi and partly in Pitney; Huntstile partly in North Petherton and partly in Andersfield. Woolston is in North Cadbury parish which is part of Catsash, but is itself in Bruton Hundred. Maperton is in Catsash, but its hamlet, Clapton, is in Bruton. Littleton is in Somerton Hundred, though a hamlet of Compton Dundon which is part of Whitley.

The County Boundary itself has undergone some changes since 1086. In the north, part of Bristol lying south of the river Avon and involving the DB sites of Bishopsworth, Bedminster and Knowle was transferred to Gloucestershire [85] On the eastern border, south-east of Monkton Combe, a portion of Wiltshire later lay west of the Avon, its boundary following the Midford brook, skirting Midford and incorporating a part of Limpley Stoke. This leaves Freshford and 'Woodwick' apparently detached from Bath Forum Hundred. The 1086 boundary was probably the Avon.

Further south, Kilmington and Yarnfield were transferred to Wiltshire (in 1895-96). In 1086 they would even, as part of Somerset, have formed a detached part of Norton Ferris Hundred unless the 1086 boundary followed the river Stour south of Kilmington.

On the southern edge of the County, Horethorne Hundred lost Goathill, Poyntington, Sandford Orcas, Weathergrove, Adber and Trent to Dorset in 1896.

Throughout the Middle Ages and until 1844 Holwell was a detached part of this Hundred surrounded by Dorset. If such a detachment existed in 1086, it is concealed under another entry (86). Also lost to Dorset in 1896 was Seaborough from Crewkerne Hundred. On the other hand, Churchstaunton was gained from Devon in 1896, and Wambrook, not mentioned in DB, from Dorset.

APPENDIX I Notes

References are to works cited in the Bibliography at the head of the General Notes; references to notes are to the Places Notes. Ellis misprints many of the Hundred names, in particular the ending æ (ae) as et instead of the diphthong; attention is drawn in the notes below only to some of the mistakes.

1   The best treatment of the Hundreds is in Anderson, but he is heavily influenced by Eyton's reconstructions and does not seem to have made an independent analysis of the Exon. Book nor of the Tax Returns.

2   On the Tax Returns see Finn, LE p.97 ff.

3   Thurlbear appears twice as nos. 19 and 38 of the Tax Return; it is named both a manor and a Hundred there.

4   Written *manehefuę* in the MS.

5   See Anderson p.73 note 1.

6   *Regis* interlined.

7   Presumably Combe St. Nicholas, a holding of Bishop Giso. Eyton i p.92 identifies it with Combe Hay.

8   Accepted by Anderson p. 48.

9   *Winestoc* is visible in the MS. Ellis prints *Winest. . .*

10   Written *Andresfelt* in the MS.

11   Annexed to Cheddar in Exchequer DB 1,2 and presumably standing for it in the second Exon. list.

12   Written *Sunmertonę;* in the MS; Ellis has *Suumertonę.*

13   Written *Licget* in the MS: Ellis has *Lieget.*

14   Written *Cochę.* in the MS and lined through for deletion.

15   Written *Blaternę* in the MS.

16   In the order of both the Exchequer and Exon. Books, Curry Rivel appears in the schedule of *Terra Regis* in a position that suggests that the first *Chori* is Curry Rivel (Exon. 89 a 1 = Exch. 1,5). It has tentatively been taken here as representing Bulstone, and the second *Chori* as Abdick.

17   In the second Exon. List, *Chori* no. 3 could be *Chari* (Cary?), the MS being rubbed at this point.

18   Eyton i pp.91-92.

19   SRS 3 p.xi.

20   1,27.

21   35,24 note.

22   Like the Frome group of Hundreds, they appear to have been surveyed as a unit, the places of all three being intermingled in the text. The Tax Return groups them in the same way.

23   Portbury, Hartcliffe, Keynsham and Bedminster Hundred entries tend to intermingle in the text (see below). One of the Bedminsters of the second Exon. list could be Keynsham, leaving Hartcliffe without a precursor.

24   Anderson p.36 suggests a slip for Manhefuę (Minehead). See Eyton i p.92.

25   8,34 note.

26   Exon. 165 a 1 = Exch. 8,17.

27   Sheriff of Somerset, he may have enjoyed special privileges in these holdings.

28   For Halse, see 22, 1 note.

29   Including the two Holfords, Bagborough, Shopnoller, Tolland and Lydeard and Leigh.

30   6,19 note.

31   Chapter 6 note.

32   See Anderson p.39. Chew Stoke is *Stoche* in DB.

33   19,16 note. Similarly in the Tax Return for the Yeovil group Osbern pays tax for 2 hides and 3 virgates in the Hundred of *Liet* (Coker) which is a royal holding and for which there is no Tax Return. See 5,3 note, and for the composition of *Liet* see below.

34   Exon. folio 489 records £514 0s. 11d. accounted for, but the individual returns amount to £487 2s. 11½d. See Eyton i pp. 89-90.

35   The Hundred Names in the second Exon. list are entered in a variety of hands suggesting that the list was compiled as information from various Hundreds became available. The scribe receiving the Hundredal return probably added its name to the list and then proceeded to enter its contents under each major landholder. The purpose of the first Exon. list is unknown, but it is clearly contemporary.

36   Exchequer 5,3-4 = Exon. 137 a 1-2.

37   Chapter 21, Roger of Courseulles' land, runs as follows:

Exon.	Exch.	Exon. List II	
422a1-423a2	21,3-10	1	North Petherton
423a3-426a5	21,11-35	5	Cannington
426b1-427a1	21,36-38	7	South Petherton
427a2-429a3	21,39-53	8	Williton
429a4-429b2	21,1-2; 54-55	?	Abdick and Bulstone
430a1-431b2	21,56-69	10	Carhampton
431b3-431b4	21,70-71	?	Bulstone
431b5-432a1	21,72-73	12	Milverton
432a2-432b2	21,74-77	26	Andersfield
432b3-433a2	21,78-80	25/27	Winterstoke/Axbridge
433a3-433b2	21,81-84	30	Taunton
433b3	21,85	?33	Somerton (21,85 note)
434a1-434b1	21,86-90	49-51	Frome Group
434b2-434b3	21,91-92	52-54	Bruton Group
435a1-435a4	21,93-96	58	Stone
435b1-435b2	21,97-98		Late entries.

38   The relation of Abdick and Bulstone Hundreds is in later times rather complex, with Abdick forming the southern half of the joint Hundred, but containing Buckland St. Mary, Broadway, Rapps, West Dowlish and Cricket Malberbie as outlying parts of Bulstone. The evidence to be derived from the Tax Returns for the two is far from clear, but it seems to support the later line of division; but of the detached parts of Bulstone, only Buckland St. Mary can be found in the Return and then in Abdick. In the text of Exon. and Exchequer DB, Abdick and Bulstone places seem intermixed.

39   8,5 = 161 b 3.

40   8,11 = 163 b 3.

41   5,20-34 = 141 b 2-143 b 2.

42   See note 23.

43   47,9 = 490 b 3.

44   5,19 = 141 b 1.

45   For Milton see 46,19 = 479 a 4.

46   46,11 = 479 a 3.

47   16,9 note.

48   8,27 note.

49   1,2 and 6,15 notes.

50   21,78.

51   1,21 note.

52   5,29 note.

53   5,17 note.

54   Yatton occasionally occurs as a Hundred in later documents, Anderson pp.46-47. East Harptree is later detached from the Hundred of Winterstoke, probably as a

result of boundary changes on the Mendips, which were probably not extensively cultivated in 1086. Parts still remain heathland.

55 8,25 note.

56 8,32 note.

57 Chapter 6 note.

58 Litton is later detached from the Hundred, but may well have been integral in 1086, see note 54.

59 See Anderson, p.63. Some of the manors of Kingsbury West continue to occur as individual Hundreds after 1086.

60 8,21-22 notes.

61 The hidage of Cutcombe, Minehead, Dunster, Avill, Myne and Bratton is also 10 hides 1 virgate and is taken by Whale (*Principles* p.22) to constitute the Hundred. The lordship hidage of Cutcombe, Minehead, Alcombe, Dunster and Staunton is 4 hides 2½ virgates, closer to the 5 hides less ½ virgate of the Tax Return.

62 Dulverton Hundred may well have included Ashway, Broford and Pixton, which form a group at 21,50-53. It may have also contained Brushford, 19,16 note.

63 Dulverton and Brompton Regis both occur as Hundreds in later times, Anderson p.72 and note 2.

64 21,49 note.

65 For Halse see 22,1 note.

66 24,28 note.

67 11,1 note. It was probably removed from Loxley Hundred as being the only non-Glastonbury manor in the Hundred, becoming at first a free manor.

68 Anderson p.52.

69 45,17 note.

70 Anderson p.51.

71 Glastonbury is not named as a Hundred until later; in 1086 it no doubt contained only the 12 hides given in DB (8,1) and was untaxed. It later expanded to include Baltonsborough, West Pennard and North Wootton; see Anderson p.45.

72 19,30-31 note.

73 1,22 note.

74 For Deadmans Well see 1,1; for Huntstile 46,11. For the composition of the Hundred, see VCH iii p.57.

75 For Ilchester see 1,10 and 8,37 notes. For the contents of the Hundred, see VCH iii p.176.

76 19,77-78 note. The boundary between Stone and Tintinhull Hundreds appears to have fluctuated. Draycott is included in Stone in the 1841 Census, SRS 3 p.332.

77 Their status seems to have been uncertain in recent times: maps of the early 19th century show them either in Kingsbury East or in South Petherton Hundreds.

78 5,1 note.

79 See FA iv p.282; KQ 24.

80 Since, however, Hardington (1,24) falls after Coker in the text and Pendomer and Closworth close a list of Houndsborough places they may have been in *Liet* in 1086. If so, Sutton Bingham (22,23) would naturally fall in the Hundred as well. But at the time of the Tax Return, *Liet* may only have included Coker (5,3 note), the other places being in the Yeovil Tax Return. See Anderson p. 59.

81 Both Brent and Wrington were Glastonbury holdings. Brent sometimes occurs as a Hundred in later times; Anderson p.50.

82 VCH iii p.14.

83 Those of the 1841 Census.

84 Brean became detached from Bempstone by the intrusion of Brent.

85 Part of Bishopsworth remained in Somerset. Also transferred were Brislington and part of Whitchurch, neither mentioned in DB.

86 Probably Milborne Port, 1,10 note.

APPENDIX II

Two texts from a Bath Cartulary.

Three Cartularies of the Benedictine Abbey of St. Peter at Bath are known to have survived from the Middle Ages. They are listed in Davis MCGB p. 5 and are found (a) in manuscript 111 of the Parker Library at Corpus Christi College, Cambridge; (b) in Hale MS 185 of the Library of the Honourable Society of Lincoln's Inn, London; and (c) in British Museum Egerton MS 3316. This last, acquired by the Museum in 1945, is unpublished and contains predominantly Edward III material with additions to 1506, the earliest document being a charter of William Rufus. The Corpus Christi register was transcribed and that from Lincoln's Inn calendared by W. Hunt for the Somerset Record Society in 1893 (SRS vol. 7) and is referred to as BC in the notes of this edition.

All three cartularies contain much to interest the student of Somerset Domesday since they comprise grants, confirmations and miscellaneous documents that between them give the bounds and villages of the DB holdings and their later history. The Corpus Christi MS, however, contains two items more closely related to the Domesday Inquest. They are printed below as Bath A. and B., the first a genuine Domesday satellite (material from the inquests on which Domesday was based), the second a summary of the Abbey's lands mainly derived from the Exchequer text. The importance of the texts was first noticed by Baring in 1912 (op. cit.) and they have been discussed in an important article by R. Lennard (op. cit.) and by V.H. Galbraith (op. cit. pp. 88-91).

The main part of the Corpus Christi Cartulary (described by M.R. James op. cit. vol. i pp. 236-247) was originally a volume in itself, now MS pages 57-129, of which page 57 was the first of the Cartulary, illuminated with a portrait of a bearded king. The MS is finely written with 27 lines to a page in single column in an early 12th century hand. Despite changes of handwriting, the script is very uniform. The last charters date from the reign of Henry II.

The pages reproduced below are numbers 93 and 128-9 of the MS. These latter are the last in the original hand, separated from what has preceded by an entry in a 13th century hand in double column at the foot of page 127 which was originally blank.

Hunt's transcription, made for him by Mr. A. Rogers of the Cambridge University Library, has been checked against the MS by kind permission of the Librarian of the Parker Library. A few minor errors of transcription or impression have been corrected and the abbreviations of the Latin extended more uniformly. *Agr'* has been extended to *agros* (*agras* being possible though both mean 'acres' here); *tantundem* has been preferred to *tantumdem*. To the left of the Latin are given the modern form of the place-name, the chapter and section reference to this edition and the corresponding Exon. column reference. The numbering of each section is that of the present editors.

BATH A

Introduction

This text, discussed in the important article by Lennard in 1943 (his conclusions supported by Galbraith), details seven manors held by the Abbot of Bath. In language and material it is very similar to the Exon. version of Domesday. The seven manors seem to have been gathered together because in them the Abbot held lordship land. As in the Exon. book, they are listed Hundred by Hundred, but without Hundred rubrication. The order is Bath Hundred, Keynsham, and the Frome group of Hundreds. In Exon. the places are entered in the order Keynsham Hundred, Bath, 'Frome'. Within each Hundred, however, the places are in the same order as in Exon., omitting manors without lordship land. The text is a copy in early 12th century hand of an earlier document. That the latter was contemporary with the DB inquests is shown by the entry for Lyncombe where Walter *Hosatus* is shown as holding 1 hide. This sub-division is neither mentioned in Exon. nor in Exchequer DB, but Walter is a DB landholder elsewhere in Bath Hundred. It is possible that the original was frag-mentary when copied. Two lordship manors, 'Eversy' and Ashwick, both in 'Frome' Hundred and therefore expected to follow Corston in the text, are omitted, although Lennard (pp. 32-33) suggests that, having been held personally by Abbot Wulfwold before 1066, they had not yet returned to the Abbey's lordship. But although values are omitted from all the last three entries, the final one, Corston, lacks other detail as well by comparison with the Exon. Book. On balance it seems likely that the original MS broke off at this point.

The close relation of Bath A. to Exon. is evident in the exact correspondence of the great majority of figures (nearly 80) found in each text and in the similarity of many phrases. The place-names too have the termination in *-a* preferred by the Exon. scribes. Despite this overall similarity, both texts have their own formulae:

Bath A	Exon.
se defendebat pro...	*reddebat gildum pro...*
Tempore Regis Edwardi	*die qua rex Eduuardus fuit*
	vivus et mortuus
de his habet abbas...	*inde habet abbas...*
cocetos (except Priston)	*bordarios*
homines (holding ploughs and hides)	*villani* (holding ploughs and hides)

Moreover, whereas Bath A. lists lordship hides and villagers' hides followed by lordship ploughs and villagers' ploughs, Exon. regroups the information so that lordship hides and ploughs are given first. These differences show that one text was not simply a mechanical abstract from the other, but suggest that one was adapted to the formulae of the other.

Both texts contain information not found in the other (noted below, after the text). That in Bath A. is usually of the type passed over by Exon., as for example at Lyncombe where Exon. omits the details of Osward's and Walter's holdings. Such fuller details of the TRE holdings sometimes appear in the *Terrae Occupatae* entries in Exon., while details of further undertenancies are found in another Domesday satellite, Evesham A. reproduced in the Worcester volume of this series.

The Exon. Book, on the other hand, gives the main TRE holder in most cases and not only supplies the values for the manors where Bath A. has none, but alters several recorded there. Some of the differences may be simple figure errors; others suggest a re-examination of values between the compilation of the two texts. Lennard with patience and ingenuity established that Bath A. was likely to have been composed first. The discrepancies between the texts suggest that Bath A. represents part of an early stage of the DB enquiry and the additional information found in Exon. was probably added at a later stage of the Inquest. In other respects, the Exon. Book seems to be a condensation and regularisation of the information contained in Bath A. The Exon. version of the same facts is usually shorter and a standard arrangement has been imposed on all the Bath entries. Thus the Lyncombe entry in Bath A. has been re-ordered to conform to Exon. norms. Mills in the Exon. book have been placed after animals and people, not between them as in Bath A. This seems intended to make clearer the boundary of the mill value-clause. In some figure discrepancies the Exon. scribe seems to have omitted copying a final minim stroke, a common source of error. The additional information in the Bath text is genuinely integrated in it and cannot have been added from local knowledge to a copy of the Exon. text. Furthermore, if the Bath A. compiler had had Exon. available to him, he would have been able to include values for all the manors. When he compiled his text, the only values available seem to have been for Bath Hundred.

The substitution of *bordarii* for *coceti* by Exon. seems to be part of the process of standardisation, though *coscets* and *coceti* also occur in the text of Exon. elsewhere, and their status seems to have been similar (see General Notes to 8,30). The treatment of Bath A. *pascua* is more complex:

	Bath A	Exon.
1. Weston	*i leugam pascuae*	*i leugam nemusculi*
2. Bathford	*i leugam pascuae*	*i leugam nemusculi*
3. Monkton Combe	*dimidiam leugam pascuae*	*i leugam nemusculi*
4. Lyncombe	*cc agros pascuae*	*cc agros pascuae*
5. Priston	*de nemore et pascua c agros xiii minus*	*lxxx agros pascuae*
6. Stanton Prior	*lx agros pascuae*	*xxx agros nemusculi et xxx agros pascuae*

These differences,being not simply of nomenclature, suggest an additional survey before the compilation of Exon.

The document is thus valuable in suggesting something of the complexity of the process of inquest and compilation in the Domesday survey. It also shows, as do the duplicate entries within the text of Domesday itself, the frequency of figure errors, and advises caution in the use of Domesday statistics.

Bath A. thus appears to be a fragmentary schedule of the lordship lands of Bath Abbey probably drawn from a larger compilation of the Abbey's lands that was made at a stage of the Inquest prior to the construction of the Exon. Book. Lennard wrote:

> On the whole it seems to me probable that the Bath text was not derived from the Exon. text but belongs to a still earlier stage of the Domesday Inquest... It may be that the text is. or is based upon, a return of demesne manors made by the Abbey itself; that this return was submitted to the Commissioners; and that they then checked and supplemented the information contained in it in the light of the jurors' verdicts.(op. cit. pp. 38-39).

Text.

Lands belonging to Bath Abbey; (Domesday Satellite)
(MS pages 128-129. Hunt BC pp. 67-68. James No. 80)

HAE SUNT TERRAE BATHONIENSIS ABBATIAE

WESTON 1
DB Som. 7,5
= 185 b 1

Abbas Bathoniensis habet unam mansionem quae vocatur Westona. Haec se defendebat tempore regis Eduuardi pro xv hidis. Has possunt arare x carrucae. De his habet abbas in dominio viii hidas et dimidiam, et homines sui vi hidas et dimidiam. Ibi habet abbas ii carrucas in dominio, et homines vi. Ibi habet abbas vii villanos et x cocetos et vii servos et i runcinum et cc oves et iiii. Et i molendinum qui reddit per annum x solidos, et xx agros prati et i leugam pascuae in longitudine et tantundem in latitudine.
Et quando abbas recepit hanc mansionem, valebat vii libras et modo valet viii.

BATHFORD 2
DB Som. 7,6
= 185 b 2

Idem abbas habet mansionem quae vocatur Forda. Haec se defendebat tempore regis Eduuardi pro x hidis. De his habet abbas in dominio v hidas, et homines v. Has omnes possunt arare ix carrucae. Ibi habet abbas ii carrucas in dominio, et homines vii. Ibi habet abbas v villanos et vii

cocetos et vi servos et i runcinum et i molendinum, qui reddit
x solidos per annum, et xii animalia et viii porcos et c et
xii oves et xii agros prati et i leugam pascuae in longitudine
et tantundem in latitudine. Et quando abbas recepit
mansionem hanc, valebat vii libras et modo valet viii.

(MONKTON)	3
COMBE	
DB Som. 7,7	
= 185 b 3	

(MONKTON)
COMBE
DB Som. 7,7
= 185 b 3

3 Abbas habet i mansionem quae vocatur Comba. Haec mansio
defendebat se tempore Regis Eduuardi pro viii hidis.
Has possunt arare viii carrucae. De his habet abbas in dominio
vi hidas i virgata minus, et homines iii hidas et i virgatam.
Ibi habet abbas iii carrucas in dominio, et homines v. Ibi habet
abbas vi villanos et viii cocetos et vi servos et i runcinum et ii
molendinos, qui reddunt per annum xiii solidos et vi denarios,
et xii porcos et lx et xii oves et xxxii agros prati et dimidiam
leugam pascuae in longitudine et tantundem in latitudine.
Et quando abbas recepit hanc mansionem, valebat viii libras
et modo valet tantundem.

LYNCOMBE
DB Som. 7,9
== 186 a 2

4 Abbas Bathoniensis habet i mansionem quae vocatur Lincoma.
Haec se defendebat tempore Regis Eduuardi pro x hidis. De
his habuit quidam tagnus Osuuardus iiii hidas et dimidiam
tempore Regis Eduuardi. Et hic tagnus non poterat auferre
terram suam de abbatia. Hic sua spontanea voluntate remisit
terram suam in abbatiam, licet has iiii hidas et dimidiam quas
superius dixi. De his habet modo Walterus hosatus i hidam
de abbate et alterae sunt in abbatia. De his x hidis praedictis habet
abbas in dominio vii, et homines sui habent iii hidas. Has omnes
insimul possunt arare vii carrucae. Ibi habet abbas in dominio
iii carrucas et homines iiii. Ibi habet abbas iiii villanos et x
cocetos et viii servos et i runcinum et ii molendinos, qui
reddunt x solidos per annum, et viii porcos et cc oves xx minus
et xxx agros prati et cc agros pascuae. Et quando abbas recepit
hanc mansionem, valebat vi libras et modo valet viii.

PRISTON
DB Som. 7,2
= 185 a 1

5 Abbas Bathoniensis habet i mansionem quae vocatur Pristona et
haec fuit de victu monachorum tempore Regis Eduuardi. Haec
mansio se defendebat pro vi hidis in vicecomitatu. Ex his
geldaverunt iiii hidae ea die qua rex Eduuardus fuit vivus et
mortuus. Has possunt arare viii carrucae. De his habet abbas
in dominio ii hidas, et homines iiii. Ibi habet abbas i carrucam,
et homines vi. Ibi habet abbas i molendinum, qui reddit per
annum vi solidos et vi denarios, et xx agros prati et de nemore et
pascua c agros xiii minus. Et homines franci habent ibi xxv
animalia et xii oves. Et vii villanos habet ibi abbas et viii
bordarios et iii servos.

STANTON
(PRIOR)
DB Som. 7,3
= 185 a 3

6 Abbas Bathoniensis habet i mansionem quae vocatur Stantona.
Haec se defendebat tempore Regis Eduuardi pro iii hidis. Has
possunt arare iiii carrucae. De his habet abbas in dominio
dimidiam hidam, et homines ii et dimidiam. Ibi habet abbas i
carrucam in dominio, et homines ii carrucas. Ibi habet abbas
iiii villanos et iii cocetos et v servos et i runcinum et xii agros
prati et lx agros pascuae.

CORSTON
DB Som. 7,13
= 186 b 2

7 Abbas Bathoniensis habet i mansionem quae vocatur Corstona.
Haec se defendebat tempore Regis Eduuardi pro x hidis.
De his habet abbas in dominio v hidas, et homines v. Has
omnes possunt arare ix carrucae. Ibi habet abbas ii carrucas
in dominio, et homines iii. Ibi habet abbas v villanos et viii
cocetos et iiii servos.

NOTES

HAE: The MS has HĘE, a second E having been added in error to an E marked clearly as a diphthong. Hunt reads *Haec.*

1
cc oves et iiii: Exon. has *cc oves.*
valebat vii libras: viii in Exon.
valet viii: x in Exon.

2
homines vii (carrucae): vi in Exon.
valebat vii libras ... valet viii: Exon. gives both values as *x.*

3
defendebat se ... pro viii hidis. Exon. has *ix* to which the detail adds up.
dimidiam leugam: i leugam in Exon.
valet tantundem: i.e. £8. Exon. has £7.

4
De his ... sunt in abbatia. There is nothing corresponding in the Exon. book. *quas superius dixi* contains an unusual first person singular, found occasionally in Exon. (see Exon. Notes to 36,7. 40,2).
Walterus Hosatus: Walter Hussey, holder of lands at Wilmington and Batheaston (7,4;10) and at Whatley (8,26).
vii carrucae: viii in Exon.
homines sui habent iii hidas: Exon. has *ii* and its land detail in consequence does not total correctly.

5
de victu monachorum: the statement is not in Exon.
in vicecomitatu: 'in the Shire' or 'in the Shire court'.
Ex his ... mortuus: not in Exon.
vi solidos et vi denarios: Exon. has *vii solidos* with *vi denarios* interlined.
de nemore et pascua c agros xiii minus: Exon. has *lxxx agros pascuae.* The wood thus appears to have been 7 acres in extent.
et homines franci ... oves: not found in Exon., perhaps accidentally omitted.
iii servos: Exon. adds *i runcinum.*
No value is given.

6
iiii carrucae: iii in Exon.
homines ii (hidas) et dimidiam: Exon. *ii,* the details of land thus not adding up correctly.
i runcinum: Exon. adds *l oves.*
lx agros pascuae: Exon. *xxx agros nemusculi et xxx agros pascuae.* There is no value given.

7
iiii servos: After this Exon. adds a number of details including the value. The text of the original probably broke off at this point. The omitted details are '1 cob; a mill which pays 30d; 6 pigs; 62 sheep; 6 acres of meadow. The value was £7; now £8.'

BATH B

Introduction

Headed *De Terris Bathae pertinentibus,* Bath B. appears to be a hidage schedule extracted from Exchequer Domesday Book. It includes Tidenham (near Chepstow) which in DB Gloucestershire is included in the land of the King, and omits Bath for which DB does not give the hidage. Apart from the entry for Tidenham (see note below), it contains nothing that could not have been derived from Exchequer DB: indeed entry 16 for Olveston and Cold Ashton seems to be a rather clumsy conflation of two separate DB entries (see Lennard p.40 note 2). The spelling of the place-names differs from DB, for example *Pristone* for DB *Prisctone,* *Wilmedune* for *Wimedone* and *Esuuiche* for *Esceuuiche,* but such differences are common in other copied texts of the period, the scribe seeming to prefer his own or local spelling. Like the Exchequer DB scribe the epitomiser refers always to *ecclesia* as the holder while Exon. and Bath A. refer to *abbas* or *abbatia.*

After entering Tidenham, the scribe seems to have entered the next 7 places from Somerset DB in Domesday order, omitting those where the Exchequer text does not give the number of lordship hides. These latter are then entered, but not in DB order. They are, however, given in distinct Hundred groups, in the order Keynsham Hundred, 'Frome', then Bath. The list ends with the two Gloucestershire holdings that are entered under the Abbey. Had the scribe had the Exon. text available to him he could have entered the lordship hides for Wilmington, Batheaston, Charlcombe and for Hugh the Interpreter's land at Bathampton.

Text.
Summary of Bath Lands based on Exchequer Domesday.
(MS page 93. Hunt BC pp. 35-36 No.30. James No. 38)

DE TERRIS BATHAE PERTINENTIBUS

TIDENHAM DB Glos. 1,56	1	Ecclesia de Batha tenet Dyddanhamme pro xxx hidis geldandis, teste R.E. De his sunt in dominio ix hidae.
PRISTON DB Som. 7,2 = 185 a 1	2	Ipsa ecclesia tenet Pristone pro vi hidis geldandis, teste R.E. De his sunt in dominio ii hidae.
STANTON (PRIOR) DB Som. 7,3 =185 a 2	3	Ipsa ecclesia tenet Stantone pro tribus hidis geldandis, teste R.E. De his in dominio dimidia hida.
WESTON DB Som. 7,5 = 185 b 1	4	Ipsa ecclesia tenet Westone pro xv hidis geldandis, teste R.E. De his sunt in dominio viii hidae et dimidia.
BATHFORD DB Som.7,6 = 185 b 2	5	Ipsa ecclesia tenet Fordam pro x hidis geldandis, t.R.E. De his sunt in dominio v hidae.
(MONKTON) COMBE DB Som. 7,7 = 185 b 3	6	Ipsa ecclesia tenet Cume pro ix hidis geldandis, t.R.E. De his sunt in dominio vi hidae.
LYNCOMBE DB Som. 7,9 =186 a 2	7	Ipsa ecclesia tenet Lincume pro x hidis geldandis, t.R.E. De his sunt in dominio vii hidae.
CORSTON DB Som. 7,13 =186 b 2	8	Ipsa ecclesia tenet Corstune pro x hidis geldandis, t.R.E. De his sunt in dominio v hidae.
WILMINGTON DB Som. 7,4 = 185 a 3	9	Ipsa ecclesia tenet Wilmedune pro tribus hidis geldandis, teste R.E.
'EVERSY' DB Som. 7,14 = 186 b 3	10	Ipsa ecclesia tenet Euestie pro una hida geldanda, t.R.E.
ASHWICK DB Som. 7,15 = 187 a 1	11	Ipsa ecclesia tenet Esuuiche pro dimidia hida geldanda, t.R.E.

BATHEASTON DB Som. 7,10 = 186 a 3	12	Ipsa ecclesia tenet Estone pro i hida et dimidia geldanda, t.R.E.
CHARLCOMBE DB Som. 7,8 = 186 a 1	13	Ipsa ecclesia tenet Cerlecome pro iiii hidis geldandis, teste R.E.
BATHAMPTON DB Som. 7,11 = 186 a 4	14	Ipsa ecclesia tenet Hamtone pro v hidis geldandis, t.R.E.
'WOODWICK' DB Som. 7,12 = 186 b 1	15	Ipsa ecclesia tenet Wdeuuiche pro ii hidis et dimidia geldandis, t.R.E.
OLVESTON / (COLD) ASHTON DB Glos. 7,1-2	16	Ipsa ecclesia tenet Aluestone pro iii hidis geldandis et Escetune pro iii hidis geldandis. In his duobus maneriis sunt x hidae, sed iiii ex his sunt a geldo liberae concessu Eaduuardi et Willelmi regis.

NOTES

1

Dyddanhamme: Tedenehā in DB Glos. 1,56 where the land is listed
under the *Terra Regis,* but with mention that the Abbot of Bath had held
it. There the lordship hides are 10 rather than the 9 here. The differences
in place-name and hidage are explained if the scribe had in front of him
the document headed *Divisiones et Consuetudines Dyddanham* which
is found in the same Cartulary (MS pp. 73-74, Hunt p.18 no. 14), and
printed also in BCS (iii 928 = Sawyer 1555). It begins *On dyddan hamme
synd xxx hida ix inlandes ⁊ xxi ge-settes landes. Inland* in OE corresponds
to *Dominium,* 'lordship'.

geldandis; 'that ought to pay tax'. The scribe has thus extended the
geld' of the DB text, which, however, normally stands for *geldantibus*
'paying tax' or *'geldabilibus'* 'taxable'.

Teste R.E. i.e. *teste Rege Eduuardo.* The scribe has misunderstood
DB T.R.E. *(tempore regis Eduuardi)* probably owing to his familiarity
with witness clauses in charters.

3

De his in dominio: The MS reads *de hís ín dominio* with the *i* of *his*
changed to *e.* The scribe appears to have written *de his in dominio*
and realising that he had omitted a verb attempted to amend *in* to
est in by alteration and abbreviation signs.

6

vi hidae: Bath A. and Exon. have 6 hides less 1 virgate.

16

a geldo liberae ... regis. The corresponding phrase in DB is *non geldant
concessu Eduuardi et Willelmi regum.*

APPENDIX III

PIRTOCHESWORDA (Exon. Tax Return 79 b 2, Williton Hundred)

John Dodgson of the Department of English, University College London, has very kindly provided the following note:

PIRTOCHESWORDA would be a difficult place-name to explain. The final element, OE *worð* latinized, is preceded by the genitive singular inflexion of an unintelligible form. Dr. F.R. Thorn has suggested (Places notes, 25,33) that the place so named was near Coleford, adjacent to Westowe (DB *Waistou*). The place-name Westowe contains the element OE *stow*. It is possible that *Pirtoches-* represents the genitival composition form of an OE place-name in *-stow;* that we have here another example of the misreading of Insular minuscule letters by scribes either unfamiliar with that script (say, by Norman scribes more at ease with the continental writing in the Carolingian minuscule that DB is written in) or transcribing badly written returns. Obviously the *d* in *-worda* represents Insular ð in *worð*. But other substitutions might result from confusion of, or unfamiliarity with, the Insular minuscule letters ƿ : ƿ (=w), Þ (=th), and of ꞃ (=r), ſ (=s), and of t, c (whence also th, ch). In *Pirtochesworda*, the scribe appears to have recognised the initial uu or ƿ of the affixed OE *worð*. But *pirtoches-* might be the result of the substitution of p for ƿ ; r for s; ch for th for Þ for ƿ ; from an OE place-name *Wistowesworð* originally written ƿistoƿesƿorð, this written form modified in three phases, 1. seen as ƿirtoÞesƿorð-, 2. transcribed as *pirtothesuuord-*, 3. miscopied as *pirtochesuuord-*. The r/s substitution could appear at any phase in the process, but ch for p has to be a result of a transcription from th (for Þ the misreading of ƿ). It is thus possible (although not proven, of course), that the spelling *Pirtochesworda* represents a place-name *Wistowesworð*, 'the private estate at, or of, Wistow(e)'. Until more is known about Somerset place-names, we have to suppose that the OE place-name *Wistow(e)* may not be identical with the name of Westowe. Although both contain OE *stow* 'a place of assembly, a community centre, *etc.*', the vowels of the protothemes are different. Westowe should represent an OE original in *wæg-* (e.g. *wæg, -es* masc., 'wall of a building'; *wæg, -e,* fem., *wæge, -an,* fem., 'a weight, a weighing balance'; *wæge, -es,* neut., 'a cup'; *wæg, -es* masc., 'a wave; water; a movement'). *Wistowe* should contain OE *wic,* 'a trading estate or settlement; a market; a factory; a dairy farm; a dependant settlement *etc.* ,' or OE *wig* 'a (heathen) shrine or temple'; either of which would make this a place-name with great potential significance.

INDEX OF PERSONS

Familiar modern spellings are given when they exist. Unfamiliar names are usually given in an approximate late 11th century form, avoiding variants that were already obsolescent or pedantic. Spellings that mislead the modern eye are avoided where possible. Two, however, cannot be avoided: they are combined in the name of 'Leofgeat', pronounced 'Leffyet' or 'Levyet'. The definite article is omittted before bynames, except where there is reason to suppose that they described the individual's occupation. The chapter numbers of listed landholders are printed in bold type. Italics indicate that persons or bynames occur only in Exon.; likewise references in italics indicate that the name, or a fuller form of it, is to be found only in Exon. In this edition these names are entered in small type in the translation, or in the Exon. Notes. It should be emphasised that this is essentially an index of personal names, not of persons.

Matthew of Mortagne	**44**
Mauger of Carteret	*10,1. 19,63.* 46,21
Mauger	1,12. 19,2-3;11;16-19;48;59. *21,92*
Bishop Maurice *of London*	15. 1,19;21. 8,37
Mereswith	21,24
Merleswein	1,4. 24,21-23;29. 31,5
Morcar	EBu 2
Count of Mortain	19. 1,4-5;9;11-12;19-20. 2,8. 8,30-31;39-40.
	10,1;6. 21,92. 46,4
Moses	5,53-54
Nicholas	34,1
Nigel *of Gournai*	5,32;38;44-45
Nigel the Doctor	*8,30.* 13,1
Nigel	5,18-19;30;55. 25,28;43
Nigel, see Roger	
Norman	1,4. 20,2. 21,47;85;92. 36,11-12
Odo of Flanders	45,6
Odo son of Gamelin	38. *21,65*
Odo	22,10
Ogis	*1,1.* 21,55;63;72. 25,8
Orde	19,25
Ordgar	21,7;75. 46,7
Ordric *brother of Leofing*	45,1
Ordric	1,21
Ordric, see Leofing	
Ordwold	*5,62*
Ordwulf	1,21. 6,9. 19,16
Osbern Giffard	39
Osbern	21,85. 42,1
Osmer's father	47,25
Osmer	47,25
Bishop Osmund of Salisbury	3
Osmund Stramin	*5,7.* 22,15
Osmund	5,56. 6,12. 19,41
Oswald	8,8;29
Osward	*8,8.* 35,12. 46,17;19
Pagnell, see Ralph	
Pancevolt, see Bernard	
Parker, see Ansketel	
Paulinus	25,26
Payne, see Edmund	
Perlo	21,47
Bishop Peter (of Lichfield and Chester)	16,7;14. 47,1
Bishop Peter, see Ranulf	
Pike, see Alwin	
Pipe	8,2
Puttock, see Alfgeat	
Rademar	24,5;7-8;25-27;33
Rahere	*47,22*
Raimer the Clerk, *brother of Walter (of Douai)*	24,35
Rainward	24,3-4;16;23-24;27(?)
Ralph *Blewitt*	26,3;5
Ralph *Crooked Hands*	6,9. 8,2;20;30
Ralph Pagnell	31
Ralph *Rufus*	5,2;48;66-67
Ralph *Trenchard*	36,7
Ralph *of Conteville*	8,33. 24,11;36-37
Ralph of Limesy	32. 10,6
Ralph of Mortimer	29
Ralph of Pomeroy	30
Ralph of Pomeroy, see Beatrix	
Ralph *of Reuilly*	31,1-3;4(?)
Ralph the priest	19,78
Ralph *a man-at-arms*	25,30

Ralph *brother of Roger* of Berkeley	45,8
Ralph	5,69. 6,1. 22,5-7. 24,20;30-32. 25,17;53. 28,1
Ralph, see Roger	
Ranulf Flambard	7,12
Ranulf nephew of Bishop Peter	*16,7*
Ranulf	21,29. 25,27;44. 35,4;13;20
Reginald *of Vautortes*	19,28;43
Reginald	37,12
Reinbald the priest	1,8;*10.* 16,1. 45,14
Richard *of Barre*	29,1
Richard *of Merri*	35,3;17
Richard *the Interpreter*	5,54. 45,14
Richard	6,1;13. 19,60. 22,4. 24,2;13. 25,15. 35,10. 36,5. 37,10-11.
Richere *of Les Andelys*	16,2
Ripe	36,3
Robert *Gernon*	21,89
Robert of Auberville	1,2. *8,17.* 24,8. 46,1-5
Robert *of Gatemore*	22,11-12
Robert *Herecom*	21,8
Robert *the Constable*	19,7;29, see Robert son of Wymarc
Robert son of Gerald	33. 1,9
Robert *son of Ivo*	19,13-14;35;66;85
Robert *son of Rozelin*	31,5
Robert *son of Walter*	19,37
Robert son of Wymarc	19,57. 25,55 see Robert the Constable
Robert	2,6. 5,54;61. 19,73. 21,3-4;11;17-18;28;31;45;78-79; 86. 22,13;18;21;25. 25,5;40. 35,16;21. 36,14. 46,7;9
Robert (another one)	5,54
Robert, see William	
Roger Arundel	22. 6,19
Roger Bushell	22,23
Roger *Whiting*	5,*4*;23;35;41
Roger of Berkeley, see Ralph	
Roger of Courseulles	21. 1,4. *8,2;4-5;8;11-14;18;20;23-24;27-28;33;41.* 10,2;6. 25,55
Roger of Courseulles' father	8,41
Roger the Breton	10,2
Roger *the Bursar*	5,34
Roger son of Nigel	*20,2-3*
Roger *son of Ralph*	5,24
Roger	1,28. 5,47; *53-54;*65. 8,31. 25,6;25-26;39;48
Roghard	6,9;13
Rolf, see Thurstan	
Rozelin, see Robert	
Rufus, see Ralph	
Rumold	44,2
Saemer	24,26. *35,2.* 46,8-9
Saered	37,12
Saeric	1,6. *5,3;64.* 22,28. 24,8. *25,40.* 46,5
Saeward's mother	*19,72*
Saeward	*19,72.* 28,1
Saewin	1,1. 19,24. 22,20
Abbot Saewold (of St. Peter's, Bath)	*7,1;5-7;9;13*
Saewulf	2,11. *5,59;64.* 8,27. 21,93;96. *24,10.* 26,8
Samson *the Chaplain*	4,1
Saswald	*2,11*
Serlo of Burcy	37. 1,9;21. *6,9. 8,17;20-21;28;30.* 27,3
Serlo of Burcy's daughter	27,3. 37,7
Sharp	25,20
Sheerwold	5,54;*62;65. 8,18;20.* 19,1. 25,5
Sibbi	5,15
Sigeric	*37,8.* 45,7
Sired	21,8

William *of Monceaux* — 5,1;3;25;42-43;63-64
William son of Guy — 28
William *son of Robert* — 21,82
William — 5,14-15;18;26. 18,1-3. 19,76. 21,6;33-34;48-49; 51-52;54;65;67-68;83;90. 22,15-16. 23,1

Winegot *the priest* — 8,12
Winulf — 19,87
Wulfa — *19,68*
Wulfa, see Aelfric
Wulfeva — 5,16. 17,4;7
Wulfgar, a monk — 8,26;35
Wulfgar — 21,43;46
Wulfgeat — 19,30
Wulfmer an Englishman — *47,13*
Wulfmer — 1,28. 5,43. 8,15;*23*
Wulfnoth — 17,8. 19,8. 24,11
Wulfred — 8,20
Wulfric — *5,61.* 6,13. 22,6. 24,19. 25,46
Wulfsi — *5,59*
Abbot Wulfward — 7,10
Wulfward *Tumbi* — 44,3
Wulfward White — 1,*28*;32;35
Wulfward *White's* wife — 1,28
Wulfward — 1,28. 2,9. 9,*3*;6. 21,71. 22,23. 32,7-8. 47,1
Wulfward, see Edward
Wulfwen — 40,1
Wulfwin — 21,51;68;82. 22,22
Abbot Wulfwold (of St. Peter's, Bath) — *7,14-15*
Wulfwold the priest — *5,43*
Wulfwold — 25,39
Wulfwy — 5,9. 8,24. 19,12
Wymarc, see Robert
Young, see Aelfric, Edric

CHURCHES AND CLERGY

Abbess:	of St. Edward's	14
Abbeys:	Athelney	19,86
	Cerne	28,2
	Glastonbury	8
	St. Peter, Muchelney	9
Abbots:	of Jumièges	1,29
	of St. Mary's, Glastonbury	8. *19,9-10*
	of St. Mary's, Montebourg	*13*
	of St. Peter's, Athelney	10. *19,86. 32,5*
	of St. Peter's, Bath	*7*
	of St. Peter's, Muchelney	9
	of St. Stephen's, Caen	12
	of St. Severus'	*18,4*
	see Leofward, Saewold, Thurstan, Wulfward, Wulfwold.	
Archbishop:	see Stigand	
Archdeacon:	see Benzelin	
Bishops:	of Bayeux	4
	of Coutances	5. 1,7;28. 8,2;25;38. 20,1. 44,2. EBe 1-3. EBu 1-2.
	of Durham	2,9
	of Salisbury	3. EDo 1
	of Wells	6. 22,20
	of Winchester	2
	see Alfwold, Giso, Maurice, Osmund, Peter, Walkelin	

Canons:	of St. Andrew's, Wells	6,*1;*16-17
Chaplains:	see Samson, Stephen	
Churches:	of St. Peter, Athelney	10. 21,98. 32,5
	of St. Peter, Bath	7
	of St. Stephen, Caen	12
	of St. John, Frome	1,8. 16,1
	of St. Mary, Glastonbury	8. 5,12;43;50. 19,9-10. 25,7-8. 37,9
	of St. Mary, Grestain	19,50
	of St. Andrew, Ilchester	8,37. 15,1
	of St. John, Milborne Port	*1,10*
	of St. Mary, Montebourg	13
	of St. Peter, Muchelney	9. 21,54(?)-55
	of *St. Mary,* North Petherton	16,7
	of the Blessed Apostle Peter, Rome 11	
	of St. Edward, Shaftesbury	14. 37,7
	of *St. Mary,* Stogumber	16,2
	of St. Peter, Winchester	2,9
	of St. Swithun, Winchester	19,7
	of Winchester	*2,11*
	of Glastonbury	*8,2*
	of St. Severus	18,4
	of Carhampton	16,6
	of Cannington	16,3
	of Crewkerne	12,1
	of Curry Rivel	16,11
	of Kilmersdon	*16,14*
	of Milverton	16,4
	of North Curry	1,19
Clergy:	**16**	
Monks:	of St. Peter's monastery, Bath	7,12
	of St. Peter's, Muchelney	9,8
	of St. Peter's,Winchester?	2,11
	see Alnoth, Wulfgar	
Nuns:	16,13	
	see Edith	
Priests:	1,7;11. *5,34.* 6,10. 16,11. 46,6	
	see Aelfric, Alfgeat, Brictmer, Erchenger, Godwin, Guy, Leofric, Ralph, Reinbald, Spirtes, Winegot, Wulfwold.	

SECULAR TITLES AND OCCUPATIONAL NAMES

Bowman *(harbalistarius)* ... Walter. Bursar *(dispensator)* ... Roger. Butler *(pincerna)* ... Alfred. Chamberlain *(camerarius)* ... Humphrey. Clerk *(clericus)* ... 6,3. 19,43. 36,7... Raimer. Constable *(stalrus, constabulus)* ... Alnoth, Robert. Cook *(cocus, coquus)* ... Ansger, Manasseh. Count *(comes)* ... Eustace, of Mortain. Countess *(comitissa)* ... Gytha, Ida. Ditcher *(fosarius, fossor)* ... Gerard. Doctor *(medicus)* ... Nigel. Earl *(comes)* ... Harold, Hugh, Leofwin, Tosti. Falconer *(accipitrarius)* ... Siward. Forester *(forestarius)* ... Aelmer,Doda, Godric. Hunter *(venator)* ... Alfward. Interpreter *(interpres)* ... Hugh, Hugolin, Richard. Porter *(portarius, portitor)* ... 19,38. Queen *(regina)* ... Edith. Reeve *(prepositus)* ... Aelfric, Alfwy, Alnoth, Godwin. Servants *(servientes)* ... 46. Sheriff *(vicecomes)* ... Baldwin, Edward, William of Mohun, Tovi. Steward *(dapifer)* ... Alfred. Usher *(hostiarius)* ... John. Young *(cild)* ... Aelfric, Edric.

The name of each place is followed by (i) the number of its Hundred and its numbered location on the map in this volume; (ii) its National Grid reference; (iii) chapter and section reference in DB. Bracketed figures here denote mention in sections dealing with a different place. Unless otherwise stated in the Places Notes the identifications of VCH and DG and the spellings of the Ordnance Survey are followed for places in England, of OEB for places abroad. Places that occur only in the Exon. Domesday or the Tax Returns are indexed Exon. or Tax Return with the folio reference, and the Exchequer DB equivalent where there is one. Other Exon. and Tax Return references are given in the margin of the text or in the Notes. Inverted commas mark lost places with known modern spelling; unidentifiable places are given in DB spelling, in italics. The National Grid reference system is explained on all Ordnance Survey maps, and in the Automobile Association Handbooks; the figures reading from left to right are given before those reading from bottom to top of the map. In Somerset, all grid references are in the 100 kilometre grid square ST except those beginning with 's' which are in square SS. Places with bracketed Grid references do not appear on 1 in. or 1:50,000 maps. Some Domesday places are now in adjacent counties; these are marked accordingly, Dorset, Glos. or Wilts. The Somerset Hundreds are numbered from West to East working Southwards on the map, and are listed after the Index. Because there is insufficient evidence to reconstruct the 1086 Hundreds fully, the 'modern' (mid-nineteenth century) Hundreds are followed, but ignoring certain later changes which are discussed in Appendix I. A name in brackets following a place-name is that of the modern parish or of a nearby major settlement, given to distinguish places of the same name.

	Map	Grid	Text		Map	Grid	Text
Adber (Dorset)	33-1	59 20	19,74. 24,37. 47,11	Babcary	22-3	56 28	19,66. 45,3
				Babington	9-2	70 51	5,49
Adsborough	18-1	27 29	25,3	Backwell	2-3	49 68	5,30
Aisholt	16-1	19 35	21,31	Badgworth	6-3	39 52	24,10
Alcombe	14-1	s97 45	25,11	Bagborough	26-1	17 33	(2,3). 25,51. 31,4
Aldwick	2-1	49 61	37,5				
Aley	16-2	18 38	25,4	'Bagley'	14-7	(s88 42)	21,61
Alford	22-1	60 32	19,65	Baltonsborough	21-2	54 34	8,22
Alfoxton	15-1	14 41	35,13	Banwell	6-4	39 59	6,9
Alhampton	13-1	62 34	8,30	Barrington	34-1	39 18	(21,97)
Aller (in Carhampton)	14-2	00 42	21,63	Barrow (nr. Castle Cary)	22-4	60 29	19,62. 24,20
Aller (nr. Langport)	29-1	39 29	32,8	Barrow Gurney	2-4	53 67	5,32
				Barton St. David	22-5	54 31	21,92. 46,21
Aller (in Sampford Brett)	15-2	(07 39)	18,3	Batcombe	13-2	69 39	8,24
Allercott	14-3	s95 39	25,23	Bath	5-1	75 64	1,(28-30);31. (5,20;66). 7,1. (40,1. 41,1) Exon. 143a2(=5,30). EW 1
Allerford	14-4	s90 46	32,4				
Allerton	11-1	40 50	24,11				
'Almsworthy'	14-5	(s82 39)	21,56				
Alstone	19-1	31 46	24,33	Bathampton	5-2	77 66	7,11
Alston Sutton	11-2	41 51	24,14	Bathealton	25-3	07 24	25,43
'Alwin's Land'	16-—	- -	21,22	Batheaston	5-3	77 67	1,30;(31). 7,10. 45,10
'Andersey'	21-1	45 50	8,1				
Ansford	22-2	63 33	24,19				
Appley	25-1	07 21	19,22. 20,2	Bathford	5-4	78 66	7,6
Ash Priors	12f-1	15 29	6,19. 22,20	Bathwick	5-5	75 65	5,37
Ashbrittle	25-2	05 21	19,20;36	Bawdrip	18-3	34 39	24,23
Ashcombe	6-1	33 61	5,13	Beckington	10-1	80 51	22,24
Ashcott	20-1	43 47	8,11;14	Bedminster (in Bristol, Glos.)	2-5	58 71	1,7
Ashill	28-1	32 17	10,6. 19,18				
Ashington	32-1	56 21	21,94	Beercrocombe	28-2	32 20	19,28
Long Ashton	2-2	54 70	5,34	Beere	16-3	24 41	16,8
Ashway	15-3	s86 31	21,50	Belluton	4-1	61 64	(1,28). 17,6
Ashwick	9-1	63 48	7,15	Berkley	10-2	81 49	22,25
Athelney	18-2	34 29	(10,6)	Bickenhall	28-3	28 18	19,27
Avill	14-6	s97 43	25,17	Bickham	14-8	s95 41	25,15
Axbridge	6-2	43 54	(1,2; 31)	'Bishopstone'	31-1	(50 17)	19,86

	Map	*Grid*	*Text*		*Map*	*Grid*	*Text*
Bishopsworth	2-6	57 68	5,20-21	Castle Cary	22-10	64 32	24,17
Blackford	22-6	65 26	8,9. 36,8	Lytes Cary	29-3	53 56	45,1-2
Blackmore	16-4	24 38	21,35	Cary Fitzpaine	29-4	54 27	22,18
Blagdon	6-5	50 58	37,1	Catcott	20-3	39 39	8,5
Blaxhold	17-1	(22 34)	21,77	Cathanger	28-8	34 22	9,8
Bleadon	6-6	34 56	2,11. EBe 1-3;	Purse Caundle	- -	- -	(19,86)
			EBu 1-2	(Dorset)			
Bossington	14-9	s89 47	10,6. 32,5	Chaffcombe	34-2	35 10	5,2
East Bower	18-4a	31 37)	24,8. 35,2.	Chard	12d-1	32 08	6,4
West Bower	18-4b	(26 36))	(46,5)	Charlcombe	5-6	75 67	7,8
Bradford on	26-2	17 22	(2,3). 19,39	Charlinch	16-6	23 37	21,12
Tone				Charlton (in	13-3	63 43	8,23
Bradney	18-5	33 38	24,24	Shepton Mallet)			
Bradon	28-4	36 20	19,17;23;25.	Charlton Adam	29-5	53 28	19,43
			47,4	Charlton	29-6	52 28	22,19
Bratton	14-10	s94 46	25,25	Mackrell			
Bratton	24-1	67 29	24,15	Charlton	24-2	72 29	33,1
Seymour				Musgrove			
Brean	11-3	29 56	24,29	Cheddar	6-7	45 53	1,2. 21,78
Brent	11-4	34 51	8,33	Upper Cheddon	26-3	23 28	(2,3). 22,2?
Brewham	23-1	72 37	(21,90).	Cheddon	26-4	24 27	(2,3). 22,2?
			25,55	Fitzpaine			
Bridgwater	**18-6**	29 37	24,21	Chelvey	2-10	46 68	44,2
Bristol (Glos.)	2-7	58 72	(5,20)	Chelwood	4-3	63 61	17,5. 34,1
Broadway	28-5	32 15	19,19	Cheriton	33-2	69 25	25,56. 28,2
Broadwood	14-11	s98 41	25,16				36,14
Brockley	2-8	46 66	45,16	Chew Magna	3-1	57 63	6,13
Broford	15-4	s91 31	21,51-52	Chew Stoke, see Stoke			
Brompton Ralph	15-5	08 32	25,7	Chewton Mendip	7-2	59 53	1,29
Brompton Regis	15-6	s95 31	1,11.	Chilcompton	7-3	64 51	3,2. 24,30
			(19,35)	Chillyhill	3-2	(56 62)	37,4
Broomfield	17-2	22 32	25,49	Chilthorne	32-3	52 19	19,79-80
'Brown'	14-12	(s99 36)	25,12	Chilton Cantelo	32-4	57 22	26,7
Brushford	15-7	s91 25	(1,12). 19,16	Chilton Polden	20-4	37 39	8,5
Bruton	23-2	68 34	1,9;(31). 21,	Chilton Trinity	18-7	29 39	21,10. 46,1
			91. (24,17.	Chilton Trivett	16-7	25 38	21,23-24
			36,1)	Chinnock	36-1	49 13	19,44;48-4?
Brympton	32-2	51 15	21,96	Chipstable	15-9	04 27	9,2
Buckland	9-3	75 51	47,19	Chiselborough	36-2	46 14	19,47
Dinham				Chubworthy	15-10	02 26	25,40
Buckland	28-6	27 13	47,1;7	Churchstanton	D-1	19 14	EDe 1
St. Mary				Clapton (in	24-3	75 29	19,68
Burnett	4-2	66 65	Exon. 114a1	Cucklington)			
			(=1,28)	Clapton (in	23-3	67 27	36,7
Burnham on Sea	11-5	30 49	24,27	Maperton)			
Butcombe	2-9	51 61	5,31	Clapton	1-1	47 74	5,27
Butleigh	20-2	52 33	8,12;18;40	in Gordano			
North Cadbury	22-7	63 27	36,5	Clatworthy	15-11	05 30	25,8
South Cadbury	22-8	63 25	36,7	Claverham	6-8	44 66	5,17
Queen Camel	22-9	59 24	1,22	Claverton	5-7	78 64	45,11
West Camel	29-2	57 24	9,7	Clayhill	18-8	26 37	21,7
Cameley	7-1	61 57	5,62	Old Cleeve	15-12	04 41	1,13
Camerton	8-1	68 57	8,31	Clevedon	1-2	40 71	44,1
Cannington	16-5	25 39	1,6;(13).	Clewer	11-6	43 51	5,19
			16,3. 46,9.	Cloford	10-3	72 44	19,53
			(47,25)	Closworth	36-3	56 10	19,52
Capland	28-7	30 18	47,5	Clutton	3-3	62 59	5,14
Capton	15-8	08 39	1,15	Coker	36-4	51 13	1,23
Carhampton	14-13	00 42	1,6;(13). 16,6.	Coleford	15-13	11 33	21,42.
			(30,2. 32,4)				25,35
Carlingcott	8-2	69 58	19,60	'Colgrim's Land'	16-—	- -	21,16

	Map	Grid	Text
Abbas Combe	33-3	70 22	14,1
Monkton Combe	5-8	77 61	7,7
Temple Combe	33-4	70 22	4,1
Combe (in Withycombe)	14-14	00 40	21,62
Combe Hay	8-3	73 59	47,20
Combe St.Nicholas	12d-2	30 11	6,2
Combe Sydenham	15-14	07 36	25,41
Combwich	16-8	25 42	17,2. 32,1
Compton Dando	4-4	64 64	5,39
Compton Dundon	20-5	49 32	8,11
Compton Durville	34-3	41 17	(1,27). 17,8. 19,3
Compton Martin	7-4	54 57	37,10
Compton Pauncefoot	22-11	64 26	36,9
Congresbury	6-9	43 63	1,21. (6,14)
Corston	8-4	69 65	7,13
Corton Denham	33-5	63 22	1,32
Cossington	20-6	35 40	8,7
Crandon	18-9	32 39	45,17
East Cranmore	10-4	68 43	} 8,32
West Cranmore	13-4	66 43	
Creech St.Michael	18-10	27 25	1,18
Crewkerne	35-1	44 09	1,20. (3,1). 12,1. (19,33)
Cricket Malherbie	28-9	36 11	19,34
Cricket St.Thomas	34-4	37 08	(1,4). 19,1
'Crook'	18-11	(32 39)	24,7
Croscombe	13-5	59 44	8,20
Crowcombe	15-15	14 36	19,7
Cucklington	24-4	75 27	19,64
Cudworth	34-5	37 10	22,10
Culbone	14-15	s84 48	5,7
North Curry	27-1	31 25	1,19
Curry Mallet	28-10	33 21	21,1-2
Currypool	16-9	22 38	21,13
Curry Rivel	28-11	39 25	1,5. 16,11. (19,17-18; 23-25;27;29. 47,5). Exon. 268a1 (=19,15)
Cutcombe	14-16	s93 39	25,9
Deadmans Well	17-3	(23 33)	1,1
Dinnington	34-6	40 12	8,36. 47,10
Discove	23-4	69 34	47,8
Ditcheat	13-6	62 36	8,30
Dodington	15-16	17 40	47,12
'Dodisham'	16-—	- -	21,20
Donyatt	28-12	33 14	19,24
Doulting	13-7	64 43	8,23
Doverhay	14-17	s89 46	21,66
Dowlish	34-7	37 12	5,1
Downhead	13-8	69 46	8,35
Downscombe	14-18	s84 39	21,57
Draycott (in Limington)	32-5	54 21	8,39. 19,12
Draycott (in Rodney Stoke)	6-10	47 50	47,15
Drayton	28-13	40 24	9,6. (21,55)
Dulverton	15-17	s91 27	1,12. (46,2)
Dundon	20-7	47 32	8,13
Compton Dundon, see Compton			
Dunkerton	8-5	71 59	36,13
Dunster	14-19	s99 43	25,2
Dunwear	18-12	31 36	24,6
Durborough	16-10	19 41	8,8
Durleigh	17-4	27 36	46,15
Durston	18-13	29 28	22,4
Dyche	16-11	16 41	35,13
Earnshill	28-14	38 21	21,71. 46,20
Easthams	35-2	45 10	(1,20). 19,33
Ston Easton	7-5	62 53	5,59. 42,3. 46,25
Easton in Gordano	1-3	51 75	5,24
'Eastrip'	23-5	(70 35)	36,3. 47,24
Eckweek	8-6	71 57	19,61. 24,32
Edington	20-8	38 39	8,5
Edingworth	11-7	35 53	8,34
'Edstock'	16-12	(23 40)	21,32
Elborough	6-11	36 59	5,11. 8,38
Eleigh	34-8	33 10	21,37
Elm	10-5	74 49	39,2
Elworthy	15-18	08 34	25,33
Embelle	15-19	11 33	21,46
Emborough	7-6	61 51	5,61
Englishcombe	8-7	71 62	5,44
Enmore	17-5	23 35	21,74
Evercreech	13-9	64 38	6,10
'Eversy'	8-8	(70 59)	7,14
Exford	14-20	s85 38	21,58-59;68. 25,19-20
Exton	15-20	s92 33	5,5
Fairoak	10-6	(80 49)	21,87
Farleigh Hungerford	8-9	80 57	21,88
Farmborough	4-5	66 60	5,18
Farrington Gurney	7-7	62 55	5,58
Fiddington	16-13	21 40	22,8
Fivehead	28-15	35 22	21,70
Foddington	22-12	57 29	19,67. 45,13;15
Ford	26-5	19 25	(2,3). 19,42
Foxcote	8-10	71 55	5,42
Freshford	5-9	78 60	5,35
Frome	10-7	77 47	1,8;(9;31). 16,1
'Gilcott'	14-21	(s99 41)	21,64
Glastonbury	21-3	50 38	8,1
Goathill (Dorset)	33-6	67 17	19,70
Goathurst	17-6	25 34	35,19
Gothelney	16-14	25 37	21,15
Greenham	25-4	07 20	19,21
Greinton	20-9	41 36	8,15

	Map	Grid	Text		Map	Grid	Text
Hadworthy	18-14	(29 34)	21,4	Illeigh, see Eleigh			
Hallatrow	7-8	63 57	5,65	Ilminster	28-17	36 14	9,3
Halse	26-6	14 27	(2,3). 22,1	Ilton	28-18	35 17	10,1
Halsway	15-21	12 37	21,41	Isle Abbotts	28-19	35 20	9,4-5
Halswell	17-7	25 33	22,17	Isle Brewers	28-20	36 21	19,8. 35,1'
Ham	20-10	42 31	8,17	Keinton	22-14	54 30	19,59.
Hamp	18-15	30 36	10,4	Mandeville			(21,92)
Hardington	9-4	74 52	5,48. (20,1)	Kenn	6-14	41 69	5,29
Hardington	36-5	51 11	1,24	Kewstoke	6-15	33 63	42,1
Mandeville				Keyford	10-8	77 47	5,55. 36,1:
East Harptree	6-12	56 55	5,9. 19,37	Keynsham	4-6	65 68	1,28
West Harptree	7-9	56 56	5,60. 24,31	Kilmersdon	9-6	69 52	16,14
Hartrow	15-22	09 34	25,39	Kilmington	24-5	77 36	(1,9). 37,7
Haselbury	36-6	47 10	47,17	(Wilts.)			
Plucknett				Kilton	15-29	16 44	25,30
Hatch	28-16	30 20	19,29	Kilve	15-30	14 42	21,47
Beauchamp				Kingsbury	12b-1	43 21	6,3
Havyatt	2-11	47 60	5,28	Episcopi			
Hawkwell	15-23	s87 25	47,13	Kingstone	34-9	37 13	8,39. 19,1(
Hay Street	7-10	(62 53)	46,24	Kingston	6-16	40 66	5,63-64
Heathfield	26-7	16 26	(2,3). 25,53	Seymour			
Hele	26-8	18 24	(2,3;5).	Kingweston	22-15	52 30	17,17
			19,40	Kittisford	25-5	07 22	22,15
Hemington	9-5	72 53	(5,48). 20,1	Knowle (in	14-23	s96 43	25,26
Henstridge	33-7	72 19	1,25.18,4	Timberscombe)			
Hill	15-24	15 42	21,47	Knowle (in	2-12	60 70	39,1
Hillfarrance	26-9	16 24	(2,3;5).	Bristol, Glos.)			
			35,22	Knowle Park	24-6	69 31	45,12
Hinton Blewitt	7-11	59 56	26,5	Knowle St.Giles	34-10	34 11	21,37
Hinton	8-11	77 58	40,1	Lamyatt	13-11	65 35	8,30
Charterhouse				Langford	25-6	11 22	1,16
Hinton	35-3	41 12	26,2	Budville			
St. George				Langham	14-24	s98 36	25,13
'Hiscombe'	31-2	(51 16)	5,3. 8,38	Langport	29-7	42 26	(1,1;19;31.
'Holcombe'	16-15	(19 35)	21,19				19,26)
Holford (nr.	26-10	14 33	(2,3). 21,	Langridge	5-10	74 69	5,36
Lydeard St.Lawrence)			83-84	Lattiford	22-16	69 26	8,19
Holford St.Mary	15-25	15 41	25,38	Laverton	10-9	77 53	26,4
'Holne'	14-—	- -	21,67	Ledforda, see Letfort			
Holnicote	14-22	s90 46	16,13. 21,65	Abbots Leigh	1-4	54 74	16,9
Holton	22-13	68 26	45,4	Leigh (in Old	15-31	02 35	35,14
Honibere	15-26	18 43	46,18	Cleeve)			
Hornblotton	13-10	59 34	8,30	Leigh (in	26-11	12 29	(2,9)
Horsey	18-16	32 39	24,25	Lydeard St. Lawrence)			
Horsey Pignes, see 'Pignes'				Leigh (in	25-7	09 24	25,47
Horsington	33-8	70 23	28,1	Milverton)			
Houndstone	32-6	52 17	19,81	Leigh (in	34-11	35 06	25,5
'Huish' (in	11-8	(31 48)	24,35-36	Winsham)			
Burnham on Sea)				Letfort,	15-—	- -	Exon. 509!
Huish (in	15-27	04 39	21,43. 31,3	Ledforda			(=1,6). Tax
Nettlecombe)							Return 79!
Huish	15-28	04 29	22,2	Lexworthy	17-8	25 35	17,3.
Champflower							21,75-76
Huntspill	19-2	31 45	24,28;34	Lilstock	15-32	16 44	46,16
Huntstile	18-17	26 33	46,11	Limington	32-7	54 22	8,41. 21,9:
Huntworth	18-18	31 34	35,3	'Litnes'	29-8	(41 26)	6,5
Hutton	6-13	35 58	5,10. 8,38	High Littleton	7-12	64 58	5,66
Idson	16-16	22 44	21,27	Stony Littleton	8-12	73 56	5,56
Ilchester	31-3	52 22	(1,10;31.	Littleton (in	29-9	49 30	21,85
			24,17)	Compton Dundon)			
St. Andrew's	31-5	52 23	8,37. 15,1	Litton	12a-1	59 54	6,17
Church (Northover, in Ilchester)							

402

	Map	Grid	Text
Lopen	34-12	42 14	19,6. 21,38. 47,3
Lovington	22-17	59 30	37,8
Loxton	6-17	37 55	17,4
Luccombe	14-25	s91 44	32,2. 38,1
Luckington	9-7	69 50	35,23
Lufton	32-8	51 16	19,82
Lullington	10-10	78 51	5,51
Luxborough	14-26	s97 38	25,27-28
Lyde	32-9	57 17	22,28
Bishops Lydeard	12f-2	16 29	6,8;(19)
East Lydeard	26-12	17 29	25,50
Lydeard St.Lawrence	26-13	12 32	(2,9)
East Lydford	22-18	57 31	8,4
West Lydford	22-19	56 31	47,21
Lyncombe	5-11	75 64	7,9
Lyng	18-19	33 28	10,5
Maidenbrooke	26-14	24 26	(2,3)
Manworthy	25-8	(08 25)	25,44
Maperton	22-20	67 26	36,10
Marksbury	4-7	66 62	8,29
Marsh Mills, see Mills			
Marston Bigot	10-11	75 44	22,26
Marston Magna	33-9	59 22	19,72-73
Martock	30-1	46 19	1,27. (35,24)
Meare	21-4	45 41	8,1
Melcombe	18-20	28 33	(24,8). 46,5
Mells	10-12	72 49	8,25
Merridge	16-17	20 34	35,20
Merriott	35-4	44 12	19,32. 47,6
St.Michael Church	18-21	30 30	46,13
'Middlecote'	10-13	(70 48)	5,50
Middlezoy	20-11	37 33	8,6
Midelney	28-21	41 22	9,1
Midgell	2-13	46 67	5,68
Milborne Port	33-10	67 18	1,10;(31.14,1). 19,71. Exon.278b1 (=19,70). (EDo 1)
Marsh Mills	16-18	19 38	35,9
Milton (in Skilgate)	15-33	(s97 27)	22,12
Milton (in Weston super Mare)	6-18	34 62	24,2. 46,19
Milton Clevedon	23-6	66 37	44,3
Milton Podimore, see Podimore			
Milverton	25-9	12 25	1,(11);26. 6,18. 16,4. (21,81)
Minehead	14-27	s96 46	25,10
Monksilver	15-34	07 37	(1,6). 21,39-40. 35,10
West Monkton	18-22	26 28	8,28
Montacute	31-4	49 16	(19,38;86)
Moortown	28-23	37 23	21,55
Moreton	7-13	(56 59)	37,11
Muchelney	28-22	42 24	9,1
Mudford	32-10	57 19	1,35.19,87. 37,12

	Map	Grid	Text
Mudford Sock, see Sock			
Myne	14-28	(s92 48)	25,24
Nettlecombe	15-35	05 37	1,14. (5,5)
Newhall	15-36	(17 40)	31,5
Newton (in Bicknoller)	15-37	10 38	25,31
Newton (in North Petherton)	18-23	30 31	17,1. 21,3. 22,7. 46,8; 17
Newton St.Loe	8-13	70 64	5,57
Northover, see Ilchester			
Norton Fitzwarren	26-15	19 25	(2,3). 19,41
Norton Malreward	3-4	59 65	5,16
Norton St.Philip	8-14	77 55	40,2
Norton sub Hamdon	36-7	47 15	19,50
Nunney	10-14	73 45	25,54
Nynehead	26-16	13 22	(2,3)
Oake	26-17	15 25	(2,3). 21,81
Oakley	32-11	53 20	35,24. Exon. 113a2 (=1,27)
Oaktrow	14-29	s94 40	25,22
Oare	14-30	s80 47	30,2
Odcombe	36-8	50 15	19,46
Orchardleigh	10-15	77 51	5,52
Otterhampton	16-19	24 43	21,17. 35,6. 47,25
Overleigh	20-12	48 35	8,16
Panborough	21-5	47 35	8,1
Pardlestone	15-38	14 41	21,47
Pawlett	18-24	30 42	24,26
Pedwell	20-13	42 36	8,11
Pendomer	36-9	52 10	19,51
Pennard	13-12	59 37	8,21
Penselwood	24-7	75 31	22,27
North Perrott	36-10	47 09	19,45
Perry	18-25	27 39	21,5-6. 22,6. 46,7
'Petherham'	16-20	(24 41)	21,21
North Petherton	18-26	29 33	1,3;(5;13). 16,7. (35,1-2)
South Petherton	34-13	43 16	1,4;(5). 16,5. (19,2)
Pightley	16-21	22 35	21,14
'Pignes'	18-27	(31 39)	46,6
'Pillocks Orchard'	16-22	(26 39)	21,25
Pilton	13-13	58 40	8,20
Pirtochesworda	15-—	- -	Tax Return 79b2
Pitcombe	23-7	67 32	36,1
Pitcote	9-8	65 49	(5,43). 46,22
Pitminster	26-18	22 19	2,10
Pitney	29-10	44 28	1,34
Pixton	15-39	s92 27	21,53
Plainsfield	16-23	19 37	35,8
Podimore	29-11	54 25	8,3
Poleshill	25-10	08 23	25,46

	Map	Grid	Text
'Ponteside'	6-19	(41 59)	21,80
Porlock	14-31	s88 46	20,3
Portbury	1-5	50 75	5,33
Portishead	1-6	46 76	5,25
Poyntington (Dorset)	33-11	65 20	19,76
Preston (in Milverton)	26-19	13 26	(1,11). 19, 35. 35,18
Preston Plucknett	32-12	53 16	45,18
Priston	4-8	69 60	7,2
Puckington	28-24	37 18	21,54
Puriton	19-3	32 41	11,1
Pylle	13-14	60 38	8,20
Quantock	17-9	(23 35)	35,21
East Quantoxhead	15-40	13 43	31,2
West Quantoxhead	15-41	11 42	25,29
Quarme	14-32	s92 36	25,14. 43,1
Raddington	15-42	01 25	22,13
Radlet	16-24	20 38	21,28. 35,7
Radstock	9-9	68 54	5,47
Rapps	28-25	33 17	32,7
Redlynch	23-8	70 33	19,58. Exon. 91a1 (=1,9)
Rexworthy	16-25	25 36	21,11
Ridgchill	2-14	53 62	16,10. 37,6 21,9
Rime	18-—	- -	21,9
Rimpton	33-12	60 21	2,12
Rodden	10-16	79 47	41,3
Rode	10-17	80 53	5,54. 45,14
Rodhuish	14-33	01 39	35,15
Runnington	25-11	11 21	25,45
St. Andrew's Church, see Ilchester			
St. Michael Church, see Michael Church			
Salisbury (Wilts.)	- -	- -	(2,9)
Saltford	4-9	68 67	5,23
Sampford Arundel	25-12	10 18	21,72
Sampford Brett	15-43	08 40	18,2
Sandford (in Wembdon)	18-28	26 37	22,5
Sandford Orcas (Dorset)	33-13	62 20	45,5
Scepeworde	- -	- -	47,22
'Seaberton'	16-26	(20 45)	25,1
Seaborough (Dorset)	35-5	42 06	3,1
Seavington	34-14	40 15	10,3. 19,2. 47,2
Selworthy	14-34	s91 46	32,3
Shapwick	20-14	41 38	8,5
Shearston	18-29	28 30	21,8
Shepton Beauchamp	34-15	40 17	19,5
Shepton Mallet	13-15	61 43	8,20
Shepton Montague	24-8	68 31	19,57
Shipham	6-20	44 57	21,79
Shopnoller	26-20	16 32	(2,3)

	Map	Grid	Text
'Shortmansford'	15-—	- -	25,42
Shovel	18-30	28 32	46,14
Skilgate	15-44	s98 27	22,11
Sock Dennis	31-6	51 21	19,85
Mudford Sock	32-13	55 19	21,95
Somerton	29-12	49 28	1,1;(2. 46,11)
Sparkford	22-21	60 26	24,18
Spaxton	16-27	22 37	35,5
Standerwick	10-18	81 50	21,86
Church Stanton, see Churchstanton			
Stanton Drew	4-10	59 63	(1,28)
Stanton Prior	4-11	67 62	7,3
Staple Fitzpaine	28-26	26 18	19,26
Staunton	14-35	s97 44	25,18
Stawell	20-15	36 38	8,10
Stawley	25-13	06 22	35,16
Steart	22-22	56 27	19,38
Stockland	16-28	23 43	21,26. 25, 31,1
Stocklinch	28-27	38 17	25,48. 47,
Stogumber	15-45	09 37	16,2
Stogursey	16-29	20 42	27,1
Chew Stoke	3-5	55 61	37,3-4. 47
Rodney Stoke	6-21	48 49	5,4
Stoney Stoke	24-9	70 32	19,57
Stoke Pero	14-36	s87 43	21,60
Stoke St. Mary	26-21	26 22	(2,3). 25,5
Stoke sub Hamdon	31-7	47 17	8,39. 19,1 13-14
Stoke Trister	24-10	73 28	19,63
Stone (in Exford)	14-37	s86 38	21,69
Stone (in Mudford)	32-14	55 18	37,12
Ston Easton, see Easton			
Stowell	33-14	68 22	5,70
'Stowey'	14-38	(s81 46)	30,1
Nether Stowey	15-46	18 39	35,11-12
Old Stowey	14-39	s95 38	25,21
Over Stratton	34-16	43 15	(1,4)
Stratton on the Fosse	9-10	65 50	5,43. 8,38
Street	34-17	35 07	25,6
Stretcholt	18-31	29 44	24,3-4
Stringston	16-30	17 42	21,34. 35,4
Long Sutton	29-13	46 25	10,2;6. 21,
Sutton Bingham	36-11	54 11	22,23
Sutton Mallet	20-16	37 36	8,5
Sutton Montis	22-23	62 24	19,56
Swainswick	5-12	75 68	5,38. 47,1
Swang	16-31	23 38	21,29
Swell	28-28	36 23	19,15
Sydenham	18-32	31 38	22,16
Syndercombe	15-47	03 30	36,4
Tadwick	5-13	74 70	45,7-8
Tarnock	11-9	37 52	24,12-13
Taunton	26-22	22 24	2,1;(2-5;8-9 19,40)
Tellisford	8-15	80 55	5,53
Templecombe, see Temple Combe			
Tetton	26-23	20 30	18,1

	Map	Grid	Text		Map	Grid	Text
'Theodoric's Land'	16-—	- -	21,30	Wheathill	22-25	58 30	37,9
				Whitcomb	33-18	63 23	1,33
'Thorent'	33-15	(70 19)	4,1	Whitelackington	28-30	37 15	22,3
Thorne (nr. Yeovil)	32-15	52 17	19,77-78	White Ox Mead	8-17	71 58	21,89
				Whitestaunton	34-19	28 10	19,4
Thorne St.Margaret	25-14	09 21	21,73	Wigborough	34-20	44 15	46,10
				Willett	15-52	10 33	25,34
Thorney	28-29	42 23	9,1	Williton	15-53	07 41	1,6;(13. 25,33)
Thornfalcon	27-2	28 23	19,31				
Thurlbear	27-3	26 21	19,30	Wilmersham	14-42	s87 43	5,6
Tickenham	1-7	45 71	26,8. 41,2	Wilmington	4-12	69 62	7,4
Timberscombe	14-40	s95 42	22,14	Wincanton	24-11	71 28	24,16
Timsbury	3-6	66 58	5,15. 45,6	Winford	2-15	54 65	5,41
Tintinhull	31-8	49 19	(8,31). 19,9	Winscombe	6-24	42 57	8,2
Tolland	26-24	10 32	(2,3). 21,82	Winsford	15-54	s90 35	1,17. (46,3)
Torweston	15-48	09 40	25,37	Winsham	12c-1	37 06	6,12
Treborough	14-41	01 36	32,6	Winterhead	6-25	43 57	5,12
Trent (Dorset)	33-16	59 18	19,75	Witham Friary	10-21	74 41	21,90. 36,2
Tuxwell	16-32	20 37	22,9. 47,9	Withiel	16-33	24 39	21,33
Twerton	8-16	72 64	5,45-46	Withycombe	14-43	01 41	5,8
Ubley	7-14	52 58	42,2	Withypool	15-55	s84 35	46,3
Uphill	6-22	31 58	37,2	Wiveliscombe	12f-3	08 27	6,6
Upton Noble	23-9	71 39	5,67	Wltune	10-—	- -	36,2
Vexford	15-49	10 35	21,44-45	Woodadvent	15-56	03 37	Tax Return 79b2
Waldron	18-33	(28 40)	21,6				
Walpole	18-34	30 41	24,5	Woodborough	8-18	69 56	39,3
Walton (nr. Glastonbury)	20-17	46 36	8,11;(14)	Woodspring	6-26	34 66	27,3
				'Woodwick'	5-16	(77 60)	7,12
Walton (in Kilmersdon)	9-11	69 51	46,23	Woolavington	20-18	34 41	8,5
				Woolley	5-17	74 68	(5,37)
Walton in Gordano	1-8	42 73	29,1	Woolmersdon	18-36	28 33	35,1
				Woolston (in Bicknoller)	15-57	09 39	25,32
Wanstrow	10-19	71 41	6,16. 36,11				
Warleigh	5-14	79 64	45,9	Woolston (in South Cadbury)	23-10	64 27	19,55. 36,7
Watchet	15-50	07 43	25,36				
Weacombe	15-51	10 40	21,48	Woolston (in Stogursey)	16-34	23 44	21,18
Weare	11-10	41 52	24,9				
Wearne	29-14	42 28	46,1	North Wootton	21-6	56 41	8,20
Weathergrove (Dorset)	33-17	61 21	5,69	Wootton Courtenay	14-44	s93 43	27,2
Wedmore	11-11	43 47	1,2. 6,15	Worle	6-27	35 62	24,1
Well, see Deadmans Well				'Worth'	34-21	(38 10)	21,36
Wellington	12c-1	14 20	6,7	Wraxall	1-10	49 71	5,40
Wellisford	25-15	09 21	46,4	Wrington	2-16	46 62	8,27
Wells	12a-2	54 45	6,1	Writhlington	9-12	70 55	47,23
Wembdon	18-35	28 37	24,22	Yarlington	23-11	65 29	19,54
Wemberham	6-23	(40 65)	6,14	Yarnfield (Wilts.)	24-12	78 38	23,1
Westbury sub Mendip	12a-3	50 48	6,11	Yatton	6-28	43 65	6,14
				Yeovil	32-16	55 16	19,83-84. 26,6
Westcombe	13-16	69 37	8,24				
King Weston, see Kingweston				Yeovilton	29-15	54 23	26,3
Weston (nr. Bath)	5-15	73 66	7,5. 41,1				
Weston Bampfylde	22-24	61 24	19,69. 36,5-6				
Weston in Gordano	1-9	44 74	5,22;26				
Westowe	26-25	12 32	(1,6). 21,49				
Whatley (nr. Frome)	10-20	73 47	8,26				
Whatley (in Winsham)	34-18	36 06	26,1				

Places not named (main entries only are included, not subdivisions of a named holding)

13,1 The Church of St. Mary of Montebourg, 5 hides.
16,12 Edith the nun, 12 acres.
21,97 Roger of Courseulles, ½ hide. (See 1,4 note)
33,2 Robert son of Gerald, 10 hides.
46,2 Robert, 1 virgate; once added to Dulverton.

Places in Somerset not indexed above

Gatemore? ... Robert (22,11 General Notes) *Herecom* (?Heathcombe) ... Robert (21,8 Places Notes)
Stowey ... Aelfric (6,13 Places Notes).

Places not in Somerset
Names starred are in the Index of Places above; others are in the Indices of Persons or of
Churches and Clergy. Bynames of persons in italics are found only in Exon.

Elsewhere in Britain
DEVONSHIRE   Exeter ... Sheriff Baldwin
DORSETSHIRE   Adber*; Purse Caundle*; Cerne ... Abbey; Goathill*; Poyntington*;
Sandford Orcas*; Seaborough*; Shaftesbury ... Church; Trent*; Weathergrove*.
COUNTY DURHAM   Durham ... Bishop.
GLOUCESTERSHIRE   Bedminster*; Berkeley ... Roger; Bristol*; Knowle*.
HAMPSHIRE   ... Aelfric Little: Boscombe ... Alstan; Winchester ... Bishop Walkelin, Churches.
MIDDLESEX   London ... *Bishop Maurice.*
WILTSHIRE   Kilmington*; Marlborough ... Alfred; Salisbury* ... Bishop Osmund, *Sheriff*
Edward (and 2,9); Yarnfield*.

Outside Britain
All places, except Rome and Flanders, are in France; the Départements to which the less well-known
belong are given under the occurrence of the name in the General Notes.

Auberville ... Robert. Barre ... *Richard.* Bayeux ... Bishop. Boulogne ... Countess Ida.
Burcy ... Serlo. Caen ... Abbot, Church. Carteret ... Mauger. Conteville ... *Ralph.*
Courseulles ... Roger, *William.* Coutances ... Bishop Geoffrey. Daumeray ... *William.*
Douai ... Walter, *alias* Walscin. Eu ... William. Falaise ... William. Flanders ... Odo.
Gournai ... *Nigel.* Grestain ... Church. Hesdin ... Arnulf. Jumièges ... Abbot. Les Andelys
... *Richere.* Lestre ... *William.* Limesy ... Ralph. Merri ... *Richard.* Mohun ... William.
Monceaux ... *William.* Montebourg ... Abbot, Church. Mortagne ... Matthew. Mortain
... Count. Mortimer ... Ralph. Pomeroy ... Ralph. Reuilly ... *Ralph.* Rivers ... *Jocelyn.*
Rome ... Church. Saint-Clair ... *Hubert.* 'Spain' (Épaignes) ... Alfred. Trelly ... Geoffrey.
Vautortes ... *Geoffrey, Hugh, Reginald.*

Maps and Map Keys

SOMERSET HUNDREDS

The figures used for Somerset Hundreds in index and map are:

1	Portbury	19	Huntspill and Puriton
2	Hartcliffe with Bedminster	20	Whitley
3	Chew	21	Glaston Twelve HIdes
4	Keynsham	22	Catsash
5	Bath Forum	23	Bruton
6	Winterstoke	24	Norton Ferris
7	Chewton	25	Milverton
8	Wellow	26	Taunton and Taunton Dean
9	Kilmersdon	27	North Curry
10	Frome	28	Abdick and Bulstone
11	Bempstone	29	Somerton
12a	Wells Forum	30	Martock
12b-d	Kingsbury East	31	Tintinhull
12e-f	Kingsbury West	32	Stone
13	Whitstone	33	Horethorne
14	Carhampton	34	South Petherton
15	Williton and Freemanners	35	Crewkerne
16	Cannington	36	Houndborough, Barwick and Coker
17	Andersfield	D	Places in Devon in 1086
18	North Petherton		

Places are mapped in their 'modern' (mid-nineteenth century) Hundred, but ignoring most detachments and the two Hundreds known to be of post-1086 formation. The probable Domesday hundredal arrangements are discussed in Appendix I. The following symbols are used on the maps :

○　　A place mentioned only in Exon. DB or in the Tax Returns.

■　　Detachments of Wells, probably forming the Domesday Hundred of Bishop Giso, most later in Kingsbury East and West Hundreds.

□　　Holdings of Glastonbury Abbey, detached from Whitley Hundred.

★　　Detached places of other Hundreds, or places belonging to Hundreds of post-1086 creation, here mapped in a geographically appropriate Hundred.

In the Map Keys, a number in brackets following an asterisked place-name indicates the Hundred to which a detached place belongs, according to the list above. BW and P denote the later Hundreds of Brent-cum-Wrington and Pitney respectively.

Hundred boundaries are taken from the maps of C. and I. Greenwood, (1820-21), John Cary (1824) and Thomas Dix, checked with parish boundaries. The list of places in each Hundred is based on the 1841 census.

The County Boundary is marked on the maps by thick lines, continuous for 1086, dotted for the modern boundary, broken where uncertain; Hundred boundaries by thin lines, broken where uncertain.

National Grid 10-kilometre squares are shown on the map border.

Each four-figure square covers one square kilometre, or 247 acres, approximately 2 hides, at 120 acres to the hide.

SOMERSET NORTHERN HUNDREDS

Portbury 1
1 Clapton in Gordano
2 Clevedon
3 Easton in Gordano
4 Abbots Leigh
5 Portbury
6 Portishead
7 Tickenham
8 Walton in Gordano
9 Weston in Gordano
10 Wraxall

Hartcliffe with Bedminster 2
1 Aldwick
2 Long Ashton
3 Backwell
4 Barrow Gurney
5 Bedminster (Glos.)
6 Bishopsworth
7 Bristol (Glos.)
8 *Brockley (7)
9 Butcombe
10 Chelvey
11 *Havyatt (BW)
12 Knowle (Glos.)
13 *Midgell (7)
14 Ridgehill
15 Winford
16 *Wrington (BW)

Chew 3
1 Chew Magna
2 Chillyhill
3 Clutton
4 Norton Malreward
5 Chew Stoke
6 Timsbury

Keynsham 4
1 Belluton
2 Burnett
3 Chelwood
4 Compton Dando
5 Farmborough
6 Keynsham
7 Marksbury
8 Priston
9 Saltford
10 Stanton Drew
11 Stanton Prior
12 Wilmington

Bath Forum 5
1 Bath
2 Bathampton
3 Batheaston
4 Bathford
5 Bathwick
6 Charlcombe
7 Claverton
8 Monkton Combe
9 Freshford
10 Langridge
11 Lyncombe
12 Swainswick
13 Tadwick
14 Warleigh
15 Weston
16 'Woodwick'
17 Woolley

Winterstoke 6
1 Ashcombe
2 Axbridge
3 Badgworth
4 Banwell
5 Blagdon
6 Bleadon
7 Cheddar
8 Claverham
9 Congresbury
10 Draycott
11 Elborough
12 East Harptree
13 Hutton
14 Kenn
15 Kewstoke
16 *Kingston Seymour (7)
17 Loxton
18 Milton
19 'Ponteside'
20 Shipham
21 Rodney Stoke
22 Uphill
23 Wemberham
24 Winscombe
25 Winterhead
26 Woodspring
27 Worle
28 Yatton

Chewton 7
1 Cameley
2 Chewton Mendip
3 Chilcompton
4 Compton Martin
5 Ston Easton
6 Emborough
7 Farrington Gurney
8 Hallatrow
9 West Harptree
10 Hay Street
11 Hinton Blewitt
12 High Littleton
13 Moreton
14 Ubley

Wellow 8
1 Camerton
2 Carlingcott
3 Combe Hay
4 Corston
5 Dunkerton
6 Eckweek
7 Englishcombe
8 'Eversy'
9 Farleigh Hungerford
10 Foxcote
11 Hinton Charterhouse
12 Stony Littleton
13 Newton St. Loe
14 Norton St. Philip
15 Tellisford
16 Twerton
17 White Ox Mead
18 Woodborough

Kilmersdon 9
1 Ashwick
2 Babington
3 Buckland Dinham
4 Hardington
5 Hemington
6 Kilmersdon
7 Luckington
8 Pitcote
9 Radstock
10 Stratton on the Fosse
11 Walton
12 Writhlington

Frome 10
1 Beckington
2 Berkley
3 Cloford
4 East Cranmore
5 Elm
6 Fairoak
7 Frome
8 Keyford
9 Laverton
10 Lullington
11 Marston Bigot
12 Mells
13 'Middlecote'
14 Nunney
15 Orchardleigh
16 Rodden
17 Rode
18 Standerwick
19 Wanstrow
20 Whatley
21 Witham Friary
Witune

Bempstone 11
1 Allerton
2 Alston Sutton
3 Brean
4 *Brent (BW)
5 Burnham on Sea
6 Clewer
7 *Edingworth (BW)
8 'Huish'
9 Tarnock
10 Weare
11 Wedmore

Wells Forum 12a
1 Litton
2 Wells
3 Westbury sub Mendip

Whitstone 13
1 Alhampton
2 Batcombe
3 Charlton
4 *West Cranmore (12a)
5 Croscombe
6 Ditcheat
7 Doulting
8 Downhead
9 *Evercreech (12a)
10 Hornblotton
11 Lamyatt
12 Pennard
13 Pilton
14 Pylle
15 Shepton Mallet
16 Westcombe

Glaston Twelve Hides 21
1 'Andersey'
2 Baltonsborough
3 Glastonbury
4 Meare
5 Panborough
6 North Wootton

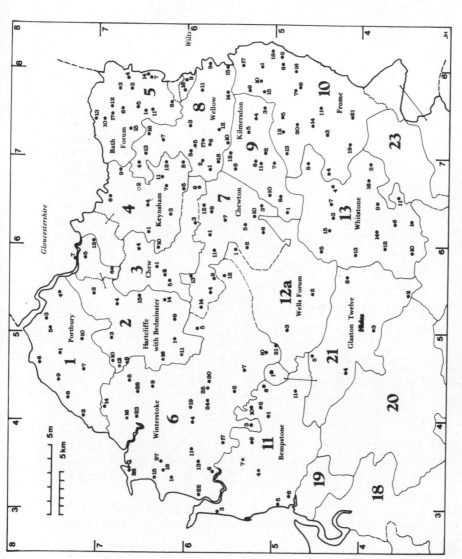

SOMERSET NORTHERN HUNDREDS